A NEW INTRODUCTION TO OLD NORSE

PART II: READER

A NEW INTRODUCTION TO OLD NORSE

PART II

READER

FIFTH EDITION

EDITED BY

ANTHONY FAULKES

VIKING SOCIETY FOR NORTHERN RESEARCH

UNIVERSITY COLLEGE LONDON

2011

ISBN: 978-0-903521-83-3

First published 2001
Second edition with corrections and additions 2002
Third edition with corrections and additions 2005
Fourth edition with corrections and additions 2007
Reprinted with minor corrections 2008
Fifth edition 2011

Printed by Short Run Press Limited, Exeter

PREFACE

This fifth edition of *A New Introduction to Old Norse* II: *Reader* has the same texts as the fourth edition, but versions of the skaldic verses in prose word order have been added after the notes to each text that contains any that are complicated enough to need them. Background notes to Text I have been contributed by Richard Perkins. Some additions to the bibliographies and minor corrections have been made by various contributors.

The texts have been prepared and annotated by the following:

I , XVII and XX: Michael Barnes.
II, XVI and XIX: Anthony Faulkes.
III, VIII, XXI and XXVII: Richard Perkins.
IV, IX, X, XI and XXIV: Rory McTurk.
V, VI, XV and XXVI: Alison Finlay.
VII: Diana Whaley.
XII and XXIII: David Ashurst.
XIII and XXII: Carl Phelpstead.
XIV: Peter Foote.
XVIII: Elizabeth Ashman Rowe.
XXV: John McKinnell.

The introductions are by the same writers, except in the case of Text I, where the introduction is by Anthony Faulkes, who has also been general editor of the whole volume, and compiled the main Glossary and Index in *Part* III, the fourth edition of which includes supplementary Glossaries and Indexes to the East Norse texts and the runic inscriptions by Michael Barnes. The general 'Introduction to the Study of Old Norse' is by Alison Finlay, the 'Note on Normalisation' is by Anthony Faulkes.

The plan of this volume was that it should include at least one extract from works in each of the main genres of Old Norse literature. This plan has now been fulfilled, and *NION* now offers an introduction to the whole range of early Scandinavian writings. Users of this book are reminded that several further complete Old Icelandic texts with glossaries are available in other Viking Society publications (see p. xxxvi below).

The first part of Text I, the extract from *Hrólfs saga*, has a comprehensive grammatical commentary. The remainder of the extract is fully glossed with virtually complete references. It is recommended that students begin with this text to ensure that they understand the grammatical structure of Old Icelandic before proceeding to others where the grammatical information in the glossary and notes is much sparser. The succeeding texts are glossed with progressively fewer references, though it is hoped that all words have been explained on their first occurrence in each extract, so that it will not be necessary for them to be read in the order in which they are printed. Idioms and constructions are explained much more fully in the Glossary than is usual in teaching books because experience has shown that it is these that cause the greatest difficulty in understanding Old Icelandic texts; and numerous cross-references are included to help elementary students identify the entry forms of words that appear in the texts in guises that are difficult to recognise—another of the persistent problems of learning this language.

A NOTE ON NORMALISATION

Texts in Old Norse manuscripts use a variety of letter forms and spellings that are very confusing for beginners learning to read in the original language.[1] For instance, 'c' and 'k', 'i' and 'j', 'þ' and 'ð' are often used indifferently for the same sounds, and various symbols or combinations of symbols are used to represent the sounds of 'o', 'ø' and 'ǫ' without distinguishing them consistently. Many abbreviations are used. Length of vowels and consonants is indicated in various ways or not at all. Capital letters, punctuation, word breaks, paragraph breaks are used according to different conventions from those that are now current, verse lines and direct speech are arranged differently on the page from the way that is now usual. Except for some special scholarly purposes, where diplomatic transcription is felt appropriate, it is now customary when printing these texts to use a single symbol for each sound, always to indicate length of vowels by the use of an acute accent (except over 'æ' and 'œ', which are by modern convention always long), and to use modern conventions for word division, capitalisation, punctuation, paragraphing and the arrangement of verse lines and direct speech. Abbreviations are usually expanded.

There are also variations in the spelling of some words that are due to differences in the dialect of the author or scribe, and others that result from changes in pronunciation from the time of the earliest written texts (twelfth century) to the time of the latest copies of Old Norse texts (seventeenth century or even later). For instance, the distinctions between the sounds 'ǫ' and 'ø', 'á' and 'ǫ́' was lost during the thirteenth century, and these sounds are now represented by 'ö' and 'á' respectively. The distinction betweeen 'e' and short 'æ' was

[1] See Stefán Karlsson, *The Icelandic Language* (2004), section 2.

lost in Old Icelandic before the time of the earliest manuscripts, but survives in some texts of Norwegian origin; on the other hand 'h' before 'l' was lost early in Norwegian, but survives still in Icelandic.

Other variations in the spelling of words arise from the development of parallel linguistic forms of words as a result of the uneven operation of sound changes, analogy with words of similar structure or with other parts of the same word, or differences in stress in certain positions. Such are the alternations of *nakkvarr/nekkverr/nǫkkurr* for the indefinite pronoun, *barðr/bariðr* for the pp. of the verb *berja*, *þykkir/þikkir/þikir* for the 3rd pers. sg. pres. of the verb *þykkja*.

The variations in the spelling in manuscripts of Old Norse texts are not random, nor are they idiosyncratic attempts to spell 'phonetically'. They are the result of the different training of scribes in scriptoria in various parts of the Old Norse world at various times. Each scriptorium had its own method of applying the Latin alphabet to the sounds of Old Norse, which was usually some variation of the methods used in Anglo-Saxon scriptoria to apply the Latin alphabet to the sounds of Old English. There survive almost no authorial manuscripts of works of Old Icelandic literature, and moreover the copies we have are often at the end of a chain of copies from the original, that were made by scribes from various scriptoria. While they would mostly try to replace the spelling conventions of the exemplar they were copying with those they had learned from their own training, they would never be able to do this consistently, so that traces of the conventions of previous scribes (and of the dialects and periods of those previous scribes) would remain, resulting in a copy with a mixture of conventions and thus with an appearance of randomness.

In the printing of Old Norse texts in German and Scandinavian editions, it has been generally customary to keep much closer to the manuscript spellings than in British and American editions, which have usually used spellings thought to represent the 'standard' pronunciation of thirteenth-century Iceland, such as is also used in most of the editions in *Íslenzk fornrit* (though in some Icelandic editions intended for the general Icelandic reader, modern Icelandic spelling is now used), even though in printing Old and Middle English and early Modern English texts for academic purposes the original spellings have generally been retained. Nevertheless, there has been a move towards keeping closer to the spelling of manuscripts, for instance in Bjarni Einarsson's edition of *Egils saga* (Viking Society for Northern Research 2003). In addition, it has been customary for editors to apply different spelling conventions to any skaldic verses included in prose texts, so as to reproduce what was supposed to have been the pronunciation at the time the verses were composed, thought in some cases to have been up to three centuries or more earlier. In the verses in *Egils saga* 2003, however, the same spellings have been used as in rendering the prose, because of the uncertainty about the verses' date and authorship.

In the texts in this Reader, editors have been given a certain amount of freedom in the spellings they adopt, with the recommendation that they keep as close to the spellings of the manuscript they are using as their base text as possible. The symbols listed in *NION* I, §§ 2.1.1–2.1.3 have been used, with the addition of 'ę' for the short 'æ' in the Norwegian texts where the distinction between 'e' and short 'æ' is made. Modern conventions for word division, capitalisation, punctuation, paragraphing and the arrangement of verse lines and direct speech are used. In the kinds of variant spellings that are due to dialect or difference of date, the editors have been encouraged to choose the spellings they deem most appropriate to the supposed date and place of composition, taking into account the usage of the scribe, but not to treat the skaldic verses differently from the prose narrative in which they are embedded, even if this interferes with the normal patterns of vowel assonance (such as characterises both end rhyme and internal rhyme in Old Norse poetry) and rhythm. It was recommended that the usage of the scribe of the manuscript should be followed in the kinds of variant spellings in the third paragraph above. On the procedures adopted in editing East Norse texts (XX) and runic inscriptions (XVII), see respectively pp. 270 and 221–22.

This policy is intended to help students become accustomed to some of the wide variety of forms (archaic, dialectal, post-classical or analogical) that appear commonly in editions (and dictionaries and grammars), and also to ensure that they are aware of the different spellings that underlie the normalised texts that have traditionally been used in teaching, and of the variations in the language between AD 900 and 1400 over the wide cultural area inhabited by Vikings in the Middle Ages. It should also make it easier for them to progress to independent reading of texts where the language is not fully normalised. All variant spellings in the texts are included in the Glossary in *NION* III, with cross-references as necessary.

Emendations to the base texts have been marked by pointed brackets ‹ › around letters added to the manuscript readings, square brackets [ ] around letters supplied that are illegible and italics for letters changed (the manuscript readings in the last case are given in footnotes).

CONTENTS

ABBREVIATIONS

BS = *The Book of the Settlements. Landnámabók,* tr. Hermann Pálsson and Paul Edwards (1972).

CCIMA = *Corpus Codicum Islandicorum Medii Aevi* I–XX (1930–56).

CSI = *The Complete Sagas of Icelanders* I–V, ed. Viðar Hreinsson *et al.* (1997).

C–V = Richard Cleasby and Gudbrand Vigfusson, *An Icelandic–English Dictionary.* 2nd ed. by William A. Craigie (1957).

DMA = *Dictionary of the Middle Ages*, ed. Joseph R. Strayer, 13 vols (1982–89).

EÓS = Einar Ól. Sveinsson, *The Age of the Sturlungs: Icelandic Civilization in the Thirteenth Century*, tr. Jóhann S. Hannesson (1953).

Gr = Michael Barnes, *A New Introduction to Old Norse*. Part I. *Grammar* (2004).

Hkr = Snorri Sturluson, *Heimskringla. History of the Kings of Norway*, tr. Lee M. Hollander (1964 and reprints).

HOIC = Jón Jóhannesson, *A History of the Old Icelandic Commonwealth*, tr. Haraldur Bessason (1974).

ÍF = *Íslenzk fornrit* I– , 1933– .

ION = E. V. Gordon, *An Introduction to Old Norse*. 2nd ed. by A. R. Taylor (1957).

Laws = *Laws of Early Iceland. Grágás* I–II, tr. Andrew Dennis, Peter Foote, Richard Perkins (1980–2000).

LP = Sveinbjörn Egilsson, *Lexicon Poeticum*, rev. Finnur Jónsson (1931).

MRN = E. O. G. Turville-Petre, *Myth and Religion of the North* (1964 and reprints).

MS = Phillip Pulsiano (ed.), *Medieval Scandinavia*: *An Encyclopedia* (1993).

NION = *A New Introduction to Old Norse.*

Oddr*ÓT* = *Saga Óláfs Tryggvasonar af Oddr Snorrason munk*, ed. Finnur Jónsson (1932).

ON = Old Norse.

PE = *Edda: die Lieder des Codex Regius nebst verwandten Denkmälern,* ed. Gustav Neckel, 4th ed., rev. Hans Kuhn (1962).

Skj = *Den norsk-islandske skjaldedigtning* A I–II, B I–II, ed. Finnur Jónsson (1912–15).

SnE, Gylfaginning = Snorri Sturluson, *Edda. Prologue and Gylfaginning*, ed. Anthony Faulkes (2005).

SnE, Háttatal = Snorri Sturluson, *Edda. Háttatal*, ed. Anthony Faulkes (1999).

SnE, Skáldskaparmál = Snorri Sturluson, *Edda. Skáldskaparmál*, ed. Anthony Faulkes (1998).

VAch = Peter Foote and David M. Wilson, *The Viking Achievement* (1970).

INTRODUCTION TO THE STUDY OF OLD NORSE

1. Old Norse or Old Icelandic?

The main aim of this Reader, and ultimately of *A New Introduction to Old Norse* as a whole, is to introduce students to representative extracts from works in each of the major genres of literature surviving in Old Icelandic, along with the necessary apparatus for reading these texts in their original language. This introduction offers a brief overview of these genres, together with an account of their context. Some bibliographical references are given at the end of each section, and more general suggestions for further reading are listed at the end of this Introduction, but these bibliographies are not exhaustive, and tend to favour works available in English. More specific introductory material and bibliographical suggestions can be found in the Introduction to each text in the Reader.

The term 'Old Norse' has traditionally been used to refer to the language, literature and culture of medieval Scandinavia in the Middle Ages. Some scholars condemn the term as an appropriation of the culture and heritage of Iceland, and prefer the label 'Old Icelandic', since virtually all the surviving literary texts were either written in Iceland, or are preserved only in Icelandic manuscripts (Jónas Kristjánsson 1994). But 'Old Norse' does capture the fact that this literary heritage ultimately represents a culture originating in mainland Scandinavia, which was taken during the Viking Age (see 2 below) not only to the Viking colonies, including Iceland, that were established in the Atlantic, but also as far afield as Greenland and North America. According to accounts in the sagas, the impetus for the settlement of these colonies came primarily from Norway, though attempts have been made to gauge the accuracy of this account by scientific means, and to argue for a strong Celtic element in the early Icelandic population. The picture of strong cultural links between Norway, Iceland and settlements in Orkney, the Hebrides and northern Britain (including Ireland) has not been seriously challenged. The language of Norway and its colonies is referred to as West Norse, to distinguish it from East Norse, the language of Sweden and Denmark. For an account of the term 'Old Norse' as it applies to the language, see Grammar, 'Introduction' 1.2.

Apart from the runic inscriptions in Text XVII, the texts included in this Reader have an Icelandic emphasis, which reflects the predominance of the Icelanders in recording the history of the Scandinavian peoples, developing new literary forms, and preserving texts of many kinds through copying and reworking over many centuries. But Texts VI, XI and XXIV originated in Norway and a selection of East Norse extracts is included in Text XX.

Even those primarily interested in the material culture — the history or archaeology — that comes within the sphere of Old Norse will find themselves extrapolating information from Icelandic texts. The study of Old Icelandic is also a starting point for runic studies, although there are virtually no genuinely medieval runic inscriptions in Iceland. But the medieval culture of Iceland is a rewarding study in itself. This remote outpost of Norway, first settled in the late ninth century, was the location for a unique political experiment; until 1262–64, when it became subject to the Norwegian crown, it remained a society without a king, ruled by an oligarchy of the most substantial landowners and chieftains. Though an Icelandic historian has recently described Iceland in this 'Free State' or 'Commonwealth' period as 'a headless, feuding society' (Helgi Þorláksson in McTurk 2005, 136), medieval Icelandic writers developed an ideology which represented it as self-sufficient and, within limits, egalitarian. The early history of their own society was represented in detail by Icelandic authors, but the historical account developed largely in the thirteenth century inevitably casts a mythologising glow over the period of settlement, and is treated with caution (if not dismissed) by modern historians. The literature of medieval Iceland is extraordinarily rich and includes at least two genres unparalleled elsewhere: the Sagas of Icelanders, highly sophisticated prose narratives relating the semi-fictionalised lives of early farmer heroes; and the highly-wrought skaldic poetry found in praise poems for Scandinavian and other rulers, usually composed by Icelandic poets, but also in less formal *lausavísur* ('occasional verses') scattered through the Sagas of Icelanders.

Though in Germany and North America Old Norse is usually taught in departments of Germanic or Scandinavian studies, in Britain it has traditionally been studied as part of a degree in English. This is a historical survival of the development of antiquarian interest in the Anglo-Saxon past which began in the seventeenth century; scholars seeking to fill gaps in their knowledge of Anglo-Saxon antiquities turned to the rich heritage of Norse texts. The Scandinavian and Anglo-

Saxon peoples were both offshoots of a common Germanic past: as well as speaking related languages, they shared a pre-Christian religion. There is evidence for this shared religion in the account of the Roman historian Tacitus, writing at the end of the first century AD, who refers in his *Germania* to the cult among the Germanic tribes of the goddess Nerthus, whose name is etymologically identical with that of the Norse god Njǫrðr. Yet extended accounts of this pagan religion are found only in Norse sources, the Prose Edda of Snorri Sturluson and the mythological poems of the Poetic Edda; early, sometimes pre-Christian references also survive in the diction of skaldic verses which Snorri's Edda was written to explicate. Tacitus also refers to the warlike ideology of these early Germanic warrior peoples, for whom 'it is infamy during life, and indelible reproach, to return alive from a battle in which their prince was slain. To preserve their prince, to defend him, and to ascribe to his glory all their own valorous deeds, is the sum and most sacred part of their oath.' This so-called 'heroic code' of extreme bravery in battle has been seen as informing poems in English such as *Beowulf* and *The Battle of Maldon*, no less than the poems of Sigurðr and other heroes in the Poetic Edda, and their literary heirs, the warrior-farmers of the Sagas of Icelanders. And *Beowulf* reveals a more tangible link with early Scandinavia, since it tells of the deeds of legendary heroes of the Danes, Swedes and other early Germanic peoples, and alludes to legendary history also reworked in Icelandic sources such as the fourteenth-century *Hrólfs saga kraka* (see Text I).

Tacitus, *Agricola and Germania*, tr. H. Mattingly (1973).
R. W. Chambers, *Beowulf: An Introduction to the Study of the Poem*. 3rd ed. (1963).
Jónas Kristjánsson, 'Er Egilssaga "Norse"?', *Skáldskaparmál* 3 (1994), 216–31.
R. I. Page, *Norse Myths* (1990, 1994).
G. Turville-Petre, *Myth and Religion of the North* (1964).
A. Wawn, *The Vikings and the Victorians* (2000).

2. The Vikings

The period *c*.750–1050, known as the Viking Age, saw widespread incursions of Scandinavian peoples, mainly Norwegians and Danes, on the cultures of Western Europe. English and Frankish sources record the impact of the *wælwulfas* 'slaughter-wolves', as they are called in the Old English poem *The Battle of Maldon*, first as pagan despoilers of the rich resources of the monasteries on the Northumbrian coast, and across the Channel north of the Seine estuary, in the late eighth century. They conquered and established colonies in Orkney, Shetland, the Hebrides and around the Irish coast in the ninth century, the time also of the settlement of the previously uninhabited Atlantic islands, Iceland and the Faroes. The further colonisation of Greenland, and exploration in North America, are recorded in the Icelandic 'Vinland sagas' (see Text XXI), though these settlements did not turn out to be permanent. The battle of Maldon in 991 was probably part of a campaign led by the Danish king Sven Forkbeard (Sveinn tjúguskegg in Icelandic texts), which culminated in his conquest of the English kingdom in 1013. England was ruled after him by his son Knut (Canute in English, Knútr in Icelandic texts); Scandinavian claims to English rule ended, however, with the defeat of the Norwegian Haraldr harðráði at Stamford Bridge in 1066.

While Viking raiders were ravaging in the west, similar activity was directed at eastern Europe and Russia from what is now Sweden. These Vikings targeted local resources, largely furs and slaves, which they obtained by seizure and the exaction of tribute. The term *Rus*, probably first used by the Finns of north-western Russia to refer to Scandinavians operating in their lands, gave what is now Russia its name. Trading routes were established to the Black Sea and as far south as Constantinople, where Scandinavians served the Byzantine Emperor as mercenary warriors in the Varangian guard.

The Anglo-Saxon and Frankish chroniclers who recorded the Viking raids from the point of view of their victims gave these heathen plunderers an understandably bad press. A more sympathetic representation had to await the development of written culture in Scandinavia following the conversion to Christianity *c.*1000 AD; Icelandic writers of the twelfth and thirteenth centuries, recreating the history of the Viking period, cast a contrastingly heroic glow over the activities of their ancestors. Some testimony contemporaneous to events survives in the form of skaldic verse, derived from eulogies to warlike leaders of the Viking Age. This must have survived for two centuries or more in oral form before it was embedded in the prose works of later writers. Sagas based on these verses and reproducing their warlike ideology record the history of the Norwegian and other Scandinavian kings, and the writers of Sagas of Icelanders elaborated the deeds of ordinary Icelandic farmers into Viking heroic epics.

Further evidence from pre-Christian times survives in the form of runic inscriptions. The runic alphabet was used in Scandinavia before the introduction of Latin alphabet. Although inscriptions appear most often on memorial stones and are brief and formulaic, they chart the movements of those commemorated, frequently travellers from Sweden via the Baltic and Russia to Constantinople. Runic inscriptions also provide valuable linguistic evidence for the early development of the Scandinavian languages (see Text XVII).

The origin of the word Viking (*víkingr*) is obscure. It may derive from the region of Norway around Oslo, known in the Middle Ages as Víkin, or from the substantive *vík* 'small bay', suggesting that Vikings were prone to lurk in coves or bays, or from Old English *wic* 'settlement', particularly used in place-names of ports, associating them rather with centres of trade — whether as legitimate traders or attackers. In *The Battle of Maldon*, *wicingas* is used synonymously with many terms identifying the Norsemen as aggressors (*wælwulfas*) and, especially, seafarers (*brimliþende, sæmenn*). In Old Icelandic texts the word *víkingr* appears tainted with the same disapproval, and is usually applied not to heroic figures but to thugs and '*berserkir*'; but *fara í víking* (to go on a Viking expedition) was a proper rite of passage for the young saga hero.

M. P. Barnes and R. I. Page, *The Scandinavian Runic Inscriptions of Britain* (2006).
S. Blöndal, *The Varangians of Byzantium*, tr. B. S. Benedikz (1978).
P. Foote and D. Wilson, *The Viking Achievement* (1970, repr. 1980).
G. Jones, *A History of the Vikings* (1984).
G. Jones, *The Norse Atlantic Saga* (1986).
J. Jesch, *Women in the Viking Age* (1991).
R. I. Page, *Runes* (1987).
Peter Sawyer, ed., *The Oxford Illustrated History of the Vikings* (1997).

3. The Early History of Iceland

The history of Iceland from its first settlement (dated to 870) down to 1118 is told in the *Íslendingabók* of Ari Þorgilsson (see Text VIII and p. 62 below), probably written about 1134. This book, which in the surviving manuscripts is called Libellus Islandorum — or rather the first, now lost version from 1122–33 on which it is based, which Ari refers to as Íslendingabók — is probably the first narrative work to be written in Icelandic, though Ari himself refers to the first recording of parts of the laws in the eleventh century. Ari uses a system of chronology that relates events in the history of Iceland to the larger picture of the Christian history of Europe. He deals with the settlement and the establishment of the law; the founding of the *Alþingi*, the annual general assembly held at Þingvellir in south-west Iceland each summer at which legislation was passed and litigation pursued; the division of the country into *fjórðungar* ('quarters' or administrative districts; see map on pp. xl–xli); the settlement of Greenland; and — as a climax — the conversion to Christianity and the history of the early bishops.

A more detailed account of the settlement of Iceland is given in *Landnámabók* ('The Book of Settlements'), which may originally have been compiled as early as 1100 by contemporaries of Ari, who has been thought to have had a role in the compilation himself (see Text XIX). It records in topographical order the arrival in Iceland of some 430 settlers, giving details of their families and descendants. Surviving versions are from the thirteenth and fourteenth centuries and later, much expanded with material from Sagas of Icelanders and elsewhere, so that their historicity is hard to assess.

Ari's account of the conversion to Christianity in about 1000 AD tells a remarkable story of the adoption of the new religion by a consensus reached by the ruling oligarchy of large landholders and chieftains. A more detailed account is given in the thirteenth-century *Kristni saga*, probably written by Sturla Þórðarson. The history of the Church in the years 1056–1176 is chronicled in another thirteenth-century work, *Hungrvaka* ('Awakener of Hunger'), relating the history of the first five bishops of Iceland. The *Biskupa sögur*, more extensive biographies of the bishops of the eleventh to the fourteenth centuries, were often written by contemporaries of the bishops themselves or other clerics (see Text XIV).

The laws of the Icelandic commonwealth are preserved in the composite collection known as *Grágás* ('Grey Goose'), found in various fragments and copies the earliest of which is from the mid-twelfth century (see Text XXVII). It is difficult to assess the relation of the surviving material to the originally oral law, recited annually at the Alþingi by the lawspeaker, part of which, according to Ari, was first committed to writing in 1117–18. With the submission of Iceland to Norway in 1262–64 *Grágás* was superseded first by a law code called *Járnsíða* and then by *Jónsbók*, of which many fine manuscripts survive. These codes were drafted in Norway.

The later secular history of Iceland down to the 1260s was told in *Sturlunga saga*, actually a compilation of sagas sometimes called *samtíðarsögur* ('Contemporary Sagas', or more accurately 'Sagas of Contemporaries') (see section 10 below and Text III), since they were written by contemporaries and sometimes eyewitnesses of the events related.

Íslendingabók. Landnámabók, ed. Jakob Benediktsson, *Íslenzk fornrit* I (1968).
Biskupa sögur I, ed. Sigurgeir Steingrímsson, Ólafur Halldórsson and P. Foote, *Íslenzk fornrit* XV (2003) (Includes *Kristni saga*, *Kristni þættir*, *Jóns saga ins helga*).
Biskupa sögur II, ed. Ásdís Egilsdóttir, *Íslenzk fornrit* XVI (2002) (Includes *Hungrvaka*, *Þórláks saga byskups*, *Páls saga byskups*).
Biskupa sögur III, ed. Guðrún Ása Grímsdóttir, *Íslenzk fornrit* XVII (1998) (Includes *Árna saga biskups*, *Lárentíus saga biskups*).
Sturlunga saga I–II, ed. Jón Jóhannesson, Magnús Finnbogason and Kristján Eldjárn (1946).
Íslendingabók – Kristni saga. The Book of the Icelanders – The Story of the Conversion, tr. S. Grønlie (2007).
The Book of Settlements, tr. Hermann Pálsson and P. Edwards (1972).
Laws of Early Iceland I–II, tr. A. Dennis, P. Foote and R. Perkins (1980–2000).
Jón Jóhannesson, *A History of the Old Icelandic Commonwealth* (1974).
Jón Viðar Sigurðsson, *Chieftains and Power in the Icelandic Commonwealth* (1999).
D. Strömbäck, *The Conversion of Iceland* (1957).
Einar Ól. Sveinsson, *The Age of the Sturlungs*, Islandica XXXVI (1953).
J. Byock, *Viking Age Iceland* (2001).
Orri Vésteinsson, *The Christianization of Iceland: Priests, Power and Social Change 1000–1300* (2000).

4. The Language

This Reader offers texts, mostly in excerpts, in the original language from the full range of Old Icelandic literary genres. Many of the best-known texts can be read in translation, and references to some available translations are included at the end of each section of this Introduction and on pp. xxxvi–xxxviii as well as in the separate introductions to each extract. But experiencing the texts in their original language repays the difficulty of learning the language in many ways. This is of course true of literature in any language. In the particular case of

Icelandic, the distinctive laconic and often ironical style of the sagas is often diluted in translation. The highly specialised linguistic requirements of poetry, particularly the highly technical demands of skaldic poetry, cannot be adequately met in translation; and leaving aside issues of literary style, there are pitfalls in attempting to assess the validity of Old Norse texts as historical sources without reference to their original form and idiom, especially where their import depends on the intricate interweaving of prose with verse citation.

A basic introduction to the Old Norse language and its relation to Modern Icelandic can be found in *A New Introduction to Old Norse. Part 1: Grammar*, Chapter 1, and a bibliography of grammatical and linguistic works on p. 267 of the same book (2nd edition). A supplementary list is included below, concentrating on dictionaries of most use to students, and works available in English.

Stefán Karlsson, *The Icelandic Language* (2004).

J. Fritzner, *Ordbog over det gamle norske Sprog* I–III (1883–96); IV, Finn Hødnebø, *Rettelser og Tillegg* (1972) (Old Norse–Danish/Norwegian).

R. Cleasby and G.Vigfusson, *An Icelandic-English Dictionary* (1874).

G. T. Zoega, *A Concise Dictionary of Old Icelandic* (1919).

Ordbog over det norrøne prosasprog/A Dictionary of Old Norse Prose (1: a–bam, 2: ban–da, 3: de–em) (1995–, in progress) (Old Norse–Danish and English).

Sveinbjörn Egilsson, *Lexicon Poeticum*, rev. Finnur Jónsson (1931) (Old Norse–Danish; poetic, particularly skaldic, vocabulary).

B. La Farge and J. Tucker, *Glossary to the Poetic Edda* (1992).

5. Sagas

The word *saga* is related to the verb *segja* 'to say', meaning to say or tell, and refers in medieval texts to almost any kind of narrative predominantly in prose (though the term is not used of some books that we would call chronicles). Icelandic medieval narratives are of many different kinds, some of them unique to Icelandic, others translations or adaptations of other European genres. Their division into different categories or types of saga is largely the work of modern scholars, however; though the terms *konungasögur* ('Kings' Sagas') and *riddarasögur* ('Knights' Sagas' or romances) occur occasionally in medieval contexts, the others are modern inventions.

The development of saga writing has sometimes been represented as a progression from the early translation of Latin Saints' Lives into the vernacular, to the full flowering of the Sagas of Icelanders, and then to a decline into a fashion for more fantastic forms; but this is misleading. The writing of one kind of saga did not cease with the development of new types, and some of the translations of 'fantastic' European romances are among the earliest sagas to be written. The reality is that most of these kinds of saga were being written concurrently throughout the medieval period, and cross-fertilised and influenced each other.

According to the Preface to Snorri Sturluson's Saga of St Óláfr, *Þat var meirr en tvau hundruð vetra tólfræð er Ísland var byggt, áðr menn tœki hér sǫgur at rita* 'It was more than 240 years after the settlement of Iceland that people began to write sagas here' (*Heimskringla* II, 422). This places the beginning of saga writing at about 1110, which agrees with modern estimates; there is evidence of vernacular writing in Iceland from the early twelfth century (for an account of this early period of Icelandic writing, see Turville-Petre 1953). Snorri's phrase *sǫgur at rita* highlights the necessary question whether there was such a thing as a pre-literary, oral saga. It is assumed that most of the sagas must go back to oral roots, but the question of the forms that oral narrative might have taken is still much debated (see Clover 1986), and discussions of the sagas as literary types must be limited to the written texts we know.

'Ór Óláfs sǫgu ins helga inni sérstǫku' in *Heimskringla* II, ed. Bjarni Aðalbjarnarson, *Íslenzk fornrit* XXVII (1945), pp. 419–51.
C. Clover, 'The Long Prose Form', *Arkiv för nordisk filologi* 101 (1986), 10–39.
P. Foote, 'Sagnaskemtan: Reykjahólar 1119', *Saga-Book* XIV, 226–39 (1953–56) (repr. in *Aurvandilstá* (1984), 65–83).
Gísli Sigurðsson, *The Medieval Icelandic Saga and Oral Tradition* (2004).
G. Turville-Petre, *Origins of Icelandic Literature* (1953).

6. Sagas of Icelanders

The best-known category of saga is the *Íslendingasögur* or Sagas of Icelanders, also known as Family Sagas. These are now taken to be the most distinctive and significant Icelandic saga form, although this was not always the case; in the nineteenth century, when the sagas were read more literally as historical sources, the Kings' Sagas were valued more highly, at least by readers outside Iceland. There are about 40 Sagas of Icelanders, narrating events that mostly took place or were said to have taken place in the period 930–1030, which is therefore often called the 'Saga Age'. Many begin with preludes reaching back before the beginning of the settlement of Iceland in 870. The sagas range in length from just a few pages to the epic scope of *Njáls saga* (see Text XXVI), 159 chapters in the standard edition. Some, such as *Gísla saga* or *Grettis saga*, are biographically structured on the life of a single individual; others, such as *Laxdœla saga* (see Text XV), deal with several generations of the same family or of the inhabitants of a district. Most of the main characters, and some of the events of the sagas, are clearly historical, though their treatment is fictional. Since the sagas were written during the thirteenth century about events some three centuries earlier, they have been compared with historical novels (see Harris 1986), but this undervalues their genuinely historical intent to reconstruct the past in a manner which the author and audience probably thought of as likely to be true. From a modern perspective we can see that thirteenth-century preoccupations, and sometimes reflections of thirteenth-century events, have been projected onto the sagas' recreation of the past, and in fact the whole project of the writing of the Sagas of Icelanders is often interpreted as a reaction to the turbulent political situation in thirteenth-century Iceland, a deliberate idealising of the distinctively Icelandic Commonwealth period at a time when Iceland was submitting to the Norwegian throne. It is also significant that the period covered by the sagas exactly spans the period of Iceland's conversion to Christianity in 1000 AD, and a major preoccupation in many sagas is either the event of the conversion itself, or the contrast of the author's attitude to the pagan past with his own Christian world view.

These sagas can be divided into sub-groups on the basis of their geographical origin within Iceland; those from the east (such as *Hrafnkels saga*) tend to be shorter, those from the north and west, such as *Kormaks saga* (see Text IV) and *Bjarnar saga Hítdœlakappa* (see Text V), more often include skaldic verses, allegedly spoken by the characters in the sagas themselves. There are also thematic groupings: the 'outlaw sagas' about Grettir, Gísli and Hǫrðr, and the poets' sagas, including those believed to be the very earliest Sagas of Icelanders, dealing with Icelanders who served as skalds at the courts of Scandinavian rulers. Also included in the Sagas of Icelanders are the so-called Vinland Sagas, dealing with the settlement of Greenland and the expeditions made from there to North America; the name derives from *Vínland*, meaning 'land of wine', the name given to one of the places visited (see Text XXI). Archaeological investigations in North America have confirmed the presence of Viking settlers at L'Anse aux Meadows in Newfoundland, although the Vinland sagas include a good deal of fanciful and confused material.

The Sagas of Icelanders are sometimes described as feud sagas. Some critics have interpreted feud as a fundamental structuring device in these sagas, others have drawn the conclusion that feud was as much a preoccupation in medieval Icelandic society as it was in the literary world of the sagas.

Íslenzk fornrit II–XIV (1933–91).

Íslendinga sögur, ed. Jón Torfason et al., 2 vols (1985–86) (Version in Modern Icelandic spelling, also available on CD-rom with searchable concordance (1996)).

The Complete Sagas of Icelanders I–V, tr. Viðar Hreinsson et al. (1997); several of the sagas in this collection are reproduced in *The Sagas of Icelanders*, introduction by R. Kellogg (2000).

T. M. Andersson, *The Problem of Icelandic Saga Origins: A Historical Survey* (1964).

T. M. Andersson and W. I. Miller, 'Introduction'. In *Law and Literature in Medieval Iceland: Ljósvetninga saga and Valla-Ljóts saga* (1989).

Einar Ól. Sveinsson, *Dating the Icelandic Sagas* (1958).

J. Harris, 'Saga as Historical Novel'. In *Structure and Meaning in Old Norse Literature. New Approaches to Textual Analysis and Literary Criticism.* Ed. John Lindow, Lars Lönnroth and Gerd Wolfgang Weber (1986), 187–219.

K. Liestøl, *The Origin of the Icelandic Family Sagas* (1930).

W. I. Miller, *Bloodtaking and Peacemaking: Feud, Law and Society in Saga Iceland* (1990).

P. M. Sørensen, *Saga and Society* (1993).

J. Tucker, ed., *Sagas of Icelanders. A Book of Essays* (1989).

Vésteinn Ólason, *Dialogues with the Viking Age: Narration and Representation in the Sagas of the Icelanders* (1998).

7. Kings' Sagas

The sagas known as *konungasögur* or Kings' Sagas are mainly historical biographies of the kings of Norway, though other Scandinavian states are represented too: *Knýtlinga saga* concerns the kings of Denmark, and *Orkneyinga saga* the rulers of Orkney, technically not kings but jarls. According to a chronological model the Kings' Sagas would have to precede the Sagas of Icelanders, since their roots lie in earlier historical works, some in Latin, some in the vernacular, written in both Norway and Iceland in the twelfth century. The *Íslendingabók* of Ari Þorgilsson (see Text VIII), from about 1130, is an example of this early historiography, and of course the surviving version concentrates on the history of Iceland; but Ari's preface tells us of an earlier version, now lost, that included *konunga ævi* ('lives of kings'). It is not clear what form these took or how detailed they were. For further details of early historiography, see the Introduction to Text VI below (pp. 62–64, and bibliography p. 66). The Kings' Sagas also have roots in hagiography (the lives of saints or *heilagra manna sögur*), since they draw on early lives of the two missionary kings of Norway, Óláfr Tryggvason, credited with the conversion of the Nordic countries, and his successor Óláfr Haraldsson *inn helgi* ('the Saint').

The fact that Icelanders were involved in historical writing from the start, in Norway as well as in Iceland, either as authors or as authoritative sources, must be linked with the fact that Icelanders had a virtual monopoly of the profession of court poet to Scandinavian rulers, composing the complex *dróttkvætt* ('court metre') or skaldic verse (see 12 below) that was used as an essential oral source by the writers of Kings' Sagas. It is said in the Prologue to Snorri Sturluson's *Heimskringla* that this poetry is the most reliable kind of historical source since the complexity of the metre renders it less prone to corruption and change than oral report not in verse would be. The stylistic technique developed in the Kings' Sagas, where a verse is cited as authority for what has been said in a prose passage, undoubtedly influenced the practice of citing verse in the Sagas of Icelanders too, where it is used to promote a realistic impression even in cases where it is not difficult to see that the verse cited has no historical authenticity.

The most distinguished example of the Kings' Saga genre is Snorri Sturluson's *Heimskringla* (see Text VII), a collection of sixteen sagas of kings of Norway from its legendary origins to the late twelfth century, structured as a triptych of which the central and longest third is the biography of King Óláfr the Saint. Snorri probably wrote the collection in the 1220s or 1230s; he had already written the saga of King Óláfr as a free-standing work before incorporating it in the collection. Snorri drew on earlier, shorter works covering all or some of the same historical span, such as *Morkinskinna* and *Fagrskinna* (see Text VI), but these are continuous narratives rather than being divided into biographies of individual kings. The writing of Kings'

Sagas after Snorri became a process of expansion, using his work as a basis but interpolating material of different kinds; ironically enough, a late compilation such as the fourteenth-century Flateyjarbók reinstates some of the more fantastic hagiographical or legendary material that Snorri had pruned from his sources. Another kind of elaboration found in both *Morkinskinna* and Flateyjarbók is the inclusion of *þættir* (the singular form is *þáttr*), often thought of as comparable to the modern short story but characterised by their context within the texture of the Kings' Sagas; they typically relate an encounter between the king in question and a visitor to his court, usually an Icelander, and help to reveal the king's character in a fictional, and often humorous mode (see *Auðunar þáttr*, Text XVI).

The assembling of the Kings' Sagas into these larger wholes tends to mask their diversity; in *Heimskringla* the mythological and legendary *Ynglinga saga*, drawing on poetic and oral sources to relate the descent of the early kings of Sweden and Norway from the pagan gods, contrasts both with the hagiographical Saga of St Óláfr and with sagas giving near-eyewitness accounts of events of the late twelfth century. *Hákonar saga Hákonarsonar*, indeed, written by Sturla Þórðarson, chronicles the life of the king who oversaw the submission of Iceland to Norway, and can be read alongside *Sturlunga saga* as a source for the thirteenth-century history of Iceland.

Flateyjarbók, ed. Guðbrandur Vigfússon and C. R. Unger, 3 vols (1860–68).
Heimskringla I–III, ed. Bjarni Aðalbjarnarson, Íslenzk fornrit XXVI–XXVIII (1941–51).
Hákonar saga Hákonarsonar, ed. G. Vigfusson, tr. G. Dasent, Icelandic Sagas II and IV, Rolls series (1887–94).
Knýtlinga saga, in *Danakonunga sögur*, ed. Bjarni Guðnason, Íslenzk fornrit XXXV (1982).
Orkneyinga saga, ed. Finnbogi Guðmundsson, Íslenzk fornrit XXXIV (1965).
Stories from the Sagas of the Kings, ed. A. Faulkes (1980).
Two Icelandic Stories, ed. A Faulkes (1967, repr. 1978).
Heimskringla, tr. L. M. Hollander (1964).
S. Bagge, *Society and Politics in Snorri Sturluson's Heimskringla* (1991).
J. Harris, 'Theme and Genre in some *Íslendinga þættir*', *Scandinavian Studies* 48, 1–28 (1976).
J. Knirk, *Oratory in the Kings' Sagas* (1981).
E. A. Rowe, *The Development of Flateyjarbók* (2004).
D. Whaley, *Heimskringla, An Introduction* (1991).

8. Legendary sagas (*fornaldarsögur*)

The category of *fornaldarsögur* ('sagas of the ancient time'), known as Legendary or Mythical–Heroic Sagas, is more miscellaneous, encompassing about thirty texts many of which are based in the remote Germanic past and include many fantastic episodes and themes. The increasing popularity of these sagas in the fourteenth and fifteenth centuries, and the fact that the Sagas of Icelanders believed to be comparatively late (such as *Grettis saga*) show a taste for this kind of material, has led the *fornaldarsögur* to be dismissed as a late and even decadent form, the suggestion being that at a time of cultural decline the Icelanders sought refuge in an escapist view of the golden age of the heroic past. More recently an opposing interpretation has been that the increased taste, from the late thirteenth century onwards, for more fictional forms, including a readiness to engage with foreign models, represents a new literary self-confidence in Iceland. As far as chronology is concerned, it is important to bear in mind that what may have been the earliest example of this genre, *Skjǫldunga saga*, a history of the earliest Danish kings which is now mostly lost, was written probably near the end of the twelfth century, before any of the Sagas of Icelanders were written. The legendary *Ynglinga saga* would also come into this category if it were not subsumed into Snorri's historical scheme. So sagas of this kind were being produced throughout the period of composition of the Sagas of Icelanders.

Some *fornaldarsögur* are prose retellings of known heroic poems; *Vǫlsunga saga*, for instance, is a rather flat paraphrase of the legendary poems of the Poetic Edda, with the story of the dragon-slaying Sigurðr at its centre. Another group closer to folktale in its origins is sometimes called 'Adventure Tales' and includes themes such as the quest, sometimes but not always for a wife and kingdom. The way in which the *fornaldarsögur* put their diverse sources to use as entertainment can be illustrated by the story of Bǫðvarr Bjarki in *Hrólfs saga kraka* (see Text I), which tells the essentially heroic story of a hero who rids the hall of the Danish King Hrólfr (the Hroþulf of *Beowulf*) of a marauding beast. A similar story is told in *Beowulf* in epic mode, but gets a burlesque treatment in the Icelandic saga.

Fornaldar sögur Norðurlanda I–IV, ed. Guðni Jónsson (1950).
Hervarar saga ok Heiðreks, ed. C. Tolkien and G. Turville-Petre (1956).
Saga Heiðreks konungs ins vitra (= *Hervarar saga*), ed. and tr. C. Tolkien (1960).

The Saga of the Volsungs, ed. and tr. R. G. Finch (1965).
Icelandic Histories and Romances, tr. R. O'Connor (2002).
The Saga of King Hrolf Kraki, tr. J. Byock (1998).
Seven Viking Romances, tr. Hermann Pálsson and P. Edwards (1985).
Ármann Jakobsson et al., eds, *Fornaldarsagornas struktur och ideologi* (2003) (includes several articles in English).
C. Clover, 'Maiden-Warriors and Other Sons', *Journal of English and Germanic Philology* 85, 35–49 (1986).
Torfi Tulinius, *The Matter of the North. The Rise of Literary Fiction in Thirteenth-Century Iceland* (2002).

9. *Heilagra manna sögur*

Other saga genres are more closely related to their European counterparts. The genre of *heilagra manna sögur* ('sagas of holy people', Saints' Lives) has the distinction of being the first kind of saga to be written in Iceland. The practice of writing was introduced to Iceland by the Church, as elsewhere in Europe, and the first documents written in the vernacular language were, not surprisingly, translations of foreign religious texts, such as Saints' Lives, for the instruction of lay people. One of the earliest surviving is *Matheus saga,* one of the *postola sögur* (Sagas of Apostles), which must date from earlier than 1150; at the other extreme *Thómas saga erkibyskups*, a life of the twelfth-century English saint Thomas Becket, whose cult was enormously popular in Iceland, is extant in several versions from the thirteenth century and later. The genre is represented in this Reader by the account of a miracle from *Maríu saga* (Text XIII). Although this group belongs to an international genre, Turville-Petre and others argue that the realistic mode and use of dialogue of the native Icelandic genres can be traced back to the style of these early translated texts: as he says (1953, xx), 'the learned literature did not teach the Icelanders what to think or what to say, but it taught them how to say it'.

Clemens saga, ed. and tr. H. Carron (2005).
The Icelandic Legend of Saint Dorothy, ed. K. Wolf (1997).
Heilagra manna sögur, ed. C. R. Unger (1877).
The Old Norse–Icelandic Legend of Saint Barbara, ed. and tr. K. Wolf (2000).
Postola sögur, ed. C. R. Unger (1874).
Matheus saga postula, ed. Ólafur Halldórsson (1994).
Thómas saga erkibyskups, ed. C. R. Unger (1869).
Jónas Kristjánsson, 'Learned Style or Saga Style?' In *Speculum Norrœnum*, ed. U. Dronke et al. (1981), 260–92.

O. Widding et al., 'The Lives of the Saints in Old Norse Prose: A Handlist'. Updated version in M. Cormack, *The Saints in Iceland: Their Veneration from the Conversion to 1400* (1963).

10. Contemporary Sagas (*samtíðarsögur*)

The genre of *Heilagra manna sögur* has connections both with the lives of the missionary kings (see above under Kings' Sagas), and with the *biskupa sögur*, lives of the bishops of Iceland from the eleventh to the fourteenth centuries. Of these, the lives of the two bishops who achieved sanctity, Þorlákr and Jón of Hólar (see Text XIV), though classic hagiographies in their rhetoric and cataloguing of miracles, have features in common with the *samtíðarsögur* ('Contemporary Sagas'). These last are mainly collected into a large compilation called *Sturlunga saga* (see Text III), and deal with more recent events in Iceland's history than the Sagas of Icelanders, in particular the extensive feuds and factional war leading up to the submission of Iceland to Norway in 1262–64. With these sagas we come closest to the modern conception of history, and they are generally accepted as historically reliable in a way that the Sagas of Icelanders are not, but their effect of realism is often created using the same carefully contrived conventions as those of the more fictional genre.

Hrafns saga Sveinbjarnarsonar, ed. Guðrún P. Helgadóttir (1987).
Sturlunga saga, ed. Jón Jóhannesson et al., 2 vols (1946).
Þorgils saga ok Hafliða, ed. U. Brown (1952).
Sturlunga saga, tr. J. McGrew and R. G. Thomas (1970–74).
Einar Ól. Sveinsson, *The Age of the Sturlungs. Icelandic Civilization in the Thirteenth Century,* tr. Jóhann S. Hannesson, Islandica XXXVI (1953).
P. Foote, 'Sturlusaga and its Background', *Saga-Book* 13, 207–37 (1950–51).
G. Nordal, '*Sturlunga saga* and the Context of Saga-Writing', in *Introductory Essays on Egils saga and Njáls saga,* ed. J. Hines and D. Slay (1992), 1–14.
G. Nordal, *Ethics and Action in Thirteenth-Century Iceland* (1998).
S. Tranter, *Sturlunga saga: The Role of the Creative Compiler* (1987).

11. *Riddarasögur*

The *riddarasögur* ('Sagas of Knights') or chivalric sagas can be divided into translations of romances popular in Europe and England, and indigenous Icelandic romances making use of the same courtly milieu and themes. As with the *fornaldarsögur*, the writing of *riddarasögur* is sometimes seen as a late development, but we know from a preface attached to the earliest surviving one, *Tristrams saga ok Ísǫndar* (see Text XII), that it was composed in 1226 at the court of King Hákon of Norway, which makes it squarely contemporaneous with the writing of the earliest Sagas of Icelanders. Although a new florid style was developed for the writing of *riddarasögur*, these early translations at least are strikingly similar to the Sagas of Icelanders in their use of an apparently impersonal narrative perspective, and while tending to stick closely to the events recorded in their originals, strip out most of the elements of description and refined analysis of emotion characteristic of their French originals.

Riddarasögur, ed. Bjarni Vilhjálmsson, 6 vols (1949–54).
Norse Romance I–III, ed. M. Kalinke (1999).
G. Barnes, 'The Riddarasögur: A Medieval Exercise in Translation', *Saga-Book* 19 (1977), 403–41.
G. Barnes, 'Arthurian Chivalry in Old Norse', in *Arthurian Literature* VII (1987), 50–102.
M. Kalinke, *King Arthur North by Northwest. The matière de Bretagne in Old Norse–Icelandic Romances* (1981).
M. Kalinke, 'Scribes, Editors, and the *riddarasögur*', *Arkiv för nordisk filologi* 97 (1982), 36–51.
H. G. Leach, *Angevin Britain and Scandinavia* (1921, repr. 1975).
P. M. Mitchell, 'Scandinavian Literature', in *Arthurian Literature in the Middle Ages*, ed. R. S. Loomis (1959), 462–71.
M. Schlauch, *Romance in Iceland* (1934, repr. 1973).
G. W. Weber, 'The Decadence of Feudal Myth: Towards a Theory of *Riddarasaga*', in *Structure and Meaning in Old Norse Literature. New Approaches to Textual Analysis and Literary Criticism*, ed. John Lindow, Lars Lönnroth and Gerd Wolfgang Weber (1986), 415–54.

12. Eddic poetry

Eddic poetry is so named after the collection of 29 poems called the Poetic Edda, preserved in a manuscript from *c.*1270 known as the Codex Regius, and dating from the ninth to the twelfth centuries. The origin of the term *edda* is uncertain. It was used of the Codex Regius collection by its seventeenth-century owner, Bishop Brynjólfur Sveinsson, who called it 'Sæmundar Edda' (mistakenly believing it to be written by the early Icelandic historian, Sæmundr Sigfússon) to distinguish it from Snorra Edda, the prose work by Snorri Sturluson. This suggests that in the seventeenth century the term was taken to imply a collection of mythological material, though it is clear that in the Middle Ages, as for Snorri Sturluson, it meant 'Art of Poetry'. The poems of the Codex Regius are arranged thematically, ten dealing with mythological material, nineteen with heroes of the legendary Germanic past. A section of perhaps eight leaves, now missing from the manuscript, would have included further heroic poems. Six mythological poems (or parts of them), one of which is not in the Codex Regius, are preserved in the fragmentary manuscript AM 748 I a 4to, from about 1300, which may have been another, similar poetical compilation, and a few others in manuscripts of Snorra Edda and elsewhere.

The metres of eddic poetry derive from the Germanic alliterative pattern essential also to Old English, Old Saxon and some Old High German verse. While the structural unit in these languages is the long line made up of two linked half-lines, eddic verse breaks up into stanzas of variable length, but most usually of eight lines (equivalent to four Old English long lines, the lines linked in pairs by alliteration). The prevailing metre, *fornyrðislag* 'old story (or 'talk') metre', normally includes two stressed syllables and a varying number of unstressed syllables in each line, and either one or two stressed syllables in the first half-line alliterate with the first stressed syllable of the second half-line. Variant metres are *málaháttr* 'speeches metre', in which each line is heavier, and made up of no fewer than five syllables, and *ljóðaháttr* 'songs-form', in which two lines of *fornyrðislag* are followed by a third, so called full line, which alliterates within itself. A basic account of eddic metres is found in Turville-Petre 1976, xiii–xvi.

The first four poems of the Edda focus on the god Óðinn, and — through his perpetual quest for wisdom — on mythological and gnomic lore. All are cast in direct speech. *Vǫluspá*, made up of Óðinn's dialogue with a sybil from the giant world, relates the events — past, present and future — in the history of the gods, ending in their downfall at *ragnarǫk* ('the doom of the gods') and the regeneration of the world and a new generation of gods. *Vafþrúðnismál* and *Grímnismál* are both catalogue poems set in narrative frameworks; *Hávamál* 'the speeches of the high one' is itself a compilation of several separate poems, incorporating catalogues of gnomic wisdom as well as events from the god's own history. *Skírnismál* narrates the winning by the god Freyr of the giant-bride Gerðr. The remaining mythological poems are concerned with Þórr, including the humorous *Hárbarðsljóð*, in which Þórr is outwitted by the cunning of Óðinn, and *Þrymskviða*, the burlesque account of Þórr's journey to Jǫtunheimr to retrieve his stolen hammer (see Text IX). *Lokasenna* is a satirical poem in which the gods are comprehensively attacked by the ambiguous god-giant Loki, who accuses each of them in turn of immorality; it ends with Þórr's forcible silencing of Loki.

Vǫlundarkviða (see Text X), which tells of the supernatural smith Vǫlundr ('Weland' in Old English, later Wayland) and his revenge against the tyrant Níðuðr, may be seen as a bridge between the mythological poems proper, and those dealing with the world of men (though it is followed by the mythological *Alvíssmál*, another catalogue set in the narrative frame of a wisdom contest, about Þórr's encounter with a dwarf).

The heroic poems of the Edda deal with legendary figures — the two Helgis, Sigurðr, Gunnarr and Hamðir (see Text XXV) whose stories must originally have been distinct, but who, even before the compilation of the Codex Regius, were beginning to be linked into a cycle. This process culminated in the fourteenth-century *Vǫlsunga saga*, a prose retelling that completes the fusion of these legends into a single family saga and attempts to smooth out the elements of contradiction and overlap introduced by the juxtaposition of originally separate poems from a variety of styles and periods. At the centre is the hero Sigurðr, slayer of the dragon Fáfnir (Siegfried in German versions of the story), who is betrothed to the valkyrie Brynhildr but marries Guðrún Gjúkadóttir, and suffers vengeance at the hand of Guðrún's brother Gunnarr, who is married to Brynhildr.

Some figures in the eddic poems, such as the Atli of *Atlakviða* (Attila the Hun) and his enemy Gunnarr, king of the Burgundians, have an identifiable historical background and elements of their stories can be found in early histories such as that of the sixth-century Jordanes (see Dronke 1969, 29–38 and 192–96). The story of Sigurðr is told with considerable differences in the Middle High German *Nibelungenlied*.

Die Lieder des Codex Regius nebst verwandten Denkmälern, ed. G. Neckel, rev. H. Kuhn (1962).

Hávamál, ed. D. Evans, with *Glossary and Index* by A. Faulkes (1986–87).

Vǫluspá, ed. S. Nordal, tr. B. Benedikz and J. McKinnell (1978).

The Poetic Edda I: *Heroic Poems*, ed. and tr. U. Dronke (1969).

The Poetic Edda II: *Mythological Poems*, ed. and tr. U. Dronke (1997).

The Poetic Edda, tr. C. Larrington (1996).
P. Acker and C. Larrington, eds, *The Poetic Edda: Essays on Old Norse Mythology* (2002).
B. Fidjestøl, *The Dating of Eddic Poetry: A Historical Survey and Methodological Investigation* (1999).
R. J. Glendinning and Haraldur Bessason, eds, *Edda. A Collection of Essays* (1983).
T. Gunnell, *The Origins of Drama in Scandinavia* (1995).
P. Hallberg, *Old Icelandic Poetry* (1975).
J. McKinnell, *Both One and Many. Essays on Change and Variety in Late Norse Heathenism* (1994).
K. von See et al., *Kommentar zu den Liedern der Edda* I–V (1993–2006).

13. Skaldic poetry

This term derives from the Old Norse word *skáld* 'poet', appropriately in that, while eddic poetry is anonymous, most skaldic poetry is attributed to a named poet. The Icelandic term for the metre most common in skaldic poetry is *dróttkvætt*, an adjective derived from *dróttkvæðr* 'poetry in court metre', referring to the aristocratic milieu of this poetic style. The earliest surviving skaldic poetry dates from the ninth century, but poems in skaldic metres, usually on religious subjects, continued to be composed throughout the fourteenth century. Skaldic poetry is famous for its convoluted syntax, elaborate diction and taxing alliterative, rhyming and syllable-counting requirements (for an exposition of these, see VII C below).

The Kings' Sagas include accounts of skalds appearing at courts, in Norway and elsewhere, to offer poems in praise of rulers, and it seems there was a premium set on length and elaborate construction (there are stories of skalds who get into trouble by offering a mere *flokkr* or sequence of verses in place of a *drápa*, a formal poem of at least twenty stanzas, including at least one refrain); but most surviving poems are experienced in more fragmentary form, in quotations in Kings' Sagas, often of no more than a single stanza, in the context of the event they refer to. Their reconstitution into long poems, few of which can be considered complete, and where the order of the stanzas is often in doubt, is the work of modern editors. On the other hand, the authors of the histories who cite these verses as corroboration for their historical narrative, and for whom they must often have been the only source, usually identify the poet by name and often give a name to the poem to which the verse belongs as well (see Texts VI and VII for the citing of verses as historical evidence). Most early court poets were Norwegian, but from *c.*1000 most skalds seem to have come from Iceland.

In the Sagas of Icelanders the citing of verse is superficially similar in that an episode may be supported by the citation of a single verse, but the verse is more often woven into the fabric of the narrative as dialogue, or the comment of an individual on the events of the saga. These verses are usually *lausavísur* or free-standing verses, specific to the occasion they refer to, though attempts have been made to reconstruct longer poems from some. Like the verses in the Kings' Sagas, some of these verses must have survived in oral form from the time of their composition (which may often have been later than the events or claimed events to which they are tied in the sagas), and have been the sources for the thirteenth-century prose narratives in which they are incorporated. But their historical authenticity is harder to establish than that of the Kings' Sagas verses, and some are taken to be 'forgeries', or in less emotive terms, embellishments composed by the saga authors themselves to enhance the apparent historicity of their narratives.

A sub-group among the Sagas of Icelanders is the so-called poets' sagas, written mostly early in the thirteenth century, which seem to indicate an interest in the biographies of Icelandic poets. But although they quote a good deal of occasional verse attributed to the poet, they seem almost to avoid the public or historical role of the court poet (see Text IV, which features love verse by the poet Kormakr, and even a stanza he shares with his beloved, Steingerðr; and Text V, in which the rival poets Bjǫrn Hítdœlakappi and Þórðr Kolbeinsson recite verses). The saga which investigates most closely the temperament and sensibility of the poet is *Egils saga Skallagrímssonar*, often supposed to be the work of Snorri Sturluson.

Another repository of skaldic poetry dismembered into single stanzas, and an invaluable source of information about it, is the Prose Edda of Snorri Sturluson (also known as Snorra Edda). In this treatise Snorri set out, according to his own account, to instruct young poets in the mysteries of skaldic verse at a time when its conventions may have become less popular and memories of the pagan religion that underpinned it were beginning to fade. The work consists of four parts: a Prologue; *Gylfaginning*, an outline of the pre-Christian Norse religion supported by quotations from eddic mythological poems; *Skáldskaparmál* ('the language of poetry') giving an account of the kennings (poetic periphrases) and *heiti* (poetic synonyms) used by the skalds, and liberally exemplified by quotations; and *Háttatal* ('catalogue of verse-forms'), which takes the form of a poem, composed by Snorri himself, in 102 stanzas, each exemplifying a variant skaldic verse-form. His Edda is thus a vital source of information on both mythology and the skaldic craft. Although it is primarily a learned work, the stories in *Gylfaginning* and *Skáldskaparmál* are told with verve and humour (see Text II below). *Háttatal* was most probably composed after Snorri's first visit to Norway in 1218–20, and the rest of his Edda may well have been written later.

While the art of skaldic poetry had acknowledged roots in the pagan religion, its conventions were adapted after the Conversion to Christian themes. Poets of the Conversion period straddle the two religions: Hallfreðr vandræðaskáld, for instance, composed for both the pagan Jarl Hákon and, later, Hákon's proselytising Christian successor, Óláfr Tryggvason, and the poet's saga dramatises the story of his own conversion (in which he demands, and gets, the king's agreement to act as his godfather) and its implications for his poetic craft. By the twelfth century Church patronage was encouraging the development of a genre of religious *drápur*, adapting the conventions of *dróttkvætt* within a literate monastic culture, in contrast to the oral context of their predecessors. Where earlier encomiastic poems survive fragmentarily as scattered references within the Kings' Sagas, twelfth-century *drápur* such as *Geisli*, composed by the Icelander Einarr Skúlason for recitation at the shrine of St Óláfr in Niðaróss (Trondheim), probably in 1153, are the earliest to survive complete. Poets continued to compose extended poems in *dróttkvætt* into the fourteenth century, fusing traditional skaldic elements with themes derived from continental material.

A development from skaldic poetry, probably originating early in the fourteenth century and remaining popular well into the nineteenth, was the distinctively Icelandic genre of *rímur*. These long narrative poems, sometimes interspersed with lyrical passages called *mansöngvar* ('love poems'), often reworked the narrative material of sagas, usually *fornaldarsögur* and *riddarasögur*. They made use of skaldic diction but with rhythms closer to those of ballads. *Óláfs ríma Haraldssonar* (Text XXII) is the earliest surviving example.

Den norsk-islandske skjaldedigtning, A I–II: *Tekst efter håndskrifterne*, B I–II: *Rettet tekst*, ed. Finnur Jónsson (1912–15).
Skaldic Poetry of the Scandinavian Middle Ages: A New Edition. II *Poetry from the Kings' Sagas* 2, ed. Kari Ellen Gade (2009); VII *Poetry on Christian Subjects*, ed. Margaret Clunies Ross (2007). (Website: www.skaldic.arts.usyd.edu.au)
Einarr Skúlason's Geisli, A Critical Edition, ed. M. Chase (2005).
Fourteenth-Century Icelandic Verse on the Virgin Mary, ed. K. Wrightson (2001).
Snorri Sturluson, *Edda: Prologue and Gylfaginning*, ed. A. Faulkes (2nd edn 2005).
Snorri Sturluson, *Edda: Skáldskaparmál*, ed. A. Faulkes, 2 vols (1998).
Snorri Sturluson, *Háttatal*, ed. A. Faulkes (1991).
Snorri Sturluson, *Edda*, tr. A. Faulkes (1987).
K. Attwood, 'Intertextual Aspects of the Twelfth-Century Christian *drápur*'. *Saga-Book* 24, 221–39.
A. Faulkes, *What was Viking Poetry For?* Inaugural Lecture, University of Birmingham (1993).
B. Fidjestøl, *Det norrøne fyrstediktet* (1982).
B. Fidjestøl, *Selected Papers* (1997).
R. Frank, *Old Norse Court Poetry*, Islandica XLII (1978).
K. E. Gade, *The Structure of Old Norse Dróttkvætt Poetry*, Islandica XLII (1994).
E. A. Kock, *Notationes Norrœnæ* (1923–41).
R. Meissner, *Die Kenningar der Skalden* (1921, repr. 1984).
G. Nordal, *Tools of Literacy. The Role of Skaldic Verse in Icelandic Textual Culture of the Twelfth and Thirteenth Centuries* (2001).
R. Perkins, 'Rowing Chants and the Origins of *dróttkvæðr háttr*'. *Saga-Book* 21 (1984–85), 155–221.
R. Poole, *Viking Poems on War and Peace: A Study in Skaldic Narrative* (1991).
G. Turville-Petre, *Scaldic Poetry* (1969).

14. Modern Icelandic

Icelandic is a conservative language and has changed less since the Middle Ages than the other Scandinavian languages, so that medieval texts are still comparatively accessible to the modern Icelandic reader. Many editions of medieval texts, including most of those in this Reader, are printed in a normalised spelling that aims to represent the language of the thirteenth century; though this differs somewhat from modern Icelandic spelling, it is much closer to modern spelling than is that of the original manuscripts (see pp. vi–viii above and Stefán Karlsson, *The Icelandic Language* (2004), section 2). Although pronunciation has changed considerably, this is masked by the fact that many teachers of Old Norse adopt modern pronunciation. For an account of differences between Old and Modern Icelandic pronunciation, see *NION* I, pp. 14–21.

Ásgeir Blöndal Magnússon, *Íslensk orðsifjabók* (1989) [etymological dictionary].
Ásta Svavarsdóttir and Margrét Jónsdóttir, *Íslenska fyrir útlendinga. Kennslubók í málfræði* (1998).
D. Neijmann, *Colloquial Icelandic. The Complete Course for Beginners* (2001).
Sverrir Hólmarson et al., *Concise Icelandic–English Dictionary* (1989).

15. Manuscripts

Attitudes to medieval literature in post-medieval Iceland were also conservative. As in other European countries, antiquarian interest in the medieval past began to develop in the Renaissance, but this went alongside an unbroken tradition of the copying of medieval texts. This continued long after the introduction of printing, with handwritten and printed texts existing side by side. Several thirteenth-century sagas are now preserved only in manuscripts from the seventeenth century and later. The spelling of texts reproduced in this Reader has been normalised, with conventional abbreviations expanded editorially; as an introduction to reading texts as they appear in early manuscripts, an extract from the fourteenth-century Möðruvallabók (Text IV) has been reproduced in facsimile as Text XVIII.

With the revival of antiquarian interest in the Nordic medieval past, and the consciousness of its preservation largely in Icelandic manuscripts, scholars in Scandinavia made collections of Icelandic manuscripts. The largest of these was built up over a lifetime by the Icelandic scholar Árni Magnússon, who was employed as assistant to the Danish Royal Antiquarian, Thomas Bartholin, and later as Professor of History at the University of Copenhagen. During a ten-year stint (1702–12) on a royal commission making a census of all the farms in Iceland he scoured the country for manuscripts and documents of all kinds; after his return to Denmark in 1713 he continued to obtain manuscripts in Norway and Denmark, as well as those he was given or sold by connections in Iceland. Many that he was unable to buy he copied, or commissioned others to copy; he also painstakingly researched the provenance of manuscripts. Despite a fire in Copenhagen in 1728 that destroyed a few dozen of Árni's manuscripts (together with all his printed books and some of his notes), Árni did more than anyone else to preserve Iceland's medieval literary heritage. His collection was bequeathed to the University of Copenhagen when he died in 1730, and was the basis for the manuscript institute there that still carries his name. As a result of negotiations in the mid-twentieth century, a large proportion of this collection (mainly manuscripts whose subject matter related specifically to Iceland) has now been returned to Iceland, where it is housed in an institute that also bears Árni's name, The Árni Magnússon Institute for Icelandic Studies. The first manuscripts to be returned were the Codex Regius of the Poetic Edda and the great Kings' Saga compilation Flateyjarbók.

Many Icelandic manuscripts have been printed in facsimile editions. Some can also be viewed on the internet at:

http://am.hi.is/WebView/
http://arnamagnaeansk.ku.dk/haandskriftssamlingen/eks/

Hreinn Benediktsson, *Early Icelandic Script* (1965).
Corpus Codicum Islandicorum Medii Aevi I–XX (1930–56).
Early Icelandic Manuscripts in Facsimile I–XX (1958–93).
Íslenzk handrit. Icelandic Manuscripts I– (1956–).
Gísli Sigurðsson and Vésteinn Ólason (eds), *The Manuscripts of Iceland* (2004).
Jónas Kristjánsson, *Icelandic Illuminated Manuscripts* (1993).
O. Bandle et al., *The Nordic Languages. An International Handbook of the History of the North Germanic Languages* I (2002).

General reference and further reading

C. Clover and J. Lindow, eds, *Old Norse–Icelandic Literature. A Critical Guide.* Islandica XLV (1985).
M. Clunies Ross, ed., *Old Icelandic Literature and Society* (2000).
P. Foote, *Aurvandilstá: Norse Studies* (1984).
E. V. Gordon, ed., *An Introduction to Old Norse*, 2nd ed. rev. A. R. Taylor (1957).
J. Jesch, *Ships and Men in the Late Viking Age: the Vocabulary of Runic Inscriptions and Skaldic Verse* (2001).
J. Jochens, *Old Norse Images of Women* (1996).
Jónas Kristjánsson, *Eddas and Sagas* (1988).
Kulturhistorisk leksikon for nordisk middelalder I–XXII (1956–78).
R. McTurk, ed., *A Companion to Old Norse-Icelandic Literature and Culture* (2005).
Sigurður Nordal, *Icelandic Culture*, tr. Vilhjálmur T. Bjarnar (1990).
P. Pulsiano, ed., *Medieval Scandinavia: An Encyclopedia* (1993).
Stefán Einarsson, *A History of Icelandic Literature* (1957).

Icelandic texts in English editions

Texts with notes and glossary:

Bandamanna saga, ed. H. Magerøy (1981).
Egils saga, ed. Bjarni Einarsson (2003).
Einar Skúlason's Geisli, A Critical Edition, ed. M. Chase (2005).
Gunnlaugs saga, ed. P. Foote and R. Quirk (1953).
Hávamál, ed. D. Evans, with *Glossary and Index* by A. Faulkes (1986–87).
Hervarar saga, ed. C. Tolkien and G. Turville-Petre (1956).
Hrafns saga Sveinbjarnarsonar, ed. Guðrún P. Helgadóttir (1987).
Snorri Sturluson, *Edda: Prologue and Gylfaginning*, ed. A. Faulkes (2nd edn 2005).
Snorri Sturluson, *Edda: Skáldskaparmál*, ed. A. Faulkes, 2 vols (1998).
Snorri Sturluson, *Háttatal*, ed. A. Faulkes (1991, repr. 1999).
Stories from the Sagas of the Kings, ed. A. Faulkes (1980).
Two Icelandic Stories, ed. A. Faulkes (1978).
Two Tales of Icelanders: Ögmundar þáttr dytts og Gunnara Helmings. Ǫlkofra þáttr, ed. I. Wyatt and J. Cook (1993).
Vafþrúðnismál, ed. T. W. Machan (1989).
Víga-Glúms saga, ed. G. Turville-Petre (1960).
Vǫluspá, ed. S. Nordal, tr. B. Benedikz and J. McKinnell (1978).
Þorgils saga ok Hafliða, ed. U. Brown (1952).

Texts with parallel translation:

Ágrip af Nóregskonungasǫgum, ed. M. J. Driscoll (1995).
The Book of the Icelanders, ed. Halldór Hermannsson, Islandica XX (1930).
Clemens saga, ed. H. Carron (2005).
The First Grammatical Treatise, ed. Einar Haugen (1972), ed. Hreinn Benediktsson (1972).
Fourteenth-Century Icelandic Verse on the Virgin Mary (2001), ed. K. Wrightson (2001).
R. Frank, *Old Norse Court Poetry*, Islandica XLII (1978).
Grottasǫngr, ed. C. Tolley (2008).
Gunnlaugs saga, ed. P. Foote, tr. R. Quirk (1957).
Guta saga, ed. C. Peel (1999).
Hákonar saga Hákonarsonar, ed. G. Vigfusson, tr. G. Dasent, Icelandic Sagas II and IV, Rolls series (1887–94).
Hávamál, ed. D. E. M. Clarke (1923).
Historia Norwegie, ed. I. Ekrem and L. B. Mortensen, tr. P. Fisher (2003).
Jómsvíkinga saga, ed. N. Blake (1962).
Norse Romance I–III, ed. M. Kalinke (1999).
The Old Norse–Icelandic Legend of Saint Barbara, ed. and tr. K. Wolf (2000).
The Poetic Edda I: *Heroic Poems*, ed. and tr. U. Dronke (1969).

The Poetic Edda II: *Mythological Poems*, ed. and tr. U. Dronke (1997).
The Poetry of Arnórr jarlaskáld, ed. and tr. D. Whaley (1998).
Saga Heiðreks konungs ins vitra (= *Hervarar saga*), ed. and tr. C. Tolkien (1960).
The Saga of the Volsungs, ed. and tr. R. G. Finch (1965).

Translations of the Sagas of Icelanders:

The Complete Sagas of Icelanders I–V, ed. and tr. Viðar Hreinsson et al. (1997).
Many of these translations are reproduced by Penguin under the heading 'World of the Sagas', as follows:
The Sagas of Icelanders, introduction by R. Kellogg (2000) [*Egils saga, Vatnsdœla saga, Laxdœla saga, Hrafnkels saga Freysgoða, Bandamanna saga, Gísla saga, Gunnlaugs saga, Refs saga, Grœnlendinga saga, Eiríks saga rauða, þættir*]
Egil's Saga, tr. B. Scudder, introduction by Svanhildur Óskarsdóttir (2004).
Gisli Sursson's Saga and the Saga of the People of Eyri, tr. Vésteinn Ólason, J. Quinn and M. Regal (2003).
Njál's saga, tr. R. Cook (2002).
Sagas of Warrior Poets, ed. D. Whaley (2002) [*Kormaks saga, Bjarnar saga Hítdœlakappa, Hallfreðar saga, Gunnlaugs saga, Víglundar saga*].
The Saga of Grettir the Strong, tr. Bernard Scudder (2005).

Other translations:

Arrow-Odd: a medieval novel, tr. Hermann Pálsson and P. Edwards (1970).
The Book of Settlements, tr. Hermann Pálsson and P. Edwards (1972).
T. M. Andersson and W. I. Miller, *Law and Literature in Medieval Iceland: Ljósvetninga saga and Valla-Ljóts saga* (1989).
Barðar saga, tr. Jón Skaptason and P. Pulsiano (1984).
The Confederates and Hen-Thorir, tr. Hermann Pálsson (1975).
Erik the Red and other Icelandic sagas, tr. G. Jones (1961).
Eyrbyggja saga, tr. P. Schach and L. M. Hollander (1959).
Fagrskinna, tr. A. Finlay (2004).
Fljotsdale saga and the Droplaugarsons, tr. E. Howarth and J. Young (1990).
Gautrek's Saga, tr. D. Fox and Hermann Pálsson (1974).
Gongu-Hrolfs saga, tr. Hermann Pálsson and P. Edwards (1981)
Guta lag, tr. C. Peel (2009).
Heimskringla, tr. L. M. Hollander (1964).
A History of Norway and the Passion and Miracles of the Blessed Óláfr, tr. D. Kunin, ed. C. Phelpstead (2001).
Hrafnkel's Saga and Other Icelandic Stories, tr. Hermann Pálsson (1971).
Hrolf Gautreksson, tr. Hermann Pálsson and P. Edwards (1972).
Icelandic Histories and Romances, tr. R. O'Connor (2002).
King Haralds Saga by Snorri Sturluson, tr. Magnus Magnusson and Hermann Pálsson (1976).

Íslendingabók – Kristni saga. The Book of the Icelanders – The Story of the Conversion. tr. S. Grønlie (2007).

Karlamagnús saga: the saga of Charlemagne and his heroes, tr. C. B. Hieatt (1975).

Knytlinga saga: History of the Kings of Denmark, tr. Hermann Pálsson and P. Edwards (1986).

Laws of Early Iceland I–II, tr. A. Dennis, P. Foote and R. Perkins (1980–2000).

Laxdaela Saga, tr. Magnus Magnusson and Hermann Pálsson (1975).

The Life of Gudmund the Good, Bishop of Hólar, tr. G. Turville-Petre and E. S. Olszewska (1942).

Morkinskinna, tr. T. M. Andersson and K. E. Gade, Islandica LI (2000).

Oddr Snorrason, *The Saga of Olaf Tryggvason*, tr. T. M. Andersson, Islandica LII (2003).

Orkneyinga Saga: The History of the Earls of Orkney, tr. Hermann Pálsson (1981).

The Poetic Edda, tr. C. Larrington (1996).

The Saga of Bjorn, Champion of the Men of Hitardale, tr. A. Finlay (2000).

The Saga of the Jomsvikings, tr. L. M. Hollander (1988).

The Saga of King Hrolf Kraki, tr. J. Byock (1998).

The Saga of King Sverri of Norway, tr. J. Sephton (1899, reissued 1994).

The Saga of Tristram and Isond, tr. P. Schach (1973).

The Saga of the Volsungs: The Norse Epic of Sigurd the Dragon Slayer, tr. J. Byock (1999).

The Sagas of Kormak and the Sworn Brothers, tr. L. M. Hollander (1949).

Saxo Grammaticus, *History of the Danes*, tr. P. Fisher, ed. H. E. Davidson (1979–80).

The Schemers and Víga-Glúm: Bandamanna saga and Víga Glúms saga, tr. G. Johnston (1999).

Seven Viking Romances, tr. Hermann Pálsson and P. Edwards (1985).

J. Simpson, *The Northmen Talk* (1965).

J. Simpson, *Icelandic Folktales and Legends*, 2nd ed. (2004).

The Skalds, A Selection of their Poems, tr. L. M. Hollander (1968).

Snorri Sturluson, *Edda*, tr. A. Faulkes (1987).

Sturlunga saga, tr. J. McGrew and R. G. Thomas (1970–74).

Sven Aggesen, *Works*, tr. E. Christiansen.

Theodoricus Monachus, *Historia de Antiquitate Regum Norwagiensium. An Account of the Ancient History of the Norwegian Kings*, tr. D. and I. McDougall (1998).

Three Icelandic Outlaw Sagas. The Saga of Gisli, the Saga of Grettir, the Saga of Hord, tr. A. Faulkes and G. Johnston (2004).

Viga-Glums saga, tr. J. McKinnell (1987).

Vikings in Russia: Yngvars saga and Eymund's saga, tr. Hermann Pálsson and P. Edwards (1989).

The Vinland sagas: Grænlendinga saga and Eirik's saga, tr. Magnus Magnusson and Hermann Pálsson (1973).

CHRONOLOGY

AD		Poets fl.
*c.*725	*Beowulf* written	
793	First viking raid on Northumbria	
*c.*850	Beginning of viking settlement in England	[Bragi the Old
*c.*870	Beginning of viking settlement in Iceland	
871	Alfred the Great becomes king of England	
*c.*885	Haraldr finehair becomes king of all Norway	[Þjóðólfr of Hvinir [Þorbjǫrn hornklofi
930	Foundation of *Alþingi*	
*c.*965	Division of Iceland into quarters	[Eyvindr skáldaspillir
*c.*985	Beginning of settlement of Greenland	[Egill, Kormakr
995	Óláfr Tryggvason becomes king of Norway	[Einarr skálaglamm
999/1000	Christianity accepted in Iceland	[Hallfreðr
*c.*1000	Discovery of America by vikings	
*c.*1005	Fifth court established	
1010	Burning of Njáll	
1014	Battle of Clontarf	[Sighvatr
1030	Fall of St Óláfr at Stikla(r)staðir	[Arnórr jarlaskáld
1056	First bishop at Skálaholt. Sæmundr the Wise born	[Þjóðólfr Arnórsson
1066	Fall of Haraldr harðráði in England. Battle of Hastings	
1067/8	Ari the Wise born	
1096	Tithe laws introduced	
1106	First bishop at Hólar	
1117–18	Laws first written down	
*c.*1125	*Íslendingabók* compiled	
1133	First monastery established (at Þingeyrar)	
*c.*1150	Earliest Icelandic manuscript fragments	
1153	Archbishopric established at Niðaróss	[Einarr Skúlason
*c.*1170	*First Grammatical Treatise*. *Hryggjarstykki*	
1179	Snorri Sturluson born	
*c.*1190–1210	*Sverris saga*	
1197	Jón Loptsson dies	
1199	Bishop Þorlákr of Skálaholt declared saint	
1200	Bishop Jón of Hólar declared saint	
1214	Sturla Þórðarson born	
1215–18	Snorri lawspeaker	
1217	Hákon Hákonarson becomes king of Norway	
1218–20	Snorri's first visit to Norway	
*c.*1220	The Prose Edda	
1222–31	Snorri lawspeaker again	
1226	*Tristrams saga*	

1237–9 Snorri's second visit to Norway
1240 Duke Skúli killed
1241 Snorri Sturluson killed 23rd September
c. 1250 Oldest surviving manuscript fragment of a saga of Icelanders (*Egils saga*)
1261 Magnús Hákonarson crowned king in Norway
1262–4 Icelanders acknowledge the king of Norway as their sovereign
1263 King Hákon dies
c. 1275 Codex Regius of eddic poems. *Morkinskinna*
c. 1280 *Njáls saga. Hrafnkels saga.* King Magnús Hákonarson dies
1284 Sturla Þórðarson dies
c. 1320 *Grettis saga*
c. 1340 Chaucer born
c. 1350 Möðruvallabók written [Eysteinn Ásgrímsson
1382 Flateyjarbók begun
1397 Norway and Iceland come under Danish rule
1550 Reformation in Iceland
1944 Iceland regains complete independence

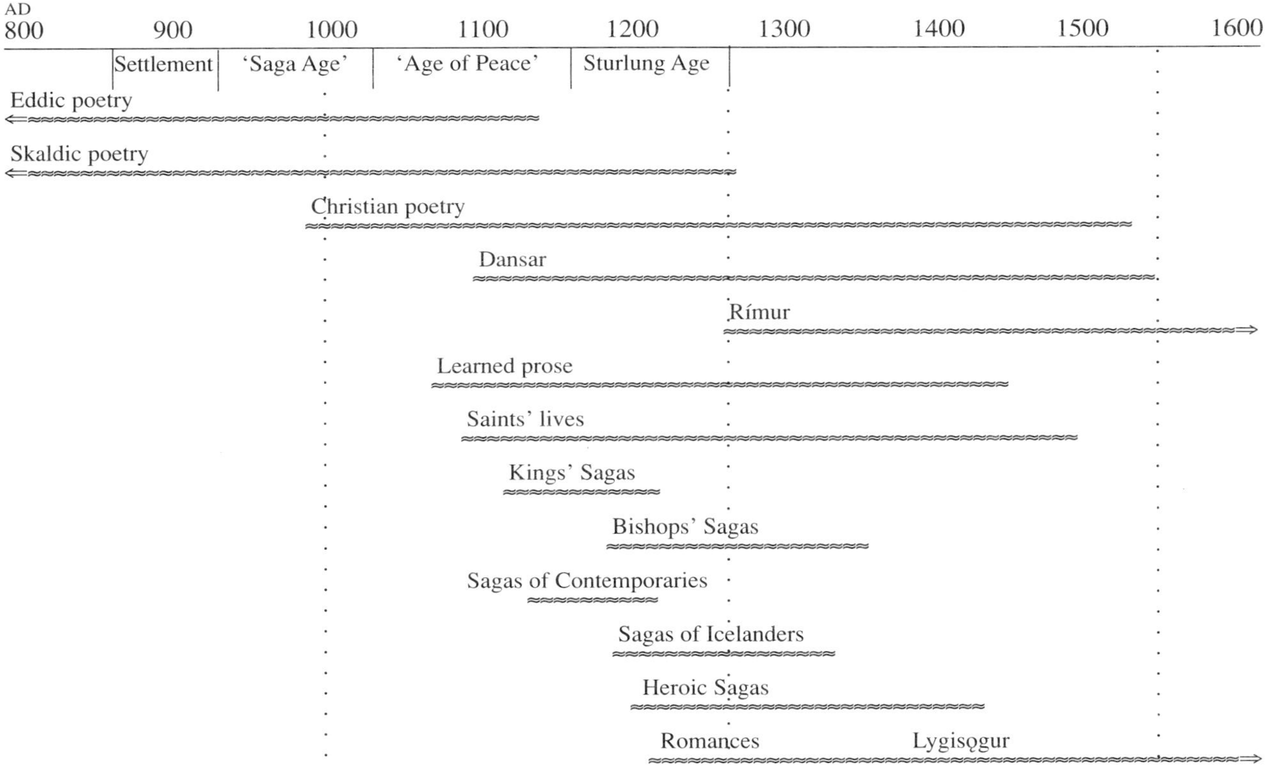

AD

800 900 1000 1100 1200 1300 1400 1500 1600

Settlement | ‘Saga Age’ | ‘Age of Peace’ | Sturlung Age

Eddic poetry

Skaldic poetry

Christian poetry

Dansar

Rímur

Learned prose

Saints’ lives

Kings’ Sagas

Bishops’ Sagas

Sagas of Contemporaries

Sagas of Icelanders

Heroic Sagas

Romances Lygisǫgur

The diagram shows the approximate periods during which the various medieval Icelandic literary genres were cultivated. The dotted lines mark the time of the conversion to Christianity (1000), the end of the Commonwealth (1262) and the Reformation (1550).

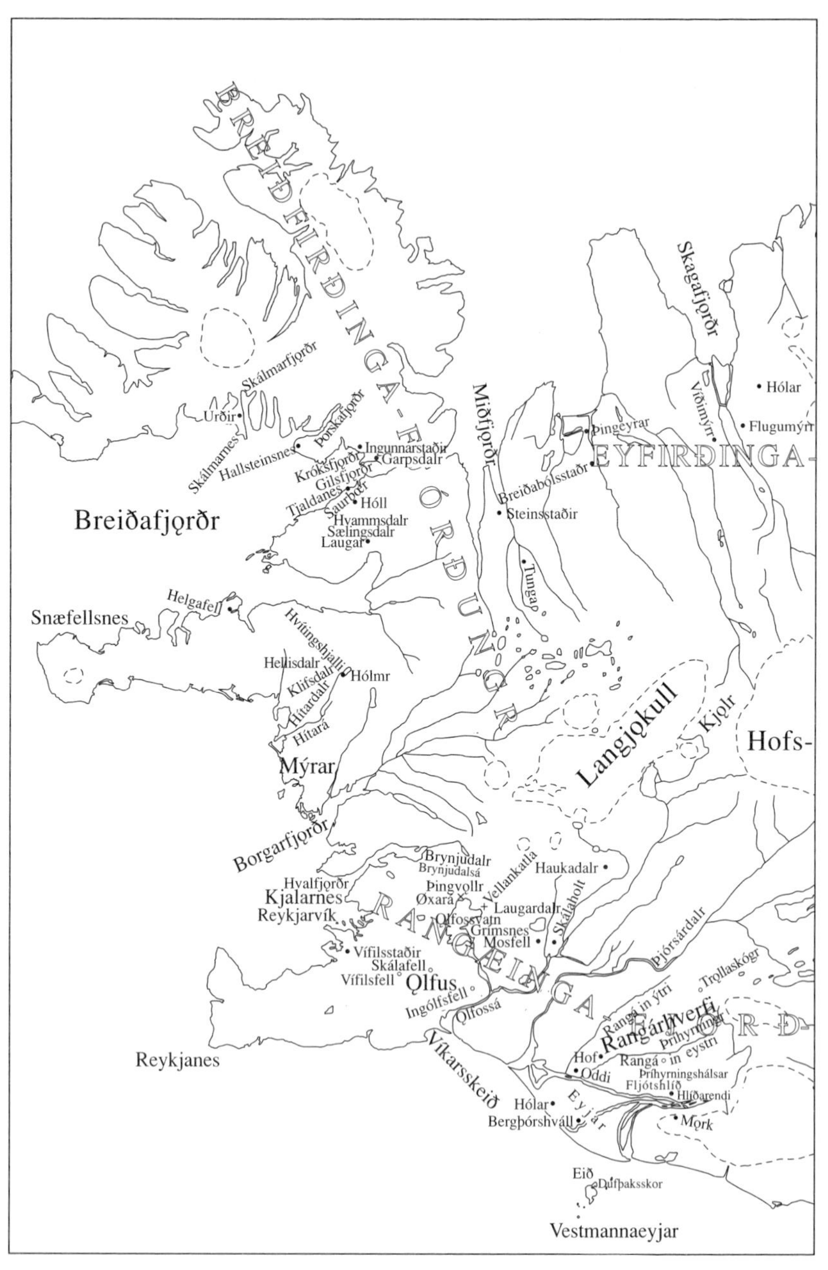

WEST ICELAND

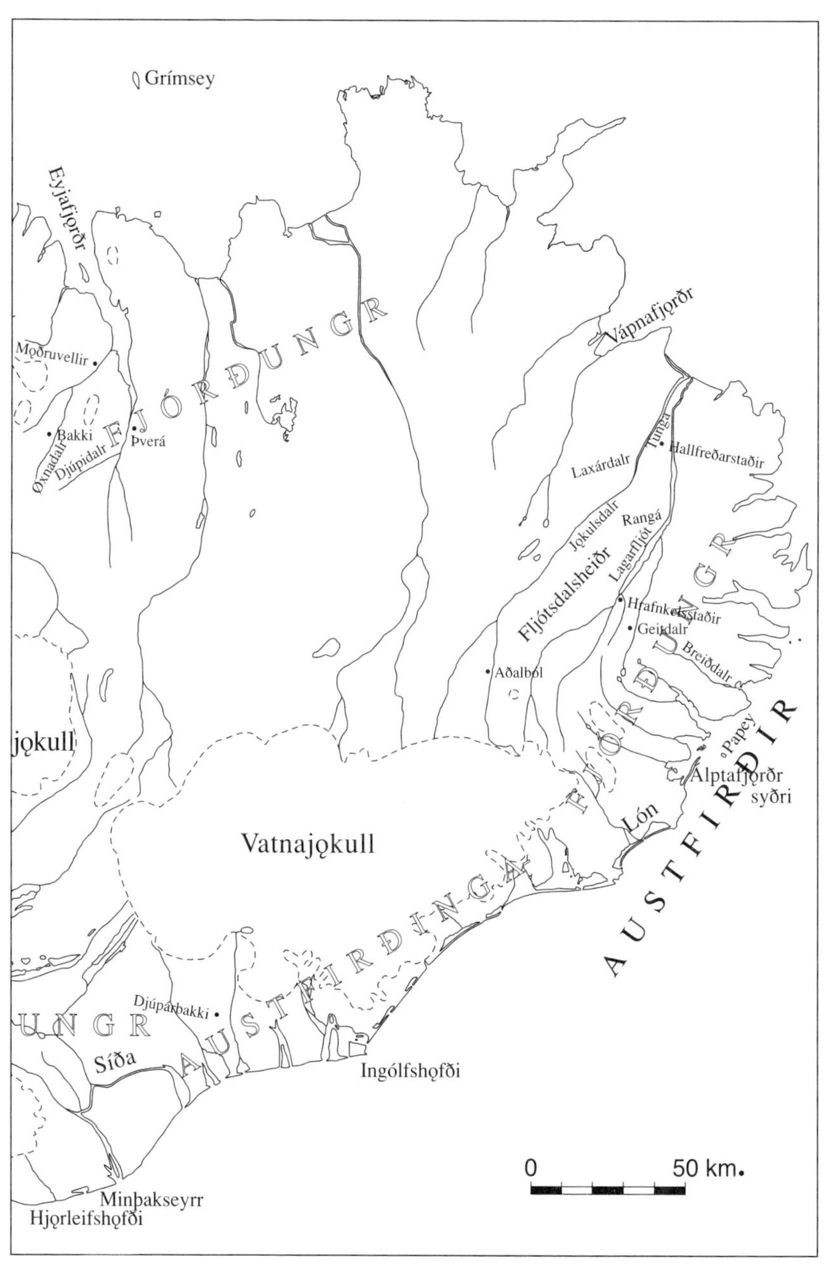

EAST ICELAND

LAWSPEAKERS OF THE MEDIEVAL ICELANDIC COMMONWEALTH

1. Úlfljótr (cf. Text VIII, note 19; *Laws* I 1–2)
2. Hrafn Hœngsson *c*.930–949
3. Þórarinn Ragabróðir Óláfsson *c*.950–969
4. Þorkell máni Þorsteinsson 970–984
5. Þorgeirr Ljósvetningagoði Þorkelsson 985–1001
6. Grímr Svertingsson 1002–1003
7. Skapti Þóroddsson 1004–1030
8. Steinn Þorgestsson 1031–1033
9. Þorkell Tjǫrvason 1034–1053
10. Gellir Bǫlverksson 1054–1062
11. Gunnarr inn spaki Þorgrímsson 1063–1065
12. Kolbeinn Flosason 1066–1071
13. Gellir Bǫlverksson (second time) 1072–1074
14. Gunnarr inn spaki Þorgrímsson (second time) 1075
15. Sighvatr Surtsson 1076–1083
16. Markús Skeggjason 1084–1107
17. Úlfheðinn Gunnarsson 1108–1116
18. Bergþórr Hrafnsson 1117–1122
19. Guðmundr Þorgeirsson 1123–1134
20. Hrafn Úlfheðinsson 1135–1138
21. Finnr Hallsson 1139–1145
22. Gunnarr Úlfheðinsson 1146–1155
23. Snorri Húnbogason 1156–1170
24. Styrkárr Oddason 1171–1180
25. Gizurr Hallsson 1181–1202
26. Hallr Gizurarson 1203–1209
27. Styrmir inn fróði Kárason 1210–1214
28. Snorri Sturluson 1215–1218
29. Teitr Þorvaldsson 1219–1221
30. Snorri Sturluson (second time) 1222–1231
31. Styrmir inn fróði Kárason (second time) 1232–1235
32. Teitr Þorvaldsson (second time) 1236–1247
33. Óláfr hvítaskáld Þórðarson 1248–1250
34. Sturla Þórðarson 1251
35. Óláfr hvítaskáld Þórðarson (second time) 1252
36. Teitr Einarsson 1253–1258
37. Ketill Þorláksson 1259–1262
38. Þorleifr hreimr Ketilsson 1263–1265
39. Sigurðr Þorvaldsson 1266
40. Jón Einarsson 1267
41. Þorleifr hreimr Ketilsson (second time) 1268
42. Jón Einarsson (second time) 1269–1270
43. Þorleifr hreimr Ketilsson (third time) 1271

I: HRÓLFS SAGA KRAKA

Hrólfs saga is one of the sagas known as heroic, mythical, or 'of ancient time' (Modern Icelandic *fornaldarsögur*). Their main distinguishing feature is that they take place before the settlement of Iceland, chiefly in northern Europe (whereas most of the 'Romance Sagas' take place in southern Europe). They are often based on poems like the heroic lays of the Poetic Edda. *Hrólfs saga* contains stories associated with the Danish Skjǫldung dynasty (also celebrated in the earlier but now mostly lost *Skjǫldunga saga*), which seem to underlie some parts of the Anglo-Saxon poem *Beowulf* too. Hrólfr kraki corresponds to Hroðulf, nephew of King Hroðgar, and the historical background of the legends about these kings was Scandinavia in the fifth and sixth centuries of our era. In *Hrólfs saga*, however, the story has come under the influence of later genres, and Hrólfr and his *kappar* ('champions') are to a certain extent based on Charlemagne and his peers; the *kastali* ('castle') mentioned in the present extract, which appears to be separate from the traditional *hǫll* ('hall'), also belongs to a later period. The double fight against the monster has certain similarities to Beowulf's fights against Grendel and Grendel's mother, and Bǫðvarr bjarki inherits some of Beowulf's characteristics from his own bear-like father. The story as it is told here, however, lacks the high seriousness of *Beowulf* and the Chansons de Geste, and contains some of the comedy and irony which feature in other medieval Icelandic tales.

All the surviving manuscripts of *Hrólfs saga* were written in the seventeenth century or later, and although the original saga is believed to have been compiled in the fourteenth, none of the manuscripts seems to preserve the original text unchanged, and their language is more like Modern than Old Icelandic. Many late forms and spellings are retained here. They are explained in the grammatical notes. The present text is based on the manuscript AM 285 4to. Where this manuscript is incoherent it is emended from AM 9 fol.

The passage begins mid-way through chapter 23 with Bǫðvarr bjarki arriving at King Hrólfr's court where he has come to seek service with the king (in the first part of the chapter Bǫðvarr has been visiting his two brothers, cf. line 149). On his way there through rain and mud he had lodged with a poor peasant and his wife who told him that their son Hǫttr was at the court and being badly treated by the courtiers; they asked Bǫðvarr to be kind to him.

King Hrólfr's courtiers had been throwing bones into the corner where Hǫttr was cowering. There is a historical example of viking bone-throwing in the *Anglo-Saxon Chronicle* under the year 1012 (the martyrdom of Archbishop Alphege or Ælfheah) and a mythical one in Snorri Sturluson's *Edda*, *Gylfaginning* ch. 44; and one might also compare the *Odyssey* XX 287–319 and XXII 284–91; Judges 15: 15.

The abbreviations used in the grammatical notes are explained at the beginning of the Glossary in Part III; the figures in brackets refer to sections of the Grammar in Part I. Unlike the Grammar and Glossary, the grammatical notes here distinguish strong masculine nouns (sm.) from weak masculine (wm.), strong feminine nouns (sf.) from weak feminine (wf.), and strong neuter nouns (sn.) from weak neuter (wn.); see 3.1.4 and 3.1.8 in the Grammar.

Bibliography

The standard edition is *Hrólfs saga kraka*, ed. D. Slay (1960). There is a text with normalised spelling in *Fornaldarsögur Norðurlanda* I–IV, ed. Guðni Jónsson (1950), I 1–105.

The saga appears in English in *Eirik the Red and other Icelandic Sagas*, tr. G. Jones (1961); and in *The Saga of King Hrolf Kraki*, tr. Jesse L. Byock, Penguin Books (1998).

On the connection with *Beowulf* see *Beowulf and the Fight at Finnsburg*, ed. F. Klaeber (1950), xviii–xx; R. W. Chambers, *Beowulf: An Introduction* (1959). On the genre, see P. Hallberg, 'Some Aspects of the Fornaldarsögur as a Corpus', *Arkiv för nordisk filologi* 97 (1982), 1–35.

For the story of Bǫðvarr bjarki (under the name Biarco) as told by Saxo Grammaticus in his Latin *Gesta Danorum*, recourse may be had to the following English translations of that work: *The First Nine Books of the Danish History of Saxo Grammaticus*, tr. Oliver Elton (1894), 68–80; Saxo Grammaticus, *The History of the Danes* I, English text, tr. Peter Fisher, ed. Hilda Ellis Davidson (1979), 54–64.

I: HRÓLFS SAGA KRAKA

Chapter 23

. . . Síðan ferr Bǫðvarr leið sína til Hleiðargarðs.[1] Hann kemr til konungs atsetu. Bǫðvarr leiðir þegar hest sinn á stall hjá konungs hestum hinum beztu ok spyrr øngvan at; gekk síðan inn í hǫll ok var þar fátt manna.

síðan adv. 'then'. **ferr** sv. 'goes': 3rd sg. pres. indic. of *fara* (3.6.10). **Bǫðvarr** sm. 1
(personal name): nom., the subject of the sentence; the adv. *síðan* occupies the first position in the sentence, so *Bǫðvarr* is in third position since the finite verb must be in first or second place (3.9.1). **leið** sf. 'way' 'journey' 'path': acc., the direct object of the sentence; *fara* does not normally take an object, but may be construed with so-called 'locative objects' (ones that indicate where something took place, cf. Eng. *he jumped the ditch*) — here we might translate 'on his way'. **sína** REFL. POSS. (referring back to the subject; 3.2.1) 'his': acc. f. sg., agreeing with *leið*. **til** prep. 'to'. **Hleiðargarðs** sm. (place-name): gen., the case always triggered by the prep. *til*; on the question of case, gender and number in compound nouns, see the analysis of *mannshǫnd* in line 6. **hann** pron. 'he': nom., the subject. **kemr** sv. 'comes': 3rd sg. pres. indic. of *koma—kom—kómu—komit*. **til** prep. 'to'. **konungs** sm. 'king's': gen., indicating possession or association, cf. the corresponding *-'s* in English. **atsetu** wf. 'residence': 2
gen., the case always triggered by the prep. *til*. **Bǫðvarr** sm. (personal name): nom., the subject. **leiðir** wv. 'leads': 3rd sg. pres. indic. of *leiða*. **þegar** adv. 'at once' 'immediately'. **hest** sm. 'horse': acc., the direct object. **sinn** REFL. POSS. (referring back to the subject) 'his': acc. m. sg., agreeing with *hest*. **á** prep. 'into'. **stall** sm. 'stable': acc., the case triggered by the prep. *á* when motion is denoted. **hjá** prep. 'alongside' 'next to'. **konungs** sm. 'king's': gen., indicating possession, cf. the corresponding *-'s* in English. **hestum** sm. 'horses': dat., the case always triggered by the prep. *hjá*. **hinum** art. 'the': dat. pl., agreeing with *hestum*. **beztu** adj. 'best': weak dat. 3
pl. sup. — weak because the noun phrase is definite ('the best horses'; 3.3.2), dat. pl. agreeing with *hestum* (note that in classical ON the weak dat. pl. of adjectives ends in *-um* (3.3.4), but that in later texts this is increasingly replaced by *-u* by analogy with all other weak pl. adj. endings); on the word-order see 3.3.5, 3.9.2. **ok** conj. 'and'. **spyrr** wv. 'asks': 3rd sg. pres. indic. of *spyrja*; the subject, *Bǫðvarr* or *hann*, is understood. **øngvan** pron. 'no one': acc. m. sg., the direct object; masculine is used since a human being is denoted and feminine gender has not been specified, masculine being the default gender (cf. **fáir** line 23). **at** prep. 'about': the prep. is here used absolutely, i.e. without a following noun or noun phrase, 'it' — Bǫðvarr's action — being understood (3.7.7); such usage is often classed as adverbial rather than prepositional. **gekk** sv. 'walked' 'went': 3rd sg. past indic. of *ganga—gekk—gengu—gengit*; the subject, *Bǫðvarr* or *hann*, is understood. **síðan** adv. 'then'. **inn** adv. 'in'. **í** prep. 'to': the combination of adv. *inn* and prep. *í* corresponds to the English prep. 'into'. **hǫll** sf. 'hall': acc., the case triggered by *í* when motion is denoted. **ok** conj. 'and'. **var** sv. 'was': 3rd sg. past indic. of *vera* (3.6.10); in this sentence the finite verb (**var**) occupies first position, as is common in ON narrative style. **þar** adv. 'there'. **fátt** adj. 'few': strong nom. n. sg., the subject; n. sg. is used because the adj. does not modify a noun with a particular number or gender; in the absence of such a noun, the adj. takes over the function of head of the noun phrase (3.3; 3.3.6 (19–21)) and is modified by *manna*. **manna** sm. 'of men': gen., indicating type, i.e. *menn* are the type or class of which few were present.

Hann sezk útarliga,[2] ok sem hann hefr setit þar nǫkkra hríð, heyrir hann þrausk nǫkkut útar í hornit í einhverjum stað. Bǫðvarr lítr þangat
6 ok sér at mannshǫnd kemr upp ór mikilli beinahrúgu, er þar lá; hǫndin var svǫrt mjǫk. Bǫðvarr gengr þangat ok spyrr hverr þar væri í beina-

4 **hann** pron. 'he': nom., the subject. **sezk** wv. 'sits down': 3rd sg. pres. indic., *-sk* form (3.6.5.3), of *setja*; the sense is reflexive, the literal meaning being 'sets/places himself'. **útarliga** adv. 'far out [i.e. near the door]'. **ok** conj. 'and'; this conj. connects the immediately preceding independent sentence with the one beginning *heyrir hann þrausk nǫkkut* at the end of line 4. **sem** conj. 'when' (3.8.2.1, end). **hann** pron. 'he': nom., the subject. **hefr** wv. 'has': 3rd sg. pres. indic. of *hafa* (3.6.7). **setit** sv. 'sat': supine (= pp. nom./acc. n. sg.) of *sitja—sat—sátu—setit*; *hefr* + *setit* forms a so-called perfect construction, the equivalent of Eng. *has sat* (3.6.2). **þar** adv. 'there'. **nǫkkra** pron. 'some' 'a little': acc. f. sg.; here used adjectivally, *nǫkkra* (an abbreviated form of *nǫkkura*) agrees with *hríð*. **hríð** sf. 'while': acc., since the phrase *nǫkkra hríð* functions here as time adverbial (3.1.2, 3.1.5 (10)). **heyrir** wv. 'hears': 3rd sg. pres. indic. of *heyra*; the finite verb is in first position because the independent sentence in which it
5 occurs is immediately preceded by a dependent sentence (3.9.1). **hann** pron. 'he': nom., the subject. **þrausk** sn. 'rummaging': acc., the direct object. **nǫkkut** pron. 'some' 'a': acc. n. sg.; here used adjectivally, *nǫkkut* agrees with *þrausk*. **útar** adv. 'farther out': comp., consisting of *út* + comp. suffix *-ar*. **í** prep. 'in'. **hornit** sn. + art. (*horn-it*) 'the corner': acc., the case triggered by *í* when motion is denoted; the English speaker may not conceive of hearing something somewhere as involving motion, but the clue is provided by the motion adv. *útar* — the hearing of *hann*, the subject, is directed farther out into the corner. **í** prep. 'in'. **einhverjum** pron. 'some': dat. m. sg.; here used adjectivally, *einhverjum* agrees with *stað*. **stað** sm. 'place': dat., the case triggered by *í* when location is denoted; note that *stað* is one of those masculine nouns that has no ending in the dat. sg. (3.1.4, 3.1.8, paradigm 2). **Bǫðvarr** sm. (personal name): nom., the subject. **lítr** sv. 'looks': 3rd sg. pres. indic. of *líta—leit—litu—litit*. **þangat** adv.
6 'thither' 'there'. **ok** conj. 'and'. **sér** sv. 'sees': 3rd sg. pres. indic. of *sjá* (3.6.10). **at** conj. 'that'. **mannshǫnd** sf. 'man's hand': nom., the subject; note that although *manns*, gen. sg. of *maðr*, is sm., the gender of the compound is determined by the second element, *hǫnd*; note further that the nom. case and sg. number of the compound is expressed by *hǫnd* alone. **kemr** sv. 'comes': 3rd sg. pres. indic. of *koma—kom—kómu—komit*. **upp** adv. 'up'. **ór** prep. 'out of'. **mikilli** adj. 'big': strong dat. f. sg., agreeing with *beinahrúgu*. **beinahrúgu** wf. 'bone-pile' 'pile of bones': dat., the case always triggered by *ór*; like *mannshǫnd* above, *beinahrúgu* is a compound, whose gender is determined and case and number expressed by the second element, *hrúgu*; in the following the structure of compounds will receive no further analysis. **er** conj. 'which'. **þar** adv. 'there'. **lá** sv. 'lay': 3rd sg. past indic. of *liggja—lá—lágu—legit*: the finite verb does not often immediately follow a subordinating conjunction, and here *þar* intervenes (3.9.1). **hǫndin** sf.
7 + art. (*hǫnd-in*) 'the hand': nom., the subject. **var** sv. 'was': 3rd sg. past indic. of *vera* (3.6.10). **svǫrt** adj. 'black': strong nom. f. sg. (3.3.2), agreeing with *hǫndin*. **mjǫk** adv. 'very' (3.9.2). **Bǫðvarr** sm. (personal name): nom., the subject. **gengr** sv. 'goes': 3rd sg. pres. indic. of *ganga—gekk—gengu—gengit*. **þangat** adv. 'thither' 'there'. **ok** conj. 'and'. **spyrr** wv. 'asks': 3rd sg. pres. indic. of *spyrja*. **hverr** pron. (interrog.) 'who': nom. m. sg.; *hverr* fulfils a double function here, (1) as a conjunction introducing the sentence, (2) as the subject (3.8.2.3); since a human being is denoted, masculine, the default gender, is used (see *øngvan*, line 3). **þar** adv. 'there'. **væri** sv. 'was': 3rd sg. past subj. of *vera* (3.6.10); the subj. is normally used in dependent interrogative sentences where the main verb of the independent sentences of which they are the object is one of 'asking'; on the word-order *hverr þar væri*, see the analysis of *lá* in line 6. **í** prep. 'in'.

hrúgunni. Þá var honum svarat ok heldr óframliga:
‘Hǫttr heiti ek, bokki sæll.’[3] 9
‘Því ertu hér,’ spyrr Bǫðvarr, ‘eða hvat gørir þú?’
Hǫttr svarar, ‘Ek gøri mér skjaldborg,[4] bokki sæll.’
Bǫðvarr segir, ‘Vesall ertu þinnar skjaldborgar!’ 12

beinahrúgunni wf. + art. (*beinahrúgu-nni*) ‘the bone-pile’ ‘the pile of bones’: dat., the 8
case triggered by *í* when location is denoted. **þá** adv. ‘then’. **var** sv. ‘was’: 3rd sg. past
indic. of *vera* (3.6.10). **honum** pron. ‘to him’: dat., the indirect object; note that in the
absence of a nominative subject, *honum* is the first (and only) noun phrase in the sentence (for an alternative analysis of the syntactic role of *honum* here, see 3.9.3); on the
word-order *þá var honum*, see the analysis of *Bǫðvarr* in line 1. **svarat** wv. ‘answered’: pp. nom. n. sg. of *svara*; in the absence of a subject with a particular gender
and number with which *svarat* could agree, n. sg. is used; nom. case is assumed since
were there a subject, e.g. *þat*, it would be in the nom.; *var svarat*, the equivalent of Eng.
was answered, forms the passive counterpart to active *NN svaraði* ‘NN answered’ (3.6.4).
ok conj. ‘and’. **heldr** adv. ‘rather’. **óframliga** adv. ‘timidly’. **Hǫttr** sm. (personal 9
name): nom., the subject complement — here in first position because it is emphasised
(3.9.1). **heiti** sv. ‘am called’: 1st sg. pres. indic. of *heita—hét—hétu—heitit*. **ek** pron.
‘I’: nom., the subject. **bokki** wm. ‘buck’ ‘fellow’: nom., the case used when someone
is being addressed. **sæll** adj. ‘happy’ ‘fortunate’: strong nom. m. sg., agreeing with
bokki; the phrase *bokki sæll* may be translated ‘good fellow’ ‘good friend’ ‘kind sir’ or
the like — it is a slightly formal term of endearment. **því** adv. (interrog.) ‘why’ (the 10
more common word for ‘why’ is *hví*). **ertu** = *ert þú*. **ert** sv. ‘are’: 2nd sg. pres. indic.
of *vera* (3.6.10). **þú** pron. ‘you’: nom., the subject. **hér** adv. ‘here’. **spyrr** wv. ‘asks’:
3rd sg. pres. indic. of *spyrja*. **Bǫðvarr** sm. (personal name): nom., the subject. **eða**
conj. ‘or’: when introducing a question *eða* is often closer in meaning to English *and* or
but — here the former. **hvat** pron. (interrog.) ‘what’: acc. n. sg., the direct object;
neuter is used because the pron. denotes a state or action — what Hǫttr is doing — and
neuter is the gender for inanimate or abstract reference. **gørir** wv. ‘are . . . doing’: 2nd
sg. pres. indic. of *gøra* (3.6.7); note that ON does not distinguish between simple (e.g.
do) and continuous constructions (e.g. *are doing*), but expresses both meanings by the
same form. **þú** pron. ‘you’: nom., the subject. **Hǫttr** sm. (personal name): nom., the 11
subject. **svarar** wv. ‘answers’: 3rd sg. pres. indic. of *svara*. **ek** pron. ‘I’: nom., the
subject. **gøri** wv. ‘am making’: 1st sg. pres. indic. of *gøra* (3.6.7); on the English
translation of the present tense, see *gørir* in line 10. **mér** pron. ‘myself’ ‘for myself’:
dat., the indirect object; note that there is no separate reflexive form of the 1st or 2nd
person pronouns, and that *mér* can thus mean both ‘me’ and ‘myself’ (3.2.1). **skjaldborg**
sf. ‘shield fortification’ ‘shield wall’: acc., the direct object; *skjaldborg* — a term denoting a battle formation in which men confront the enemy with an impenetrable wall
of shields — is used here metaphorically to denote the protective construction Hǫttr is
building out of the pile of bones. **bokki** wm. ‘buck’ ‘fellow’ (see line 9). **sæll** adj.
‘happy’ ‘fortunate’ (see line 9). **Bǫðvarr** sm. (personal name): nom., the subject. 12
segir wv. ‘says’: 3rd sg. pres. indic. of *segja*. **vesall** adj. ‘wretched’: strong nom. m.
sg., agreeing with *þú* (*ertu* = *ert þú*, cf. line 10), which has masculine reference; *vesall*
is moved into first position in the sentence to give it emphasis, and since the verb, the
ert of *ertu*, must be in either first or second position in an independent sentence, it
comes next, pushing the subject, the *þú* of *ertu*, into third place (3.9.1). **ertu** (see line
10 and the analysis of *vesall* immediately above). **þinnar** poss. adj. ‘in respect of
your’: gen. f. sg., agreeing with *skjaldborgar*. **skjaldborgar** sf. ‘shield fortification’
‘shield wall’ (see line 11): gen., dependent on the adj. *vesall* and imparting the sense ‘in
respect of’ ‘with regard to’.

Bǫðvarr þrífr til hans ok hnykkir honum upp ór beinahrúgunni. Hǫttr kvað þá hátt við ok mælti:

'Nú viltu bana mér! Gør eigi þetta, svá sem ek hefi nú vel um búizk, en þú hefr nú rofit í sundr skjaldborg mína, ok hafða ek nú gǫrt hana

15 Gør eigi þetta] at þú gørir þetta *285*.

13 **Bǫðvarr** sm. (personal name): nom., the subject. **þrífr** sv. 'grabs': 3rd sg. pres. indic.
of *þrífa—þreif—þrifu—þrifit*. **til** prep. 'at': the sense indicated is of movement towards Hǫttr — verb + prep. might be translated 'grabs hold of' or simply 'grasps'.
hans pron. 'him': gen., the case always triggered by *til*. **ok** conj. 'and'. **hnykkir** wv.
'pulls': 3rd sg. pres. indic. of *hnykkja*. **honum** pron. 'him': dat., the direct object (3.1.5
(16) and (18)). **upp** adv. 'up'. **ór** prep. 'out of'. **beinahrúgunni** wf. + art. (*beinahrúgunni*) 'the bone-pile' 'the pile of bones': dat., the case always triggered by *ór*. **Hǫttr** sm.
14 (personal name): nom., the subject. **kvað** sv. 'cried out': 3rd sg. past indic. of *kveða—
kvað—kváðu—kveðit*. **þá** adv. 'then'. **hátt** adv. 'loudly' (3.5.1). **við** prep. 'at': the
prep. is used here absolutely, 'this' or 'this treatment' being understood as following
við (3.7.7; see also *at* in line 3). **ok** conj. 'and'. **mælti** wv. 'said': 3rd sg. past indic. of
15 *mæla*. **nú** adv. 'now'. **viltu** = *vilt þú*. **vilt** wv. 'want': 2nd sg. pres. indic. of *vilja*
(3.6.7). **þú** pron. 'you': nom., the subject; *nú* occupies the first position in the sentence, so *þú* is in third position since the finite verb must be in first or second place
(3.9.1). **bana** wv. 'kill': inf. **mér** pron. 'me': dat., the direct object (3.1.5 (16) and
(18)). **gør** wv. 'do': imp. (2nd sg. pres.) of *gøra* (3.6.7); the subject of the imperative,
þú, is omitted here as in English. **eigi** adv. 'not': since in English negative verb phrases
are constructed with auxiliary *do* (e.g. *I do not drink* rather than **I drink not*), we must
translate 'do not do!'. **þetta** pron. 'this': acc. n. sg.; neuter is used because the pronoun
refers to an action — the destruction of the pile of bones — and neuter is the gender for
inanimate or abstract reference. **svá** adv. 'so': the construction here is discontinuous
— *svá*, which has its natural place before the *sem* that introduces the dependent sentence (3.8.2.4), modifies the adv. *vel*, which would normally immediately follow, but
vel itself modifies the verb phrase *um búizk*, and has been attracted to the position
preceding it inside the dependent sentence. **sem** conj. 'as' (3.8.2.4). **ek** pron. 'I':
nom., the subject. **hefi** wv. 'have': 1st sg. pres. indic. of *hafa* (3.6.7). **nú** adv. 'now'.
vel adv. 'well' (see the analysis of *svá* in this line). **um** prep. 'around': the prep. is used
here absolutely since the noun phrase it governs is expressed by the *-sk* inflexion of
búizk (3.9.8.3). **búizk** sv. 'protected myself' 'made myself secure': supine (= pp. nom./
acc. n. sg.), *-sk* form (3.6.5.3), of *búa—bjó—bjoggu—búit*: as is clear from the translation, the *-sk* suffix here imparts a reflexive sense to the verb; *hefi* + *búizk* forms a so-
16 called perfect construction, the equivalent of Eng. *have protected* (*myself*)(3.6.2). **en**
conj. 'but'. **þú** pron. 'you': nom., the subject. **hefr** wv. 'have': 2nd sg. pres. indic. of
hafa (3.6.7). **nú** adv. 'now'. **rofit** sv. 'broken': supine (= pp. nom./acc. n. sg.) of
rjúfa—rauf—rufu—rofit; *hefr* + *rofit* forms a so-called perfect construction, the equivalent of Eng. *have broken* (3.6.2). **í sundr** adv. 'asunder' 'to pieces': although formally
this phrase consists of prep. + adv., it functions as an adverb just like English *asunder*
— historically prep. + adj.; often *sundr* is used on its own with the same meaning as *í
sundr*. **skjaldborg** sf. 'shield fortification' 'shield wall': acc., the direct object of *rofit*.
mína poss. adj. 'my': acc. f. sg., agreeing with *skjaldborg*; note that the possessive
follows the noun it modifies, the usual word-order in ON (3.9.2). **ok** conj. 'and'.
hafða wv. 'had': 1st sg. past indic. of *hafa* (3.6.7). **ek** pron. 'I': nom., the subject. **nú**
adv. 'now'. **gǫrt** wv. 'made': supine (= pp. nom./acc. n. sg.) of *gøra* (3.6.7); *hafða* +
gǫrt forms a so-called pluperfect or past perfect construction, the equivalent of Eng.
had made (3.6.2). **hana** pron. 'her': acc., the direct object of *gǫrt*: note that the femi-

svá háva útan at mér, at hon hefr hlíft mér við ǫllum hǫggum ykkar,
svá ekkert hǫgg hefr komit á mik lengi, en ekki var hon þó enn svá 18
búin sem ek ætlaða hon skyldi vera.'

Bǫðvarr mælti: 'Ekki muntu nú fá skjaldborgina gǫrða lengr.'

nine 3rd person pron. is used because the reference is to the feminine noun *borg*. **svá** 17
adv. 'so'. **háva** adj. 'high': acc. f. sg., agreeing with *hana*; the nom. m. sg. form of this
adj. is *hár* (3.3.8.5, point (5)). **útan** adv. 'from without' 'externally' (3.5.1). **at** prep.
'towards' 'up to': together *útan at* might be translated 'around' — the wall extending
towards Hǫttr affords him protection from the outside world. **mér** pron. 'me': dat., the
case always triggered by *at*. **at** conj. 'that'. **hon** pron. 'she': nom., the subject; on the
feminine gender, see *hana* in line 16. **hefr** wv. 'has': 3rd sg. pres. indic. of *hafa*. **hlíft**
wv. 'protected': supine of *hlífa*. **mér** pron. 'me': dat., the direct object (3.1.5 (16) and
(18)). **við** prep. 'against'. **ǫllum** adj. 'all': dat. pl., agreeing with *hǫggum*. **hǫggum**
sn. 'blows': dat., the case triggered by *við* in the sense 'against' (3.7.4). **ykkar** poss.
adj. 'your [dual]': originally the 2nd dual poss. adj. was inflected for case, gender and
number (3.3.9), but in later ON the invariable form *ykkar* (formally gen. of the pronoun
(*þ*)*it*; 3.2.1) came to be the norm; the use of the dual here is unexpected since the
reference is to a large number of people, as the text goes on to make clear — possibly
Hǫttr is categorising Bǫðvarr as one entity and the courtiers as another, but more likely
this is a modern Icelandic usage, where the originally dual 1st and 2nd person forms are
used to denote all numbers higher than one; note that the possessive follows the noun it
modifies, the usual word-order in ON. **svá** conj. 'so': *svá* is normally an adverb, but it 18
regularly combines with a following *at* to form a two-word conjunction introducing
sentences of result or purpose ('so that'; 3.8.2.2); occasionally the *at* is omitted, as here,
and *svá* then adopts the role of conjunction. **ekkert** pron. 'no': nom. n. sg.; here used
adjectivally, *ekkert* (a later form of *ekki*) agrees with *hǫgg*. **hǫgg** sn. 'blow': nom., the
subject. **hefr** wv. 'have': 3rd sg. pres. indic. of *hafa*. **komit** sv. 'come' 'landed':
supine of *koma—kom—kómu—komit*. **á** prep. 'on'. **mik** pron. 'me': acc., the case
triggered by *á* when motion is denoted. **lengi** adv. 'for a long time'. **en** conj. 'but'.
ekki adv. 'not': although formally the nom./acc. n. sg. form of the pron. *engi* 'no one'
'none', *ekki* is often used synonymously with the adv. *eigi* 'not'. **var** sv. 'was': 3rd sg.
past indic. of *vera* (3.6.10). **hon** pron. 'she': nom., the subject: *ekki* occupies first
position in the sentence (for reasons of emphasis), so the subject comes in 3rd place
since only one element may precede the finite verb (3.9.1); on the use of the feminine
gender, see line 16: *hana*. **þó** adv. 'all the same' 'nevertheless'. **enn** adv. 'yet'. **svá**
adv. 'so'. **búin** sv. 'prepared' 'constructed': pp. nom. f. sg., agreeing with *hon*, of 19
búa—bjó—bjoggu—búit. **sem** conj. 'as'. **ek** pron. 'I': nom., the subject. **ætlaða** wv.
'intended': 1st sg. past indic. of *ætla*. **hon** pron. 'she': nom., the subject. **skyldi** pret.-
pres. vb. 'should': 3rd sg. past; formally *skyldi* may be either indic. or subj. (3.6.7), but
in a dependent sentence describing a hypothetical situation, i.e. what was intended, it is
likely to be subj. **vera** sv. 'be': inf. (3.6.10). **Bǫðvarr** sm. (personal name): nom., the 20
subject. **mælti** wv. 'said': 3rd. sg. past indic. of *mæla*. **ekki** adv. 'not' (see the analysis
of *ekki* in line 18). **muntu** = *munt þú*. **munt** pret.-pres. vb. 'will': 2nd sg. pres. indic.
of *munu* (3.6.7). **þú** pron. 'you': nom., the subject; on the word-order adv. + finite verb
+ subject, see the analysis of *hon* in line 18. **nú** adv. 'now'. **fá** sv. 'get': inf. of *fá—
fekk—fengu—fengit*. **skjaldborgina** sf. + art. (*skjaldborg-ina*) 'the shield fortification'
'the shield wall': acc., the direct object. **gǫrða** wv. 'made' 'constructed': pp. acc. f. sg.
(a later form of *gǫrva)*, agreeing with *skjaldborgina*, of *gøra*; *fá* + *gǫrða* forms a periphrastic construction, the equivalent of Eng. *get made* (3.9.7.1). **lengr** adv. 'any longer':
comp.

Hǫttr mælti, 'Skaltu nú bana mér, bokki sæll?'

Bǫðvarr bað hann ekki hafa hátt, tók hann upp síðan ok bar hann út ór hǫllinni ok til vatns nǫkkurs sem þar var í nánd, ok gáfu fáir at þessu gaum. Hann þváði hann upp allan.[5]

Síðan gekk Bǫðvarr til þess rúms sem hann hafði áðr tekit, ok leiddi

21 **Hǫttr** sm. (personal name): nom., the subject. **mælti** wv. 'said': 3rd sg. past indic. of
mæla. **skaltu** = *skalt þú*. **skalt** pret.-pres. vb. 'shall': 2nd sg. pres. indic. of *skulu*
(3.6.7); the usual implication of *skulu* is intention, so that although 'shall' is the English
cognate of *skalt*, an idiomatic English translation would be 'do [you] intend to' 'are
[you] going to'. **þú** pron. 'you': nom., the subject. **nú** adv. 'now'. **bana** wv. 'kill': inf.
mér pron. 'me': dat., the direct object (3.1.5 (16) and (18)). **bokki** wm. 'buck' 'fellow'
22 (see line 9). **sæll** adj. 'happy' 'fortunate' (see line 9). **Bǫðvarr** sm. (personal name):
nom., the subject. **bað** sv. 'bade' 'told': 3rd sg. past indic. of *biðja—bað—báðu—beðit*.
hann pron. 'him': acc., the direct object of **bað** (but see the analysis of *hafa* in this line).
ekki adv. 'not' (see line 18). **hafa** wv. 'behave' 'act': inf. (3.6.7); the basic meaning of
hafa is 'have', but when construed with an adv. and nothing further it takes on the sense
of behaving in the manner denoted by the adv; *bað hann ekki hafa* is an acc + inf.
construction, in which acc. *hann* can be analysed both as the direct object of *bað* and
the subject of *hafa* (3.9.4). **hátt** adv. 'loudly', 'noisily' (3.5.1). **tók** sv. 'took' 'lifted':
3rd sg. past indic. of *taka—tók—tóku—tekit*. **hann** pron. 'him': acc., the direct object.
upp adv. 'up'. **síðan** adv. 'then'. **ok** conj. 'and'. **bar** sv. 'carried': 3rd sg. past indic.
of *bera—bar—báru—borit*. **hann** pron. 'him': acc., the direct object. **út** adv. 'out'.
23 **ór** prep. 'from'. **hǫllinni** sf. + art. (*hǫll-inni*) 'the hall': dat., the case always triggered
by *ór*. **ok** conj. 'and'. **til** prep. 'to'. **vatns** sn. 'lake': gen., the case always triggered
by *til*. **nǫkkurs** pron. 'some' 'a certain': gen. n. sg.; here used adjectivally, *nǫkkurs*
agrees with *vatns* and follows it. **sem** conj. 'which'. **þar** adv. 'there'. **var** sv. 'was':
3rd sg. past indic. of *vera* (3.6.10); on the word-order *sem þar var*, see the analysis of *lá*
in line 6. **í** prep. 'in'. **nánd** sf. 'proximity': dat., the case triggered by *í* when location
is denoted; idiomatic English for *í nánd* would be 'near by'. **ok** conj. 'and'. **gáfu** sv.
'gave' 'paid': 3rd pl. past indic. of *gefa—gaf—gáfu—gefit*. **fáir** adj. 'few': strong nom.
m. pl., the subject; although *fáir* is the sole element in the noun phrase and thus has no
noun to agree with, it takes nom. m. pl. form because the referent is plural and probably
exclusively male, and masculine is in any case the default gender where people in gen-
24 eral are denoted (3.3; 3.3.6 (19–21)). **at** prep. 'to'. **þessu** pron. 'this': dat. n. sg. — dat.
case is automatic after *at*; on the neuter gender, see *þetta* in line 15. **gaum** sm. 'heed',
'attention': acc., the direct object. **hann** pron. 'he': nom., the subject. **þváði** wv.
'washed': 3rd sg. past indic. of *þvá*; more commonly this verb is strong (3.6.9.3). **hann**
pron. 'him': acc., the direct object. **upp** adv. 'up' 'thoroughly'. **allan** adj. 'all': acc. m.
sg., agreeing with *hann*; more idiomatic English for *allan* would be the adverbial phrase
25 'all over'. **síðan** adv. 'then'. **gekk** sv. 'went': 3rd sg. past indic. of *ganga—gekk—
gengu—gengit*. **Bǫðvarr** sm. (personal name): nom., the subject. **til** prep. 'to'. **þess**
pron. 'that': gen. n. sg.; here used adjectivally, *þess* agrees with *rúms*. **rúms** sn. 'seat'
'place': gen., the case always triggered by *til*. **sem** conj. 'which'. **hann** pron. 'he':
nom., the subject. **hafði** wv. 'had': 3rd sg. past indic. of *hafa*. **áðr** adv. 'previously'
'before'. **tekit** sv. 'taken': supine of *taka—tók—tóku—tekit*. **ok** conj. 'and'. **leiddi**
26 wv. 'led': 3rd sg. past indic. of *leiða*. **eptir** prep. 'after'. **sér** refl. pron. (referring back
to the understood subject, *Bǫðvarr*; 3.2.1; 3.2.6 (6) and (10)) 'him': dat., the case triggered by *eptir* in the sense 'after [motion]' 'following'. **Hǫtt** sm. (personal name): acc.,
the direct object. **ok** conj. 'and'. **setr** wv. 'places': 3rd sg. pres. indic. of *setja* (3.6.9.3).

eptir sér Hǫtt ok setr hann þar hjá sér. En hann er svá hræddr at skelfr á honum leggr ok liðr, en þó þykisk hann skilja at þessi maðr vill hjálpa sér. Eptir þat kveldar ok drífa menn at hǫllunni ok sjá Hrólfs kappar at Hǫttr var settr í bekk upp ok þykir þeim sá maðr hafa gǫrt

hann pron. 'him': acc., the direct object. **þar** adv. 'there'. **hjá** prep. 'next to'. **sér** refl.
pron. 'him': dat., the case always triggered by *hjá*; on the use of the refl. pron., see the
previous *sér* in this line. **en** conj. 'but'. **hann** pron. 'he': nom., the subject. **er** sv. 'is':
3rd sg. pres. indic. of *vera*. **svá** adv. 'so'. **hræddr** adj. 'frightened': strong nom. m.
sg., agreeing with *hann*. **at** conj. 'that'. **skelfr** sv. 'trembles': 3rd. sg. pres. indic. of
skjálfa—skalf—skulfu—skolfit. **á** prep. 'on'. **honum** pron. 'him': dat., the case trig- 27
gered by *á* when location is denoted; body-part possession is often indicated in ON by
á + dat., corresponding to a possessive adj. in English — thus *á honum* here should be
rendered 'his'. **leggr** sm. 'hollow bone [of arm or leg]': nom., the subject. **ok** conj.
'and'. **liðr** sm. 'joint': nom., the subject; the conjoined nouns *leggr ok liðr* are used
here by synecdoche for the whole body, the sense being that Hǫttr trembled all over —
that may be in part why the verb *skelfr* is sg., even though together *leggr ok liðr* make a
pl. subject, but another possible reason is that *skelfr* precedes the subject, and that the
writer was not clear in his mind at that point what form the subject was going to take
(3.9.8.2). **en** conj. 'but'. **þó** adv. 'nevertheless'. **þykisk** wv. 'thinks': 3rd. sg. pres.
indic., *-sk* form (3.6.5.3), of *þykja* (3.6.9.3); the sense is reflexive, the literal meaning
being 'thinks himself' — the *-sk* takes the place of the direct (reflexive) object in an
acc. + inf. construction 'thinks himself to . . . [i.e. thinks that he . . .]' (3.9.4). **skilja** wv.
'understand': inf. **at** conj. 'that'. **þessi** pron. 'this': nom. m. sg.; here used adjectivally, *þessi* agrees with *maðr*. **maðr** sm. 'man': nom., the subject. **vill** wv. 'wants':
3rd sg. pres. indic. of *vilja* (3.6.7); indic., rather than subj., is used because the dependent sentence describes not a hypothetical situation, but what Hǫttr understands to be a
fact. **hjálpa** sv. '[to] help': inf. of *hjálpa—h(j)alp—hulpu—hólpit*. **sér** refl. pron. 28
(referring back to *Hǫttr*, the subject of the higher sentence, rather than *þessi maðr*;
3.2.1) 'him': dat., the direct object (3.1.5 (16) and (18)). **eptir** prep. 'after'. **þat** pron.
'that': acc., the case triggered by *eptir* in the sense 'after [time]'; on the neuter gender,
see *þetta* in line 15. **kveldar** wv. 'evening draws on': 3rd sg. pres. indic. of *kvelda*; the
construction is impersonal in the sense that no subject is conceived or expressed (3.9.3).
ok conj. 'and'. **drífa** sv. 'drift': 3rd. pl. pres. indic. of *drífa—dreif—drifu—drifit*. **menn**
sm. 'men': nom., the subject. **at** prep. 'to' 'towards'. **hǫllunni** sf. + art. (*hǫllu-nni*;
3.1.7.4 (3)) 'the hall': dat., the case always triggered by *at*. **ok** conj. 'and'. **sjá** sv.
'see': 3rd pl. pres. indic. of *sjá* (3.6.10). **Hrólfs** sm. (personal name): gen., indicating
possession or association. **kappar** wm. 'champions' 'warriors': nom., the subject. **at** conj. 29
'that'. **Hǫttr** sm. (personal name): nom., the subject. **var** sv. 'was': 3rd. sg. past indic.
of *vera*. **settr** wv. 'placed' 'put': pp. nom. m. sg. of *setja*, agreeing with *Hǫttr*. **í** prep.
'in(to)' 'on'. **bekk** sm. 'bench': acc., the case triggered by *í* when motion is denoted.
upp adv. 'up'. **ok** conj. 'and'. **þykir** wv. 'seems': 3rd sg. pres. indic. of *þykja* (3.6.9.3).
þeim pron. 'to them': dat., representing the experiencer, i.e. the person experiencing
the process denoted by the verb (3.9.4); the construction *þykir þeim* is impersonal in the
sense that there is no nominative subject (3.9.3) — though see *maðr* in this line. **sá**
pron. 'that': nom. m. sg.; here used adjectivally, *sá* agrees with *maðr*. **maðr** sm. 'man':
nom., the subject: we have here a hybrid construction, nom. + inf., where *sá maðr* is
taken as the subject of the immediately following inf. clause rather than as the object of
þykir (3.9.4); on a more abstract level the whole of the inf. clause *sá maðr hafa gǫrt sik
œrit djarfan* can be analysed as the subject of *þykir* in that this is what 'seems' to
'them'. **hafa** wv. 'have': inf. **gǫrt** wv. 'made': supine of *gøra*.

sik œrit djarfan, er þetta hefr til tekit. Illt tillit hefr Hǫttr, þá hann sér kunningja sína, því hann hefr illt eitt af þeim reynt; hann vill lifa gjarnan ok fara aptr í beinahrúgu sína, en Bǫðvarr heldr honum, svá at hann náir ekki í burt at fara, því hann þóttisk ekki jafnberr fyrir hǫggum

30 **sik** refl. pron. (referring back to the subject, *sá maðr*; 3.2.1; 3.2.6 (6) and (10)) 'himself': acc., the direct object. **œrit** adv. 'enough', 'sufficiently'. **djarfan** adj. 'bold' 'arrogant': strong acc. m. sg., the object complement agreeing with *sik*, which has masculine singular reference; an idiomatic translation of *þykir þeim sá maðr hafa gǫrt sik œrit djarfan* would be 'it seems to them the man has shown considerable arrogance'. **er** conj. 'who'. **þetta** pron. 'this': acc. n. sg., the direct object; on the neuter gender, see *þetta* in line 15. **hefr** wv. 'has': 3rd sg. pres. indic. of *hafa*. **til** prep.: the prep. is used here absolutely, i.e. without a following noun or noun phrase (3.7.7), its function being to modify the sense of the verb. **tekit** sv. 'taken' 'undertaken' 'done': supine of *taka—tók—tóku—tekit*; it is the prep. *til*, used in close collocation with *taka* 'take', that gives the sense 'undertaken' 'done'. **illt** adj. 'bad' 'expressing dislike': strong acc. n. sg., agreeing with *tillit*. **tillit** sn. 'look' 'glance': acc., the direct object. **hefr** wv. 'has': 3rd. sg. pres. indic. of *hafa*. **Hǫttr** sm. (personal name): nom., the subject. **þá** conj. 'when': *þá* is normally an adverb meaning 'then', but it regularly combines with a following *er* to form a two-word conjunction with the meaning 'when'; sometimes the *er* is omitted, as here, and *þá* then adopts the role of conjunction (3.8.2.1). **hann** pron.

31 'he': nom., the subject. **sér** sv. 'sees': 3rd sg. pres. indic. of *sjá* (3.6.10). **kunningja** wm. 'acquaintances': acc., the direct object. **sína** REFL. POSS. (referring back to the subject; 3.2.1) 'his': acc. m. pl., agreeing with *kunningja*. **því** conj. 'because': *því* is normally an adverb meaning 'therefore', but it regularly combines with a following *at* to form a two-word conjunction introducing sentences of reason or cause (3.8.2.2); sometimes the *at* is omitted, as here, and *því* then adopts the role of conjunction. **hann** pron. 'he': nom., the subject. **hefr** wv. 'has': 3rd sg. pres. indic. of *hafa*. **illt** adj. 'bad' 'evil': strong acc. n. sg., the direct object; on the absence of a noun with which *illt* can agree and the use of the n. sg., see *fátt* in line 3. **eitt** adj. 'alone': strong acc. n. sg., agreeing with *illt*; this is the same word as the numeral 'one', and although used here adjectivally, it corresponds most naturally to the Eng. adverbs 'only', 'just'. **af** prep. 'of' 'from'. **þeim** pron. 'them': dat., the case always triggered by *af*. **reynt** wv. 'experienced': supine of *reyna*. **hann** pron. 'he': nom., the subject. **vill** wv. 'wants': 3rd sg. pres. indic. of *vilja* (3.6.7). **lifa** wv. '[to] live': inf. **gjarnan** adv.: the function of *gjarnan* here is to emphasise *vill* — we might translate the sentence 'he wants very

32 much to live'. **ok** conj. 'and'. **fara** sv. 'go': inf. of *fara* (3.6.10). **aptr** adv. 'back'. **í** prep. 'in(to)'. **beinahrúgu** wf. 'bone-pile' 'pile of bones': acc., the case triggered by *í* when motion is denoted. **sína** REFL. POSS. (referring back to the subject, *hann*) 'his': acc. f. sg., agreeing with *beinahrúgu*. **en** conj. 'but'. **Bǫðvarr** sm. (personal name): nom., the subject. **heldr** sv. 'holds': 3rd sg. pres. indic. of *halda—helt—heldu—haldit*. **honum** pron. 'him': dat., the direct object. **svá** adv. 'so'. **at** conj. 'that': see *svá* (1) in

33 line 18. **hann** pron. 'he': nom., the subject. **náir** wv. 'gets' 'manages' 'is able': 3rd sg. pres. indic. of *ná*. **ekki** adv. 'not': see *ekki* in line 18. **í burt** adv. 'away'. **at** inf. marker 'to'. **fara** sv. 'go': inf. of *fara*. **því** conj. 'because': see *því* in line 31. **hann** pron. 'he': nom., the subject. **þóttisk** wv. 'thought' 'felt': 3rd sg. past indic., *-sk* form (3.6.5.3) of *þykja* (3.6.9.3); the *-sk* suffix here corresponds to a dative experiencer (as in *honum þótti* 'to him seemed'), while *hann*, the subject of the infinitive clause (with omitted infinitive; 3.9.5.2) *hann ekki* [*vera*] *jafnberr* 'he not [to be] equally exposed [i.e. he would not be equally exposed]' is moved into the higher sentence and becomes the subject of *þóttisk* (3.9.4). **ekki** adv. 'not'. **jafnberr** adj. 'equally exposed': strong

þeira, ef hann næði þangat at komask. Hirðmenn hafa nú sama vanða, ok kasta fyrst smám beinum um þvert gólfit til Bǫðvars ok Hattar.[6] Bǫðvarr lætr sem hann sjái eigi þetta. Hǫttr er svá hræddr at hann tekr eigi á mat né drykk, ok þykir honum þá ok þá sem hann muni vera lostinn. Ok nú mælir Hǫttr til Bǫðvars:

34 sama vanða] samt vanða sinn *285*.

nom. m. sg., agreeing with *hann* (see the analysis of *þóttisk* in this line). **fyrir** prep.
'before' 'to'. **hǫggum** sn. 'blows': dat., the case triggered by *fyrir* when location in
front of is denoted. **þeira** poss. adj. 'their': the gen. of the 3rd pl. personal pronoun 34
used with adjectival function (3.3.8.5 (6)). **ef** conj. 'if'. **hann** pron. 'he': nom., the
subject. **næði** wv. 'managed' 'were able': 3rd sg. past subj. of *ná*; the subjunctive is
normally used in sentences introduced by *ef* where the verb is in the past tense. **þangat**
adv. 'thither' 'there'. **at** inf. marker 'to'. **komask** sv. 'come' 'get': inf., *-sk* form, of
koma—kom—kómu—komit; the *-sk* suffix imparts a reflexive sense to the verb, the
literal meaning being 'move oneself'. **hirðmenn** sm. 'courtiers': nom., the subject.
hafa wv. 'have' 'maintain': 3rd pl. pres. indic. of *hafa*. **nú** adv. 'now'. **sama** adj. 'the
same': weak acc. m. sg., agreeing with *vanða*; the weak form of this adjective suffices
to express definite sense, though it is often found in conjunction with the def. art. **vanða**
wm. 'custom' 'practice': acc., the direct object. **ok** conj. 'and'. **kasta** wv. 'throw': 3rd 35
pl. pres. indic. of *kasta*. **fyrst** adv. 'at first'. **smám** adj. 'small': dat. pl., agreeing with
beinum. **beinum** sn. 'bones': dat., with instrumental sense (3.1.5 (20)). **um** prep.
'over'. **þvert** adj. 'transverse': strong acc. n. sg., agreeing with *gólfit*; the sense of
þvert is adverbial ('over the floor crossways') and strong forms of this adj. are normally
used whether the noun phrase in which it occurs is definite or indefinite. **gólfit** sn. +
art. (*gólf-it*) 'the floor': acc., the case always triggered by *um*. **til** prep. 'to'. **Bǫðvars**
sm. (personal name): gen., the case always triggered by *til*. **ok** conj. 'and'. **Hattar** sm.
(personal name): gen., the case always triggered by *til*. **Bǫðvarr** sm. (personal name): 36
nom., the subject. **lætr** sv. 'acts': 3rd sg. pres. indic. of *láta—lét—létu—látit*. **sem**
conj. 'as though'. **hann** pron. 'he': nom., the subject. **sjái** sv. 'sees': 3rd sg. pres. subj.
of *sjá* (3.6.10; *sjái* is a later variant of *sé*); the subjunctive is used in sentences introduced by *sem* with the meaning 'as though', because what is expressed is unreal —
Bǫðvarr does see what is happening, but he pretends not to. **eigi** adv. 'not'. **þetta**
pron. 'this': acc. n. sg., the direct object; on the neuter gender, see *þetta* in line 15.
Hǫttr sm. (personal name): nom., the subject. **er** sv. 'is': 3rd sg. pres. indic. of *vera*.
svá adv. 'so'. **hræddr** adj. 'afraid': strong nom. m. sg., agreeing with *Hǫttr*. **at** conj.
'that'. **hann** pron. 'he': nom., the subject. **tekr** sv. 'takes': 3rd sg. pres. indic. of
taka—tók—tóku—tekit. **eigi** adv. 'not'. **á** prep. 'on(to)': *tekr á*, literally 'takes on(to)', 37
means 'touches'. **mat** sm. 'food': acc., the case triggered by *á* when motion is denoted.
né conj. 'nor' (3.8.1). **drykk** sm. 'drink': acc., the case triggered by *á* when motion is
denoted (*eigi á mat né* [*á*] *drykk*). **ok** conj. 'and'. **þykir** wv. 'seems': 3rd sg. pres.
indic. of *þykja* (3.6.9.3). **honum** pron. 'to him': dat., the case marking the experiencer
of the 'seeming'. **þá** adv. 'then'. **ok** conj. 'and'. **þá** adv. 'then': *þá ok þá* means 'at
every moment'. **sem** conj. 'as though'. **hann** pron. 'he': nom., the subject. **muni**
pret.-pres. vb. 'will' 'must': 3rd sg. pres. subj. of *munu* (3.6.7); on the use of the subjunctive, see *sjái* in line 36. **vera** sv. 'be': inf. **lostinn** sv. 'hit': pp. nom. m. sg., 38
agreeing with *hann*, of *ljósta—laust—lustu—lostit*; *vera* + *lostinn* form a passive construction, the equivalent of Eng. *be hit* (3.6.4). **ok** conj. 'and'. **nú** adv. 'now'. **mælir**
wv. 'speaks' 'says': 3rd. sg. pres. indic. of *mæla*. **Hǫttr** sm. (personal name): nom., the
subject. **til** prep. 'to'. **Bǫðvars** sm. (personal name): gen., the case always triggered
by *til*; on the word-order of *nú mælir Hǫttr*, see *Bǫðvarr* in line 1.

'Bokki sæll, nú ferr at okkr stór knúta, ok mun þetta ætlat okkr til nauða.'[7]

39 **bokki** wm. 'buck' 'fellow' (see line 9). **sæll** adj. 'happy' 'fortunate' (see line 9). **nú** adv. 'now'. **ferr** sv. 'travels' 'comes': 3rd sg. pres. indic. of *fara* (3.6.10). **at** prep. 'towards'. **okkr** pron. 'us [dual]': dat., the case always triggered by *at*. **stór** adj. 'big': strong nom. f. sg., agreeing with *knúta*. **knúta** wf. 'knuckle-bone': nom., the subject; when the subject comes after the verb, as here (see *Bǫðvarr* in line 1), it is common for it to be postponed, allowing phrases dependent on the verb, like *at okkr*, to follow it immediately. **ok** conj. 'and'. **mun** pret.-pres. vb. 'will': 3rd sg. pres. indic. of *munu* (3.6.7). **þetta** pron. 'this': nom. n. sg., the subject: on the neuter gender, see *þetta* in line 15. **ætlat** wv. 'intended': pp. nom. n. sg., agreeing with *þetta*, of *ætla*; *mun . . . ætlat* is a contracted form of *mun . . . vera ætlat* (3.9.5.2), a passive construction, the equivalent of Eng. *will be intended* (3.6.4). **okkr** pron. 'for us [dual]': dat., the case of
40 the intended beneficiary (a type of indirect object). **til** prep. 'for' 'as'. **nauða** sf. 'difficulties' 'harm': gen., the case always triggered by *til*; pl. *nauðir* commonly corresponds to an Eng. sg.; a more idiomatic translation of *mun þetta ætlat okkr til nauða* is 'this will be intended to harm us'.

Bǫðvarr bað hann þegja. Hann setr við holan lófann ok tekr svá við knútunni ok fylgir þar leggrinn með. Bǫðvarr sendir aptr knútuna ok setr á þann sem kastaði, ok rétt framan í hann með svá harðri svipan at hann fekk bana. Slær þá myklum ótta yfir hirðmennina.

Kemr nú þessi fregn fyrir Hrólf konung[8] ok kappa hans upp í kastalann, at maðr mikilúðligr sé kominn til hallarinnar ok hafi drepit einn hirðmann hans, ok vildu þeir láta drepa manninn. Konungr spyrr, hvárt hirðmaðrinn hefði verit saklauss drepinn.

'Því var næsta,' sǫgðu þeir.

Komsk þá fyrir Hrólf konung ǫll sannindi hér um. Hrólfr konungr sagði þat skyldi fjarri, at drepa skyldi manninn.

'Hafi þit hér illan vanða upp tekit, at berja saklausa menn beinum; er mér í því óvirðing, en yðr stór skǫmm, at gøra slíkt. Hefi ek jafnan rœtt um þetta áðr, ok hafi þit hér at øngvan gaum gefit, ok hygg ek at þessi maðr muni ekki alllítill fyrir sér, er þér hafið nú á leitat; ok kallið hann til mín, svá ek viti hverr hann er.'

Bǫðvarr gengr fyrir konung ok kvaddi hann lystiliga. Konungr spyrr hann at nafni.

'Hattargriða kalla mik hirðmenn yðar, en Bǫðvarr heiti ek.'

Konungr mælir, 'Hverjar bœtr viltu bjóða mér fyrir hirðmann minn?'

Bǫðvarr svarar, 'Til þess gørði hann, sem hann fekk.'

Konungr mælir, 'Viltu vera minn maðr ok skipa rúm hans?'

Bǫðvarr svarar, 'Ekki neita ek at vera yðar maðr, ok munu vit ekki skiljask svá buit, vit Hǫttr, ok dveljask nær þér báðir, heldr en þessi hefr setit; elligar vit fǫrum burt báðir.'

Konungr segir, 'Eigi sé ek at honum sœmð, en ekki spara ek mat við hann.'

Bǫðvarr gengr nú til þess rúms sem honum líkaði, en ekki vildi hann þat skipa sem hinn hafði áðr. Hann kippti upp í einhverjum stað þremr mǫnnum, ok síðan settusk þeir Hǫttr þar niðr ok innar í hǫllinni en þeim var skipat. Heldr þótti mǫnnum ódælt við Bǫðvar, ok var þeim inn mesti íhugi á honum.

Ok sem leið at jólum, gørðusk menn þar ókátir. Bǫðvarr spurði Hǫtt hverju þat sætti; hann sagði honum at dýr eitt hafi komit þar tvá vetr í samt, mikit ok ógurligt.

'Ok hefr vængi á bakinu ok flýgr jafnan. Tvau haust hefr þat nú hingat vitjat ok gǫrt mikinn skaða. Á þat bíta ekki vápn,[9] en kappar konungs koma ekki heim, þeir sem eru einna mestir.'

Bǫðvarr mælti, 'Ekki er hǫllin svá vel skipuð sem ek ætlaða, at eitt dýr skal hér eyða ríki ok fé konungsins.'

Hǫttr sagði, 'Þat er ekki dýr, heldr er þat it mesta trǫll.'

Nú kemr jólaaptann. Þá mælir konungr:

'Nú vil ek at allir menn séu kyrrir ok hljóðir í nótt, ok banna ek ǫllum mínum mǫnnum at ganga í nǫkkurn háska við dýrit, en fé ferr eptir því sem auðnar, því ek vil eigi missa menn mína.'[10]

Allir heita hér góðu um, at gøra eptir því sem konungr bauð.

Bǫðvarr leynisk í burt um nóttina; hann lætr Hǫtt fara með sér, ok gørði hann þat nauðugr ok kallar sér stýrt til bana. Bǫðvarr segir betr muni til takask. Þeir ganga í burt frá hǫllinni, ok verðr Bǫðvarr at bera Hǫtt, svá er hann hræddr. Nú sjá þeir dýrit, ok því næst œpir Hǫttr slíkt sem hann má ok kvað dýrit mundi gleypa hann. Bǫðvarr bað bikkju þá þegja ok kastar honum niðr í mosann, ok þar liggr hann ok eigi með ǫllu óhræddr, ok eigi þorir hann heldr heim at fara. Nú gengr Bǫðvarr í móti dýrinu; þat hœfir honum, at sverðit er fast í umgjǫrðinni, er hann vildi bregða því. Bǫðvarr eggjar nú fast sverðit ok þá bragðar í umgjǫrðinni,[11] ok nú fær hann brugðit umgjǫrðinni svá sverðit gengr ór slíðrunum, ok leggr þegar undir bœgi dýrsins ok svá fast at þegar stóð í hjartanu, ok datt þá dýrit til jarðar dautt niðr. Eptir þat ferr hann þangat sem Hǫttr liggr. Bǫðvarr tekr hann upp ok berr hann þangat sem dýrit liggr dautt. Hǫttr skelfr ákaft. Bǫðvarr mælir:

'Nú skaltu drekka blóð dýrsins.'

Hann er lengi tregr, en þó þorir hann víst eigi annat. Bǫðvarr lætr hann drekka tvá sopa stóra; hann lét hann ok eta nǫkkut af dýrshjartanu.[12] Eptir þetta tók Bǫðvarr til hans ok áttusk þeir við lengi. Bǫðvarr mælti:

'Helzt ertu nú sterkr orðinn, ok ekki vænti ek þú hræðisk nú hirðmenn Hrólfs konungs.'

Hǫttr svarar, 'Eigi mun ek þá hræðask upp frá þessu ok ekki þik.'

'Vel er þá orðit, Hǫttr félagi,' segir Bǫðvarr. 'Fǫrum nú til ok reisum upp dýrit ok búum svá um at menn hyggi kvikt muni vera.'

Þeir gøra nu svá. Eptir þat fara þeir heim ok hafa kyrrt um sik, ok veit enginn maðr hvat þeir hafa iðjat.

Konungr spyrr um morguninn hvat þeir viti til dýrsins, hvárt þat hafi nǫkkut þangat vitjat um nóttina. Honum var sagt at fé allt væri heilt í grindum ok ósakat. Konungr bað menn forvitnask hvárt engin sæi líkindi til at þat hefði heim komit. Varðmenn gørðu svá ok kómu skjótt aptr ok sǫgðu konungi at dýrit fœri þar ok heldr geyst at borginni. Konungr bað hirðmenn vera nú hrausta ok duga nú hvern eptir því sem hann hefði hug til, ok ráða af óvætt þennan; ok svá var gǫrt, sem konungr bauð, at þeir bjuggu sik til þess. Konungr horfði á dýrit ok mælti síðan:

'Øngva sé ek fǫr á dýrinu, en hverr vill nú taka kaup til ok ganga í móti því?'

Bǫðvarr mælti, 'Þat væri næsta hrausts manns forvitnisbót. Hǫttr félagi, rektu af þér illmæli þat at menn láta, sem enginn krellr eðr dugr muni í þér vera. Farþú nú ok dreptu dýrit. Máttu sjá at enginn er allfúss til annarra.'

'Já,' svaraði Hǫttr, 'ek mun til þessa ráðask.'

Konungr mælti, 'Ekki veit ek hvaðan þessi hreysti er at þér komin, Hǫttr, ok mikit hefr um þik skipazk á skammri stundu.'

Hǫttr mælti, 'Gef mér til sverðit Gullinhjalta,[13] er þú heldr á, ok skal ek þá fella dýrit eða fá bana.'

Hrólfr konungr mælti, 'Þetta sverð er ekki beranda nema þeim manni sem bæði er góðr drengr ok hraustr.'

Hǫttr sagði, 'Ætla svá til, konungr, at mér muni svá háttat.'

Konungr mælti, 'Hvat má vita, nema fleira hafi skipzk um hagi þína en sjá þykir? Því fæstir menn þykjask þik kenna, at þú sért hinn sami maðr. Nú tak við sverðinu ok njót manna bezt, ef þetta er til unnit.'

Síðan gengr Hǫttr at dýrinu alldjarfliga ok høggr til þess, þá hann kemr í hǫggfœri. Dýrit fellr niðr dautt. Bǫðvarr mælir:

'Sjáið nú, herra, hvat hann hefr til unnit.'

Konungr segir, 'Víst hefr hann mikit skipazk, en ekki hefr Hǫttr einn dýrit drepit; heldr hefr þú þat gǫrt.'

Bǫðvarr segir, 'Vera má at svá sé.'

Konungr mælir, 'Vissa ek, þá þú komst hér, at fáir mundi þínir jafningjar vera, en þó þyki mér þat þitt verk frægiligast, at þú hefr gert hér annan kappa þar er Hǫttr er, ok óvænligr þótti til mikillar gæfu. Nú vil ek hann heiti eigi Hǫttr lengr ok skal hann heita Hjalti upp frá þessu; skaltu nú heita eptir sverðinu Gullinhjalta.'

Ok endar hér þennan þátt frá Bǫðvari ok brœðrum hans.

Notes

[1] As its name suggests, *Hrólfs saga kraka* has the story of the Skjǫldung king Hrólfr kraki (cf. note 8 below) as its main theme and ends with the king's defeat and death in a great battle fought against his half-sister Skuld and her husband Hjǫrvarðr. But as implied by the text itself, the saga consists of different episodes (*þættir*; sg. *þáttr*), at least the fourth of which (chs 17–23) is substantially digressive in content from the rest of the saga. This fourth part tells the story of Bǫðvarr and his brothers and how Bǫðvarr becomes King Hrólfr's trusted retainer (cf. line 149). Bǫðvarr's father is Bjǫrn ('Bear'), the son of a king in northern Norway, his mother is Bera ('She-bear'). Bjǫrn's stepmother, Hvít, lays a curse on him so that by day he is transformed into a bear. In this embodiment he is killed and the pregnant Bera is forced to eat a small portion of the bear meat. She subsequently gives birth to three sons, Elgfróði, who is an elk from the navel downwards, Þórir who has dog's paws instead of feet and Bǫðvarr who appears normal but later displays bear-like qualities. When they reach adulthood, Elgfróði adopts the life of a brigand and Þórir becomes king of Gautland, while Bǫðvarr sets out to join the court of King Hrólfr at Hleiðargarðr. Close to the king's residence he lodges with a poor farmer and his wife who tell him how their son Hǫttr is at Hrólfr's court and how the king's courtiers pelt him with bones; they beg Bǫðvarr to throw only small bones at their son. The hero then continues on his way.

Bǫðvarr corresponds to the Bodvarus of the lost *Skjǫldunga saga* and the Biarco of Saxo Grammaticus's *Gesta Danorum*. He is scarcely to be regarded as a historical figure. In the final chapters of *Hrólfs saga*, Bǫðvarr is accorded the nickname *bjarki* and this may have been a more original name for the hero. The name *Bǫðvarr* probably arose as a prefix to Bjarki's name, a genitive singular of *bǫð*, 'battle'; *bǫðvar-Bjarki* would mean 'battle-Bjarki'. The figure of Bǫðvarr also corresponds in many ways to that of the eponymous hero of the Old English poem *Beowulf*.

Bǫðvarr's bear-like qualities manifest themselves for example in the names of his mother and father, his (nick)name *bjarki* which means 'little bear' and the fact that he fights part of the final battle against Skuld and Hjǫrvarðr in the form of a bear. In this respect he also shares similarities with Beowulf, whose name ('bee-wolf') is probably a noa-expression for a bear.

Hleiðargarðr is the *Lethra* of Saxo Grammaticus's *Gesta Danorum* and the modern Danish (*Gammel*) *Lejre*. The present-day village is on the Danish island of Zealand (Sjælland) some 40 km. west of Copenhagen and a short distance inland from the city cathedral town and port of Roskilde. The area is replete with visible evidence of habitation stretching back to the Stone Age (including grave-mounds and ship-settings). Excavations at Lejre in the 1980s revealed the remains of two large halls, the one built partially on top of the other. The later of these, measuring some 48 × 11 metres, is probably to be dated to the mid-ninth century and is one of the largest Viking-Age halls hitherto discovered in Scandinavia. The earlier hall, of similar size, has been dated to around AD 660 — later, that is, than the lifetime of the historical Hrólfr (see note 8 below). While the association of Lejre with the Skjǫldung dynasty is not perhaps to be regarded as a certainty, it was one made already in the late medieval period by Danish and Icelandic chroniclers and historians. And in the twentieth century R. W. Chambers could write in his *Beowulf: An Introduction* (p. 19): 'We may be fairly sure that the spot where Hrothgar built his "Hart-Hall" and where Hrothulf [i.e. the Norse Hrólfr] held that court to which the North ever after looked for its pattern of chivalry was Leire, where the grave mounds rise out of the waving cornfields.'

[2] It appears that the author of the saga conceives the entrance to the hall as being in one of its shorter ends. The king's seat (*hásæti*) would have been halfway along on the right hand side (cf. the 'Plan of a Norse hall' in *ION* 229). Other seats would have been assigned according to status. Thus those nearer the door would have been more lowly than others and when Bǫðvarr chooses such a place (i.e. *sezk útarliga*) he would modestly (and perhaps circumspectly) have been placing himself amongst those of lower rank. But having become one of the king's men, he selects for himself and Hǫttr places (and three men's places instead of two) further away from the door than those allocated to them (lines 70–71: *innar í hǫllinni en þeim var skipat*) and than the one occupied by the man Bǫðvarr has killed. And generally places closer to the king's would have been of higher status than others. Thus in lines 63–65, Bǫðvarr makes it a condition of his becoming Hrólfr's courtier that he and Hǫttr are allocated places closer (*nær*) to the king than that occupied by the man he has killed. Later in the saga (ch. 24) and recognized as Hrólfr's most esteemed champion,

Bǫðvarr is honoured with a place at the king's immediate right hand, with Hǫttr (now called Hjalti) to his immediate right.

[3] In addressing Bǫðvarr with the words *bokki sæll* (also in lines 11, 21, 39), Hǫttr is being very deferential: *bokki* has the sense of 'important person' or 'man of stature', and the adjective *sæll* is best translated idiomatically by some such phrase as 'by your leave' (cf. ch. 75 of *Grettis saga* (*ÍF* VII, 239–40) where a serving-woman uses it in addressing her mistress who has just scolded her). After his transformation into a new, confident person later in the passage, Hǫttr's tone changes and in his first words to King Hrólfr he uses the familiar second person singular imperative (line 130; cf. note 7 below).

[4] *skjaldborg*: we hear of 'shield-walls' not only in Norse but also in medieval English and German sources (Old English *scildburh*; Old High German *sciltburg*) and they were a feature of battles and sieges. The word might refer either to a defensive line or enclosure of overlapping shields or to a movable screen intended to protect warriors from attack from above (for example, in sieges). In some cases the *skjaldborg* may have resembled the Roman *testudo*, with warriors holding shields above their heads. In the final chapter of the saga (ch. 34) King Hrólfr appears to fight his final battle initially from within a shield-wall. Hǫttr's structure of bones is, of course, a travesty of the real thing.

[5] The present extract from *Hrólfs saga kraka*, which tells how Hǫttr is transformed from a frightened wretch into a formidable warrior has been analysed by Jens Peter Schjødt (*Initiation Between Two Worlds. Structure and Symbolism in Pre-Christian Scandinavian Religion* (2008), 312–26; cf. also 238 and 290 note 31). Schjødt finds in it reminiscences of pre-Christian initiation rites for warriors (as described, for instance, by Tacitus in his account of the Germanic tribe the Chatti in ch. 31 of his *Germania*). Thus when at Bǫðvarr's bidding Hǫttr drinks two gulps of the beast's blood and eats a morsel of its heart (lines 102–03), it is largely that which changes him into a new person. And when here in line 24 Bǫðvarr gives Hǫttr a thorough cleansing in a lake, Schjødt suggests that we have a vestige of a purification rite which might be seen as a stage in Hǫttr's separation from his former way of life. Schjødt also sees Hǫttr's 'killing' of the already dead beast (lines 138–39), in reality already dispatched by Bǫðvarr, as part of the

initation process. And the process might be thought of as being sealed by the change of Hǫttr's name to Hjalti (lines 147–48).

[6] On bone-throwing, see, in addition to the introduction, Ian McDougall, 'Serious entertainments: an examination of a peculiar type of Viking atrocity', in *Anglo-Saxon England* 22 (1993), 201–25. McDougall draws attention to a number of references to bone-throwing in medieval sources, including the sagas and the provincial laws of mainland Scandinavia. Perhaps the most pertinent of these is a passage in Sven Aggesen's *Lex castrensis* (written *c.*1182; cf. *MS* 2–3), which purports to represent the rules of Canute the Great's bodyguard and states how any member judged to have transgressed the rules of the company was to be seated apart from the others (cf. line 5: *útar í hornit*) so that they could pelt him with bones. (McDougall's translation: 'Further, if obstinate arrogance should, through three offences, mark anyone off as incapable of being corrected, and should he refuse to repent, they have decreed that he should be seated as far as possible away from everyone else, to be pelted with bones as anyone pleases.') While the historical reliability of this information offered by Sven is not unimpeachable, neither is it without interest in the present context. Cf. also *The works of Sven Aggesen*, tr. Eric Christiansen (1992), 35.

[7] The use of the first and second person personal pronouns in this extract deserves special comment. In the earliest Icelandic the functions of the second person nominative forms were singular for *þú*, dual (two and two only) for *(þ)it*, and plural (more than two) for *(þ)ér*, with corresponding functions for the oblique cases (acc., gen. and dat.). For first person personal pronouns, the functions were singular for *ek*, dual for *vit*, plural for *vér*, again with corresponding functions in the oblique cases. Cf. *Gr* 3.2.1. As the language developed over the centuries, however, the dual sense gradually disappeared and the old dual forms (*(þ)it*, *vit* (and their oblique forms) came to have plural sense. At the same time, quite possibly under the influence of German usage, the old plural forms (*vér*, *(þ)ér*, and their oblique forms) came to be used in honorific senses. The result was that *ek* and *þú* (with their oblique forms) retained their singular sense, the older dual forms (*(þ)it*, *vit* and their oblique forms) assumed plural sense, while the older plural forms (*vér*, *(þ)ér*, and their oblique forms) were used in honorific contexts. In the present text, representing a saga probably written in the fourteenth or perhaps first half of the fifteenth century but preserved in a manuscript of the

mid-seventeenth century, there is a mixture, indeed something of a confusion, of the two systems. Bǫðvarr (lines 63, 64, 65: *vit*) and Hǫttr (line 39: *okkr* (twice)) are probably each using the old dual in referring collectively to their two selves. On the other hand, in line 17, Hǫttr appears to use the old dual *ykkar* with plural sense (cf. grammatical note to that line). And when the king scolds his courtiers in lines 52–56, he uses not only the old dual form *þit* on the one hand but also the old plural forms *þér* and *yðr* on the other, all with plural (but not honorific) sense. In addressing King Hrólfr in lines 59 and 63, Bǫðvarr uses the honorific *yðar*, although in line 64 he switches to a more familiar singular *þér* (dat.). And the plural imperative (*sjáið*) with which Bǫðvarr addresses the king in line 140 also presupposes an honorific sense. By contrast, when Hǫttr asks the king to give him the sword Gullinhjalti in line 130, it is with the more familiar singular imperative (*gef*) (cf. also the singular imperative *ætla* in line 134); cf. note 3 above. See further the introduction to Text XXIV (pp. 340–41); Helgi Guðmundsson, *The Pronominal Dual in Icelandic* (1972); Stefán Karlsson, *The Icelandic Language*, tr. Rory McTurk (2004), 28.

[8] *Hrólfr konungr*: this is the king after whom the saga is named and its main character. Hrólfr appears in a number of medieval sources, particularly Icelandic and Danish ones (e.g. as Rolvo in Saxo's *Gesta Danorum*), but also in the Old English poems *Widsiþ* (as Hroþwulf) and *Beowulf* (as Hroþulf). (In *Beowulf* it is, however, Hroþulf's uncle Hroþgar (Hróarr in the Norse sources) who plays a central role in the first part of the poem and who receives Beowulf's visit.) Traditions about Hrólfr must go back to a historical king of the Skjǫldung dynasty whose reign probably fell in the first half of the sixth century. Otherwise little is known about the figure. There are hints in the Old English sources that at some stage Hroþulf usurped the dynasty's throne. And it is not impossible that some of the events recounted in the final chapters of *Hrólfs saga* (e.g. Hjǫrvarðr's attack on Hrólfr in chs 31–34) have a basis in reality.

[9] Immunity from weapons was thought to be enjoyed by all sorts of beings (e.g. monsters, wizards and witches) in Norse legend and folklore, not least in the sagas. In *Beowulf* Grendel cannot be killed by the sword.

[10] The pagan Yule-tide was a dangerous time when hauntings traditionally took place; see Schjødt, *Initiation between two worlds*.

Structure and symbolism in pre-Christian Scandinavian religion (2008), 322, footnote 58.

[11] At the beginning of ch. 23 of *Hrólfs saga* we are told how Bǫðvarr acquires his sword in a cave on the direction of his mother and how he makes a scabbard for it out of birch. The sword has special qualities: it could only be urged (*eggjat*) to action on a limited number of occasions and when drawn would always be the death of a man. We hear of it elsewhere in Norse tradition too. It was called Laufi and Saxo describes it as being unusually sharp and long. Various sources tell how in later times a certain Miðfjarðar-Skeggi broke into the grave-mound of King Hrólfr where Bǫðvarr was also buried and tried unsuccessfully to remove Laufi, though he did come away with Hrólfr's sword Skǫfnungr (see e.g. *ÍF* I, 212, 213, *BS* 81; cf. note 13 below). Other swords in Norse legend have temperaments of their own and show a reluctance to be drawn.

[12] It was a widespread belief that by drinking a creature's blood or eating part of its body one acquired the characteristics of that creature, for example, strength, courage, wisdom. Earlier in ch. 23, Bǫðvarr's brother Elgfróði lets blood from his own leg and after Bǫðvarr has drunk it, he immediately becomes considerably stronger. And the animal-like features of Bera's three sons (ch. 20; see note 1 above) are the result of her eating, while pregnant, a morsel of the meat of the bear into which Bjǫrn has been transformed.

[13] The name of this sword has been compared with the Old English words *gylden hilt* (or proper noun *Gyldenhilt*) used in line 1677 of *Beowulf* of the sword that Beowulf finds in the lair of Grendel's mother, with which he kills her and cuts off Grendel's head and which eventually passes into the hands of the Danish king Hroþgar (cf. note 8 above). This is one of the interesting (if enigmatic) correspondences between the accounts of Bǫðvarr and Beowulf. Cf. R. W. Chambers, *Beowulf: An Introduction* (pp. 54–61, 473, 475). Rather than referring to the hilt of a sword, the word *hjalt* in Old Norse was used either of the guard (the part between the blade and the hilt) or the pommel (i.e. the knob or boss at the end of the hilt). The personal name *Hjalti* is indeed probably derived from the word *hjalt* in this sense (cf. lines 147–48). The sword normally worn by Hrólfr, called Skǫfnungr, was described in ch. 30 of the saga as 'the best sword ever carried in Scandinavia'.

II: Snorri Sturluson, EDDA: SKÁLDSKAPARMÁL

Skáldskaparmál is the second part of the Prose Edda, written by Snorri Sturluson in Iceland, probably after his first visit to Norway in 1218–20, and he may have been intermittently engaged on the work until his death in 1241. It is a treatise on poetry, claiming to be addressed to young poets; *Skáldskaparmál* ('the language of poetry') is mainly about poetic diction, and *Háttatal* ('enumeration of verse-forms'), the third part, is about metre and formal devices such as alliteration and rhyme. *Gylfaginning*, the first part, and the first section of *Skáldskaparmál*, given here, contain a series of mythological narratives that give the background to many of the kennings (periphrastic expressions, often metaphorical, for various concepts which sometimes require knowledge of the mythology of heathen Scandinavia for their understanding). A purportedly historical introduction to the mythology is provided in a Prologue to *Gylfaginning*, and in this first section of *Skáldskaparmál* the mythological narratives told to explain various kennings lead up to a story about the origin of the mead of poetry.

Like most of the rest of the Prose Edda, the first section of *Skáldskaparmál* is in dialogue form, the questions being asked by Ægir, a personification of the sea, and the stories being told by the god Bragi, according to Snorri a god of poetry. The setting is a feast, as in the eddic poem *Lokasenna*, and the dialogue, between one of the gods and a visitor to their hall, is reminiscent of both *Gylfaginning* and *Vafþrúðnismál*, another of the eddic poems.

The first story has a close parallel in the skaldic poem *Haustlǫng* by Þjóðólfr of Hvinir, a Norwegian poet of the ninth century, which is quoted by Snorri in other parts of his Edda, and the story of the origin of the mead of poetry is paralleled in *Hávamál* verses 104–10. There are allusions to all the stories told in this selection in skaldic kennings, but even though there are analogues for some of them from mythologies outside the Norse area, it is uncertain how ancient they are.

The text here is based on the Codex Regius (GkS 2367 4to; = R). Emendations are from Codex Wormianus (AM 242 fol.) or Codex Trajectinus (MS No. 1374, University Library, Utrecht).

Bibliography

Editions: Snorri Sturluson: *Edda. Prologue and Gylfaginning*. Ed. A. Faulkes. Clarendon Press (1982), repr. Viking Society for Northern Research (1988, 2000).

Snorri Sturluson: *Edda. Skáldskaparmál*. Ed. A. Faulkes. 2 vols. Viking Society for Northern Research (1998).

Snorri Sturluson: *Edda. Háttatal*. Ed. A. Faulkes. Clarendon Press (1991), repr. Viking Society for Northern Research (1999).

Translation: Snorri Sturluson. *Edda*. Tr. A. Faulkes. Everyman (1987).

II: Snorri Sturluson: EDDA

Skáldskaparmál

E[inn ma]ðr er nefndr Ægir eða Hlér. Hann bjó í ey þeiri er nú er kǫlluð [Hlé]sey. Hann var mjǫk fjǫlkunnigr. Hann gerði ferð sína til Ásgarðs, en er Æsir vissu ferð hans var honum fagnat vel ok þó margir hlutir með sjónhverfingum. Ok um kveldit er drekka skyldi, þá lét Óðinn bera inn í hǫllina sverð, ok váru svá bjǫrt at þar af lýsti, ok var ekki haft ljós annat meðan við drykkju var setit. Þá gengu Æsir at gildi sínu ok settusk í hásæti tólf Æsir, þeir er dómendr skyldu vera ok svá váru nefndir: Þórr, Njǫrðr, Freyr, Týr, Heimdallr, Bragi, Viðarr, Váli, Ullr, Hœnir, Forseti, Loki; slíkt sama Ásynjur: Frigg, Freyja, Gefjun, Iðunn, Gerðr, Sigyn, Fulla, Nanna. Ægi þótti gǫfugligt þar um at sjásk. Veggþili ǫll váru þar tjǫlduð með fǫgrum skjǫldum. Þar var ok áfenginn mjǫðr ok mjǫk drukkit. Næsti maðr Ægi sat Bragi, ok áttusk þeir við drykkju ok orðaskipti. Sagði Bragi Ægi frá mǫrgum tíðindum þeim er Æsir hǫfðu átt.

Hann hóf þar frásǫgn at 'þrír Æsir fóru heiman, Óðinn ok Loki ok Hœnir, ok fóru um fjǫll ok eyðimerkr ok var illt til matar. En er þeir koma ofan í dal nakkvarn, sjá þeir øxna flokk ok taka einn uxann ok snúa til seyðis. En er þeir hyggja at soðit mun vera, raufa þeir seyðinn ok var ekki soðit. Ok í annat sinn er þeir raufa seyðinn, þá er stund var liðin, ok var ekki soðit. Mæla þeir þá sín á milli hverju þetta mun gegna. Þá heyra þeir mál í eikina upp yfir sik at sá er þar sat kvazk ráða því er eigi soðnaði á seyðinum. Þeir litu til ok sat þar ǫrn ok eigi lítill. Þá mælti ǫrninn:

'"Vilið þér gefa mér fylli mína af oxanum, þá mun soðna á seyðinum."

'Þeir játa því. Þá lætr hann sígask ór trénu ok sezk á seyðinn ok leggr upp þegar it fyrsta lær oxans tvau ok báða bógana. Þá varð Loki reiðr ok greip upp mikla stǫng ok reiðir af ǫllu afli ok rekr á kroppinn erninum. Ǫrninn bregzk við hǫggit ok flýgr upp. Þá var fǫst stǫngin við kropp arnarins ok hendr Loka við annan enda. Ǫrninn flýgr hátt svá at fœtr taka niðr grjótit ok urðir ok viðu, [en] hendr hans hyggr hann at slitna munu ór ǫxlum. Hann kallar ok biðr allþarfliga ǫrninn friðar, en hann segir at Loki skal aldri lauss verða nema hann veiti honum svardaga at koma Iðunni út of Ásgarð með epli sín,[1] en Loki vil þat. Verðr hann þá lauss ok ferr til lagsmanna sinna ok er eigi at sinni sǫgð fleiri tíðindi um þeira ferð áðr þeir koma heim. En at ákveðinni stundu teygir Loki Iðunni út um Ásgarð í skóg nokkvorn ok segir at hann hefir fundit epli þau er henni munu gripir í þykkja, ok bað at hon skal hafa með sér sín epli ok bera saman ok hin. Þá kemr þar Þjazi jǫtunn í arnarham ok tekr Iðunni ok flýgr braut með ok í Þrymheim til bús síns.

'En Æsir urðu illa við hvarf Iðunnar ok gerðusk þeir brátt hárir ok gamlir. Þá áttu þeir Æsir þing ok [spyrr hverr annan] hvat síðarst vissi til Iðunnar, en þat var sét síðarst at hon gekk ór Ásgarði með Loka. Þá var Loki tekinn ok fœrðr á þingit ok var honum heitit bana eða píslum. En er hann varð hræddr þá kvazk hann mundu sœk‹j›a eptir Iðunni í Jǫtunheima ef Freyja vill ljá honum valshams er hon á. Ok er hann fær valshaminn flýgr hann norðr í Jǫtunheima ok kemr einn dag til Þjaza jǫtuns. Var hann róinn á sæ, en Iðunn var ein heima. Brá Loki henni í hnotar líki ok hafði *í* klóm sér ok flýgr sem mest. [E]n er Þjazi kom heim ok saknar Iðunnar, tekr hann arnarhaminn ok flýgr eptir Loka ok dró arnsúg í flugnum. En er Æsirnir sá er valrinn flaug með hnotina ok hvar ǫrninn flaug, þá gengu þeir út undir Ásgarð ok báru þannig byrðar af lokarspánum, ok þá er valrinn flaug inn of borgina, lét hann fallask niðr við borgarvegginn. Þá slógu Æsirnir eldi í lokarspánu en ǫrninn mátti eigi stǫðva er hann missti valsins. Laust þá eldinum í fiðri arnarins ok tók þá af fluginn. Þá váru Æsirnir nær ok drápu Þjaza jǫtun fyrir innan Ásgrindr ok er þat víg allfrægt.

'En Skaði, dóttir Þjaza jǫtuns, tók hjálm ok brynju ok ǫll hervápn ok ferr til Ásgarðs at hefna fǫður síns. En Æsir buðu henni sætt ok yfirbœtr, ok hit fyrsta at hon skal kjósa sér mann af Ásum ok kjósa at fótum ok sjá ekki fleira af. Þá sá hon eins manns fœtr forkunnar fagra ok mælir:

'"Þenna kýs ek, fátt mun ljótt á Baldri."[2]

'En þat var Njǫrðr ór Nóatúnum. Þat hafði hon ok í sættargjǫrð sinni at Æsir skyldu þat gera er hon hugði at þeir skyldu eigi mega, at hlœgja hana. Þá gerði Loki þat at hann batt um skegg geitar nokkvorrar ok ǫðrum enda um hreðjar sér ok létu þau ymsi eptir

51 o *R*.

ok skrækti hvárttveggja við hátt. Þá lét Loki fallask í kné Skaða ok þá hló hon. Var þá gjǫr sætt af Ásanna hendi við hana.

'Svá er sagt at Óðinn gerði þat til yfirbóta við hana at hann tók augu Þjaza ok kastaði upp á himin ok gerði af stjǫrnur tvær.'

Þá mælir Ægir: 'Mikill þykki mér Þjazi fyrir sér hafa verit, eða hvers kyns var hann?'

Bragi svarar: 'Ǫlvaldi hét faðir hans, ok merki munu þér at þykkja ef ek segi þér frá honum. Hann var mjǫk gullauðigr, en er hann dó ok synir hans skyldu skipta arfi, þá hǫfðu þeir mæling at gullinu er þeir skiptu at hverr skyldi taka munnfylli sína ok allir jafnmargar. Einn þeira var Þjazi, annarr Iði, þriði Gangr. En þat hǫfum vér orðtak nú með oss at kalla gullit munntal þessa jǫtna, en vér felum í rúnum eða í skáldskap svá at vér kǫllum þat mál eða orðta‹k›, tal þessa jǫtna.'

Þá mælir Ægir: 'Þat þykki mér vera vel fólgit í rúnum.'

Ok enn mælir Ægir: 'Hvaðan af hefir hafizk sú íþrótt er þér kallið skáldskap?'

Bragi svarar: 'Þat váru upphǫf til þess at guðin hǫfðu ósætt við þat fólk er Vanir heita, en þeir lǫgðu með sér friðstefnu ok settu grið á þá lund at þeir gengu hvárirtveggju til eins kers ok spýttu í hráka sín*um*. En at skilnaði þá tóku goðin ok vildu eigi láta týnask þat griðamark ok skǫpuðu þar ór mann. Sá heitir Kvasir. Hann er svá vitr at engi spyrr hann þeira hluta er eigi kann hann órlausn. Hann fór víða um heim at kenna mǫnnum frœði, ok þá er hann kom at heimboði til dverga nokkvorra, Fjalars ok Galars, þá kǫlluðu þeir hann með sér á einmæli ok drápu hann, létu renna blóð hans í tvau ker ok einn ketil, ok heitir sá Óðreyrir, en kerin heit*a* Són ok Boðn. Þeir blendu hunangi við blóðit ok varð þar af mjǫðr sá er hverr er af drekkr verðr skáld eða frœðamaðr. Dvergarnir sǫgðu Ásum at Kvasir hefði kafnat í mannviti fyrir því at engi var þar svá fróðr at spyrja kynni hann fróðleiks.

'Þá buðu þessir dvergar til sín jǫtni þeim er Gillingr heitir ok konu hans. Þá buðu dvergarnir Gillingi at róa á sæ með sér. En er ‹þeir› fóru fyrir land fram, røru dvergarnir á boða ok hvelfði skipinu. Gillingr var ósyndr ok týndisk hann, en dvergarnir réttu skip sitt ok reru til lands. Þeir sǫgðu konu hans þenna atburð, en hon kunni

91 sína *R*. 97 heitu *R*.

illa ok grét hátt. Þá spurði Fjalarr hana ef henni mundi hugléttara ef hon sæi út á sæinn þar er hann hafði týnzk, en hon vildi þat. Þá mælti hann við Galar bróður sinn at hann skal fara upp yfir dyrrnar er hon gengi út ok láta kvernstein falla í hǫfuð henni, ok talði sér leiðask óp hennar, ok svá gerði hann. Þá er þetta spurði Suttungr bróðurson Gillings, ferr hann til ok tók dvergana ok flytr á sæ út ok setr þá í flœðarsker. Þeir biðja Suttung sér lífsgriða ok bjóða honum til sættar í fǫðurgjǫld mjǫðinn dýra, ok þat verðr at sætt með þeim. Flytr Suttungr mjǫðinn heim ok hirðir þar sem heita Hnitbjǫrg, setr þar til gæzlu dóttur sína Gunnlǫðu. Af þessu kǫllum vér skáldskap Kvasis blóð eða dverga drekku eða fylli eða nakkvars konar lǫg Óðreris eða Boðnar eða Sónar eða farskost dverga, fyrir því at sá mjǫðr f[lut]ti þeim fjǫrlausn ór skerinu, eða Suttunga mjǫð eða Hnitbjarga lǫgr.'

Þá mælir Ægir: 'Myrkt þykki mér þat mælt at kalla skáldskap með þessum heitum, en hvernig kómu þeir Æsir at Suttunga miði?'

Bragi svarar: 'Sjá saga er til þess at Óðinn fór heiman ok kom þar er þrælar níu slógu hey. Hann spyrr ef þeir vili at hann brýni ljá þeira. Þeir játa því. Þá tekr hann hein af belti sér ok brýndi, en þeim þótti bíta ljárnir myklu betr ok fǫluðu heinina. En hann mat svá at sá er kaupa vildi skyldi gefa við hóf, en allir kváðusk vilja ok báðu hann sér selja, en hann kastaði heininni í lopt upp. En er allir vildu henda þá skiptusk þeir svá við at hverr brá ljánum á háls ǫðrum. Óðinn sótti til náttstaðar til jǫtuns þess er Baugi hét, bróðir Suttungs. Baugi kallaði illt fjárhald sitt ok sagði at þrælar hans níu hǫfðu drepizk, en talðisk eigi vita sér ván verkmanna. En Óðinn nefndisk fyrir honum Bǫlverkr. Hann bauð at taka upp níu manna verk fyrir Bauga, en mælir sér til kaups einn drykk af Suttunga miði. Baugi kva*zk* enskis ráð eiga af miðinum, sagði at Suttungr vildi einn hafa, en fara kvezk hann mundu með Bǫlverki ok freista ef þeir fengi mjǫðinn. Bǫlverkr vann um sumarit níu mannsverk fyrir Bauga, en at vetri beiddisk hann Bauga leigu sinnar. Þá fara þeir báðir ‹til Suttungs›. Baugi segir Suttungi bróður sínum kaup þeira Bǫlverks, en Suttungr synjar þverliga hvers dropa af miðinum. Þá mælir Bǫlverkr til Bauga at þeir skyldu freista véla nokkvorra, ef þeir megi ná miðinum, en Baugi lætr þat vel

135 kvað *R*. ráðs *R*.

vera. Þá dregr Bǫlverkr fram nafar þann er Rati heitir ok mælir at Baugi skal bora bjargit ef nafarrinn bítr. Hann gerir svá. Þá segir Baugi at gǫgnum er borat bjargit, en Bǫlverkr blæss í nafars raufina ok hrjóta spænirnir upp í móti honum. Þá fann hann at Baugi vildi svíkja hann, ok bað bora gǫgnum bjargit. Baugi boraði enn. En er Bǫlverk‹r› blés annat sinn, þá fuku inn spænirnir. Þá brásk Bǫlverkr í orms líki ok skreið í nafars raufina, en Baugi stakk eptir honum nafrinum ok missti hans. Fór Bǫlverkr þar til sem Gunnlǫð var ok l*á* hjá henni þrjár nætr, ok þá lofaði hon honum at drekka af miðinum þrjá drykki. Í inum fyrsta drykk drakk hann all‹t› ór Óðreri, en í ǫðrum ór Boðn, í inu‹m› þriðja ór Són, ok hafði hann þá allan mjǫðinn. Þá brásk hann í arnarham ok flaug sem ákafast. En er *Suttungr* sá flug arnarins, tók hann sér arnarham ok flaug eptir honum. En er Æsir sá hvar Óðinn flaug þá settu þ*eir* út í garðinn ker sín, en er Óðinn kom inn of Ásgarð þá spýtti hann upp miðinum í kerin, en honum var þá svá nær komit at Suttungr mundi ná honum at hann sendi aptr suman mjǫðinn, ok var þess ekki gætt. Hafði þat hverr er vildi, ok kǫllum vér þat skáldfífla hl*u*t. En Suttunga mjǫð gaf Óðinn Ásunum ok þeim mǫnnum er yrkja kunnu. Því kǫllum v[ér] skáldskapinn feng Óðins ok fund ok drykk hans ok gjǫf hans ok drykk Ásanna.'

Notes

[1] According to *Gylfaginning* ch. 26, Bragi's wife Iðunn had charge of the golden apples from which the gods needed to take bites so as to remain eternally young.

[2] Baldr is described in *Gylfaginning* ch. 22 as the most beautiful of the gods and Skaði naturally hopes that she has chosen him.

151 ljá *R*. 155 Þjazi *R*. 156 þú *R*. 160 lit *R*.

III: Sturla Þórðarson: ÍSLENDINGA SAGA

Sturla Þórðarson (1214–84) belonged to the great Sturlung family and was nephew of Snorri Sturluson (d. 1241). His *Íslendinga saga* is the longest single saga in the compilation known as *Sturlunga saga*, which was probably made about 1300 and covers the history of Iceland from 1117 to 1264 with special attention to the thirteenth century. Other sagas in the collection (and by other authors than Sturla) are, for example, *Þorgils saga ok Hafliða* (covering the period 1117–21), *Hrafns saga Sveinbjarnarsonar* (about a chieftain and notable physician from the Western Fjords killed in 1213), *Þórðar saga kakala* (about Sturla's cousin, Þórðr kakali Sighvatsson, and with a description of a famous sea-battle fought in Húnaflói in 1244) and *Svínfellinga saga* (about family feuds in south-eastern Iceland in the years 1248–52). The sagas of the *Sturlunga*-compilation (often referred to as 'Sagas of Contemporaries') have significant value as contemporary historical sources for the turbulent period leading up to the country's submission to Norway in 1262–64. This, perhaps paradoxically, was also a time of intense literary activity during which many of the Sagas of Icelanders were written.

Sturla's *Íslendinga saga* covers the period 1183–1262 and was probably composed towards the end of his life, between 1271 and 1284. Sturla's other literary works include *Hákonar saga gamla*, a biography of the Norwegian king Hákon Hákonarson (r. 1217–63; written 1264–65); *Magnúss saga lagabœtis*, about Hákon's son Magnús (r. 1263–80), probably completed shortly after his death; a redaction of *Landnámabók*; and perhaps *Kristni saga*, which describes the conversion of Iceland and the early history of its church. Further, he may have written a version of *Grettis saga*. Sturla was also a poet and, for example, composed skaldic poetry in praise of the kings Hákon Hákonarson and his son Magnús lagabœtir. He probably played a significant part in the compilation of the law-code *Járnsíða* which replaced the laws of the Commonwealth in 1271–73 (but which was itself replaced in 1281 by another called *Jónsbók*). Like other members of the Sturlung family, Sturla was closely involved in the often tumultuous political events of thirteenth-century Iceland (described not least in *Íslendinga saga*); but unlike several of them (for example, Snorri Sturluson), he survived the violence of the age and died of natural causes on the day after his seventieth birthday.

The protagonist of the story told in this extract, Gizurr Þorvaldsson (1208–68), played a central part in the history of Iceland in the period leading up to the end of the Commonwealth. After returning from Norway in 1252, Gizurr established himself at the farm Flugumýrr (modern Icelandic Flugumýri) in Skagafjǫrðr in northern Iceland, in territory which Þórðr Sighvatsson kakali had entrusted to Eyjólfr Þorsteinsson and Hrani Koðránsson. At the same time Gizurr sought to cement his relationship with Sturla Þórðarson by marrying his son Hallr to Sturla's daughter Ingibjǫrg. The wedding was celebrated at Flugumýrr in October 1253, and it was here, after many of the guests (including Sturla) had departed, that Eyjólfr and Hrani with a band of followers made their attack and eventually set fire to the farm. The extract describes the burning and the loss of Gizurr's wife Gróa and their three sons. Gizurr escaped, however, to take a dreadful revenge, and within two years many of the attackers of Flugumýrr, including Eyjólfr and Hrani, were dead by the actions of Gizurr and his allies.

Sturla's account of the burning has been admired for its vivid detail and objective narrative skill. It should be remembered that he had left the scene of the event only shortly before Eyjólfr's attack and that his own thirteen-year-old daughter Ingibjǫrg, the bride, was one of the major figures in the drama as, fatally, was his newly-acquired son-in-law, Hallr, son of Gizurr. He was probably, however, writing his account some twenty years after the event. Accounts of the burning at Flugumýrr (though not necessarily Sturla Þórðarson's) may well have influenced the story of the burning of Njáll and his sons as told in chapters 127–130 of *Njáls saga.*

The context of the episode given here may be summarised as follows. As noted above, Þórðr Sighvatsson kakali had put Eyjólfr and Hrani Koðránsson in control of the territory (in effect the whole of Iceland) which had been assigned to him by King Hákon Hákonarson. Eyjólfr had control over the westerly part of the area, including Skagafjǫrðr, and Hrani the easterly part with Eyjafjǫrðr. When Gizurr arrived back from Norway in 1252, however, the farmers of Skagafjǫrðr accepted him as their leader and the following year Gizurr drove Eyjólfr out of Skagafjǫrðr and settled at Flugumýrr. Eyjólfr moved to Mǫðruvellir in Hǫrgárdalr. Goaded on by his wife Þuríðr (the daughter of Sighvatr Sighvatsson who had been killed by Gizurr at the Battle of Ørlygsstaðir in 1238), Eyjólfr, together with Hrani Koðránsson, attacked Gizurr at Flugumýrr in an episode the latter part of which is described in this selection. The intention was to kill Gizurr, but as will be seen, he escaped. After Gizurr went abroad in 1254, hostilities continued between Eyjólfr and Gizurr's ally, Oddr Þórarinsson, and in these Eyjólfr appears to have had the support of Heinrekr Kársson (bishop of Hólar, 1247–60). Eyjólfr and Hrafn Oddsson, a prominent chieftain from north-western Iceland, killed Oddr at his home in Skagafjǫrðr early in 1255. Oddr's brother Þorvarðr allied himself with Þorgils Bǫðvarsson skarði, Sturla Þórðarson and a third chieftain and attacked and killed Eyjólfr at Þveráreyrar on 19th July, 1255.

At the point where the selection begins, Gizurr and his companions in the farm at Flugumýrr have put up a stout and lengthy resistance to Eyjólfr and his band of assailants before the expedient of fire is resorted to. Time was not on the side of Eyjólfr and his band, who were in hostile territory (cf. lines 122–23). Their power base was in Eyjafjǫrðr and eastwards from there, and they had to do something to resolve the impasse.

Sturlunga saga, and with it *Íslendinga saga*, is preserved in two medieval vellums, Króksfjarðarbók (AM 122 a fol.; written *c.*1350–70) and Reykjarfjarðarbók (AM 122 b fol.; written *c.*1375–1400). Both manuscripts (particularly the latter) are now defective and, in reconstructing lost parts of their texts, recourse must be had to the many copies in paper manuscripts (including a good one in the British Library) which were derived from them when they were more complete than now. The text of the selection here follows Króksfjarðarbók (ff. 101vb28–102vb26) but with certain emendations and additions mostly based on British Library Add. 11,127.

Bibliography

Facsimile edition: Jakob Benediktsson (ed.), *Sturlunga saga: Manuscript no. 122 a fol. in the Arnamagnæan Collection*, Early Icelandic manuscripts in facsimile I (1958). [= Króksfjarðarbók]

Critical edition: Kr. Kålund (ed.), *Sturlunga saga*, 2 vols. (1906–11).

Popular editions: Jón Jóhannesson, Magnús Finnbogason and Kristján Eldjárn (eds), *Sturlunga saga*, 2 vols. (1946). Örnólfur Thorsson (ed.), *Sturlunga saga*, 3 vols. (1988).

English translation: Julia McGrew and R. George Thomas (tr.), *Sturlunga saga*, 2 vols. (1970–74).

Background reading:

Gunnar Karlsson, *Samband við miðaldir* (1992), 164–71.
Jónas Kristjánsson, *Eddas and sagas* (1988), Index, s.v. Sturla Þórðarson.
W. P. Ker, *Epic and romance*, 2nd ed. (1908), 246–74.
MS, under *Hákonar saga gamla Hákonarsonar; Landnámabók; Magnúss saga lagabœtis; Sturla Þórðarson; Sturlung Age; Sturlunga saga.*
Guðrún Nordal, 'Sturlunga saga and the context of saga-writing', in *Introductory essays on Egils saga and Njáls saga*, ed. John Hines and Desmond Slay (1992), 1–14.

III: Sturla Þórðarson: ÍSLENDINGA SAGA

Gizurr Þorvaldsson's escape from the burning at Flugumýrr, 1253

Chapter 172

. . . Ok þá er Eyjólfr sá at þeim sóttisk seint, ‹en uggði› at heraðsmenn myndi at koma, þá báru þeir eld at. Jón af Bakka hafði haft tjǫrupinn[1] með sér, ok þá tóku þeir gærur af þǫnum ‹er þar váru úti›[2] ok báru þar í eld ok tjǫruna. Sumir tóku tǫðu ok tráðu í gluggana ok lǫgðu þar eld í, ok varð þá reykr mikill brátt í húsunum ok svælumikit.

Gizurr lagðisk niðr í skálanum með setstokkinum ǫðrum megin ok lagði nasirnar ok hǫfuðit við gólfit[3] ok þar Gróa, kona hans, hjá honum.[4] Þorbjǫrn nef lá þar hjá þeim, ok horfðusk þeir Gizurr at hǫfðunum.[5] Þorbjǫrn heyrði at Gizurr bað fyrir sér á marga vega háleitliga til Guðs, svá at eigi kvazk hann slíkan formála heyrt hafa, en hann þóttisk eigi sinn munn mega í sundr hefja fyrir reyk. Ok eptir þat stóð Gizurr upp, ok helt Gróa á honum. Gizurr gekk í anddyrit syðra, ok var honum þá erfitt mjǫk, bæði af reyk ok hita, ok var þat þá í hug at leita út heldr en vera lengr inni svældr.

Gizurr glaði stóð við dyrrin ok talaði við Kolbein grǫn ok bauð Kolbeinn honum grið, því at þeir hǫfðu fyrr þat við mælzk at hvárr skyldi ǫðrum grið gefa, hvárr sem vald hefði til.[6] Gizurr Þorvaldsson stóð at baki nafna sínum meðan þeir tǫluðu þetta, ok svalaði honum heldr meðan. Gizurr glaði beiddisk at hann mundi kjósa mann með sér til griða. Kolbeinn játaði því, þegar frá væri Gizurr ok synir hans.

Þá kom þar til Gró í anddyrit Ingibjǫrg Sturludóttir ok var í náttserk einum ok berfœtt.[7] Hon var þá þrettán vetra gǫmul ok var bæði mikil vexti ok skǫrulig at sjá. Silfrbelti hafði vafizk um fœtr henni, er hon komsk ór hvílunni fram; var þar á pungr ok þar í gull hennar mǫrg. Hafði ‹hon› þat þar með sér. Gróa varð fegin henni mjǫk ok segir at eitt skyldi yfir þær ganga báðar.

Ok er Gizuri hafði heldr svalat, þá var honum þat í hug at hlaupa eigi út. Hann var í línklæðum ok í brynju, stálhúfu á hǫfði, sverðit Brynjubít í hendi. Gróa var ok í náttserk einum. Gizurr gekk at henni Gró ok tók fingrgull tvau ór brókabeltispungi sínum ok fekk henni í hǫnd, því at hann ætlaði henni líf en sér dauða. Annat fingrgullit hafði átt Magnús biskup, fǫðurbróðir hans, en annat Þorvaldr, faðir hans.[8] Kvazk hann vilja at þeira gripa nyti vinir hans, ef svá fœri sem hann vildi. Gizurr fann þá á Gró at henni fannsk mikit um skilnaðinn þeira. Leitaði Gizurr þá innar eptir húsunum ok með honum Guðmundr, frændi hans. Hann vildi aldri við hann skilja. Þeir kómu at litlustofu ok ætluðu þar út at leita. Þá heyrði hann þar mannamál úti ok bǫlvan. Brott hvarf hann þaðan.

Chapter 173

Nú verðr þar frá at hverfa. Þær Gróa ok Ingibjǫrg gengu nú út at durunum. Gróa bað Ingibjǫrgu útgǫngu. Þat heyrði Kolbeinn grǫn, frændi hennar,[9] ok bað hana út ganga til sín. Hon kvazk eigi þat vilja, nema hon køri mann með sér. Kolbeinn kvað eigi þat mundu. Gróa bað hana út ganga, — 'en ek verð at leita sveinsins Þorláks, systursonar míns,' segir hon — Þorleifr hreimr var faðir hans.[10] Sveinninn hafði út hlaupit áðr, ok loguðu um hann línklæðin er hann kom ofan á vǫllinn. Hann var tíu vetra gamall. Komsk hann til kirkju.[11]

Þat er sumra manna sǫgn at Þorsteinn genja hryndi Gró inn í eldinn, ok þar fannsk hon í anddyrinu.[12]

Kolbeinn grǫn hljóp inn í eldinn eptir Ingibjǫrgu ok bar hana út til kirkju. Tóku þá húsin mjǫk at loga.

Hallr Gizurarson kom litlu síðar at þeim inum syðrum durunum ok Árni beiskr með honum, fylgðarmaðr hans.[13] Þeir váru báðir mjǫk þreyttir ok móðir af hita. Borði var skotit um þverar dyrrnar.[14] Hallr horfði lítt á ok hljóp þegar út yfir borðit. Hann hafði sverð í hendi ok ekki fleira vápna. Einarr Þorgrímsson var nær staddr er Hallr hljóp út, ok hjó í hǫfuð honum með sverði, ok var þat banasár.[15] Ok er hann fell, hjó annarr á fótinn hœgra fyrir neðan kné svá at nær tók af. Þórólfr munkr frá Þverá, ǫlgerðarmaðr, var nýgenginn áðr út ok var þar í túninu.[16] Hann tók gæru, er þar lá, ok skaut undir Hall, þá er þeir Einarr gengu frá honum. Hann kippti ǫllu saman, Halli ok gærunni, á leið til kirkjunnar, þá er þeir hugðu eigi at. En Hallr var fáklæddr ok kom kuldi í sár hans. Munkrinn var ok berfœttr, ok kól hann ok. Gat hann þó komit þeim báðum í kirkju of síðir.[17]

Árni beiskr hljóp þegar út eptir Halli. Hann drap fótum í borðit — var þá við aldr — ok fell, er hann kom út. Þeir spurðu, hverr þar fœri svá hrapalliga.

'Árni beiskr er hér,' segir hann, 'ok mun ek ekki griða biðja. Sé ek ok, at sá liggr hér skammt frá mér er mér líkar eigi illa at ek hafa slíka fǫr ok hann.'[18]

Kolbeinn mælti þá: ‘Man engi nú Snorra Sturluson, ef þú fær grið.’[19] Báðir unnu þeir Kolbeinn á honum ok Ari Ingimundarson; ok fleiri hjoggu þeir hann, ok lét hann þegar líf sitt.

Þá fell ofan skálinn, fyrst norðan af skálanum suðr um loptit er í var skálanum. Þessir menn urðu þar undir: Ísleifr Gizurarson, Ketilbjǫrn, bróðir hans, Bjǫrn Óláfsson, Steinn smiðr, Kolbjǫrn, Ásgrímr. Guðlaugr piltr, Ketill sútari, Kormakr bryti létusk í klefanum. Sokki Ormsson lézk í litlustofu. Páll hét lausamaðr einn er fannsk dauðr í borðhúsi í stofunni. Snauðir menn kǫfnuðu níu í gestahúsi ok hét maðr Þorfinnr, faðir Þórólfs tinsmiðs. Hálfr þriði tugr manna lézk í brennunni.

Halldórr Guðmundarson[20] gekk út suðrdyrr af búrinu, ok var þar fyrir Eyjólfr Þorsteinsson ok gaf honum grið. Ok er hann kom mjǫk at kirkjunni, var þar fyrir sá maðr er Þorkell smiðr hét, er síðan var veginn á Mǫðruvǫllum.[21] Hann tók til hans ok kvað eigi svá ótt í kirkjuna, en annarr hjó til hans með sverði við forkirkjuna ok kom framan á hálsinn inum hœgra megin, ok hraut blóðit allt á kirkjuna. Var þat mikill áverki. Komsk hann við þat í kirkju.

Nú tóku ǫll húsin at loga, nema eldhús brann eigi ok litlastofa ok skyrbúr.

Chapter 174

Nú er at segja frá Gizuri Þorvaldssyni at hann kom at skyrbúri, ok hann Guðmundr, frændi hans, fylgði honum.[22] Gizurr bað hann fara frá sér, kvað heldr mega einn fá nokkut undanbragð ef þess vildi auðna, þar sem þeir fengu eigi báðir. Þar kom þá ok Jón prestr Halldórsson,[23] ok kvað Gizurr þá báða skyldu brott fara frá sér at sinni. Gizurr steypti þá af sér brynjunni ok stálhúfunni, en hafði sverðit í hendi. Þeir Jón prestr leituðu til suðrdura af búrinu ok fengu báðir grið. Gizurr Þorvaldsson gekk í búrit. Hann sá hvar skyrker stóð á stokkum í búrinu. Þar hleypti ‹hann› sverðinu Brynjubít ofan í skyrit svá at þat sǫkk upp um hjǫltin. Gizurr sá at þar var ker í jǫrðu hjá, lítit, ok var í sýra.[24] En skyrkerit stóð þar yfir ofan ok hulði mjǫk sýrukerit þat er í jǫrðunni var. Þar var rúm þat er maðr mátti komask í kerit, ok fór Gizurr þar í kerit þat er ‹í› jǫrðunni var ok settisk niðr í sýruna í línklæðum einum, ok tók honum sýran í geirvǫrtur. Kalt var í sýrunni.

Skamma hríð hafði hann þar setit áðr hann heyrði mannamál ok heyrði at um var talat, ef hann fyndisk, at þrír menn váru til ætlaðir til áverka við hann, ok skyldi sitt hǫgg hǫggva hverr ok fara ekki ótt at, ok vita hvernig hann yrði við. Hrani[25] var til ætlaðr ok Kolbeinn grǫn ok Ari Ingimundarson. Nú kómu þeir í búrit með ljósi ok leituðu allt. Þeir kómu at kerinu er Gizurr sat í kerinu,[26] ok lǫgðu í kerit þrír menn með spjótum eða fjórir. Þeir þrættu um: sǫgðu sumir, at fyrir yrði, en sumir ekki. Gizurr hafði lófana fyrir kviði sér sem hógligast, at þeir skyldi sem sízt kenna at fyrir yrði. Hann skeindisk á lófunum ok svá framan á beinum á skǫfnungunum. Váru þat lítil sár ok mǫrg. Svá hefir Gizurr sagt sjálfr, áðr þeir kœmi í búrit, at hann skalf af kulða, svá at svaglaði í kerinu; en er þeir kómu í búrit, þá skalf hann ekki. Tvisvar leituðu þeir um búrit, ok fór svá í hvárttveggja sinn. Eptir ‹þat gengu› þeir í brott ok út ok bjoggusk í brott.

Gengu menn þá til griða, þeir er lífs váru, Guðmundr Fálkason, Þórðr djákni, Óláfr er síðan var kallaðr gestr, ok hafði Einarr Þorgrímsson unnit á honum.[27] Þá var í dagan. Stigu brennumenn þá á bak ok riðu út ór garði. Fótar-Ǫrn[28] reið síðast ok segir Eyjólfi at hann sá mann ganga til kirkju ok var leiddr, ok kvazk hyggja at Gizurr væri; kvað þat eitt ráð at snúa aptr. Þeir svǫruðu margir, kváðu þat ekki vera mega. Varð ok ekki af, at þeir sneri aptr.

Gizurr hafði þá gengit til kirkju, sem Ǫrn ætlaði, því at svá var honum kalt orðit at hann þolði eigi lengr þar at vera. Ok er Gizurr kom í kirkju, váru klæði borin at honum, ok vermði sú kona hann á lærum sér er Hallfríðr hét ok var kǫlluð Garðafylja, er síðan var heimakona með Kálfi Brandssyni á Víðimýri.[29] Hann var háss orðinn mjǫk af reyk ok kulða. Gizurr hresstisk brátt ok bar sik vel ok drengiliga eptir slíka mannraun ok harma. Hallr, son hans, andaðisk þá er nær var hálfljóst

. . .

Notes

[1] Jón and his son, Ljótr ('Ugly') were probably the last to join Eyjólfr's party. His farm lay in Øxnadalr, only a little to the east of Øxnadalsheiðr, the high ground to be crossed before Skagafjǫrðr, where Flugumýrr lay, was reached. It is natural, then, that it was he who should provide the *tjǫrupinnr*, particularly if it were a relatively heavy object (see below). After the burning, in October 1253, a band of men under Gizurr ravaged Bakki while Jón was absent. And in late January of the following year, they surprised him while he was sleeping in his house (rather than in the church there where he had slept since the burning) and killed him. The meaning of the word *tjǫrupinnr* is uncertain. It may refer to a piece of wood covered in tar which could be used in starting a fire. But it more probably refers to a small barrel (or other vessel) containing tar (cf. older English *pin*, 'small cask, keg').

[2] There would have been sheepskins stretched out to dry outside the farm at Flugumýrr.

[3] Gizurr did this to be able to breathe the fresher air near the floor.

[4] Gróa Álfsdóttir was Gizurr's second wife, whom he had only married in 1252. She was certainly mother of Hallr (line 51) and Ísleifr (line 74), and possibly also of Ketilbjǫrn (line 74).

[5] Þorbjǫrn nef was son of Þórðr Narfason, brother of Helga, mother of the bride, Ingibjǫrg Sturludóttir.

[6] On *grið*, cf. *Laws*, I 183–84, 210, 260. Gizurr glaði appears to have been a close companion and supporter of Gizurr Þorvaldsson for at least a quarter of a century. He survived the burning at Flugumýrr, quite possibly by accepting Kolbeinn's offer mentioned here. His home was at Lang(a)holt in Flói in southern Iceland. His by-name *glaði* means 'the Cheerful'. Kolbeinn Dufgusson grǫn was one of the incendiaries. He was subsequently apprehended and killed at Espihóll in Eyjafjǫrðr in January, 1254, by one of a band of men under Gizurr Þorvaldsson. Gizurr composed a skaldic verse commemorating the killing. Cf. lines 40–41 and note 9.

[7] Ingibjǫrg Sturludóttir was the daughter of Sturla Þórðarson, the author of *Íslendinga saga*, by Helga Þórðardóttir. She was newly wed to Hallr Gizurarson.

[8] Þorvaldr Gizurarson (d. 1235), Gizurr's father, is known for, among other things, his foundation (1226) of the Augustinian monastery on the island of Viðey (off modern Reykjavík), of which he was first prior. See *HOIC*, 197–98 and Index.

[9] Kolbeinn's father Dufgus was a nephew of Þórðr Sturluson, father of Sturla Þórðarson, father of Ingibjǫrg. Cf. line 15 and note 6.

[10] Þorleifr Ketilsson hreimr (died 1289; married to Gróa's sister) had left the wedding-feast the day before the night of the burning (i.e. on Tuesday, 21st October, 1253), apparently leaving his son at Flugumýrr. He also joined Gizurr in the revenge for the burning. Þorleifr later distinguished himself by being elected lawspeaker (*lǫgsǫgumaðr*) on three occasions (1263–1265, 1268, 1271) and was the last person to hold the position.

[11] Most of the churches of thirteenth-century Iceland were attached to farms and privately owned. It is natural that there should have been one at an important farm like Flugumýrr. In situations like the one described here, churches would have been regarded as places of sanctuary.

[12] This refers to the gruesome scene where Gizurr returns to the farm soon after the burning and finds the remains of his wife and his son, Ísleifr. Þorsteinn genja may well be identical with Þorsteinn Guðmundarson, who after the event praised the stout resistance presented by the defenders at Flugumýrr.

[13] Árni beiskr was the man who dealt Snorri Sturluson his death-blow at Reykholt on 23rd September, 1241. He was killed by Kolbeinn grǫn Dufgusson and Ari Ingimundarson at Flugumýrr.

[14] A board had been put across the doorway by the attackers to prevent escape from the burning building.

[15] Einarr Þorgímsson was from Øxnahóll in Øxnadalr (cf. note 1). He was killed there in January, 1254, by Óláfr gestr in Gizurr's revenge for the burning (cf. lines 119–20).

[16] Þórólfr munkr frá Þverá was presumably from Þverá, often called Munka-Þverá, in Eyjafjǫrðr. A Benedictine monastery was established there in 1155 (cf. *HOIC*, 194). Ale was specially brewed for great

feasts such as this one at Flugumýrr and Þórólfr had presumably played at least some part in this.

[17] *þeim báðum* must refer to Hallr and Þórólfr himself.

[18] Árni's reference to Hallr here presupposes a situation prior to the events described in lines 58–63; in other words, the narrative is here going back in time. Sturla recognised the difficulties of telling of a number of more or less simultaneous events. Earlier in the description of the events at Flugumýrr, he explicitly writes: 'Now a number of things happened simultaneously, but one can only tell about one thing at a time' (*Nú urðu margir atburðir senn, ok má þó frá einum senn segja*).

[19] It is appropriate that Kolbeinn should draw attention to Snorri Sturluson's killing. His father was Snorri's nephew as well as Þórðr Sturluson's. Cf. lines 15–16, 40 and notes 6 and 9.

[20] Guðmundarson: so Króksfjarðarbók; but some manuscripts have Ǫgmundarson here, and earlier in *Íslendinga saga* (ch. 172), a Halldórr Ǫgmundarson is mentioned amongst the defenders of Flugumýrr 'er síðan var kallaðr hálshǫgg' (who afterwards was known as 'neck-chop'); cf. lines 85–86.

[21] Mǫðruvellir was a farm in Hǫrgárdalr (not to be confused with Mǫðruvellir in Eyjafjǫrðr, about 33 km. further south) some 50 km. north-eastwards from Flugumýrr. In late January, 1254, three of the incendiaries were seized at Mǫðruvellir and killed. One of the three is named Þorgils Sveinsson, and it is quite possible that 'Þorkell' here is an error for 'Þorgils'.

[22] Excavations of the eleventh-century farmhouse at Stöng in southern Iceland have revealed the remains of a *skyrbúr* and evidence of large vats, some half-buried in the earthen floor, and similar remains have also been found at the Augustinian monastery on the island of Viðey off modern Reykjavík (cf. note 8 above). *Skyr* was a common dish in Scandinavia of the Middle Ages and is still widely consumed in present-day Iceland (often eaten with sugar and milk or cream); it consists of milk, soured and thickened, and is sometimes likened to yoghurt.

Although modern *skyr* has something of the consistency of cream-cheese, medieval sources refer to it being drunk.

[23] Probably not the same as Prest-Jóan, who was involved in the killing of Kolbeinn grǫn (cf. note 6 above).

[24] *Sýra* was sour whey; this was a common drink in medieval Iceland and would have been stored in large quantities on farms. It was often mixed with water to make a drink called *blanda*.

[25] Hrani Koðránsson, of Grund in Eyjafjǫrðr, one of the incendiaries, was subsequently killed in revenge (May, 1254) on the island of Grímsey by a band of men under the leadership of Oddr Þórarinsson, an ally of Gizurr Þorvaldsson.

[26] The repetition of the antecedent *kerinu* is perhaps for emphasis, though *er Gizurr sat í* may mean 'while Gizurr was sitting in [it]' rather than 'which Gizurr was sitting in'.

[27] Óláfr gestr survived the burning at Flugumýrr; cf. note 15 above.

[28] We learned earlier that Fótar-Ǫrn acted as look-out for Eyjólfr's band. We are also told that during the attack he spent most of his time on his horse. The latter circumstance might be consistent with the suggestion that he may have been called Fótar-Ǫrn because he had something wrong with his leg or foot.

[29] Kálfr Brandsson had himself been at the wedding-feast but had presumably left before the attack by Eyjólfr. He later married Guðný, another daughter of Sturla Þórðarson. In 1259 he also allied himself with Gizurr Þorvaldsson against his enemy, Þórðr Andrésson. Like his father and grandfather before him, he lived at Víðimýrr, a major farm in Skagafjǫrðr.

IV: KORMAKS SAGA

The other Family Sagas with which *Kormaks saga* has most in common are *Hallfreðar saga*, *Bjarnar saga Hítdœlakappa*, *Gunnlaugs saga ormstungu* and *Laxdœla saga*. In all of these apart from *Laxdœla saga* the hero, as in *Kormaks saga*, is a poet; and in all five sagas the hero seems to hesitate between, on the one hand, the idea of committing himself in marriage to a woman with whom he is intimately involved in Iceland and, on the other, the lure of the *útanferð* ('journey abroad'), the need (as the hero sees it) to travel abroad to win fame and fortune. *Kormaks saga* is exceptional among these sagas in that its hero's hesitation is attributed to supernatural causes, as this extract shows; and in the fact that the hero, Kormakr, does not travel abroad until relatively late in the history of his relations with Steingerðr, the woman with whom he is involved. *Kormaks saga* also resembles *Gunnlaugs saga* but differs from *Hallfreðar saga*, *Bjarnar saga* and *Laxdœla saga* in that its hero's journey abroad does not lead to his marrying another woman. *Kormaks saga* nevertheless raises the question of whether the supernatural explanation of Kormakr's failure to marry Steingerðr is to be seen as symbolic of an emotional ambivalence in his character, such as the heroes of the other four sagas all have, in greater or lesser degree.

Opinions have been divided as to whether these stories with the motif of the wavering hero owe more to European romances such as the story of Tristan and Isolde, a prose version of which was made in Norwegian in the thirteenth century as *Tristrams saga ok Ísǫndar*, or to Germanic stories such as that of Sigurðr Fáfnisbani ('the slayer of Fáfnir'), a relatively full version of which is preserved in *Vǫlsunga saga*, a thirteenth-century Icelandic *fornaldarsaga* based largely on the heroic lays of the Poetic Edda. See Bjarni Einarsson, *Skáldasögur* ('sagas of poets', 1961; English summary, pp. 280–99). *Kormaks saga* is probably the oldest of the five Family Sagas listed above (see Paul Bibire's review of Bjarni Einarsson's *To skjaldesagaer* (1976) in *Saga-Book* XX:3 (1980), 238–40, p. 239), and may have influenced the other four. All five are anonymous, but probably written in the west or north-west of Iceland.

There has also been disagreement about whether or not the verses of *Kormaks saga* were composed along with the prose by the author of the saga at the time of its composition, i.e. early in the thirteenth century. The claim that the author of the prose also composed the verse is made in spite of the apparent discrepancy in content between some of the verses and the prose (e.g. in the first verse in the extract here, it is Kormakr's shield that the scythe strikes against, rather than a sword as in the prose). Those who decide that the saga author did not compose the verse then debate whether the verses were made by the persons to whom they are attributed in the saga or indeed by any other poet or poets living between the time in which the events of the saga are set (the tenth century) and the author's time. See, besides the works already cited, Theodore M. Andersson, 'Skalds and troubadours', *Mediaeval Scandinavia* 2 (1969), 7–41; Bjarni Einarsson, 'The lovesick skald: a reply to Theodore M. Andersson', *Mediaeval Scandinavia* 4 (1971), 21–41; Einar Ól. Sveinsson, 'Kormakr the Poet and his Verses', *Saga-Book* XVII:1 (1966), 18–60; Peter Hallberg, *Old Icelandic poetry: eddic lay and skaldic verse*, tr. Paul Schach and S. Lindgrenson (1975), 141–53.

Kormaks saga is preserved in its entirety in Möðruvallabók (AM 132 fol.; = M), a mid fourteenth-century collection of Family Sagas. A small part of the saga (beginning half-way through chapter 3 and ending at a point corresponding to the end of line 56 of this extract) is also preserved on one of the three surviving leaves of the late fourteenth-century manuscript AM 162 F fol. (= 162; the other two leaves preserve parts of *Bjarnar saga Hítdœlakappa*). The saga has been edited from these manuscripts by Theodor Möbius (1886) and by Einar Ól. Sveinsson (*ÍF* VIII, 1939, 201–302), and it is in the latter edition that the full text of the saga is most readily available. The present extract is based mainly on the text of that edition, though it has been collated with that of M as edited in facsimile by Einar Ól. Sveinsson (in *CCIMA* V, ff. 121v–122r). The interpretations of the verses reflected in the present text differ in several respects from those of Möbius and Einar Ólafur, and indeed from those of Finnur Jónsson in his critical edition of the verses in *Skj* B I 73–74. The readings from 162 given in the textual notes are derived from those supplied in the two editions of *Kormaks saga* just mentioned, as well as from those given by Finnur Jónsson in his diplomatic edition of the verses in *Skj* A I 82–83. Readings from 162 are, however, given only in cases where the text of M is in one way or another problematic.

The spelling of Kormakr's name with a short *a* (*Kormakr* as opposed to *Kormákr*), recommended by Einar Ól. Sveinsson in his article of 1966 referred to above, in preference to the long *á* spelling used in his 1939 edition of the saga, has been adopted here.

In this extract, which corresponds to chs 5–6 in *ÍF*, to a single chapter in M, Steingerðr's father Þorkell takes steps to end Kormakr's visits to his daughter, of which he disapproves. A literal transcription of the text of M can be found in extract XVIII, and a facsimile of the two pages of the manuscript at http://vsnrweb-publications.org.uk/NION-2-facs.pdf.

Bibliography

Edition: *Vatnsdœla saga*, ed. Einar Ól. Sveinsson, *ÍF* VIII, 201–302.

Translations: *The Sagas of Kormák and the Sworn Brothers*, tr. Lee M. Hollander (1949), 1–72; *Kormak's saga*, tr. Rory McTurk, in *CSI* I, 179–224. McTurk's translation has been reprinted in revised form, and with notes, in *Sagas of Warrior-poets: Kormak's saga, the Saga of Hallfred Troublesome-poet, the Saga of Gunnlaug Serpent-Tongue, the Saga of Bjorn, Champion of the Hitardal People, Viglund's Saga*, ed. Diana Whaley (2002), 3–67, 269–74.

Russell Poole, ed., *Skaldsagas: Text, Vocation and Desire in the Icelandic Sagas of Poets* (2001).

IV: KORMAKS SAGA

Chapter 5: Fall Þorveigarsona

Þorveig hét kona; hún var mjǫk fjǫlkunnig. Hún bjó á Steinsstǫðum í Miðfirði. Hon átti tvá sonu. Hét hinn ellri Oddr en hinn yngri Guðmundr; þeir váru hávaðamenn miklir. Oddr venr kvámur sínar í Tungu til Þorkels ok sitr á tali við Steingerði. Þorkell gerir sér dátt við þá brœðr ok eggjar þá at sitja fyrir Kormaki. Oddr kvað sér þat ekki ofrefli.

Þat var einnhvern dag er Kormakr kom í Tungu; var Steingerðr í stofu ok sat á palli. Þorveigarsynir sátu í stofunni ok váru búnir at veita Kormaki tilræði er hann gengi inn, en Þorkell hafði sett ǫðrum megin dyra sverð brugðit, en ǫðrum megin setti Narfi ljá í langorfi. En þá er Kormakr kom at skáladyrum, skaraði ofan ljáinn ok mœtti hann sverðinu, ok brotnaði í mikit skarð. Þá kom Þorkell at ok kvað Kormak mart illt gera ok var málóði; snýr inn skyndiliga ok kveðr Steingerði af stofunni. Ganga þau út um aðrar dyrr, ok lýkr hann hana í einu útibúri; kvað þau Kormak aldri sjásk skulu. Kormakr gengr inn ok bar hann skjótara en þá varði, ok varð þeim bilt.

Kormakr litask um ok sér eigi Steingerði, en sér þá brœðr er þeir st‹r›uku vápn sín, snýr í brott skyndiliga ok kvað vísu:

Hneit við Hrungnis fóta
hallvitj‹ǫ›ndum stalli,
inn var ek Ilmi at finna,
engisa*x*, of *g*enginn;
vita skal hitt, ef h*æt*ir
hand-Viðris mér grandi,
— ne Yggs fyr lið leggjum —
líti‹l›s meira vítis.

Kormakr finnr ‹eigi› Steingerði, ok kvað vísu:

Braut hvarf ór sal sæta,
sunds erum hugr á Gunni,
hvat merkir nú, herkis,
hǫll þverligar alla?

21 engi sár *M*. fenginn *M*. 22 hann hættir *M*.

Rennda ek allt it innra
Eir ‹h›árgeirs at þeiri,
h*ú*ns erum Hǫrn at finna,
hús brágeislum, fúsir.

Eptir þat gekk Kormakr at húsi‹nu› er Steingerðr var í ok braut upp húsit ok talaði við Steingerði.

Hon mælti, 'Þú breytir óvarliga, sœkir til tals við mik, því at Þorveigarsynir eru ætlaðir til hǫfuðs þér.' Þá kvað Kormakr:

Sitja sverð ok hvetja
sín andskotar mínir,
eins karls synir, inni;
er*u*t þeir banar mínir.
En á víðum velli
vega tveir at mér einum;
þá er sem ær at úlfi
órœknum fjǫr sœki.

Þar sat Kormakr um daginn.

Nú sér Þorkell at þetta ráð er farit er hann hafði stofnat. Nú biðr hann Þorveigarsonu at sitja fyrir Kormaki í dal einum fyrir útan garð sinn.

Þá mælti Þorkell: 'Narfi skal fara með ykkr, en ek mun vera heima ok veita yðr lið, ef þér þurfuð.'

Um kveldit ferr Kormakr í brott, ok þegar er hann kemr at dalnum, sá hann menn þrjá ok kvað vísu:

Sitja menn ok meina
mér eina Gná steina;
þeir hafa víl at vinna
er mér varða Gná borða;
því meira skal ek þeiri
er þeir ala meira
ǫfund um órar gǫngur
unna sǫlva Gunni.

Þá hljópu Þorveigarsynir upp ok sóttu at Kormaki lengi. Narfi skrjáði

33 hlíns erumk *M*. 42 erat *M*.

um it ýtra. Þorkell sér heiman at þeim sœkisk seint, ok tekr vápn sín. Í því bili kom Steingerðr út ok sér ætlan fǫður síns; tekr hon hann hǫndum, ok kemsk hann ekki til liðs með þeim brœðrum. Lauk svá því máli at Oddr fell, en Guðmundr varð óvígr ok dó þó síðan. Eptir þetta fór Kormakr heim, en Þorkell sér fyrir þeim brœðrum.

Litlu síðar ferr Kormakr at finna Þorveigu ok kvezk ekki vilja byggð hennar þar í firðinum.

'Skaltu flytja þik í brott at ákveðinni stundu, en ek vil allra bóta varna um sonu þína.'

Þorveig mælti, 'Þat er líkast at því komir þú á leið at ek verða heraðflótta, en synir mínir óbœttir, en því skal ek þér launa at þú skalt Steingerðar aldri njóta.'

Kormakr segir, 'Því mantu ekki ráða, in vánda kerling.'

‹Chapter 6›

Síðan ferr Kormakr at finna Steingerði jafnt sem áðr; ok eitt sinn, er þau tala um þessa atburði, lætr hon ekki illa yfir. Kormakr kveðr vísu:

Sitja menn ok meina
mér ásjánu þína;
þeir hafa lǫgðis Loddu
linna fœtr at vinna;
því at upp skulu allar,
ǫlstafns, áðr ek þér hafna,
lýsigrund, í landi,
linns, þjóðár rinna.

'Mæl þú eigi svá mikit um,' segir Steingerðr. 'Mart má því bregða.'

Þá kvað Kormakr vísu:

Hvern myndir þú, *H*rundar,
Hlín, skapfrǫmuð, línu,
— líknsýnir mér lúka
ljós — þér at ver kjósa?

Steingerðr segir:

88 Grundar *M*.

Brœðr mynda ek blindum,
bauglestir, mik festa;
yrði goð, sem gerðisk,
góð mér ok skǫp, Fróða.

Kormakr segir, 'Nú kaustu sem vera ætti; opt hefi ek higat mínar kvámur lagðar.'

Nú biðr Steingerðr Kormak stunda til fǫður hennar ok fá hennar, ok fyrir sakir Steingerðar gaf Kormakr Þorkatli gj*afar*. Eptir þetta eigu margir menn hlut í, ok þar kom um síðir at Kormakr bað Steingerðar, ok var hon honum fǫstnuð ok ákveðin brullaupsstefna, ok stendr nú kyrrt um hríð. Nú fara orð á milli þeirra, ok verða í nokkurar greinir um fjárfar, ok svá veik við breytiliga, at síðan þessum ráðum var ráðit, fannsk Kormaki fátt um, en þat var fyrir þá sǫk at Þorveig seiddi til at þau skyldi eigi njótask mega.

Þorkell í Tungu átti son roskinn er Þorkell hét ok var kallaðr tanngnjóstr; hann hafði verit útan um stund. Þetta sumar kom hann út ok var með fǫður sínum.

Kormakr sœkir ekki brullaupit eptir því sem ákveðit var, ok leið fram stundin. Þetta þykkir frændum Steingerðar óvirðing er hann bregðr þessum ráðahag, ok leita sér ráðs.

93 Bráðr *M*. 100 gjǫfum *M*.

Verses in prose word order

Lines 18–25: Engisa*x* hneit við stalli fóta Hrungnis hallvitj‹ǫ›ndum; ek var of *g*enginn inn at finna Ilmi; hitt skal vita líti‹l›s meira vítis, ef h*æt*ir mér grandi hand-Viðris; ne leggjum Yggs fyr lið.

Lines 27–34: Sæta hvarf braut ór sal; erum hugr á Gunni herkis sunds; hvat merkir nú þverligar alla hǫll? Ek rennda brágeislum allt it innra hús at þeiri Eir ‹h›árgeirs; erum fúsir at finna Hǫrn h*ú*ns.

Lines 39–46: Andskotar mínir, synir eins karls, sitja inni ok hvetja sverð sín; þeir er*u*t banar mínir. En tveir vega at mér einum á víðum velli; þá er sem ær sœki fjǫr at órœknum úlfi.

Lines 54–61: Menn sitja ok meina mér eina Gná steina; þeir er varða mér Gná borða hafa víl at vinna; því meira skal ek unna þeiri Gunni sǫlva er þeir ala meira ǫfund um gǫngur órar.

Lines 78–85: Menn sitja ok meina mér ásjánu þína; þeir hafa fœtr linna Loddu lǫgðis at vinna; því at allar þjóðár í landi skulu rinna upp áðr ek hafna þér, lýsigrund linns ǫlstafns.

Lines 88–91: Hvern skapfrǫmuð *H*rundar myndir þú kjósa þér at ver, Hlín línu? Líknsýnir lúka mér ljós.

Lines 93–96: Ek mynda festa mik br*æ*ðr Fróða blindum, bauglestir; yrði goð ok skǫp góð mér, sem gerðisk.

V: BJARNAR SAGA HÍTDŒLAKAPPA

Bjarnar saga Hítdœlakappa, like *Kormaks saga*, belongs to the group of poets' sagas which tell of the rivalry between men for a woman's love. In the case of *Bjarnar saga*, the hero's rival, Þórðr Kolbeinsson, is a historically-attested court poet, whose eulogistic verses are preserved in texts of the Kings' Sagas; the more fictitious poetic reputation of the hero Bjǫrn Arngeirsson depends entirely on the frequently scurrilous verses preserved in his saga. The feud arises from competition for the love of Oddný Þorkelsdóttir, originally betrothed to Bjǫrn but married instead to Þórðr, who treacherously spreads a false report of the hero's death during his youthful adventures in Russia and England. On Bjǫrn's return to Iceland his justifiable antagonism to Þórðr inaugurates a lifelong hostility, involving an adulterous relationship with Oddný and a series of slanderous exchanges between the two poets, reflecting the details of life in a farming community in Borgarfjǫrðr in the west of Iceland. Slander, especially in verse, was an offence heavily punished by law in Iceland, a law also breached by Bjǫrn's erection of *níð* — a carved representation of Þórðr involved in a homosexual encounter. The sexual connotations of the insult correspond metaphorically to Bjǫrn's sexual appropriation of Þórðr's wife, as does the saga's unusually negative representation of Þórðr as a paradoxical blend of coward and aggressor. The feud finally modulates into the physical violence conventionally found in the Sagas of Icelanders, culminating in the scene reproduced below, in which Þórðr, assisted by a host of minor characters who have been drawn into the feud — including Þórðr's nominal son Kolli, who learns only in the course of battle that Bjǫrn is his real father — finally gets the better of the hero.

The saga is poorly preserved, mainly in the seventeenth-century paper manuscript AM 551 D a 4to (= 551). The first five chapters are missing, although a summary text survives in an expanded version of Snorri Sturluson's separate *Saga of St Óláfr.* Two leaves survive of the medieval manuscript (AM 162 F fol., = 162; late fourteenth century) from which the seventeenth-century copy was made; the first part of the text below (to line 45) is found on the second of these leaves. The saga's relatively unsophisticated structure and absence of overt influence from other sagas suggest an early date of composition, around 1220, although an attempt has recently been made to establish it as a late and derivative work (Bjarni Guðnason 1994). The text refers to earlier traditions which served as its sources, and to the twelfth-century cleric Runólfr Dálksson, who may have written a short biography of Bjǫrn. Most of the verses cited must also be older than the prose.

The full text of the saga can be found in *ÍF* III. The following extract is based on that edition, with some modifications from the edition of John LeC. Simon (1966).

Bibliography

Bjarnar saga Hítdœlakappa. In *Borgfirðinga sǫgur*, ed. Sigurður Nordal and Guðni Jónsson (1938; reprinted with supplement 1951). *ÍF* III.

John LeC. Simon, ed., *A Critical Edition of Bjarnar saga hítdælakappa*. Unpublished Ph.D thesis, University of London (1966).

Bjarnar saga Hítdœlakappa, ed. R. C. Boer (1893).

The Saga of Bjorn, Champion of the Hitardal People, tr. Alison Finlay. In *CSI* I, 255–304.

The Saga of Bjorn, Champion of the Men of Hitardale, tr. Alison Finlay (1999).

Bo Almqvist, 'The death forebodings of Saint Óláfr, King of Norway, and Rögnvaldr Brúsason, Earl of Orkney. A folkloristic and philological study'. In *Viking Ale: Studies on folklore contacts between the Northern and Western worlds*, ed. Éilís Ní Dhuibhne-Almqvist and Séamas Ó Cathaín (1991), 30–64, and notes 243–55. Reprinted from *Béaloideas* 42–44 (1974–76), 1–40.

Theodore M. Andersson, *The Icelandic Family Saga: An Analytic Reading* (1967). Harvard Studies in Comparative Literature 28.

Theodore M. Andersson and William Ian Miller, *Law and Literature in Medieval Iceland: Ljósvetninga saga and Valla-Ljóts saga* (1989).

Bjarni Guðnason, 'Aldur og einkenni Bjarnarsögu Hítdælakappa'. In *Sagnaþing helgað Jónasi Kristjánssyni sjötugum 10. apríl 1994*, ed. Gísli Sigurðsson, Guðrún Kvaran and Sigurgeir Steingrímsson (1994), 69–86.

Ursula Dronke, '*Sem jarlar forðum*. The influence of *Rígsþula* on two saga episodes'. In *Speculum Norrœnum: Norse Studies in Memory of Gabriel Turville-Petre*, ed. Ursula Dronke, Guðrún P. Helgadóttir, Gerd Wolfgang Weber and Hans Bekker-Nielsen (1981), 56–72.

Preben Meulengracht Sørensen, *The Unmanly Man: Concepts of Sexual Defamation in Early Northern Society* (1983). The Viking Collection 1.

W. H. Vogt, 'Die Bjarnar saga hítdœlakappa. Lausavísur, frásagnir, saga'. *Arkiv för nordisk filologi*, 27 (1921), 27–79.

Russell Poole, ed., *Skaldsagas: Text, Vocation and Desire in the Icelandic Sagas of Poets* (2001).

Alison Finlay, 'Interpretation or Over-Interpretation? The dating of two *Íslendingasǫgur*', *Gripla* XIV (2004), 61–91.

V: BJARNAR SAGA HÍTDŒLAKAPPA

Chapter 32

Þat er sagt í ǫðru lagi frá Birni, at hann var snimma á fótum þann morgin ok mataðisk, en Sigmundr, húskarl hans, var farinn upp í dal. Birni þótti illar húsgǫngur, er hann átti sǫkótt, ok þótti aldri ørvænt á hverri stundu hann þurfti manna við, ok var hann nokkut brúnvǫlr ok sagði Þórdísi, konu sinni, at hann myndi fara á Hvítingshjalla ok skera mǫn á hrossum Þorsteins, áðr hann sendi þau vestr;[1] ok þó kvað hann heldr hafa harkat um draumana um nóttina ok kvazk þó ógǫrla vita fyrir hverju þat mun vera. Hann kvazk mjǫk opt á þá leið dreyma sem nú ok kvað þó nú mest um vera.

Hon mælti, 'Þat vilda ek at þú fœrir hvergi frá húsi í dag, ok ertu óvarr um þik, þar er fjándmenn þínir sitja umhverfum þik; eða hvat dreymði þik?'

'Ekki læt ek drauma ráða fǫrum mínum,' segir hann.

'Eigi vilda ek at þú fœrir frá húsi, ok værir sem varastr um þik ok hefir þat fyrir engum spillt; en mér virðisk sem raunillar hafi verit svefnfararnar í nótt, ok seg mér hvat fyrir bar.' En Bjǫrn kvað vísu:[2]

Undr er, ef ekki bendir,
opt vakir drengr at lengrum,
ógn hef ek fyrða fregna,
framvísar mér dísir,
því at armleggjar orma
Ilmr dagleygjar hilmis
heim ór hverjum draumi
hjalmfaldin býðr skaldi.

'Þetta hefir mik opt dreymt,' sagði hann, 'ok nú með mestu móti í nótt.'

Hon latti hann frá húsi at fara, en hann lét ekki letjask. Húskarlar, þeir sem heima váru, fóru í skóg at hǫggva við, ok var Bjǫrn einn roskinna manna. Nú býr hann til hrossanna ok hefir manskæri mikil á linda ok hǫtt á hǫfði ok skjǫld á hlið; sverð hafði hann í hendi, er Þorfinnr Þvarason átti.[3] Bjǫrn var mikill maðr vexti ok vænn ok freknóttr, rauðskeggjaðr, skrofhárr ok dapreygðr ok manna bezt vígr.[4]

22 dagleggjar *162*.

Sveinn fimmtán vetra gamall fór með honum. Ok er þeir gengu ór túni, kvað Bjǫrn vísu:

Út geng ek með lið lítit,
lítt sé ek hers við víti;
sverð fylgir menmyrði[5]
mítt ok skjǫldr enn hvíti;
en fyrir einum runni
ægis dýrs of Mýrar,
vǫndr skal hjalts ór hendi
hrøkkva, fyrr en ek støkkva.

Þeir fóru þá gǫtu er liggr til Hvítingshjalla; en þeir eigu at fara yfir Hítará, skammt frá því er hon fellr ór vatninu. Ok er þeir hafa farit um hríð, þá sér sveinninn sex menn fara í móti þeim frá stakkgarði af Hvítingshjalla. Bjǫrn spyrr sveininn ef hann sæi hrossin[6] á hjǫllunum, kvað auðsæ vera munu fyrir litar sakir. Hann kvazk sjá hrossin ok svá sex menn fara í mót þeim. Bjǫrn kvað þá enn vísu:

Tv*ei*r eru‹m›, vǫrðr,[7] en várum,
vápn-Eirar, vel fleiri;
opt ‹v›ar ‹s›kald und skildi
skól‹kinn›i‹s› at jólum;
enn hraustg*e*ði á hausti,
hoddlestis, kom vestan,
sveit vara *s*eggja lítil
snarfengs, með lið drengja.

Bjǫrn hafði kyrtil góðan ok var í hosum ok vafit silkiræmu um fót sér, þeiri er hann hafði skipt um við inn helga Óláf konung.[8] Hann brá sverðinu er Þorfinnr Þvarason átti, ok mælti:

'Illt sverð á hér góðr drengr,' segir hann.

Kálfr sér þá brátt, þar sem hann var kominn, ok heldr eptir þeim ok mælti:

'Eigi er minni ván,' segir hann, 'at skipti með oss gæfunni; þeir þóttusk mik hafa í hættu settan,[9] en ek hygg at ek veiða nú þann bjǫrn, er vér vildum allir veiða.'

48 Tvær *551*. 52 hraustgoði *551*. 54 leggja *551*.

'Skammt eigu þeir nú hingat, Bjǫrn,' segir sveinninn, 'því at þeir fara hart.'

Bjǫrn svarar, 'Því auðveldara mun okkr at taka hrossin sem fleiri beina at.'

Sveinninn mælti, 'Ekki munu þetta *friða*rmenn vera; þeir eru allir með vápnum. Ok enn sé ek fleiri menn, því at sumir fara eptir okkr ok enn vápnaðir.'

'Eigi skyldir þú of mikit um gera,' segir Bjǫrn; 'kann vera, at þat sé réttamenn.'[10]

Sveinninn mælti, 'Ek sé enn fleiri menn, ok fara frá Hólmi; ok er okkr þat eitt ráð at snúa til Hellisdals, ok fǫrum síðan Klifsdal ok forðum okkr.'[11]

Bjǫrn mælti, 'Ekki hefi ek enn eltr verit hér til, ok svá mun enn, ok mun ek eigi aptr hverfa; fǫrum eptir Klifsandi til Klifsjǫrva, ok gjarnan vilda ek fara til Grásteins ins mikla, ef vit mættim þangat komask.'

'Eigi má ek þat vita,' segir sveinninn, 'hvé okkr má þat endask, því at menn sœkja at okkr ǫllum megin, ok sé ek þat gǫrla, at sex eru hvar saman, þótt sumir eigi lengra til okkar en sumir; ok sé ek nú alls eigi færi menn en fjóra ok tuttugu.'

Bjǫrn spyrr, 'Hvern veg er þeim mǫnnum varit, er okkr eru næstir?'

Sveinninn segir, ok þóttisk Bjǫrn kenna Kálf at frásǫgn hans.[12] Kálfr var maðr mikill ok svartr, ok átti skammt til þeira á bak þeim, er Kolli ok synir Eiðs kómu fyrir þá. Dálkr ferr at frá Hólmi ok er sýnu first þeim ok þeir er honum fylgja. Bjǫrn mælti við sveininn:

'Far þú nú upp í hjallann eptir hrossunum, en ek mun hér bíða; ekki mun stoða at fara lengra.'

Nú settisk Bjǫrn niðr, en sveinninn ferr at taka hrossin ok vildi víkja ok mátti eigi, því at þá hafði tekizk fundr þeira.

Þeir koma fyrst at Birni, Kálfr við sétta mann, Kolli ok synir Eiðs með honum við sex menn. Þorvaldr Eiðsson skýtr spjóti at Birni þegar er hann náir til hans. Bjǫrn tók spjótit á lopti ok sendi aptr til eiganda. Þat kom á Þorvald miðjan, ok fell hann dauðr til jarðar. Þeir hǫfðu komizk á milli hans ok Grásteins, svá at Bjǫrn komsk eigi þangat. Þórðr vildi hefna bróður síns ok hjó til Bjarnar mikit hǫgg; en Bjǫrn helt á skildinum svá at handleggr hans var í mundriðanum, ok kom hǫggit á skjǫldinn ok varð svá mikit, at handleggr Bjarnar gekk í sundr, ok fell skjǫldrinn niðr. Þá þreif Bjǫrn sporð skjaldarins hinni hendinni

69 fyrirmenn *551*.

ok rak í hǫfuð Þórði, svá at hann fekk þegar bana; en sumir menn segja at hann legði hann með sǫxunum til bana.[13] Kolli sótti Bjǫrn fast, nær í mesta lagi einna manna í sífellu, þótt vér kunnim eigi at greina hvert sárafar hann veitti honum. Kálfr mælti, kvað honum nú fyrir allt eitt koma, þótt hann felldi nokkura menn, ok kvað hann skyldu nú eigi undan ganga.

'Er oss nú eigi mannfátt,' segir hann.

Sumir mæltu at slá skyldi hring um Bjǫrn ok varðveita hann, at hann komisk hvergi í brott, ok bíða Þórðar Kolbeinssonar at vega at honum til lykða. Ok meðan þeir rœddusk þetta við, þá leysti Bjǫrn manskæri af linda sér, ok váru þau nýhvǫtt er hann fór heiman, bæði mikil ok bitrlig. Nú kom Dálkr til með sex menn ok vill þegar sœkja at Birni, því at hann var hraustr karlmaðr, ok þóttisk hann varla á‹n› hólmsǫk við Bjǫrn, er hann átti sonar síns at hefna. En Bjǫrn bregðr sverðinu Þorfinns, er hann hafði heiman haft, ok høggr á fót Dálki svá hart at fótrinn brotnaði, en eigi beit, ok varð Dálkr óvígr ok fluttr á brott þangat sem honum var óhætt.

Ok því næst kom Þórðr Kolbeinsson; ok er Bjǫrn sá hann, þá mælti hann:

'Seinn til slíks móts, lítill sveinn.'[14]

'Sá skal þér þó nú nær standa í dag,' segir Þórðr, 'ok hǫggva þik klækishǫgg.'

'Þau ein muntu hǫggva,' segir Bjǫrn, 'meðan þú lifir.'

Þórði varð mismælt, ok vildi hann sagt hafa at sá skyldi hann hǫggva klámhǫggvi þann dag.[15] Bjǫrn grípr nú skærin, því at hann veit at sverðit dugir ekki, ok hleypr at Þórði ok ætlar at reka á honum skærin. Þórðr veiksk undan, en fyrir varð húskarl Þórðar er Grímr hét, ok fekk þegar bana. Ok í því bili hjó Kálfr til Bjarnar ok veitti honum mikit sár, ok fell Bjǫrn nú, svá at hann stóð á knjám ok varðisk með skærunum af mikilli hugprýði, því at hann var inn mesti fullhugi, sem opt hǫfðu raunir á orðit, ok veitti þeim mǫrg sár er hann sóttu. Þeir sóttu hann nú svá fast, ok engi meir en Kolli.

Bjǫrn mælti, 'Fast sœkir þú mik í dag, Kolli,' segir Bjǫrn.

'Eigi veit ek hverjum í er at þyrma,' segir hann.

'Svá er ok,' segir Bjǫrn, 'móðir þín mun þetta fyrir þik hafa lagt at þú skyldir mér harðasta atgǫngu veita; en sjá þykkjumk ek at annat mun þér betr gefit en ættvísin.'[16]

Kolli segir, 'Eigi þykkir mér þú þat snimma sagt hafa, ef mér er nokkurr vandi á við þik.'

Ok þegar gengr Kolli brott ok hættir atsókninni.

Bjǫrn varðisk mjǫk lengi með skærunum, svá at hann stóð á knjám, ok allir undruðusk þeir hví hann mátti slíka vǫrn veita, næsta vápnlauss maðr, svá margir sem þeir sóttu hann, ok þóttusk þó allir hafa fullleiksa, er honum urðu næstir. Nú er þat sagt at Þórðr hjó til Bjarnar, ok beit af honum þjóhnappana, ok fellr Bjǫrn þá. Þórðr vill þá eigi láta hǫggva á milli ok høggr af Birni hǫfuð í ǫðru hǫggvi ok gengr á milli bols ok hǫfuðs,[17] ok þá kvað Þórðr vísu:

Láskat, snarr at snerru,
(segg þann bitu eggjar,
hinn er fyrir heiði sunnan
hugprýði mér *frýði*)
at, morðvanda*r*, myndak,
meiðs hlutum rán af beiði
(bitu þann fyrir sǫk sanna
sverð) hans bani verða.

Þórðr tók hǫfuð Bjarnar ok batt við álar sér; lét þar hanga við sǫðul sinn.[18] Kálfr kvazk vilja at þeir kœmi í Hólm ok lýsti þar víginu, ok lézk vilja fœra þeim men, er Bjǫrn hafði haft á sér. Dálkr svarar ok kvað þat óskylt vera ok kappsamligt, kvað þat betr sóma at sýna sik í yfirbótum við frændr Bjarnar eptir þetta verk heldr en auka vansemð við þá. Þórðr lagði þar hvártki til. Kálfr reið þegar af vetfangi. Ok er þeir riðu í brott ok váru komnir ofan yfir Klifsand, þá flugu móti þeim hrafnar nokkurir, ok þá orti Þórðr vísu þessa:

Hvert stefni þér, hrafnar,
hart með flokk enn svarta?
Farið ljóst matar leita
landnorðr frá Klifsandi.
Þar liggr Bjǫrn, en Birni
blóðgǫgl of skǫr stóðu;
þollr hné hjalms á hjalla
Hvítings ofar lítlu.

152 kviða *551*. 153 ek morðvandan *551*.

Notes

[1] The trimming of horses' manes has aristocratic and heroic resonances. Þrymr, lord of the giants, is said to trim his horses' manes and twist golden collars for his dogs as he sits on his ancestors' burial mound (*Þrymskviða* 6); it is also named as one of the activities (along with making shafts for their spears and driving horses) which the murdered young sons of the great king Atli have not lived to perform (*Atlakviða* 37). The horses are a gift from Bjǫrn to the influential chieftain, Þorsteinn Kuggason, who had attempted to bring about a settlement between Bjǫrn and Þórðr.

[2] The verse includes a strange blend of pagan and Christian symbolism. The helmeted woman who invites the poet home — that is, to his death — suggests the valkyrie, one of the supernatural 'shield-maidens' whose function was to help Óðinn in his task of choosing warriors doomed to die. The chosen heroes would join the god in Valhǫll and engage in perpetual warfare in preparation for the final battle against the predestined enemies of gods and men. But this apparition is explicitly associated with the 'ruler of day's fire', clearly a kenning for the Christian God, though it has been argued that the kenning may refer to Óðinn, or to a deity blending pagan and Christian conceptions. There is a parallel in a number of verses in *Gísla saga* in which the poet describes two women, one benign and one hostile, who appear to him in dreams; in one of these the expression *bjóða heim* 'invite home' is used, as in Bjǫrn's verse. It has been argued that the 'good' dream-woman is the poet's *fylgja* or protective spirit.

[3] Þorfinnr Þvarason, Bjǫrn's cousin, is said earlier in the saga to have borrowed Bjǫrn's famous sword, though no reason is given. Þorfinnr has little role in the saga other than to account for the hero's weaponless state.

[4] It is not uncommon for sagas to include a description of the hero shortly before his death, a passage described by Theodore M. Andersson as a 'necrology' (1967, 60–62), and generally used to present him in a positive light. It has been suggested that skalds were stereotypically portrayed as dark and ugly; Bjǫrn does not conform to this type, but

shares his red hair and freckled colouring with another hero with poetic leanings, Grettir. There are some indications that red hair or beard was associated with shrewdness and wit; Snorri goði in *Eyrbyggja saga* is also red-bearded, and *Rauðgrani* 'Red-beard' was one of Óðinn's names. The purpose of the reference to Bjǫrn's poor sight must be to motivate the dialogue between him and the boy who describes the approaching attackers (lines 44–85).

[5] The man-kenning *menmyrðir* must refer to Bjǫrn himself, although it seems inappropriate that the verse stresses his ownership of the sword and shield he is carrying (Bjǫrn's own weapons have, according to the prose narrative, been borrowed by his father, and he is carrying the inadequate sword of his cousin Þorfinnr Þvarason). This has been cited as one instance of the disparity between verse and prose in this part of the saga (Vogt 1921, 54, 65); it would be more accurate, in fact, to refer it to the multiplicity of traditions, in both verse and prose, about Bjǫrn's last battle and the weapons he carried to it (Finlay 2004).

[6] At this point the text preserved in the second of the two surviving medieval manuscript fragments breaks off; the remaining text comes from the seventeenth-century paper copy of this manuscript which is the major source for the saga.

[7] Again it is inappropriate, though not unprecedented, for Bjǫrn to address the boy accompanying him with a full-blown warrior kenning (*vǫrðr vápn-Eirar*). The author seems determined to push the idea of an unequal encounter to its extremity. Bjǫrn is attacked by no fewer than twenty-four, and while the saga's presumed source, the verse, emphasizes the vulnerability of the warrior stripped of all but one of his supporters, the prose pares this down to the point where Bjǫrn's companion, though adequate as an audience for his last verse, is negligible as a combatant, and in fact leaves the scene before the fight begins. The 'bold man' who 'brought a band from the west in autumn' may be Bjǫrn's powerful ally Þorsteinn Kuggason.

[8] Chapter 9 of the saga relates how Bjǫrn accidentally exchanges garters with King (later Saint) Óláfr of Norway as they dress after a communal

bath; Bjǫrn continues to wear the garter all his life and is buried with it after his death. When his bones are later disinterred the garter is found uncorrupted — a testimony to the king's sanctity — and is claimed to be still in existence at the time of the saga's writing, used as a belt on a set of mass vestments. Another version of this story exists in some manuscripts of Snorri's *Saga of St Óláfr*.

[9] *í hættu*: 'in danger [of missing him]'. This must be the sense of Kálfr's remark. It is improbable that he should be the first attacker to catch up with Bjǫrn in view of the detailed account of Þórðr's disposition of forces, which places Kálfr not on the way to Hvítingshjalli, but in the opposite direction, towards Vellir. The subsequent narrative, however, makes it clear that Kálfr is overtaking Bjǫrn from behind; the six men the boy sees in front of them must be the sons of Eiðr, Kolli and their companions. Kálfr's pun on the meaning of the name Bjǫrn, 'bear', is taken up later as the attackers encircle their disarmed opponent (line 109).

[10] Bjǫrn's insistence that the attackers are men of peace is clearly a heroic pretence, since he has already drawn his sword.

[11] The names appear in this order in the manuscripts, but have apparently been mistakenly reversed, as the route to Hellisdalr lies through Klifsdalr.

[12] For the literary convention of characters identified from a distance by their clothing, see *Laxdœla saga* ch. 63; Andersson and Miller (1989), 141 n. 38, 172 n. 90. See note 4 above.

[13] This reference to two conflicting versions of the narrative is the strongest indication of the existence of differing traditions, presumably oral, about Bjǫrn's life before the writing of the saga. In his examination of the relationship between verse and prose in the saga, Vogt (1921) suggests that the author was attempting to reconcile the testimony of the verse *Út geng ek með lið lítit*, lines 34–41, which says that Bjǫrn is carrying a sword and shield, with that of a narrative in which he is unarmed except for the mane-shears (his weapons having been borrowed by his father).

[14] Bjǫrn's slighting epithet *lítill sveinn* is also used of Þórðr in verses earlier in the saga.

[15] Bo Almqvist, analysing this and other slips of the tongue in saga literature, argues that in folk-belief a slip of the tongue was a portent of death, and speculates that 'it is not impossible that the folk tradition upon which the saga was based ascribed the slip of the tongue to Björn' (1991, 248 note 30). But Almqvist also acknowledges that in literary manifestations of the theme, the person whose tongue slips is frequently made to reveal an accidental truth, in this case the cowardly strain in Þórðr's own character. Þórðr intends to threaten Bjǫrn with a *klámhǫgg*, a blow struck from behind on the thighs or buttocks, shaming both because it implies that the victim was turning to flee, and also, as Meulengracht Sørensen argues, as 'a symbolic action with a sexual component, corresponding to that of *níð*; the mutilated man was deprived of his manhood' (1983, 68). The law-code *Grágás* includes *klámhǫgg* among injuries categorised as *in meiri sár,* 'major wounds'. By involuntarily substituting the word *klækishǫgg,* 'coward's blow', similar in sound and structure but opposite in meaning, Þórðr turns the shame upon himself.

[16] This dramatic revelation to Kolli of his relationship with Bjǫrn concludes the 'paternity theme' (Dronke 1981) running through the saga. Once again traditional heroic motifs are called upon; in the Old High German *Hildebrandslied*, father and son fight to the death.

[17] This phrase might conceivably have something to do with the ancient ritual of passing between a severed head and trunk in order to prevent the dead person from returning.

[18] The cutting off of an enemy's head as a trophy is frequently mentioned in the sagas. *Orkneyinga saga* tells of Jarl Sigurðr of Orkney tying the head of his defeated enemy, Melbrikta 'Tooth', to his saddle 'for his own glory', but wounding his leg on Melbrikta's protruding tooth and eventually dying of the wound. The custom is thought to be of Irish origin.

Verses in prose word order

Lines 17–24: Undr er, ef framvísar dísir bendir mér ekki—drengr vakir opt at lengrum, hef ek fregna ógn fyrða — því at hjalmfaldin armleggjar orma Ilmr dagleygjar hilmis býðr skaldi heim ór hverjum draumi.

Lines 34–41: Ek geng út með lítit lið; ek sé lítt við víti hers; sverð mítt ok enn hvíti skjǫldr fylgir menmyrði; en fyrr en ek støkkva of Mýrar fyrir einum runni ægis dýrs, skal vǫndr hjalts hrøkkva ór hendi.

Lines 48–55: Eru‹m› tv*eir*, vǫrðr vápn-Eirar, en várum vel fleiri; ‹s›kald ‹v›ar opt und skildi at skól‹kinn›i‹s› jólum; enn hraustg*e*ði kom vestan á hausti með lið drengja; *s*eggja sveit snarfengs hoddlestis vara lítil.

Lines 149–56: Láskat, snarr at snerru (eggjar bitu þann segg, hinn er *frýði* mér hugprýði fyrir sunnan heiði) at myndak verða bani hans; hlutum rán af beiði meiðs morðvanda*r*; sverð bitu þann fyrir sanna sǫk.

Lines 165–172: Hrafnar, hvert stefni þér hart með enn svarta flokk? Farið ljóst leita matar landnorðr frá Klifsandi. Þar liggr Bjǫrn, en blóðgǫgl stóðu of skǫr Birni; hjalms þollr hné litlu ofar á Hvítingshjalla.

VI: FAGRSKINNA

Fagrskinna is a history of Norway written in the early thirteenth century in Norway, possibly by an Icelander. It covers in a more compressed form the same time-span as Snorri Sturluson's *Heimskringla*, excluding the legendary *Ynglinga saga*: the period from the reign of the ninth-century Hálfdan svarti to 1177. Whether Snorri knew *Fagrskinna* is uncertain, but *Fagrskinna* and *Heimskringla* certainly share many features and at times the wording is identical, though the author of *Fagrskinna* falls short of Snorri's sophistication and skill. The author's taste for set-piece battles is well illustrated in the extract reproduced here; he gives full value to the account of this climactic scene found in his source, but dispenses with its hagiographic dwelling on the missionary efforts of Óláfr Tryggvason and does not aspire to the psychological and political depth of Snorri's account of the manœuvrings preceding the battle.

The name *Fagrskinna*, 'beautiful parchment', was applied in the seventeenth century to a now lost manuscript of the work, which was apparently known in medieval times as *Nóregs konunga tal*, 'Catalogue of the kings of Norway'. Compared with the earlier prose Latin and vernacular histories which were its sources, the work is a well-constructed and serious attempt at historical objectivity, avoiding excesses of piety and fantastic elements, as witness the measured treatment in this extract of the legend of Óláfr Tryggvason's survival of the Battle of Svǫlðr. The high proportion of verses, many of them unknown elsewhere, which are interwoven with the prose text and drawn on for authenticating detail, shows this author as a pioneer of the historiographical techniques perfected by Snorri.

The text survives in two versions, both now existing only in seventeenth-century and later copies of two medieval manuscripts. The older version (B, *c.*1250) is the basis of the text edited in Bjarni Einarsson's edition in *ÍF* XXIX and is that followed in this extract. This version, however, has numerous gaps which are filled by reference to the later version (A, *c.*1300); the latter third of the extract below follows the A version because of a lacuna in B. Although the surviving copies are Icelandic, the survival of many Norwegian word-forms reflects the origin of the text in Norway (see below).

The place of *Fagrskinna* in early Norse historiography

Histories of Norway and other Scandinavian topics were among the first texts to be written in Iceland, and provide important evidence of the transition from Latin to vernacular composition and of the shifting of the literary focus from continental Scandinavia to Iceland. The interrelationship of the various texts is difficult to disentangle, since some are completely lost, and others are now found only in later copies and reworkings that have often incorporated material from supposedly later works. The following is a summary account of historians and texts relevant to *Fagrskinna*:

Adam of Bremen, *Gesta Hammaburgensis ecclesiae pontificum*. The author was an eleventh-century canon who wrote (*c*.1073), in Latin, on matters of concern to the Archbishop of Bremen. Book 4 includes material, valuable because of its early date but sometimes of dubious accuracy, about the pre-Christian practices of the Scandinavian peoples.

Sæmundr Sigfússon 'inn fróði' (the Wise), an Icelandic scholar (d. 1133), is referred to as an authority in many historical texts. His lost work probably took the form of a chronological summary of the lives of the Norwegian kings. It is presumed to have been in Latin, since Ari, whose work was composed later, is referred to by Snorri Sturluson as the first writer of history in the vernacular.

Ari Þorgilsson is best known for his surviving short vernacular history of Iceland, now known as *Íslendingabók*; but the manuscript gives the surviving book a Latin title, *Libellus Islendorum*, and refers to an earlier, now lost, version as *Íslendingabók*, which it seems to say included lives of kings and genealogies. Whether these were in Latin or the vernacular, and whether they were more than brief regnal lists, is not known. The first version was written between 1122 and 1133 (see the introduction to VIII below).

Theodoricus monachus, *Historia de Antiquitate Regum Norwagiensium* 'The Ancient History of the Norwegian Kings'. This is an account in Latin, brief but with many digressions, of the Norwegian kings from Haraldr hárfagri to Sigurðr Jórsalafari (d. 1130). Theodoricus (Þórir) was probably a Benedictine monk at Niðarhólmr in Trondheimsfjord in Norway who wrote the work for presentation to Archbishop Eysteinn (1161–88) of Niðaróss (modern Trondheim). Theodoricus claims to be the first to write down the material he records, naming as sources the memories preserved by Icelanders and in particular their poems, though he may not have known these directly. He may also have had access to regnal lists and chronologies such as those attributed to Ari and Sæmundr.

Historia Norwegiae. A Latin text found only in a fragmentary manuscript from 1500 or later, but originally written probably in Norway before 1200. After a geographical preface, it deals briefly with the history of Norway down to 1015, and probably concluded with an account of its conversion to Christianity.

Ágrip af Nóregskonunga sǫgum. A short history (*ágrip* 'summary') in Norse, surviving, though incompletely, in an Icelandic copy (*c*.1230) of a Norwegian manuscript. The text was probably written sometime before 1200, and probably originally covered the reigns from Hálfdan svarti to 1177, though it now breaks off in the middle of the twelfth century. It is believed that the author made use of Theodoricus and of *Historia Norwegiae*, but the relative dating of the three texts is difficult to establish; it also incorporates vernacular poetry.

Oddr Snorrason, *Óláfs saga Tryggvasonar*. Oddr Snorrason was a monk at Þingeyrar in the north of Iceland who wrote a Latin life of Óláfr Tryggvason *c*.1190 (according to some *c*.1170). It now survives only in three different redactions (one fragmentary) of an Icelandic translation. Oddr made use of the early Latin histories as well as oral traditions, including skaldic verse. It is clear that Oddr's work is the main source for *Fagrskinna*'s account of Óláfr, though the relationship is made problematic by the late date of the surviving translation, some versions of which may in turn have been influenced by *Fagrskinna* itself, as well as other later texts.

Gunnlaugr Leifsson, *Óláfs saga Tryggvasonar*. Gunnlaugr, also a monk at Þingeyrar, wrote another Latin life of Óláfr Tryggvason which probably used and expanded Oddr's version. It is now lost, but some passages survive translated into Icelandic in the form of interpolations in *The Greatest saga of Óláfr Tryggvason* (*Óláfs saga Tryggvasonar en mesta*). This early fourteenth-century work is based on a version of the saga of Óláfr Tryggvason in *Heimskringla*, expanded with material relevant to the king's life from a variety of texts.

Morkinskinna. In its present state this history, covering approximately the years 1035–1177, is found in an Icelandic manscript from about 1275, of which about a third is apparently missing. This version is considered to be a reworking, including interpolations from *Ágrip* and additional skaldic stanzas, of an older text written *c*.1220, which may have lacked the many digressive anecdotes or *þættir* about Icelanders abroad; some argue, however, that these are integral to the work. The early *Morkinskinna* was an important source for the latter parts of *Fagrskinna* and *Heimskringla*.

Heimskringla. Snorri Sturluson is generally accepted as the author. He is believed to have written it *c*.1230, reworking his own earlier *Óláfs saga helga* as the centrepiece. It covers the same chronological range as *Fagrskinna*, with the addition of the largely legendary *Ynglinga saga*, but on a more ambitious scale, with the biographies of individual kings presented as self-contained sagas. Snorri made wide use of existing prose sources although they are rarely overtly acknowledged; his account of the battle of Svǫlðr depends as heavily as *Fagrskinna* does on Oddr's *Óláfs saga Tryggvasonar*, but is more economically narrated, and more fully supported by Snorri's account of the events preceding it.

Snorri famously articulated the importance of skaldic verse as historical source material and cites it extensively, though there is proportionately more in *Fagrskinna*. Scholars disagree as to whether Snorri knew *Fagrskinna*; it may not have been known in Iceland before the composition of *Heimskringla*, though Snorri could have encountered it during his first visit to Norway. There are many similarities of structure and wording, but these can often be attributed to common sources, such as Oddr's *Óláfs saga*. It has been suggested that Snorri came to know *Fagrskinna* only at a late stage in the composition of *Heimskringla*.

The Battle of Svǫlðr

This extract (chapter 24 of the *ÍF* edition) tells of the defeat and death at Svǫlðr of King Óláfr Tryggvason in 999/1000, at the end of a five-year reign. He was celebrated as the bringer of Christianity to northern lands, as *Fagrskinna* relates: 'He was the first of the kings of Norway to hold the true faith in God, and from his direction and power all the kingdom of Norway became Christian, and the Orkneys, Faroes, Shetland, Iceland and Greenland.' This is an overstatement, since it was only the coastal areas of Norway that were touched by Óláfr's proselytising; it was left to his more celebrated namesake, King Óláfr Haraldsson (the Saint) to complete the conversion. Hagiographic legends concerning both kings began to spring up almost immediately after their deaths, and there is considerable transference of material from one body of legend to another: for instance, the famous tale of the breaking of Einarr þambarskelfir's bow at Svǫlðr, found in *Heimskringla* but not in *Fagrskinna*, is told of Óláfr Haraldsson at the Battle of Nesjar in the early thirteenth-century *Legendary Saga of St Óláfr*.

Fagrskinna's main source for the life of Óláfr was the hagiographic account by the Icelandic monk Oddr Snorrason, but *Fagrskinna* minimises the hagiographic element and heavily compresses the narration of the king's life, though the account of the battle, with its colourful heroic and rhetorical devices, is more expansive. We know of the events leading up to the battle from a variety of contradictory sources and traditions, most of which the author of *Fagrskinna* ignores.

The language of *Fagrskinna*

Although the text exists in late Icelandic copies, its Norwegian provenance is clear from the prevalence of Norwegian spellings. These are found in both versions, though the distribution is somewhat different in the two. At the time of the settlement of Iceland, the language was that taken there by settlers mostly from the western districts of Norway; by the thirteenth century, significant dialectal divergences can be detected in manuscripts. The following are the most conspicuous Norwegian features, and are retained where they occur in the extract edited here:

œy for *ey*. Where Icelandic *ey* is produced by *i*-mutation of *au*, the corresponding Norwegian form is *œy* or *øy* (*lœypizk*, Icel. *hleypizk*; *lœyniliga*, Icel. *leyniliga*).

a for *ǫ*. The vowel produced by *u*-mutation of *a*, rendered in Old Icelandic by *ǫ*, often does not occur in Norwegian where the *u* is, or would normally be, retained; in this text the *u* is often lost (*faðr*, Icel. *fǫður*; *annr*, Icel. *ǫnnur*). The absence of mutation (i.e. the spelling with *a*) is more consistent in the B version (compare *frásǫgur*, line 320, from A, with *faðr*, line 42, and *hafuð*, line 76, from B).

l, r, n for *hl, hr, hn*. The voiceless initial consonant groups *hl, hr, hn,* were voiced to *l, r, n* in Norwegian (*ló*, Icel. *hló*; *ræddr*, Icel. *hræddr*). In one of the verses attributed to Hallfreðr *hnekkir* is required for alliteration with *hertryggðar* and *hyggja*, so the *h* is added here to the manuscript form *nekkir* (line 178).

ú for *ó*. The negative prefix, more commonly *ó-* in Icelandic, was more commonly *ú-* in Norwegian; see here *úkristni* alongside *ókristni*.

sunr for *son(r)*. The Icelandic form *-son* is probably a reduction, because of its frequent unstressed use in nominal compounds, of the form represented in Norwegian as *sunr*.

hánum for *honum*. The Icelandic form *honum* derives from mutation of *á* to *ó* under the influence of a nasal consonant and following back vowel; the vowel was then reduced to *o* because it was frequently unstressed.

meðr and *viðr* for *með* and *við*. These forms are more prevalent in the A version (the latter part of this extract).

Other Norwegianisms (frequent occurrence of *æ* for *e,* vowel harmony in unaccented syllables, *y* for *i, gh* for *g*) are also found in this text but are not represented in this extract.

Where the text is extant in both versions, the earlier (B) version has been followed, but some emendations have been adopted from the A version without annotation.

Bibliography

Fagrskinna: Nóregs kononga tal, ed. Finnur Jónsson (1902–03). Samfund til Udgivelse af Gammel Nordisk Litteratur 30.

Fagrskinna: *Nóregs konunga tal*, in *Ágrip af Nóregskonunga sǫgum. Fagrskinna — Nóregs konunga tal*, ed. Bjarni Einarsson (1985). *ÍF* XXIX.

Fagrskinna, A Catalogue of the Kings of Norway, tr. Alison Finlay (2004).

Adam of Bremen, *Gesta Hammaburgensis ecclesiae pontificum*, ed. W. Trillmich and R. Buchner in *Quellen des 9. und 11. Jahrhunderts zur Geschichte der hamburgischen Kirche und des Reiches* (1978), 135–499.

Adam of Bremen, *History of the Archbishops of Hamburg-Bremen*, tr. Francis J. Tschan (1959).

Ari Þorgilsson, *Íslendingabók*, in *Íslendingabók. Landnámabók*, ed. Jakob Benediktsson (1968). *ÍF* I.

The Book of the Icelanders (Íslendingabók) by Ari Thorgilsson, ed. and tr. Halldór Hermannsson (1930). Islandica 20.

Theodoricus monachus, *Historia de antiquitate regum Norwagiensium*, in *Monumenta Historica Norvegiæ*, ed. G. Storm (1880, repr. 1973), 1–68.

Theodoricus monachus, *Historia de antiquitate regum Norwagiensium. An account of the Ancient History of the Norwegian Kings*, tr. David and Ian McDougall (1998).

Historia Norwegiae. In *Monumenta Historica Norvegiæ*, ed. G. Storm (1880, repr. 1973), 69–124. Translation in *A History of Norway and The Passion and Miracles of the Blessed Óláfr*, tr. Devra Kunin, ed. Carl Phelpstead (2001).

Ágrip af Nóregskonungasǫgum. A Twelfth-Century Synoptic History of the Kings of Norway, ed. and tr. M. J. Driscoll (1995).

Saga Óláfs Tryggvasonar af Oddr Snorrason munk, ed. Finnur Jónsson (1932).

Oddr Snorrason, *Óláfs saga Tryggvasonar*, in *Færeyinga saga. Óláfs saga Odds*. Ed. Ólafur Halldórsson (2006). *ÍF* XXV.

Óláfs saga Tryggvasonar en mesta I–III, ed. Ólafur Halldórsson (1958–2000). Editiones Arnamagnæanæ.

The Saga of King Olaf Tryggwason who Reigned over Norway A.D. 955 to A.D. 1000, tr. John Sephton (1895). [*The Greatest Saga of Óláfr Tryggvason*]

Morkinskinna, ed. Finnur Jónsson (1932). Samfund til Udgivelse af Gammel Nordisk Litteratur 53.

Morkinskinna: The Earliest Icelandic Chronicle of the Norwegian Kings (1030–1157), tr. T. M. Andersson and Kari Ellen Gade (2000). Islandica 51.

T. M. Andersson, 'Kings' Sagas (Konungasögur)'. In *Old Norse-Icelandic Literature. A Critical Guide*, ed. Carol J. Clover and John Lindow (1985). Islandica 45.

Gustav Indrebø, *Fagrskinna* (1917). Avhandlinger fra Universitetets historiske Seminar 4.

Bjarni Einarsson, 'Fagrskinna', *MS* 177.

VI: FAGRSKINNA

Chapter 24: The Death of Óláfr Tryggvason

Sveinn Danakonungr þóttisk missa mikilla eigna þeira er vera skyldu í tilgjǫf Gunnhildar konu hans, því at Þyri hafði eignir þær er Haraldr konungr, faðir hennar, hafði gefit henni. En Búrizleifr þóttisk þá mjǫk svikinn, þó at hann hefði tilgjǫf þá er Þyri skyldi hafa, því at konan kom eigi til hans.[1] Af atkalli Gunnhildar ok áeggjun sendi Sveinn konungr menn eptir Þyri ok lét fylgja henni nauðgri á Vinðland til fundar Búrizleifs konungs, ok gerði hann brullaup til hennar. En hon vildi eigi eiga heiðinn mann þá heldr en fyrr, ok var hon svá nætr sjau með konunginum at hon þá at þeim hvárki mat né drykk, ok með ráðum fóstrfaðr síns gat hon lœypizk á braut á skóg einn ok svá til þess er hon kom til sjóvar, ok fengu þau þar eitt lítit skip ok fóru til Danmarkar. En hon þorði þar eigi at leggja, því at hon uggði at Sveinn konungr, bróðir hennar, myndi þegar láta fylgja henni til Vinðlands aptr, ef hann vissi at hon væri þar komin. Hon fór þá lœyniliga til Nóregs á fund Óláfs konungs ok bað hann leggja til hjálpræði með sér. Hann tók við henni ok gerði sér at eiginkonu án ráði Sveins konungs, bróður hennar.

Hon bað Óláf konung opt at hann skyldi heimta fé hennar at Búrizleifi konungi á Vinðlandi, ok kallaðisk hafa lítit af því er hon átti með réttu at hafa. Þá gerði konungr ferð sína ór landi, bauð út liði miklu ok hafði sex tigu skipa, fór austr til Vinðlands í gegnum Danakonungs ríki fyrir útan hans þǫkk ok vilja. Óláfr konungr fær mikit fé, ok allt eignaðisk hann þat er hann vildi, ok olli því mest liðveizla Ástríðar, dóttur Búrizleifs konungs, er átti Sigvaldi jarl at Jómi.

Þá er Óláfr konungr fór af Vinðlandi, sigldi hann yfir til Danmarkar lítinn byr ok fagrt veðr, ok fóru þau skip fyrir er smæri váru, en þau síðar er stœrri váru, fyrir því at þau þurftu meira veðrit en þau er smæri váru. Við einn hólma fyrir Vinðlandi váru saman komnir margir stórir hǫfðingjar. Þessi hólmi heitir Svǫlðr.[2] Í þessum flota var Sveinn Danakonungr, er miklar sakar þóttisk eiga við Óláf konung. Sú var ein at Óláfr átti Þyri, systur hans, ok fengit hennar at ólœyfi hans. Annr sǫk var at hann sagði at Óláfr hafði sezk í skattlǫnd hans, Nóregs ríki, er Haraldr konungr, faðir hans, hafði lagt undir sik.[3] Sigvaldi jarl var þar með Danakonungi fyrir þá sǫk at hann var Danakonungs jarl. Í þessum flota var ok mikill hǫfðingi, Óláfr svænski Svíakonungr, er hefna þóttisk eiga á Óláfi konungi mikillar svívirðingar. Hann hafði slitit festarmálum ok lostit með glófa sínum Sigríði, móður Óláfs konungs, dóttur Skǫglar-Tósta.[4] Þá samu Sigríði átti þá Sveinn Danakonungr, ok var hon mjǫk fýsandi at Sveinn Danakonungr gerði Óláfi konungi mein eða svívirðing. Ok í þessu liði var Eiríkr jarl Hákonarsunr, er mestar sakar þóttisk eiga við Óláf konung ok hans menn, er verit hafðu nær drápi faðr hans, Hákonar, ok flæmt ór landi alla sunu hans ok sezk í ríkit eptir.

Ástríðr hafði fengit Óláfi konungi ellifu skip, ok skyldi þetta lið fylgja konunginum til þess er hann kœmi um Danmǫrk. En þat var mest til at þau Búrizleifr ok Ástríðr tóku svá vel við Óláfi konungi, at Geila hafði verit dóttir Búrizleifs konungs ok systir Ástríðar, er Óláfr konungr hafði átta þá er hann var á Vinðlandi.[5] Óláfr Tryggvasunr hafði alls eitt skip ok sjau tigu skipa, sem segir Halldórr ókristni:[6]

Œyna fór ok einu,
unnviggs, konungr sunnan,
sverð rauð mætr at morði
meiðr, sjau tigum skeiða,
þá er húnlagar h*reina*
hafði jarl[7] um krafða,
sætt gekk seggja *á*ttar
sundr, Skánunga fundar.

Þessir hǫfðingjar hafðu úvígjan her ok lágu í hǫfn einni innan at hólmanum, en skip Óláfs konungs sigldu hit ýtra fyrir, þá er hǫfðingjarnir váru uppi á hólmanum ok sá til er flotinn sigldi austan. Þeir sá at smá skip sigldu fyrir. Nú sjá þeir eitt mikit skip ok mjǫk glæsiligt.

Þá mælti Sveinn konungr, 'Farum til skipa sem tíðast, þar siglir nú Ormr enn langi austan.'[8]

Þá svaraði Eiríkr jarl, 'Bíðum enn, fleiri hafa þeir stór skip en Orm enn langa.'

Ok svá var. Þetta skip átti Styrkárr af Gimsum. Þá sá þeir enn annat skip mikit ok vel búit, hǫfðaskip.

Þá mælti Sveinn konungr, 'Nú man hér fara Ormr enn langi, ok verðum eigi of seinir í móti þeim.'

54 hanum *MS.* 55 skræfðan, krafðan *MSS.* 56 ættar *MS.*

Þá svaraði Eiríkr jarl, 'Eigi man þetta vera enn Ormr enn langi; fá hafa enn farit stór skip þeira, en mǫrg munu til vera.'

Svá var þat sem jarlenn sagði. Nǫkkur skip fóru þá um áðr en skip sigldi með stafaðu segli. Þat var skeið ok miklu meira en annr skip þau er siglt hafðu. Þá er Sveinn konungr sá at þetta skip hafði engi hafuð, stóð hann upp, mælti ok ló við:

'Ræddr er Óláfr Tryggvasunr nú, eigi þorir hann at sigla með hǫfðum dreka síns; farum nú ok leggjum at sem harðast.'

Þá svaraði Eiríkr jarl, 'Eigi er þetta, herra, Óláfr konungr. Kenni ek þetta skip, opt hefi ek þat sét, þat á Erlingr Skjálgssunr,[9] ok er betr at vér leggim um skut hánum til þessar orrostu.[10] Þeir drengir eru þar innan borðs at vér megum víst vita ef vér hittum Óláf Tryggvasun. Betra er oss skarð í flota hans en skeið þessi svá búin.'

Þá mælti Óláfr Svíakonungr, 'Eigi skyldum vér æðrask at leggja til bardaga við Óláf, þó at hann hafi skip mikit. Er þat skǫmm ok neisa, ok man þat spyrjask á ǫll lǫnd, ef vér liggjum hér með óvígjan her, en hann siglir þjóðleið fyrir útan.'

Þá svaraði Eiríkr jarl, 'Herra, lát sigla þetta skip; ek man segja þér góð tíðendi, at eigi man Óláfr Tryggvasunr um oss hafa siglt, ok þenna dag munum vér kost eiga at berjask við hann. Nú eru hér margir hǫfðingjar ok væntir mek þeirar ríðar at allir vér skulum hafa œrit at vinna fyrr en vér skiljumsk.'

Þá mæltu þeir enn, er fram kom eitt mikit skip, 'Þetta man vera Ormr enn langi, ok eigi vill Eiríkr jarl,' sagðu Danir, 'berjask ok hefna faðr síns, ef hann vill eigi nú.'

Jarlenn svaraði reiðr mjǫk, ok lét vera eigi minni ván at Danum myndi eigi vera óleiðari at berjask en hánum eða hans mannum. Þá var eigi langt at bíða þess er þrjú skip sigla ok eitt miklu mest, ok hafði drekahafuð gyllt.

Þá mæltu allir at jarlenn hafði satt sagt, 'ok hér ferr nú Ormr enn langi.'

Eiríkr jarl svaraði, 'Eigi er þetta Ormr enn langi,' ok bað þá þó til leggja ef þeir vildi. Þá tók Sigvaldi jarl skeið sína ok reri út til skipanna, lét skjóta upp skildi hvítum.[11] Þeir laða seglum ok bíða. Þetta et mikla skip er Tranan, er stýrði Þorkell nefja, konungs frændi.[12] Þeir spyrja Sigvalda hver eru tíðendi.

Hann sagði þeim þau tíðendi af Sveini Danakonungi, 'þau er Óláfi Tryggvasyni er skylt at vita, ok þarf hann þess, at hann varisk.'

Þá létu þeir Þorkell fljóta skipen ok bíða. Því næst sá þeir Sveinn konungr sigla fjǫgur skip ok eitt miklu mest ok á drekahafuð, þau er gull eitt váru á at sjá. Þá mæltu allir senn:

'Furðu mikit skip er Ormr enn langi. Ekki langskip man jafnfrítt í verǫldu vera, ok mikil rausn er at láta gera slíkan grip.'

Þá mælti Sveinn Danakonungr, 'Hátt mun Ormr enn langi bera mik. Hánum skal ek stýra í kveld fyrr en sól setisk,' ok hét á lið sitt at búask skyldi.

Þá mælti Eiríkr jarl svá at fáir menn hœyrðu, 'Þó at Óláfr Tryggvasunr hefði ekki meira skip en þat er nú má sjá, þá man Sveinn konungr við Danaher einn aldrigi þessu skipi stýra.'

Sigvaldi, er hann sá hvar skipen sigldu, bað þá Þorkel nefju draga Ormenn undir hólmenn, lét veðret þeim betr standa at sigla á hafet ok at fara landhallt við stór skip ok lítinn byr. Þeir gerðu svá, heimtu undir hólmann þessi fjǫgur, fyrir því at þeir sá sum sín skip undir hólmann róa, ok grunaði þá at vera myndi nǫkkur tíðendi, beita á veðr þeim nær hólmanum, lóðu seglum ok taka til ára. Þetta et mikla skip er kallat Ormr enn skammi. Þá sá þeir hǫfðingjarnir hvar sigla þrjú skip allstór ok et fjórða síðast. Þá mælti Eiríkr jarl við Svein konung ok við Óláf Svíakonung:

'Standið nú upp ok til skipa; nú man ek eigi þræta at Ormr enn langi siglir, ok þar megu þér nú hitta Óláf Tryggvasun.'[13]

Þá þagnaðu þeir allir ok varð at ótti mikill, ok margr maðr ræddisk þar við sinn bana.

Óláfr Tryggvasunr sá hvar menn hans hafðu lagt undir hólmann, ok þóttisk vita at þeir myndu hafa spurt nǫkkur tíðendi, vendir ok þessum skipum inn at hólmanum ok lóðu seglum. Sigvaldi stýrði skeið sinni inn með hólmanum í móti liði konunganna, er innan fóru. Fyrir þessa sǫk kvað Stefnir þetta um Sigvalda:[14]

Mankat ek nefna
— nær man ek stefna:
niðrbjúgt er nef
á níðingi —
þann er Svein konung
sveik ór landi,
en Tryggva sun
á tálar dró.

Sveinn Danakonungr ok Óláfr Svíakonungr ok Eiríkr jarl hafðu gǫrt þat ráð á milli sín, ef þeir felldi Óláf Tryggvasun, at sá þeira er þessu væri næstr skyldi eignask skip hans ok allt lutskipti þat sem fengisk í orrostu, en veldi Nóregskonungs skyldi hafa at þriðjungi hverr við annan.

Þá sá Óláfr konungr ok menn hans at þeir váru sviknir, ok at sjór allr var þakðr í nánd þeim af herskipum, en Óláfr konungr hafði lítit lið, sem segir Hallfrøðr, er lið hafði siglt í fra hánum:[15]

Þar hygg ek mjǫk til misstu
— mǫrg kom drótt á flótta —
gram þann er gunni framði,
gengis Þrœnzkra drengja.
Nœfr vá einn við jǫfra
allvaldr tvá snjalla
— fræg*r* er til slíks at segja
*s*iðr — ok jarl enn þriðja.

Þá lagði í sinn stað hverr þeira þriggja hǫfðingja, Sveinn Danakonungr með sitt lið, Óláfr Svíakonungr með Svíaher; þriðja stað bjó Eiríkr jarl sitt lið.

Þá mælti við Óláf konung einn vitr maðr, Þorkell dyrðill:

'Hér er ofrefli liðs, herra, við at berjask. Dragum upp segl vár ok siglum út á haf eptir liði váru. Er þat engum manni blœyði at hann ætli hóf fyrir sér.'

Þá svaraði Óláfr konungr hátt, 'Leggi saman skipen ok tengið, herklæðisk menn ok bregðið sverðum. Ekki skulu mínir menn á flótta hyggja.'

Þetta orð váttaði Hallfrøðr á þá lund:

Geta skal máls þess, er mæla
menn at vápna sennu
dolga fangs við drengi
dáðǫflgan b*ǫ*r kváðu.
Baðat hertryggðar hyggja
‹h›nekkir sína rekka
— þess lifa þjóðar sessa
þróttar orð — á flótta.

160 frægð, frægt *MSS*. 161 þíðr, suðr *MSS*. 176 búr *MS*.

Þá spurði Óláfr Tryggvasunr menn sína, 'Hverr er hǫfðingi fyrir þessu liði, er hér liggr næst oss?'

Þeir svaraðu, 'Þat hyggjum vér at Sveinn Danakonungr sé.'

Þá mælti Óláfr konungr, 'Eigi skulum vér óttask þat lið, því at aldrigi báru Danir sigr í orrostu, þá er þeir barðusk á skipum við Norðmenn.'

Enn spurði Óláfr konungr, 'Hverir liggja þar út í frá ok hafa mǫrg skip?'

Hánum var sagt at þar var Óláfr Svíakonungr. Óláfr konungr segir: 'Ekki þurfum vér at óttask Svía, rossæturnar. Þeim man vera blíðara at sleikja blótbolla sína en ganga upp á Orm enn langa undir vápn yðr.'[16]

Þá spurði enn Óláfr Tryggvasunr, 'Hverir eigu þau skip en stóru, er þar liggja út í frá flotanum?'

Hánum var sagt at þat var Eiríkr jarl Hákonarsunr með Járnbarðann, er allra skipa var mest.[17] Þá mælti Óláfr konungr:

'Mjǫk hafa þeir tignum mannum í þenna her skipat í móti oss, ok af þessu liði er oss ván harðrar orrostu. Þeir eru Norðmenn sem vér ok hafa opt sét blóðug sverð ok margt vápnaskipti, ok munu þeir þykkjask eiga við oss skapligan fund, ok svá er.'

Þessir fjórir hǫfðingjar, tveir konungar ok tveir jarlar, leggja til orrostu við Óláf Tryggvasun, ok er Sigvalda lítt við orrostuna getit. En þó segir Skúli Þorsteinssunr í sínum flokki at Sigvaldi var þar:[18]

Fyglða ek Frísa dolgi,[19]
fekk ungr þar er spjǫr sungu
— nú finnr ǫld at eldumk —
aldrbót, ok Sigvalda,
þá er til móts við mœti
malmþings í dyn hjalma
sunnr fyrir Svǫlðrar mynni[20]
sárlauk roðinn bárum.

Þessi orrosta varð harðla snǫrp ok mannskœð. Fellu Danir mest, því at þeir váru næstir Norðmannum. Þeir heldusk eigi við ok leggja í frá ór skotmáli, ok fór þessi herr, sem Óláfr Tryggvasunr sagði, meðr alls engan orðstír, en eigi at síðr[21] var hǫrð orrosta ok lǫng; fell af hvárumtveggja mikit lið ok mest af Svíum, ok þar kom at Óláfr svænski sá þat at bezta ráði fyrir sér ok sínu liði at vera sem fjarst ok lét síga á hǫmlur aptr undan, en Eiríkr jarl lá viðr síbyrðt. Óláfr konungr Tryggvasun

207 munni, myðe *MSS.*

hafði lagt Orm enn langa í millum Orms ins skamma ok Trǫnunnar, en hin smæstu skipin ýzt. En Eiríkr jarl lét frá hǫggva hvert sem roðit var, en lagði at þeim er eptir váru.

Nú er smæri skip Óláfs konungs ruðusk, stukku mennirnir undan ok gengu upp á hin stœrri skipin. Varð í því mikit mannspjall í hvárntveggja flokkenn. En svá sem liðit fell af skipum Eiríks jarls, þá kom annat eigi minna í staðenn af Svíum ok Danum, en ekki kom í staðenn þess liðs er fell af Óláfi konungi. Ruðusk þá skip hans ǫll ǫnnr nema Ormr enn langi eigi, fyrir því at hann var borði hæstr ok bazt skipaðr, en meðan liðit var til, þá hafði þangat á gengit, ok hafði hann haldit sinni fullri skipan at manntali, þó at sumir létisk fyrir hánum. En þá er roðinn var Ormr enn skammi ok Tranan, þá lét Eiríkr þau í frá hǫggva, en síðan lagðisk Járnbarðinn síbyrðr viðr Orm enn langa, sem segir Halldórr úkristni:[22]

Fjǫrð kom heldr í harða,
hnitu rœyr saman drœyra,
tungl skǫ́rusk þá tingla
tangar, Ormr enn langi,
þá er borðmiki*nn* Barða
brynflag‹ð›s reginn lagði
— jarl vann hjalms und holmi
hríð — við Fáfnis síðu.[23]

Gerðisk snarpra sverða,
slitu drengir frið lengi,
þá er gullin spjǫr gullu,
gangr um Orm enn langa.
Dolgs kváðu fram fylgja
fráns leggbita hánum
svænska menn at sennu
sunnr *ok* danska runna.

Hykkat ek vægð at vígi
— vann drótt jǫfur sóttan,
fjǫrð kom‹sk› jarl at jǫrðu —
ógnharðan sik spǫrðu,

234 borðmikill *MS*. 245 í *MS*.

þá er fjarðmýils fœrðuð
folkharðr á trǫð Barða
— lítt var Sifjar sóti
svangr — viðr Orm enn langa.

Þessi orrosta var svá hǫrð, fyrst af sókn drengiligri ok þó mest af vǫrnenni, er alla vega lǫgðu skip at Ormenum, en þeir er vǫrðusk gengu svá í mót at þeir stigu niðr af borðunum ok í sjóinn ok sukku niðr með vápnum sínum ok gættu eigi annars en þeir berðisk á landi ok vildu æ fram.[24] Svá kvað Hallfrøðr:[25]

Sukku niðr af Naðri,
naddfárs í bǫð sárir,
baugs, gerðut við vægjask,
verkendr Heðins serkjar.
Vanr man Ormr, þótt Ormi
alldýrr konungr stýri,
þar er hann skríðr meðr lið lýða,
lengi slíkra drengja.

Þá fellu menninir fyrst um mitt skipit, þar sem borðen váru lægst, en fram um stafnenn ok aptr í fyrirrúminu heldusk menninir lengst viðr. Þá er Eiríkr jarl sá at Ormrinn var auðr miðskipa, þá gekk hann upp meðr fimmtánda mann, ok er þat sá Úlfr enn rauði ok aðrir stafnbúar, þá gengu þeir ór stafninum framan ok svá hart at þar er jarlenn var at jarlenn varð undan at røkkva ok aptr á skip sitt, ok þá er hann kom á Barðann, þá eggjaði jarlenn sína menn at sœtti at vel, ok gengu þá upp í annat sinn meðr miklu liði. Var þá Úlfr ok allir stafnbúarnir komnir at lyptingunni, en roðit var allt skipit fram. Sótti þá lið Eiríks jarls allumveginn at þeim Óláfi konungi, svá sem Halldórr úkristni segir:[26]

Hét á heiptar nýta
hugreifr — með Óleifi
aptr stǫkk þjóð um þoptur —
þengill sína drengi,

250 fjarðmykils *MS*, mýils *Oddr Snorrason*.

þá er hafvita hǫfðu
hallands um gram snjallan
— varð um Vinða myrði
vápnreið — lokit skeiðum.

Þá sótti Eiríkr jarl aptr at fyrirrúminu meðr sína menn ok var þar hǫrð viðrtaka. Óláfr konungr hafði verit þann dag allan í lyptingunni á Orminum. Hann hafði gylltan skjǫld ok hjálm, þunga ringabrynju ok svá trausta at ekki festi á henni, ok er þó svá sagt at ekki skorti vápnaburðenn at lyptingunni, fyrir því at allir menn kenndu konungenn, af því at vápn hans váru auðkennd ok hann stóð hátt í lypting. En í hjá konungenum stóð Kolbjǫrn stallari meðr þvílíkan vápnabúnað sem konungrenn hafði. Nú fór þessi orrosta sem líkligt var, þar sem hvárttveggja hǫfðu raustir á hizk, at þeir létusk þó er fámennari váru, ok þá er allt var fallit lið Óláfs konungs, þá ljóp hann sjálfr fyrir borð, ok brá skildinum upp yfir hafuð sér ok svá Kolbjǫrn stallari, en hans skjǫldr varð undir honum á sjónum, ok kom hann sér eigi í kafit, ok þeir menn er váru á smám skipum tóku hann ok hugðu at konungrinn væri sjálfr. Hann fekk þó grið af jarlenum. En eptir þat, þá ljópu allir fyrir borð, þeir er eptir lifðu ok þó flestir sárir, ok þeir er griðin fengu váru af sundi teknir. Þat var Þorkell nefja, Karlshafuð ok Þorsteinn ok Einarr þambarskelfir.[27]

En eptir þat er orrostunni var lokit, þá eignaðisk Eiríkr jarl Orm enn langa ok ǫnnr skip Óláfs ok margs manns vápn, þeira er drengiliga hafðu borit til dauðadags. Þat hefir Hallfrøðr váttat, at Þorkell nefja flýði svá at ǫll váru skip Óláfs konungs roðin:[28]

Ógrœðir sá auða
armgrjóts Tranu fljóta
— hann rauð geir at gunni
glaðr — ok báða Naðra,
áðr en hjaldrþorinn heldi,
hugframr *í* bǫð ramri,
snotr á snœrivitni
sunds Þórketill[29] undan.

Þessi orrosta hefir frægust verit á Norðrlandum, af því at sagt er um

311 æ *MS.*

vǫrn drengiliga, þar næst af atsókn ok sigrenum, er þat skip varð unnit á djúpum sæ er engi maðr ætlaði vápnum sótt verða, en þó mest fyrir sakar þess er þvílíkr hǫfðingi fell er þá var frægastr á danska tungu. Svá mikit gerðu menn sér um at vingask í allri umrœðu við Óláf konung at mestr lutr manna vildi eigi hœyra at hann myndi fallit hafa, nema létu at hann var í Vinðlandi eða í Suðrríki, ok eru margar frásǫgur um þat gǫrvar. En hans ástvinir ræddusk at þat myndi logit vera, ok lýsti Hallfrøðr því vandræðaskáld, sá maðr er svá mikit hafði unnt konungenum at menn segja at eptir fall konungsins fekk hann vanheilsu af harmi, þá er hánum vannsk til dauðadags.[30] Þetta vitni bar Hallfrøðr:[31]

Veit ek eigi hitt, hvár‹t› H*ei*ta
hungrdœyfi skal ek lœyfa
dynsæðinga dauðan
dýrbliks eða þó kvikvan,
alls sannliga segja
— sárr mun gramr at hváru,
hætt er til hans at frétta —
hvárttveggja mér seggir.

Samr var árr um ævi
oddflag‹ð›s hinn er þat sagði,
at lofða gramr lifði,
læstyggs burar Tryggva.
Vera kveðr ǫld ór éli
Óláf kominn stála;
menn geta máli sǫnnu —
mjǫk er verr en svá — ferri.

Ok enn kvað hann þetta:

Mundut þess, er þegnar
þróttharðan gram sóttu,
— fer ek meðr lýða lí*ði*
landherðar — skǫp verða,

325 hætta *MS*. 344 lifi *MS*, líði *Heimskringla*.

at mundjǫkuls myndi
margdýrr koma stýrir
— geta þykkjat mér gotnar
glíkli‹g›s — ór her slíkum.

Ok enn kvað hann:

Enn segir auðar kenni
austr ór malma gnaustan
seggr frá sárum tyggja
sumr eða brott of komnum.
Nú er sannfregit sunnan
siklings ór styr miklum,
kann ek eigi margt at manna,
morð, veifanar orði.

Ok enn sagði hann:[32]

Norðmanna hygg ek nenninn
— nú er þengill fram genginn,
dýrr hné dróttar stjóri —
dróttin und lok sóttan;
grams dauði brá gœði
góðs úfárar þjóðar.
Allr glepsk f‹r›iðr af falli
flug‹s›tyggs sunar Tryggva.

351 kennir *MS*.

Notes

[1] Fagrskinna, ch. 19, outlines the abortive betrothal of Þyri, arranged by Jarl Sigvaldi of Jómsborg as part of a peace settlement between King Sveinn of Denmark and Búrizleifr, King of the Wends:

> Next Sigvaldi sent word to his father-in-law, King Búrizleifr, and said that King Sveinn had come to Jómsborg, and that he himself was willing to arbitrate between them or else allow King Sveinn to go back to Denmark. In turn, he persuaded King Sveinn to make peace with King Búrizleifr according to the settlement that Sigvaldi decided between them. If he was not willing to do that, then he would come into the presence and power of King Búrizleifr. They came to terms in this way, that each of the kings agreed to Jarl Sigvaldi's judgement, and when they had settled this by a binding agreement between them, the jarl pronounced the terms of their settlement, saying first that King Sveinn should marry Gunnhildr, daughter of King Búrizleifr, and her dowry should be that part of Wendland which the Danes had conquered in the realm of the king of the Wends. On the other hand, King Búrizleifr was to marry Þyri, daughter of King Haraldr and sister of King Sveinn. She had previously been married to Styrbjǫrn, son of King Óláfr of the Swedes; her father, King Haraldr, was still alive then. He had given her extensive estates on Fyn and south in Falster and Bornholm. Jarl Sigvaldi made a division in this way: Búrizleifr was to keep that part of Wendland which had previously been apportioned to the estates of Gunnhildr, Búrizleifr's daughter, whom King Sveinn was to marry, and King Haraldr's daughter Þyri was now to have that; and Gunnhildr Búrizleifsdóttir was now to possess all those estates in Denmark which Þyri had owned, and receive all her bridal gift in Denmark, and Þyri all her bridal gift in Wendland, except that the jarl reserved from the division Jómsborg and all the districts that he specified. Then King Búrizleifr and Jarl Sigvaldi prepared a great feast in Jómsborg, and at that feast the wedding of King Sveinn and the betrothal of King Búrizleifr were celebrated.
>
> After that, King Sveinn went home to his kingdom with his wife Gunnhildr. They later had two sons, the elder called Knútr ríki (the Great), the younger Haraldr.
>
> When King Sveinn came back from Wendland, he sent word to his sister Þyri, and told her everything he had agreed in Wendland with King Búrizleifr. Þyri was not pleased at this news, for she was Christian, and said that she would rather die among Christians than come into the power of a heathen king and violate her Christianity. She stayed on her estates and looked after her property for some years after that.

[2] The site of the battle is uncertain. *Fagrskinna* and *Heimskringla* agree in locating it by an unidentified island, Svǫlðr, in the southern Baltic, while *Ágrip* and Adam of Bremen say that it took place in Øresund, between Sjælland and Skåne.

[3] Sveinn's father, Haraldr Gormsson, had seized power in Norway in alliance with Jarl Hákon, after the death in battle of King Haraldr gráfeldr (976). Óláfr Tryggvason established himself as king on the death of Jarl Hákon (995).

[4] *Heimskringla* (*Óláfs saga Tryggvasonar*, ch. 61) relates Óláfr Tryggvason's breach of his betrothal to the pagan Sigríðr (mother of King Óláfr of Sweden), on her refusal to accept Christianity, calling her *hundheiðin* 'absolutely heathen, ?heathen as a dog' and slapping her face with his glove. The words *með glófa sínum* occur only in the A version of *Fagrskinna*.

[5] Óláfr's marriage to Geila during his early Viking adventures is mentioned only briefly in *Fagrskinna*, but *Heimskringla*, in which she is called Geira, gives a probably fictitious account of the marriage and of Geira's death three years later.

[6] This verse is also cited in *Heimskringla* and Oddr Snorrason's saga of Óláfr. Nothing is known of the poet Halldórr ókristni other than the verses cited in the Kings' Sagas, four of them in *Fagrskinna*; some or all of these belong to a poem in honour of Jarl Eiríkr, to which Snorri refers. This verse supports the timing of the battle during Óláfr's return from Wendland (*sunnan*), rather than on his way south as Adam and *Ágrip* assert, and is the source for the statement in the prose that Óláfr commanded 71 ships. This is contradicted in other sources; *Historia Norwegiae* assigns the 71 ships to Óláfr's opponents, and according to Theodoricus, 'it is said that with only eleven ships he engaged in battle against seventy'. *Fagrskinna* is vague about the size of the *úvígr herr* opposing Óláfr, although he is still overwhelmed by force of numbers, presumably because the actual battle involves only the small number of Óláfr's ships lured into Sigvaldi's trap.

[7] It is unclear whether this jarl is Eiríkr Hákonarson — referred to elsewhere in Halldórr's verses, as here, as *jarl* without further qualification — or the treacherous Sigvaldi. The verse is also cited in *Heimskringla* (*ÍF* XXVI, 352), where Snorri explicitly uses it as a source for his account of Sigvaldi's apparent support for Óláfr: 'This verse says that King Óláfr and Jarl Sigvaldi had 71 ships when they sailed from the south.' See note 14 below.

[8] *Fagrskinna* (ch. 23) recounts the building of *Ormr inn langi*, Óláfr's famous 'Long Serpent':

> King Óláfr had a ship built at Hlaðahamrar. It was much larger and more splendidly built than other longships. It had thirty-four rowing-benches. On it were placed dragon-heads decorated with gold, and that ship was called Ormr inn langi (the Long Serpent). On this ship there was to be no man younger than twenty and none older than sixty. Many things were forbidden to the men who were to be on the Ormr, and none was to be on it unless he was an impressive man in some way, and many examples show that on that ship were only heroes, and no cowards or weaklings.

[9] Erlingr Skjálgsson was Óláfr Tryggvason's brother-in-law.

[10] *leggim um skut hánum til þessar orrostu*: go into this battle round his stern, that is, after he has sailed on, avoiding a confrontation with him.

[11] *lét skjóta upp skildi hvítum*: showing a white shield was a token of peaceful intentions.

[12] Þorkell nefja was Óláfr Tryggvason's half-brother, according to *Heimskringla* (*Óláfs saga Tryggvasonar*, ch. 52).

[13] The long, tension-building scene in which the leaders wrongly identify one ship after another as the Long Serpent is an obvious literary device, and has been traced to the ninth-century *De Gestis Karoli Magni* by the Monk of St Gall, where it occurs in an account of the approach of Charlemagne's army against the Langobards. Its treatment in *Fagrskinna* is somewhat confused and repetitive. In the more succinct version of *Heimskringla,* there are four rather than six false alarms; the sightings help to identify two of the leaders serving with the king, as well as his two lesser named ships, the Trana 'Crane' and Ormr inn skammi 'the Short Serpent', both of which were introduced earlier in the narrative of Óláfr's reign. *Fagrskinna* mentions both these ships here for the first time, and is undecided whether Þorkell nefja commands the Trana or Ormr inn skammi. According to *Heimskringla,* Ormr inn skammi was commanded by Þorkell nefja, the Trana by Þorkell dyrðill, the king's uncle (mentioned in *Fagrskinna* simply as 'a wise man').

[14] This *fornyrðislag* verse, attributed to the poet Stefnir Þorgilsson, is also found in Oddr Snorrason's saga, which also quotes a Latin version of it said to have been composed by Oddr. *Heimskringla* does not cite the verse but, like Oddr's saga, gives a clearer account of Sigvaldi's treachery. He is sent by the alliance against Óláfr to lure him from Wendland, assuring him that there is no army lying in wait for him. *Fagrskinna* presents him less ambiguously as a subordinate of King

Sveinn of Denmark, and Skúli Þorsteinsson's verse (below) associates him with Eiríkr's force. The allusion in the verse to Sigvaldi's tricking Sveinn into leaving his country is to the story recorded in ch. 19 of *Fagrskinna* (see note 1 above) of Sigvaldi feigning sickness in order to capture King Sveinn and carry him off to an enforced settlement with the Wends.

[15] Hallfreðr vandræðaskáld ('troublesome poet') was an Icelandic poet who composed extensively in honour of King Óláfr, and also, paradoxically, for the king's enemies, the jarls Hákon and Eiríkr. *Hallfreðar saga* records his conversion to Christianity by Óláfr, who agreed to act as his godfather, and his probably fictitious love affairs. This and the subsequent verse are also found in Oddr Snorrason's saga and *Heimskringla*, and these and the other verses of Hallfreðr's in this extract are believed to belong to the *erfidrápa* 'memorial lay' composed by Hallfreðr after the king's death. *Hallfreðar saga* relates his composition of another poem in Óláfr's honour during his lifetime; nine surviving verses or half-verses about the king's early viking adventures, preserved in *Fagrskinna* and elsewhere, are attributed to this poem.

[16] These are conventional gibes at the stereotypically pagan Swedes. A verse in *Hallfreðar saga* includes a similar taunt (*ÍF* VIII, 188):

heldr mun hœli-Baldri
hrævinns fyr því minna,
vǫn erumk slíks, at sleikja
sinn blóttrygil innan.

[The boastful Baldr of the carrion-maker (god of the sword = warrior, man) will find it less trouble — so I expect — to lick out the inside of his sacrifice-bowl (than to fight).]

[17] Eiríkr's ship Járnbarðinn ('the Iron-Beak') or Barði (as the ship is named in Halldórr's next verse), is mentioned earlier in *Fagrskinna*, but without description. The related neuter noun *barð* was used of a ship's prow and of the edge of a steep hill.

[18] Skúli Þorsteinsson was an Icelandic poet, grandson of Egill Skalla-Grímsson. *Egils saga* ends with a reference to his presence at Svǫlðr: 'hann var stafnbúi Eiríks jarls á Járnbarðanum, þá er Óláfr konungr Tryggvason fell' (*ÍF* II, 300). Little is known of him in historical sources, and of his poetry only this verse and a number of half-stanzas

preserved in *Snorra Edda* survive, most of them probably belonging to the *flokkr* referred to here, about the poet's deeds.

[19] *Frísa dolgr* 'enemy of Frisians' is presumably Eiríkr.

[20] *Svǫlðrar mynni* 'mouth' suggests that Svǫlðr may actually have been a river; Icelandic authors, presumably unfamiliar with the topography, seem to have interpreted the references to it in verse sources as the name of the island referred to in the subsequently cited verse of Halldórr (line 236).

[21] At this point a lacuna begins in the older (B) text. The remainder of this extract follows the A version, and some changes in the spelling conventions are noticeable: *viðr*, *meðr* instead of *við*, *með*, and definite article forms with *i* rather than *e* (*inn* for *enn*); on the other hand, the mutated vowel *ǫ* before *u* occurs more frequently.

[22] The next three verses are also found in Oddr Snorrason's saga and the first two of them also in *Heimskringla.*

[23] *Fáfnir*, the name of the legendary dragon killed by Sigurðr, refers to Ormr inn langi.

[24] The suggestion that the defenders fought so furiously that they stepped overboard as if they were fighting on land is presumably an over-literal interpretation of Hallfreðr's following verse, 'sukku niðr af Naðri'.

[25] Also in Oddr Snorrason's saga and in *Heimskringla.*

[26] Also in Oddr Snorrason's saga and in *Heimskringla.*

[27] MS *þambaskelmir*, emended in accordance with *Heimskringla* and other texts. *Heimskringla,* following Oddr's saga, includes a colourful anecdote in which the breaking of Einarr the master-archer's bow by an enemy arrow signals Óláfr's downfall:

> 'Hvat brast þar svá hátt?' Einarr svarar, 'Nóregr ór hendi þér, konungr.' ['What broke so loudly there?' Einarr answered, 'Norway, out of your hands, King.']

The story may be inspired by a misinterpretation of the element *þǫmb* 'belly', which could also mean 'bowstring', in the nickname *þambarskelfir* (see VII B:2, note 12). As recorded here, Einarr survives the battle to become a significant figure in the histories of Óláfr Haraldsson and his successors (cf. *Haralds saga Sigurðarsonar* in *Heimskringla*, extract VII B below).

[28] This verse is also in *Heimskringla* and Oddr Snorrason's saga.

[29] *Þórketill* is an archaic form of Þorkell, its trisyllabic form necessary to preserve the metre of the verse. The use of such archaic forms tends to confirm the authentic age of the verse, although they are common enough to be imitated by later poets.

[30] Legends of Óláfr's survival and possible future return to Norway are widespread, and sprang up almost immediately after the battle, as the reference in Hallfreðr's verse testifies. According to Theodoricus, 'some say that the king then escaped from there in a skiff, and made his way to foreign parts to seek salvation for his soul.' Oddr Snorrason's saga records a tradition that he ended his life as a monk in Syria or 'Girkland', i.e. the Byzantine empire. The author of *Fagrskinna* more sceptically sees in the rumours evidence for the sense of loss suffered by the king's followers.

[31] The next four verses are also found in *Heimskringla*. Only the first half-verse is found in Oddr Snorrason's saga.

[32] This verse is found only in *Fagrskinna*, except for the last two lines, which are quoted as the second half of the poem's *stef* 'refrain' in *Hallfreðar saga* and Oddr Snorrason's saga.

Verses in prose word order

Lines 50–57: Œyna konungr fór sunnan sjau tigum skeiða ok einu, mætr meiðr unnviggs rauð sverð at morði þá er jarl hafði um krafða húnlagar h*reina* Skánunga fundar; sætt seggja *á*ttar gekk sundr.

Lines 154–61: Þar hygg ek gram þann er framði gunni misstu mjǫk til gengis Þrœnzkra drengja; mǫrg drótt kom á flótta. Nœfr allvaldr vá einn við tvá snjalla jǫfra ok jarl enn þriðja; fræg*r s*iðr er til slíks at segja.

Lines 173–80: Geta skal máls þess, er menn kváðu dáðǫflgan bǫr dolga fangs mæla við drengi at vápna sennu. Hertryggðar ‹h›nekkir baðat sína rekka hyggja á flótta; þess sessa þjóðar þróttar orð lifa.

Lines 201–08: Ek fyglða Frísa dolgi ok Sigvalda, fekk ungr aldrbót þar er spjǫr sungu — nú finnr ǫld at eldumk — þá er bárum roðinn sárlauk til móts við mœti malmþings í dyn hjalma sunnr fyrir Svǫlðrar mynni.

Lines 230–37: Fjǫrð kom Ormr enn langi í heldr harða — rœyr drœyra hnitu saman — þá tungl tingla tangar skǫ́rusk, þá er brynflag‹ð›s reginn lagði borðmiki*nn* Barða við síðu Fáfnis; jarl vann hjalms hríð und holmi.

Lines 138–45: Snarpra sverða gangr gerðisk um Orm enn langa; drengir slitu frið lengi þá er gullin spjǫr gullu. Kváðu svænska menn *ok* danska dolgs runna fylgja hánum fram sunnr at fráns leggbita sennu.

Lines 246–53: Hykkat ek vægð at vígi — drótt vann jǫfur sóttan, jarl kom‹sk› at fjǫrðjǫrðu — ógnharðan spǫrðu sik þá er folkharðr fœrðuð Barða á fjarðmýils trǫð viðr Orm enn langa — lítt var Sifjar sóti svangr.

Lines 259–66: Heðins baugs serkjar verkendr, sárir í naddfárs bǫð, sukku niðr af Naðri; gerðut vægjask við. Ormr man lengi vanr slíkra drengja þar er hann skríðr meðr lið lýða, þótt alldýrr konungr stýri Ormi.

Lines 277–84: Hugreifr þengill hét á sína heiptar nýta drengi — þjóð stǫkk með Óleifi aptr um þoptur — þá er hǫfðu lokit skeiðum hallands hafvita um snjallan gram; vápnreið varð um Vinða myrði.

Lines 306–13: Ógrœðir armgrjóts sá Tranu ok báða Naðra fljóta auða — glaðr, hann rauð geir at gunni — áðr en hjaldrþorinn Þórketill, hugframr *í* ramri bǫð á snœrivitni, heldi snotr sunds undan.

Lines 325–32: Veit ek eigi hitt, hvár‹t› skal ek lœyfa hungrdœyfi H*ei*ta dýrbliks dynsæðinga dauðan eða þó kvikvan, alls seggir segja mér hvárttveggja sannliga; sárr mun gramr at hváru; hætt er at frétta til hans.

Lines 333–40: Var samr árr oddflag‹ð›s hinn er þat sagði um ævi læstyggs burar Tryggva at lofða gramr lifði. Ǫld kveðr Óláf vera kominn ór éli stála; menn geta ferri sǫnnu máli; mjǫk er verr en svá.

Lines 342–49: Mundut verða skǫp þess, er þegnar sóttu þróttharðan gram — ek fer meðr lí*ð*i landherðar lýða — at margdýrr mundjǫkuls stýrir myndi koma ór slíkum her; þykkjat mér gotnar geta glíkli‹g›s.

Lines 351–58: Enn segir sumr seggr kenni auðar frá sárum tyggja eða brott of komnum ór malma gnaustan austr. Nú er morð siklings sannfregit sunnan ór miklum styr; kann ek eigi margt at veifanar orði manna.

Lines 360–67: Ek hygg nenninn dróttin Norðmanna sóttan und lok; nú er þengill genginn fram; dýrr dróttar stjóri hné; dauði góðs grams brá gœði úfárar þjóðar. Allr f‹r›iðr glepsk af falli flug‹s›tyggs sunar Tryggva.

VII: Snorri Sturluson: HEIMSKRINGLA

Snorri's cycle of sixteen sagas about Norwegian kings is often regarded as supreme among the *konungasögur* 'Kings' Sagas'. Works such as *Morkinskinna*, *Fagrskinna* and sagas of individual kings including Óláfr Tryggvason and Óláfr Haraldsson have chronological precedence, and they provided Snorri both with material and with literary models (see the list of historiographical antecedents in the introduction to extract VI above). Nevertheless, *Heimskringla* is outstanding for its scope, balance, literary verve, and shrewd penetration of human nature and political motive.

Heimskringla may be seen as a triptych, in which the great saga of Óláfr Haraldsson (St Óláfr), adapted from Snorri's earlier separate saga, is flanked by sagas about his predecessors and successors. Extract A, from the concluding saga of the first 'third' of *Heimskringla*, shows something of the variety of the work. The narrative follows the adventures of Óláfr Tryggvason in the British Isles before his coming to power in Norway *c.*995, as he engages in routine raiding and acquires, through a mix of supernatural influences and his own practical flair, a new religion, a distinguished wife and a famous dog. Many of the plot motifs have a distinctly folkloristic tinge — test, assumed identity, prophecy, rivalry in love and a 'helpful animal' — and can be paralleled, for instance, in I. Boberg's *Motif-Index of Early Icelandic Literature* (1966). The theme of Icelandic independence under threat — of contemporary interest to Snorri writing probably in the years around 1230 — is then dramatised in the famous *landvættir* incident (ch. 33). Extract B, from the racy *Haralds saga Sigurðarsonar*, is set in the mid eleventh century. It illustrates on a small scale Snorri's gift for constructing powerful narrative, as he builds an expectation of treachery through skilful disposition of information and through manipulation of viewpoint as we follow the jealous gaze of Haraldr watching his rival from a balcony, and enter the darkened chamber with the doomed Einarr. Within *Haralds saga* as a whole the episode contributes to the portrayal of the power-hungry monarch who so well deserved his nickname *harðráði* 'the hard-ruler, the ruthless', and it explores themes which run throughout *Heimskringla*: law, leadership, and the precarious balance of power between the royal descendants of Haraldr hárfagri, the dynasty of the Hlaðajarlar, the *lendir menn* and the free farmers. Both extracts also illustrate the construction of prose narratives from the suggestions of skaldic verses, of which Snorri cites over six hundred in the work as a whole.

Most of the events told in the two extracts appear in others of the Sagas of Kings, but never with the same literary or ideological emphasis. There is, for instance, a strongly clerical flavour to the account of Óláfr's baptism in Oddr Snorrason's *Óláfs saga Tryggvasonar* and *The Greatest Saga of Óláfr Tryggvason* (*Óláfs saga Tryggvasonar en mesta*; this is partly dependent on *Heimskringla*). The *Morkinskinna* account of the death of Einarr þambarskelfir contains some of the same fine dramatic strokes as Snorri's, including Einarr's words, *Myrkt er í málstofu konungs*, 'it is dark in the king's council-chamber', but the circumstances leading up to his killing are quite different, and, as in *Fagrskinna*, the narrative is much more favourable to King Haraldr. Snorri's account bears a strong resemblance to that in the fragmentary *Hákonar saga Ívarssonar* (an unusual early thirteenth-century Icelandic biography of an eleventh-century Norwegian chieftain who was neither a king nor a saint), but being more streamlined it has greater dramatic impact.

Snorri Sturluson had much experience of the world, which to some extent conditioned his view of the past. An ambitious Icelandic magnate honoured with office at the Norwegian court, lawyer, poet and mythographer, he lived at a time when struggles between the leading Icelandic families, tensions between ecclesiastical and secular powers and pressure from Norway were opening the way for Iceland's formal submission to the Norwegian crown in 1262–64. His fascination with the complexities of political and social relationships is as apparent in *Heimskringla* as it is in Snorri's own life as glimpsed through *Sturlunga saga* and other prose works (see further Bagge 1991; Whaley 1991).

The present text is based on the manuscript readings presented in Finnur Jónsson's four-volume *Heimskringla* (1893–1901, I 307–18 and III 132–37), supplemented by Bjarni Aðalbjarnarson's edition (*Íslenzk fornrit* XXVI 264–72 and XXVIII 122–26). Of the manuscripts, Kringla, a thirteenth-century vellum of which only one leaf survives, is considered to have, in general, the text closest to Snorri's original; and it is from its opening words *Kringla heimsins* 'the circle of the world', that the grandiose modern title of the work derives. The text of Kringla is preserved in seventeenth-century copies, especially AM 35, 36 and 63 fol. (which cover the three parts of

Heimskringla respectively and are referred to in the notes as K), and 18 fol. in the Royal Library Stockholm (Stock. papp. fol. nr 18). The 'K' readings have been adopted except where an alternative is clearly superior. The manuscripts most closely related to K are AM 39 fol. (= 39) and Codex Frisianus or Fríssbók (= F), while a second group is formed by Jöfraskinna (surviving mainly in two paper copies known as J1 and J2) and AM 47 fol. (= 47), known as Eirspennill, which contains little more than the final third of *Heimskringla*.

Chapter headings are taken from 18; most are supported in at least one other manuscript, often J2.

Bibliography

Editions: *Heimskringla. Nóregs konunga sögur af Snorri Sturluson* I–IV, ed. Finnur Jónsson (1893–1901); Snorri Sturluson, *Heimskringla* I–III, ed. Bjarni Aðalbjarnarson, *ÍF* 26–28 (1941–51).

Translations: Snorri Sturluson, *Heimskringla. Part One: The Olaf Sagas* I–II, tr. Samuel Laing, revised Jacqueline Simpson (1964); *Part Two: Sagas of the Norse Kings*, tr. Samuel Laing, revised Peter Foote, Everyman's Library (1961). *Heimskringla or the Lives of the Norse Kings*, tr. Erling Monsen and A. H. Smith (1932); *Heimskringla. History of the Kings of Norway by Snorri Sturluson*, tr. Lee M. Hollander (1964, repr. 1977).

Background:

Diana Whaley, *Heimskringla: An Introduction*. Viking Society for Northern Research (1991).

Sverre Bagge, *Society and Politics in Snorri Sturluson's* Heimskringla (1991).

Bo Almqvist, *Norrön niddiktning* I: *Nid mot furstar* (1965).

Hákonar saga Ívarssonar, ed. Jón Helgason and Jakob Benediktsson, Samfund til Udgivelse af Gammel Nordisk Litteratur 62 (1952).

R. Meissner, *Die Kenningar der Skalden* (1921).

For other Kings' Sagas see Introduction and Bibliography to VI above.

VII A: ÓLÁFS SAGA TRYGGVASONAR

Chapter 30: Hernaðr Óláfs konungs

Síðan helt Óláfr Tryggvason til Englands ok herjaði víða um landit. Hann sigldi allt norðr til Norðimbralands ok herjaði þar. Þaðan helt hann norðr til Skotlands ok herjaði þar víða. Þaðan sigldi hann til Suðreyja ok átti þar nǫkkurar orrostur. Síðan helt hann suðr til Manar ok barðisk þar. Hann herjaði ok víða um Írland. Þá helt hann til Bretlands ok herjaði víða þat land, ok svá þar er kallat er Kumraland. Þaðan sigldi hann vestr til Vallands ok herjaði þar. Þá sigldi hann vestan ok ætlaði til Englands. Þá kom hann í eyjar þær er Syllingar heita, vestr í hafit frá Englandi. Svá segir Hallfreðr vandræðaskáld:[1]

Gerðisk ungr við Engla
ofvægr konungr bægja.
Naddskúrar réð nœrir
Norðimbra sá morði.
Eyddi ulfa greddir
ógnblíðr Skotum víða
(gerði seims) með sverði
(sverðleik í Mǫn skerðir).

Ýdrógar lét œgir
eyverskan her deyja
— Týr var tjǫrva dýrra
t*ír*ar gjarn — ok Íra.
Barði brezkrar jarðar
byggvendr ok hjó tyggi
— gráðr þvarr geira hríðar
gjóði — kumrskar þjóðir.

Óláfr Tryggvason var fjóra vetr í hernaði síðan er hann fór af Vinðlandi til þess er hann kom í Syllingar.

22 týjar *K*; *most manuscripts have* tírar.

Chapter 31: Skírðisk Óláfr konungr í Syllingum

Óláfr Tryggvason, þá er hann lá í Syllingum, spurði hann at þar í eyjunni var spámaðr nǫkkurr, sá er sagði fyrir óorðna hluti, ok þótti mǫrgum mǫnnum þat mjǫk eptir ganga. Gerðisk Óláfi forvitni á at reyna spádóm manns þess. Hann sendi þann af mǫnnum sínum er fríðastr var ok mestr, ok bjó hann sem vegligast, ok bað hann segja at hann væri konungr, því at Óláfr var þá frægr orðinn af því um ǫll lǫnd at hann var fríðari ok gǫfugligri ok meiri en allir menn aðrir. En síðan er hann fór ór Garðaríki hafði hann eigi meira af nafni sínu en kallaði sik Óla ok kvazk vera gerzkr.

En er sendimaðr kom til spámannsins ok sagðisk vera konungr, þá fekk hann þessi andsvǫr:

'Ekki ertu konungr, en þat er ráð mitt at þú sér trúr konungi þínum.'

Ekki sagði hann fleira þessum manni. Fór sendimaðr aptr ok segir Óláfi, ok fýsti hann þess at meir at finna þenna mann er hann heyrði slík andsvǫr hans, ok tók nú ifa af honum at hann væri eigi spámaðr. Fór þá Óláfr á hans fund ok átti tal við hann ok spurði eptir hvat spámaðr segði Óláfi fyrir, hvernug honum myndi ganga til ríkis eða annarrar hamingju.

Einsetumaðrinn svaraði með helgum spádómi:

'Þú munt verða ágætr konungr ok ágæt verk vinna. Þú munt mǫrgum mǫnnum til trúar koma ok skírnar. Muntu bæði þér hjálpa í því ok mǫrgum ǫðrum. Ok til þess at þú ifir eigi um þessi mín andsvǫr, þá máttu þat til marks hafa: þú munt við skip þín svikum mœta ok flokkum, ok mun á bardaga rœtask, ok muntu týna nǫkkuru liði ok sjálfr sár fá, ok muntu af því sári banvænn vera ok á skildi til skips borinn. En af þessu sári muntu heill verða innan sjau nátta ok brátt við skírn taka.'

Síðan fór Óláfr ofan til skipa sinna, ok þá mœtti hann þar ófriðarmǫnnum þeim er hann vildu drepa ok lið hans. Ok fóru þeira viðskipti svá sem einsetumaðr hafði sagt honum, at Óláfr var sárr borinn á skip út, ok svá at hann var heill á sjau nóttum. Þóttisk þá Óláfr vita at þessi maðr myndi honum sanna hluti sagt hafa ok þat, at hann var sannr spámaðr, hvaðan af sem hann hefði þann spádóm.

Fór þá Óláfr annat sinn at finna þenna mann, talaði þá mart við hann, spurði vendiliga hvaðan honum kom sú speki er hann sagði fyrir óorðna hluti. Einsetumaðr segir at sjálfr Guð kristinna manna lét hann vita allt þat er hann forvitnaðisk, ok segir þá Óláfi mǫrg stórmerki

Guðs. Ok af þeim fortǫlum játti Óláfr at taka skírn, ok svá var at Óláfr var skírðr þar ok allt fǫruneyti hans.[2] Dvalðisk hann þar mjǫk lengi ok nam rétta trú, ok hafði þaðan með sér presta ok aðra lærða menn.

Chapter 32: Óláfr fekk Gyðu

Óláfr sigldi ór Syllingum um haustit til Englands, lá þar í hǫfn einni, fór þá með friði, því at England var kristit ok hann var ok kristinn. En þar fór um landit þingboð nǫkkut, ok allir menn skyldu til þings koma.

En er þing var sett, þá kom þar dróttning ein er Gyða er nefnd, systir Óláfs kvárans er konungr var á Írlandi í Dyflinni. Hon hafði gipt verit á Englandi jarli einum ríkum. Var sá þá andaðr, en hon helt eptir ríkinu. En sá maðr var í ríki hennar er nefndr er Alvini, kappi mikill ok hólmgǫngumaðr. Hann hafði beðit hennar, en hon svaraði svá at hon vildi kjør af hafa, hvern hon vildi eiga af þeim mǫnnum er í hennar ríki váru, ok var fyrir þá sǫk þings kvatt at Gyða skyldi sér mann kjósa. Var þar kominn Alvini ok búinn með inum beztum klæðum, ok margir aðrir váru þar vel búnir. Óláfr var þar kominn ok hafði vásklæði sín ok loðkápu ýzta, stóð með sína sveit út í frá ǫðrum mǫnnum.

Gyða gekk ok leit sér á hvern mann þann er henni þótti nǫkkut mannsmót at. En er hon kom þar sem Óláfr stóð, ok sá upp í andlit honum ok spyrr hverr maðr hann er, hann nefndi sik Óla.

'Ek em útlendr maðr hér,' segir hann.

Gyða mælti, 'Viltu eiga mik, þá vil ek kjósa þik.'

'Eigi vil ek neita því,' segir hann.

Hann spurði hvert nafn þessarar konu var, ætt eða øðli.

'Ek em,' segir hon, 'konungsdóttir af Írlandi. Var ek gipt higat til lands jarli þeim er hér réð ríki. Nú síðan er hann andaðisk, þá hefi ek stýrt ríkinu. Menn hafa beðit mín ok engi sá er ek vilda giptask. En ek heiti Gyða.'

Hon var ung kona ok fríð. Tala þau síðan þetta mál ok semja þat sín á milli. Festir Óláfr sér Gyðu.

Alvina líkar nú ákafliga illa. En þat var siðr á Englandi, ef tveir menn kepptusk um einn hlut, at þar skyldi vera til hólmganga. Býðr Alvini Óláfi Tryggvasyni til hólmgǫngu um þetta mál. Þeir leggja með sér stefnulag til bardaga, ok skulu vera tólf hvárir. En er þeir finnask, mælir Óláfr svá við sína menn at þeir geri svá sem hann gerir. Hann hafði mikla øxi. En er Alvini vildi hǫggva sverði til hans, þá laust hann sverðit ór hǫndum honum ok annat hǫgg sjálfan hann, svá at Alvini fell. Síðan batt Óláfr hann fast. Fóru svá allir menn Alvina at þeir váru barðir ok bundnir ok leiddir svá heim til herbergja Óláfs. Síðan bað hann Alvina fara ór landi brott ok koma eigi aptr, en Óláfr tók allar eigur hans. Óláfr fekk þá Gyðu ok dvalðisk á Englandi en stundum á Írlandi.

Þá er Óláfr var á Írlandi, var hann staddr í herferð nǫkkurri, ok fóru þeir með skipum. Ok þá er þeir þurftu strandhǫggva, þá ganga menn ‹á land› ok reka ofan fjǫlða búsmala. Þá kømr eptir einn bóndi ok bað Óláf gefa sér kýr þær, er hann átti. Óláfr bað hann hafa kýr sínar, ef hann mætti kenna.

'Ok dvel ekki ferð vára.'

Bóndi hafði þar mikinn hjarðhund. Hann vísaði hundinum í nautaflokkana, ok váru þar rekin mǫrg hundruð nauta. Hundrinn hljóp um alla nautaflokkana ok rak brott jafnmǫrg naut sem bóndi sagði at hann ætti, ok váru þau ǫll á einn veg mǫrkuð. Þóttusk þeir þá vita at hundrinn myndi rétt kennt hafa. Þeim þótti hundr sá furðu vitr. Þá spyrr Óláfr ef bóndi vildi gefa honum hundinn.

'Gjarna,' segir bóndi.

Óláfr gaf honum þegar í stað gullhring ok hét honum vináttu sinni. Sá hundr hét Vígi ok var allra hunda beztr. Átti Óláfr hann lengi síðan.[3]

Chapter 33: Frá Haraldi Gormssyni

Haraldr Gormsson Danakonungr spurði at Hákon jarl hafði kastat kristni en herjat land Danakonungs víða. Þá bauð Haraldr Danakonungr her út ok fór síðan í Nóreg. Ok er hann kom í þat ríki er Hákon jarl hafði til forráða, þá herjar hann þar ok eyddi land allt ok kom liðinu í eyjar þær er Sólundir heita. Fimm einir bœir stóðu óbrenndir ‹í Sogni› í Læradal, en fólk allt flýði á fjǫll ok markir með þat allt er komask mátti.

Þá ætlaði Danakonungr at sigla liði því til Íslands ok hefna níðs þess, er allir Íslendingar hǫfðu hann níddan. Þat var í lǫgum haft á Íslandi, at yrkja skyldi um Danakonung níðvísu fyrir nef hvert er á var landinu.[4] En sú var sǫk til, at skip þat, er íslenzkir menn áttu, braut í Danmǫrk, en Danir tóku upp fé allt ok kǫlluðu vágrek, ok réð fyrir bryti konungs, er Birgir hét. Var níð ort um þá báða. Þetta er í níðinu:[5]

Þá er sparn á mó M*arnar*
morðkunnr Haraldr sunnan,
varð þá Vinða myrðir[6]
vax eitt, í ham faxa,
en bergsalar Birgir
bǫndum rækr í landi
— þa‹t› sá ǫld — í jǫldu
óríkr fyrir *l*íki.[7]

Haraldr konungr bauð kunngum manni at fara í hamfǫrum til Íslands ok freista hvat hann kynni segja honum.[8] Sá fór í hvalslíki. En er hann kom til landsins, þá fór hann vestr fyrir norðan landit. Hann sá at fjǫll ǫll ok hólar váru fullir af landvéttum, sumt stórt en sumt smátt.[9] En er hann kom fyrir Vápnafjǫrð, þá fór hann inn á fjǫrðinn ok ætlaði á land at ganga. Þá fór ofan ór dalnum dreki mikill ok fylgðu honum margir ormar, pǫddur ok eðlur ok blésu eitri á hann. En hann lagðisk í brott ok vestr fyrir land, allt fyrir Eyjafjǫrð. Fór hann inn eptir þeim firði. Þar fór móti honum fugl svá mikill at vængirnir tóku út fjǫllin tveggja vegna, ok fjǫlði annarra fugla, bæði stórir ok smáir. Braut fór hann þaðan ok vestr um landit ok svá suðr í Breiðafjǫrð ok stefndi þar inn á fjǫrð. Þar fór móti honum griðungr mikill ok óð á sæinn út ok tók at gella ógurliga. Fjǫlði landvétta fylgði honum. Brott fór hann þaðan ok suðr um Reykjanes ok vildi ganga upp á Víkarsskeiði. Þar kom í móti honum bergrisi ok hafði járnstaf í hendi, ok bar hǫfuðit hæra en fjǫllin, ok margir aðrir jǫtnar með honum.[10]

Þaðan fór hann austr með endlǫngu landi.

'Var þá ekki,' segir hann, 'nema sandar ok ørœfi ok brim mikit fyrir útan, en haf svá mikit millim landanna,' segir hann, 'at ekki er þar fœrt langskipum.'

Þá var Brodd-Helgi í Vápnafirði, Eyjólfr Valgerðarson í Eyjafirði, Þórðr gellir í Breiðafirði, Þóroddr goði í Ǫlfusi.[11]

Síðan snøri Danakonungr liði sínu suðr með landi, fór síðan til Danmerkr, en Hákon jarl lét byggva land allt ok galt enga skatta síðan Danakonungi.

138 mǫrnis *K*, Mǫrnar *Jómsvíkinga saga (291)*. 145 ríki *K*, líki *J1, F, Jómsvíkinga saga (291)*.

Notes

[1] The following two stanzas belong to a sequence of verses about Óláfr's viking exploits which also appears in Oddr Snorrason's *Óláfs saga Tryggvasonar* and in *Fagrskinna* and is edited by Finnur Jónsson in *Skj* A I 156–59, B I 148–50, where the two are printed as stanzas 8 and 9. Oddr Snorrason and the *Fagrskinna* author quote 8a and 9b as a single stanza, then 8b (lines 7–8 then 5–6) and 9a as another. Bjarne Fidjestøl suggests that Snorri's ordering and his prefatory prose represent a rearrangement in the interests of greater geographical coherence (*Det norrøne fyrstediktet*, 1982, 106–09).

[2] According to the *Anglo-Saxon Chronicle* (E and F versions), Óláfr (Anlaf) was confirmed at Andover in 994, with King Æthelred as his sponsor.

[3] The faithful Vígi is portrayed as pining to death after his master's fall in Oddr Snorrason's saga and *The Greatest Saga of Óláfr Tryggvason*.

[4] One verse per head (literally 'nose') of the population would of course have resulted in an impossibly long poem, unless only the chieftains were meant; but it is likely that each person was supposed to contribute a single free-standing verse (*lausavísa*). As Almqvist (1965, 164–65 and 232) suggests, this may be a play on the idea of a poll-tax.

[5] This verse is also quoted in AM 291 4to, a manuscript of *Jómsvíkinga saga*. Almqvist (1965, 119–85 and 221–35) gives a full discussion of the verse and the whole episode.

[6] Almqvist (1965, 182–84) suggests that *Vinða myrðir* 'slayer of Wends' and *morðkunnr* 'battle-famed' may be ironic, taunting the Danes for their lack of success against the Wends.

[7] Birgir is *fyrir* 'in front', and *í . . . jǫldu líki* 'in a mare's form' neatly parallels *í ham faxa* 'in the shape of a horse', hence implying a jibe about passive homosexuality of the sort common in *níð* 'slander'. The association of horses with sexual energy is also traditional.

[8] The following episode is virtually unique to *Heimskringla*. Elsewhere Snorri frequently prefers more rational explanations to supernatural ones, but here he vividly dramatises the hazards of sailing a fleet to a land whose coast is unfamiliar and inhabitants hostile. In *The Greatest Saga of Óláfr Tryggvason* these are merely presented in the form of

sober arguments which dissuade Haraldr from his intended invasion.

[9] The *landvættir* (or *landvéttir*: 'land-beings' or 'land-spirits') appear in other sources, including *Landnámabók*, as supernatural guardians or rulers of the land.

[10] The resemblance of the four main creatures — a dragon, a huge bird, an ox and a giant — to the Evangelist symbols of Christian iconography has been pointed out, e.g. by Einar Ól. Sveinsson in *Minjar ok Menntir, Afmælisrit helgað Kristjáni Eldjárn* (1976), 117–29, but Almqvist (1965, 136–47 and 225–27) argues for origins in the native concepts of fetches, shape-shifters and dream figures. Whether or not these four are to be counted among the *landvættir* is unclear. The case against is put by Almqvist (1965, 147–50 and 227–28), who is supported by Jón Hnefill Aðalsteinsson, 'Landvættir, verndarvættir lands', in *Skæðagrös* (1997), 83. The four figures were adopted to support the armorial bearings of Iceland in 1919.

[11] The neat representation of all four quarters of Iceland by fabulous defenders and a parallel set of prominent chieftains is characteristic of Snorri's often systematic approach. Almqvist points out (1965, 146–47 and 227) the match of Þórðr gellir's nickname, which means 'bellower' and is recorded as a name for an ox, with the bellowing ox of Breiðafjǫrðr.

Verses in prose word order

Lines 11–18: Ungr, ofvægr konungr gerðisk bægja við Engla. Sá nœrir naddskúrar réð morði Norðimbra. Ógnblíðr greddir ulfa eyddi Skotum víða með sverði. Skerðir seims gerði sverðleik í Mǫn.

Lines 19–26: See Section C below.

Lines 138–45: Þá er morðkunnr Haraldr sparn sunnan á mó M*arnar* í ham faxa, varð myrðir Vinða þá vax eitt, en óríkr Birgir, rækr bǫndum bergsalar í landi, fyrir í *l*íki jǫldu. Ǫld sá þa‹t›. [Understand *varð* to be repeated before *fyrir*.]

VII B: HARALDS SAGA SIGURÐARSONAR

Chapter 40: Frá Einari þambarskelfi

Einarr þambarskelfir var ríkastr lendra manna í Þrándheimi.[12] Heldr var fátt um með þeim Haraldi konungi. Hafði Einarr þó veizlur sínar, þær sem hann hafði haft meðan Magnús konungr lifði. Einarr var mjǫk stórauðigr. Hann átti Bergljótu, dóttur Hákonar jarls, sem fyrr var ritat.[13] E‹i›ndriði var þá alroskinn, sonr þeira. Hann átti þá Sigríði, dóttur Ketils kálfs ok Gunnhildar, systurdóttur Haralds konungs. Eindriði hafði fríðleik ok fegrð af móðurfrændum sínum, Hákoni jarli eða sonum hans, en vǫxt ok afl hafði hann af fǫður sínum, Einari, ok alla þá atgørvi er Einarr hafði um fram aðra menn. Hann var inn vinsælsti maðr.[14]

Chapter 42: Frá Haraldi konungi

Haraldr konungr var ríklundaðr, ok óx þat sem hann festisk í landi‹nu›, ok kom svá at flestum mǫnnum dugði illa at mæla í móti honum eða draga fram annat mál en hann vildi vera láta. Svá segir Þjóðólfr skáld:[15]

Gegn skyli herr sem hugnar
hjaldrvitjaðar sitja
dolgstœranda dýrum
dróttinvandr ok standa.
Lýtr folkstara feiti
(fátt er til nema játta
þat sem þá vill gotnum)
þjóð ǫll (konungr bjóða).

Chapter 43: Frá Einari þambarskelfi

Einarr þambarskelfir var mest forstjóri fyrir bóndum allt um Þrándheim. Helt hann upp svǫrum fyrir þá á þingum er konungs menn sóttu. Einarr kunni vel til laga. Skorti hann eigi dirfð til at flytja þat fram á þingum, þó at sjálfr konungr væri við. Veittu honum lið allir bœndr. Konungr reiddisk því mjǫk, ok kom svá at lykðum at þeir þreyttu kappmæli. Segir Einarr at bœndr vildu eigi þola honum ólǫg, ef hann bryti lands-rétt á þeim. Ok fór svá nǫkkurum sinnum milli þeira. Þá tók Einarr at hafa fjǫlmenni um sik heima, en þó miklu fleira ‹þá› er hann fór til býjar svá at konungr var þar fyrir. Þat var eitt sinn at Einarr fór inn til býjar ok hafði lið mikit, langskip átta eða níu ok nær fimm hundruðum manna. En er hann kom til bœjar, gekk hann upp með lið þat. Haraldr konungr var í garði sínum ok stóð út‹i› í loptsvǫlum ok sá er lið Einars gekk af skipum, ok segja menn at Haraldr kvað þá:[16]

Hér sé ek upp enn ǫrva
Einar, þann er kann skeina
þjal*f*a, þambarskel*fi*,
þangs, fjǫlmennan ganga.
Fullafli bíðr fyllar
(finn ek opt, at drífr minna)
hilmis stóls (á hæla
húskarla lið jarli).

Rjóðandi mun ráða
randa bliks ór landi
oss,[17] nema Einarr kyssi
øxar munn enn þunna.

Einarr dvalðisk í býnum nǫkkura daga.

Chapter 44: Fall Einars ok Eindriða

Einn dag var átt mót, ok var konungr sjálfr á mótinu. Hafði verit tekinn í býnum þjófr einn ok var hafðr á mótinu. Maðrinn hafði verit fyrr með Einari, ok hafði honum vel getizk at manninum. Var Einari sagt. Þá þóttisk hann vita at konungr myndi eigi manninn láta undan ganga fyrir því at heldr þótt Einari þœtti þat máli skipta. Lét þá Einarr vápnask lið sitt, ok ganga síðan á mótit. Tekr Einarr manninn af mótinu með valdi. Eptir þetta gengu at beggja vinir ok báru sáttmál milli þeira. Kom þá svá at stefnulagi var á komit. Skyldu þeir hittask sjálfir.

Málstofa var í konungsgarði við ána niðri. Gekk konungr í stofuna við fá menn, en annat lið hans stóð úti í garðinum. Konungr lét snúa fjǫl yfir ljórann, ok var lítit opit á. Þá kom Einarr í garðinn með sitt lið. Hann mælti við Eindriða, son sinn:

'Ver þú með liðinu úti, við engu mun mér þá hætt.'

39 þjalma *K*, þjalfa *Hulda, Hrokkinskinna, Flateyjarbók*; -skelmi *K*, -skelfi *39, Fagrskinna (B), Hulda*.

Eindriði stóð úti við stofudyrrin. En er Einarr kom inn í stofuna, mælti hann:

'Myrkt er í málstofu konungsins.'

Jafnskjótt hljópu menn at honum, ok lǫgðu sumir en sumir hjoggu. En er Eindriði heyrði þat, brá hann sverðinu ok hljóp inn í stofuna. Var hann þegar felldr ok báðir þeir.

Þá hljópu konungsmenn at stofunni ok fyrir dyrrin, en bóndum fellusk hendr, því at þeir hǫfðu þá engan forgǫngumann. Eggjaði hverr annan, segja at skǫmm var er þeir skyldu eigi hefna hǫfðingja síns, en þó varð ekki af atgǫngunni. Konungr gekk út til liðs síns ok skaut á fylking ok setti upp merki sitt, en engi varð atganga bóandanna. Þá gekk konungr út á skip sitt ok allt lið hans, røri síðan út eptir ánni ok svá út á fjǫrð leið sína.

Bergljót, kona Einars, spurði fall hans.[18] Var hon þá í herbergi því er þau Einarr hǫfðu haft út í bœnum. Gekk hon þegar upp í konungsgarð, þar sem bóndaliðit var. Hon eggjaði þá mjǫk til orrostu, en í því bili røri konungr út eptir ánni. Þá mælti Bergljót:

'Missum vér nú Hákonar Ívarssonar, frænda míns. Eigi mundu banamenn Eindriða róa hér út eptir ánni, ef Hákon stœði hér á árbakkanum.'

Síðan lét Bergljót búa um lík þeira Einars ok Eindriða. Váru þeir jarðaðir at Óláfskirkju hjá leiði Magnúss konungs Óláfssonar.

Eptir fall Einars var Haraldr konungr svá mjǫk óþokkaðr af verki þessu at þat einu skorti á, er lendir menn ok bœndr veittu eigi atferð ok heldu bardaga við hann, at engi varð forgǫngumaðr til at reisa merki fyrir bóandaherinum.

Notes

[12] Einarr þambarskelfir Eindriðason's adult life spans the first half of the eleventh century, and he plays a prominent role in the sagas of several rulers of Norway (see the *Fagrskinna* extract in this volume). The meaning of his nickname has been debated, but 'bow-string trembler' or 'paunch-shaker' are among the possible interpretations (B. Fidjestøl argues for the former in *Nordica Bergensia* 14 (1997), 6–8). *Lendir menn*, literally 'landed men', were powerful royal officers who had been granted rights to revenues and entertainment from farms in a certain territory. *Veizla*, literally 'grant, allowance', hence 'feast', was applied to the entertainment of the *lendr maðr* and his followers, and extended to encompass broader rights and the farms from which they were extracted. According to *Óláfs saga helga* ch. 21 in *Heimskringla*, Einarr's *veizlur* in Þrándheimr go back to the reign of the earls Eiríkr and Sveinn at the beginning of the eleventh century, as does his marriage to their sister Bergljót.

[13] See *Óláfs saga Tryggvasonar* (in *Heimskringla*) ch. 19.

[14] Ch. 41, an account of Ormr jarl and other descendants of the earls of Hlaðir, still a notable force in Norway at this time, is omitted here.

[15] The stanza is from *Sexstefja* 'Poem with six refrains'; its second half comprises the only one of these that is preserved. It is also quoted in *Hákonar saga Ívarssonar* p. 7 and in the manuscripts Hulda and Hrokkinskinna.

[16] The next stanza is also in *Hákonar saga Ívarssonar* p. 8, Fagrskinna (manuscripts B, A), Hulda, Hrokkinskinna and Flateyjarbók; in *Snorra Edda* the second half (only) is quoted to illustrate the use of *húskarlar* to refer to *hirðmenn* 'king's followers, retainers'. The following half-stanza is also in *Hákonar saga Ívarssonar* p. 9, Fagrskinna (manuscripts B, A), Hulda, Hrokkinskinna and Flateyjarbók.

[17] The pronoun *oss* 'us' seems to be used here for sg. 'me' — perhaps an instance of the 'royal we', though such use of pl. personal pronouns for sg. is common in skaldic poetry. Alternatively, the sense could be 'me and mine'.

[18] Bergljót was the daughter of Earl Hákon inn ríki ('the mighty') Sigurðarson. Her fleeting appearance as a 'female inciter' figure here

is emphasised in manuscripts 39, F and 47, where this sentence begins a new chapter, headed *Frá Bergljót* (39), *Frá Bergljótu H. dóttur* (47; untitled in F). On this figure, see J. M. Jochens, 'The female inciter in the Kings' Sagas', *Arkiv för nordisk filologi* 102 (1987), 100–19. Bergljót's scene is absent from *Morkinskinna* and *Fagrskinna*.

Verses in prose word order

Lines 15–22: Gegn herr hjaldrvitjaðar skyli sitja ok standa dróttinvandr, sem hugnar dýrum dolgstœranda. Ǫll þjóð lýtr feiti folkstara; fátt er til nema játta þat sem konungr vill þá bjóða gotnum.

Lines 37–44: Hér sé ek enn ǫrva Einar þambarskel*fi*, þann er kann skeina þjal*fa* þangs, ganga upp fjǫlmennan. Fullafli bíðr fyllar stóls hilmis; finn ek opt, at minna lið húskarla drífr á hæla jarli.

Lines 45–48: Rjóðandi bliks randa mun ráða oss ór landi, nema Einarr kyssi enn þunna munn øxar.

VII C: THE ART AND CRAFT OF THE SKALDIC STANZA

This section offers a brief introduction to the techniques of skaldic poetry as illustrated by a stanza from VII A above. It was composed, according to medieval sources, by Hallfreðr vandræðaskáld ('trouble-some poet') in praise of King Óláfr Tryggvason at the end of the tenth century. It has been chosen here because it typifies in so many ways the court poetry which is the best-known application of the skaldic art. The text follows the *Heimskringla* version (see VII A above, and Glossary and Notes; also *Den norsk-islandske Skjaldedigtning*, ed. Finnur Jónsson (1912–15), A I 158–9 for text in manuscript spelling with variant readings).

Ýdr*óg*ar lét *__æ__g*ir
eyverskan her d*ey*ja
— **T**_ýr_ var **t**jǫrva d*ýr*ra
t_ír_ar gjarn — ok *Ír*a.
B_arð_i **b**rezkrar j*arð*ar
b_ygg_vendr ok hjó t*yggi*,
— **gr**_áð_r þvarr **g**eira hr*íð*ar
g_jóð_i — kumrskar þ*jóð*ir.

Stanza reordered as if prose:

Œgir ýdrógar lét eyverskan her ok Íra deyja. Týr dýrra tjǫrva var gjarn tírar. Tyggi barði byggvendr brezkrar jarðar ok hjó kumrskar þjóðir. Gráðr þvarr gjóði hríðar geira.

Translation:

The foe of the bow-string [warrior] caused the island army and the Irish to die. The Týr of precious swords [warrior] was eager for glory. The prince beat the inhabitants of the 'British' land and felled the Cumbrian peoples. Hunger diminished for the osprey of the storm of spears [battle > raven].

Metrical features:

The metre is *dróttkvætt* 'court metre', that of some five-sixths of the skaldic corpus. Its main features, setting aside certain licences, varia-tions and complications, are these:

i. The stanza (*vísa*) consists of eight lines (*vísuorð*). The two half-stanzas (*vísuhelmingar* or *helmingar*, sg. *helmingr*) are metrically independent and often syntactically so. (In some cases they are also preserved as separate entities.)

ii. Each line has six syllables.

iii. Each line ends with a trochee (⏗ x, i.e. heavy, stressed syllable followed by an unstressed one).

iv. Lines are linked in pairs by alliteration, shown here in bold: two alliterating sounds (*stuðlar*) in each odd line and one (the *hǫfuðstafr* 'chief stave/post') in the first stressed syllable of each even line. Any vowel or diphthong alliterates with any other, though preferably an unlike one (as in lines 1–2 of the stanza above, where it will also be noted that the pattern of alliteration helps to mark the clause boundaries).

v. Individual lines contain pairs of internal rhymes or *hendingar*, indicated here by italics. These link the sounds in stressed syllables, the second rhyme in the line always falling on the penultimate syllable. The rhyme involves the vowel (or diphthong) in each syllable and one or more postvocalic consonant(s), but where there is no postvocalic consonant belonging to the same syllable, the rhyme consists of vowel only. There are two types of internal rhyme. Odd lines normally have half-rhyme (*skothending*) in which the vowels are different but one or more of the postvocalic consonants are identical. Even lines have full rhyme (*aðalhending* 'chief rhyme') in which vowels and one or more postvocalic consonant(s) are identical. Quite frequently an *aðalhending* is introduced into an odd line, as in lines 3 and 5 of the stanza above.

vi. There are further constraints on the patterns of stress within the line, and on the distribution of alliteration and internal rhyme.

Clause arrangement and word order:

The highly inflected nature of the Old Norse language means that syntactic relations can usually be made clear by grammatical endings and are less heavily dependent on word order than they are in languages such as modern English; and the skalds exploit this potential flexibility to an often quite extraordinary extent. Within clauses there are frequent departures from the 'normal', 'prose' order, though because the syntax is usually quite straightforward this rarely causes real difficulties. It is in the arrangement of clauses within the *helmingr* that skaldic style differs most from the everyday. Although skalds frequently use a straightforward sequential pattern, each clause finishing before the next starts (pattern *ab*, or *abc* etc.), they also play with clause boundaries, suspending a clause while interrupting with another and hence making what can be termed 'frame' patterns (as in the first *helmingr* of the specimen stanza, where the clauses form a pattern *aba*) or 'interlace' patterns (*abab* etc.). Combined patterns are also possible, as in the second *helmingr* of the specimen stanza. This could be analysed in two ways: i) as 'sequence' and 'frame' in the pattern *abcb*, since the *a* clause *barði . . . byggvendr* could be understood as complete, with an understood 'he' as subject of *barði*; or ii) as 'frame' and 'interlace' in the pattern *abacb*, since once *tyggi* in line 6 has been reached, it can be taken as subject of *barði* in the *a* clause as well as of *hjó* in the *b* clause. This is the analysis represented above in 'Stanza re-ordered as if prose'. By breaking the linear flow of language, the skalds can allow phrases to float free, resonating with more than one clause in the helming, and they can also produce special effects, for instance mimicking simultaneous actions or expressing the brokenness of intense emotion.

Content:

The stanza promotes a general military ideology and the reputation of a specific, though unnamed, viking leader, who is grammatical subject of four out of the five verbs. The defeated enemy is always referred to by collective terms, and is always the grammatical and conceptual object. The claims about the slaughter of these enemies are extremely generalised, as are the intercalated clauses about the hero's desire for glory and the waning of the raven's hunger (because, it is understood, the hero provides carrion), and all these belong to an informal repertoire of motifs which are constantly deployed, and ingeniously varied, by skalds.

Diction:

Much of the skalds' virtuosity goes into expressing recurrent key concepts such as 'man, ruler, battle, ship, sword, gold, woman' by means of

i. Poetic appellations known as *heiti*, such as *tjǫr(r)* 'sword' (or possibly 'spear'), and *tyggi* 'ruler, prince' in the stanza by Hallfreðr. *Heiti* are words which are rare or non-occurring in prose, and often redolent with connotations in addition to the main concepts to which they refer. Thus *hilmir* 'ruler, prince' has etymological associations with *hjalmr* 'helmet' and therefore may hint at a 'helmet-provider', 'helmet-bearer' or 'defender', while *huginn* 'raven' contains a mythological allusion since it is a generalised application of a proper name referring to one of Óðinn's two raven scouts.

ii. Kennings, stereotyped and more or less figurative periphrases consisting of at least two elements, usually *heiti*, one functioning as the 'base word' and the other as the 'determinant' or qualifier. The base word is in whatever grammatical case is required by the syntax, while the determinant is either in the genitive case and separate from the base word, as in *grœðis hestr* 'ocean's horse' = ship, or is compounded with the base word, as in *skýrann* 'cloud-hall' = sky. Some kennings, including one in the Hallfreðr stanza, are 'double' (*tvíkennt*) since the determinant of a kenning is itself a kenning. Where this device is repeated, the kenning is 'extended', 'driven' or perhaps 'inlaid' (*rekit*).

The kennings in the specimen stanza are:

ýdrógar œgir: 'bow-string's terrifier / foe' = warrior.

Týr tjǫrva dýrra: 'Týr (god) of precious swords = warrior': the adj. *dýrra* 'precious' is not essential to the working of the kenning.

geira hríð: 'spears' storm' = battle, its *gjóðr* 'osprey' = raven; a *tvíkennt* expression.

The elements are juxtaposed according to certain stereotyped patterns which are almost infinitely variable. Here battle is 'spears' storm', but almost any word for weather could be substituted, and any word for weapons or armour.

The difficulty of skaldic poetry:

Skaldic poetry has a reputation for tortuous and riddling complexity, and some poems, for example the best of the tenth-century pagan compositions, are indeed extremely challenging to the textual skills, mythical knowledge and historical imagination of modern readers. Verses such as the specimen here, however, are (local textual problems aside) readily interpretable. Although the skalds liked to surprise by novelty and by ingenious variation on themes, their art is very much based on the fulfilment of expectations, grammatical and poetic. In the verse above, for example, the past tense *lét* 'caused' is extremely likely to be completed by an infinitive, so that although *deyja* is separated from it by three words, the audience will be listening or looking for such a completion. The god-name *Týr* similarly sets up the expectation of a 'warrior' or 'man' kenning with a term for battle, weapon, ship or treasure as its determinant, and this is fulfilled almost immediately by *tjǫrva* 'of swords' (cf. Meissner 1921, 259–63, 273–79). Again, since many skaldic battle poems refer to the beasts of battle (raven, eagle or wolf) being fed or cheered (since the hero makes carrion of his enemies), *gráðr* 'hunger, greed' triggers anticipation of a motif of this kind. It is therefore fully possible for modern readers, like the original early Nordic audiences, to acquire a set of frameworks for interpretation, above all by gaining experience of the poetry, but also by consulting reference works on poetic diction such as Snorri Sturluson's *Edda*, the medieval *þulur* or lists of *heiti* (printed in *Skj* A I 649–90; B I 656–80), *LP*, or Meissner 1921, though in all these cases we should beware of a too normative approach, and in the last two cases the examples are sometimes based on heavily emended texts.

Preservation:

On the preservation of skaldic poetry in general, see p. xxv above. The specimen stanza, together with others in praise of Óláfr, is preserved in the *Óláfs saga Tryggvasonar* by Oddr Snorrason ch. 82, *Fagrskinna* ch. 23, *Óláfs saga Tryggvasonar* ch. 30 in *Heimskringla*, and *Óláfs saga Tryggvasonar en mesta* ch. 77 (cf. note 1 on p. 87 above; on these sources see p. 60 above). In the first two sources, this and others of Hallfreðr's verses about Óláfr are cited continuously, whereas in the last two they are punctuated by prose narrative and are in a somewhat different order. The two *helmingar* of the specimen above do not form a single stanza in Oddr's saga and *Fagrskinna* but are the second *helmingar* of two different stanzas.

Editions:

The entire corpus of skaldic poetry from the beginnings to c.1400 is edited in *Den norsk-islandske Skaldedigtning*, ed. Finnur Jónsson (1912–15), A 1–II (edited text) and B I–II (diplomatic text). A new nine-volume edition, with English translation and notes, is in preparation as *Skaldic Poetry of the Scandinavian Middle Ages: A New Edition*, of which two volumes are now published: II *Poetry from the Kings' Sagas* 2, ed. Kari Ellen Gade (2009) and VII *Poetry on Christian Subjects*, ed. Margaret Clunies Ross (2007).

VIII: Ari Þorgilsson: ÍSLENDINGABÓK

Ari Þorgilsson was probably born in 1068 on the Snæfellsnes peninsula of Iceland and died in 1148. He lost his father and grandfather while still a boy and at the age of seven went to live with a maternal relative, Hallr Þórarinsson of Haukadalr (cf. line 184) in the south-western part of the country. At Haukadalr he must have come into contact with some of the most prominent, learned and travelled Icelanders of the time, in particular various members of the great Mosfellingar family (cf. note 35 below) to which belonged the first bishops of Iceland, Ísleifr Gizurarson and his son, Gizurr Ísleifsson, who would have resided at Skálaholt some 25 km. away. And Ísleifr's son Teitr (cf. line 8) actually lived in Haukadalr where he ran a small school. Ari became one of Teitr's pupils and he refers to him as his *fóstri* 'fosterer' and the wisest man he knew. It must have been at Haukadalr and under the influence of men like Teitr and Hallr that Ari developed his interest in history and related subjects. Ari tells us in ch. 9 of *Íslendingabók* that he spent fourteen winters at Haukadalr, which means he must have quit the place in about 1089. We have no precise knowledge of how and where he spent the remaining years of his long life. But he was an ordained priest and it can reasonably be inferred that he lived for some of this time at least in his ancestral area of Snæfellsnes. He could well have held a chieftaincy (*goðorð*) there.

Ari's only preserved work, the second version of his *Íslendingabók*, covers less than twenty pages in its main manuscript. Its contents may be summarised as follows.

The Prologue (= lines 1–6) tells us of the circumstances surrounding the writing of the first (now lost) version of the work and, in rather unclear terms, of the changes made in producing the second version. There follows a genealogy (which may well be a later interpolation) of Haraldr hárfagri going back to the Swedish king Óláfr trételgja. Then comes a list of contents of the book's ten chapters. Chapter 1 (lines 7–34) deals with the settlement of Iceland, presenting Ingólfr as the first settler. Chapter 2 names four main settlers of the east, south, west and north of the country and tells (lines 35–43) how a Norwegian called Úlfljótr first 'brought law' out to Iceland. Chapter 3 (lines 44–63) deals with the establishment of the Alþingi. Chapter 4 gives an account of certain changes made in the Icelandic calendar (see *HOIC*, 44–45). Chapter 5 describes the events which led to the division of the country into quarters (see *HOIC*, 49–52). A short chapter 6 (lines 64–74) and a lengthier chapter 7 (lines 75–149) cover respectively the discovery and settlement of Greenland by Eiríkr enn rauði and the formal acceptance of Christianity by the Icelandic Alþingi. Chapter 8 tells of the so-called 'foreign' or 'missionary' bishops who visited Iceland in the tenth and eleventh centuries (see *HOIC*, 138–44) and of events during the long lawspeakership of Skapti Þóroddsson (1004–30), including the establishment of the so-called Fifth Court (see *HOIC*, 70–74; *Laws* I, 83–88, 244–45). Ísleifr Gizurarson, the first man to be formally consecrated as bishop of Iceland (1056–80), is the subject of Chapter 9 (see *HOIC*, 144–46). And the final chapter 10 (of which lines 150–97 form a major part) deals with Gizurr Ísleifsson (bishop of Iceland from 1082 to 1106; bishop of Skálaholt from 1106 to 1118). Although the last words of ch. 10 are *Hér lýksk sjá bók* ('This book ends here'), two further items follow in both the extant manuscripts: (i) genealogies from original settlers of Iceland down to these five bishops: Ísleifr Gizurarson and his son Gizurr, Jón Ǫgmundarson (cf. line 191), Þorlákr Rúnólfsson (cf. line 1) and Ketill Þorsteinsson (cf. also line 1); (ii) a genealogy from the mythical Yngvi Tyrkjakonungr down to Ari himself, ending with the words *en ek heitik Ari*, 'and I am called Ari'.

As noted, Ari's information in his Prologue on the changes he made in the first version of his work to produce the second is rather unclear and there has been much modern scholarly discussion on the matter. This has led to only uncertain and differing conclusions. The primary issue to be addressed in this context is whether the second version of *Íslendingabók* represents an abridgement or an expansion of the first (cf. notes 1 and 3 below).

It is normally assumed that Ari had virtually no written sources about the early history of Iceland. But he may well have used Sæmundr Sigfússon's now lost work on the Norwegian kings which, it is assumed, was written in Latin (see p. 62 above; cf. line 145). And there is evidence to suggest that he knew such written works on non-Icelandic matters as Adam of Bremen's *Gesta Hammaburgensis ecclesiae pontificum* (cf. again p. 62), various works by the Venerable Bede and, quite clearly, a life of the martyr King Edmund, whoever its author (cf. lines 12–14). But it was primarily oral sources that he relied on for information about Icelandic history. He obviously learnt a great deal from acquaintances from his time at Haukadalr: Teitr Ísleifsson would have been of particular importance to him in this respect (cf. lines 8–9, 36, 144), as well as Hallr Þórarinsson, Sæmundr Sigfússon (cf. lines 2, 145) and bishop Gizurr Ísleifsson himself. He also received information from people from his home area in the west of Iceland, his uncle Þorkell Gellisson (cf. lines 10, 73–74) and Þóríðr Snorradóttir (cf. line 11). At least two lawspeakers, Markús Skeggjason (cf. line 152) and Úlfheðinn (cf. line 55) would have been his informants (cf. note 51 below).

The preserved version of *Íslendingabók* was, then, based on an earlier one which Ari says he wrote for the bishops Þorlákr Rúnólfsson and Ketill Þorsteinsson and subsequently showed to them and to the priest Sæmundr Sigfússon. From the wording of his statement and other factors it is clear that the first version must have been written between 1122 (when Ketill became bishop) and 1133 (when both Þorlákr and Sæmundr died). The preserved version of *Íslendingabók* refers to the lawspeakership of Goðmundr Þorgeirsson (lines 170–71) which ran from 1123 to 1134. If this reference is original to the second version, then it must, of course, have been written in or after 1134. But there are good reasons for assuming that it is a later interpolation. Further there are reasons for thinking that Ari wrote his first version fairly early on in the period 1122–33 and produced the second version within four or five years of it.

Ari's work has great importance for the study of Icelandic history and literature. It is, in effect, the oldest original prose work in Icelandic and decades passed before other works of historiography were written in that language. *Íslendingabók* exercised considerable influence on later Icelandic literature, as did *Landnámabók*, the original (and now lost) version of which is probably also from his hand. Snorri Sturluson, writing some hundred years later, makes particular reference to him in the prologue to his *Heimskringla*. It is Ari's specific mention of his oral sources and his careful attention to chronology in *Íslendingabók* that give his work such value. It is true that he does not always tell his story well. For example, his description of the foundation of the Alþingi (lines 44–55) is somewhat inconsequential. But his account of the conversion of Iceland shows him as an excellent narrator. And however desultory Ari's narrative may occasionally seem, the value of his whole book can hardly be overestimated.

Although there are various minor witnesses, we have to rely mainly on two seventeenth-century paper manuscripts written by Jón Erlendsson (died 1672) for our text of the second version of *Íslendingabók*. AM 113 b fol. (the better of the two) and AM 113 a fol. both go back directly to a lost original probably written about 1200 or perhaps a little earlier (and thus, of course, not Ari's original). AM 113 a fol. was written in 1651, AM 113 b fol. probably rather later. The text of the selections here is based on AM 113 b fol. (designated 'A') as follows: (a): f. 1r2–11; (b): ff. 1v4–2r14; (c): ff. 2r23–3r9; (d): f. 4r25–v13; (e): ff. 4v14–6v10; (f): ff. 8r17–9v2. Most of the emendations are from AM 113 a fol. (designated 'B').

Bibliography

Facsimile edition: Jón Jóhannesson (ed.), *Íslendingabók Ara fróða. AM 113 a and 113 b, fol.* Íslenzk handrit. Icelandic manuscripts I (1956). [Contains a useful 'Introduction' in English]

Critical edition: Ari Þorgilsson hinn fróði, *Íslendingabók*, ed. Anne Holtsmark (1951); rev. Hallvard Magerøy and Tor Ulset (1978).

Normalised edition with English translation: Ari Thorgilsson, *The Book of the Icelanders (Íslendingabók)*, ed. and tr. Halldór Hermannsson (1930).

Íslenzk fornrit edition (*ÍF* I): *Íslendingabók*. In *Íslendingabók, Landnámabók*, ed. Jakob Benediktsson (1968).

Background reading:

Björn Þorsteinsson, *Thingvellir. Iceland's National Shrine*, tr. Peter Foote (1987).

The Book of the Settlements. Landnámabók, tr. Hermann Pálsson and Paul Edwards (1972).

Finn Gad, *The History of Greenland*, I. *Earliest Times to 1700*, tr. Ernst Dupont (1970).

Jónas Kristjánsson, *Eddas and Sagas*, tr. Peter Foote (1988), Index, under 'Ari Þorgilsson the Wise'.

Gwyn Jones, *The Norse Atlantic Saga*, 2nd ed. (1986).

Knud J. Krogh, *Viking Greenland* (1967).

MS, under *Íslendingabók*.

Dag Strömbäck, *The Conversion of Iceland*, tr. Peter Foote (1975).

G. Turville-Petre, *Origins of Icelandic Literature* (1953), 88–108.

VIII: Ari Þorgilsson: ÍSLENDINGABÓK

(a) Prologue[1]

‹Í›slendingabók gørða ek fyrst byskupum órum, Þorláki ok Katli, ok sýndak bæði þeim ok Sæmundi presti.[2] En með því at þeim líkaði svá at hafa eða þar viðr auka, þá skrifaða ek þessa of et sama far, fyr útan áttartǫlu ok konungaævi,[3] ok jók*k* því er mér varð síðan kunnara ok nú er gerr sagt á þessi en á þeirri. En hvatki es *mi*‹s›sagt es í frœðum þessum, þá er skylt at hafa þat heldr, er sannara reynisk . . .

(b) The settlement of Iceland[4]

Chapter 1

‹Í›sland byggðisk fyrst úr Norvegi á dǫgum Haralds ens hárfagra,[5] Hálfdanar sonar ens svarta, í þann tíð — at ætlun ok tǫlu þeira Teits fóstra míns,[6] þess manns er ek kunna spakastan, sonar Ísleifs byskups; ok Þorkels fǫðurbróður míns Gellissonar, er langt munði fram;[7] ok Þóríðar Snorra dóttur goða,[8] es bæði vas margspǫk ok óljúgfróð — es Ívarr, Ragnars sonr loðbrókar,[9] lét drepa Eadmund enn helga Englakonung.[10] En þat vas sjau tegum ‹vetra› ens níunda hundraðs eptir burð Krists, at því es ritit es í sǫgu hans.[11]

Ingólfr hét maðr nórœnn, es sannliga er sagt at fœri fyrst þaðan til Íslands, þá es Haraldr enn hárfagri var sextán vetra gamall, en í annat sinn fám vetrum síðarr.[12] Hann byggði suðr í Reykjarvík. Þar er Ingólfshǫfði kallaðr fyr austan Minþakseyri, sem hann kom fyrst á land, en þar Ingólfsfell fyr vestan Ǫlfossá, es hann lagði sína eigu á síðan.

Í þann tíð vas Ísland viði vaxit á miðli fjalls ok fjǫru.[13]

Þá váru hér menn kristnir, þeir er Norðmenn kalla papa.[14] En þeir fóru síðan á braut, af því at þeir vildu eigi vesa hér við heiðna menn, ok létu eptir bœkr írskar ok bjǫllur ok bagla; af því mátti skilja at þeir váru menn írskir.[15]

En þá varð fǫr manna mikil mjǫk út hingat úr Norvegi til þess unz konungrinn Haraldr bannaði, af því at honum þótti landauðn nema. Þá sættusk þeir á þat, at hverr maðr skyldi gjalda konungi fimm aura,[16] sá er eigi væri frá því skiliðr ok þaðan fœri hingat. En svá er sagt at

4 jóki *A*. 5 nú sagt *A*.

Haraldr væri sjau tegu vetra konungr ok yrði áttrœðr. Þau hafa upphǫf verit at gjaldi því es nú er kallat landaurar.[17] En þar galzk stundum meira en stundum minna, unz Óláfr enn digri[18] gørði skýrt at hverr maðr skyldi gjalda konungi hálfa mǫrk, sá er fœri á miðli Norvegs ok Íslands, nema konur eða þeir menn es hann næmi frá. Svá sagði Þorkell oss Gellissonr.

(c) The establishment of the Alþingi[19]

Chapter 2

. . . En þá es Ísland vas víða byggt orðit, þá hafði maðr austrœnn fyrst lǫg út hingat úr Norvegi sá er Úlfljótr hét — svá sagði Teitr oss — ok váru þá Úlfljótslǫg kǫlluð — hann var faðir Gunnars er Djúpdœlir eru komnir frá í Eyjafirði[20] — en þau váru flest sett at því sem þá váru Golaþingslǫg eða ráð Þorleifs ens spaka Hǫrða-Kárasonar[21] váru til, hvar við skyldi auka eða af nema eða annan veg setja. Úlfljótr var austr í Lóni. En svá es sagt at Grímr geitskǫr væri fóstbróðir hans, sá er kannaði Ísland allt at ráði hans, áðr Alþingi væri átt. En honum fekk hverr maðr penning til á landi hér, en hann gaf fé þat síðan til hofa.[22]

Chapter 3

‹A›lþingi vas sett at ráði Úlfljóts ok allra landsmanna þar er nú es. En áðr vas þing á Kjalarnesi, þat es Þorsteinn Ingólfs sonr landnámamanns, faðir Þorkels mána lǫgsǫgumanns, hafði þar, ok hǫfðingjar þeir es at því hurfu.[23] En maðr hafði sekr orðit of þræls morð eða leysings, sá er land átti í Bláskógum; hann es nefndr Þórir kroppinskeggi; en dóttursonr hans es kallaðr Þorvaldr kroppinskeggi, sá es fór síðan í Austfjǫrðu ok brenndi þar inni Gunnar, bróður sinn. Svá sagði Hallr Órœkj*u*sonr.[24] En sá hét Kolr es myrðr var. Við hann es kennd gjá sú es þar es kǫlluð síðan Kolsgjá, sem hræin fundusk. Land þat varð ‹síðan› allsherjarfé, en þat lǫgðu landsmenn til Alþingis neyzlu. Af því es þar almenning at viða til Alþingis í skógum ok á heiðum hagi til hrossa hafnar. Þat sagði Úlfheðinn oss.

Svá hafa ok spakir menn sagt at á sex tegum vetra yrði Ísland albyggt svá at eigi væri meirr síðan.

51 Órœkjasonr *A*. 53 síðan *B*.

Því nær tók Hrafn lǫgsǫgu,[25] Hœngs sonr landnámamanns, næstr Úlfljóti, ok hafði tuttugu sumur; hann var úr Rangárhverfi. Þat var sex tegum vetr*a* eptir dráp Eadmundar konungs, vetri eða tveim áðr Haraldr enn hárfagri yrði dauðr, at tǫlu spakra manna. Þórarinn Ragabróðir, sonr Óleifs hjalta, tók lǫgsǫgu næstr Hrafni ok hafði ǫnnur tuttugu; hann vas borgfir*zk*r.

(d) The settlement of Greenland[26]

Chapter 6

‹L›and þat es kallat es Grœnland fannsk ok byggðisk af Íslandi. Eiríkr enn rauði hét maðr breiðfirzkr es fór út heðan þangat ok nam þar land er síðan es kallaðr Eiríksfjǫrðr.[27] Hann gaf nafn landinu ok kallaði Grœnland ok kvað menn þat myndu fýsa þangat farar, at landit ætti nafn gott.[28]

Þeir fundu þar manna vistir bæði austr ok vestr á landi,[29] ok keiplabrot ok steinsmíði þat es af því má skilja at þar hafði þess konar þjóð farit es Vínland hefir byggt ok Grœnlendingar kalla Skrælinga.[30]

En þat vas, es hann tók byggva landit, fjórtán vetrum eða fimmtán fyrr en kristni kvæmi hér á Ísland, at því er sá talði fyrir Þorkeli Gellissyni á Grœnlandi er sjálfr fylgði Eiríki enum rauða út.[31]

(e) The Alþingi accepts Christianity[32]

Chapter 7

‹Ó›láfr rex Tryggva sonr, Óláfs sonar, Haralds sonar ens hárfagra, kom kristni í Nóreg ok á Ísland.[33]

Hann sendi hingat til lands prest þann er hét Þangbrandr ok hér kenndi mǫnnum kristni ok skírði þá alla es við trú tóku.[34] En Hallr á Síðu, Þorsteins sonr, lét skírask snimhendis, ok Hjalti Skeggjasonr úr Þjórsárdali ok Gizurr enn hvíti Teits son, Ketilbjarnar sonar, frá Mosfelli, ok margir hǫfðingjar aðrir.[35] En þeir váru þó fleiri es í gegn mæltu ok neittu. En þá er hann hafði hér verit einn vetr eða tvá, þá fór hann á braut ok hafði vegit hér tvá menn eða þrjá þá er hann hǫfðu nítt.[36] En hann sagði konunginum Óláfi es hann kom austr allt þat es hér hafði yfir hann gingit, ok lét ørvænt at hér mundi kristni enn takask.

60 vetrum *A*. 63 borgfirðir *A*.

En hann[37] varð við þat reiðr mjǫk ok ætlaði at láta meiða eða drepa ossa landa fyrir, þá es þar váru austr.

En þat sumar et sama kvámu útan heðan þeir Gizurr ok Hjalti, ok þágu þá undan við konunginn, ok hétu honum umbsýslu sinni til á nýja leik at hér yrði enn við kristninni tekit, ok létu sér eigi annars ván en þar mundi hlýða. En et næsta sumar eptir fóru þeir austan, ok prestr sá es Þormóðr hét, ok kvámu þá í Vestmannaeyjar es tíu vikur váru af sumri,[38] ok hafði allt farizk vel at. Svá kvað Teitr þann segja es sjálfr var þar.[39] Þá vas þat mælt et næsta sumar áðr í lǫgum at menn skyldi svá koma til Alþingis es tíu vikur væri af sumri, en þangat til kvámu viku fyrr.

En þeir fóru þegar inn til meginlands ok síðan til Alþingis ok gátu at Hjalta at hann vas eptir í Laugardali með tólfta mann, af því at hann hafði áðr sekr orðit fjǫrbaugsmaðr et næsta sumar á Alþingi of goðgá.[40] En þat vas til þess haft, at hann kvað at Lǫgbergi kviðling þenna:[41]

Vil ek eigi goð geyja;
grey þykir mér Freyja.[42]

En þeir Gizurr fóru unz þeir kvámu í stað þann í hjá Ǫlfossvatni, es kallaðr es Vellankatla, ok gørðu orð þaðan til þings, at á mót þeim skyldi koma allir fulltingsmenn þeira, af því at þeir hǫfðu spurt at andskotar þeira vildi verja þeim vígi þingvǫllinn. En fyrr en þeir fœri þaðan, þá kom þar ríðandi Hjalti ok þeir er eptir váru með honum. En síðan riðu þeir á þingit, ok kvámu áðr á mót þeim frændr þeira ok vinir, sem þeir hǫfðu æst. En enir heiðnu menn hurfu saman með alvæpni ok hafði svá nær at þeir myndi berjask at ‹eigi› of sá á miðli.

En annan dag eptir gengu þeir Gizurr ok Hjalti til Lǫgbergs ok báru þar upp erindi sín. En svá er sagt, at þat bæri frá, hvé vel þeir mæltu. En þat gørðisk af því, at þar nefndi annarr maðr at ǫðrum vátta, ok sǫgðusk hvárir úr lǫgum við aðra, enir kristnu menn ok enir heiðnu, ok gingu síðan frá Lǫgbergi.

Þá báðu enir kristnu menn Hall á Síðu at hann skyldi lǫg þeira upp segja, þau es kristninni skyldi fylgja. En hann leystisk því undan við þá, at hann keypti at Þorgeiri lǫgsǫgumanni, at hann skyldi upp segja; en hann vas enn þá heiðinn.[43] En síðan er menn kvámu í búðir,[44] þá

106 þingvellinn *A*. 110 eigi] *a space is left for this word in A.*

lagðisk hann niðr Þorgeirr ok breiddi feld sinn á sik ok hvíldi þann dag allan ok nóttina eptir ok kvað ekki orð. En of morguninn eptir settisk hann upp ok gørði orð at menn skyldi ganga til Lǫgbergis.

En þá hóf hann tǫlu sína upp, es menn kvámu þar, ok sagði at honum þótti þá komit hag manna í ónýtt efni ef menn skyldi eigi hafa allir lǫg ein á landi hér, ok talði fyrir mǫnnum á marga vega at þat skyldi eigi láta verða, ok sagði at þat mundi at því ósætti verða, es vísaván vas at þær barsmíðir gørðisk á miðli manna es landit eyddisk af. Hann sagði frá því, at konungar úr Norvegi ok úr Danmǫrku hǫfðu haft ófrið ok orrostur á miðli sín langa tíð, til þess unz landsmenn gørðu frið á miðli þeira, þótt þeir vildi eigi. En þat ráð gørðisk svá, at af stundu sendusk þeir gersemar á miðli; enda helt friðr sá meðan þeir lifðu.[45]

'En nú þykkir mér þat ráð,' kvað hann, 'at vér látim ok eigi þá ráða er mest vilja í gegn gangask, ok miðlum svá mál á miðli þeira, at hvárirtveggju hafi nakkvat síns máls, ok hǫfum allir ein lǫg ok einn sið. Þat mon verða satt, es vér slítum í sundr lǫgin, at vér monum slíta ok friðinn.'

En hann lauk svá máli sínu at hvárirtveggju játtu því, at allir skyldi ein lǫg hafa, þau sem hann réði upp at segja.

Þá vas þat mælt í lǫgum at allir menn skyldi kristnir vesa ok skírn taka, þeir er áðr váru óskírðir á landi hér. En of barna útburð skyldu standa en fornu lǫg ok of hrossakjǫts át.[46] Skyldu menn blóta á laun, ef vildu, en varða fjǫrbaugsgarðr ef váttum of kvæmi við. En síðar fám vetrum var sú heiðni af numin sem ǫnnur.

Þenna atburð sagði Teitr oss at því er kristni kom á Ísland.

En Óláfr Tryggvason fell et sama sumar at sǫgu Sæmundar prests.[47] Þá barðisk hann við Svein Haraldsson Danakonung ok Óláf enn sœnska Eiríks son at Uppsǫlum Svíakonungs, ok Eirík, es síðan vas jarl at Norvegi, Hákonarson.[48] Þat vas þremr tegum vetr*a* ens annars hundraðs eptir dráp Eadmundar, en þúsundi eptir burð Krists at alþýðu tali.[49]

(f) Events during Gizurr's episcopacy[50]

Chapter 10

. . . Gizurr byskup vas ástsælli af ǫllum landsmǫnnum en hverr maðr annarra þeira es vér vit*i*m hér á landi hafa verit. Af ástsæld hans ok af

148 vetrum *A*. 151 vitam *A*.

tǫlum þeira Sæmundar með umbráði Markúss lǫgsǫgumanns[51] vas þat í lǫg leitt, at allir menn tǫlðu ok virðu allt fé sitt ok sóru at rétt virt væri, hvárt sem vas í lǫndum eða í lausaaurum, ok gørðu tíund af síðan.[52] Þat eru miklar jartegnir, hvat hlýðnir landsmenn váru þeim manni, es hann kom því fram at fé allt vas virt með svardǫgum þat es á Íslandi vas, ok landit sjálft ok tíundir af gǫrvar ok lǫg á lǫgð, at svá skal vesa, meðan Ísland es byggt. Gizurr byskup lét ok lǫg leggja á þat, at stóll byskups þess es á Íslandi væri skyldi í Skálaholti vesa, en áðr vas hvergi, ok lagði hann þar til stólsins Skálaholtsland ok margra kynja auðœfi ǫnnur, bæði í lǫndum ok í lausum aurum.[53] En þá es honum þótti sá staðr hafa vel at auðœfum þróazk, þá gaf hann meir en fjórðung byskupsdóms síns til þess at heldr væri tveir byskupsstólar á landi hér en einn, svá sem Norðlendingar æstu hann til.[54] En hann hafði áðr látit telja búendr á landi hér, ok váru þá í Austfirðingafjórðungi sjau hundruð heil, en í Rangæingafjórðungi tíu, en í Breið‹firð›ingafjórðungi níu, en í Eyfirðingafjórðungi tólf, en ótalðir váru þeir es eigi áttu þingfararkaupi at gegna of allt Ísland.[55]

‹Ú›lfheðinn Gunnars sonr ens spaka tók lǫgsǫgu eptir Markús ok hafði níu sumur; þá hafði Bergþórr Hrafnssonr sex, en þá hafði Goðmundr Þorgeirssonr tólf sumur.[56] Et fyrsta sumar es Bergþórr sagði lǫg upp vas nýmæli þat gǫrt at lǫg ór skyldi skrifa á bók at Hafliða Mássonar of vetrinn eptir at sǫgu ok umbráði þeira Bergþórs ok annarra spakra manna þeira er til þess váru teknir.[57] Skyldu þeir gørva nýmæli þau ǫll í lǫgum er þeim litisk þau betri en en fornu lǫg. Skyldi þau segja upp et næsta sumar eptir í lǫgréttu ok þau ǫll halda es enn meiri hlutr manna mælti þá eigi gegn. En þat varð at fram fara, at þá vas skrifaðr Vígslóði ok margt annat í lǫgum ok sagt upp í lǫgréttu af kennimǫnnum of sumarit eptir.[58] En þat líkaði ǫllum vel, ok mælti því manngi í gegn.

Þat vas ok et fyrsta sumar es Bergþórr sagði lǫg upp, þá var Gizurr byskup óþingfœrr af sótt. Þá sendi hann orð til Alþingis vinum sínum ok hǫfðingjum at biðja skyldi Þorlák Rúnólfs son Þorleiks sonar, bróður Halls í Haukadali,[59] at hann skyldi láta vígjask til byskups. En þat gerðu allir svá sem orð hans kvámu til, ok fekksk þat af því, at Gizurr hafði sjálfr fyrr mjǫk beðit, ok fór hann útan þat sumar en kom út et næsta eptir ok vas þá vígðr til byskups.

Gizurr vas vígðr til byskups þá es hann var fertøgr.[60] Þá vas Gregóríus septimus páfi.[61] En síðan vas hann enn næsta vetr í Danmǫrku ok kom of sumarit eptir hingat til lands. En þá es hann hafði verit fjóra vetr ok tuttugu byskup, svá sem faðir hans, þá vas Jóan Ǫgmundarsonr vígðr til byskups fyrstr til stóls at Hólum;[62] þá vas hann vetri miðr en hálf*sex*tøgr. En tólf vetrum síðar, þá es Gizurr hafði alls verit byskup sex vetr ens fjórða tegar, þá vas Þorlákr vígðr til byskups; hann lét Gizurr vígja til stóls í Skálaholti at sér lifanda. Þá vas Þorlákr tveim vetrum meir en þrítøgr, en Gizurr byskup andaðisk þremr tegum nátt*a* síðar í Skálaholti á enum þriðja degi í viku ‹quinto› kalendas Junii[63]

. . .

193 hálffertøgr *A*. 196 náttum *A*.

Notes

[1] On the Prologue to *Íslendingabók* and the difficulties it presents, see Turville-Petre 1953, 88–102; Jón Jóhannesson 1956, xiv–xxiii. The problems revolve around: (a) the meaning of *fyr útan*; (b) what the words *áttartala* and *konungaævi* refer to; and to some extent (c) the meaning of *of et sama far*. On these problems see note 3 below and *NION* III, s.v. **far**.

[2] Sæmundr Sigfússon was a member of the Oddaverjar family, with its ancestral home at Oddi, just east of where the River Rangá in ýtri flows into Þverá (south-western Iceland) (cf. *HOIC* 231–32, 362). He studied on the Continent and is credited with a now lost synoptic work about the kings of Norway believed to have been written in Latin. After his death, he became a legendary figure in Icelandic folklore and, for example, the poems of the Elder Edda were wrongly attributed to him (cf. Jónas Kristjánsson 1988, 25–26). Like Ari Þorgilsson, he was nicknamed *inn fróði*, 'the Learned'. Cf. p. 62 above; Turville-Petre 1953, 81–87; *MS*, s.v. *Sæmundr Sigfússon inn fróði*.

[3] *of et sama far*: 'on the same subject'; or 'covering the same ground' (so *ION* 207); or possibly 'in the same way'.

The majority of scholars understand *fyr útan* to mean 'without', i.e. that *áttartala* and *konungaævi*, which were to be found in the earlier version of *Íslendingabók*, have been omitted in the second, preserved, version. But others have suggested that they mean 'apart from' and that the *áttartala* and *konungaævi* are an addition to the earlier version and are to be found in the preserved version.

áttartǫlu is formally singular but is probably used here in a collective sense; the element *-ævi* in *konungaævi* is plural. The first word may be roughly translated 'genealogies', the second 'lives of kings'. Precisely what are referred to here is less certain and depends to some extent on the interpretation *fyr útan* in line 3. If *fyr útan* is taken to mean 'apart from' and the items referred to are assumed to be present in the preserved version of *Íslendingabók*, then the word *áttartala* might refer (for example) to the genealogies of the bishops following ch. 10 (referred to by Ari himself as *kyn byskupa Íslendinga ok áttartala*), and *konungaævi* might refer to various chronological statements in the present *Íslendingabók* relating events in Icelandic history to the lives of foreign kings (cf. lines 7–14, 145–49). If the items in question were in the earlier version but have been removed in the preserved one, then this matter becomes a much more speculative one, and one which has received much scholarly attention (cf. note 20 below).

[4] On the discovery and settlement of Iceland, see *BS*; Jones 1986, especially 27–72; *MS*, s.v. *Iceland*; *HOIC* 1–34.

[5] While it is not possible to give exact dates, Haraldr hárfagri probably lived from about 855 to about 935. He is said to have been descended from the Swedish Yngling dynasty and his father, Hálfdan inn svarti, was king of Vestfold. Haraldr succeeded to the throne as a young man and, partly in alliance with the earl of Hlaðir, Hákon Grjótgarðsson, extended a hegemony widely in Norway. Sometime in the 890s he won a decisive sea-battle at Hafrsfjorden (near Stavanger) and in so doing established control of the south-western part of the country. He may, to a certain extent, therefore, be regarded as the first ruler of all Norway, though when written sources represent his tyranny as a major cause of emigration by Norwegian chieftains to Iceland, there is doubtless some exaggeration involved. Cf. *MS*, s.v. *Haraldr hárfagri ("fair-hair") Hálfdanarson.*

[6] Teitr, a son of Ísleifr Gizurarson, was Ari's main mentor and teacher (cf. *fóstri*). It is he whom Ari refers to most frequently as an informant (cf. lines 36, 93, 144). He seems to have had several other pupils as well as Ari. He died in 1110.

[7] Þorkell Gellisson is also mentioned in *Laxdœla saga*. He is said to have lived at the important farm of Helgafell on Snæfellsnes. See also note 31 below.

[8] Þóríðr died in 1112 at the age of 88. Her father, Snorri goði Þorgrímsson (d. 1031), appears in *Eyrbyggja saga* as a major character and in several other sources.

[9] Ívarr was a prominent Viking chieftain of the second half of the ninth century. The sources about him include, in addition to Icelandic ones, *The Anglo-Saxon Chronicle*, Irish annals, Adam of Bremen's

Gesta (cf. p. 62 above) and Saxo Grammaticus's *Gesta Danorum*. He was presumably a leader of the large Danish army which invaded East Anglia in 865 (cf. note 10 below). He also took part in an attack on York at about the same time in which the rival English kings Ælla and Osbert were killed. *The Annals of Ulster* describe him as the 'king of the Northmen of all Ireland and Britain'. He died in about 873. The legendary Ragnarr loðbrók could well represent a combination of two different historical figures, one of whom is likely to have been a parent of the historical Ívarr. However this may be, Ari probably conceived *loðbrók* as a nickname for Ragnarr and then in some such sense as 'shaggy breeches'. Cf. Rory McTurk, *Studies in Ragnars saga loðbrókar and its major Scandinavian analogues* (1991).

[10] Edmund the Martyr, king of the East Angles, resisted the Danish invasion of his kingdom, was taken prisoner and, when he rejected Ívarr's demands for tribute and allegiance, was put to death (20th November 869) by being shot with arrows. On the apparent discrepancy between the date of Edmund's death in 869 and that given by Ari in lines 13–14 (i.e. 870), see note 49 below.

[11] It is uncertain what written work about St Edmund is referred to. *De miraculis Sancti Eadmundi*, written shortly before 1100 by the English cleric Hermannus, is perhaps the most likely, though Abbo of Fleury's *Passio Sancti Eadmundi* (written *c.*988) is another possibility. Cf. Strömbäck 1975, 19 note 1.

[12] Ingólfr is traditionally regarded as the first Scandinavian settler in Iceland and founder of modern Reykjavík. Ari gives no name for his father but some later sources refer to him as the son of Ǫrn, others of Bjǫrnólfr, the latter perhaps more correctly. Cf. *HOIC* 13 footnote 35.

[13] Modern research supports the suggestion here that, at the time of its settlement, Iceland was much more extensively wooded than in Ari's own. In the intervening period, over-exploitation by man and overgrazing by livestock led to deforestation. The birch continues to be the main type of tree in Iceland, but various kinds of willow, as well as the rowan and juniper, are also found quite widely.

[14] *papar* (the word goes back ultimately to Latin *papa*, 'father') were Irish anchorite monks who had found their way to the Scottish islands, the Faroes and Iceland. Their presence in these places is suggested by place-names containing the element *pap-* (e.g. *Papa Stour* in Shetland, *Papey* off eastern Iceland). The Irish monk Dicuil, writing about 825, gives an account of an island in the far north he calls *Thile* which was visited by clerics some thirty years earlier. Most scholars have identified this with Iceland and Irishmen would thus have been first to set foot in Iceland, as early as the beginning of the ninth century. See *Dicuili Liber de mensura orbis terrae*, ed. and tr. J. J. Tierney (1967), 75–77; *HOIC* 3–7; Strömbäck (1975), 60–67; *A History of Norway and The Passion and Miracles of the Blessed Óláfr*, tr. Devra Kunin, ed. with introduction and notes by Carl Phelpstead (2001), 8 and 84–85.

[15] It is not certain that books actually written in Irish are meant; books which were 'Irish' in their appearance, style and decoration may rather be intended. Cf. Ian McDougall, 'Foreigners and Foreign Languages in Medieval Iceland', *Saga-Book* XXII (1986–89), 180–82. The Irish monks would doubtless have counted their books great treasures. *Bagall* is a loan-word probably either from Old Irish (*bachall*) or Old English (cf. Middle English *bag*(*h*)*el*), both words themselves being ultimately derived from Latin *baculus*. The Icelandic word is often translated 'crozier' but may refer rather to the long stout walking-sticks (Latin *cambutta*) used by Irish monks. For illustrations of medieval croziers (though of a later date) found in Iceland, see *HOIC* 398 and Björn Þorsteinsson 1987, 52. *Bjǫllur* probably means small hand-bells. Such items have been found in Iceland and some of them, though they must derive from a date later than any Irish presence there, may have associations with the British Isles. See further P. W. Joyce, *A Social History of Ancient Ireland* (1903), I 343, 352–54, 372–78.

[16] An ounce (*eyrir*) was a weight of about 27 g., and while basically used of silver as a medium of exchange, was also transferred to measure other media (homespun in ells, for instance) by a system of equivalences. There were eight ounces (*aurar*) to a mark (*mǫrk*) (cf. line 32 below). Cf. *HOIC* 328–35; *Laws* II 386, 389–90.

[17] *Landaurar*, 'land dues', were primarily a toll which Icelanders were obliged to pay the king of Norway on arrival in that country. It was abolished by *Gamli sáttmáli*, 'the Old Pact', of 1262–64 which brought Iceland under Norwegian rule. But the word is also used in some sources of a tax imposed on those leaving Norway for other places. See *HOIC* 109–17, 282–87; *Laws* II 211 note 100.

[18] Óláfr enn digri or Óláfr helgi Haraldsson is one of the most important figures of the Viking Age and the sources about him are numerous and diverse. He was a great-great-grandson of Haraldr enn hárfagri, born in Norway in about 995. He appears to have participated in wide-ranging Viking raids at an early age which took him to places as far apart as Finland and Spain. He was involved in the Danish attacks on England in the years 1009–1014 and was baptised in Rouen in Normandy at about this time. He returned to Norway in 1015 and established himself as the first effective ruler of the whole country. During his reign, Óláfr consolidated his power by the elimination of various petty chieftains and strengthening the civil administration of the country. He also continued the process of the conversion in which Óláfr Tryggvason had earlier played such an important part (cf. note 33 below). Because of external threats, primarily from Canute the Great, he was forced to seek asylum with Yaroslav in Russia in 1028 but returned two years later with a small army only to be defeated and killed at the Battle of Stiklarstaðir (modern Stiklestad) in Trøndelag on 29th July 1030. Although never officially canonised, Óláfr became the object of a considerable cult after his death and is regarded as patron saint of Norway. His shrine in the cathedral at Trondheim became a place of pilgrimage and a number of churches (not least in the British Isles) are dedicated to him. See *MS*, s.v. *Óláfr, St.*; *Óláfs saga helga*.

[19] On Ari's account of Úlfljótr's Law and the establishment, site and institutions of the Alþingi, see *HOIC* 35–93; *Laws* I 1–6, 53–138; Björn Þorsteinsson 1987; *MS*, s.v. *Alþingi*. Some scholars take Ari's statements about Úlfljótr's Law as historically suspect (see note 21 below). Certainly the clauses found in various sources purporting to be from Úlfljótr's Laws (cf. Halldór Hermannsson in Ari Thorgilsson 1930, 76–77) are probably most reasonably regarded as antiquarian reconstructions from the twelfth or thirteenth century.

[20] Certain critics who think that Ari omitted the *áttartala* found in the earlier version of *Íslendingabók* when he made his second version (see note 3 above) have pointed to the words in this parenthesis as a possible vestige of material he unwittingly left behind when otherwise removing genealogical material (see Jón Jóhannesson 1956, xxi).

[21] Golaþingslǫg was the law for western and southern Norway (cf. *MS* 385–86). It has been argued that Golaþingslǫg was not established until about 950, i.e. at a time later than the events here described. Further, the fact that the preserved Golaþingslǫg and laws of the Icelandic Commonwealth are so different makes it seem improbable that the former influenced the latter at an earlier stage of the development of both.

Þorleifr is a shadowy figure who appears in a number of Kings' Sagas. Some sources make him a relation of Úlfljótr or connect him with the establishment of Golaþingslǫg.

[22] What Ari says of Grímr's mission here is not entirely clear. The purpose of his search may have been to find a suitable meeting-place for the Alþingi. But it may have been to collect views on the very establishment of the assembly. The statement that each man gave Grímr a penny is also problematic. If he indeed gave the money to the temples (*hof*), this would suggest a close association between these institutions and the political administration of Iceland in heathen times. Cf. *HOIC* 38–39, 54–55.

[23] It is disputed whether the reference is to a local assembly or to some sort of forerunner to the Alþingi. For a review of the arguments, see Halldór Hermannsson in Ari Thorgilsson 1930, 78; *HOIC* 35–40. A local assembly called Kjalarnessþing certainly existed during the Commonwealth period (see *HOIC* 76–77).

[24] Little or nothing is known of this informant of Ari's. He may have hailed from eastern Iceland.

[25] The lawspeaker of the medieval Icelandic Commonwealth was elected for a period of three years, though he could always be re-elected. It was his duty to recite all sections of the law at Lǫgberg (see note 41 below) during his term of office and the Assembly Procedures

Section (*þingskaparþáttr*) every year. He received a fee and half of the fines imposed by judgments at the General Assemby. Cf. Strömbäck 1975, 15 and note; *HOIC* 47–49; *Laws* I 187–88, 249–50; II 384–85.

[26] On the discovery and settlement of Greenland by Scandinavians, see *BS* 48–50; *HOIC* 98–101; Krogh 1967; Gad 1970; Jones 1986, 73–114; *MS*, s.v. *Greenland, Norse in.*

[27] The main sources for Eiríkr the Red and his family are *Íslendingabók, Landnámabók, Grœnlendinga saga* and *Eiríks saga rauða* (cf. Jones 1986, 142–235). Eiríkr is said to have lived in the inner part of Eiríksfjǫrðr at Brattahlíð (Qassiarsuk), where extensive Norse archaeological remains have been found. Eiríksfjǫrðr, together with Einarsfjǫrðr immediately to the south of it, formed the central part of Eystribyggð ('Eastern Settlement'), the more southerly of the two medieval Scandinavian settlements in Greenland. The other settlement, Vestribyggð ('Western Settlement'), lay in the area to the east of Greenland's present-day capital, Nuuk. Both settlements were on the southern part of the west coast of Greenland. See maps in *ÍF* IV.

[28] It is easier to understand the reasoning attributed to Eiríkr here if we remember that, as well as denoting the colour green, Old Norse *grœnn* can mean 'good; hopeful; advantageous', where no notion of physical colour is present (cf. C–V 218). Thus in *Finnboga saga* ch. 6 (*ÍF* XIV 262), the superlative of the adjective is used with an understood noun *kostr*, the expression meaning 'the best alternative': *sá mun grænstr at segja satt.* Further, the noun *kostr* is used in the compound *land(s)kostir*, 'quality, potential of (a) land for settlement' (cf. *Eiríks saga rauða* ch. 11 (*ÍF* IV (1985), 430); *Vatnsdœla saga* ch. 15 (*ÍF* VIII 40–41).

[29] *austr ok vestr á landi* is probably a reference to the two Scandinavian settlements in Greenland, Eystribyggð and Vestribyggð (cf. note 27 above).

[30] The first element of the compound *keiplabrot* appears to be genitive plural of *keipull*, attested otherwise only in *SnE, Skáldskaparmál* 128. Different etymologies have been suggested for *keipull*: it may be a

loan-word (cf. Latin *caupulus*, Old English *cuopel*, 'small ship'; Welsh *ceubol*, 'ferry-boat'). Or it may be a diminutive of *keipr*, 'boat'. It is not certain that the word *keipull* by itself necessarily denoted a skin boat, though doubtless it was remains of skin boats of some kind that Eiríkr and his men found. But for these, the word *húðkeipr* was the most precise term, e.g. in *Flóamanna saga* ch. 23 (*ÍF* XIII 289), and was used of the vessels of the Skrælingar in *Grœnlendinga saga* ch. 4 (*ÍF* IV (1985), 255–56, alongside *keipr*) and *Eiríks saga rauða* ch. 11 (*ÍF* IV (1985), 428).

The artefacts referred to by Ari in this paragraph were probably left behind by some early culture of Inuit, most probably the Dorset culture, which had visited and moved on from the areas of Greenland in question centuries before the arrival of the Scandinavians. Certainly vestiges of Dorset-culture settlement have been found in both the Eastern and Western Settlements by modern archaeologists. *Vínland* (literally 'Wine-land') refers to some area on the eastern side of the North American continent visited by Scandinavians from about AD 1000 onwards. The name is also known to us from Adam of Bremen's *Gesta* (see p. 62 above) and e.g. *Grœnlendinga saga* and *Eiríks saga rauða*. Although we do not know its exact definition, it may have included Newfoundland, on the northern tip of which island a Scandinavian site has been discovered at L'Anse aux Meadows. While there is archaeological evidence to suggest that there may have been contacts between Scandinavians and Dorset-Inuits in Newfoundland, we have no need to assume that in using the word *Skrælingar* here Ari is referring specifically to Dorset-Inuits. The word seems to have been applied indiscriminately by medieval Scandinavians to any non-Scandinavian people they encountered in Greenland or North America. Moreoever, it is perfectly possible that the Scandinavians had not met with the Inuit in Greenland at the time from which Ari has his information; the Thule-Inuit (ancestors of the Inuit of modern Greenland) probably did not enter the northern part of the country from the Canadian islands until about AD 1100 at the earliest.

[31] Þorkell's visit to Greenland, which must have taken place in the period *c.*1050–70 (cf. *ÍF* I 14 note 3), is mentioned only here. For another example of Ari mentioning his informants' own sources, see lines 93–94 below and note 39.

[32] On the conversion of Iceland, see Turville-Petre 1953, 48–69; *HOIC* 118–38; Strömbäck 1975; *MS*, s.v. *Conversion*. In addition to this account by Ari, the chief primary sources are Theodoricus monachus's *Historia de antiquitate regum Norwagiensium*, *Historia Norwegiae*, *Ágrip*, Oddr Snorrason's *Óláfs saga Tryggvasonar*, Snorri Sturluson's *Heimskringla*, *Njáls saga*, *Kristni saga* and *Óláfs saga Tryggvasonar en mesta*. The account in *Kristni saga* is particularly detailed.

[33] At an early age (he was born *c*.968) Óláfr Tryggvason took part in Viking expeditions and *The Anglo-Saxon Chronicle* tells of his attacks on England in the early 990s (which involved the extortion of Danegeld). According to some sources, he was baptised in the Isles of Scilly (cf. pp. 89–90 above). He became king of Norway in 995 and during his short reign strove to further the cause of Christianity not only in Norway itself but also in the Scandinavian colonies in the west. In Norway his success was only partial. He died fighting King Sveinn Haraldsson (see lines 145–49 below and Text VI above). Cf. Strömbäck 1975, 31–37; *MS*, s.v. *Óláfr Tryggvason*; *Óláfs saga Tryggvasonar*.

Ari uses a number of Latin words (such as *rex* instead of *konungr*) and Latinisms in *Íslendingabók* (cf. line 197 below). This he may have done under the influence of specific Latin sources.

[34] Þangbrandr (also known as Theobrand(us)) is mentioned in a number of sources (cf. note 32 above), some of which cite what are ostensibly contemporary verses about him. He appears to have been of either Flemish or Saxon origin. The element *Þangbrand-* appears in a number of Icelandic place-names, suggesting perhaps that he travelled widely in the country; see *HOIC* 128–31; Strömbäck 1975, 25–26.

[35] Hjalti Skeggjason was Gizurr enn hvíti's son-in-law, and plays an important part in *Njáls saga*. Gizurr belonged to what was perhaps one of the most distinguished Icelandic families of the Commonwealth period, the descendants of Ketilbjǫrn the Old, the original settler of a large part of south-western Iceland which included Mosfell, Skálaholt and Haukadalr. As seen here, he played an important part in the introduction of Christianity into Iceland and is a major figure in *Njáls*

saga. Among his descendants were his son Ísleifr, first bishop of Iceland (1056–80), Gizurr, second bishop of Iceland (1082–1106) and first bishop of Skálaholt (1106–18), and Gizurr Þorvaldsson (1208–68), who played an important part in the history of Iceland leading up to the end of the Commonwealth (see Text III above). The family (or parts of it) are sometimes referred to as the Mosfellingar, sometimes as the Haukdœlir.

[36] *þá er hann hǫfðu nítt*, 'who had insulted him'; probably more specifically 'who had composed scurrilous verses about him' The noun *níð* has roughly the sense of 'defamation', often of a sexual character; cf. Preben Meulengracht Sørensen, *The Unmanly Man. Concepts of Sexual Defamation in Early Northern Society*, tr. Joan Turville-Petre (1983), 28–32, 79–81; *Laws* II 197 note 16. Some of the verses said to have been composed about Þangbrandr have been preserved.

[37] I.e. Óláfr Tryggvason.

[38] The first day of summer was Thursday, 9th–15th April (cf. *Laws* II 15 note 84). Gizurr and Hjalti's arrival in Iceland must have been 18th–24th June and thus more or less coincided with the beginning of the Assembly (Alþingi) (cf. *Laws* I 57).

[39] Strömbäck (1975, 19) cites this sentence as an instance of how meticulous Ari could be in referring to his informants and their sources: 'We may note, for example, that he establishes the fact that the two chieftains who were to bring Christianity to Iceland first landed in mid-June . . . in Vestmannaeyjar by referring to one of his best-informed source-men [i.e. Teitr; cf. lines 8–9, 36, 144], who had himself been told this by *a man who was there on the islands* at the time.'

[40] *Fjǫrbaugsgarðr*, 'lesser outlawry', involved banishment from Iceland for three years (see *Laws* I 250). Under the laws of the Commonwealth, the penalty for reciting shaming slander (*níð*; see note 36 above) about another person was full outlawry (*skóggangr*); see *Laws* II 197–99.

[41] On *Lǫgberg*, see *Laws* I 251; *HOIC* 41–44; Björn Þorsteinsson 1987, 41–42 and passim. It was at Lǫgberg that the recital of the laws by the lawspeaker took place (cf. note 25 above).

[42] *At geyja goð* probably means 'to blaspheme (the) gods'; cf. the word *goðgá* (line 99) which must mean 'blasphemy' (the second element of this word comes from the same root as *geyja*). The verse is ironical: 'I do not wish to blaspheme the gods; (but) Freyja seems to me to be a bitch.' It is in the metre *málaháttr* with internal and end-rhymes (cf. *ION* 317; *SnE, Háttatal* st. 83, or, in some versions, st. 80, 81, 85, 88, and p. 87). On the voluptuous fertility-goddess Freyja, see *MRN* 175–79; *MS*, s.v. *Freyr and Freyja*. In Oddr*ÓT*, *Njáls saga* (ch. 102) and *Óláfs saga Tryggvasonar en mesta* two further lines are added: *Æ mun annat tveggja / Óðinn grey eða Freyja*, 'One of the two, either Óðinn or Freyja, will always be a bitch.' Cf. Strömbäck 1975, 13–14.

[43] It seems probable that Hallr was simply bribing Þorgeirr; Oddr*ÓT* says that Óláfr Tryggvason had given Gizurr and Hjalti a substantial sum of money before they left Norway 'to make friends with chieftains'. Cf. Strömbäck 1975, 30–31.

[44] *búðir* were the temporary shelters used by those attending the Alþingi at Þingvellir and assemblies elsewhere in Iceland. Their walls would have been made of turf and stone and when in use they would have been roofed with awnings of canvas or homespun. See Björn Þorsteinsson 1987, 32–34.

[45] Þorgeirr's exemplum cited here is not historical and no real events are referred to. In *Kristni saga* the names of the two fictitious kings are given as Tryggvi (of Norway) and Dagr (of Denmark).

[46] The exposure of unwanted infants (especially females) after birth (*barna útburðr*) appears to have been practised in heathen Iceland and is referred to in the sagas (e.g. *Gunnlaugs saga ormstungu* ch. 3). There was general Christian opposition to the consumption of horse-meat (*hrossakjǫts át*) in the Middle Ages, probably due to its association with heathen ritual rather than to the Mosaic Law, and, as Ari

implies, it was later forbidden in the laws of the Icelandic Commonwealth (cf. *Laws* I 49). Cf. Strömbäck 1975, 17 note 1 and 29 note 2.

[47] The location of the battle is disputed. It may have taken place off the German island of Rügen (cf. p. 58 above and **Svǫlðr** in *NION* III).

[48] Sveinn Haraldsson (Sven Forkbeard) revolted against his father, Haraldr Gormsson, to ascend the throne of Denmark in about 986. In the 990s he was involved in attacks on England, one of them together with Óláfr Tryggvason. He also laid claim to Norway and after his defeat of Óláfr Tryggvason recorded here had control of much of that country. In 1013 he led a speedy invasion of England. Ethelred the Unready was driven into exile and Sveinn was king of the country for a few months until his death at Gainsborough on 3rd February 1114. Cf. *MS*, s.v. *Sven Haraldsson (Forkbeard)*.

Óláfr enn sœnski (known in Swedish as Olof Skötkonung), son of King Erik the Victorious, ruled from *c*.995 and died *c*.1021. He is probably the first king who could be said to have ruled all Sweden, though only for a limited time. He embraced Christianity himself and attempted to impose it on his subjects, but was eventually frustrated by the heathen faction.

Eiríkr Hákonarson was son of Hákon Sigurðarson Hlaðajarl who had ruled Norway *c*.970–95. After the fall of Óláfr Tryggvason, Eiríkr and his brother Sveinn had control of parts of the country, though as subordinates of Sveinn Haraldsson. After Eiríkr was summoned to England by Canute in 1015, Óláfr Haraldsson (digri) returned to Norway and defeated Sveinn at the Battle of Nesjar. Eiríkr died in England as earl of Northumbria in about 1024.

[49] Modern chronological investigations suggest that Christianity was in fact accepted at the Alþingi in June 999, and that Óláfr Tryggvason fell in battle in the September of that same year. The apparent discrepancy arises from the fact that Ari began his year on 1st September, as was not uncommon at the time. Cf. Strömbäck 1975, 2 note 1.

By the expression *at alþýðu tali* Ari refers to the system (now common) of dating historical events from the birth of Christ. This was introduced by Dionysius Exiguus (*fl.* AD 500) and fostered by the Venerable Bede (d. 735). Systems using other dates for Christ's birth were known in medieval Iceland, including that connected with Gerlandus of Besançon (*fl.* AD 1100) which assumes that Christ was born seven years later than Dionysius and Bede reckoned.

[50] On Bishop Gizurr Ísleifsson, see *HOIC* 147–53; Turville-Petre 1953, 79–82. He was son of Ísleifr, first bishop of Iceland, and grandson of Gizurr enn hvíti who played such a notable role in the introduction of Christianity to Iceland (see lines 80, 88, 111 above). He was born in 1042, consecrated in 1082 (cf. note 60 below) and died in 1118. On laws of tithe, see *Laws* II 221–35, 398–99 and references; *HOIC* 147–50, 169–78. On the writing down of the secular laws, cf. *HOIC* 89–93; *Laws* I 9–16. And on Jón Ǫgmundarson and the foundation of the see of Hólar, see Turville-Petre 1953, 109–42, 197–99; *HOIC* 153–56; *MS*, s.v. *Jóns saga ens helga*. Cf. note 62 below and Text XIV.

[51] Earlier in chapter 10 of *Íslendingabók*, Ari mentions Markús as his informant for the terms of office of all the lawspeakers before his own time and gives Markús's sources for the lawspeakers before his (Markús's) time. Markús was a poet and composed, for example, a memorial poem in honour of King Eirik Ejegod of Denmark (d. 1103).

[52] Iceland was the first of the Scandinavian countries to introduce tithes, at the Alþingi in 1096 or 1097. The amount was one per cent of a man's unencumbered possessions; one quarter was sent to the bishop, a second quarter to the priest, a third to the local church and a fourth to the poor.

[53] The land at Skálaholt had originally been part of Gizurr's family estate (cf. note 35 above). After the death of his mother, Gizurr had it established by law that the bishop of Iceland should live at Skálaholt. Before that, no particular place of residence had existed.

[54] The diocese of Skálaholt was to cover the eastern, southern and western quarters, while that of Hólar (established in 1106) was to cover the northern quarter. But the northern quarter was the largest and most populous, so Gizurr was giving up claim to more than one fourth of the tithes he had previously received. See *HOIC* 151.

[55] For the boundaries of the four quarters of medieval Iceland, see the map in *Laws* I 280. Rangæingafjórðungr is often called Sunnlendingafjórðungr, Breiðfirðingafjórðungr Vestfirðingafjórðungr and Eyfirðingafjórðungr Norðlendingafjórðungr. Most (but not all) scholars regard the word *hundrað*, 'hundred', used here as referring to the so-called 'long' or 'duodecimal' hundred (i.e. 120) rather than the 'decimal' hundred (i.e. 100) (cf. C–V 292–93; *Gr* 3.4.1). If this is right, then the total number of farmers who paid assembly attendance dues in Iceland was about 4,560, otherwise about 3,800. These figures have been used to calculate the total population of Iceland at the end of the eleventh century and have produced estimates as high as 80,000.

Þingfararkaup was paid by every householder with means above a prescribed level if he or a proper substitute did not attend the General Assembly and was received by those who did attend (cf. *HOIC* 61; *Laws* II 366 and references; Björn Þorsteinsson 1987, 25).

[56] The words *en þá hafði Goðmundr Þorgeirssonr tólf sumur* are probably not original to the second version of *Íslendingabók*, that is, they were very likely added to it later, either by Ari himself or by someone else. Cf. p. 107 above.

[57] Hafliði Másson (d. 1130) lived at Breiðabólsstaðr (in modern Vestur-Húnavatnssýsla). He was one of the most powerful chieftains of his time. His feud with Þorgils Oddason over the years 1117–21 is the subject of *Þorgils saga ok Hafliða*, one of the sagas of the compilation known as *Sturlunga saga* (cf. p. 29 above). The text written at Breiðabólsstaðr in the winter of 1117–18, referred to by modern scholars as 'Hafliðaskrá', is mentioned in the Konungsbók version of *Grágás*, the laws of the Icelandic Commonwealth, where it is said that 'everything in the book which Hafliði had made is to be accepted unless it has since been modified, but only those things in the accounts given by other legal experts which do not contradict it, though anything in them which supplies what is left out there or is clearer is to be accepted'; cf. *Laws* I 190–91, 4–5, 9–16.

[58] It was probably read out by clerics rather than by the lawspeaker, Bergþórr, because the latter could not read.

[59] It was at Hallr's home in Haukadalr that Ari was brought up (cf. p. 105 above). Hallr has been referred to as 'one of the main channels through which tradition flowed from ancient to medieval Iceland' (Turville-Petre 1953, 89). He died at the age of ninety-four in 1089. Although he could neither read nor write, he had an excellent memory and could, for example, remember his baptism by the missionary Þangbrandr. He had been in the service of King Óláfr Haraldsson of Norway and was renowned for his good works.

[60] Gizurr's consecration was attended with certain difficulties. Gizurr would normally have been consecrated by the archbishop of Hamburg–Bremen, under whose authority the church in Iceland came. In the Investiture Controversy between the papacy and the German Empire (cf. *DMA* VI, 498–500 and references), however, the archbishop of the time, Liemarus, had allied himself with the Emperor (Henry IV) against Pope Gregory VII (see note 61 below) who had then suspended and excommunicated him (1074). Gizurr, who supported the Pope, was therefore forced to travel to visit Gregory to seek advice, and it was at his bidding that Gizurr was consecrated by archbishop Hartwig of Magdeburg (on 4th September 1082). It was partly these circumstances which were the cause of the relatively long interval between Ísleifr's death (5th July 1080) and Gizurr's consecration. Cf. *HOIC* 147.

[61] Gregory VII (originally Hildebrand) is regarded as one of the great reforming popes of the Middle Ages. His letters attest to his concern for the fortunes of the Church in places as far apart as Spain, Norway and Hungary.

[62] Jón Ǫgmundarson was born about 1052 and was first bishop of Hólar from 1106 until his death in 1121. Hafliði Másson may have been involved in the choice of Hólar as a suitable location for the centre of the northern see (cf. *HOIC* 153). As bishop, Jón established a school at Hólar and also planned the foundation of the first Icelandic monastery at Þingeyrar, though this was not established until 1133. He strove against the remnants of heathen practice and belief which were still alive in his diocese. For example, he forbade the naming of the days of the week after the pagan gods and this prohibition is reflected in present-day Icelandic (see XIV:79–82 below). The Alþingi

officially endorsed the cult of Jón as a saint in 1200. See references in note 50 above.

[63] *quinto kalendas Junii* is short for *quinto die ante kalendas Junii*, 'the fifth day before the calends of June'. According to the Roman calendar, the calends (*kalendae*) of a month was its first day. The ordinal numeral *quintus* is inclusive, counting the days at both ends (i.e. the day referred to and the day of the calends). The date is, therefore, 28th May. The addition of the word *quinto* is made on the basis of *Hungrvaka,* a synoptic history of the early bishops of Iceland. On the Roman calendar, see e.g. Benjamin Hall Kennedy, *The Revised Latin Primer*, ed. and revised by James Mountford (1962), 215–17.

IX: ÞRYMSKVIÐA

Þrymskviða, an eddic poem in which the god Þórr, disguised as the goddess Freyja, recovers his hammer from the giant Þrymr, who has refused to give it back unless he is granted Freyja in marriage, is preserved only in the Codex Regius of the Poetic Edda, GkS 2365 4to. This manuscript dates from the second half of the thirteenth century, but gives clear signs of having been copied from an older exemplar. Few scholars would now accept E. V. Gordon's view (*ION*, 136) that *Þrymskviða* 'was probably composed about 900'; compelling reasons have been adduced for regarding it as much younger than that, perhaps even from the first half of the thirteenth century. One of these is the fact that it departs occasionally from the traditional rules of Old Norse alliterative poetry; in its first two lines it uses end-rhyme, and in line 112, which echoes line 104, it appears to sacrifice alliteration for an effect of near-repetition. With its frequent use of repetition, indeed (most notably at lines 10, 35 and 45), it may show the influence of European ballad poetry, Scandinavian examples of which are not reliably attested until the thirteenth century. Furthermore, the fundamentally comic tone and subject-matter of *Þrymskviða* strongly suggest that, in the many cases where it shows close similarity of wording to other eddic poems, it is more likely to have been the borrower than the lender, since the contexts in which the relevant words occur in the other poems are mostly serious, and the borrowing of a serious passage for comic purposes in a poetic tradition is a more likely development than the reverse process. This at least suggests that *Þrymskviða* is relatively late among the surviving eddic poems, even if it does not tell us much about its precise date. Examples are *Þrymskviða* line 5 (repeated at lines 10, 35 and 45), which is word for word the same as the line in *Brot af Sigurðarkviðu* (st. 6) introducing Guðrún Gjúkadóttir's question to her brothers about the whereabouts of her husband Sigurðr, whom they have slain; *Þrymskviða* line 23 (echoed at line 25), which is identical with the sybil's rhetorical question about the end of the world in *Vǫluspá* (st. 48); *Þrymskviða* lines 53–55, which are identical with the lines in *Baldrs draumar* (st. 1) describing the debate among the gods and goddesses as to the reason for Baldr's ominous dreams; and *Þrymskviða* lines 108–09, which recall the description in *Guðrúnarkviða I* (st. 27) of how Brynhildr Buðladóttir's eyes flashed fire at the sight of Sigurðr's dead body. In at least one case, rather than placing a serious passage from an earlier eddic poem in a comic context, *Þrymskviða* may be building on a situation in such a poem where elements of comedy are already present. It is especially tempting, for example, to regard Loki's words to Þórr in line 69, *þegi þú*, as an echo of *Lokasenna*, where the phrase occurs altogether sixteen times, and is four times used by Þórr in addressing Loki with the accompanying insult *rǫg vættr* 'effeminate creature' (*Lokasenna*, st. 57, 59, 61, 63); in *Þrymskviða* it is used by Loki in addressing Þórr at the very moment when Þórr is afraid of being accused of effeminacy himself, as a result of having to dress up as a bride. The comic tone of *Þrymskviða* does not in itself justify the view that the poem is of late, post-pagan date. 'It does not follow that those who told humorous tales about the gods had ceased to believe in them' (Turville-Petre 1953, 19). On the other hand, the fact that virtually no record is found outside *Þrymskviða,* either in Snorri Sturluson's Prose Edda or elsewhere, of a myth of Þórr's loss and recovery of his hammer, might suggest, together with the tone of the poem, that *Þrymskviða* was composed as a relatively late, comic, literary response to pre-Christian Scandinavian mythology, and that the story it tells was largely the product of literary invention.

It was considerations of this kind that led Peter Hallberg (1954, 51–77) to argue that Snorri Sturluson (died 1241) was the author of *Þrymskviða*. Snorri, with his vast knowledge of Old Norse mythology and poetry, would certainly have been well equipped to compose a convincing pastiche of a mythological eddic poem. In doing so in the case of *Þrymskviða*, according to Hallberg, Snorri invented the 'myth' of Þórr's loss and recovery of his hammer, but was too conscientious a scholar to include any reference to it in his Prose Edda, which was intended as, among other things, a compendium of ancient myths. Taking the view that Snorri was especially fascinated by the idea of an awe-inspiring glance of the eye, Hallberg compared lines 108–09 of *Þrymskviða* to the description of Þórr hooding his eyes in *Gylfaginning* 37/18–21 and to the description of King Eiríkr Bloodaxe's piercing gaze in *Arinbjarnarkviða* (st. 5), a poem attributed in *Egils saga Skallagrímssonar*, of which Hallberg believed Snorri was the author, to the tenth-century poet Egill Skallagrímsson, the saga's hero (see *ÍF* II 259). It has recently been argued by Baldur Hafstað (1994) that Snorri was the author of *Arinbjarnarkviða* itself, as well as of *Egils saga*.

This view, if it can be accepted, might lend some slight support to Hallberg's argument.

Those who wish to argue for a late date for *Þrymskviða* cannot afford to ignore (as Hallberg seems to do) the fact that it makes frequent use of the particle *um* (or *of*) before verbs, whether in the past tense (as in lines 2, 5, etc.), the past participle (as in lines 26, 81, 93, 128, etc.) or the infinitive (as in line 101, cf. line 109). In *Þrymskviða* this particle occurs in contexts where, in Primitive Norse, the verbs in question would have had a prefix; in the case of *um komit*, line 93, for example, the prefix would have been **ga-*, cognate with the prefix *ge-* found in certain circumstances in verbs and other parts of speech in Old English and Modern German. Whereas in Old Norse, as the Glossary confirms, the *of/um* particle is meaningless, the prefixes it has replaced would in the prehistory of Old Norse have modified to a greater or lesser extent the senses of the words in which they occur; the prefix **ga-*, for example, might have imparted a perfective aspect or perhaps the sense of 'together' to the verb in which it occurred, so that the primitive Norse equivalent of *um komit* in *Þrymskviða* line 93 might have meant 'come together', 'assembled'. The fact that, from a historical-linguistic point of view, the *of/um* particle seems to be used 'correctly' in *Þrymskviða*, i.e. in positions where, in Primitive Norse, a prefix would have occurred, strongly suggests that the poem is considerably older than Hallberg (for example) would claim. On the other hand, while it is uncertain how knowledgeable Old Norse speakers were of ancient forms of their language (see Einar Ól. Sveinsson 1966, especially 38–42), the possibility that the *Þrymskviða* poet was using the particle as a deliberate means of archaising his style should not be discounted (though see Fidjestøl 1999, 228); and John McKinnell has recently argued (2000, 2, 14; 2001, 333, 335) that the poet has here been influenced by the use of the prefix *ge-* in late Old English verse. These considerations may not weigh heavily enough to allow for a date of as late as the thirteenth century for the composition of *Þrymskviða*, however, and Hallberg's view that the poem dates from that century, and particularly his view that it was composed by Snorri Sturluson, should be treated with caution.

Bibliography

Stanza numbers of Eddic poems correspond to those in *PE* (1962).

Beowulf and the Fight at Finnsburg, ed. Fr. Klaeber, 3rd ed. (1950).

Margaret Clunies Ross, 'Reading *Þrymskviða*', in *The Poetic Edda: Essays on Old Norse Mythology*, ed. Paul Acker and Carolyne Larrington (2002), 177–94.

Einar Ól. Sveinsson, 'Kormakr the Poet and his Verses', *Saga-Book* XVII:1 (1966), 18–60.

Bjarne Fidjestøl, *The Dating of Eddic Poetry: a Historical Survey and Methodological Investigation*, ed. Odd Einar Haugen, Bibliotheca Arnamagnæana XLI (1999).

John Frankis, 'Sidelights on Post-Conquest Canterbury: towards a Context for an Old Norse Runic Charm (*DR* 419)', *Nottingham Medieval Studies* 44 (2000), 1–27.

Baldur Hafstað, 'Er Arinbjarnarkviða ungt kvæði?' in *Sagnaþing helgað Jónasi Kristjánssyni sjötugum 10. apríl 1994*, ed. Gísli Sigurðsson *et al.* (1994), 19–31.

Peter Hallberg, 'Om Þrymskviða', *Arkiv för nordisk filologi* 69 (1954), 51–77.

Hervarar saga ok Heiðreks, ed. G. Turville-Petre (1956).

Jonna Louis-Jensen, '"Halt illu frān Būfa!" — til Tolkningen af Kvinneby-Amuletten fra Öland', in *Northern Lights: Following Folklore in North-Western Europe. Aistí in adhnó do Bho Almqvist: Essays in Honour of Bo Almqvist*, ed. Séamas Ó Catháin *et al.* (2001), 111–26 (with English summary, p. 124).

John McKinnell, 'Myth as Therapy: the Usefulness of *Þrymskviða*', *Medium Ævum* 69 (2000), 1–20.

John McKinnell, 'Eddic poetry in Anglo-Scandinavian Northern England', ch. 19 in *Vikings and the Danelaw. Select Papers from the Proceedings of the Thirteenth Viking Congress, Nottingham and York, 21–30 August 1997*, ed. James Graham-Campbell *et al.* (2001), 327–44.

Jón Karl Helgason, '"Þegi þú, Þórr!": Gender, Class, and Discourse in *Þrymskviða*', in *Cold Counsel: Women in Old Norse Literature and Mythology: a Collection of Essays*, ed. Sarah M. Anderson with Karen Swenson (2002), 159–66.

Preben Meulengracht Sørensen, *The Unmanly Man: Concepts of Sexual Defamation in Early Northern Society*, tr. Joan Turville-Petre (1983).

Richard Perkins, '*Þrymskviða*, Stanza 20, and a Passage from *Víglundar saga*', *Saga-Book* XXII:5 (1988), 279–84.

Richard Perkins, 'The Eyrarland Image: *Þrymskviða*, stanzas 30–31', in *Sagnaþing helgað Jónasi Kristjánssyni sjötugum 10. apríl 1994*, ed. Gísli Sigurðsson *et al.* (1994), 653–64.

Folke Ström, Níð, ergi *and Old Norse Moral Attitudes*, The Dorothea Coke Memorial Lecture in Northern Studies delivered at University College London 10 May 1973 (1974).

Sǫrla þáttr, in *Fornaldarsögur Norðurlanda*, ed. Guðni Jónsson (1950), I 365–82.
G. Turville-Petre, *Origins of Icelandic literature* (1953).
Þiðriks saga af Bern, ed. Henrik Bertelsen (1905–11).

The notes below are highly selective. Entries for mythical and legendary figures and locations mentioned in the poem will be found in Rudolf Simek, *Dictionary of Northern Mythology*, tr. Angela Hall (1993), in Andy Orchard, *Dictionary of Norse Myth and Legend* (1997), and in John Lindow, *Handbook of Norse Mythology* (2001). Although it has entries for only the major mythological figures, much useful information, including an entry on *Þrymskviða* itself (by Alfred Jakobsen), will be found in *MS*. John Lindow's descriptive bibliography, *Scandinavian Mythology: an Annotated Bibliography*, Garland Folklore Bibliographies 13 (1988), supplied as it is with a 90-page Index, will also be found helpful. Readers of German will find indispensable the commentary on *Þrymskviða* in Klaus von See *et al.*, *Kommentar zu den Liedern der Edda* II: *Götterlieder* (*Skírnismál*, *Hárbarðsljóð*, *Hymiskviða*, *Lokasenna*, *Þrymskviða*) (1997), 508–75.

IX: ÞRYMSKVIÐA

Reiðr var þá Ving-Þórr   er hann vaknaði
ok síns hamars   um saknaði;
skegg nam at hrista,   skǫr nam at dýja,
réð Jarðar burr   um at þreifask.

Ok hann þat orða   alls fyrst um kvað:
'Heyrðu nú, Loki,   hvat ek nú mæli,
er engi veit   jarðar hvergi
né upphimins: Áss er stolinn hamri!'

Gengu þeir fagra   Freyju túna,
ok hann þat orða   alls fyrst um kvað:
'Muntu mér, Freyja,   fjaðrhams ljá,[1]
ef ek minn hamar   mættak hitta?'

Freyja kvað:
'Þó mynda ek gefa þér,   þótt ór gulli væri,
ok þó selja,   at væri ór silfri.'

Fló þá Loki,   fjaðrhamr dunði,
unz fyr útan kom   Ása garða
ok fyr innan kom   jǫtna heima.

Þrymr sat á haugi,   þursa dróttinn,[2]
greyjum sínum   gullbǫnd snøri
ok mǫrum sínum   mǫn jafnaði.

Þrymr kvað:
'Hvat er með Ásum?   Hvat er með álfum?
Hví ertu einn kominn   í Jǫtunheima?'

'Illt er með Ásum,   ‹illt er með álfum›;
hefir þú Hlórriða   hamar um fólginn?'

'Ek hefi Hlórriða   hamar um fólginn
átta rǫstum   fyr jǫrð neðan;
hann engi maðr   aptr um heimtir,
nema fœri mér   Freyju at kvæn.'

Fló þá Loki,   fjaðrhamr dunði,
unz fyr útan kom   jǫtna heima
ok fyr innan kom   Ása garða;
mœtti hann Þór   miðra garða,
ok þat hann orða   alls fyrst um kvað:

'Hefir þú erindi   sem erfiði?
Segðu á lopti   lǫng tíðindi;
opt sitjanda   sǫgur um fallask
ok liggjandi   lygi um bellir.'

'Hefi ek erfiði   ok ørindi;
Þrymr hefir þinn hamar,   þursa dróttinn;
hann engi maðr   aptr um heimtir
nema hánum fœri   Freyju at kván.'

Ganga þeir fagra   Freyju at hitta,
ok hann þat orða   alls fyrst um kvað:
'Bittu þik, Freyja,   brúðar líni.
Vit skulum aka tvau   í Jǫtunheima.'[3]

Reið varð þá Freyja   ok fnasa*ð*i;
allr Ása salr   undir bifðisk;
stǫkk þat it mikla   men Brísinga.[4]
'Mik veiztu verða   vergjarnasta,
ef ek ek með þér   í Jǫtunheima.'

Senn váru Æsir   allir á þingi
ok Ásynjur   allar á máli,
ok um þat réðu   ríkir tívar
hvé þeir Hlórriða   hamar um sœtti.

32 ok unz *R*.   48 fnasasi *R*.

Þá kvað þat Heimdallr,   hvítastr Ása —
vissi hann vel fram,   sem Vanir aðrir[5] —
'Bindu vér Þór þá   brúðar líni;
hafi hann it mikla   men Brísinga.

Látum und hánum   hrynja lukla
ok kvennváðir   um kné falla,
en á brjósti   breiða steina,
ok hagliga   um hǫfuð typpum.'

Þá kvað þat Þórr,   þrúðugr Áss:[6]
'Mik munu Æsir   argan[7] kalla,
ef ek bindask læt   brúðar líni.'

Þá kvað þat Loki   Laufeyjar sonr:
'Þegi þú, Þórr,[8]   þeira orða;
þegar munu jǫtnar   Ásgarð búa,
nema þú þinn   hamar þér um heimtir.'

Bundu þeir Þór þá   brúðar líni
ok inu mikla   meni Brísinga;
létu und honum   hrynja lukla,
ok kvennváðir   um kné falla,
en á brjósti   breiða steina,
ok hagliga   um hǫfuð typðu.

Þá kvað þat Loki   Laufeyjar sonr:
'Mun ek ok með þér   ambótt vera;
vit skulum aka tvau   í Jǫtunheima.'[9]

Senn váru hafrar   heim um reknir,
skyndir at skǫklum,   skyldu vel renna.
Bjǫrg brotnuðu,   brann jǫrð loga,
ók Óðins sonr   í Jǫtunheima.

Þá kvað þat Þrymr, þursa dróttinn:
'Standið upp, jǫtnar, ok stráið bekki!
Nú fœrið mér Freyju at kván,
Njarðar dóttur ór Nóatúnum.

Ganga hér at garði gullhyrndar kýr,
øxn alsvartir jǫtni at gamni;
fjǫlð á ek meiðma, fjǫlð á ek menja,
einnar mér Freyju ávant þykkir.'

Var þar at kveldi um komit snimma,
ok fyr jǫtna ǫl fram borit;
einn át oxa, átta laxa,
krásir allar þær er konur skyldu;
drakk Sifjar verr sáld þrjú mjaðar.

Þá kvað þat Þrymr, þursa dróttinn:
'Hvar sáttu brúðir bíta hvassara?
Sáka ek brúðir bíta in breiðara,
né in meira mjǫð mey um drekka.'

Sat in alsnotra ambótt fyrir,
er orð um fann við jǫtuns máli:
'Át vætr Freyja átta nóttum,
svá var hon óðfús í Jǫtunheima.'

Laut und línu, lysti at kyssa,
en hann útan stǫkk endlangan sal.
'Hví eru ǫndótt augu Freyju?
Þykki mér ór augum ‹eldr um› brenna.'

Sat in alsnotra ambótt fyrir,
er orð um fann við jǫtuns máli:
'Svaf vætr Freyja átta nóttum,
svá var hon óðfús í Jǫtunheima.'

Inn kom in arma   jǫtna systir,[10]
hin er brúðfjár[11]   biðja þorði.
'Láttu þér af hǫndum   hringa rauða,
ef þú ǫðlask vill   ástir mínar,
ástir mínar,   alla hylli.'

Þá kvað þat Þrymr,   þursa dróttinn:
'Berið inn hamar   brúði at vígja;
leggið Mjǫllni   í meyjar kné;
vígið okkr saman   Várar hendi.'[12]

Hló Hlórriða   hugr í brjósti
er harðhugaðr   hamar um þekði.
Þrym drap hann fyrstan,   þursa dróttinn,
ok ætt jǫtuns   alla lamði.

Drap hann ina ǫldnu   jǫtna systur,
hin er brúðfjár   of beðit hafði;
hon skell um hlaut   fyr skillinga
en hǫgg hamars   fyr hringa fjǫlð.
Svá kom Óðins sonr   endr at hamri.

Notes

[1] *fjaðrhams*: what seems to be involved here is a flying suit which can be worn without the wearer himself (or herself) changing into the form of a bird. While the motif of transformation into a bird for purposes of flight is common enough in Old Norse mythology and elsewhere, the idea of a detachable and transferable flying apparatus is relatively rarely attested. See McKinnell 2000, 2, 14, and McKinnell 2001, 335–36.

ljá: if four is taken as the minimum number of syllables per half-line in the metre to which *Þrymskviða* conforms, i.e. *fornyrðislag* (cf. *ION* §180), the monosyllable *ljá*, following here the disyllable *fjaðrhams*, means that the half-line in which it occurs is of the 'short' type, having only three syllables. Such 'short types' are also known as 'reduced' half-lines (see *ION* §178), since they reflect a reduction in syllable number resulting from various sound changes that took place in the course of the development of Old Norse from Primitive Norse. While reduced half-lines were apparently regarded as 'permissible variants', there can be little doubt that the metre of the poem would have sounded more regular if, in this line, the older (disyllabic) form *léa* had been employed in recitation. This consideration may be used together with the one involving the *of*/*um* particle (see the introduction above) as an argument either for the poem's antiquity or, alternatively, for the view that the poet was making deliberate use of archaism. See also the notes to lines 65, 69 and 115 below.

[2] *Þrymr sat á haugi*: E. V. Gordon, in his note to this line (*ION*, 241), emphasises the royal and chieftainly associations of mounds. It may also be worth noting here that in the eddic poem *Hlǫðskviða* (*PE* 302–12), st. 14, Hlǫðr, the illegitimate son of King Heiðrekr, is referred to as sitting on a mound by one of the other characters in the poem in what appears to be a disparaging statement; this at any rate was the view of G. Turville-Petre, who in commenting on this stanza acknowledged that a king's authority might be symbolised by his sitting on a mound, but mainly emphasised that 'it was the practice of herdsmen to watch their stock from a mound, and there was no trade more deeply despised than that of the herdsman' (see *Hervarar saga ok Heiðreks* 1956, 87).

þursa dróttinn: this phrase, which is repeated in lines 41, 85, 98, 119 and 125, also occurs in the Canterbury and Sigtuna runic charms, dating probably from the eleventh and tenth centuries respectively, where it is used in each case as a hostile term of address with reference to the disease or infection against which the charm is directed. On these see John Frankis 2000 and Jonna Louis-Jensen 2001. On the possible significance of this usage for the interpretation of *Þrymskviða*, see note 12 below.

[3] It is not clear whether it is Þórr or Loki who is speaking here. For a compelling argument that it is Þórr, see Perkins 1988. The view that it is Þórr is apparently also accepted by McKinnell 2000, 5; see further note 9 below.

[4] *men Brísinga*: Freyja's necklace. From parts of Snorri's *Skáldskaparmál* for which Snorri cites as sources the poems *Húsdrápa* and *Haustlǫng*, by Úlfr Uggason (tenth century) and Þjóðólfr of Hvinir (ninth century) respectively, it is possible to piece together a story of how Loki stole the Brísingamen from Freyja and how the god Heimdallr recovered it after he and Loki had contended for it in the form of seals (see *SnE, Skáldskaparmál* 19–20, 32). The anonymous fourteenth-century *Sǫrla þáttr* tells how Freyja obtained a necklace as a result of sleeping in turn with each of the four dwarves who made it; how Loki stole this necklace at Óðinn's request by biting Freyja in the form of a flea while she was asleep, thus causing her to move so that he could unclasp it from her neck; and how Óðinn returned the necklace to Freyja after she had undertaken to start a fight between two kings that would constantly renew itself until a Christian warrior should intervene and kill them (this is the battle known as Hjaðningavíg, of which Snorri gives an account, also in *SnE, Skáldskaparmál* 72–73). The *Brísinga men* of Old Norse sources may or may not be identical with the *Brōsinga mene* of *Beowulf*, line 1199, which according to that poem (lines 1197–1201) was carried off to a 'bright stronghold' by one Hāma, who was escaping the hostility of Eormenric, and who 'chose eternal gain' (see *Beowulf and the Fight at Finnsburg* 1950, 45, 177–79). This story has an analogue in the mid-thirteenth-century Norwegian *Þiðriks saga af Bern*, based on Low German sources. *Þiðriks saga* does not mention any *Brísinga men*, but tells in chs 345 and 430 how Heimir (cf. Hāma) was forced to flee the enmity of Erminrikr (cf. Eormenric) and entered a monastery, bringing with him, among other

things, ten pounds' worth of movable property (*Þiðriks saga af Bern*, 1905–11, II 176–77, 375–77). For the view that in *Þrymskviða* the Brísingamen is a symbol of female sexuality, corresponding to the hammer as a symbol of male sexuality, see McKinnell 2000, 3–7, and cf. note 12 below.

[5] *sem Vanir aðrir*: the natural meaning of these words is 'like other Vanir', but since Heimdallr was one of the Æsir, not one of the Vanir, as the preceding line confirms, this half-line might perhaps be translated 'like those others, the Vanir'. But if the poem was written in Christian times, the lines may reflect the confusion of the author about the categories of Norse mythology.

[6] *þrúðugr Áss*: another 'reduced' half-line of only three syllables, where an older, disyllabic form of *Áss* (cf. Primitive Norse **ansuʀ*) would have allowed perfect metrical regularity; cf. note 1 above.

[7] *argan*: for valuable studies of what is conveyed by this adjective in Old Norse, see Ström 1974, and Meulengracht Sørensen 1983.

[8] *þegi þú, Þórr*: since the two syllables of *þegi* are 'resolved', counting metrically as one (see *ION* §177), this amounts to another 'reduced' half-line of only three syllables, in which an older, disyllabic form of *Þórr* (cf. Primitive Norse **þunraʀ*) would have allowed perfect metrical regularity; cf. note 1 above.

[9] Note the exact repetition here of line 47. There the use of the neuter plural form *tvau*, which would be expected where the two referred to are of different sexes, is plainly justified by the fact that a god (whether Þórr or Loki, cf. note 3 above), is addressing a goddess, Freyja. Here, however, the god Loki is addressing another god, Þórr. As McKinnell (2000, 5) points out, the use of *tvau* here has usually been interpreted in terms of gender role, i.e. as mockery of Þórr, with Loki addressing Þórr as a woman now that he is dressed like one; this is clearly the view of Perkins (1988, 282, 284). McKinnell (2000, 5–6) argues interestingly that it is to be explained rather in terms of Loki literally turning into a female, and Þórr, though disguised as a female, actually remaining male.

[10] *jǫtna systir*, here and in line 127, may be just a kenning for 'troll-wife' rather than meaning literally 'giants' sister'.

[11] *hin er brúðfjár* (cf. also line 128): since *hin er* might very well have been pronounced as one syllable (with substitution of older *es* for *er* permitting the elided form *hin's*), this (like the identical first half of line 128) is probably to be taken as a metrically 'reduced' half-line, in which the older, disyllabic element *-féar* (as opposed to the monosyllabic *-fjár*) in *brúðfjár* would have allowed perfect metrical regularity; cf. note 1 above.

[12] Richard Perkins (1994) argues that Þórr's hammer is a phallic symbol, and that the placing of a hammer in the bride's lap was a feature of pagan Scandinavian wedding ceremonies. His view that *Þrymskviða* is about the loss and recovery of Þórr's virility may be interestingly compared with McKinnell's view (2000) of the poem in terms of Jungian psychology as being about the male fear of lost manhood (symbolised by the stolen hammer) and the female fear of male betrayal (symbolised by the broken necklace), cf. note 4 above. Frankis (2000, 2–5), on the other hand, suggests that the verb *vígja* 'to bless' as used in line 122 may carry with it something of the sense of 'consign to perdition', in which, he believes, the same verb is used in the Canterbury runic charm, where the object of the verb, *þik*, has the same referent as the phrase *þursa dróttinn* (cf. *Þrymskviða*, lines 19, 41, 85, 98, 119 and 125), which immediately follows it, and which evidently refers to the blood-poisoning against which the charm is directed. In this view, Þórr's recovery of his hammer and his use of it to destroy Þrymr immediately afterwards would presumably symbolise recovery from, or the successful treatment of, some kind of medical condition.

Vár, according to *SnE*, *Gylfaginning* 29/36–38, 'listens to people's oaths and private agreements that women and men make between each other. Thus these contracts are called *várar*. She also punishes those who break them.'

X: VǪLUNDARKVIÐA

Vǫlundarkviða, which immediately follows *Þrymskviða* in the Codex Regius, has long been regarded as one of the oldest eddic poems, i.e. as dating from the ninth century. A recent argument that it shows the influence of late Old English verse (see McKinnell 2001, 331–35), however, implies a date of composition in the tenth century or even later. It tells how Vǫlundr and his two brothers meet and marry three swan-maidens, who after nine years fly away and leave them. While two of the brothers, Egill and Slagfiðr, go in search of their wives, Vǫlundr stays behind, working at the craft of ring-making, and hoping for his wife's return. He is then robbed by King Níðuðr of one of the rings he has made, is captured by him and hamstrung, and forced to serve him as a smith. After discovering that the stolen ring has been given to the king's daughter, Bǫðvildr, Vǫlundr takes revenge, first by beheading the king's two young sons and presenting their parents and Bǫðvildr with some bowls, gems and brooches made from the boys' skulls, eyes and teeth respectively; and secondly by seducing Bǫðvildr, after assuring her that he will repair the ring, the breaking of which she has feared to reveal to anyone but him. Able now to fly, Vǫlundr responds from the air to a question from Níðuðr about the fate of his two sons by first enjoining him to swear not to harm the woman by whom he, Vǫlundr, may have a child, and then telling him how he has disposed of the two princes, and that Bǫðvildr is pregnant. He flies off, leaving the distraught Níðuðr to hear from Bǫðvildr herself about the nature of her relations with Vǫlundr.

This story finds a lengthy parallel in that of Velent (= Vǫlundr), which forms part of *Þiðreks saga af Bern*, a thirteenth-century Old Norse prose presentation of what are mainly German narrative traditions. Velent, the son of the giant Vaði, is trained in smithcraft by two dwarves, of whose intention to kill him, however, he learns from his father before the latter's death. Velent kills the dwarves and takes possession of their tools and precious metal. He builds a kind of submarine by hollowing out a tree-trunk and fitting it with glass windows, and arrives in this vessel in the realm of King Níðungr, whose service he enters and who at first treats him well. The king's smith, Amilias, challenges him to make a sword that will cut through some armour that Amilias himself undertakes to make. Taking up the challenge, and dissatisfied with the first sword he makes, Velent reduces it to dust by filing, feeds the file-dust to some poultry, and makes another sword from the birds' droppings. Still not fully satisfied, he follows the same procedure with the second sword, thus making a third, which he calls Mímungr. With Mímungr, he cuts through Amilias's armour and kills him, in accordance with the terms of the challenge. He replaces him as the king's smith, and becomes famous as such. His fortunes then change, however. King Níðungr, marching to meet an invading army, realises after five days' march that he has not brought with him his victory stone, and fears defeat as a result. He promises his daughter and half his kingdom to the man who can bring him the stone by the following morning, and Velent, the only one to undertake the task, manages by riding on his horse Skemmingr to fetch the stone on time. On his return, however, the king's steward attempts to bribe Velent into giving him the stone so that he, rather than Velent, can claim the king's reward, whereupon Velent kills the steward. He conveys the stone to the king, whose victory is thus assured, but the king, angered by the killing of the steward, who had been his favourite retainer, makes Velent an outlaw. Velent then tries to take revenge on the king by poisoning him, but is foiled in the attempt, and is punished for it by having tendons cut in both his legs, so that he is unable to walk. He adjusts to this situation by feigning willingness to comply with the king's requirement that he resume work as his smith. When two of the king's three sons ask him to make missiles for them he says that they must first visit him walking backwards soon after a fall of snow, which they do the next day after snow has fallen in the night. Velent kills them, and makes various items of household equipment for the king from their bones, including cups from their skulls. When the king's daughter breaks her finest ring (not one of Velent's in this account) and fears to admit it to her parents, Velent tells her maid that the princess herself must visit him before he will repair it. When she does so, he locks her in the smithy with him and has intercourse with her. Having sent for his brother Egill, a skilled archer, Velent obtains from him the feathers of some birds he has shot, and uses them to make a feather-costume, which enables him to fly. In it he flies onto a tower, from which he reveals to Níðungr what he has done with his sons' bones, and taunts him with the likelihood that he has made his daughter pregnant. He then flies off. The king orders Egill on pain of death to shoot at Velent, but Egill aims deliberately at Velent's left armpit, knowing that Velent has secreted there a bladder filled with the blood of the king's slain sons. He punctures the bladder, and Níðungr, seeing the blood, believes Velent dead. When Níðungr dies soon afterwards, his surviving son succeeds him, and Velent establishes friendly relations with him and marries his sister, who by now has given birth to Velent's son, Viðga, to whom Velent passes on in due course the sword Mímungr and a shield on which a golden serpent is depicted.

While there are obviously close similarities between these two accounts, the differences between them make it safest to assume a common source for them both, rather than a direct relationship between them. Echoes of the story they tell are found in various Old English poems: in *Deor*, where Welund (= Vǫlundr, Velent) and Beadohild (= Bǫðvildr) are dwelt on as examples of patience under suffering — Welund because of his subjection to bondage by Niðhad (= Níðuðr), and Beadohild because her discovery that she was pregnant caused her even more distress than the death of her brothers; in *Waldere*, where Weland's (*sic*) skills as a smith are praised, and from which it emerges that Þeodric (= Þiðrikr) intended to give Widia (= Viðga), the grandson of Niðhad and son of Weland, the sword Mimming (= Mímungr), because he, Widia, had once saved Þeodric; and in *Beowulf*, where a fine battle-dress is described as 'the work of Weland'. In a verse passage in King Alfred's Old English translation of Boethius's *De consolatione Philosophiae* reference is made to 'the bones of the wise Weland, that goldsmith who was long ago most famous'; and in the medieval German Latin poem *Waltharius* there is mention of a coat of mail made by Weland, *Wielandia fabrica*, that shields Waltharius (= Waldere) from his attackers. Pictorial representations of the story are found in carvings on the whalebone casket of Northumbrian origin known as the Franks casket, dated to *c.*700, and preserved in the British Museum; on the picture stone Ardre VIII, dated *c.*800, on the Swedish island of Gotland; and in stone carvings from northern England dating from the ninth and tenth centuries, found variously on a hogback tomb preserved fragmentarily in Bedale Church, North Yorkshire, and on stone crosses preserved, more or less fragmentarily, in the Parish Church and the City Museum of Leeds, West Yorkshire, and in Sherburn Church, near Filey, North Yorkshire. Weland and Wade (= Vaði) have come to be associated through local legend with specific places in England, Denmark, and Germany; and Chaucer twice mentions Wade, once in *Troilus and Criseyde* and once in *The Canterbury Tales*, referring in the latter instance, in the Merchant's Tale, to 'Wades boot' (Wade's boat) in a context of 'muchel craft' — an allusion, surely, to the underwater boat made, according to *Þiðriks saga*, by Velent, son of Vaði. This list of reflexes of the story is by no means exhaustive.

Bibliography

Ásgeir Blöndal Magnússon, 'Um ögurstund', in *Sjötíu ritgerðir helgaðar Jakobi Benediktssyni 20. júlí 1977*, 2 vols, ed. Einar G. Pétursson and Jónas Kristjánsson (1977), I 20–29.

Finn Hødnebø, *Ordbog over Det gamle norske Sprog af Dr. Johan Fritzner: rettelser og tillegg* (= vol. IV of the four-volume 4th edition of Fritzner's dictionary, published in 1973) (1972).

Hans Kuhn, *Edda: die Lieder des Codex Regius nebst verwandten Denkmälern, herausgegeben von Gustav Neckel:* II. *Kurzes Wörterbuch*, 3rd revised edition of Neckel's *Kommentierendes Glossar* (1968).

Beatrice La Farge and John Tucker, *Glossary to the Poetic Edda: based on Hans Kuhn's Kurzes Wörterbuch* (1992).

Alec McGuire and Ann Clark, *The Leeds Crosses*. Drawings by Peter Brears (1987).

John McKinnell, 'Eddic Poetry in Anglo-Scandinavian Northern England', ch. 19 in *Vikings and the Danelaw: Select Papers from the Proceedings of the Thirteenth Viking Congress, Nottingham and York, 21–30 August 1997*, ed. James Graham-Campbell *et al.* (2001), 327–44.

John McKinnell, 'The context of *Vǫlundarkviða*', in *The Poetic Edda: Essays on Old Norse Mythology*, ed. Paul Acker and Carolyne Larrington (2002), 195–212.

The Poetic Edda II: *Mythological Poems*, ed. Ursula Dronke (1997), 239–328.

Paul Beekman Taylor, '*Vǫlundarkviða*', in *MS*, 711–13.

Tvær kviður fornar: Völundarkviða og Atlakviða með skýringum, ed. Jón Helgason (1966).

Þiðriks saga af Bern, ed. Henrik Bertelsen, 2 vols (1905–11), I lxxvi–viii, 73–139.

Þorgils saga ok Hafliða, ed. Ursula Brown (1952).

The notes below are more selective than in the case of *Þrymskviða*. Exhaustive notes on *Vǫlundarkviða* will be found in Dronke's edition (in *The Poetic Edda* II (1997) and (in Icelandic) in that of Jón Helgason (*Tvær kviður fornar* (1966)), both listed in the Bibliography above. Entries on 'Völund' and '*Völundarkvida*' (*sic*) will be found in Andy Orchard's *Dictionary of Norse Myth and Legend* (1997), and reference may also be made to John Lindow's *Scandinavian Mythology: an Annotated Bibliography*, Garland Folklore Bibliographies 13 (1988).

X: VǪLUNDARKVIÐA

Frá Vǫlundi

Níðuðr hét konungr í Svíþjóð. Hann átti tvá sonu ok eina dóttur; hon hét Bǫðvildr. Brœðr ‹váru› þrír, synir Finnakonungs. Hét einn Slagfiðr, annarr Egill, þriði Vǫlundr. Þeir skriðu ok veiddu dýr. Þeir kvámu í Úlfdali ok gerðu sér þar hús. Þar er vatn er heitir Úlfsjár. Snemma of morgin fundu þeir á vatnsstrǫndu konur þrjár, ok spunnu lín. Þar váru hjá þeim álptahamir þeira. Þat váru valkyrjur. Þar váru tvær dœtr ‹H›lǫðvés konungs, Hlaðguðr svanhvít ok Hervǫr alvitr. En þriðja var Ǫlrún, Kíars dóttir af Vallandi. Þeir hǫfðu þær heim til skála með sér. Fekk Egill Ǫlrúnar, en Slagfiðr Svanhvítar, en Vǫlund‹r› Alvitrar. Þau bjuggu sjau vetr. Þá flugu þær at vitja víga ok kvámu eigi aptr. Þá skreið Egill at leita Ǫlrúnar, en Slagfiðr leitaði Svanhvítar, en Vǫlundr sat í Úlfdǫlum. Hann var hagastr maðr, svá at menn viti, í fornum sǫgum. Níðuðr konungr lét hann hǫndum taka, svá sem hér er um kveðit.

Frá Vǫlundi ok Níðaði

Meyjar flugu sunnan, myrkvið í gǫgnum,
Alvitr unga, ørlǫg drýgja;
þær á sævar strǫnd settusk at hvílask,
drósir suðrœnar, dýrt lín spunnu.

Ein nam þeira Egil at verja,
fǫgr mær fira, faðmi ljósum;
ǫnnur var Svanhvít, svanfjaðrar dró;
en in þriðja, þeira systir,
varði hvítan háls *Vǫl*undar.

Sátu síðan sjau vetr at þat,
en inn átta allan þráðu,
en enn níunda nauðr um skilði;
meyjar fýstusk á myrkvan við,
Alvitr unga, ørlǫg drýgja.

11, 13 Svanhvítrar *CR*. 25 Ǫnundar *CR*.

Kom þar af veiði ve*ð*reygr skyti;
Slagfiðr ok Egill sali fundu auða;
gengu út ok inn ok um sásk.
Austr skreið Egill at Ǫlrúnu,
en suðr Slagfiðr at Svanhvítu.

En einn Vǫlundr sat í Úlfdǫlum;
Hann sló gull rautt við gimfastan,[1]
lukði hann alla lindbauga vel;
svá beið hann sinnar ljós‹s›ar
kvánar, ef hánum koma gerði.

Þat spyrr Níðuðr, Níara dróttinn,
at einn Vǫlundr sat í Úlfdǫlum;
nóttum *fó*ru seg‹g›ir, negldar váru brynjur,
skildir bliku þeira við inn skarða mána.

Stigu ór sǫðlum at salar gafli,
gengu inn þaðan endlangan sal;
sá þeir á bast bauga dregna,
sjau hundruð allra, er sá seggr átti.

Ok þeir af tóku, ok þeir á létu,
fyr einn útan, er þeir af létu.

Kom þar af veiði veðreygr skyti,
Vǫlundr, líðandi um langan veg.
Gekk brúnni beru hold steikja;
hár brann hrísi, allþur‹r› fura,
viðr enn vin‹d›þurri, fyr Vǫlundi.

Sat á berfjalli, bauga talði,
álfa ljóði, eins saknaði;
hugði hann at hefði Hlǫðvés dóttir,
Alvitr unga, væri hon aptr komin.

31 vegreygr *CR*. 34 skreiðr *CR*. 43 váru *CR*.

Sat hann svá lengi   at hann sofnaði,
ok hann vaknaði   vilja lauss;
vissi sér á hǫndum   hǫfgar nauðir,
en á fótum   fjǫtur um spenntan.

‘Hverir ro jǫfrar,   þeir er á lǫgðu
bestibyrsíma[2]   ok mik bundu?’

Kallaði nú Níðuðr,   Níara dróttinn:
‘Hvar gaztu, Vǫlundr,   vísi álfa,
vára aura   í Úlfdǫlum?’

‘Gull var þar eigi   á Grana[3] leiðu,
fjarri hugða ek várt land   fjǫllum Rínar;
man ek at vér meiri   mæti áttum,
er vér heil hjú   heima várum.

‘Hlaðguðr ok Hervǫr   borin var Hlǫðvé,
kunn var Ǫlrún,   Kíars dóttir.’

Hon inn um gekk   ennlangan sal,
stóð á gólfi,   stillti rǫddu:
‘Era sá nú hýrr, er ór holti ferr.’

Níðuðr konungr gaf dóttur sinni Bǫðvildi gull‹h›ring þann er hann tók af bastinu at Vǫlundar. En hann sjálfr bar sverðit er Vǫlundr átti. En dróttning kvað:

‘Tenn hánum teygjask,   er hánum er tét sverð
ok hann Bǫðvildar   baug um þekkir;
ám*u*n eru augu   ormi þeim enum frána;
sníðið ér hann   sina magni
ok setið hann síðan   í sævar stǫð.’[4]

Svá var gǫrt, at skornar váru sinar í knésfótum, ok settr í hólm einn er þar var fyrir landi, er hét Sævarstaðr.[5] Þar smíðaði hann konungi

83 amon *CR*. 85 settið *CR*.

alls kyns gørsimar. Engi maðr þorði at fara til hans nema konungr einn.

Vǫlundr kvað:

'Skínn Níðaði sverð á linda,
þat er ek hvesta, sem ek haga*s*t kunna,
ok ek herðak sem mér hœgst þótti:
sá er mér, frán‹n› mækir, æ fjarri borinn;
sékka ek þann Vǫlundi til smiðju borinn.
Nú berr Bǫðvildr brúðar minnar
— bíðka ek þess bót — bauga rauða.'

Sat hann, né hann svaf, ávalt, ok hann sló hamri;
vél gørði hann heldr hvatt Níðaði.

Drifu ungir tveir á dýr sjá,
synir Níðaðar, í sævar stǫð.

Kómu þeir til kistu, krǫfðu lukla,
opin var illúð, er þeir í sá;
fjǫlð var þar menja, er þeim mǫgum sýndisk
at væri gull rautt ok gørsimar.

'Komið einir tveir, komið annars dags!
Ykkr læt ek þat gull um gefit verða.
Segiða meyjum né salþjóðum,
manni øngum, at it mik fyndið.'

Snemma kallað‹i› seggr ‹á› annan,
Bróðir á bróður: 'Gǫngum baug sjá!'

Kómu til kistu, krǫfðu lukla,
opin var illúð, er þeir í litu.
Sneið af hǫfuð húna þeira,
ok undir fen fjǫturs fœtr um l*ag*ði;
en þær skálar, er und skǫrum váru,
sveip hann útan silfri, seldi Níðaði.

92 hagazt *CR*. 115 logði *CR*.

En ór augum jarknasteina
sendi hann kunnigri konu Níðaðar;
en ór tǫnnum tveggja þeira
sló hann brjóstkringlur, sendi Bǫðvildi.

Þá nam Bǫðvildr baugi at hrósa,
er brotit hafði:
'Þoriga ek at segja, nema þér einum.'

Vǫlundr kvað:

'Ek bœti svá brest á gulli,
at feðr þínum fegri þykkir,
ok mœðr þinni miklu betri,
ok sjálfri þér at sama hófi.'

Bar hann hana bjóri, því at hann betr kunni,
svá at hon í sessi um sofnaði.
'Nú hefi ek hefnt harma minna,
allra nema einna íviðgjar*n*ra.

'Vel ek,' kvað Vǫlundr, 'verða ek á fitjum[6]
þeim er mik Níðaðar námu rekkar.'
Hlæjandi Vǫlundr hófsk at lopti.
Grátandi Bǫðvildr gekk ór eyju,
tregði fǫr friðils ok fǫður reiði.

Úti stendr kunnig kván Níðaðar,
ok hon inn um gekk endlangan sal;
en hann á salgarð settisk at hvílask:
'Vakir þú, Níðuðr, Níara dróttinn?'

'Vaki ek ávalt, vilja laus‹s›,
sofna ek minnst sízt mína sonu dauða;
kell mik í hǫfuð, kǫld eru mér ráð þín,
vilnumk ek þess nú, at ek við Vǫlund dœma.

133 íviðgjarira *CR*. 143 vilja ek *CR*.

'Seg þú mér þat, Vǫlundr,   vísi álfa:
af heilum hvat varð   *hú*num mínum?'

'Eiða skaltu mér áðr   alla vinna,
at skips borði   ok at skjaldar rǫnd,
at mars bœgi   ok at mækis egg,
at þú kveljat   kván Vǫlundar,
né brúði minni   at bana verðir,
þótt vér kván e‹i›gim,   þá er þér kunnið,
eð‹a› jóð eigim   innan hallar.

'Gakk þú til smiðju   þeirar er þú gørðir,
þar fiðr þú belgi   blóði stokkna.
Sneið ek af hǫfuð   húna þinna,
ok undir fen fjǫturs   fœtr um lagðak.

'En þær skálar,   er und skǫrum váru,
sveip ek útan silfri,   senda ek Níðaði;
en ór augum   jarknasteina
senda ek kunnigri   kván Níðaðar.

'En ór tǫnnum   tveggja þeira
sló ek brjóstkringlur,   senda ek Bǫðvildi;
nú gengr Bǫðvildr   barni aukin,
eingadóttir   ykkur beggja.'

'Mæltira þú þat mál   er mik meirr tregi,
né ek þik vilja, Vǫlundr,   verr um níta;
erat svá maðr hár   at þik af hesti taki,
né svá ǫflugr   at þik neðan skjóti,
þar er þú skollir   við ský uppi.'

Hlæjandi Vǫlundr   hófsk at lopti,
En ókátr Níðuðr   sat þá eptir.

148 sonum *CR*.

‘Upp rístu, Þak‹k›ráðr, þræll minn inn bezti,
bið þú Bǫðvildi, meyna bráhvítu,
ganga fagrvarið við fǫður rœða.’

‘Er þat satt, Bǫðvildr, er sǫgðu mér:
sátuð it Vǫlundr saman í hólmi?’

‘Satt er þat, Níðaðr, er sagði þér:
sátu vit Vǫlundr saman í hólmi
eina ǫgurstund[7] — æva skyldi!
Ek vætr hánum ‹vinna› kunnak,
ek vætr hánum vinna máttak.’

Notes

[1] *við gimfastan*: the Codex Regius here has *við gimfástaɴ*. La Farge and Tucker (1992, 85), following Hans Kuhn (1968, 75), understand *gimfastan* as the masculine accusative singular of a compound adjective *gimfastr* 'fireproof', formed from *gim*, n., a poetic word for 'fire', and from the adjective *fastr*, meaning 'fast' in the sense of 'firm', 'fixed'. On this basis they take *gimfastan* to refer here to the fireproof quality of an anvil, a suggestion which involves assuming the implicit presence in the sentence of the noun *steði*, m., 'anvil' in its accusative singular form, *steðja*. The phrase *við gimfastan ‹steðja›* would thus mean 'on a fireproof anvil'. Another possible reading is *við gim fastan*, which would involve taking *gim* as the accusative singular of a masculine noun **gimr* 'gem', which is not otherwise attested in Old Norse (where, however, the compound *gimsteinn*, m. 'precious stone' is found). Since *gim*, m., is the usual Old English word for 'gem', 'jewel', McKinnell (2001, 331), who adopts this reading, sees *gim* here as one example of Old English influence on *Vǫlundarkviða*. The meaning of the phrase, in this reading, would be 'round the firmly-held gem' (cf. also *The Poetic Edda* II, ed. U. Dronke (1997), 245, 308). A third possibility is to read *við gim fástan*, with *gim* taken once again as the accusative singular of a masculine noun meaning 'gem' and as qualified by *fástan*, the masculine accusative singular of the superlative form, *fástr*, of the adjective *fár* (found most often in compounds such as *dreyrfár* 'blood-coloured'), meaning 'multicoloured' or 'highly coloured', 'bright'. This reading, which would give the meaning 'round the brightest (of) gem(s)', is the one adopted in Jón Helgason's edition, *Tvær kviður fornar* (1966), 59. Of these three possibilities, it is the first that is favoured here.

[2] *bestibyrsíma*: previous commentators have found the element *-byr-* problematic, and have preferred to discount it by emending to *bestisíma*, taking *-síma* as the accusative singular of *sími*, m., 'rope', 'cord', 'bond' (or of *síma*, n., 'thread'), and as forming together with *besti*, n., 'bast', 'bark-fibre' (= *bast*, n., cf. line 47) a compound noun *bestisími*, m. (or *bestisíma*, n.), meaning 'bast rope', 'cord made of bark-fibre'. It may be noted, however, that Hødnebø (1972, 67), gives under *byrr*, m. ('fair wind [for sailing]', 'favourable wind'), the phrase *binda byr við*

as meaning 'to delay', 'hold back', though it is not clear from the example he gives whether these meanings are to be understood in a transitive or intransitive sense: 'bundu eigi lengi síðan byr við ok riðu aptr síðan skyndiliga.' What seems to emerge from this example (which is from *Þorgils saga ok Hafliða*, cf. the edition of Ursula Brown (1952, 37, 89)) is that the phrase means 'to restrict (or tie) one's time of departure to (the opportunity afforded by) a fair wind', i.e. to delay or postpone a projected journey until such time as conditions are favourable. If the phrase may be taken as indicating that the noun *byrr* had associations of delay or restraint (as well as of auspiciousness), it is conceivable that *byrsími*, m., or *byrsíma*, n., might be interpreted as meaning 'a rope or cord used for the purpose of (temporarily) restraining someone', i.e. for tying someone up (until the time is ripe for his or her release). On this basis it may be very tentatively suggested that what is present here is the accusative singular of either *bestibyrsími*, m., or *bestibyrsíma*, n., meaning 'a restrictive rope or cord made of bast or bark-fibre'.

[3] *Grana*: Grani was the horse ridden by Sigurðr Fáfnisbani (see the introduction to IV, above), and used by him for, among other things, transporting the gold he won as a result of slaying the dragon Fáfnir; see *PE*, 188. *Grana leið* 'Grani's path' therefore presumably means Gnitaheiðr (*PE* 180), which together with the mention of the mountains of the Rhine in the next line suggests that there has been some contamination of the story of Vǫlundr with that of Sigurðr.

[4] *sævar stǫð*: 'landing place by the sea'. The landing place in question seems to have been on an island, to judge from the phrases *ór eyju* and *í hólmi*, the former occurring in line 137 and the latter in lines 179, 181. Although *sær* can mean 'lake' as well as 'sea', the latter meaning seems the more likely one in the present context, in view of the possible tidal connotations of the word *ǫgurstund*, see the note on that word below. The writer of the prose narrative accompanying *Vǫlundarkviða* in the Codex Regius has clearly understood the expression *sævar stǫð* as a place-name (see note 7, below), and as the name of an island, see lines 86-87.

[5] Here the expression *sævar stǫð* (see the previous note) appears to

have been understood as a place-name, with the noun *stǫð*, f., 'landing place', 'place where boats are beached', being replaced by the noun *staðr*, m. 'place of settlement', here suffixed to *Sævar-*.

[6] *verða ek á fitjum*: 'if I could get (*or* rise?) on upward-pushing feet'. One meaning of *fit*, f., is the 'web' of the kind found on the feet of certain aquatic birds, which might suggest that Vǫlundr is here speaking of himself as partaking of the nature of such a bird, and envisaging leaving the island referred to in line 137 either by swimming or flying. Another meaning is the 'hind flipper' of a seal or walrus; according to Jón Helgason (*Tvær kviður fornar* 1966, 74), the expression *verða á fitjum* would express well the idea of a seal moving into an upright position by sitting up on its hind flippers. Given the German connections of the story (see the Introduction) it is likely that the noun *fit* also carries here something of the sense of Middle Low German *vittek* 'wing' (cf. *Tvær kviður fornar* 1966, 74, and La Farge and Tucker 1992, 61).

[7] *ǫgurstund*: Ásgeir Blöndal Magnusson (1977) argues convincingly that this word as used here reflects two meanings: (1) 'the (brief) period of time between the reaching by the tide of its highest level and its beginning to ebb', for which the Modern Icelandic dialect expression *að bíða eftir ögrinu* 'to wait for the turning of the tide' provides evidence; and (2) 'a time of great distress', which finds support in evidence from *c.*1500, cited by Ásgeir Blöndal and also by Jón Helgason (*Tvær kviður fornar* 1966, 80), that *ögr*, *ögur*, n., could mean 'heavy heart'. The meaning here may well be no more than 'a brief time of great distress', though it is perfectly possible that the tidal associations are present here as well; cf. note 4, above.

XI: ÞIÐREKS SAGA

This extract from *Þiðreks saga af Bern* (cf. the introduction to X, above) has been chosen for the Reader partly because of the relative simplicity of its style, which makes it easy for beginners to read, and partly because it offers an opportunity for comparison of German treatments of the story of the fall of the Burgundians (called the Niflungar in the extract) with the Old Norse ones. The German traditions of this event are chiefly represented by the *Nibelungenlied*, an epic poem in Middle High German dating from *c.*1205, and the Old Norse ones by the anonymous mid thirteenth-century Icelandic prose *Vǫlsunga saga* and its eddic sources, most especially (as far as the extract is concerned) the anonymous poems *Atlakviða* and *Atlamál*. What is described in the extract is the reception by Grímhildr of her brothers at the court of her husband, the Hunnish king Attila, where she has urged him to invite them (see *Þiðriks saga*, ed. H. Bertelsen, II, 279–80); in *Þiðreks saga* his court is located at Soest in Westphalia, as the name Susa in the extract (line 11) shows. In the *Nibelungenlied* the reason for the invitation is the wish of Kriemhilt (as Grímhildr is there named) to be avenged on her brothers for the slaying of her former husband Siegfried, who corresponds to the Sigurðr (or in *Þiðreks saga* Sigurðr sveinn) of Old Norse sources. In *Vǫlsunga saga* and its relevant sources, the invitation comes from Atli (the Attila of the extract), whose motive is lust for the treasure that Sigurðr had won by his slaying the dragon Fáfnir, and which, after Sigurðr had married Guðrún (the Grímhildr of the extract), had been acquired by her brothers (i.e. the Burgundians) when they brought about his death. Guðrún had then reluctantly married Atli, who now covets the treasure. Of these two versions of the story, the Old Norse one is thought to be the older. *Þiðreks saga*, itself an Old Norse work, though containing mainly German narrative material, is in general closer to the German version than to the Old Norse one, but falls somewhere between the two. From the extract it is clear, for example, that while Grímhildr deeply mourns the death of her former husband, which is consistent with the revenge motive of the German version, she is also interested in whether her brothers have brought the treasure of the Niflungar with them, which is consistent with the emphasis in the Old Norse version on her new husband's lust for it. The present discussion, which is aimed at providing an immediate context for the extract below, concentrates on the events and characters of the story as it is told in *Þiðreks saga*; neither the extract itself, nor what is said here specifically about *Þiðreks saga*, should be allowed to give rise to assumptions about the content of the story as told elsewhere, whether in the German or Old Norse versions. Parts of the story not covered by the extract are referred to by volume and page numbers of Bertelsen's edition.

In the extract (lines 15–18), it is said that fires were prepared for the Niflungar on their arrival at Attila's court, and that they dried themselves. This is to be understood in the light of the fact, reported shortly before the extract begins, that they had encountered bad weather on their way to Soest and got wet (II, 295). It is also perhaps intended to recall the fact that, earlier on their journey, their ship had capsized while they were crossing the Rhine, after which they dried themselves by fires at the castle of Roðingeirr, Margrave of Bakalar (Pöchlarn) (who also features in the extract; see below) (II, 286–92). On that occasion the business of drying themselves had exposed the bright armour they were wearing, as it also does in the scene described in the extract (lines 18–19). The brothers of Grímhildr mentioned in the extract are Gunnarr, Gíslher and Gernoz (see lines 28–30 and 54). Hǫgni is their half-brother, having been conceived as a result of their mother sleeping with a supernatural being in the temporary absence of their father (I, 319–23). In referring to himself (as he seems to be doing in line 25 of the extract) as *óvin*, a word which can mean 'devil' as well as 'enemy', Hǫgni is probably alluding partly to his semi-supernatural, illegitimate origins and partly to the fact that Grímhildr has little reason to feel friendly towards him, because it was he who had killed her husband Sigurðr sveinn, as she had suspected from the start; he had in fact speared him between the shoulder-blades (II, 264–68), where Grímhildr, in the extract (line 35), recalls that he was wounded. Fólkher is a kinsman of the Niflungar, as the extract makes clear (line 55), and Aldrian (line 44) is the son of Attila and Grímhildr (II, 308). Þiðrekr, for whom the Ostrogothic king Theoderic (d. 526) is the historical prototype, is of course the main character of *Þiðreks saga*, from which the extract is taken; and Roðingeirr and Hildibrandr (lines 56–57) are among the many heroic figures with whom Þiðrekr becomes associated in the course of his career, which, as T. M. Andersson (1986, 368–72) has shown, constitutes the backbone of the saga's plot. Hildibrandr had been Þiðrekr's foster-father when he was a boy (I, 34), and Roðingeirr, who had been present with Þiðrekr at the marriage of Grímhildr to Attila and been given by Gunnarr on that occasion the sword Gramr, which had belonged to Sigurðr sveinn (II, 278–79), gave the sword to Gíslher (II, 294) when the Niflungar visited him, as described above, on their way to Attila's court, on which journey he then joined them (II, 295). Ironically and tragically, it is with this same sword that Gíslher kills Roðingeirr in the battle that follows what is described in the extract (II, 320–21). Þiðrekr, it is emphasised near the end of the extract (line 73), was the first to warn the Niflungar — albeit obliquely — of the hostile intentions of Grímhildr and her husband. That they hardly needed any warning, however, is apparent from Hǫgni's no less oblique words to Grímhildr on his arrival (line 25), and from the fact that, earlier in the story, he had suspected treachery and advised his half-brothers against accepting the invitation (II, 281–84).

There are three main manuscripts of *Þiðreks saga*: a Norwegian vellum (Stock. Perg. fol. nr 4) marred by several lacunae and dating from the late thirteenth century, and two complete Icelandic paper manuscripts (AM 177 fol. and AM 178 fol.), both dating from the seventeenth century. The Norwegian manuscript, Stock. Perg. fol. nr 4, is referred to by Bertelsen and here as *Mb*. The present extract, which is in normalised spelling, has been prepared with the help of Bertelsen's and Guðni Jónsson's editions and collated with the relevant part of the text as it appears in the facsimile edition of *Mb* produced by P. Petersen and published in 1869. It is from this facsimile edition that the readings from *Mb* given below in footnotes are taken. The editor is grateful to David Ashurst for supplying photocopies of the relevant pages, 119r–120r, from the copy of this edition held in the British Library, and for guidance as to the meaning of Hǫgni's words to Grímhildr in reply to her question about the treasure of the Niflungar.

Bibliography

Theodore M. Andersson, 'The epic source of Niflunga saga and the Nibelungenlied', *Arkiv för nordisk filologi* 88 (1973), 1–54.

Theodore M. Andersson, *The Legend of Brynhild* (1980).

Theodore M. Andersson, 'An interpretation of *Þiðreks saga*', in *Structure and Meaning in Old Norse Literature: New Approaches to Textual Analysis and Literary Criticism*, ed. John Lindow *et al.* (1986), 347–77.

Theodore M. Andersson, 'Composition and Literary Culture in *Þiðreks saga*', in *Studien zum Altgermanischen: Festchrift für Heinrich Beck*, ed. Heiko Uecker (1994), 1–23.

M. J. Driscoll, review of *The Saga of Thidrek of Bern*, tr. E. R. Haymes (see below), *Journal of English and Germanic Philology* 89 (1990), 389–93.

R. G. Finch, 'Þiðreks saga af Bern', in *MS* 662–63.

Das Nibelungenlied, ed. Helmut de Boor (on the basis of Karl Bartsch's edition, first published in 3 vols, 1870–80), 13th ed., revised (1956).

The Nibelungenlied, tr. A. T. Hatto (1969).

Photo-lithographisk Aftryk af Pergamentscodex No. IV Folio i det kongelige Bibliothek i Stockholm, indeholdende Didrik af Berns Saga. Udført i Opmaalingscontorets photographiske Anstalt af P. Petersen (Christiania, 1869).

The Poetic Edda I: *Heroic Poems*, ed. Ursula Dronke (1969).

The Saga of Thidrek of Bern, tr. Edward R. Haymes (1988) (cf. the review of M. J. Driscoll, above).

The Saga of the Volsungs: the Norse Epic of Sigurd the Dragon Slayer, tr. Jesse L. Byock (1990).

Þiðreks saga af Bern, ed. Guðni Jónsson, 2 vols (1954).

Þiðriks saga af Bern, ed. Henrik Bertelsen, 2 vols (1905–11).

Vǫlsunga saga. The Saga of the Volsungs, ed. and tr. R. G. Finch (1965).

XI: ÞIÐREKS SAGA

Frá drottning‹u› Grímhildi

Drottning Grímhildr stendr í einum turn ok sér fǫr brœðra sinna ok þat, at þeir ríða nú í borgina Susa. Nú sér hon þar margan nýjan skjǫld ok marga hvíta brynju ok margan dýrligan dreng.

Nú mælti Grímhildr, 'Nú er þetta it grœna sumar fagrt. Nú fara mínir brœðr með margan nýjan skjǫld ok marga hvíta brynju, ok nú minnumk ek hversu mik harmar in stóru sár Sigurðar sveins.'

Nú grætr hon allsárliga Sigurð svein ok gekk í móti þeim Niflungum ok bað þá vera vel komna ok kyssir þann er henni var næstr, ok hvern at ǫðrum. Nú er þessi borg náliga full af mǫnnum ok hestum, ok þar eru ok fyrir í Susa mǫrg hund‹r›*u*ð manna ok svá hesta, svá at ei fær tǫlu á komit.

Frá brœðrum Grímhildar

Attila konungr tekr vel við sínum mágum, ok er þeim fyl*g*t í hallirnar, þær sem búnar eru, ok ger‹v›ir fyrir þeim eldar. En Niflung‹ar› fara ekki af sínum brynjum, ok ekki láta þeir sín vápn at sinni.

Nú kemr Grímhildr inn í hǫllina, þar er fyrir váru hennar brœðr við eld ok þurka sik. Hon sér hversu þeir lypta upp sínum kyrtlum ok þar undir eru hvítar brynjur. Nú sér Hǫgni sína systur Grímhildi ok tekr þegar sinn hjálm ok setr á hǫfuð sér ok spennir fast ok slíkt it sama Fólkher.

Frá Grímhildi ok brœðrum

Þá mælti Grímhildr: 'Hǫgni, sitt‹u› heill. Hvárt hefir þú nú fœrt mér Niflungaskatt þann er átti Sigurðr sveinn?'

‹Þá svarar Hǫgni,› 'Ek fœri þér,' segir hann, 'mikinn óvin; þar fylgir minn skjǫldr ok minn hjálmr með mínu sverði, ok eigi lei‹f›ða ek mína brynju.'

Nú mælti Gunnarr konungr við Grímhildi: 'Frú systir, gakk hingat ok sit hér.'

Nú gengr Grímhildr at sínum unga brœðr Gíslher ok kyssir hann ok sitr í hjá honum ok milli ‹ok› Gunnars konungs, ok nú grætr hon sárliga.

11 hundað *Mb*. 14 fylkt *Mb*.

Ok nú spyrr Gíslher, ‘Hvat grætr þú, frú?’

Hon svarar, ‘Þat kann ek vel þér segja. Mik harmar þat mest nú sem jafnan þau stóru sár, er hafði Sigurðr sveinn sér miðil herða ok ekki vápn var fest á hans skildi.’

Þá svarar Hǫgni, ‘Sigurð svein ok hans sár látum nú vera kyrr ok getum eigi. Attila konung af Húnalandi, gerum hann nú s*v*á ljúfan sem áðr var þér Sigurðr sveinn. Hann er hálfu ríkari, en ekki fær nú at gert at grœða sár Sigurðar sveins. Svá verðr þat nú vera sem áðr er orðit.’

Þá stendr upp Grímhildr ok gengr í brott.

Því næst kemr þar Þiðrekr af Bern ok kallar at Niflungar skulu fara til borðs. Ok honum fylgir son Attila konungs, Aldrian. Nú tekr Gunnarr konungr sveininn Aldrian ok berr í faðmi sér út. En Þiðrekr konungr af Bern ok Hǫgni eru svá góðir vinir, at hvárr þeira leggr hǫnd sína yfir annan ok ganga svá út ór hǫllinni ok alla leið þar til er þeir koma til konungs hallar. Ok á hverjum turn ok á hverri hǫll ok á hverjum garði ok á hverjum borgarvegg standa nú kurteisar konur, ok allar vilja Hǫgna sjá, svá frægr sem hann er um ǫll lǫnd af hreysti ok drengskap. Nú kómu þeir í ‹hǫll Attila konungs›.

Frá Attila konung‹i ok› brœðrum Grímhildar

Attila konungr sitr nú í sínu hásæti ok setr á hœgra veg sér Gunnar konung, sinn mág, ok þar næstr sitr junkherra Gíslher, þá Gernoz, þá Hǫgni, þá Fólkher, þeira frændi. Á vinstri hlið Attila konungs sitr Þiðrekr konungr af Bern ok Roðingeirr margreifi, þá meistari Hildibrandr. Þessir allir sitja í hásæti með Attila konungi. Ok nú er skipat þessi hǫll fyrst með inum tignustum mǫnnum ok þá hverjum at ǫðrum. Þeir drekka þat kveld gott vín, ok hér er nú in dýrligsta veizla ok með alls konar fǫngum er bezt megu vera, ok eru nú kátir. Ok nú er svá mikill fjǫlði manna kominn í borgina, at hvert hús er fullt náliga í borginni. Ok þessa nótt sofa þeir í góðum friði ok eru nú allkátir ok með góðum umbúnaði.

Þá er morgnar ok menn standa upp, kemr til Niflunga Þiðrekr konungr ok Hildibrandr ok margir aðrir riddar‹ar›. Nú spyrr Þiðrekr konungr hversu þeim hafi sofizk þá nótt. Þá svarar Hǫgni ok lætr sér hafa vel sofnat:

38 sjá *Mb.*

'En þó er mitt skap ekki betra en til meðallags.'

Nú mælir Þiðrekr konungr, 'Ver kátr, minn góði vin Hǫgni, ok glaðr ok með oss vel kominn ok vara þik hér í Húnalandi, fyrir því at þín systir Grímhildr grætr enn hvern dag Sigurð svein, ok alls muntu þess við þurfa, áðr en þú komir heim.'

Ok nú er Þiðrekr inn fyrsti maðr, er varat hefir Niflunga. Þá er þeir eru búnir, ganga þeir út í garðinn. Gengr á aðra hlið Gunnari konungi Þiðrekr konungr, en á aðra meistari Hildibrandr, ok með Hǫgna gengr Fólkher. Ok nú eru allir Niflungar upp staðnir ok ganga um borgina ok skemta sér.

XII: SAGA AF TRISTRAM OK ÍSǪND

The *Saga af Tristram ok Ísǫnd*, also known as *Tristrams saga ok Ísǫndar*, occupies an important position in the history of medieval literature. In part this is because it provides the only complete, though condensed, account of the twelfth-century *Roman de Tristan* by Thomas (of Britain, or d'Angleterre), which now exists otherwise only in fragments, but which formed the basis for Gottfried von Strassburg's unfinished masterpiece, *Tristan und Isold*. From the nineteenth century to the present day the saga has therefore been a major source for the study of the Tristan legend. And the legend itself continues to fascinate now, as it did in the Middle Ages, because it is the quintessential tale of a compulsive love that transcends all other loyalties.

The importance of this saga specifically for Old Norse–Icelandic studies is that it was probably the first of the large-scale works to be translated from French at the behest of Hákon Hákonarson, king of Norway 1217–63. As such it helped to create an enthusiasm in the north for stories of the romance type — which show a concern for love as well as fighting, for the fantastic, for emotions quite freely expressed, for beauty and other sensory delights, for elegant manners, for costly display, and not least for accomplishments such as the knowledge of languages and music. The romance translations made for King Hákon, which embody these characteristics, make up a significant corpus in their own right. They would still do so, assuming that they had survived, even if they had not exerted influence beyond Norway; but in fact they soon arrived in Iceland, where themes and concerns from them were drawn into the Sagas of Icelanders, and where native imitations started to be written and to develop a character of their own. Eventually the romantic sagas, generally known today as *riddarasögur* (Sagas of Knights), came to be one of the dominant genres of Old Icelandic literature.

As regards the saga's origin, the main piece of evidence is the prologue found in the seventeenth-century Icelandic manuscript AM 543 4to, which contains the earliest complete version of the work now extant. This states that the translation was made at Hákon's command in 1226 by a certain Brother Robert. Such attributions always leave room for scepticism, but in this case there is wide agreement that the statements of the prologue are highly plausible, for in most of its parts the saga bears a strong stylistic likeness to other romance translations made for King Hákon that are preserved in Iceland, and also — most significantly — to *Strengleikar*, a collection of short pieces based on Breton *lais*, which has survived in a Norwegian manuscript from *c.*1270 and is probably close to its original form. It is apparent, nevertheless, that the *Saga af Tristram ok Ísǫnd* as we have it is by no means identical to Brother Robert's version and that it has been modified, as one would expect, during the centuries of its transmission in Iceland. It was probably Robert himself who pushed the material in the direction of native sagas by concentrating on the story and omitting the many long passages of reflection that may be said to adorn, or alternatively to clog, the French text; but the very few leaves of the saga surviving from medieval manuscripts, which are themselves Icelandic and no earlier than the mid-fifteenth century, render Thomas's words at somewhat greater length than is the case with the later manuscripts, and thus show that the saga has undergone at least one further round of shortening. There are signs too of material being added from sources other than Thomas. The consequence is that the work contains many discontinuities and inconsistencies, some of which are mentioned in the notes to the extract given here; but often enough, when Thomas or Gottfried seem bent on maximum elaboration, the saga strikes to the heart of the matter in a way that is astute, honest and humane (see note 11 below, for example).

One of the most noticeable features of the *Saga af Tristram ok Ísǫnd* is the style in which many of its parts are written. It is not unlikely that this so-called 'court style', which is common to the Hákonian romances, was established by Brother Robert, or perhaps developed for the very first time, in this particular saga. The most obvious characteristics are the following: the frequent use of constructions based on present participles, which is regarded as unidiomatic in classical Old Norse; a good deal of alliteration, whether in formal pairs or in longer *ad hoc* strings; the habitual use of synonymous doublets, with or without alliteration; and repetitions of an underlying lexical item in varied forms. There is also the occasional recourse to rhyme and other forms of wordplay. These mannerisms derive from medieval Latin prose and can also be observed, in different concentrations, in the 'learned style' translations of Latin texts and in the 'florid style' of later religious works; but in the court romances they are integrated with the relatively plain manner displayed by native

Icelandic sagas, eschewing simile and working for the most part in sentences that are not especially complex. No doubt the purpose of the verbal decorations was to dignify the prose in general, and in particular to indicate the importance of passages where such decorations are in high density.

All the stylistic features just mentioned, except rhyme, are well represented in the extract given here, which comes from the last third of the saga when Tristram and Ísǫnd have been forced to part, Tristram to live in Brittany and Ísǫnd to remain with her husband in Cornwall. The description of the Hall of Statues is not extant in the fragments of Thomas's work (nor did Gottfried reach so far in the story), but the episode must originally have been present in the poem because one of the fragments (lines 941–1196) begins with Tristan recalling his love and kissing his beloved's image, corresponding to a point in ch. 81 of the saga. Grotesque though the episode may seem to modern taste, it clearly caught the Icelandic imagination, as shown by the fact that it is echoed in several native romances (cf. Schach 1968), notably in *Rémundar saga keisarasonar* ch. 7.

The passage has been transcribed from the manuscript mentioned above, AM 543 4to. Norwegianisms of the types listed on page 65 above do not occur in the manuscript orthography of the extract except for the occasional appearance of *y* in place of *i*; this feature has been retained here only for the name Bryngvet, which is consistently spelled thus. In general the spelling of the manuscript is post-medieval but has been normalised in line with the usage of *ÍF*, and the following substitutions have been made: *konungr* for *kóngur*, *inn* for *hinn* etc., *lifanda* for the Norwegian neuter form *lifandi* and *eigi* for *ei*.

Bibliography

Primary:

Saga af Tristram ok Ísönd samt Möttuls saga, ed. Gísli Brynjólfsson (1878).

Tristrams saga ok Ísondar, ed. Eugen Kölbing (1878).

Saga af Tristram og Ísönd, ed. Bjarni Vilhjálmsson in *Riddarasögur* I (1951), 1–247.

Paul Schach, 'An Unpublished Leaf of *Tristrams Saga*: AM 567 Quarto, XXII, 2', *Research Studies* (Washington State University) 32 (1964), 50–62.

Paul Schach, 'The Reeves Fragment of *Tristrams saga ok Ísöndar*', in *Einarsbók. Afmæliskveðja til Einars Ól. Sveinssonar. 12 desember 1969*, ed. Bjarni Guðnason, Halldór Halldórsson and Jónas Kristjánsson (1969), 296–308.

Saga af Tristram og Ísönd, ed. Vésteinn Ólason (1987).

Tristrams saga ok Ísöndar, ed. and tr. Peter Jorgenson in *Norse Romance*, ed. Marianne E. Kalinke, I (1999) 23–226.

The Saga of Tristram and Ísönd, tr. Paul Schach (1973).

Gottfried von Strassburg, *Tristan und Isold*, ed. Friedrich Ranke (1961).

Rémundar saga keisarasonar, ed. Bjarni Vilhjálmsson in *Riddarasögur* V (1951), 161–339.

Strengleikar: An Old Norse Translation of Twenty-one Old French Lais, ed. and tr. Robert Cook and Mattias Tveitane (1979). Norrøne Tekster 3.

Thomas, *Le Roman de Tristan*, ed. Joseph Bédier (1902).

Background:

Geraldine Barnes, 'The *Riddarasögur*: A Medieval Exercise in Translation', *Saga-Book* 19 (1974–77), 403–41.

Geraldine Barnes, 'The *Riddarasögur* and Medieval European Literature', *Medieval Scandinavia* 8 (1975), 140–58.

Foster W. Blaisdell Jr., 'The So-called "Tristram-Group" of *Riddarasögur*', *Scandinavian Studies* 46 (1974), 134–39.

Alison Finlay, '"Intolerable Love": *Tristrams saga* and the Carlisle *Tristan* Fragment', *Medium Ævum* LXXIII.2 (2004), 205–24.

Peter Hallberg, 'Is There a "Tristram-Group" of *Riddarasögur*?', *Scandinavian Studies* 47 (1975), 1–17.

Sylvia C. Harris, 'The Cave of Lovers in the *Tristramssaga* and Related Tristan Romances', *Romania* 98 (1977), 306–30 and 460–500.

Henry Goddard Leach, 'Tristan in the North', in *Angevin Britain and Scandinavia* (1921), 169–98.

Paul Schach, 'The Style and Structure of *Tristrams saga*', in *Scandinavian Studies: Essays Presented to Dr Henry Goddard Leach on the Occasion of His Eighty-fifth Birthday*, ed. Carl F. Bayerschmidt and Erik J. Friis, (1965), 63–86.

Paul Schach, 'Some Observations on the Influence of *Tristrams saga ok Ísöndar* on Old Icelandic Literature', in *Old Norse Literature and Mythology. A Symposium*, ed. Edgar C. Polomé (1968), 81–129.

Maureen F. Thomas, 'The Briar and the Vine: Tristan Goes North', *Arthurian Literature* 3 (1983), 53–90.

XII: SAGA AF TRISTRAM OK ÍSǪND

Chapter 80

Nú lætr Tristram skunda smíðinni þat er hann má, ok líkar honum þar vel undir fjallinu. Smíða þar trésmiðir ok gullsmiðir, ok var nú allt kompásat ok búit saman at fella. Tristram lofaði þá smiðunum heim at fara, ok fylgði þeim til þess ‹er› þeir váru ór eynni komnir ok síðan h‹eim› til síns fóstrlands. Nú hefir Tristram øngvan félaga þar hjá sér nema jǫtuninn;[1] ok báru þeir nú allt starf smiðanna ok felldu saman hválfhúsit, svá sem efnit var áðr af smiðunum til búit, allt steint ok gyllt með inum bezta hagleik.[2] Ok mátti þá berliga sjá smíðina fullgǫrva, svá at enginn kunni betr œskja.

Undir miðju hválfinu reistu þeir upp líkneskju eina, svá hagliga at líkams vexti ok andliti at enginn ásjáandi maðr kunni annat at ætla en kvikt væri í ǫllum limunum, ok svá frítt ok vel gǫrt at í ǫllum heiminum mátti eigi fegri líkneskju finna.[3] Ok ór munninum stóð svá góðr ilmr at allt húsit fylldi af, svá sem ǫll jurtakyn væri þar inn‹i›, þau sem dýrust eru. En þessi inn góði ilmr kom með þeiri list ór líkneskjunni, at Tristram hafði gǫrt undir geirvǫrtunni jafnsítt hjartanu eina boru á brjóstinu, ok setti þar einn bauk fullan af gullmǫlnum grǫsum, þeim sœtustum er í váru ǫllum heiminum. Ór þessum bauk stóðu tveir reyrstafir af brenndu gulli, ok annarr þessara skaut ilm út undan hnakkanum þar sem mœttisk hárit ok holdit, en annarr með sama hætti horfði til munnsins. Þessi líkneskja var, at skǫpun, fegrð ok mikilleik, svá lík Ísǫnd dróttningu svá sem hon væri þar sjálf standandi, ok svá kviklig sem lifandi væri. Þessi líkneskja var svá hagliga skorin ok svá tignarliga klædd sem sómði inni tignustu dróttningu. Hon hafði á hǫfði sér kórónu af brenndu gulli, gǫrva með alls konar hagleik — ok sett með inum dýrustum gimsteinum ok ǫllum litum.[4] En í því laufinu sem framan var í enninu stóð einn stórr smaragdus, at aldri bar konungr eðr dróttning jafngóðan. Í hœgri hendi líkneskjunnar stóð eirvǫndr eðr valdsmerki, í inum efra endanum með flúrum gǫrt, innar hagligustu smíðar: leggr viðarins var allr klæddr af gulli ok settr með fingrgullssteinum; gulllaufin váru it bezta Arabíagull; en á inu efra laufi vandarins var skorinn fugl með fjǫðrum ok alls konar li*t*um fjaðranna ok fullgǫrt at vængjum, blakandi sem hann væri kvikr ok

18 bauk] bauðk. 32 lifum, *but corrected in the manuscript.*

lifandi. Þessi líkneskja var klædd inum bezta purpura með hvítum skinnum; en þar fyrir var hon klædd purpurapelli, at purpurinn merkir harm, hrygð, válk ok vesǫlð er Ísǫnd þolði fyrir ástar sakir við Tristram. Í hœgri hendi helt hon fingrgulli sínu, ok þar var á ritat orð þau er Ísǫnd dróttning mælti í skilnað þeira: 'Tristram,' kvað hon, 'tak þetta fingrgull í minning ástar okkar, ok gleym eigi hǫrmum okkar, válk‹i› ok vesǫlðum, er þú hefir þolat fyrir mínar sakir ok fyrir þínar.'[5]

Undir fótum hennar var einn fótkistill steyptr af kopar í líking þess vánda dvergs er þau h*afði* rœgt fyrir konunginum ok hrópat;[6] líkneskjan stóð á brjósti honum því líkast sem hon skipaði honum undir fœtr sér, en hann lá opinn undir fótum hennar því líkt sem hann væri grátandi. Hjá líkneskjunni var gǫr af brenndu gulli lítil skemtan, rakki hennar, hǫfuð sitt skakandi ok bjǫllu sinni hringjandi, gǫrt með miklum hagleik.[7] En ǫðru‹m› megin dvergsins stóð ein líkneskja lítil, eptir Bryngvet, fylgismey dróttningar; hon var vel skǫpuð eptir fegrð sinni ok vel skrýdd inum bezta búnaði, ok helt sér í hendi keri með loki, bjóðandi Ísǫnd dróttningu með blíðu andliti. Umbergis kerit váru þau orð er hon mælti: 'Ísǫnd dróttning, tak drykk þennan, er gǫrr var á Írlandi Markis konungi.'[8] En ǫðru‹m› megin í herberginu, sem inn var gengit, hafði hann gǫrt eina mikla líkneskju í líking jǫtunsins, svá sem hann stœði þar sjálfr einfœttr ok reiddi báðum hǫndum járnstaf sinn yfir ǫxl sér at verja líkneskjuna; en hann var klæddr stóru bukkskinni ok loðnu — ok tók kyrtillinn honum skammt ofan, ok var hann nakinn niðr frá nafla — ok gnísti tǫnnum, grimmr í augum, sem hann vildi berja alla þá er inn gengu.[9] En ǫðru‹m› megin dyranna stóð eitt mikit león steypt af kopar ok svá hagliga gǫrt at enginn hugði annat en lifanda væri, þeir er þat sæi. Þat stóð á fjórum fótum ok barði hala sínum um eina líkneskju, er gǫr var eptir ræðismanni þeim er hrópaði ok rœgði Tristram fyrir Markis konungi.[10]

Enginn kann at tjá né telja þann hagleik er þar var á þeim líkneskjum er Tristram lét þar gøra í hválfinu. Ok hefir hann nú allt gǫrt þat er hann vill at sinni, ok fær nú í vald jǫtunsins ok bauð honum, sem þræli sínum ok þjónustumanni, þetta svá vel at varðveita at ekki skyldi þar nærri koma; en hann sjálfr bar lyklana bæði at hválfhúsinu ok líkneskjunum. En jǫtunninn hafði allt fé sitt frjálst annat. Ok líkaði þetta Tristram vel, er hann hefir slíku á leið komit.

42 hǫfðu.

Chapter 81

Sem Tristram hafði lokit starfi sínu, þá reið hann heim til kastala síns sem hann var vanr, etr ok drekkr ok sefr hjá Ísodd, konu sinni, ok var kærr með félǫgum sínum.[11] En eigi er honum hugr at eiga líkamslosta við konu sína, en þó fór hann leynt með, því engi maðr mátti ætlan hans né athœfi finna, því allir hugðu ‹at› hann byggði hjónskapliga sem hann skyldi með henni. En Ísodd er ok svá lunduð at hon leyndi fyrir hverjum manni svá tryggiliga at hon birti hvárki fyrir frændum sínum né vinum.[12] En þá er hann var í burtu ok gørði líkneskjur þessar, þá þótti henni mjǫk kynligt, hvar hann var eða hvat hann gørði.

Svá reið hann heim ok heiman um einn leynistíg at enginn varð varr við hann, ok kom svá til hválfhússins. Ok jafnan sem hann kom inn til líkneskju Ísǫndar, þá kyssti hann hana svá opt sem hann kom, ok lagði hana í fang sér ok hendr um háls sem hon væri lifandi, ok rœddi til hennar mǫrgum ástsamligum orðum um ástarþokka þeira ok harma. Svá gørði hann við líkneskju Bryngvetar, ok minntisk á ǫll orð þau er hann var vanr at mæla við þær. Hann minntisk ok á alla þá huggan, skemtan, gleði ok ynði er hann fekk af Ísǫnd, ok kyssti hvert sinn líkneskit, er hann íhugaði huggan þeira; en þá var hann hryggr ok reiðr, er hann minntisk á harm þeira, vás ok vesalðir, er hann þolði fyrir sakir þeira er þau hrópuðu, ok kennir þat nú líkneskju hins vánda ræðismanns.

Notes

[1] The giant, Moldagog, is introduced in ch. 73 as the owner and defender of the land. Tristram defeats him in single combat by chopping off one of his legs, at which point the giant swears loyalty to Tristram and surrenders his treasures along with his territory; in return Tristram fashions a wooden leg for his new vassal (ch. 76).

[2] Ch. 78 says that the main structure of the vaulted building had been made by an earlier giant who abducted the daughter of a certain Duke Orsl and brought her to the place, where he inadvertently killed her because of his size and weight (*sakir mikilleik‹s› hans ok þunga*) while trying to have sex. The fragments of Thomas's poem do not contain this story, but versions of it are told by Wace and Geoffrey of Monmouth.

[3] *Kvikt* and subsequent words modifying *líkneskja* have the neuter form, perhaps by attraction to *annat*. But *fullgǫrt* in line 33 (modifying *fugl*) and *gǫrt* in line 46 (modifying *skemtan* or *rakki*) are also neuter where one would expect masculine or feminine forms, and it is probably to be explained as the use of 'natural' gender (or rather referring to animals and statues as neuter, as often in English) and the tendency to looseness in grammar that is common in seventeenth-century manuscripts and was reversed by nineteenth-century purists. In all three cases the adjective is separated from its noun. Cf. Gr 3.9.8.2.

[4] The words *kórónan var* are to be understood in front of *sett*.

[5] The full account of the parting is in ch. 67.

[6] In the Norwegian original there would have been perfect alliteration on *rægt* and *hrópat* (*rópat*; the initial breathing in such words is early lost in Norwegian, see p. 65 above); likewise on the phrase *hryggr ok reiðr* in the final sentence of the extract. The dwarf, who appears for the first time in ch. 54, tries to gather evidence against the lovers by sprinkling flour between their beds so that King Markis will see Tristram's footprints (ch. 55). He is with the king when the lovers are discovered embracing in an orchard — the event that brings about their separation (ch. 67). There is no indication in the rest of the saga that he is ever punished for his enmity towards Tristram and Ísǫnd, or that he regrets it at all; nevertheless his tears, as depicted in the sculpture, are to be understood primarily as signifying remorse, though with

overtones of cowardice. In much Old Norse literature it is shameful for males to weep except when mourning a person of rank, but in the romances it is common even for heroes to weep at moments of strong emotion, as Tristram himself does when he parts from Ísǫnd (ch. 68).

[7] Ísǫnd's dog, a gift from Tristram, came originally from Elfland (*Álfheimar*, ch. 61). In the saga he is portrayed as a large animal that hunts wild boar and deer when Tristram and Ísǫnd are living together in the woods (chs 63 and 64); but Gottfried (line 16,659) specifies two separate animals and represents the one of elvish origin as a small lapdog (line 15,805). Ch. 61 of the saga lays much emphasis on the delights of sensory perception, commenting on the silkiness and wonderful colours of the dog's coat, and saying that the sound of his bell transported Tristram 'so that he hardly knew whether he was the same man or another one' (*svá at hann kenndi varla hvárt hann var inn sami eða annarr*).

[8] Ísǫnd's mother prepares a wine-like love potion and tells Bryngvet to serve it to Ísǫnd and King Markis on their wedding-night; but before Bryngvet can do so another servant finds it and unwittingly gives some to Ísǫnd and Tristram, thus causing all the pain that ensues from their love (ch. 46). Bryngvet perseveres with her instructions and serves more of the potion to Markis and his bride; on the evidence of the statue it appears that she hoped to rectify the situation by allowing Ísǫnd to fall in love with Markis, but ch. 46 says only that she gave the potion to the king without his knowledge, and that Ísǫnd did not drink it on that occasion.

[9] The giant's trouserless condition is not mentioned elsewhere. Possibly it is meant to recall what was said of the chamber's previous owner and his size (note 2 above); but in any case its message is clearly 'Keep out, or else'.

[10] Maríadokk, the steward referred to, is introduced as Tristram's friend and bed-partner, and as the man who first discovered the adulterous affair: he woke up in the night, noticed that Tristram was missing, went out in search of him and heard him talking with Ísǫnd (ch. 51). In the same chapter the saga states that it was not until a long time after this event that 'malicious persons' (*ǫfundarmenn*) told Markis

what was going on, and Maríadokk is not actually named as one of the tell-tales. Gottfried, however, states in his poem that the corresponding character, Marjodoc, quickly went to the king and pretended to have heard rumours (lines 13, 637–51). The end-on approach of the lion, which appears only in this passage, no doubt involves maximum disgrace for the steward.

[11] After parting with Ísǫnd, Tristram marries Ísodd, daughter of the duke of Brittany. The saga states bluntly that he does so either in the hope that new love will drive out old or because he wants a wife 'for benefit and pleasure' (*til gagns ok gamans*, ch. 69), this and the next sentence standing in place of much logic-chopping in Thomas (lines 235–420). On his wedding night, however, Tristram decides not to consummate the marriage because thoughts of Ísǫnd intrude, and he pretends to be ill (ch. 70). The assertion that his sickness was nothing else than pining for the other Ísǫnd (*ekki var ǫnnur sótt Tristrams en um aðra Ísǫnd*, ch. 70) confirms that in the saga, as in the poems of Thomas and Gottfried, the two women originally had the same name.

[12] Ísodd has promised Tristram not to tell anyone that they do not have sex (ch. 70). Ch. 96 suggests that at one point she thinks he wants to become a priest or monk — possibly a joke. Eventually a chance event forces her to tell her brother Kardín, who then construes Tristram's behaviour as an insult to the family (chs 82 and 83); but Kardín abandons any thought of a feud with Tristram when he sees the statue of Bryngvet, which he initially mistakes for a real woman, and falls in love (ch. 86). This, in fact, is the only narrative function fulfilled by the episode of the statues.

XIII: MARÍU SAGA

A Miracle of the Virgin Mary

Biographies of the saints and stories of miracles demonstrating their sanctity were among the most popular and influential literary forms of the Middle Ages. The earliest written texts brought to Iceland by Christian missionaries included Latin hagiographic narratives, and scholars have argued that they exerted seminal influence on the origins of Icelandic literature (see Turville-Petre 1953; Jónas Kristjánsson 1981 and 1986; Foote 1994).

Among the saints a special and pre-eminent place was accorded to Mary, the mother of Jesus. Her cult gained increasing importance in twelfth- and thirteenth-century Europe and in the thirteenth century the Marian prayer *Ave Maria* (known as *Maríuvers* in Old Norse) became one of the few texts all Christians were required to know by heart. Twice as many churches were dedicated to Mary as to the next most popular saint in pre-Reformation Iceland (St Peter) and she was the patron saint of Hólar Cathedral. Several Marian feasts were prominent in the Icelandic calendar and four were provided with sermons in the *Old Icelandic Homily Book*. A sizeable corpus of Marian poetry in Old Icelandic also survives (on the cult of Mary in Iceland see Cormack 1994, 126–29; some Marian poetry is accessible in Wrightson 2001).

Maríu saga is an Icelandic prose account of the life of the Virgin Mary that, unusually for this type of text, intersperses biographical narrative with theological reflection on a wide range of more or less closely related topics. The deeply learned saga-writer drew on a number of source texts including the Gospels of Matthew and Luke, the apocryphal Gospel known as Pseudo-Matthew, and especially *Evangelium de nativitate Mariae*, an apocryphal account of the birth and early life of Mary believed during the Middle Ages to be by St Jerome. For historical background the writer used Books 16 and 17 of *Antiquities of the Jews* by the first-century Jewish historian Flavius Josephus; and other sources include various books of the Old and New Testaments and texts by Saints Jerome, Gregory the Great, Augustine and John Chrysostom.

A detailed description of the Fourth Lateran Council in chapter 23 of *Maríu saga* indicates that the saga must have been written after

1215. *Guðmundar saga* records that a saga of the Virgin Mary was written by a priest called Kygri-Bjǫrn Hjaltason (died 1237/38) and as there is no evidence of any *Maríu saga* other than the one which survives circulating in Iceland before the sixteenth century it seems probable that Kygri-Bjǫrn composed the surviving text. This would mean it was written sometime between 1216 and 1236 (in which year Kygri-Bjǫrn was elected bishop of Hólar; he then went abroad, possibly to have his election confirmed, and died shortly after his return). Turville-Petre has suggested a slightly narrower dating of between 1224 and 1236 (Turville-Petre 1972, 107).

Fourteen of the nineteen surviving manuscripts of *Maríu saga* include collections of miracle stories involving the Virgin Mary (the other five manuscripts are fragments and may originally have included miracle stories too). An additional twenty-five manuscripts contain only miracle stories, without the saga, but as these are fragmentary manuscripts it remains unclear whether the saga and miracles were ever transmitted separately. The miracle collections vary in size, contents and origin; they appear in manuscripts dating from *c.*1225–50 onwards.

Unger's edition of *Maríu saga* (1871) prints two slightly different texts of the saga (from Holm perg. 11 4to and AM 234 fol.) and over 200 miracle stories, many of them in more than one version. Three different versions of a miracle of the Virgin are given below in texts normalised from Unger's edition (this miracle story, also known from Latin and Old French sources, is briefly discussed in Widding 1965, 132–35). The three versions illustrate three different prose styles. The earliest of the three is found in AM 232 fol., a fourteenth century manuscript (*c.*1350). The writer has rendered the narrative in a concise and straightforward style free of rhetorical elaboration and like that characteristic of the Sagas of Icelanders. The version in AM 635 4to, a paper manuscript from the early eighteenth century (*c.*1700–25), translates more closely from Latin, attempting greater fidelity to the style and language of the original and also providing much more circumstantial detail than AM 232 fol. The third text comes from Holm perg. 11 4to (*c.* 1325–75; some readings have been adopted from Holm perg. 1 4to (*c.* 1450–1500)). This is written in the so-called florid style, a 'high' style developed during the second half of the thirteenth century especially in religious writing. Characteristic features of the florid style found in the extract below include extensive use of adjectives and adverbs, the use of doublets, and use of the present participle where Saga Style would prefer a clause with a finite verb. A delight in rhetorical amplification that is another characteristic of the Florid Style is also notable in this, the longest of the three accounts of the miracle.

Bibliography

C. R. Unger, ed., *Mariu saga: Legender om Jomfru Maria og hendes jertegn* (1871). [The standard edition]

Ásdís Egilsdóttir, Gunnar Harðarson, Svanhildur Óskarsdóttir, eds, *Maríukver: sögur og kvæði af heilagri guðsmóður frá fyrri tíð* (1996). [An edition of the saga, selected miracles and a variety of other medieval Icelandic Marian texts, in modernised Icelandic]

Margaret Cormack, *The Saints in Iceland: Their Veneration from the Conversion to 1400*, Subsidia hagiographica 78 (1994).

Margaret Cormack, 'Sagas of Saints', in Margaret Clunies Ross, ed., *Old Icelandic Literature and Society* (2000), 302–25.

Peter Foote, 'Saints' Lives and Sagas', in Hans Bekker-Nielsen and Birte Carlé, eds, *Saints and Sagas: A Symposium* (1994), 73–88.

Jónas Kristjánsson, 'Learned Style or Saga Style?' in Ursula Dronke *et al.*, eds, *Speculum Norroenum: Norse Studies in Memory of Gabriel Turville-Petre* (1981), 260–92.

Jónas Kristjánsson, 'The Roots of the Sagas', in Rudolf Simek, *et al.*, eds, *Sagnaskemmtun: Studies in Honour of Hermann Pálsson on his 65th Birthday, 26 May 1986* (1986), 183–200.

G. Turville-Petre, *Origins of Icelandic Literature* (1953).

G. Turville-Petre, 'The Old Norse Homily on the Assumption and *Maríu saga*,' *Mediaeval Studies* 9 (1947), 131–40; reprinted in his *Nine Norse Studies* (1972), 102–17.

Ole Widding *et al.*, 'The Lives of the Saints in Old Norse Prose: A Handlist,' *Mediaeval Studies* 25 (1963), 294–337. [Lists manuscripts of *Maríu saga* and the associated miracle stories on pp. 321–24]

Ole Widding, 'Jartegn og Maríu saga. Eventyr', in Hans Bekker-Nielsen *et al.*, *Norrøn fortællekunst: kapitler af den norsk–islandske middelalderlitteraturs historie* (1965), 127–36.

Ole Widding, 'Norrøne Marialegender på europæisk baggrund', *Opuscula* X, *Bibliotheca Arnamagnæana* XL (1996), 1–128. [A detailed comparison of the contents of the surviving Norse miracle collections and analysis of their relations to contemporary Latin collections; English summary on pp. 125–28]

Kellinde Wrightson, ed., *Fourteenth-Century Icelandic Verse on the Virgin Mary. Drápa af Maríugrát. Vitnisvísur af Maríu. Maríuvísur I–III* (2001).

XIII: MARÍU SAGA

A Miracle of the Virgin Mary

AM 232 fol.:

Munklífi eitt var í fjalli því, er Tumba[1] heitir. Þar stóð Mikjáls kirkja hjá munklífinu. Í musterin*u* var Maríu líkneskja, ok svá ger sem Dróttinn sæti í knjám henni, ok var silkidúkr breiddr yfir hǫfuð þeim. Þar kómu opt reiðar stórar ok eldingar, ok laust eitt sinn svá kirkjuna, at hon brann ǫll, en líkneskja Maríu var heil, ok svá stallrinn, er hon stóð á. Hvergi var á silkidúkinn runnit, er á líkneskjunni var. Munkar lýstu þessi jartegn, ok lofuðu allir Guð, þeir er heyrðu. Vér eigum þess Guð at biðja, at hann leysi oss svá frá eilífum eldi sem líkneskit frá þessum eldshita.

AM 635 4to:

Eldr brenndi eigi líkneski várrar frú

Í fjalli því, er Tumba heitir í sjónum, er kirkja hins helga Michaelis engils. Í þeim stað er mikill fjǫlði munka, er þar þjóna Guði. Þat bar til einn tíma, at með leyndum Guðs dómi[2] sló elding kirkjuna ok brenndi hana alla. Þar var líkneskja Guðs móður Marie ger með tré. Yfir hǫfðinu líkneskjunni var einn silkidúkr. Sem eldrinn kom til þess staðar, er skriptin stóð í, brenndi hann allt umkringis, en sjálfa líknes-kjuna tók ekki, sem hann óttaðisk at koma henni nær, svá at eigi brann þat silkitjald sem var yfir líkneskjunni, ok eigi døkknaði þat sjálft af reyk eðr hita. Eitt flabellum gert með páfuglafjǫðrum, er studdisk við líkneskit, brann ok eigi. Gerði Guð þessa jartegn at sýna viðrkvæmiligt vera, at eigi mætti eldrinn granda líkneskju þeirar, sem með hjarta ok líkam helt heilagt skírlífi með ǫðrum dygðum, svá at engi hiti lostasemi mátti tendrask með henni. Svá hlífði Guðs móðir, sem þér heyrðuð, sinni líkneskju í eldinum sýnandi með því, at hon má auðveldliga með Guðs miskunn frelsa frá helvítis eldi þá sem henni þjóna.

2 musterinn.

Holm perg. 11 4to:

Eldr grandaði eigi líkneski várrar frú.

Svá er sagt, at eitt munklífi með miklum mannfjǫlða í regluligum lifnaði hreins skírlífis stendr á fjalli því, er Tumba heitir. Þar er Michials kirkja hjá munklífinu. Í því musteri var líkneski várrar frú sancte Marie sœmiliga með tré formeruð á þann hátt, sem Dróttinn várr sæti í knjám henni ok væri dúkr af silki breiddr yfir hǫfuð þeim. Í sǫgðum stað kómu opt stórar reiðarþrumur ok eldingar, ok einn tíma kom svá hryggiliga til efnis, at kirkjuna laust, svá at hon brann ǫll ok hvert þat herbergi, sem þar stóð nærri umbergis. En fyrr sǫgð líkneskja Guðs móður var heil ok óskǫdd, svá sem eldrinn hefði hana óttazk, týnandi allri sinni grimmðarnáttúru svá framarliga, at engis kyns reykjarþefr eða eldsbrunalitr hafði heldr snortit sagðan dúk en sjálfa líkneskjuna, slíkt sama fótstallinn, er hon stóð á. Lýstu munkar þessi jartegn, ok lofuðu allir Guð, er heyrðu. Þat var viðrkvæmiligt ok vel trúanligt, sem birtisk í sǫgðu stórtákni, at þess*a* heims eldr þyrði eigi at snerta þeirar líkneskju, sem bæði var hrein mær í hug ok líkama, flekklaus með ǫllum greinum af hverjum sem einum bruna veraldligra girnda. Nú sem Guðs móðir sancta María, vernda‹n›di sína líkneskju, sem vér sǫgðum, af þeim eldsbruna, gefr oss fullkomliga skilja, at sér þjónandi menn má hon auðveldliga frelsa af eilífum eldi, því[3] sém ‹vér› iðuliga verandi í hennar þjónustu standandi, at hon sé oss veitandi sem vér erum mest þurfandi, sem ‹er› alla hluti fáandi, af sínum sœtasta syni þiggjandi, þeim er lifir ok ríkir með feðr ok helgum anda útan enda. Amen.

40 þessi *Holm perg. 11 4to.* 43 verndandi *Holm perg. 1 4to*; verndaði *Holm perg. 11 4to.* 46 vér iðuliga *Holm perg. 1 4to*; iduligast *Holm perg. 11 4to.*

Notes

[1] A church was built on Mount Tumba, near Avranches in south Normandy, after an apparition of the Archangel St Michael there in the eighth century. In AD 1000 a Benedictine monastery was established on the mount, which now takes its name, le Mont-Saint-Michel, from the Archangel who appeared there.

[2] In Latin *occulto Dei iudicio*, a phrase often used of events in which God moved in a mysterious way. Cf. Job 11: 7–9; Romans 11: 33. Cf. also XIV:11 below.

[3] *því* ('for this reason') seems to introduce the main clause in this immensely complicated sentence.

XIV: JÓNS SAGA HELGA

The first native bishop in Iceland was Ísleifr Gizurarson. He was consecrated in 1056 as bishop of the whole population. He was succeeded in 1081 by his son, Gizurr (died 1118), whose patrimony, Skál(a)holt, in the south of the country, was made the official episcopal seat by an act of the Alþingi. About 1100 Bishop Gizurr agreed that the people of the Northern Quarter should have a bishop of their own, with a cathedral at Hólar in Hjaltadalr (Skagafjǫrðr). With the approval of clergy and people he selected a middle-aged priest from the South of Iceland, Jón Ǫgmundarson (born 1052), as the first bishop of Hólar. Jón duly went abroad to seek archiepiscopal and papal sanction and in 1106 was consecrated in Lund (then of course in Denmark) by Ǫzurr (Asser), bishop there since 1089 but now newly installed as archbishop and metropolitan of the Scandinavian churches. Jón returned to Iceland by way of Norway where he collected a cargo of timber for the new church he intended to build as his cathedral. We have no contemporary record of his activities as diocesan of the Northern Quarter. He died in 1121.

In 1193 Bishop Þorlákr Þórhallsson of Skálholt died and miracles attributed to his intercession were soon reported. His cult was formally established by the Alþingi in 1199. This seems to have prompted the Northerners to seek a saint for themselves. Invocation of Jón Ǫgmundarson, their first bishop, was deemed successful, and Jón's *dies natalis,* 23 April, was made a day of national observance in 1200. Soon after, as was essential, a work on the new saint's *vita et acta* was composed in Latin by Gunnlaugr Leifsson, Benedictine monk of Þingeyrar (born *c.*1140, died 1219; cf. note 4 to extract below). At the same time, a similar book was composed in Icelandic; the author apparently borrowed some material from Gunnlaugr's work. This *Jóns saga Hólabyskups ins helga* is known in three recensions but only one of them exists as a unified work. This is the so-called S text, found whole in AM 234 fol., written *c.*1340, and in fragments in other manuscripts, the oldest in AM 221 fol., written *c.*1300. This recension is in a plain style and is an abridgment of an early work which is also represented in the so-called H recension. This is known only in two manuscripts, paper from the early seventeenth century, Holm papp. 4:o nr 4 and AM 392 4to, independent copies of a late medieval exemplar. Its style is like that of the S recension but it is generally fuller and probably often closer to the early text that was their common original. Unfortunately, it is defective at the beginning and has a large lacuna in the middle. The third recension, called L, is a revision, made *c.*1320–30, of a text more like H than S. It survives incomplete in Holm perg. fol. nr 5, written *c.*1365; part of the text missing there is supplied by fragments in AM 219 fol. from about 1400. The saga in this form has a good many passages rewritten in the Latinate style that became fashionable in Iceland towards 1300 and flourished especially between about 1320 and 1350 (cf. the introduction to extract XIII above). It is also unique in introducing two whole *þættir,* one concerning Sæmundr inn fróði Sigfússon (1056–1133), which is not found elsewhere, and one concerning Gísl Illugason, known separately in the compilation of kings' sagas found in the codexes called Hulda and Hrokkinskinna but adapted in L to suit the hagiographer's purpose.

The text printed below follows the S recension but with preference given to H in lines 17, 115–16, 128, 133–38 and 142, and to L in lines 155, 165–91 (see notes below). In this last passage typical features of 'florid' style and vocabulary are *sagðra* 168, 172, *hvern* 169, *prédikandi* 176, *undir stjórn ok yfirboði* 177, *ritandi* 178, *mektugir* 182, *jungfrú* 185, *sǫgðum* 186, *kynnandi* 190.

Bibliography

The text here is based on that in *Biskupa sögur* I (2003), *ÍF* XV, 202–20. There is a translation in *Origines Islandicae*, ed. and tr. Gudbrand Vigfusson and F. York Powell (1905, repr. 1976), I 534–67, and several extracts, including some of the text printed here, but from the L redaction, in *The Northmen Talk*, tr. Jaqueline Simpson (1965), 65–76.

Chapter 8

Á þessu sumri hóf Jón byskup yfirfǫr sína yfir ríki sitt ok tók at stýra Guðs kristni med mikilli stjórn. Hirti hann vánda menn af því veldi er honum var gefit af Guðs hálfu, en styrkti góða menn ok siðláta í mǫrgum góðum hlutum.

Inn helgi Jón byskup hafði skamma stund at stóli setit at Hólum áðr en hann lét leggja ofan kirkju þá er þar var. Sjá kirkja hafði gjǫr verit næst þeiri er Oxi Hjaltason hafði gjǫra látit. Þat hyggja menn at sú kirkja hafi mest gjǫr verit undir tréþaki á ǫllu Íslandi er Oxi lét gjǫra, ok lagði til þeirar kirkju mikil auðræði ok lét hana búa innan vel ok vandliga ok þekja blýi alla. En sú kirkja brann upp ǫll med ǫllu skrúði sínu *at* leyndum dómi Guðs.[1] Enn helgi Jón byskup lét gjǫra kirkju at Hólum mikla ok virðuliga, sú er stendr þar í dag, ok hefir hún þó verit bæði þakið ok margir hlutir aðrir at gjǫrvir síðan.[2] Enn helgi Jón byskup sparði ekki til þessar kirkjugjǫrðar þat er þá væri meiri Guðs dýrð en áðr ok þetta hús væri sem fagrligast gjǫrt ok búit. Hann valði þann mann til kirkjugjǫrðarinnar er þá þótti einnhverr hagastr vera. Sá hét Þóroddr ‹Gamlason›,[3] ok var bæði at inn helgi Jón sparði eigi at reiða honum kaupit mikit ok gott, enda leysti hann ok sína sýslu vel ok góðmannliga. Þat er sagt frá þessum manni at hann var svá næmr þá er hann var í smíðinni, þá heyrði hann til er prestlingum var kennd íþrótt sú er grammatica heitir, en svá loddi honum þat vel í eyrum af miklum næml*ei*k ok athuga at hann gjǫrðisk enn mesti íþróttamaðr í þess konar námi.

Þá er Jón hafði skamma stund byskup verit, þá lét hann setja skóla heima þar at staðnum vestr frá kirkjudyrum ok lét smíða vel ok vandliga, ok enn sér merki húsanna.[4] En til þess at stýra skólanum ok kenna þeim mǫnnum er þar settisk í, þá valði hann einn enn bezta klerk ok enn snjallasta af Gautlandi. Hann hét Gísli ok var Finnason. Hann reiddi honum mikit kaup til hvárstveggja, at kenna prestlingum ok at veita slíkt upphald heilagri kristni með sjálfum byskupi sem hann mátti sér við koma í kenningum sínum ok formælum. Ok ávalt er hann prédikaði fyrir fólkinu, þá lét hann liggja bók fyrir sér ok tók þar af slíkt er hann talaði fyrir fólkinu, ok gjǫrði hann þetta mest af forsjá ok lítillæti, at

11 ok *S*. 17 *from H and L*. 22 næmlæk *S*.

þar hann var ungr at aldri þótti þeim meira um vert er til hlýddu at þeir sæi þat at hann tók sínar kenningar af helgum bókum en eigi af einu saman brjóstviti. En svá mikil gipt fylgði þó hans kenningum at menninir þeir er til hlýddu kómusk við mjǫk ok tóku mikla skipan ok góða um sitt ráð. En þat er hann kenndi í orðunum þá sýndi hann þat í verkunum. Kenningar hans váru linar ok léttbærar ǫllum góðum mǫnnum, en vitrum mǫnnum þóttu vera skapligar ok skemtiligar, en vándum mǫnnum varð ótti at mikill ok sǫnn hirting. Um allar stórhátíðir þá var þar fjǫlmenni mikit, því at þannug var þá mikit erendi margra manna, fyrst at hlýða tíðum, svá fagrliga sem þær váru fram fœrðar, þar með boðorðum byskups ok kenningum þeim hinum dýrðligum er þar var þá kostr at heyra, hvárt sem heldr váru fram fluttar af sjálfum byskupi eða þessum manni er nú var frá sagt.

Skamma stund hafði enn helgi Jón byskup verit áðr hann tók at fœra siðu manna ok háttu mjǫk í annat efni en áðr hafði verit, gjǫrðisk hirtingasamr við ósiðamenn, en var blíðr ok hœgr ǫllum góðum mǫnnum, en sýndi á sjálfum sér at allt þat er hann kenndi í orðunum, þá fylldi hann þat í verkunum. Sýndisk svá vitrum mǫnnum þeim er gjǫrst vissu hans ráð at hann yrði sjaldan afhuga því er sjálfr Dróttinn mælti til sinna lærisveina: 'Luceat lux vestra coram hominibus ut videant opera vestra bona et glorificent patrem vestrum qui in celis est.'[5] Þessi orð mæla svá: 'Lýsi ljós yðart fyrir mǫnnum til þess at þeir sjái góð verk yður ok dýrki þeir fǫður yðarn þann er í himnum er.'

Enn helgi Jón byskup lagði ríkt við þat sem síðan hefir haldizk, at menn skyldu sœkja til tíða á helgum dǫgum eða á ǫðrum vanðatíðum, en bauð prest*u*num at segja optliga þá hluti er þeir þyrftu at vita. Hann bauð mǫnnum at hafa hversdagliga háttu sem kristnum mǫnnum sómir, en þat er at sœkja hvern dag síð ok snemma kross eða kirkju ok flytja þar fram bœnir sínar með athuga. Hann bauð at menn skyldu hafa, hverr í sínu herbergi, mark ins helga kross til gæzlu sjálfum sér. Ok þegar er maðrinn vaknaði, þá skyldi hann signa sik ok syngja fyrst Credo in Deum ok segja svá trú sína almáttkum Guði ok ganga svá síðan allan daginn vápnaðr med marki heilags kross, því er hann merkti sik með þegar er hann vaknaði, en taka aldrigi svá mat eða svefn eða drykk at maðr signi sik eigi áðr. Hann bauð hverjum manni at kunna Pater noster ok Credo in Deum ok minnask sjau sinnum tíða sinna á

55 til þess *repeated over column break.* 59 prestinum *S.*

hverjum degi, en syngja skylduliga hvert kveld áðr hann sofnaði Credo in Deum ‹ok› Pater noster.[6]

Ok at vér lúkum þessu máli í fám orðum, þá fekk hann svá samit siðu sinna undirmanna á skǫmmu bragði með Guðs fulltingi at heilug kristni í Norðlendingafjórðungi hefir aldrigi staðit með slíkum blóma, hvárki áðr né síðan, sem þá stóð meðan fólkit var svá sælt at þeir hǫfðu slíks byskups stjórn yfir sér. Hann bannaði ok með ǫllu alla óháttu ok forneskju eða blótskapi, gjǫrninga eða galdra ok reis í móti því með ǫllu afli, ok því hafði eigi orðit af komit með ǫllu meðan kristnin var ung. Hann bannaði ok alla hindrvitni þá er fornir menn hǫfðu tekit af tunglkvámum eða dœgrum eða eigna daga heiðnum mǫnnum eða guðum, sem er at kalla Óðins dag eða Þórs, ok alla þá hluti aðra er honum þóttu af illum rótum rísa.[7]

Leikr sá var mǫnnum tíðr er ófagrligr er, at kveðask skyldu at, karlmaðr at konu en kona at karlmanni, klækiligar vísur ok hæðiligar ok óáheyriligar. En þat lét hann af takask ok bannaði með ǫllu at gjǫra. Mansǫngs kvæði eða vísur vildi hann eigi heyra kveðin ok eigi láta kveða.[8] Þó fekk ‹hann› því eigi með ǫllu af komit.

Þat er sagt ífrá at hann kom á hljóð at Klœngr Þorsteinsson, sá er síðan varð byskup í Skálaholti, en var þá prestlingr ok ungr at aldri, las bók þá er kǫlluð er Ovidius Episto‹la›rum.[9] Í þeiri bók býr mansǫngr mikill. En hann bannaði honum at lesa þess konar bœkr ok kallaði þó hverjum manni mundi œrit hǫfugt at gæta sín við líkamligri munúð ok rangri ást, þó at hann kveykti eigi upp hug sinn til þess meðr ne einum siðum eða þess konar kvæðum.

Hann var ok iðinn at því at sníða af mǫnnum ljóta ‹lǫstu›, ok svá fór hann kœnliga með því at sá kom náliga engi á hans fund at eigi fengi hann á nǫkkura lund leiðréttan fyrir sakir guðligrar ástar ok kostgæfi þeirar er hann lagði á hverjum manni at hjálpa. Ok ef hann lagði mǫnnum harðar skriptir á hendr fyrir sakir mikilla glœpa, en þeir gengi undir vel ok lítillátliga, þá var skammt at bíða áðr helgasta hans brjóst, þat er heilagr andi hafði valit sér til byggðar, þá samharmaði þeira meinlætum ok létti ‹hann› þá nǫkkut skriptunum. Ok þá sǫmu menn[10] er hann hafði fyrr barða fyrir sakir guðligrar ástar ok umvandanar, þeim hinum sǫmum líknaði hann þá miskunnsamliga er þeir váru við skilðir sína annmarka. Ok sá er alla sína undirmenn elskaði sem brœðr eða

101 samharmaði] + hann *S*.

syni, þá fœddisk hann af engra manna annmǫrkum eða vanhǫgum, en samfagnaði því er ǫðrum gekk vel en harmaði þat allt er annan veg varð. Hann var maðr svá huggóðr at varla mátti hann sjá eða vita þat er mǫnnum var til meins, en svá ǫrr ok mildr við fátœka menn at varla hafði hans maki fengizk. Hann var sannr faðir allra fátœkra manna. Huggaði hann ekkjur ok fǫðurlausa, ok engi kom svá harmþrunginn á hans fund at eigi fengi á nǫkkurn veg huggan af hans tilstilli. Svá var hann ástsæll við allt fólk at engi vildi náliga honum í móti gjǫra, ok var þat meirr fyrir sakir guðligrar ástar þeirar er allir menn unnu honum en líkamligrar hræzlu. ‹Skǫrugliga flutti hann fram alla þá hluti er til byskupligs embættis kómu,›[11] ok þar er hann braut sína fýsi í marga staði en gjǫrði Guðs vilja, ef hann fann þat at þat var eigi allt eitt fyrir sakir líkamligs eðlis, þá launaði Guð honum þat svá í hǫnd þegar at hann okaði undir hann alla hans undirmenn í heilagri hlýðni.

En heilagr Johannes lifði líf sitt eptir guðligri setningu ok góðra manna dœmum, var á bœnum nætr ok daga, vakði mikit ok fastaði lǫngum ok deyddi sik í mǫrgum hlutum til þess at þá mætti hann meira ávǫxt gjalda Guði en áðr af þeim hlutum ǫllum er honum váru á hendi fólgnir. Ok til þess at hann mætti þá vera frjálsari en áðr tíðir at veita eða formæli eða aðra hluti þá fram at fœra er Guðs kristni væri mest upphald at, þá valði hann menn til forráða fyrir staðinn með sér þá er fyrir skyldu sjá staðarins eign, með húsfreyju þeiri gǫfugri er hann hafði áðr átta ‹er Valdís hét›.[12] Einn af þeim mǫnnum var prestr virðuligr sá er Hámundr hét Bjarnarson. Hann var afi Hildar nunnu ok einsetukonu sem enn man getit verða síðar í þessu máli. Næst Hámund*i* var at ráðum prestr sá er Hjalti hét ok var frændi byskups. Af leikmǫnnum var sá maðr me‹st› í ráðum er var gǫfugr at ætt. Hann hét Ǫrn ok var son Þorkels af Víðimýri. Þessir menn hǫfðu aðra menn at undir sér, þá er sumir ǫnnuðusk um eign staðarins eða lǫnd, en sumir um vinnu eða aðra iðju á staðnum, sumir at hirða verkfœri eðr greiða fyrir um verkreiða, ‹sumir› til ferða, sumir til atflutninga til staðarins, sumir at þjóna fátœkum mǫnnum, ok var byskup áminnandi at þat væri myskunnsamliga gjǫrt, sumir at taka við gestum ok veita þeim beina,[13] því at á hverri hátíð sóttu menn á fund byskups, hundrað manna eða stundum tvau hundruð eða nǫkkuru fleiri, því at hinn heilagi Jón byskup hafði

115–16 *inserted from H.* 128 *inserted from H.* 130 Hámunda *S.* 133–38 Þessir . . . beina *thus H.*

þat í formælum sínum at honum þótti því at einu til fulls ef hverr maðr í ‹hans sýslu ok allra helzt innan› heraðs, sá er fǫng hefði á, kœmi *um* sinn hit sjaldnasta at vitja staðarins at Hólum á tólf mánuðum. Ok fyrir þá sǫk varð þar svá fjǫlmennt at skírdegi eða páskum at þar skorti þá eigi fjǫgur hundruð manna allt saman, karlar ok konur. Ok þó at margir af þessum mǫnnum hefði vistir með sér, þá váru hinir fleiri er á byskups kosti váru, ok af honum váru saddir bæði andligri fœzlu ok líkamligri, ok styrktir með byskupligri blezan fóru með fagnaði til sinna heimkynna.

Margir siðlátir menn réðusk þangat heim til staðarins ok gáfu fé með sér, en sumir fœddu sik sjálfir til þess at hlýða kenningum byskups ok tíðagjǫrð, ok gjǫrðu sér hús umhverfis kirkjugarðinn.

Heilagr Jón byskup tók marga menn til læringar ok fekk til góða meistara at kenna þeim, Gísla Finnason, er fyrr gátum vér, at kenna grammaticam, en ‹einn franzeis,› Ríkina prest, kapulán sinn ok ástvin, at kenna sǫng eða versagjǫrð, því at hann var ok hinn mesti lærdómsmaðr.[14] Þá var þat ekki hús náliga er eigi væri nǫkkut iðnat í þat er til nytsemðar var. Þat var hinna ellri manna háttr at kenna hinum yngrum, en hinir yngri rituðu þá er náms varð í milli. Þeir váru allir samþykkir, ok eigi deildu þeir ok engi ǫfundaði annan. Ok þegar er til var hringt tíða, þá kómu þeir þar allir ok fluttu fram tíðir sínar með miklum athuga. Var ekki at heyra í kórinn nema fagr sǫngr ok heilagt bœnahald. Hinir ellri menn kunnu sér at vera vel siðaðir, en smásveinar váru svá hirtir af meistǫrum sínum at þeir skyldu eigi treystask með gáleysi at fara.

Allir hinir sœmiligstu kennimenn í Norðlendingafjórðungi váru nǫkkura hríð til náms at Hólum, þá sem várr aldr, segir bróðir Gunnlaugr, mátti muna, sumir af barndómi, sumir á fulltíða aldri. Margir af sagðra meistara lærisveinum ǫnduðusk á várum dǫgum. En einn af þeim varð Ísleifr Hallsson, hvern Jón byskup œskti at verða skyldi byskup næst eptir hann ok ténaðarmann[15] síns byskupsdóms ef hann mœddi elli, en hann andaðisk fyrr en herra byskup. En at ek nefna nǫkkura sagðra lærisveina, þá er ek sá mínum augum, var einn af þeim Klœngr er síðan var byskup í Skál‹a›holti. Var hann tólf vetra gamall á hendi fólginn Jóni byskupi af móður sinni til frœðináms, ok varð hann hinn bezti klerkr ok var lengi síðan sœmiligr kennimaðr í Hólakirkju, hinn mesti upphaldsmaðr kristninnar, prédikandi fagrliga

142 *inserted from H.* heraðinu *S.* til *S.* 155 *inserted from L.* 165–91 *from L.*

Guðs orð undir stjórn ok yfirboði tveggja Hólabyskupa, Ketils ok Bjarnar. Hafði hann marga vaska lærisveina undir sér, ritandi bœkr margar ok merkiligar, þær sem enn tjásk at Hólum ok víða annars staðar. Vilmundr var þar ok lærðr, er fyrstr var ábóti á Þingeyrum, svá ok Hreinn er þar var hinn þriði ábóti. Margir váru ok þar aðrir í skóla, þeir er síðan urðu mektugir kennimenn, Ísleifr Grímsson, frændi byskups, Jón svarti, Bjarni Bergþórsson, Bjǫrn, er síðan var hinn þriði byskup at Hólum, ok margir aðrir þeir er langt er frá at segja. Þar var ok í frœðinæmi hreinferðug jungfrú er Ingunn hét. Øngum þessum var hon lægri í sǫgðum bóklistum. Kenndi hon mǫrgum grammaticam ok frœddi hvern er nema vildi. Urðu því margir val menntir undir hennar hendi. Hon rétti mjǫk latínubœkr, svá at hon lét lesa fyrir sér, en hon sjálf saumaði, tefldi eða ‹vann› aðrar hannyrðir meðr heilagra manna sǫgum, kynnandi mǫnnum Guðs dýrð eigi at eins meðr orðum munnnáms heldr ok meðr verkum handanna.[16]

187 margir val *repeated.*

Notes

[1] *at leyndum dómi Guðs* = Latin *occulto Dei iudicio*. Cf. XIII:13 above and note.

[2] According to H and L, Bishop Jón shipped a cargo of Norwegian timber to Iceland on his return voyage from Lund. (Icelanders had the right to free timber from Norwegian forests that were royal property; cf. *Laws* II 211.) This information is omitted in S. Oxi Hjaltason's church was probably built about 1050. It is not known when it burned down and when it was replaced by the church Bishop Jón demolished to make way for his new cathedral. Jón's church stood, though repaired from time to time, until about 1290.

[3] Þóroddr is called Gamlason in H and L. He has been identified as the Þóroddr *rúnameistari* mentioned in connection with a grammatical treatise, possibly the man of the same name who was a householder in Dalasýsla (western Iceland) in the first half of the twelfth century.

[4] *ok enn sér merki húsanna* is absent in H. L has *hvern* [sc. *skóla*] *vér sám með várum augum, segir bróðir Gunnlaugr, er latínusǫguna hefir saman sett.*

[5] 'Let your light so shine before men, that they may see your good works, and glorify your Father which is in heaven' (Matt. 5: 16).

[6] The Apostles' creed and the Lord's prayer were obligatory learning; see *Laws* I 26. In the course of the thirteenth century the Hail Mary was included as part of this basic Christian knowledge. The ultimate source for the seven canonical hours observed daily by men in secular orders and members of monastic foundations was Psalm 119: 164 (Vulgate 118: 164), 'Seven times a day do I praise thee . . .' (so in the Authorised Version). Laymen were also encouraged to observe them as far as possible.

[7] The reform which abolished old weekday names that had reference to pagan deities is attributed to St Silvester (pope 313–35). It became common form in the Latin liturgical calendar but elsewhere in Western Europe was effective, at least in large part, only in Icelandic and Portuguese.

[8] Exchange of scurrilous or lewd verses, often impromptu, is attested in various sources though, naturally enough, few texts of this kind have survived. Such pastimes were always frowned on by churchmen. *Mansǫngr*, literally 'maid-song', referred to love-poetry in general; making and repeating such verse could be counted an offence punishable at law; see *Laws* II 198. The term *mansǫngr* was later used of the conventional introduction to *rímur*, often addressed to a lady or ladies, but not always with love as the theme. See e.g. W. A. Craigie, *Specimens of Icelandic Rímur* I (1952), 291–93; T. Gunnell, *The Origins of Drama in Scandinavia* (1995), 85–86, 144, 346–48.

[9] Ovid's verse-epistles are *Epistulae Heroidum* and *Epistulae ex Ponto*, and presumably the title in S and H refers to the former (on the fateful loves of notable ladies). For the summary remark in S, *Í þeiri bók býr mansǫngr mikill*, H has: *En í þeiri bók kennir þeim er les brǫgð til þess er horfir til saurlífis ok munaðsemi*; and L has: *En í þeiri bók talar meistari Ovidius um kvenna ástir ok kennir meðr hverjum hætti menn skulu þær gilja ok nálgask þeira vilja*. These descriptions and the account of Bishop Jón's reaction are much more appropriate to Ovid's *Ars amatoria*, as the title in L, *de arte*, makes explicit. The switch to *[liber] Epistolarum* in the joint source of S and H may stem from some editorial delicacy. All Ovid's works, including the *Art of Love*, were common school reading in the Middle Ages.

[10] The object of *líknaði* is *þá sǫmu menn . . . þeim inum sǫmum*. The first phrase is acc., the second dat.; *líkna* normally takes the dat., and the explanation of the discrepancy is presumably that the writer did not know what verb was to come when he began writing the sentence. Cf. Text I, footnote to line 27 above, and Gr 3.9.8.2.

[11] The words *Skǫrugliga . . . kómu* are introduced from H.

[12] These men and Bishop Jón's wife, Valdís, are not mentioned in other sources.

[13] *Þessir menn* (line 133) . . . *veita þeim beina*: thus H. S has: *Þessir menn ǫnnuðusk mest þat er til staðarins kom ok skipuðu mǫnnum til sýslu, sumum til atflutningar við staðinn um þá hluti er ‹við þótti› þurfa. Sumir váru settir til verknaðar, sumir at þjóna fátœkum mǫnnum, ok var byskup vandr at því at þat væri miskunnsamliga gjǫrt,*

sumir at taka við gestum. L says only: *Sumir menn váru skipaðir at taka meðr gestum*.

[14] Ríkini has a German name and was probably Frankish rather than French. The description, *einn franzeis*, is in L, not in S; H lacks this paragraph and the rest of the extract.

[15] *-mann*: the case form is influenced by *hvern*, and would be correct in an acc. and inf. construction after *œskti*. It is possibly an instance of anacoluthon rather than an instance of the acc. form *mann* for nom. *maðr*, a substitution sometimes found in late fourteenth-century manuscripts.

[16] Lines 165–91 are from the L recension. A comparable passage in S is an abridgment of a similar text. Ketill Þorsteinsson was bishop of Hólar 1122–45, Bjǫrn Gilsson 1147–62. Vilmundr Þórólfsson was the first abbot of Þingeyrar, 1133–48; Hreinn Styrmisson was the third abbot there, 1166–71. The identity of Ísleifr Grímsson and Jón svarti is uncertain. Bjarni Bergþórsson is thought to be a priest of that name who is mentioned in other sources as an expert in *computus* (mathematics and astronomy) and nicknamed *inn tǫlvisi*; he died in 1173. Ingunn was probably the Inguðr Arnórsdóttir who is recorded as an informant in a list in Oddr*ÓT*, a list which is thought to be derived from Gunnlaugr Leifsson's work on the same king.

XV: LAXDŒLA SAGA

Laxdœla saga is generally thought to have been written about the middle of the thirteenth century, because of its fully developed style and structure, the reference made in it to earlier sagas and other written sources, and the apparent influence on it of European romance. At its centre is the 'love triangle' story involving Kjartan, Guðrún and Bolli, which echoes, and probably draws upon, the plot common to poets' sagas such as *Kormaks saga* and *Bjarnar saga Hítdœlakappa* (see Finlay 1997), but its range is much wider. It is the saga that perhaps most fully deserves the label 'Family Saga': not only is the descent of all the important characters traced from the one Norwegian chieftain, Ketill flatnefr, but many of the disputes that arise in its course involve family relationships, often the problematic ones between half- and foster-brothers, and marriage and divorce are among its prevailing themes. This in itself has the consequence that the role and concerns of women are unusually prominent in the saga, and the author's evident interest in and sympathy for a woman's point of view has led to speculation that the author may have been a woman (e.g. Kress 1986). It is not out of the question, of course, that a male author could enter into this point of view (an alternative candidate for authorship is Óláfr Þórðarson hvítaskáld, nephew of Snorri Sturluson and author of a treatise on prosody), particularly if, for whatever reason, he was writing for a predominantly female audience.

The feminine perspective is clear from the beginning of the saga in the unusually prominent role given to Unnr in djúpúðga, daughter of Ketill flatnefr, who takes on the conventionally masculine task of founding a settlement and a dynasty in Iceland; she is the ancestress of the Laxdœlir ('people of Laxárdalr'), the family from whom the saga derives its name, and to which Kjartan and Bolli belong. The saga relates the evolution of this family over several generations before Guðrún Ósvífrsdóttir (whose family is descended from one of Unnr's brothers) is introduced. The unusual elaboration of this early part of the saga, which goes far beyond the brevity of the conventional saga prelude, has prompted much discussion of the saga's structure; it is generally felt to introduce and define themes that play a part in the central conflict of the saga. Some have gone so far as to argue that, rather than building up a background against which Kjartan and Bolli can be seen as idealised and heroic figures (as Madelung 1972, for example, suggests), the opening chapters present Unnr as an exemplary figure, representing family loyalty and generosity, against which the behaviour of the three central figures is measured and found wanting (Conroy and Langen 1988). Ursula Dronke argues for a further moral decline in what she calls the 'Age of Pewter' (1979, 137) after the death of Kjartan.

The position of Guðrún as the focus of the saga is established not only by her dominant personality — believed to be partly modelled on two heroic women in the poems of the Poetic Edda, her namesake Guðrún Gjúkadóttir and the valkyrie Brynhildr, who is also cheated of the man she should have married — but also by the saga's marking out of her four marriages as a narrative sequence. This is achieved by Guðrún's four dreams in Chapter 33, which foreshadow the four marriages that the saga subsequently relates. The tidily predicted sequence is interrupted by her love for and loss of Kjartan, a pattern repeated in her dialogue at the very end of the saga with her son Bolli, who asks her ambiguously which man (*maðr* 'man', but possibly also 'husband') she has loved most. At first she responds with a comparison of the four men she has married; but her final reply, *Þeim var ek verst er ek unna mest* ('I treated worst the one I loved best'), must surely refer to Kjartan — though the question is debated to this day.

The earliest surviving (but fragmentary) manuscripts of *Laxdœla saga* are from the end of the thirteenth century. The only complete medieval version of the saga is in the mid-fourteenth-century Möðruvallabók, in which other Sagas of Icelanders (including *Kormaks saga* and *Njáls saga*) are also preserved (see Text XVIII). Editions of the saga are based on this text. The extract edited here follows the text of Möðruvallabók as it is represented in the editions of Kålund and Einar Ól. Sveinsson. The textual notes show where readings other than those of Möðruvallabók have been adopted; these readings are from late paper manuscripts, and may in many cases be scribal corrections. The Möðruvallabók text shows signs of later alteration which sometimes obscures the original reading; examples of this have not been noted here if the likely original reading is indicated by the evidence of other manuscripts.

Bibliography

Laxdœla saga, ed. Einar Ól. Sveinsson (1934). *ÍF* V.

Laxdœla saga, ed. Kr. Kålund (1889–91).

The Saga of the People of Laxardal, tr. Keneva Kunz. In *CSI* V 1–120. Other translations of the saga are reviewed in Auerbach 1998–2001.

Loren Auerbach, 'Female Experience and Authorial Intention in *Laxdœla saga*'. *Saga-Book* XXV (1998–2001), 30–52.

Heinrich Beck, '*Laxdœla saga* — A Structural Approach'. *Saga-Book* XIX (1974–77), 383–402.

Patricia Conroy and T. C. S. Langen, '*Laxdœla saga*: Theme and Structure'. *Arkiv för nordisk filologi* 103 (1988), 118–41.

Robert Cook, 'Women and Men in Laxdœla Saga'. *Skáldskaparmál* 2 (1992), 34–59.

Ursula Dronke, 'Narrative insight in *Laxdœla saga*'. In *J. R. R. Tolkien, Scholar and Story-teller: Essays in Memoriam*. Ed. Mary Salu and Robert T. Farrell (1979), 120–37.

Alison Finlay, 'Betrothal and Women's Autonomy in *Laxdœla saga* and the Poets' Sagas'. *Skáldskaparmál* 4 (1997), 107–28.

Hjalmar Falk, *Altwestnordische Kleiderkunde* (1919).

Judith Jesch, *Women in the Viking Age* (1991).

Jenny Jochens, *Women in Old Norse Society* (1995).

Helga Kress, '"You will find it all rather monotonous"; on Literary Tradition and the Feminine Experience in *Laxdœla saga*'. In *The Nordic Mind. Current Trends in Scandinavian Literary Criticism*. Ed. Frank Egholm Andersen and John Weinstock (1986), 181–95. [Originally published in Icelandic in *Konur skrifa, til heiðurs Önnu Sigurðardóttur* (1980), 97–109.]

Laws of Early Iceland I–II, tr. A. Dennis *et al.* (1998–2000).

Margaret Arendt Madelung, *The Laxdœla Saga: Its Structural Patterns* (1972). University of North Carolina Studies in the Germanic Languages and Literatures, 74.

XV: LAXDŒLA SAGA

Chapter 34: Af Þorvaldi

Þorvaldr hét maðr, sonr Halldórs Garpsdalsgoða. Hann bjó í Garpsdal í Gilsfirði, auðigr maðr ok engi hetja.[1] Hann bað Guðrúnar Ósvífrsdóttur á Alþingi þá er hon var fimmtán vetra gǫmul. Því máli var *eigi fjarri tekit*, en þó sagði Ósvífr at þat myndi á kostum finna, at þau Guðrún váru eigi jafnmenni. Þorvaldr talaði óharðfœrliga, kvazk konu biðja, en ekki fjár. Síðan var Guðrún fǫstnuð Þorvaldi, ok réð Ósvífr einn máldaga, ok svá var skilt, at Guðrún skyldi ein ráða fyrir fé þeira þegar er þau koma í eina rekkju, ok eiga alls helming, hvárt er samfarar þeira væri lengri eða skemmri. Hann skyldi ok kaupa gripi til handa henni svá at engi jafnfjáð kona ætti betri gripi, en þó mætti hann halda búi sínu fyrir þær sakar. Ríða menn nú heim af þingi. Ekki var Guðrún at þessu spurð, ok heldr gerði hon sér at þessu óg*eti*t, ok var þó kyrrt.[2] Brúðkaup var í Garpsdal at tvímánuði. Lítt unni Guðrún Þorvaldi ok var erfið í gripakaupum; váru engar gersimar svá miklar á Vestfjǫrðum at Guðrúnu þœtti eigi skapligt at hon ætti, en galt fjándskap Þorvaldi ef hann keypti eigi, hversu dýrar sem metnar váru. Þórðr Ingunnarson[3] gerði sér dátt við þau Þorvald ok Guðrúnu ok var þar lǫngum, ok fell þar m*ǫrg* umrœða á um kærleika þeira Þórðar ok Guðrúnar. Þat var eitt sinn at Guðrún beiddi Þorvald gripakaups. Þorvaldr kvað hana ekki hóf at kunna ok sló hana kinnhest.[4] Þá mælti Guðrún:

'Nú gaftu mér þat er oss konum þykkir miklu skipta at vér eigim vel at gǫrt, en þat er litarapt gott, ok af hefir þú mik ráðit brekvísi við þik.'

Þat sama kveld kom Þórðr þar. Guðrún sagði honum þessa svívirðing ok spurði hann hverju hon skyldi þetta launa. Þórðr brosti at ok mælti: 'Hér kann ek gott ráð til. Gerðu honum skyrtu ok brautgangs hǫfuðsmátt ok seg skilit við hann fyrir þessar sakar.'[5]

Eigi mælti Guðrún í móti þessu, ok skilja þau talit. Þat sama vár segir Guðrún skilit við Þorvald ok fór heim til Lauga. Síðan var gǫrt féskipti þeira Þorvalds ok Guðrúnar, ok hafði hon helming fjár alls, ok var nú meira en áðr. Tvá vetr hǫfðu þau ásamt verit. Þat sama vár seldi Ingunn land sitt í Króksfirði þat sem síðan heitir á Ingunnarstǫðum, ok fór vestr á Skálmarnes; hana hafði átt Glúmr Geirason,

3–4 svarat *M*. 13 ógott (?) *M*. 19 mjǫk *M*. 24 þú] *written twice in M*.

sem fyrr var ritat. Í þenna tíma bjó Hallsteinn goði á Hallsteinsnesi fyrir vestan Þorskafjǫrð; hann var ríkr maðr ok ‹meðallagi› vinsæll.

Chapter 35: Af Kotkeli ok Grímu

Kotkell hét maðr er þá hafði út komit fyrir litlu. Gríma hét kona hans; þeira synir váru þeir Hallbjǫrn slíkisteinsauga ok Stígandi. Þessir menn váru suðreyskir. Ǫll váru þau mjǫk fjǫlkunnig ok inir mestu seiðmenn. Hallsteinn goði tók við þeim ok setti þau niðr at Urðum í Skálmar‹firði›, ok var þeira byggð ekki vinsæl.

Þetta sumar fór Gestr ‹til þings ok fór› á skipi til Saurbœjar sem hann var vanr. Hann gisti á Hóli í Saurbœ. Þeir mágar léðu honum hesta, sem fyrr var vant.[6] Þórðr Ingunnarson var þá í fǫr með Gesti ok kom til Lauga í Sælingsdal. Guðrún Ósvífrsdóttir reið til þings ok fylgði henni Þórðr Ingunnarson. Þat var einn dag er þau riðu yfir Bláskógaheiði — var á veðr gott — þá mælti Guðrún:

'Hvárt er þat satt, Þórðr, at Auðr, kona þín, er jafnan í brókum ok setgeiri í, en vafit spjǫrrum mjǫk í skúa niðr?'[7]

Hann kvazk ekki hafa til þess fundit.

'Lítit bragð mun þá at,' segir Guðrún, 'ef þú finnr eigi, ok fyrir hvat skal hon þá heita Bróka-Auðr?'

Þórðr mælti, 'Vér ætlum hana litla hríð svá hafa verit kallaða.'

Guðrún svarar, 'Hitt skiptir hana in meira, at hon eigi þetta nafn lengi síðan.'

Eptir þat kómu menn til þings; er þar allt tíðindalaust. Þórðr var lǫngum í búð Gests ok talaði jafnan við Guðrúnu. Einn dag spurði Þórðr Ingunnarson Guðrúnu hvat konu varðaði ef hon væri í brókum jafnan svá sem karlar. ‹Guðrún svarar:›

'Slíkt víti á konum at skapa fyrir þat á sitt hóf sem karlmanni, ef hann hefir hǫfuðsmátt ‹svá› mikla at sjái geirvǫrtur hans berar, brautgangssǫk hvárttveggja.'[8]

Þá mælti Þórðr, 'Hvárt ræðr þú mér at ek segja skilit við Auði hér á þingi eða í heraði, ok gera ek þat við fleiri manna ‹ráð›, því at menn eru skapstórir, þeir er sér mun þikj‹a› misboðit í þessu?'

Guðrún svarar stundu síðar, 'Aptans bíðr óframs sǫk.'

Þá spratt Þórðr þegar upp ok gekk til Lǫgbergs ok nefndi sér vátta at hann segir skilit við Auði, ok fann þat til saka at hon skarsk í setgeirabrœkr sem karlkonur.[9] Brœðrum Auðar líkar illa ok er þó kyrrt.

Þórðr ríðr af þingi med þeim Ósvífrssonum. En er Auðr spyrr þessi tíðindi, þá mælti hon:

Vel er ek veit þat,
var ek ein um látin.

Síðan reið Þórðr til féskiptis vestr til Saurbœjar með tólfta mann ok gekk þat greitt, því at Þórði var óspart um hversu fénu var skipt. Þórðr rak vestan til Lauga mart búfé. Síðan bað hann Guðrúnar; var honum þat mál auðsótt við Ósvífr, en Guðrún mælti ekki í móti. Brullaup skyldi vera at Laugum at tíu viku‹m› sumars; var sú veizla allskǫrulig. Samfǫr þeira Þórðar ok Guðrúnar var góð. Þat eitt helt til at Þorkell hvelpr ok Knútr fóru eigi málum á hendr Þórði Ingunnarsyni, at þeir fengu eigi styrk til. Annat sumar eptir hǫfðu Hólsmenn selfǫr í *Hvamms-dal*; ‹var› Auðr at seli. Laugamenn hǫfðu selfǫr í Lambadal; sá gengr v‹est›r í fjǫllin *af Sælingsdal*. Auðr spyrr þann mann er smalans gætti hversu opt hann fyndi smalamann *frá Laugum*. Hann kvað þat jafnan vera, sem líkligt var, því at *háls einn* var á milli *seljanna*. Þá mælti Auðr: 'Þú skalt hitta í dag smalamann frá Laugum, ok máttu segja mér hvat manna er at vetrhúsum eða í seli, ok rœð allt vingjarnliga til Þórðar, sem þú átt at gera.'

Sveinninn heitr at gera svá sem hon mælti. En um kveldit, er smalamaðr kom heim, spyrr Auðr tíðinda. Smalamaðrinn svarar:

'Spurt hefi ek þau tíðindi er þér munu þykkja góð, at nú er breitt hvílugólf milli rúma þeira Þórðar ok Guðrúnar, því at hon er í seli en hann heljask á skálasmíð, ok eru þeir Ósvífr tveir at vetrhúsum.'

'Vel hefir þú njósnat,' segir hon, 'ok haf sǫðlat hesta tvá er menn fara at sofa.'

Smalasveinn gerði sem hon bauð, ok nǫkkuru fyrir sólarfall sté Auðr á bak, ok var hon þá at vísu í brókum. Smalasveinn reið ǫðrum hesti ok gat varla fylgt henni, svá knúði hon fast reiðina. Hon reið suðr yfir Sælingsdalsheiði ok nam eigi staðar fyrr en undir túngarði at Laugum. Þá sté hon af baki, en bað smalasveininn gæta hestanna meðan hon gengi til húss.

Auðr gekk at durum ok ‹var opin hurð›; hon gekk *til eldhúss* ok at lokrekkju þeiri er Þórðr lá í ok svaf. Var hurðin fallin aptr en eigi lokan fyrir. Hon gekk *í* lokrekkju*na*, en Þórðr svaf ok horfði í lopt

82 Lamba- *M*. 84 at baki dalnum *M*. 85 Þórðar *M*. 86 dalrinn *M*. ánna *M*. 103 inn *M*. 105 at lockreckiunni *M*.

upp. Þá vakði Auðr Þórð, en hann snerisk á hliðina er hann sá at maðr var kominn. Hon brá þá saxi ok lagði at Þórði ok veitti honum áverka mikla ok kom á hǫndina hœgri; varð hann sárr á báðum geirvǫrtum. Svá lagði hon til fast at saxit nam í beðinum staðar. Síðan gekk Auðr brott ok til hests ok hljóp á bak ok reið heim eptir þat.

Þórðr vildi upp spretta er hann fekk áverkann, ok varð þat ekki, því at hann mœddi blóðrás. Við þetta vaknaði Ósvífr ok spyrr hvat títt væri, en Þórðr kvazk orðinn fyrir áverkum nǫkkurum. Ósvífr spyrr ef hann vissi hverr á honum hefði unnit, ok stóð upp ok batt um sár hans. Þórðr kvazk ætla at þat hefði Auðr gǫrt. Ósvífr bauð at ríða eptir henni; kvað hana fámenna til mundu hafa farit, ok væri henni skapat víti. Þórðr kvað þat fjarri skyldu fara; sagði hana slíkt hafa at gǫrt sem hon átti.

Auðr kom heim í sólarupprás, ok spurðu þeir brœðr hennar hvert hon hefði farit. Auðr kvazk farit hafa til Lauga ok sagði þeim hvat til tíðinda hafði gǫrzk í fǫrum hennar. Þeir létu vel yfir ok kváðu of lítit mundu at orðit. Þórðr lá lengi í sárum, ok greru vel bringusárin, en sú hǫndin varð honum hvergi betri til taks en áðr.

Kyrrt var nú um vetrinn. En eptir um várit kom Ingunn, móðir Þórðar, vestan af Skálmarnesi. Hann tók vel við henni. Hon kvazk vilja ráðask undir áraburð Þórðar; kvað hon Kotkel ‹ok konu hans ok sonu› gera sér óvært í fjárránum ok fjǫlkynngi, en hafa mikit traust af Hallsteini goða. Þórðr veiksk skjótt við þetta mál ok kvazk hafa skyldu rétt af þjófum þeim þótt Hallsteinn væri at móti; snarask þegar til ferðar við tíunda mann. Ingunn fór ok vestr með honum. Hann hafði ferju ór Tjaldanesi. Síðan heldu þau vestr til Skálmarness. Þórðr lét flytja til skips allt lausafé þat er móðir hans átti þar, en smala skyldi reka fyrir innan fjǫrðu. Tólf váru þau alls á skipi; þar var Ingunn ok ǫnnur kona. Þórðr kom til bœjar Kotkels með tíunda mann; synir þeira Kotkels váru eigi heima. Síðan stefndi hann þeim Kotkeli ok Grímu ok sonum þeira um þjófnað ok fjǫlkynngi ok lét varða skóggang; hann stefndi sǫkum þeim til Alþingis ok fór til skips eptir þat.

Þá kómu þeir Hallbjǫrn ok Stígandi heim er Þórðr var kominn frá landi, ok þó skammt; sagði Kotkell þá sonum sínum hvat þar hafði í gǫrzk meðan þ*eir* váru eigi heima. Þeir brœðr urðu óðir við þetta ok kváðu menn ekki hafa fyrr gengit í berhǫgg við þau um svá mikinn

140 þat *M*.

fjándskap. Síðan lét Kotkell gera seiðhjall mikinn; þau fœrðusk þar á upp ǫll; þau kváðu þar ‹harðsnúin› frœði. Þat váru galdrar.[10] Því næst laust á hríð mikilli. Þat fann Þórðr Ingunnarson ok hans fǫrunautar, ‹þar sem hann var á sæ staddr›, ok til hans var gǫrt veðrit. Keyrir skipit vestr fyrir Skálmarnes. Þórðr sýndi mikinn hraustleik í sæliði. Þat sá þeir menn er á landi váru at hann kastaði því ǫllu er til þunga var, útan mǫnnum. Væntu þeir menn er á landi váru Þórði þá landtǫku, því at þá var af farit þat sem skerjóttast var. Síðan reis boði skammt frá landi, sá er engi maðr munði at fyrr hefði uppi verit, ok laust skipit svá at þegar horfði upp kjǫlrinn. Þar drukknaði Þórðr ok allt fǫruneyti hans, en skipit braut í spán, ok rak þar kjǫlinn er síðan heitir Kjalarey; skjǫld Þórðar rak í þá ey er Skjaldarey er kǫlluð. Lík Þórðar rak þar þegar á land ok hans fǫrunauta; var þar haugr orpinn at líkum þeira, þar er síðan heitir Haugsnes.

143 frœði] + sín, en *M*.

Notes

[1] Þorvaldr and his father Halldórr, together with their location in Garpsdalr and Þorvaldr's marriage to Guðrún, are mentioned in *Landnámabók* (*ÍF* I 160).

[2] The medieval collection of laws *Grágás*, written mostly in the thirteenth century but incorporating earlier material, confirms that betrothal was a contract between the prospective husband and the bride's male relatives (*Laws* II 53). Some saga narratives, however, represent women protesting at not being consulted (e.g. *Laxdœla saga* ch. 23), or suggest that a marriage arranged without the bride's consent could end in disaster (*Njáls saga* chs 9–11). Jenny Jochens (1995, 44–48) argues that this emphasis on consent arose as a response to the Church's insistence on marriage as a contract between equal partners.

[3] Þórðr was the son of the poet Glúmr Geirason (referred to in line 34), some of whose verses in honour of the son and grandson of King Haraldr hárfagri of Norway are cited in the Kings' Sagas, but his second name derives from the name of his mother Ingunn. He is said in *Laxdœla saga* (*ÍF* V 87) to be *sakamaðr mikill* 'much given to lawsuits'; his taste for litigation is evident in this extract and leads to his downfall.

[4] In other sagas too, the disgrace of a slap in the face triggers a wife's rebellion against her husband (*Bjarnar saga Hítdœlakappa* ch. 12, *Eyrbyggja saga* ch. 14, *Njáls saga* chs 11, 16, 48).

[5] *Grágás* (*Laws* II 63–66) refers to the possibility of divorce instigated by either party (though in this later, Christian, context the permission of the bishop is to be sought in many cases). On the basis of observations made by Arab and other visitors to Viking cultures (Jesch 91–92), as well as numerous references to divorce in the Sagas of Icelanders, this situation is generally thought to represent the remaining traces of a more liberal pre-Christian system of divorce virtually on demand, on grounds such as dishonour, or sexual or other incompatibility (Jochens 55–60). The wearing of women's clothes, such as the low-cut shirt referred to here, by a man was an offence in law (see note 8 below), but nowhere else is this referred to as grounds for divorce.

[6] The Gestr referred to is Gestr Oddleifsson, well-known in *Laxdœla saga* and elsewhere for his ability to foretell the future (in Chapter 33 he interprets the dreams of Guðrún as foreshadowing her four marriages). It is said on his introduction to the saga that he is in the habit of staying at Hóll with Þórðr and his two brothers-in-law (the *mágar* referred to here) on his way to the Alþingi.

[7] *Brœkr* 'breeches' here denotes an exclusively male garment. Falk (1919, 121) considers that the word could also apply to a garment worn by women (and that this is what makes Skarpheðinn's gift to Flosi of *brœkr blár* in chapter 123 of *Njáls saga* insulting), but that the feminine version would be open around the legs; in this case it is the additional specification of a piece let in to form the seat (*setgeiri í*) that identifies it as masculine wear. The word *spjarrar* has sometimes been taken to refer to the integral socks attached to one kind of (men's) trousers (*leistabrœkr*), but probably means bands of cloth wrapped around the lower legs; this is mentioned elsewhere as male dress.

[8] Wearing clothes proper to the opposite sex is prohibited in *Grágás* (*Laws* II 69–70), but is not said there to be grounds for divorce: 'If women become so deviant that they wear men's clothing, or whatever male fashion they adopt in order to be different, and likewise if men adopt women's fashion, whatever form it takes, then the penalty for that, whichever of them does it, is lesser outlawry.'

[9] *karlkonur*, plural of *karlkona* 'masculine woman', is found only in Möðruvallabók (other manuscripts have *karlmaðr* 'man' or *karlar* 'men'). The word does not occur in any other text.

[10] The most detailed account of the practice of the magic rite called *seiðr*, in chapter 4 of *Eiríks saga rauða*, also refers to a pedestal or platform on which the witch sits, in that case surrounded by women, one of whom chants a traditional poem, corresponding to the *galdrar* referred to here. The songs of the magician-family are said later in *Laxdœla saga* to sound pleasant (*fǫgr var sú kveðandi at heyra*); on this later occasion they cause the victim's immediate death, but more usually *seiðr* operates by influencing the weather, as in the case of Þórðr.

XVI: AUÐUNAR ÞÁTTR

The word *þáttr* (pl. *þættir*) in Old Icelandic meant literally 'a strand in a rope', but early developed various metaphorical meanings with the basic sense of 'a subsidiary part of something'. As a literary term it meant a short prose narrative constituting a chapter or integral episode in a saga. Though a few narratives that are classed as *þættir* are found as independent stories in manuscripts, the majority are found as parts of sagas, particularly Sagas of Kings. One group is associated with the missionary kings Óláfr Tryggvason and Óláfr Haraldsson, the saint, and the sagas of these kings contain various *þættir* relating to the victory of Christianity over heathendom in the late tenth and eleventh centuries. But the largest group of *þættir* is found in sagas of Haraldr harðráði (king of Norway 1046–66); some of these relate to the conflict between Haraldr harðráði and his kinsman Magnús góði Óláfsson during the period of their joint rule over Norway *c.*1046 (see *MS*, s.v. *þáttr*).

Many of the *þættir* may be older than the sagas in which they are preserved, and may originally have been independent stories. Linguistic archaisms in some of them (e.g., in *Auðunar þáttr, of, fyr, þars* and the suffixed pronoun *-k*) suggest that they may come from the earliest period of saga-writing in Iceland, the late twelfth century; there is little to support the idea that they were orally composed, but they are all anonymous. The majority that have survived have Icelanders as their main characters (there are 49 so-called *Íslendinga þættir*, 'Tales of Icelanders', in *CSI*), though these are often unhistorical and their adventures fictional. The story is often about how an insignificant Icelander travels abroad to a foreign (usually Norwegian) court and surmounts various difficulties to get the better of the foreigners, including the ruler himself, and returns to Iceland having made his fortune. Though the settings are historical, the events are mostly of minor historical significance. But the way in which these stories must have supported the developing feeling of Icelandic identity and national pride is obvious.

Auðunar þáttr follows this last pattern. Though nothing that happens in the story is impossible (gifts of polar bears from the Arctic to European rulers were not all that uncommon in the Middle Ages), it clearly has affinities to folk-tales (see *ÍF* VI, c–civ). Great emphasis is laid on the hero's *gæfa* or *gipta* 'luck', 'good fortune' (a sort of innate power emanating from a person predisposing his undertakings to success), though Auðunn is also presented as having a deal of skill in managing the eminent persons with whom he comes into contact. Auðunn is not known from other sources, though the *þáttr* says he came from the Western Fjords of Iceland (line 2) and the historical Þorsteinn Gyðuson (d. 1190; mentioned in *Sturlunga saga, Guðmundar saga biskups* and Icelandic annals; he lived on Flatey in Breiðafjǫrðr) is said to be descended from him (line 191 below). The story is supposed to take place about 1050–60 (the hostilities between Norway and Denmark referred to in line 33 continued, off and on, from soon after Magnús Óláfsson's death in 1047 until 1064; the events of these years are described in detail in *Morkinskinna, Fagrskinna* and *Heimskringla*; see Gwyn Jones, *A History of the Vikings* (1984), 406–08).

Auðunar þáttr survives in three versions. One is in *Morkinskinna* (GkS 1009 fol., written *c.*1275), a history of the kings of Norway from 1035–1177 probably first compiled *c.*1220 (see p. 63 above). A second is in *Flateyjarbók* (GKS 1005 fol.), a huge compilation of Kings' Sagas and other texts, written *c.*1387–1395, with additions made *c.*1450–1500; *Auðunar þáttr* is among these additions, in the saga of the kings Magnús Óláfsson and Haraldr harðráði in a redaction deriving mainly from the original *Morkinskinna* compilation. The third version appears in two later compilations of Kings' Sagas, *Hulda* (AM 66 fol., *c.*1350–1375) and *Hrokkinskinna* (GKS 1010 fol., *c.*1400–1450), which are also derived from the original *Morkinskinna* compilation, but have a text more similar to that in *Flateyjarbók* than to that in GkS 1009 fol. (see *MS*, s.v. *Hulda–Hrokkinskinna*). The version in GkS 1009 fol. seems likely to be closest to the original of the three, though it has probably been shortened, while each of the three versions contains some details that are not in either of the others.

Bibliography

The *Morkinskinna* text is printed with original spelling in *Morkinskinna*, ed. Finnur Jónsson (1932), 180–87, and in normalised spelling in *ION* 129–35 and *ÍF* VI, 359–68; the *Flateyjarbók* text is in *Flateyjarbók*, ed. Sigurður Nordal (1944–45), IV 195–200.

There is a translation in *CSI* I 369–74 and translation and discussion in Arnold R. Taylor, 'Auðunn and the Bear', *Saga-Book* XIII (1946–53), 78–96. The *Morkinskinna* version is also translated in *Eirik the Red and Other Icelandic Sagas*, tr. Gwyn Jones (The World's Classics, 1961), 163–70, and the *Flateyjarbók* version in *Hrafnkel's Saga and Other Icelandic Stories*, tr. Hermann Pálsson (Penguin Books 1971), 121–28. See also *MS*, s.v. *Auðunar þáttr vestfirzka*; Joseph Harris, 'Theme and Genre in Some *Íslendinga þættir*', *Scandinavian Studies* 48 (1976), 1–28.

There is a translation of the whole of the *Morkinskinna* compilation in *Morkinskinna: The Earliest Icelandic Chronicle of the Norwegian Kings (1030–1157)* by Theodore M. Andersson and Kari Ellen Gade (2000).

XVI: AUÐUNAR ÞÁTTR

Frá því er Auðunn enn vestfirzki fœrði Sveini konungi bjarndýri

Maðr hét Auðunn, vestfirzkr at kyni ok félítill. Hann fór útan vestr þar í fjǫrðum með umbráði Þorsteins, búanda góðs, ok Þóris stýrimanns, er þar hafði þegit vist of vetrinn með Þorsteini. Auðunn var ok þar o*k* starfaði firir honum Þóri ok þá þessi laun af honum, útanferðina ok hans umsjá. Hann Auðunn lagði mestan hluta fjár þess er var fyr móður sína áðr hann stigi á skip, ok var kveðit á þriggja vetra bjǫrg. Ok nú fara þeir út heðan, ok fers‹k› þeim vel, ok var Auðunn of vetrinn eptir með Þóri stýrimanni — hann átti bú á Mœri. Ok um sumarit eptir fara þeir út til Grœnlands ok eru ‹þar› of vetrinn. Þess er við getit, at Auðunn kaupir þar bjarndýri eitt, gjǫrsimi mikla, ok gaf þar firir alla eigu sín*a*. Ok nú of sumarit eptir þá fara þeir aptr til Nóregs ok verða vel reiðfara; hefir Auðunn dýr sitt með sér ok ætlar nú at fara suðr til Danmerkr á fund Sveins konungs ok gefa honum dýrit. Ok er hann kom suðr í landit þar sem konungr var firir, þá gengr hann upp af skipi ok leiðir eptir sér dýrit ok leigir sér herbergi. Haraldi konungi var sagt brátt at þar var komit bjarndýri, gørsimi mikil, ok á íslenzkr maðr. Konungr sendir þegar menn eptir honum, ok er Auðunn kom firir konung, kveðr hann konung vel. Konungr tók vel kveðju hans ok spurði síðan:

'Áttu gjǫrsimi mikla í bjarndýri?'

Hann svarar ok kvezk eiga dýrit eitthvert.

Konungr mælti, 'Villtu selja oss dýrit við slíku verði sem þú keyptir?'

Hann svaraði, 'Eigi vil ek þat, herra.'

'Villtu þá,' sagði konungr, 'at ek gefa þér tvau verð slík, ok mun þat réttara, ef þú hefir þar við gefit alla þína eigu?'

'Eigi vil ek þat, herra,' sagði hann.

Konungr mælti, 'Villtu gefa mér þá?'

Hann svaraði, 'Eigi, herra.'

Konungr mælti, 'Hvat villtu þá af gjǫra?'

Hann svaraði, 'Fara,' segir ‹hann›, 'til Danmerkr ok gefa Sveini konungi.'

Haraldr konungr sagði: 'Hvárt er at þú ert maðr svá óvitr at þú hefir eigi heyrt ófrið þann er í milli er landa þessa, eða ætlar þú giptu þína

4 of *M*. 11 sínu *M*. 13 með *written twice over line break M*. 25 þína *written twice over line break M*.

svá mikla at þú munir þar komask með gjǫrsimar er aðrir fá eigi komizk klakklaust þó at nauðsyn eigi til?'

Auðunn svaraði, 'Herra, þat er á *y*ðru valdi, en øngu játum vér ǫðru en þessu er vér hǫfum áðr ætlat.'

Þá mælti konungr, 'Hví mun eigi þat til at þú farir leið þína sem þú vill, ok kom þá til mín er þú ferr aptr, ok seg mér hversu Sveinn konungr launar þér dýrit, ok kann þat vera at þú sér gæfumaðr.'

'Því heit ek þér,' sagði Auðunn.

Hann ferr nú síðan suðr með landi ok í Vik austr ok þá til Danmerkr; ok er þá uppi hverr penningr fjárins, ok verðr hann þá biðja matar bæði fyr sik ok fyr dýrit. Hann kømr á fund ármanns Sveins konungs þess er Áki hét, ok bað hann vista nokkverra bæði fyr sik ok fyr dýrit.

'Ek ætla,' sagði hann, 'at gefa Sveini konungi dýrit.'

Áki lézk selja mindu honum vistir ef hann vildi. Auðunn kvezk ekki til hafa firir at gefa.

'En ek vilda þó,' sagði hann, 'at þetta kvæmisk til leiðar at ek mætta dýrit fœra konungi.'

'Ek mun fá þér vistir sem it þurfið til konungs fundar, en þar í móti vil ek eiga hálft dýrit, ok máttu á þat líta at dýrit mun deyja fyrir þér, þars it þurfuð vistir miklar, en fé sé farit, ok er búit við at þú hafir þá ekki dýrsins.'

Ok er hann lítr á þetta, sýnisk honum nǫkkvot eptir sem ármaðrinn mælti firir honum, ok sættask þeir á þetta, at hann selr Áka hálft dýrit, ok skal konungr síðan meta allt saman. Skulu þeir fara báðir nú á fund konungs, ok svá gjǫra þeir, fara nú báðir á fund konungs ok stóðu fyr borðinu. Konungr íhugaði hverr þessi maðr mindi ‹vera› er hann kenndi eigi, ok mælti síðan til Auðunar:

'Hverr ertu?' sagði hann.

Hann svaraði, 'Ek em íslenzkr maðr, herra,' sagði hann, 'ok kominn nú útan af Grœnlandi ok nú af Nóregi, ok ætlaðak at fœra yðr bjarndýr þetta; keyptak þat með allri eigu minni, ok nú er þó á orðit mikit fyrir mér: ek á nú hálft eitt dýrit' — ok sagði konungi síðan hversu farit hafði með þeim Áka ármanni hans. Konungr mælti:

'Er þat satt, Áki, er hann segir?'

'Satt er þat,' sagði hann.

Konungr mælti, 'Ok þótti þér þat til liggja, þar sem ek settak þik mikinn mann, at hepta þat eða *tá*lma er maðr gjǫrðisk til at fœra mér

36 ǫðru *M*. 59 íhugaði *written twice over line break M*. 70 melma *M*.

gørsimi ok gaf fyr alla eign, ok sá þat Haraldr konungr at ráði at láta hann fara í friði, ok er hann várr óvinr? Hygg þú at þá, hvé sannligt þat var þinnar handar, ok þat væri makligt at þú værir drepinn. En ek mon nú eigi þat gjǫra, en braut skaltu fara þegar ór landinu ok koma aldrigi aptr síðan mér í augsýn. En þér, Auðunn, kann ek slík*a* þǫkk sem þú gæfir mér allt dýrit, ok ver hér með mér.'

Þat þekkisk hann ok er með Sveini konungi um hríð.

Ok er liðu nǫkkverjar stundir, þá mælti Auðunn við konung:

'Braut fýsir mik nú, herra.'

Konungr svarar heldr seint, 'Hvat villtu þá,' segir hann, 'ef þú vil eigi með oss vera?'

Hann sagði, 'Suðr vil ek ganga.'

'Ef þú vildir eigi svá gott ráð taka,' sagði konungr, 'þá mindi mér fyr þikkja í, er þú fýsisk í brott.'

Ok nú gaf konungr honum silfr mjǫk mikit, ok fór hann suðr síðan með Rúmferlum, ok skipaði konungr til um ferð hans, bað hann koma til sín er ‹hann› kvæmi aptr. Nú fór hann ferðar sinnar unz hann kemr suðr í Rómaborg. Ok er hann hefir þar dvalizk sem hann tíðir, þá ferr hann aptr; tekr þá sótt mikla, gjǫrir hann þá ákafliga magran. Gengr þá upp allt féit þat er konungr hafði gefit honum til ferðarinnar, tekr síðan upp stafkar‹l›s stíg ok biðr sér matar. Hann er þá kollóttr ok heldr ósælligr. Hann kemr aptr í Danmǫrk at páskum þangat sem konungr er þá staddr, en ei‹gi› þorði hann at láta sjá sik ok var í kirkjuskoti ok ætlaði þá til fundar við konung er hann gengi til kirkju um kveldit. Ok nú er hann sá konunginn ok hirðina fagrliga búna, þá þorði hann eigi at láta sjá sik. Ok er konungr gekk til drykkju í hǫllina, þá mataðisk Auðunn úti, sem siðr ‹er› til Rúmferla meðan þeir hafa eigi kastat staf ok skreppu. Ok nú of *a*ptaninn, er konungr gekk til kveldsǫngs, ætlaði Auðunn at hitta hann, ok svá mikit sem honum þótti fyrr fyr, jók nú miklu á, er þeir váru drukknir hirðmenninir. Ok er þeir gengu inn aptr, þá þekði konungr mann ok þóttisk finna, at eigi hafði frama til at ganga fram at hitta hann. Ok nú er hirðin gekk inn, þá veik konungr út ok mælti:

'Gangi sá nú fram er mik vill finna; mik grunar, at sá muni vera maðrinn.'

Þá gekk Auðunn fram ok fell til fóta konungi, ok varla kenndi konungr hann. Ok þegar er konungr veit hverr hann er, tók konungr í hǫnd honum Auðuni ok bað hann ‹vel› kominn.

75 slíku *M*. 98 optaninn *M*.

'Ok hefir þú mikit skipazk,' sagði hann, 'síðan vit sámsk,' — leiðir hann eptir sér inn. Ok er hirðin sá hann, hlóg*u* þeir at honum, en konungr segir:

'Eigi þurfu þér at honum at hlæja, því at betr hefir hann sét fyr sinni sál heldr en ér.'

Þá lét konungr gjǫra honum laug ok gaf honum síðan klæði, ok er hann nú með honum.

Þat er nú sagt einhverju sinni of várit, at konungr býðr Auðuni at vera með sér álengðar ok kvezk mindu gjǫra hann skutilsvein sinn ok leggja til hans góða virðing. Auðunn sagði:

'Guð þakki yðr, herra, sóma þann allan, er þér vilið til mín leggja, en hitt er mér í skapi, at fara út til Íslands.'

Konungr sagði, 'Þetta sýnisk mér undarliga kosit.'

Auðunn mælti, 'Eigi má ek þat vita, herra,' sagði hann, 'at ek hafa hér mikinn sóma með yðr, en móðir mín troði stafkarls stíg út á Íslandi, því at nú er lokit ‹bjǫrg› þeiri er ek lagða til áðr ek fœra af Íslandi.'

Konungr svaraði, 'Vel er mælt,' sagði hann, 'ok mannliga, ok muntu verða giptumaðr; sjá einn var svá hlutrinn, at mér mindi eigi mislíka at þú fœrir í braut heðan, ok ver nú með mér þar til er skip búask.'

Hann gørir svá.

Einn dag, er á leið várit, gekk Sveinn konungr ofan á bryggjur, ok váru menn þá at at búa skip til ýmissa landa, í Austrveg eða Saxland, til Svíþjóðar eða Nóregs. Þá koma þeir Auðunn at einu skipi fǫgru, ok váru menn at at búa skipit. Þá spurði konungr:

'Hversu lízk þér, Auðunn, á þetta skip?'

Hann svaraði, 'Vel, herra.'

Konungr mælti, 'Þetta skip vil ek þér gefa ok launa bjarndýrit.'

Hann þakkaði gjǫfina eptir sinni kunnustu. Ok er leið stund ok skipit var albúit, þá mælti Sveinn konungr við Auðun:

'Þó villdu nú á braut, þá mun ek nú ekki letja þik, en þat hefi ek spurt at illt er til hafna firir landi *y*ðru, ok eru víða ørœfi ok hætt skipum. Nú brýtr þú ok týnir skipinu ok fénu, lítt sér þat þá á, at þú hafir fundit Svein konung ok gefit honum gjǫrsimi.'

Síðan seldi konungr honum leðr‹hosu› fulla af silfri.

'Ok ertu þá enn eigi félauss með ǫllu, þótt þú brjótir skipit, ef þú fær haldit þessu. Verða má svá enn,' segir konungr, 'at þú týnir þessu

108 sámdsk *M*. 109 hlóga *M*. 115–16 at vera með *written twice M*. 121 at ek vita hafa *M*. 138 *written* ǫðru *M; corrected in manuscript*. 139 fénun *M*.

fé; lít*t* nýtr þú þá þess er ‹þú› fannt Svein konung ok gaft honum gjǫrsimi.'

Síðan dró konungr ‹hring› af hendi sér ok gaf Auðuni ok mælti: 'Þó at svá illa verði at þú br‹j›ótir skipit ok týnir fénu, eigi ertu félauss ef þú kemsk á land, því at margir menn hafa gull á sér í skipsbrotum; ok sér þá at þú hefir fundit Svein konung, ef þú heldr hringinum. En þat vil ek ráða þér,' segir hann, 'at þú gefir eigi hringinn, nema þú þikkisk eiga svá mikit gott at launa nǫkkverjum gǫfgum manni; þá gef þeim hringinn, því at tignum mǫnnum sómir at þiggja. Ok far nú heill.'

Síðan lætr hann í haf ok kømr í Nóreg ok lætr flytja upp varnað sinn, ok þurfti nú meira við þat en fyrr er hann var í Nóregi. Hann ferr nú síðan á fund Haralds konungs ok vill efna þat er hann hét honum áðr hann fór til Danmerkr, ok kveðr konung vel. Haraldr konungr tok vel kveðju hans.

'Ok sezk niðr,' sagði hann, 'ok drekk hér með oss.'

Ok svá gjǫrir hann. Þá spurði Haraldr konungr:

'Hverju launaði Sveinn konungr þér dýrit?'

Auðunn svaraði, 'Því, herra, at hann þá at mér.'

Konungr sagði, 'Launat minda ek þér því hafa. Hverju launaði hann enn?'

Auðunn svaraði, 'Gaf hann mér silfr til suðrgǫngu.'

Þá sagði Haraldr konungr, 'Mǫrgum manni gefr Sveinn konungr silfr til suðrgǫngu eða annarra hluta, þótt ekki fœri honum gørsim*ar*. Hvat er enn fleira?'

'Hann bauð mér,' sagði Auðunn, 'at gørask skutilsveinn hans ok mikinn sóma til mín at leggja.'

'Vel var þat mælt,' sagði konungr, 'ok launa mindi hann enn fleira.'

Auðunn sagði, 'Gaf hann mér knǫrr með farmi þeim er hingat er bezt varit í Nóreg.'

'Þat var stórmannligt,' sagði konungr, 'en launat minda ek þér því hafa. Launaði hann því fleira?'

Auðunn sagði, 'Gaf hann mér leðrhosu fulla af silfri ok kvað mik þá eigi félausan ef ek helda því, þó at skip mitt bryti við Ísland.'

Konungr sagði, 'Þat var ágætliga gǫrt, ok þat minda ek ekki gǫrt hafa; lauss minda ek þikkjask, ef ek gæfa þér skipit. Hvárt launaði hann fleira?'

144 lítr *M*. 167 gørsimur *M*. 171 var þat var *M*.

'Svá var víst, herra,' sagði Auðunn, 'at hann launaði; hann gaf mér hring þenna er ek hefi á hendi, ok kvað svá mega at berask at ek týnda fénu ǫllu, ok sagði mik þá eigi félausan, ef ek ætta hringinn, ok bað mik eigi lóga, nema ek ætta nǫkkverjum tignum ‹manni› svá gott at launa at ek vilda gefa. En nú hefi ek þann fundit, því at þú áttir kost at taka hvárttveggja frá mér, dýrit ok svá líf mitt, en þú lézt mik fara þangat í friði sem aðrir náðu eigi.'

Konungr tók við gjǫfinni með blíði ok gaf Auðuni í móti góðar gjafar áðr en þeir skilðisk. Auðunn varði fénu til Íslandsferðar ok fór út þegar um sumarit til Íslands ok þótti vera inn mesti gæfumaðr.

Frá þessum manni, Auðuni, var kominn Þorsteinn Gyðuson.

XVII: RUNIC INSCRIPTIONS

The terms 'rune' and 'runic' have been used to mean many different things, as the relevant entries in the *Oxford English Dictionary* will confirm. It is important to stress that here (as in all serious linguistic work) 'runes' and 'runic' refer to a set of symbols used for writing language — and nothing else. Like Roman, Greek or Cyrillic letters, runes denote speech sounds: they are an alphabetic type of script, and can in principle be used to write any language (indeed a fair number of medieval runic inscriptions are in Latin). Runes do *not* constitute a language in themselves. Neither are they to be associated with mystical poems or with fortune-telling, supernatural powers or similar mumbo-jumbo. It should further be noted that runes are an epigraphic script: they are found carved or scratched into stone, wood, bone, metal, etc., but were not normally written with ink on parchment. This means that the messages they carry are laconic; runic inscriptions do not preserve lengthy pieces of literature.

The origin of the runic alphabet has been the subject of much speculation, but as yet there is no consensus about when, where and for what reasons it was brought into being. The oldest extant rune-inscribed artefacts are dated to AD 200 or a little earlier. From the third century we have a reasonable number. Most have been found in southern Scandinavia, with a concentration in the area which now comprises Denmark, but a few have an eastern European provenance. These early inscriptions tend to consist of one or two words only and are hard to classify typologically. Names appear to be common, but it is often difficult to decide whether a particular name refers to the object on which it is carved, the owner, or the maker. Some of the inscriptions seem to belong to the world of trade. None obviously reflects a religious milieu. On the basis of the available evidence it has been suggested that the runic alphabet originated in southern Scandinavia in the first century of the Christian era. It is argued that Germanic peoples from this region trading with the Roman Empire perceived the need for a system of writing. That they did not simply adopt the Roman alphabet is put down to their distance from Roman culture. By no means all subscribe to this thesis, however. Some have sought to derive the runes from the Greek alphabet, others from various North Italic scripts. It has also been argued that several features of early runic writing, for example the fact that it can run right to left as well as left to right, point to a much earlier date of origin than the physical evidence implies. One theory has it that runic script derives from archaic Greek epigraphy and may be as old as the fifth or fourth century BC. All we can say for certain is that the runes must be somewhat older than the earliest datable inscriptions because of the latter's relatively wide geographical distribution. It also seems likely that there is some connection between the runes and classical Roman capitals: the correspondences of form and sound are too striking to be ignored (e.g. ᚱ /r/, ᚺ /h/, ᛁ /i/, ᛏ /t/, ᛒ /b/, and, less immediately transparent, ᚠ /f/, ᚲ /k/, ᚢ /u/, ᛊ /s/).

The runic alphabet of the period AD *c*.200–700 is known as the older *fuþark* (*fuþark* after its first six characters), and is preserved complete or in fragmentary form in nine inscriptions. These early recordings of the runic alphabet show considerable homogeneity in the form of the individual runes and, not least, the order in which they appear. The fact that variation exists, however, means it is more helpful for the student to present a reconstructed older *fuþark*, based on typical forms and the most commonly attested order.

ᚠ ᚢ ᚦ ᚨ ᚱ ᚲ ᚷ ᚹ ᚺ ᚾ ᛁ ᛃ ᛇ ᛈ ᛉ ᛊ ᛏ ᛒ ᛖ ᛗ ᛚ ᛜ ᛟ ᛞ

f u þ a r k g w h n i j æ p z s t b e m l ŋ o d

Fig. 1 The older *fuþark*

The ŋ symbol indicates that this rune denoted the velar nasal sound of southern English ***sing*** (possibly sometimes a following /g/ as well, as in northern English).

Virtually all meaningful inscriptions written with the older runes in Scandinavia are in a form of language that pre-dates Old Norse. No examples will therefore be given here. Students who wish to familiarise themselves with this early linguistic stage should consult Antonsen (1975) or Krause (1966).

The runic alphabet did not remain unchanged. In Frisia and Anglo-Saxon England it was expanded to take account of sound changes in the forms of Germanic spoken in these areas (the best account of English runes and their uses is Page, 1999). For reasons that are by no means clear, the Scandinavians went the opposite way from their Anglo-Saxon cousins. At a time when the number of distinctive speech sounds in their language was rising, they ejected eight runes from the *fuþark* and simplified the forms of many of the characters they retained. This reform, which took place no later than *c*.700, seems to have been universally accepted. The new alphabet, known to modern scholars as the younger *fuþark*, appears in two fairly distinct variants, one more drastically simplified than the other. The simpler runes are known as 'short-twig', and are found chiefly in Sweden, Norway and their colonies in the period *c*.700–1000 (less appropriate names sometimes used of these characters are 'Swedish-Norwegian runes' and 'Rök runes' — the latter after the famous Rök stone from Östergötland, Sweden). The more complex runes are called 'long-branch' and are associated with Denmark throughout the Viking Age and early medieval period and with Sweden after *c*.1000 (less appropriate names here are 'Danish runes' or 'normal runes'). In Norway post-1000 rune-writers replaced certain short-twig with long-branch characters. The resulting alphabet is often known as the 'Norwegian mixed *fuþark*'. In illustrating these different manifestations of the younger *fuþark*, reconstructed alphabets are once again presented, based on common usage; the order of the runes is always the same.

ᚠ ᚢ ᚦ ᚬ ᚱ ᚴ ᚽ ᚿ ᛁ ᛆ/ᛅ ᛌ ᛐ ᛓ/ᛒ ᛙ ᛚ ᛧ

f u þ ã r k h n i a s t b m l ʀ

Fig. 2 The short-twig younger *fuþark*

ᚠ ᚢ ᚦ ᚬ ᚱ ᚴ ᚼ ᚾ ᛁ ᛅ ᛋ ᛏ ᛒ ᛘ/ᛙ ᛚ ᛦ

f u þ ã r k h n i a s t b m l ʀ

Fig. 3 The long-branch younger *fuþark*

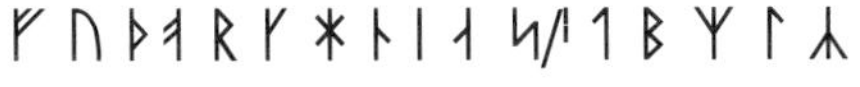

ᚠ ᚢ ᚦ ᚮ ᚱ ᚴ ᚼ ᚿ ᛁ ᛆ ᛋ/ᛌ ᛐ ᛒ ᛘ ᛚ ᛦ

f u þ o r k h n i a s t b m l y

Fig. 4 The Norwegian mixed *fuþark*

The **ã** symbol indicates that this rune denoted a nasal *a*-sound (for most of the Viking Age, at least), as in French ***man**ger*.

Towards the end of the Viking Age Christianity became the official religion in Scandinavia, bringing with it the Roman alphabet and medieval European culture. Conceivably, knowledge of an alphabet in which it was possible to denote speech sounds more precisely than the runic — with its limited inventory of sixteen characters — encouraged rune-writers to seek ways of expanding their medium. Whatever the cause, between about 1000 and 1200 various expedients were adopted to increase the range of runic characters available. In some cases diacritic dots were placed on runes (ᚵ, for example, tended to denote a voiced velar — and perhaps palatal — as distinct from ᚴ, which stood for the unvoiced counterpart(s); ᛂ was used for front unrounded vowels lower than /i/). Another method was to differentiate existing variants, so that what had been two forms of the same rune became two separate characters, each denoting a different sound (ᛆ was thus restricted to /a/ and ᚮ to /o/, while ᛅ came to denote /æ/ and ᚯ /ɔ/ or /ø/). The upshot of these reforms was what is generally known as the medieval *fuþark*. That the example given in Fig. 5 below is a modern construct must be strongly emphasised. While complete older and younger *fuþark*s of various kinds are attested, medieval alphabet inscriptions tend to be based firmly on the sixteen runes of the younger *fuþark*. Odd supplementary characters may be included, but seldom more than one or two. Quite possibly rune-writers did not consider the medieval additions to the *fuþark* to be new runes, simply variations on the existing sixteen.

ᚠ ᚢ ᚦ ᚮ ᚱ ᚴ ᚼ ᚿ ᛁ ᛆ ᛌ ᛏ ᛒ ᛘ ᛚ ᛦ ᚡ ᚧ ᚤ ᚵ ᛂ ᛅ ᛍ ᛋ ᛑ ᛔ ᛕ ᚯ

f u þ o r k h n i a s t b m l y f̈ þ̈ ü k̈ ï æ c z ẗ b̈ p ǫ

Fig. 5 The medieval *fuþark*

Double dots are used here in transliterating dotted runes, to indicate that not all these supplementary characters had a fixed sound value. ᚤ, for example, might denote /ø/ or /y/, and even /o/ in some areas, while ᛂ regularly stood for both /æ/ and /e/ until the differentiation of ᛆ and ᛅ. Occasionally a dotted rune may even have the same value as its undotted counterpart.

During the Viking and Middle Ages many different types of runic inscription were made. Best known are perhaps the commemorative rune stones which span the period *c.*750–1100. After 1100 the raised stone with its emphasis on the commissioner(s) — the living — goes out of fashion and is replaced by the grave-slab which concentrates attention on the dead. Inscriptions are also found on a variety of loose objects: wood, bone, metal — even leather and pottery. Some of these are charms, some marks of ownership, some brief letters; yet others take the form of statements, express wishes, or record crude jokes; not a few seem to be pure gobbledygook. There is also a substantial corpus of runic graffiti. Those carved into the walls or furniture of churches are often of a pious nature, some of the other examples are more racy. Church furniture may also carry more formal inscriptions, recording, for example, who made an object or its purpose.

After some four hundred years of coexistence with the Roman alphabet, runes dropped out of fashion in Scandinavia. It is impossible to give anything like a precise date for their demise since in one or two places they continued to be used for particular purposes long after they had been forgotten elsewhere — in Gotland until *c.*1600, in Iceland until well into the seventeenth century, and in the Swedish province of Dalarna — there increasingly mixed with letters of the Roman alphabet — as late as the nineteenth century.

Runic inscriptions are important. Although often extremely laconic, many of them were composed in the pre-manuscript period and — unlike most manuscript texts — are originals. They can throw light on Scandinavian history, culture and language, not least the last. Runic writing tends to be more orthophonic (i.e. true to the pronunciation) than its Roman-alphabet counterpart, presumably because runes were not learnt in a school or scriptorium and carvers adopted a less disciplined approach to orthography. Through runic writing we can thus learn at first hand something of the forms of Scandinavian in use during the Viking and Middle Ages.

Each of the runic texts below is presented in four different ways: (1) by a normalised representation of the runes; (2) as a transliteration (in bold); (3) as an edited text (in italics); (4) in English translation.

The normalisation of runes is a process akin to printing handwritten texts in the Roman alphabet: in principle each rune appears in one form only. However, variants that are diagnostic of a particular type of alphabet are retained.

The aim of the transliteration is to make the text more accessible to the reader without knowledge of runes, while preserving as much of possible of the original orthography. What is transliterated is therefore in each case the distinctive rune (so that, for example, ᚴ is always rendered as **k**, ᛋ and ᛌ as **s**, and so on). While it is sensible to give one's transliteration a helpful phonological profile (rendering ᚠ ᚢ ᚦ as **fuþ**, for example, rather than, say, as **xyz**) it cannot be over-emphasised that we are not dealing here with phonetic transcription: ᚴ is rendered as **k** whether it denotes /k/, [g] or [ɣ] (a voiced velar spirant, as the *g* in ON or modern Icelandic *eiga*, cf. *NION* I 11, 17), ᚢ is given as **u** whichever rounded vowel it stands for (/u/, /o/, /y/, /ø/ or the semivowel [w]), etc. Nor is modern punctuation or spacing introduced in the transliteration; the text is given line by line as it appears in the original. Separation marks are however reproduced as **:** for convenience whatever their actual form. Round brackets indicate that a rune, group of runes or separator is uncertain, square brackets that the material within them is conjectured or supplied from an earlier drawing or photograph. A slur over two or more transliterated runes marks a bind-rune (a runic ligature).

The distance of some of the edited texts from the Old Norse of grammars and dictionaries makes normalisation problematic. In the selection offered here Norwegian and Norwegian-inspired inscriptions have been treated like the Icelandic texts in *NION* II. For Danish and Swedish inscriptions the normalisation practice of Peterson (1994) has been used as a guideline, but the editor has felt free to depart from it to indicate notable phonological features. Long vowels are marked with an acute accent, as in Old Icelandic; ʀ stands for the reflex of Germanic /z/, most recently identified as a voiced palatal fricative with sibilant quality. Note that *æ* can denote a short as well as a long vowel.

Bibliography

Elmer H. Antonsen, *A Concise Grammar of the Older Runic Inscriptions* (1975).

Michael P. Barnes, 'The origins of the younger *fuþark* — a reappraisal'. In *Runor och runinskrifter* (1987), 29–45. Kungl. Vitterhets Historie och Antikvitets Akademien, Konferenser 15.

Michael Barnes, 'Standardisation and variation in Migration- and Viking-Age Scandinavian'. In *Útnorðr: West Nordic Standardisation and Variation*, ed. Kristján Árnason (2003), 47–66.

Solbritt Benneth *et al.*, eds, *Runmärkt: från brev till klotter — runorna under medeltiden* (1994).

Anders Bæksted, *Islands runeindskrifter* (1942). Bibliotheca Arnamagnæana II.

DR = Lis Jacobsen and Erik Moltke, eds, *Danmarks runeindskrifter* 1–2 (1941–42).

Klaus Düwel, *Runenkunde* (3rd ed., 2001).

Katherine Holman, *Scandinavian Runic Inscriptions in the British Isles: Their Historical Context* (1996). Senter for middelalderstudier, Norges teknisk-naturvitenskapelige universitet, Skrifter 4.

Sven B. F. Jansson, *Runes in Sweden* (2nd ed., 1987).

Wolfgang Krause, *Die Runeninschriften im älteren Futhark* 1–2 (1966). Abhandlungen der Akademie der Wissenschaften in Göttingen, philologisch-historische Klasse, dritte Folge, 65.

Erik Moltke, *Runes and Their Origin: Denmark and Elsewhere* (1985).

NIyR = Magnus Olsen *et al.*, eds, *Norges innskrifter med de yngre runer* 1–6 (1941, in progress).

R. I. Page, *Runes* (1987).

R. I. Page, *An Introduction to English Runes* (2nd ed., 1999).

Lena Peterson, *Nordiskt runnamnslexikon* (5th ed., 2007). [The 4th ed. of this work (2002) is available at http://www.sofi.se/SOFIU/runlex/]

Lena Peterson, *Svenskt runordsregister* (2nd ed. 1994). Runrön 2.

SR = *Sveriges runinskrifter* 1–15 (1900, in progress). (This series is subdivided by province — e.g. vol. 2 is *Östergötlands runinskrifter*, vols 6–9 *Upplands runinskrifter* — and edited by a variety of scholars.)

XVII: RUNIC INSCRIPTIONS

A: KÄLVESTEN

(Photo: Michael Barnes)

ᛌᛐᛁᚴᚢᛧ·ᚴᛆᚱᚦᛁ·ᚴᚢᛓᛚᚦᛆᚢ·
ᛆᚠᛐᛆᚢᛁᚿᛐᛌᚢᚿᚢᛌᛁᚿ·ᛌᛆᚠᛁᛆᛚᛆᚢᛌᛐᚱ
ᛙᛧᛆᛁᚢᛁᛌᛚᛁ·ᚢᛁᚴᛁᚴᛧᚠᛆᚦᛁ
ᛆᚢᚴᚱᛁᛙᚢᛚᚠᛧ

stikuʀ:karþi:kublþau͡:
aftauintsunusin:safialaustr
miʀaiuisli:uikikʀfaþi
aukrimulfʀ

Styggur(?) gærði kumbl þau aft Øyvind sunu sinn. Sá fial austr meʀ Øyvísli. Víkingʀ fáði auk Grímulfʀ.

'Stygguʀ(?) made these memorials after Øyvindʀ his son. He fell east with Øyvísl. Víkingʀ wrote and Grímulfʀ.'

This inscription is designated Ög 8 in *SR*. It is from Östergötland in central southern Sweden and dated to the ninth century.

In runic writing it is not uncommon for a single character to denote the final sound of one word and the initial sound of the next, as in **aukrimulfʀ**. It is necessary only that the two sounds denoted can be expressed by one and the same rune. The spellings **kubl** and **uikikʀ** reflect the omission of homorganic nasals that is a feature of runic spelling. When /m/ occurs immediately before /p/ or /b/, and /n/ before /k/, /g/, /t/ or /d/, rune-writers often do not designate the nasal; the **b** in **kubl** thus indicates /mb/, the second **k** in **uikikʀ** /ng/. On the possible use of **i** for /y/, see Bryggen (2) below.

The word *kumbl* is almost always plural and is thought to denote a monument made up of more than one element. In the earliest Viking-Age inscriptions, as in those from before the Viking Age, there seems to be no way of distinguishing between 'that' and 'this': *þau* defines *kumbl*, but not obviously as something close at hand or more distant. *Aft* is a short form of the preposition *eptir*, parallel to *fyr* for *fyrir* and *und* for *undir*. The short forms are on the whole earlier than their longer counterparts. *Sunu* is an old acc. sg. form with the original *-u* preserved (as it may also possibly be in the *-u-* in *Stygguʀ*, though the etymology of this name is uncertain). The demonstratives *sá*, *sú* are regularly used in Viking-Age runic inscriptions to denote 'he', 'she'. *Fial* is an East

Scandinavian variant of West Scandinavian *fell*. The preposition **miʀ**, apparently reflecting a spoken form lacking [ð], is attested only in a handful of runic inscriptions from Sweden. Outside the Swedish province of Hälsingland, use of the verb *fá* to denote the making of a runic inscription is an indicator of considerable age; it is a term found in older *fuþark* inscriptions (in the form **fa(i)hido** '[I] made') and in the earliest of those in the younger *fuþark*. *Auk* is an older form of *ok* with the diphthong preserved (the conjunction is related to the verb *auka* 'increase'). For personal names in the above text and for personal and place-names in Glavendrup, Jelling, Andreas II and Gripsholm below, see Peterson 2007.

The Kälvesten inscription is notable for being the earliest to document a Scandinavian expedition to the east. Rune forms and language combine to suggest a date in the first half of the ninth century.

B: GLAVENDRUP

(Photo and © National Museum of Denmark)

(Side A)

ᚱᛅᚴᚾᚼᛁᛚᛏᚱ·ᛋᛅ
ᛏᛁ·ᛋᛏᛅᛁᚾᚦᚬᚾᛋᛁ·ᛅᚢᚠᛏ
ᛅᛚᛅ·ᛋᛅᚢᛚᚢᛅᚴᚢᚦᛅ
ᚢᛁᛅᛚ(ᛁ)ᚦᛋᚼᛅᛁᚦᚢᛁᛅᚱᚦᛅᚾᚦᛁᛅᚴᚾ

(Photo and © National Museum of Denmark)

(Side B)

ᛅᛚᛅ·ᛋᚢᚾᛁᛦ·ᚴᛅᚱᚦᚢ
ᚴᚢᛒᛚ·ᚦᛅᚢᛋᛁ·ᛅᚠᛏ·ᚠᛅᚦᚢᚱ
ᛋᛁᚾ·ᛅᚢᚴ·ᚼᚬᚾᛋ·ᚴᚢᚾᛅ·ᛅᚢᚠᛏ
ᚢᛅᚱ·ᛋᛁᚾ·ᛁᚾ·ᛋᚢᛏᛁ·ᚱᛅᛁᛋᛏ·ᚱᚢᚾ
ᛅᛦ·ᚦᛅᛋᛁ·ᛅᚠᛏ·ᛏᚱᚢᛏᛁᚾ·ᛋᛁᚾ
ᚦᚢᚱ·ᚢᛁᚴᛁ·ᚦᛅᛋᛁ·ᚱᚢᚾᛅᛦ

(Photo and © National Museum of Denmark)

(Side C)

ᛅᛏ᛫ᚱᛁᛏᛅ᛫ᛋᛅ᛫ᚢᛅᚱᚦᛁ᛫ᛁᛋ᛫ᛋᛏᛅᛁᚾᚦᛅᚾᛋᛁ
ᛅᛁᛚᛏᛁ᛫ᛁᚦᛅ ᛅᚠᛏ᛫ᚬᚾᚬᚾ᛫ᛏᚱᛅᚴᛁ

(Side A)

raknhiltr:sa
ti:stainþãnsi:auft
ala:sauluakuþa
uial(i)þshaiþuiarþanþiakn

(Side B)

ala:suniʀ:karþu
kubl:þausi:aft:faþur
sin:auk:hãns:kuna:auft
uar:sin:in:suti:raist:run

aʀ:þasi:aft:trutin:sin
þur:uiki:þasi:runaʀ

(Side C)

at:rita:sa:uarþi:is:stainþansi
ailti:iþa aft:ãnãn:traki

Ragnhildr satti stæin þennsi aft Alla, Sǫlva goða, véa liðs, hæið-verðan þegn. Alla syniʀ gærðu kumbl þausi aft faður sinn auk hans kona aft ver sinn. En Sóti ræist rúnaʀ þassi aft dróttin sinn. Þórr vígi þassi rúnaʀ. At retta(?) sá verði es stæin þennsi ailti(?) eða aft annan dragi.

'Ragnhildr placed this stone after Alli, leader of the SǫlvaR, priest of the host, a noble thane. Alli's sons made these memorials after their father and his wife after her husband. But Sóti carved these runes after his lord. Þórr hallow these runes. May he be reckoned a pervert(?) who removes(?) this stone or drags it [for use as a memorial] after another.'

This inscription has the number 209 in *DR*. It is from Fyn and dated to the tenth century.

For notes on *kumbl* and *auk*, see the Kälvesten inscription above.

There is disagreement about what the sequences **au**, **ai** and **ia** denote in Danish inscriptions of the mid- and late Viking Age. Some argue that after the East Scandinavian monophthongisation /au/ > /ø:/, /ei/ > /e:/, /øy/ > /ø:/, digraphic spellings were used to denote vowel sounds for which the younger *fuþark* had no specific symbols, **au** denoting /ø/ or /ɔ/ and **ia** or **ai** /æ/. Others believe that in the case of **ia**, at least, some kind of diphthongisation is reflected (cf. Swedish dialectal *jär* as a reflex of *hér* 'here'). The question cannot easily be resolved. We may note that **au** became a common way of indicating /ɔ/ throughout the Scandinavian runic world — including the West where there was no monophthongisation — and that the Glavendrup inscription consistently spells historical /au/ and /ei/ digraphically, indicating perhaps that the carver still used the historical diphthongs in his speech. In the East Scandinavian of the Viking Age the demonstrative pronoun meaning 'this/these' usually consisted of the basic pronoun *sá*, *sú*, *þat* plus the deictic (pointing) particle *-sa* or *-si*. Hence *þennsi* (acc. m. sg.), *þassi* (< *þaʀ* + *si*, acc. f. pl.), *þausi* (acc. n. pl.). Acc. *faður* lacks labial mutation (cf. *NION* I 39–41), as commonly in East Scandinavian.

The sequence **ala:sauluakuþauial(i)þshaiþuiarþanþiakn** has been taken in different ways. *DR* sees *sǫlva* as an epithet, 'the pale', agreeing with *Alla*; *goða* is reckoned to be modified by *véa* (gen. pl.), giving 'priest of (the) temples'; that leaves *liðs hæiðverðan þegn*, which is said to mean 'noble thane of the retinue', with 'thane' a rank in a king's or nobleman's body of retainers. Further permutations are possible. In favour of the interpretation offered on p. 223 above are the references to **nuʀa kuþi** 'leader of the Ness-dwellers(?)' in the Helnæs and Flemløse I inscriptions (*DR* 190; 192; cf. also Icelandic *Ljósvetninga-goði*), and the suspicion that *liðs* would probably follow *hæiðverðan þegn* if it modified the phrase, as *véa* supposedly follows *goða*. With the order *liðs hæiðverðan þegn*, which implies definition of *þegn*, we would perhaps also expect the adjective to have weak inflexion. It is unfortunate that this part of the inscription is so hard to interpret, for it clearly contains information on the structure of tenth-century Danish society. As construed on p. 223 above, the man commemorated was *goði* (secular leader?) of a group of people, *véi* (priest? — cf. Gothic *weiha* with that meaning) of a body of men, and a *þegn* — perhaps the holder of some military rank. That the offices enumerated are three may be significant. The making of the monument is attributed to three agencies (Alli's sons, Ragnhildr and Sóti), and the Tryggevælde inscription (*DR* 230), apparently commissioned by the same Ragnhildr and also carved by Sóti, describes a (different) monument made up of three elements.

Whatever Alli's functions, it is clear they were not performed in a Christian society. That is amply confirmed by the invocation *Þórr vígi þassi rúnaʀ*; almost certainly by the final part of the inscription too, though important elements of this are obscure. We may surmise with Niels Åge Nielsen (*Runestudier*, 1968, 14–15) that **rita** is a way of writing *retta*, from earlier **hretta* and related to Old Icelandic *skratti* 'unmanly sorcerer', but the meaning of **ailti** is hard to determine. Conceivably we are dealing here with the verb *elta* 'chase'. Whatever the exact interpretation, the warning against tampering with the rune-stone has several parallels (*Runestudier*, 16–52), and all seem to stem from entirely heathen milieux. To this may be added the heathen ship-setting that forms part of the Glavendrup monument.

C: JELLING II

(Side A)

ᚼᛅᚱᛅᛚᛏᚱ:ᚴᚢᚾᚢᚴᛦ:ᛒᛅᚦ:ᚴᛅᚢᚱᚢᛅ
ᚴᚢᛒᛚ:ᚦᛅᚢᛋᛁ:ᛅᚠᛏ:ᚴᚢᚱᛘᚠᛅᚦᚢᚱᛋᛁᚾ
ᛅᚢᚴᛅᚠᛏ:ᚦᚨᚢᚱᚢᛁ:ᛘᚢᚦᚢᚱ:ᛋᛁᚾᛅ:ᛋᛅ
ᚼᛅᚱᛅᛚᛏᚱ[:]ᛁᛅᛋ:ᛋᚨᛦ·ᚢᛅᚾ·ᛏᛅᚾᛘᛅᚢᚱᚴ

(Photo: Michael Barnes)

(Side B)

ᛅᛚᛅ·ᛅᚢᚴ·ᚾᚢᚱᚢᛁᛅᚴ

(Side C)

·ᛅᚢᚴ:ᛏ(ᚬ)ᚾᛁ[·](ᚴᛅᚱᚦᛁ)[·]ᚴᚱᛁᛋᛏᚾᚬ

(Side A)

haraltr:kunukʀ:baþ:kaurua
kubl:þausi:aft:kurmfaþursin
aukaft:þãurui:muþur:sina:sa
haraltr[:]ias:sãʀ:uan:tanmaurk

(Side B)

ala:auk:nuruiak

(Side C)

:auk:t(ã)ni[:](karþi)[:]kristnã

Haraldr konungʀ bað gǫrva kumbl þausi aft Gorm faður sinn auk aft Þórví móður sína. Sá Haraldr es séʀ vann Danmǫrk alla auk Norveg auk dani gærði kristna.

'King Haraldr ordered these memorials to be made after Gormʀ, his father, and after Þórví, his mother. That Haraldr who won for himself all Denmark and Norway and made the Danes Christian.'

This inscription has the number 42 in *DR*. It is from northern Jutland and dated to the period *c.*960–80.

For notes on the spellings **kunukʀ**, **kubl** and **auk**, and on the word *kumbl* itself, see Kälvesten above; for digraphic spellings of expected monophthongs and the forms *þausi* and *faður*, see Glavendrup.

Conceivably **ã** was inserted into **þãurui** as a means of indicating the nasal quality of the root vowel (*þór-* < **þunra-*); it is otherwise hard to understand why the name should have been written in this way. **nuruiak** represents the earliest recorded form of the name 'Norway'; it is noteworthy that it lacks the dental spirant denotation of OE *Norðweg*.

The *Haraldr konungʀ* of the inscription is the Danish King Haraldr Blue-tooth, who ruled from somewhen around the middle of the tenth century until *c.*985; *Gormʀ* is his predecessor, King Gormr the Old, and *Þórví* the famed Þyri *Danmarkar bót* ('Denmark's betterment', an epithet that perhaps has its origins in the Jelling I inscription — *DR* 41 — made by Gormr in her memory). All three figures appear in various of the Icelandic Kings' Sagas. Here Haraldr speaks to us directly. The stone, he states, is raised in memory of his father and mother, but he goes on to claim mighty achievements for himself, to the extent that the inscription is more a celebration of his own life than that of his parents. Scholars have wondered why Haraldr would have waited so long before erecting the memorial, and it has been suggested the part of the inscription that records Haraldr's deeds was added later (for which there is some physical evidence). It is also possible that an earlier inscription in memory of Gormr and Þórví was replaced by Jelling II. The claim that Haraldr won for himself the whole of Denmark is probably to be understood to mean that he consolidated the strong position that Gormr had established, perhaps extending his power eastwards (it is far from clear what *Danmǫrk* encompassed in the tenth century). That he won Norway receives some support from Einarr Skálaglamm's poem *Vellekla* (980s?), where it is said that Norway north of the Oslofjord area lay under Earl Hákon (stanza 17) and that *konungr mykmarkar Hlǫðvinjar* 'the King of Jutland' commanded the earl to defend the Dannevirke (protective wall in southern Jutland) against the enemy (stanza 27). There are different accounts of when and in what circumstances Haraldr became Christian (940s? *c.*960?). The statement *dani gærði kristna* must refer to the introduction of Christianity as the official religion of 'Denmark', an event that presumably took place not long after Haraldr's conversion. Individual families will have been Christian before this and others will have remained heathen for a time afterwards. (The most important sources for Danish history in the tenth century are presented and translated into Danish in Jørgen Bjernum, *Kilder til vikingetidens historie*, 1965. See further the collection of articles entitled 'Jelling problems' in *Mediaeval Scandinavia* 7, 1974, 156–234; Moltke 1985, 202–20; Else Roesdahl, *The Vikings*, 1992, 161–65.)

D: ANDREAS II

(Photo: Michael Barnes)

ᛌᚬᚿᛐ:ᚢᛚᚠ:ᚽᛁᚿ:ᛌᚢᛆᚱᛐᛁ:ᚱᛆᛁᛌᛐᛁ:ᚴᚱᚢᛌ:ᚦᚬᚿᛆ:ᛆᚠᛐᛁᚱ:ᛆᚱᛁᚿ:ᛓᛁᛆᚢᚱᚴ:ᚴᚢᛁᚿᚢ:ᛌᛁᚿᛆ

sãnt:ulf:hin:suarti:raisti:krus:þãna:aftir:arin:biaurk:kuinu:sina

Sandulfr hinn svarti reisti kross þenna eptir Arinbjǫrg, kvinnu sína.

'Sandulfr the black raised this cross after Arinbjǫrg, his wife.'

This inscription is MM (Manx Museum) no. 131, from the far north of the Isle of Man. Together with the bulk of the Manx runic corpus it has been dated, chiefly on art-historical grounds, to the tenth century.

For notes on the digraphic spelling of /ɔ/, see Glavendrup.

Sandulfr, the subject of the sentence, lacks the nom. m. sg. *-r* ending. Several of the Manx inscriptions show aberrant grammatical forms, and this has been attributed to prolonged contact with speakers of other languages (notably Gaelic). The long prepositional form **aftir** (see Kälvesten above) appears to conflict with the tenth-century dating of the inscription. Other runological and linguistic features of the Manx inscriptions too suggest they may be later than conventionally supposed, but art historians continue to insist on the tenth century (see Katherine Holman, 'The dating of Scandinavian runic inscriptions from the Isle of Man', *Innskrifter og datering/Dating Inscriptions*, 1998, 43–54). *Kvinna* 'woman' 'wife' is a variant form of *kona* (whose gen. pl. is *kvenna*).

While 'stones' were raised in Denmark, Norway and Sweden, the Norse settlers in the Isle of Man (and some of the other colonies in the British Isles) opted for crosses. The Irish tradition of raising crosses without legend and the Norse habit of raising rune-stones seem to have merged. Whether this apparent blending of Gaelic and Norse culture is enough to explain the extraordinarily high level of runic activity in Man (over 30 inscriptions or fragments thereof survive) is uncertain. It may simply be that fashions spread more easily in a relatively small island community.

E: GRIPSHOLM

(Photo: Scott Wolter)

×ᛏᚢᛚᛅ:ᛚᛁᛏ:ᚱᛅᛁᛋᛅ:ᛋᛏᛅᛁᚾ:ᚦᛁᚾᛋᛅᛏ:ᛋᚢᚾ:ᛋᛁᚾ:ᚼᛅᚱᛅᛚᛏ:ᛒᚱᚢᚦᚢᚱ:
ᛁᚾᚴᚢᛅᚱᛋ:ᚦᛅᛁᛦᚠᚢᚱᚢ:ᛏᚱᛁᚴᛁᛚᛅ:ᚠᛁᛅᚱᛁ:ᛅᛏ:ᚴᚢᛚᛁ:ᛅᚢᚴ:ᛅ:ᚢᛋᛏᛅᚱᛚᛅᚱ:
ᚾᛁ:ᚴᛅᚠᚢ:ᛏᚢᚢ:ᛋᚢᚾᛅᚱ:ᛚᛅ:ᛅᛋᛁᚱᚴ:ᛚᛅᚾ:ᛏᛁ

:tula:lit:raisa:stain:þinsat:sun:sin:haralt:bruþur:
inkuars:þairfuru:trikila:fiari:at:kuli:auk:a:ustarlar:
ni:kafu:tuu:sunar:la:asirk:lan:ti

Tolla lét ræisa stæin þennsa at sun sinn Harald, bróður Ingvars.

Þæiʀ fóru drængila
fiarri at gulli
auk austarla
ærni gáfu.
Dóu sunnarla
á Serklandi.

'Tolla had this stone raised after her son, Haraldr, Ingvarr's brother. They went manfully, far in search of gold, and in the east gave [food] to the eagle. Died in the south in Serkland.'

This inscription runs in one continuous line along the body of the carved snake. It is designated Sö 179 in *SR* and is from Södermanland in eastern Sweden, dated to the eleventh century.

The pronoun *þæiʀ* was initially forgotten and added below the line. Although the rune-writer makes regular use of separation points, the division is not always between words. In two cases a single character denotes the final sound of one word and the initial sound of the next (**þinsat** = *þennsa at*, **a:ustarlar:ni** = *austarla ærni*, see Kälvesten above), and while the separation in **sunar:la:asirk:lan:ti** might be thought to have morphemic (relating to word-structure) or phonological rationale, that in **a:ustarlar** is harder to fathom.

The small number of runes available to those who carved in the younger *fuþark* makes a sequence like **tula** difficult to interpret. Initial **t** may stand for /t/ or /d/, **u** for any rounded vowel, and **l** for a long or short consonant. The guess that the stone's commissioner was called *Tolla* is prompted by the thought that **tula** may conceal a hypocoristic name. These are often derived from full names and tend to exhibit weak inflexion and a long medial consonant. *Tolla* is a plausible hypocoristic form of *Þorlaug*, *Þorleif*/*Þorlǫf* or *Þorljót*. The preposition *at* 'after' 'in memory of' is most probably an assimilated form of *aft*; it triggers the accusative and is not to be confused with the *at* that triggers the dative (see *NION* I 186; cf. *NION* III, **at**[1]). The adverb suffix *-la* (*drængila*, *austarla*, *sunnarla*) is also found in Old West Norse (e.g. *harðla* 'very', *síðla* 'late'), but is less common there.

Over twenty-five Swedish rune-stones commemorate men who accompanied Ingvarr on an expedition to the east. There is also an Icelandic saga telling of his exploits, *Yngvars saga víðfǫrla*. Though this seems to be largely fiction, some of what it says agrees with other sources. Thus saga and rune-stones agree that the expedition headed east, and the 1041 date the saga gives for Ingvarr's death is confirmed by three Icelandic annals. We are probably safe in assuming that all the Ingvarr stones are from the 1040s. This great expedition met its end in 'Serkland'. The name occurs in Swedish runic inscriptions other than those raised in memory of Ingvarr's followers, in skaldic verse, and in Icelandic prose literature. Scholars differ about the location of Serkland. An influential view connects *serk-* with the name Saracen and holds that Ingvarr and his followers made their way to what is now Syria and Iraq by way of the Russian rivers (see, however, Kirsten Wolf's article '*Yngvars saga víðfǫrla*' and accompanying bibliography in Phillip Pulsiano and Kirsten Wolf, eds, *Medieval Scandinavia, An Encyclopedia*, 1993, 740).

Apart from the raiser formula (the initial statement detailing who commissioned the stone, after whom, and their relationship), the inscription is composed in *fornyrðislag*, the metre of most of the Eddic poems. Alliteration in the first two lines is on *f-* (*fóru, fiarri*), in lines three and four on vowels (*austarla, ærni*), and in the last two on *s-* (*sunnarla, Serklandi*). Verse is common enough in eleventh-century Swedish inscriptions (see Frank Hübler, *Schwedische Runendichtung der Wikingerzeit*, 1996).

F: MAESHOWE no. 23

ᛌᛁᛆ·ᚼᚯᚢᚼᚱ·ᚢᛆᚱ·ᚠᛦᚱ·ᛚᛆᚦᛁᚿ·ᚼᛅᛚᛏᚱ· ᛚᚮᚦᛒᚱᚮᚴᛆᚱ·ᛌᛦᚿᛁᚱ·ᚼᛅᚿᛆᚱ
ᚦᛅᛁᚱᚢᚯᚱᚮ·ᚼᚢᛆᛏᛁᚱ·ᛌᛚᛁᛏᚢᚯᚱᚮ· ᛘᛅᚿ·ᛌᛅᛘᚦᛅᛁᚱᚢᚯᚱᚮᚠᛦᚱᛁᛌᛁᚱ

sia:hǫuhr:uar:fyr:laþin:hæltr: loþbrokar:synir:hænar
þæiruǫro:huatir:slituǫro: mæn:sæmþæiruǫrofyrisir

Sjá haugr var fyrr hlaðinn heldr Loðbrókar. Synir hennar, þeir vǫ́ru hvatir, slíkt vǫ́ru menn, sem þeir vǫ́ru fyrir sér.

'This mound was built before Loðbrók's. Her sons, they were bold. Such were men, as they were of themselves [i.e. they were the sort of people you would really call men].'

(Photo: Bengt A. Lundberg,
Central Board of National Antiquities, Stockholm)

This inscription is edited in Michael P. Barnes, *The Runic Inscriptions of Maeshowe, Orkney* (1994), 178–86. It is carved into two adjacent stones (the splits in the two lines of runes are indicated by spaces in the transcription and transliteration above) of one of the walls of the prehistoric chambered cairn known as Maeshowe on the Orkney Mainland. The likelihood is that most of the thirty-three runic inscriptions in the cairn were the work of Norwegian passers-by rather than native Orcadians and that they were all made towards the middle of the twelfth century.

In medieval runic inscriptions **h** is commonly used to denote [ɣ] (see p. 216 above). The spelling **laþin** indicates Norwegian or at least non-Icelandic authorship (contrast Icel. *hlaðinn*). The use of *heldr* in the sense 'than' is well documented (cf. Johan Fritzner, *Ordbog over det gamle norske Sprog*, 1883–1972, I 782–83). The thrice-repeated **uǫro** 'were' indicates a labially mutated root vowel. In normalised Old Icelandic this word is usually written *váru*, reflecting early thirteenth-century coalescence of /ɔ:/ (a long low back rounded vowel, cf. *NION* I 8–9) with its non-mutated counterpart /a:/. Not all have agreed that the sequence **slituǫro** is to be interpreted *slíkt vǫ́ru*. It has been read as part of a compound *sléttvǫrumenn* 'smooth-hide men', judged to be used in playful antithesis to the name Loðbrók 'shaggy breeches'. If **slit** does denote *slíkt* we must assume a pronunciation [sli:xt], with the unvoiced velar spirant [x] (as in Scots *lo**ch***, cf. *NION* I 11–12, 17–18) perhaps confused with preaspiration — if indeed that feature existed in twelfth-century Scandinavian.

The inscription apparently makes reference to the legendary character Ragnarr loðbrók and his famous sons, but uses the feminine pronoun *hennar* in the process. Three possible explanations for this suggest themselves. (1) The grammatical gender of *brók* (f.) has overridden natural gender. (2) To the carver, Loðbrók was not Ragnarr's nickname but the name of a woman. (3) A (puerile) joke is being made at Ragnarr's expense based on the feminine gender of *brók*. Given the jocular nature of many of the Maeshowe graffiti, the last explanation is perhaps the most plausible.

G: BRYGGEN (BERGEN)

(1) B 279; *NIyR* 651

(Photo: J. E. Knirk; © Museum of Cultural History, University of Oslo, Norway)

ᚦᚮ͡ᚱᚴᛅᛚᛚᛘᛦᚿᛐᛅᚱᛂᛌᛂᚿᛐᛂᚱᚦᛂᚱᛔᛁᛔᛅᚱ

þo͡rkællmyntærïsïntïrþïrb̈ib̈ar

Þorkell myntari sendir þér pipar.

'Þorkell moneyer sends you pepper.'

(2) B 17

(Side A)

ᚭᛌᛐ:ᛘᛁᚿ:ᚴᛁᛌ:ᛘᛁᚴ
ᚴᛁ

(Side B)

ᚠ:ᚢᚦᚭᚱᚴ:ᚼᚿᛁᛆᛌ:ᛐᛒᛘᛚᛦ

(Side A)

ost:min:kis:mik
ki

(Side B)

f:uþork:hnias:tbmly

Ást mín, kyss mik.

'My love, kiss me' (accompanied by an enigmatic **ki** — perhaps the beginning of a second **kis** — and followed or preceded by the complete younger runic alphabet).

(3) B 380

(Photo: J. E. Knirk; © Museum of Cultural History, University of Oslo, Norway)

(Side A)

ᚼᚿᛁᚴ:ᛌᚿᚦᚢ:ᛆᚴ:ᛁᚼᚢᚼᚢᛘ:ᚴᛆᚦᛆᛘ

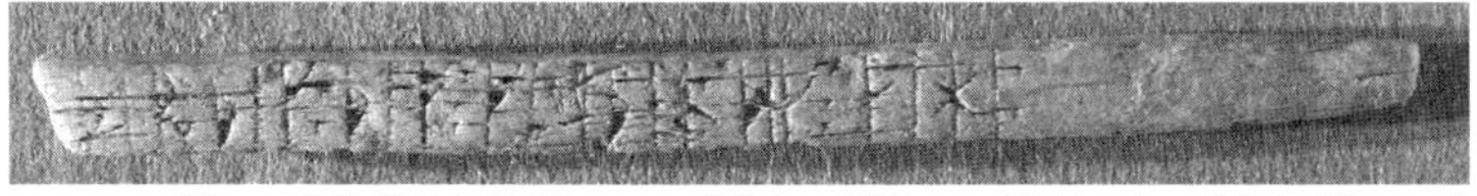

(Photo: J. E. Knirk; © Museum of Cultural History, University of Oslo, Norway)

(Side B)

ᚦᛆᚱ:ᚦᛁᚴ:ᚦᛁᚴ:ᚴᛁ:ᛆᚦᚿᚼ:ᚦᛁᚴ:ᚿᛁᚼᛁ:

(Side A)

hæil:sïþu:ok:ihuhum:k̈oþom

(Side B)

þor:þik:þik̈:k̈i:oþïn:þik:æihi:

Heil(l) sé þú
ok í hugum góðum.
Þórr þik þiggi.
Óðinn þik eigi.

'Be you hale and in good spirits. Þórr receive you. Óðinn own you.'

Most of the Bryggen inscriptions have received only preliminary publication. They have an archaeological number prefixed by B. Those included in the corpus edition *Norges innskrifter med de yngre runer* have an *NIyR* number as well. A selection of the Bryggen runic finds was discussed by Aslak Liestøl in his article 'Runer frå Bryggen', *Viking* 27 (1963), 5–53. Vol. 6 of *NIyR* deals with the inscriptions in Latin and with those classified as business letters and owners' tags. The whole corpus is available on the internet at http://www.nb.no/baser/runer/ribwww/english/runeindex.html

In terms of age the Bryggen inscriptions, which can be reasonably precisely dated by fire layers, stretch from the late twelfth to the early fifteenth century. They are written on a variety of materials, most commonly wood but also bone, leather, metal, stone and pottery. Their content is also varied. Three fairly typical examples are presented here: (1) is from the world of commerce, (2) expresses a lover's heartfelt desire, (3) is of uncertain import but carries echoes of Norse poetry.

(1) is carved on a small piece of wood and was found above the 1198 fire layer. It was presumably a note or label accompanying a parcel of pepper despatched by Þorkell. Notable in this inscription is the doubling of **l** to mark a long consonant — a Roman-alphabet practice sometimes adopted by medieval rune-writers. The spelling **myntærï** suggests weakening of both vowels in the *-ari* suffix.

(2) is carved on both sides of a piece of wood. It was found above the 1248 fire layer. The spelling **ost** indicates a pronunciation in the region of /ɔ:st/ (for /ɔ:/ see p. 234 above), implying rounding of /a:/,

a characteristic feature of most mainland Scandinavian dialects by the late Middle Ages. It is strange to find *kyss* written **kis** in the thirteenth century. As long as there was no separate rune for /y(:)/, either **u** or **i** were in theory possible symbols for this high front rounded vowel since /y/ shared the features [high] and [front] with /i/ and [high] and [rounded] with /u/ (cf. Kälvesten above). In fact **u** was the rune normally used to denote /y(:)/ in the Viking Age; it seems to have become the preferred symbol for all rounded vowels. Whether **kis** reflects unrounding of /y/, known from a few modern Norwegian dialects, is uncertain. Another Bryggen inscription, B 118, writes the same word **kys**.

Partial or complete *fuþark*s are very common in the Bryggen material. Some have attributed their use to a belief in the magic powers of the runic alphabet — the conviction that it could help ward off evil or, as here, achieve a particular aim. This is highly uncertain. *Fuþark*s may have been carved for practice, to demonstrate literacy, or for other mundane reasons (cf. Karin Seim, *De vestnordiske futhark-innskriftene fra vikingtid og middelalder — form og funksjon*, 1998, 198–335). Notable in this *fuþark* is the use of separation points. Why there should be a separator after the initial **f** is uncertain. The division of the younger *fuþark* into three groups of six, five and five runes respectively is, however, a well-established practice — and the basis of a widespread type of runic cryptography (cf. Page 1999, 80–88).

(3) is carved on both sides of a piece of wood. It was found under the 1198 fire layer. On the use of **h** to denote [ɣ], see Maeshowe no. 23 above. The sequence **sïþu** is presumably to be construed as 2nd sg. pres. subj. of *vera* '[to] be' + pronoun. The verb-form lacks the usual *-r* ending, however, and is possibly to be seen as a cross between subjunctive and imperative.

The text appears to be in verse. The metre has been identified as *galdralag*, a variant of *ljóðaháttr* notorious for its irregularity (see *SnE*, *Háttatal* 100–01). Certainly side A of the inscription not only has alliteration, but carries distinct echoes of *Hymiskviða* 11 (*PE* 90):

Ver þú heill, Hymir,
í hugum góðum.

How far side B's text is to be seen as a continuation of A's is unclear, as is its purpose. It is hard to suppose that belief in the Norse gods persisted in Bergen into the late twelfth century. Perhaps the writer intended a curse, along the lines of the well-documented *troll hafi/ taki* . . . 'the trolls have/take . . .'. At the time the inscription was made Óðinn and Þórr might well have been regarded as trolls. Alternatively there may be a further literary allusion here (cf., e.g., *Hárbarðsljóð* 60, *PE* 87). If the allusion is specific, however, it must be to literature that has not survived.

XVIII: MÖÐRUVALLABÓK

The Möðruvallabók Text of Chapter Five of *Kormaks saga*: A Palaeographical Commentary

The manuscript known as Möðruvallabók (AM 132 fol., Stofnun Árna Magnússonar á Íslandi) got its name in the late nineteenth century from Möðruvellir in Eyjafjörður, where Magnús Björnsson (d. 1662), the first known owner of the book, lived. (For information about the book's contents and history, see Einar Ól. Sveinsson 1933.) Möðruvallabók is datable only by the forms of its language, spelling and letters, which suggest that it was written in the middle of the fourteenth century. Mistakes in the names of places in eastern Iceland indicate that the manuscript was not written in that part of the country, and a reference to Miðfjörður as being in the west shows that it was probably put together in northern Iceland, for a scribe from southern or western Iceland would think of Miðfjörður as lying to the north. Möðruvallabók contains eleven Sagas of Icelanders and must have been expensive to produce, for it is both large (consisting of 200 leaves measuring 34 × 24 cm) and elaborately decorated with coloured initials ornamented with romanesque foliage or simple pen flourishes. The book was produced by a team of scribes; one wrote the text (leaving blank spaces for the chapter headings and the initials, as well as for the verses in *Egils saga*), another copied in the missing verses and a third wrote the chapter headings and drew and coloured the initials. A fourth scribe wrote part of the text of *Egils saga* on folio 83 recto.

Chapter Five of *Kormaks saga* begins towards the bottom of the second column on fol. 121 verso. The initial 'Þ' is three lines high, indicating that it begins an 'ordinary' chapter. 'Important' chapters, such as the first chapter of a saga, were usually given larger initials four, five or six lines high, a graphic indication of their 'larger' significance.

The text is written in what is called Gothic formal textual script or Gothic book hand (to distinguish it from the half-cursive script used in documents). Compared with Carolingian scripts, the letters are compressed vertically, the vertical elements have been made uniform, the serifs and curved elements have been broken into angles, and the bows of different letters that face each other are 'fused' or overlapped. Characteristic letter shapes are the 'two-storey a', whose neck bends to touch its bow, and the tall letters such as 'l' and 'k', whose ascenders start with a serif on the left instead of looping round to the right, as in half-cursive. Unlike their European counterparts, Icelandic scribes of Gothic script did not always use round 's' in final position, and they preferred an angular form of the Carolingian 'f' (ꝼ), except in Latin words, where they used the proper Gothic 'f' that stands on the guide line. In the first half of the fourteenth century, the upper arm becomes looped, and in the second half of the fourteenth century, the bottom arm becomes looped as well (ꝼ). As with the Carolingian scripts, 'i' and 'j' are not dotted, and 'u' and 'v' are used interchangeably for both the consonant and the vowel (even to the extent of sometimes putting an accent over 'v' to indicate a long vowel). Capital initials are not regularly used at the beginning of sentences and in proper nouns; instead, they occur at the beginning of chapters, paragraphs, verses and speeches. Occasionally they are used to signal important nouns, some of which may be names.

In the following transcription, letters in italics are expansions of abbreviations. Facsimiles of the two manuscript pages can be seen at http://vsnrweb-publications.org.uk/NION-2-facs.pdf. Compare the normalised text in extract IV.

fol. 121v, col. 2, line 28:

Þorveig h*et* kona. h*on* v*ar* **fall þorueig*ar*sona** | ði

Observe the 'round r' after the 'o' in *Þorveig* (ꝛ); the shape results from writing an 'r' using the right-hand curve of the 'o' for the upright. Round 'r' is generally used after a letter with a bow, such as 'o' or 'd' (which has the form ð). The letter above the first 'h' is a 't', though it looks like an 'r'. Icelandic abbreviations generally have one of the omitted consonants above the word, with no indication of what the omitted vowel is or whether it goes before or after the superscript consonant. The abbreviation for *hon* ('h' with superscript 'o') breaks the rule just given for superscript letters, but it is because 'h' with a horizontal stroke through the ascender (the stroke is a general sign of abbreviation) is the abbreviation for the extremely common word *hann*. A different abbreviation must therefore be used for *hon*. The line breaks off to leave space for the chapter heading, which is in red ink. The virgule before the 'ði' at the very end shows that these letters belong with 'haf' in the line above (i.e. *hafði*, the last word of Chapter 4).

line 29:

miog fiolkun*n*ig h*on* bio asteinstodum í

Note that 'ǫ' is written without the hook, long vowels are usually written without accent marks, and there is no point at the end of the sentence. All these absences are common. The second 'n' in *fjǫlkunnig* is not written but is indicated by a horizontal stroke above, which here signifies a nasal consonant. (In such abbreviations, the stroke is often to the left of the 'n' that is written, making it difficult to see whether the transcription should be 'n*n*' or '*n*n'.) No space separates the preposition *á* from its object *Steinsstǫðum*; this is a frequent practice. Also frequent is the practice of using a single consonant to represent two, resulting in 'steinstodum' for *Steinsstǫðum*.

line 30:

miðfirði. h*on* atti .íj. sonu. h*et* hin*n* ellri

Note the regular 'r' after the 'i'. Roman numerals were usually set off by a point before and after, and the last 'i' took the form of 'j'. The usual abbreviations for *hon* and *hét* appear, as well as the nasal stroke for the second 'n' in *hinn*.

line 31:

oddr en hin*n* yng*ri* guðmundr þ*ei*r v*aro* hauaðam*en*n

Note the round 'r' after the letters with bows: 'd' (ð) in *Oddr* and *Guðmundr* and 'þ' in *þeir*. There were several variants of 'y', but all have a dot to distinguish them from 'ij'. Note the superscript 'i' above the 'g' in 'yng'; generally a superscript vowel stands for 'r' or 'v' plus that vowel, and here it stands for 'ri'. Two more very common abbreviations appear here: 'þr' with a stroke through the ascender of the 'þ' stands for *þeir*, and 'v' with a superscript 'o' stands for *varo* (i.e. *váru*). The stroke over 'mn' simply signals an abbreviation; it is not a nasal stroke, although it looks like one.

line 32:

miklir. Oddr venr kuam*ur* sinar itungu til

As mentioned in the introduction, Icelandic scribes did sometimes use initial capitals for names, but it can be difficult to tell whether a letter is meant to be large or not. The 'O' here is definitely large, and some would read the 'o' at the beginning of line 31 as large as well, though it is not as large as this one. Note the abbreviation sign over the 'm' in *kvámur*; shaped something like ∞, it actually evolved from a round 'r', which as a superscript letter was the Latin abbreviation for 'ur' and was so used in Icelandic.

line 33:

þ*or*k*els*. & sitr a tali v*ið* St*ein*g*erði*. þ*or*k*ell* g*er*ir ser dádt v*ið* þa b*ræðr*

The abbreviation for all case forms of *Þorkell* is 'þ' with a stroke through the ascender followed by 'k' with a stroke through the ascender. These strokes are general signals of abbreviation and do not indicate nasal consonants.

There is no indication of case; here it is expanded to *Þorkels* because the preceding *til* always takes the genitive. Note the shape of the ampersand. It is actually a ligature of 'e' and 't', i.e. *et*, the Latin word for 'and'. Although it is borrowed from Latin, Icelandic scribes most likely thought of it as *ok* rather than *et*, and it may be transcribed *ok*, which is how the scribe spells the word on fol. 122r, col. 1, line 34. The scribe's usual abbreviation for *Steingerðr* (irrespective of case) appears here: a capital 'S', a small 't', and an abbreviation sign something like a flattened 'S' (cf. the more rounded form of this sign in line 36 below). The 'v' with superscript 'i' is a common abbreviation for *við*. The zigzag over the 'g' in *gerir* (called a 'tittle', and much like the abbreviation sign in *Steingerðr*) stands for a front vowel or diphthong plus 'r'. The abbreviation for *bræðr* is 'bb'; the idea is that if one 'b' stands for *bróðir*, then two b's stand for the plural. Note that in the text of extract IV, the vowel *æ* of *bræðr* is archaised/normalised to *brœðr*.

line 34:

& eggiar þa at sitia f*irir* k*ormaki*. Oddr q*ua*ð ser þ*at* ecki

The abbreviation for *fyrir* is 'f' with a superscript 'i'. This word was often spelled *firir* (the unrounded first vowel resulting from low-stress conditions, cf. *þikkja* for *þykkja* and *mindi* for *myndi*), so without an unabbreviated example to guide us, we cannot be certain which spelling the scribe would use. If the scribe does use *firir* when spelling it out in full, the abbreviated form should be expanded to *firir* as well (a principle that applies to any abbreviated word). *Kormakr* is abbreviated by a stroke through the ascender of its first letter. The expansion here in the dative is controlled by the preceding preposition. The spelling of *kvað* is unusual; the standard form would be 'kð' with either a sign something like a 'w', which means 'v' or 'r' plus 'a', or a superscript 'a', also indicating 'v' or 'r' plus the vowel, but the scribe here employs both. Although 'qv' is a common alternative for 'kv', the spelling *kuað* on fol. 122r, col. 1, line 4 suggests that the use of 'q' here is because it affords space for an abbreviation sign (and also avoids confusion with the 'k' abbreviation for *Kormakr*). It therefore might be more representative of the scribe's orthography to expand the abbreviation with 'q' as *kuað*, but 'q' is retained here to show what is actually on the page. Finally, what looks like a 'þ' with a superscript 'a' is more likely to be 'þ' with a stroke through the ascender, which is a very common abbreviation for *þat*. This abbreviation appears more clearly in the next line.

line 35:

ofrefli. þ*at* var ein*n*huern dag er k*ormakr* ko*m* i tun

Apart from the abbreviation for *þat*, the most interesting thing to see in this line is how the nasal stroke signifies an 'n' in *einnhvern* and an 'm' in *kom*.

line 36:

gu. v*ar* St*eingerðr* i stofu & sat a palli. þorueig*ar* s*ynir* sátv

Note the superscript ‘r’ in *var* and *Þorveigar*, indicating ‘ar’. Note also the doubled ‘s’; as with the doubled ‘b’ in line 34, a single ‘s’ is an abbreviation for *son*, and two s’s stand for the plural *synir*. This abbreviation is set off by a point before and after.

line 37:

i stofun*n*i & v*aro* bun*ir* at v́eita k*ormaki* t*il* ræði er h*ann* gengi

The front-vowel-plus-r sign appears over ‘bun’; here the front vowel is an ‘i’. The accent over the ‘v’ must be treated as a graphical flourish, but in fol. 122r, col. 1, line 3 it represents a long vowel, cf. fol. 122r, col. 1, line 34. The scribe often abbreviates names by putting a point after the first letter, but here he has put a point before and after the ‘k’ as well, as he did with the abbreviation for *synir* in the previous line. Note that the elements of the compound word *tilræði* are separated by a space (cf. the running together of a preposition and its object in line 29). The very common abbreviation for *hann* (‘h’ with a stroke through the ascender) appears at last.

line 38:

in*n*. en þ*or*k*ell* hafdi sett odr*um* megin dyra sv*er*ð

Do not mistake the two t’s of *sett* for ‘ct’, despite the almost non-existent cross-bar of the first ‘t’. The round ‘r’ with a stroke through the tail in ‘odr’ is the Latin sign for ‘rum’, here yielding *odrum*. The scribe spells *dura* as *dyra* (an extension of the i-mutation forms occurring in other parts of the paradigm); note the dot over the ‘y’ (see note to line 31 above). The front-vowel-plus-r sign appears over ‘svð’; here the front vowel is an ‘e’.

line 39:

brugðit. en oðr*um* megin setti N*arfi* lia i langorfi.

What looks like a majuscule ‘H’ is actually a majuscule ‘N’. This letter shape is inherited from early Carolingian script and developed from the fashion of making the angle of the cross-bar of the ‘N’ shallower and shallower, until at last it was horizontal rather than diagonal. Note also how the letters of *langorfi* are spread rather far apart; presumably the scribe was stretching the word so that it would reach to the end of the line.

line 40:

en þa er k*ormakr* ko*m* at skaladyrum. skaraði ofan

The ‘r’ over the ‘e’ is not an abbreviation; it is simply the second letter of the word written superscript, perhaps to save space. This turned out not to be necessary, for when the scribe came to write *skaraði ofan*, he had to space the letters widely to fill the line. Scribes frequently faced the problem of whether to right-justify the line by stretching one word or compressing two.

line 41:
liai*n*n. & mætti h*ann* suerðínu & brotnaði i mik*it*

The accent over the ‘i’ in *sverðinu* does not represent a long vowel; it may be intended to help the reader distinguish between the minim of the ‘i’ and the minims of the ‘n’. The final ‘it’ of *mikit* is indicated by a stroke through the ascender of the ‘k’; this is another common use of that sign.

fol. 122r, col. 1, line 1:
skarð. þa ko*m* þ*or*k*ell* at & q*ua*ð k*ormak* mart illt g*er*a & var

The expansion *Kormak* in the accusative case is determined by its being the object of the preceding verb.

line 2:
maloði. snyr in*n* skyndiliga & kueðr St*eingerði* af sto

Similarly, the expansion *Steingerði* in the dative case is determined by the preceding verb. The letters ‘sto’ at the end of the line are the first part of the word *stofunni*. Note that the scribe does not use a hyphen to indicate a word divided at the line break.

line 3:
fun*n*i. ganga þau v́t v*m* aðrar dyr*r*. & lykr h*ann* hana

Here we see an accent placed over ‘v’ to indicate a long vowel. The small capital ‘ʀ’ with a dot over it is a combination of two abbreviations for the same thing: small capital consonants (most frequently ‘ɢ’, ‘ɴ’ and ‘ʀ’) were used to represent geminates, but doubled consonants could also be indicated by a dot over a single capital consonant.

line 4:
ieinu vtiburi. kuað þau k*ormak* alldri siaz s*ku*lu. kor*makr*

The letters ‘slu’ with a stroke through the ‘l’ is the usual abbreviation for *skulu*. Perhaps to fill out the line, the scribe uncharacteristically spells out the first syllable of *Kormakr* and indicates the rest of the word with a general abbreviation sign.

line 5:

gengr in*n* & bar h*ann* skiotara at en þa varði. & v*ar*ð

line 6:

þei*m* bilt. k*ormakr* litaz v*m*. & ser e*igi* stei*ngerð*i. en ser þa b*ræðr*

An 'e' with a superscript 'i' was a common abbreviation for *eigi*.

line 7:

er þ*ei*r stuku vapn sín. snyr i brott skyndiliga.

The scribe clearly writes *stuku* (which would normally represent *stukku*, the past plural of *støkkva*), but this may be an error for *struku* (the past plural of *strjúka*), which gives better sense.

line 8:

& q*uað* v*isu*. Hneit v*ið* hrungnis fota. halluitindum

The abbreviation '.q.v.' for the phrase *kvað vísu* is common. Note the large initial marking the start of the verse, as well as the 'v' (for *vísa*) in the space between the columns (cf. lines 12, 19, 28). The scribe clearly writes *halluitindum*, but this is an error for *halluitiondum* (i.e. *hallvitjǫndum*).

line 9:

stalli. in*n* v*ar* ek ilmi at fin*n*a. engi sar of fengin*n*

The words *sár* and *fenginn* are subject to emendation because it is difficult to interpret the line as it stands, but the letters are all quite clear.

line 10:

vita s*ka*l hitt ef h*ann* hætt*ir*. handuiðris m*er* grandi ne

The letters 'sl' with a stroke through the 'l' is the usual abbreviation for *skal*.

line 11:

yggs f*ir* líð leggiu*m*. litis meira vitiss. k*ormakr* fin*n*r. Stei*ngerði*

Note the small capital 'ɢ' (without a dot) for the geminate in *yggs*. The spelling 'litis' is an error for *lítils*. The sense of the passage shows that the scribe (or his exemplar) has left out *eigi* or *ecki* from the phrase *Kormakr finnr Steingerði*.

line 12:

& q*uað* v*isu*. Braut huarf or sal sæta. sun*n*z erum

Note the use of 'z' to represent 'ds'. Most often it represents 'ts' (which is how the two sounds in *sunds* would have been pronounced).

line 13:
hugr a gun*n*i. huat m*er*kir nu h*er*kiss haull þu*er*

line 14:
ligar alla renda ek allt it iðra. eirar geirs at

The scribe (or his exemplar) has left out the 'h' in *hárgeirs*.

line 15:
þ*ei*ri. hlins eru*m*c haurn at fin*n*a. h*us* brageislu*m* fu

What looks like 'ɔ' by the 'h' is actually the Latin abbreviation for 'us' and was so used in Icelandic.

line 16:
sir. Ept*ir* þ*að* geck k*ormakr* at h*us*i er St*eingerðr* v*ar* i & braut vpp h*us*it

The scribe or his exemplar has omitted the suffixed article *-nu* from *húsi*.

line 17:
& talaði v*ið* St*eingerði*. h*on* m*ælti*. þu breyt*ir* ouarliga. sæk*ir* t*il* tals

The letters 'mli' with a stroke through the 'l' is a common abbreviation for *mælti*. Note that the last letter of *tals* is superscript to keep it within the column.

line 18:
v*ið* mik þ*via*t þ*or*veigar s*ynir* ero ætlaðer t*il* hofuðs þ*er*. þa

line 19:
q*uað* k*ormakr*. Sitia suerð & huetia. sin andskot*ar* minir

line 20:
eins karls synir in*n*i erað þ*ei*r banar min*ir*. en*n* a

line 21:
viðu*m* velli. vega tueir at mer einu*m*. þa er se*m* ærat

line 22:
vlfi oræknu*m* fior sæki. þar sat k*ormakr* v*m* dagin*n*. Nu sér

line 23:

þ*or*k*ell*. at þ*et*ta ráð er farit er h*ann* hafði stofnat. Nu

The letters 'þta' with a stroke through the ascender of the 'þ' is the usual abbreviation for *þetta*.

line 24:

biðr h*ann* þ*orveigar sonu* at sitia f*irir* k*ormaki* i dal einu*m* f*irir* vtan garð

line 25:

sin*n*. þa mæl*t*i þ*or*k*ell*. Narui s*ka*l fara m*eð* ykr. en ek mu*n*

The sign that looks like a '3' after the 'm' of *með* developed from the semi-colon (;). It is a Latin abbreviation used to represent several combinations of letters, including 'et'. In Iceland it was adopted as an abbreviation for 'eð'.

line 26:

vera heima & veita yðr lið ef þ*er* þurfit. v*m* kue

line 27:

lldit f*er*r k*ormakr* i br*o*tt & þeg*ar* er h*ann* ke*m*r at dalnu*m* sa h*ann* m*en*n

Note the superscript 'o' above 'btt'. A superscript vowel usually stands for 'r' or 'v' plus that vowel, and here it stands for 'ro'.

line 28:

.ííj. & q*uað* v*isu*. Sitia m*en*n & meina. m*er* eína gnásteina

line 29:

þ*ei*r hafa vilat vin*n*a er m*er* v*ar*ða gna borða. þ*vi* meira

line 30:

s*ka*l ek þ*ei*ri. er þ*ei*r ala meíra aufund v*m* varar gong*ur*.

line 31:

yn*n*a saulua gun*n*i. þa hliopu þ*orueigar* s*ynir* vpp & sottu at

Note the ligature of the two p's; this is a space-saving device like the use of 'ꝛ' after 'o'.

line 32:

k*ormaki* lengi. Narui skriaði v*m* it ytra. þ*or*k*ell* ser hei*m*an

line 33:
at þei*m* sækiz seint & tekr v́apn sín i þ*vi* bili ko*m* st*eingerðr*

The stroke over the ‘v’ is a flourish and not an indication of a long vowel.

line 34:
v́t & ser ætlan foður síns. tekr h*on* h*ann* hondu*m*. ok

In contrast to the ‘v́’ in the previous line, the stroke over the ‘v’ here is an indication of a long vowel.

line 35:
ke*mz* h*ann* ecki t*il* liðs m*eð* þei*m* b*ræðrum* lauk sua þ*vi* ma

line 36:
li at oddr fell en Guðm*und*r v*ar*ð ouigr & do þo siða*n*

line 37:
ept*ir* þ*et*ta for k*ormakr* hei*m*. en þ*or*k*ell* ser f*irir* þei*m* b*ræðrum* litlu si

line 38:
ðar*r* fer*r* k*ormakr* at fin*n*a þorv*eigu*. & kuez ecki. vilia by

line 39:
gð hen*n*ar þar i firðinu*m*. s*ka*ltu flytia þik i brott

Note the abbreviation for *skaltu*: the usual abbreviation for *skal* (cf. line 10 above), followed by ‘tu’.

line 40:
at aqueðin*n*i stundu. en ek vil allra bota v*ar*na

The spelling of *ákveðinni* with a ‘q’ shows that the scribe freely uses both ‘q’ and ‘k’ before ‘v’ (‘u’) even when he does not need to use ‘q’ in order to have space above the letter for an abbreviation.

line 41:
v*m* sonu þina. þ*orveig* m*ælti*. þ*at* er likaz at þ*vi* komi*r* þu a leið

The abbreviation ‘m.’ could stand for either *mælir* or *mælti*, but because the scribe writes *mælti* in lines 17 and 25, we assume that *mælti* is meant here as well. The last letters of the line are difficult to read because the word was compressed to fit the tiny space left at the end of the column.

col. 2, line 1:
at ek v*er*ða h*er*að flotta en s*ynir* min*ir* obætt*ir*. en þvi s*ka*l

line 2:
ek þer launa at þu s*ka*lt st*eingerðar* alld*ri* níota. k*ormakr* s*egir*. þuí

Note the superscript 'i' after the 'd' in 'alld'. A superscript vowel usually stands for 'r' or 'v' plus that vowel, and here it stands for 'ri'. The stroke above the 'i' in *njóta* is probably meant to distinguish the 'i' from the 'n'; it does not indicate a long vowel. The abbreviation 's.' could stand for either *segir* or *sagði*, and as 'seg*ir*' is found in line 9 below, 's.' is expanded as *segir* here as well.

line 3:
mantu ecki raða en vanda k*er*ling. Siðan f*er*r

Note that *Siðan* does not start a new chapter in this version of the text.

line 4:
k*ormakr* at fin*n*a St*eingerði* ia*m*t se*m* aðr. ok eitt sin*n* er þau tala

The nasal consonant supplied in the expansion of 'iat' is 'm' because the scribe's spelling of *jafnt* without 'f' suggests that that his pronunciation of this word was /yamt/ rather than /yant/.

line 5:
v*m* þ*ess*a atburði. lætr h*on* ecki illa if*ir*. k*ormakr* q*uað* v*isu*. Sitia

A ligature of 'þ' and long 's', with a stroke through the ascender, is the abbreviation for *þess*. Here the following 'a' gives the case ending.

line 6:
m*en*n & meina. m*er* asianu þína. þ*ei*r hafa laugdis

line 7:
loddu. lin*n*a fætr at vin*n*a. þ*via*t vpp s*ku*lu allar a/l

Note the ligature of 'a' and 'v'. The scribe does not often use ligatures, and in this case may have done so in order to fit the last word into the text column. Instead of 'ǫ', itself a ligature of 'a' and 'o', the spelling 'au' or 'av' was often used in Icelandic for the labial mutation of *a* (cf. *haull* in col. 1, line 13, above).

line 8:

stafns aðr ek þ*er* hafna. lysigrund i l*an*di. lin*nz*

The letters 'ld' with a general abbreviation stroke stand for *land*.

line 9:

þioðár ren*na*. Mælþu e*igi* sua mikit v*m* seg*ir* St*eingerðr*

Note the uncial (i.e. Continental early medieval Latin) form of the capital 'M'.

line 10:

mart ma þ*vi* bregða. þa q*uað* k*ormakr* v*isu*. Hv*er*n munder

line 11:

þu grundar hlin skapfraumuð linu. liknsy

line 12:

nir m*er* luka. lios þ*er* at ver kiosa. St*eingerðr segir*. Braðr

line 13:

munda ek blindu*m*. bauglest*ir* mik festa. yrði

The exaggerated serif of the 'd' in *blindum* makes the minim before it look like an 'í', but it is not.

line 14:

goð se*m* g*er*ðiz. goð m*er* & skaup f*ro*ða. k*ormakr segir*. Nu kaustu

The 'z' at the end of *gerðiz* stands for 'st', which is a late alternative for the *-sk* suffix (see *NION* I, § 3.6.5.3).

line 15:

se*m* v*er*a ætti opt hefi ek higat minar kuamur

line 16:

lagðar. Nu biðr st*eingerðr* k*ormak* stunda t*il* foður hen*na*r

line 17:

& fa hen*na*r & f*irir* saker st*eingerðar* gaf k*ormakr* þ*or*k*atli* giofu*m*. ep

The abbreviation for *hennar* ('hnar' with a stroke through the ascender of the 'h') is unusual. Perhaps influenced by the dative case of *Þorkatli*, the scribe has put *gjafar* in the dative.

line 18: t*ir* þ*et*ta eigu marg*ir* m*en*n hlut i & þar ko*m* v*m* siðir

line 19:
at k*ormakr* bað St*eingerðar*. & var h*on* h*onu*m fostnut & aqueðin

line 20:
brullaupsstefna & stendr nu kyrt v*m* hrið nu

line 21:
fara orð a milli þ*eir*ra. & v*er*ða i nockurar grein*ir*

The letters 'þra' with a stroke through the ascender of 'þ' are the common abbreviation for *þeirra*.

line 22:
v*m* fiarfar. & sua veík v*ið* breytiliga at siðan

There is a rather thick accent mark over the 'i' of *veik* which lends it the appearance of a long 's', but the sense calls for *veik* and not *vesk*, which is meaningless.

line 23:
þ*ess*um raðu*m* v*ar* raðit. fanz k*ormaki* fatt v*m*. en þ*at* v*ar* f*irir*

line 24:
þa sauk at þ*orveig* seiddi t*il* at þau skylldi e*igi* nio

line 25:
taz mega. þ*or*k*ell* i tungu atti son roskin*n* er

line 26:
þ*or*kell het. & v*ar* kallaðr tangniostr.h*ann* hafði v*er*

line 27:
it vtan v*m* stund. þ*et*ta sumar ko*m* h*ann* v́t. & v*ar* m*eð*

line 28:
foður sínu*m*. k*ormakr* sæk*ir* e*igi* brullaupit. ept*ir* þ*vi* se*m* a

line 29:
kueðit v*ar* & leið f*ra*m*m* stundin. þ*et*ta þik*ir* fræn

line 30:
du*m* St*eingerðar* oui*r*ðíng er h*ann* bregðr þ*ess*um raða hag & lei

line 31:
Bersi het **kuanfang bersa** | ta ser raðs.

As with the first line of Chapter Five, the first line of the next chapter includes a large decorated initial to signal the start of the new chapter, the heading for which is in red in the centre of the line, and the end of the last line of the previous chapter fills the space at the end of the line and is marked off by a virgule.

As has emerged from the preceding commentary, Icelandic scripts changed over time. (For illustrations of these scripts down to 1300, see Hreinn Benediktsson 1965.) The earliest script was the Carolingian minuscule that was current when Latin letters were first taught to Icelanders. This script was used through the first quarter of the thirteenth century, and was gradually superseded by a Carolingian Insular script that was used through the rest of the century. By the fourteenth century, various kinds of Gothic script had become predominant. A formal textual Gothic was used for de luxe books, but for letters, charters and other documents a half-cursive Gothic was used, and this informal script gave rise to a formal half-cursive that was used in books. Not surprisingly, most manuscripts show signs of the transition from one script to another, signs that help establish the date of the manuscripts. The formal textual Gothic script of Möðruvallabók suggests a date of the fourteenth or fifteenth century, and the presence of all three kinds of 'f' (ꝼ) on fol. 121v, col. 2, lines 29 and 30; with the upper arm looped on fol. 121v, col. 2, lines 35 and 37; and with the lower arm looped as well (ꝼ) on fol. 121v, col. 2, line 36) somewhat narrows the date to closer to the middle of the fourteenth century.

Scripts changed slowly, making it difficult to pinpoint the date of an undated manuscript on that basis alone, but the Icelandic language itself and its spelling evolved somewhat more rapidly, providing additional evidence for a manuscript's age. Keep in mind that scribes often worked from written texts, and sometimes they would retain the earlier forms that they saw in their exemplars, although in general their copies reflect contemporary forms. This text of *Kormaks saga* is definitely from the fourteenth century; *es* has been replaced by *er*, 'þ' is absent from non-initial positions, and 'd' has begun to replace 'ð'. Yet there are none of the changes that arose in the second half of the century: *á* is not written 'aa' (cf. fol. 121v, col. 2, line 29), 'e' does not become 'ei' before 'ng' and 'nk' (cf. fol. 121v, col. 2, line 37), and *enn* or *inn* has not been replaced by *hinn* as the definite article (*en* is used on fol. 122r, col. 2, line 3, though *hinn* appears, before an adjective, on fol. 121v, col. 2, lines 30 and 31).

It is the combination of these various factors that has led to the dating of Möðruvallabók to the middle of the fourteenth century. On the basis of its orthography, it could be from the first half of the century, but the double-looped 'ꝥ' makes it more likely to be just a little later. The chronological range of these palaeographic and linguistic forms is reflected in the way the date is given in the recent analysis by Degnbol *et al.* 1989, which uses the formulation '*c.*1330–1370' instead of the near-equivalent '*c.*1350'.

Bibliography

Einar Ól. Sveinsson, ed. 1933. *Möðruvallabók (Codex Mödruvallensis): MS. No. 132 fol. in the Arnamagnæan Collection in the University Library of Copenhagen*. Corpus codicum islandicorum medii aevi 5.

Degnbol, Helle, Bent Chr. Jacobsen, Eva Rode and Christopher Sanders, eds 1989. *Ordbog over det norrøne prosasprog / A Dictionary of Old Norse Prose. Registre / Indices.*

Hreinn Benediktsson. 1965. *Early Icelandic Script as Illustrated in Vernacular Texts from the Twelfth and Thirteenth Centuries*. Íslenzk handrit / Icelandic Manuscripts II.

XIX: LANDNÁMABÓK

Landnámabók (The Book of the Settlements) is thought to have been first compiled in the first half of the twelfth century, probably by several collaborators including Ari Þorgilsson, who also wrote *Íslendingabók* (The Book of the Icelanders, see Text VIII above), and Kolskeggr Ásbjarnarson (see *ÍF* I 395; both these men were nick-named *inn fróði* 'the learned', or, in the case of the latter, *inn vitri* 'the wise'). It must have been based on information provided by contemporary landowners in various parts of Iceland. It contains accounts of the first settlers in each area of Iceland in the late ninth and early tenth centuries, beginning with Ingólfr Arnarson (cf. Text VIII above, note 12) in the southwest of the country, and going round the coast clockwise until it came back to the southwest (though the original work seems to have begun in the south, at the eastern limit of the Southern Quarter). It covers about 430 settlers (men and women), contains 3,500 personal names and about 1500 farm-names. The genealogies of settlers are traced both down to the time of the compilers and back to their origins in Norway or other parts of northern Europe. Since there was no state taxation of landholdings in the Icelandic Commonwealth, the original purpose of the work, insofar as it was not simply historical, may be presumed to have had something to do with assertion of inheritance rights, or more generally to do with the establishment of a national identity.

The work does not survive in its original form, but a version of it, known as Styrmisbók, was made by the priest and historian Styrmir Kárason (died 1245; lawspeaker at the Alþingi 1210–14 and 1232–35; prior of the monastery on Viðey near Reykjavík 1235–45). From this were derived the five surviving redactions. Only a fragment of the Melabók version survives, on parts of two poorly preserved leaves written at the end of the fourteenth or beginning of the fifteenth century. This version was probably compiled by Snorri Markússon of Melar in Melasveit (d. 1313) and seems to have been based fairly closely on Styrmisbók, with some additions from Sagas of Icelanders. Sturlubók was compiled by the historian Sturla Þórðarson (died 1284), nephew of Snorri Sturluson, but is only preserved in AM 107 fol., written by Jón Erlendsson (died 1672). It is this version that first introduced the changed geographical arrangement of the work, beginning now with the settlement of Ingólfr. Sturla also added a great deal of new material from Sagas of Icelanders and other histories or pseudo-historical writings (while some early Sagas of Icelanders may have themselves included material from Styrmisbók). Hauksbók was compiled by *lǫgmaðr* (one of the two highest government officials in Iceland) Haukr Erlendsson (died 1334) in 1306–08. Part of this redaction survives in Haukr's own hand in AM 371 4to, part in AM 105 fol., written again by Jón Erlendsson. Haukr used both Styrmisbók and Sturlubok, and also introduced material from other sources, including Sagas of Icelanders. Skarðsárbók was compiled by Björn Jónsson of Skarðsá (died 1655) in the 1630s, and survives in various copies, the most important of which is AM 104 fol., written by Ásgeir Jónsson (died 1707). It was based principally on Sturlubók and Hauksbók. Finally, there is Þórðarbók, compiled by Þórður Jónsson (died 1670) probably between 1644 and 1651, and preserved in what is largely Þórður's autograph in AM 106 and 112 fol. It is based on Skarðsárbók and Melabók and some other sources, and can be used for reconstructing the lost Melabók text.

The extract below comprises chapters 6–9 of the Sturlubók version (AM 107 fol., ff. 2v21–5v5; S), with some corrections from Hauksbók (H). They tell mainly of the settlement of Ingólfr, held to be the first Icelandic settler, in south-west Iceland, where he lived at what is now the capital of Iceland, Reykjavík (there is a parallel to most of this in *Flóamanna saga* chs 2–3, *ÍF* XIII 233–37). Like many other settlers, he initially appropriated a huge area, comprising the whole of the south-western peninsular of Iceland, but this was subsequently divided up among a number of later arrivals.

Bibliography

Landnámabók is edited by Jakob Benediktsson in *ÍF* I. This is based on Sturlubók, with all the divergent passages in Hauksbók printed on facing pages, and with the whole of what survives of Melabók printed on the lower part of the relevant pages. Variants and additional material from Skarðsárbók and Þórðarbók are indicated in textual notes, while the whole of Skarðsárbók with full variants and most of the additional passages from Þórðarbók are printed in the same editor's *Skarðsárbók. Landnámabók Björns Jónssonar á Skarðsá* (1958 and 1966). The Sturlubók, Hauksbók and Melabók versions are all included in full in *Landnámabók* (1900), ed. Finnur Jónsson. All the primary manuscripts are reproduced in facsimile in *Landnámabók. Ljósprentun handrita*, ed. Jakob Benediktsson (1974), which has an introduction in English as well as in Icelandic. Sturlubók is translated into English in *BS*.

There is discussion in English in Jakob Benediktsson, '*Landnámabók. Some Remarks on its Value as a Historical Source*', *Saga-Book* XVII (1969), 275–92; *MS* 373–74; G. Turville-Petre, *Origins of Icelandic Literature* (1953), ch. 4.

XIX: LANDNÁMABÓK

‹Chapter 6›: Frá Bjǫrnólfi

‹B›jǫrnólfr hét maðr, en annarr Hróaldr; þeir váru synir Hrómundar Gripssonar. Þeir fóru af Þelamǫrk fyrir víga sakir ok staðfestusk í Dalsfirðí á Fjǫlum. Sonr Bjǫrnólfs var Ǫrn, faðir þeira Ingólfs ok Helgu, en Hróalds son var Hróðmarr, faðir Leifs.

Þeir Ingólfr ok Leifr fóstbrœðr fóru í hernað með sonum Atla jarls ens mjóva af Gaulum, þeim Hásteini ok Hersteini ok Hólmsteini. Með þeim fóru ǫll skipti vel, ok er þeir kvámu heim, mæltu þeir til samfara með sér annat sumar. En um vetrinn gørðu þeir fóstbrœðr veizlu sonum jarlsins. At þeiri veizlu strengði Hólmsteinn heit at hann skyldi eiga Helgu Arnardóttur eðr øngva konu ella. Um þessa heitstrenging fannsk mǫnnum fátt, en Leifr roðnaði á at sjá, ok varð fátt um með þeim Hólmsteini er þeir skilðu þar at boðinu.

Um várit eptir bjoggusk þeir fóstbrœðr at fara í hernað ok ætluðu til móts við sonu Atla jarls. Þeir fundusk við Hísargafl, ok lǫgðu þeir Hólmsteinn brœðr þegar til orrostu við þá Leif. En er þeir hǫfðu barizk um hríð, kom at þeim Ǫlmóðr enn gamli, son Hǫrða-Kára, frændi Leifs, ok veitti þeim Ingólfi. Í þeiri orrostu fell Hólmsteinn, en Hersteinn flýði.

Þá fóru þeir Leifr í hernað. En um vetrinn eptir fór Hersteinn at þeim Leifi ok vildi drepa þá, en þeir fengu njósn af fǫr hans ok gørðu mót *honu*m. Varð þá enn orrosta mikil, ok fell þar Hersteinn.

Eptir þat dreif at þeim fóstbrœðrum vinir þeira ór Firðafylki. Váru þá menn sendir á fund Atla jarls ok Hásteins at bjóða sættir, ok sættusk þeir at því at þeir Leifr guldu eignir sínar þeim feðgum.

En þeir fostbrœðr bjoggu skip mikit er þeir áttu, ok fóru at leita lands þess er Hrafna-Flóki hafði fundit ok þá var Ísland kallat. Þeir fundu landit ok váru í Austfjǫrðum í Álptafirði enum syðra. Þeim virðisk landit betra suðr en norðr. Þeir váru einn vetr á landinu ok fóru þá aptr til Nóregs.

Eptir þat varði Ingólfr fé þeira til Íslandsferðar, en Leifr fór í hernað í vestrvíking. Hann herjaði á Írland ok fann þar jarðhús mikit.[1] Þar gekk hann í, ok var myrkt þar til er lýsti af sverði því er maðr helt á. Leifr drap þann mann ok tók sverðit ok mikit fé af honum; síðan var

2 *Space is left for a large ornamented capital at the beginning of each chapter, and also at line 104.* 4 Fjǫlum *H*, Fjǫllum *S*. 22 honum *H*, þeim *S*.

hann kallaðr Hjǫrleifr. Hjǫrleifr herjaði víða um Írland ok fekk þar mikit fé; þar tók hann þræla tíu er svá hétu: Dufþakr ok Geirrøðr, Skjal‹d›bjǫrn, Halldórr ok Drafdittr; eigi eru nefndir fleiri. En eptir þat fór Hjǫrleifr til Nóregs ok fann þar Ingólf fóstbróður sinn. Hann hafði áðr fengit Helgu Arnardóttur, systur Ingólfs.

‹Chapter 7›

‹Þ›enna vetr fekk Ingólfr at blóti miklu ok leitaði sér heilla um forlǫg sín, en Hjǫrleifr vildi aldri blóta. Fréttin vísaði Ingólfi til Íslands. Eptir þat bjó sitt skip hvárr þeira mága til Íslandsferðar; hafði Hjǫrleifr herfang sitt á skipi en Ingólfr félagsfé þeira, ok lǫg‹ð›u til hafs er þeir váru búnir.

‹Chapter 8›

‹S›umar þat er þeir Ingólfr fóru til at byggja Ísland, hafði Haraldr hárfagri verit tólf ár konungr at Nóregi; þá var liðit frá upphafi þessa heims *sex* þúsundir vetra ok sjau tigir ok þrír vetr, en frá holdgan Dróttins átta hundruð ok sjau tigir ok fjǫgur ár. Þeir hǫfðu samflot þar til er þeir sá Ísland; þá skilði með þeim.

Þá er Ingólfr sá Ísland, skaut hann fyrir borð ǫndugissúlum sínum til heilla;[2] hann mælti svá fyrir at hann skyldi þar byggja er súlurnar kœmi á land. Ingólfr tók þar land er nú heitir Ingólfshǫfði, en Hjǫrleif rak vestr fyrir land ok fekk hann vatnfátt. Þá tóku þrælarnir írsku þat ráð at knoða saman mjǫl ok smjǫr, ok kǫlluðu þat óþorstlátt; þeir nefndu þat minþak. En er þat var til búit, kom regn mikit, ok tóku þeir þá vatn á tjǫldum. En er minþakit tók at mygla, kǫstuðu þeir því fyrir borð, ok rak þat á land þar sem nú heitir Minþakseyrr. Hjǫrleifr tók land við Hjǫrleifshǫfða, ok var þar þá fjǫrðr, ok horfði botninn inn at hǫfðanum.

Hjǫrleifr lét þar gjǫra skála tvá, ok er ǫnnur toptin átján faðma, en ǫnnur nítján. Hjǫrleifr sat þar um vetrinn. En um várit vildi hann sá; hann átti einn uxa ok lét hann þrælana draga arðrinn. En er þeir Hjǫrleifr váru at skála, þá gerði Dufþakr þat ráð at þeir skyldu drepa uxann ok segja at skógarbjǫrn[3] hefði drepit, en síðan skyldu þeir ráða á þá Hjǫrleif ef þeir leitaði bjarnarins. Eptir þat sǫgðu þeir Hjǫrleifi þetta. Ok er þeir fóru at leita bjarnarins ok dreifðusk í skóginn, þá

49 vi. *H*, íij. *S*.

settu þrælarnir at sérhverjum þeira ok myrðu þá alla, jafnmarga sér. Þeir hljópu á brutt með konur þeira ok lausafé ok bátinn. Þrælarnir fóru í eyjar þær er þeir sá í haf til útsuðrs, ok bjoggusk þar fyrir um hríð.

Vífill ok Karli hétu þrælar Ingólfs; þá sendi hann vestr með sjó at leita ǫndvegissúlna sinna. En er þeir kvámu til Hjǫrleifshǫfða, fundu þeir Hjǫrleif dauðan. Þá fóru þeir aptr ok sǫgðu Ingólfi þau tíðindi; hann lét illa yfir drápi þeira Hjǫrleifs. Eptir þat fór Ingólfr vestr til Hjǫrleifshǫfða, ok er hann sá Hjǫrleif dauðan, mælti hann:

'Lítit lagðisk hér fyrir góðan dreng, er þrælar skyldu at bana verða, ok sé ek svá hverjum verða ef eigi vill blóta.'

Ingólfr lét búa grǫft þeira Hjǫrleifs ok sjá fyrir skipi þeira ok fjárhlut. Ingólfr gekk þá upp á hǫfðann ok sá eyjar liggja í útsuðr til hafs; kom honum þat í hug at þeir[4] mundu þangat hlaupit hafa, því at bátrinn var horfinn; fóru þeir at leita þrælanna ok fundu þá þar sem Eið heitir í eyjunum. Váru þeir þá at mat er þeir Ingólfr kvámu at þeim. Þeir vurðu felmsfullir ok hljóp sinn veg hverr. Ingólfr drap þá alla. Þar heitir Dufþaksskor er hann[5] lézk. Fleiri hljópu þeir fyrir berg þar sem við þá er kennt síðan. Vestmannaeyjar heita þar síðan er þrælarnir váru drepnir, því at þeir váru Vestmenn. Þeir Ingólfr hǫfðu með sér konur þeira er myrðir hǫfðu verit; fóru þeir þá aptr til Hjǫrleifshǫfða; var Ingólfr þar vetr annan.

En um sumarit eptir fór hann vestr með sjó. Hann var enn þriðja vetr undir Ingólfsfelli fyrir vestan Ǫlfusá. Þau missari fundu þeir Vífill ok Karli ǫndvegissúlur hans við Arnarhvál fyrir neðan heiði.

‹Chapter 9›

‹I›ngólfr fór um várit ofan um heiði; hann tók sér bústað þar sem ǫndvegissúlur hans hǫfðu á land komit; hann bjó í Reykjarvík; þar eru enn ǫndugissúlur þær í eldhúsi. En Ingólfr nam land milli Ǫlfusár ok Hvalfjarðar fyrir útan Brynjudalsá, milli ok Øxarár ok ǫll nes út.

Þá mælti Karli: 'Til ills fóru vér um góð heruð er vér skulum byggja útnes þetta.'

Hann hvarf á brutt ok ambátt með honum. Vífli gaf Ingólfr frelsi, ok byggði hann at Vífilstoptum; við hann er kennt Vífilsfell; þar bjó ‹hann› lengi, varð skilríkr maðr. Ingólfr lét gjǫra skála á Skálafelli; þaðan sá hann reyki við Ǫlfusvatn ok fann þar Karla.

101 kennt Vífilsfell *first written* kendr Vífilsd(alr) *in S*. 102 Skála- *H*, Skalla- *S* (skála *also witten with* -ll- *in S in line 62*).

‹I›ngólfr var frægastr allra landnamsmanna, því at hann kom hér at óbyggðu landi ok byggði fyrstr landit; gørðu þat aðrir landnámsmenn eptir hans dœmum.

Ingólfr átti Hallveigu Fróðadóttur systur[6] Lopts ens gamla; þeira son var Þorsteinn, er þing lét setja á Kjalarnesi áðr Alþingi var sett.[7] Son Þorsteins var Þorkell máni lǫgsǫgumaðr, er einn heiðinna manna hefir bezt verit siðaðr at því er menn vita dœmi til. Hann lét sik bera í sólargeisla í banasótt sinni ok fal sik á hendi þeim Guði er sólina hafði skapat; hafði hann ok lifat svá hreinliga sem þeir kristnir menn er bezt eru siðaðir. Son hans var Þormóðr, er þá var allsherjargoði er kristni kom á Ísland. Hans son var Hamall, faðir Más ok Þormóðar ok Torf‹a›.

Notes

[1] There is a record of such an event in Iceland in 874; see *ÍF* I cxxxvi.

[2] Such high seat pillars may have had carvings of heathen gods on them; presumably the gods were believed to guide the pillars ashore at a propitious place, and they would bave been re-used in the settler’s new home in Iceland. See particularly *Eyrbyggja saga* ch. 4 (*ÍF* IV 7–10).

[3] There have never been any brown bears in Iceland, though polar bears have sometimes reached there on drift ice.

[4] I.e. *þrælarnir* (so Þórðarbók).

[5] I.e. Dufþakr.

[6] Þórðarbók has, more correctly, *fǫðursystur*.

[7] See Text VIII above, lines 44–47 and note 23.

XX: EAST NORSE

Old Norse, as defined in *NION* I, 1.2, refers to Viking-Age and medieval Icelandic (*c*.870–1550) and Norwegian (*c*.750–1350). The term has, however, sometimes been used more widely, to include pre-Reformation Swedish and Danish, and also the Scandinavian colonial languages (besides Icelandic) that resulted from Viking-Age expansion and settlement. *ION*, for example, has separate sections devoted to 'West Norse' (Icelandic and Norwegian) and 'East Norse' (Danish and Swedish). This terminological uncertainty has various causes. Literary and historical scholars have tended to focus almost exclusively on the medieval writings of Iceland and Norway, so that for them Old Norse easily became synonymous with the shared literary idiom of those two countries. Added to that, the English word 'Norse' is not far removed from Scandinavian *norsk*(*r*) 'Norwegian' (from which language Icelandic is of course descended). Those concerned with linguistic history, on the other hand, seeking English equivalents for the Danish/Norwegian terms *vestnordisk* and *østnordisk* (Swedish *västnordiska*, *östnordiska*), tended to alight on 'West Norse' and 'East Norse', though some have preferred 'Old West Scandinavian' and 'Old East Scandinavian'.

Traditionally the East/West division is seen as the first major dialect split in Scandinavian. Prior to that, a relatively homogeneous North or North-West Germanic is supposed to have existed, a daughter language of Common or Proto-Germanic, itself descended from Indo-European. Differences between East and West emerge during the Viking Age (*c*.750–1050) and early Middle Ages (*c*.1050–1200), and are clearly manifested in the oldest preserved vernacular manuscripts from Scandinavia (Iceland and Norway *c*.1150, Denmark and Sweden *c*.1250–75).

How far the traditional view of pre-Reformation Scandinavian linguistic history reflects reality has increasingly been questioned. In the light of what is currently known about language change and diversity, it is hard to believe that a uniform speech community stretching from Helgeland in Norway to southern Jutland, from the Baltic to the North Sea, can have existed at any period. Nor is it easy to see how the radical changes of the Scandinavian syncope period (*c*.550–700), whereby a language not far removed from Common Germanic developed into an idiom close to Old Norse, could have been accomplished without considerable dialectal variation — at least while the changes were under way. The alternative is to assume that throughout the Scandinavian-speaking world a rising generation began simultaneously to alter their speech patterns in identical ways — a scenario that runs counter to the little evidence that exists and seems to be without parallel. It is possible that political and social factors in the early Viking Age worked in favour of linguistic uniformity, giving us the 'Common Scandinavian' of linguistic handbooks, but it is hard to identify precisely what factors these might have been. More likely, there was always dialectal variation of one kind or another, but the sparseness of the sources hides it from our view.

At the start of the manuscript age differences must have existed not only between West and East Norse, but between speech communities all over the Scandinavian world. That, at least, is what the earliest preserved vernacular texts indicate. Beneath the overlay of regional and scriptorium-based norms of writing, a dialect continuum can be glimpsed, running from southern Jutland through the Danish islands to Skåne and thence further north, east and west into Sweden and Norway.

Medieval writings from Denmark and Sweden may thus be expected to show features of East Norse, of regional and of local (scriptorium-based or dialectal) type. In addition there will be variation depending on the age of text or manuscript. The Scandinavian Middle Ages (*c*.1050–1550) were, like the syncope period, a time of great linguistic change. It was then that the grammars of Danish, Norwegian and Swedish lost most of their inherited inflexions, and speech was Germanised through the adoption of vast numbers of words, idioms and derivational affixes from Low German, the language of the Hanseatic traders (many of whom populated the growing Scandinavian towns such as Bergen, Lund, Stockholm).

The West Norse/East Norse dichotomy as it appears in manuscript sources comes down to a limited range of phonological and morphological criteria. The principal shibboleths are enumerated here (grammatical abbreviations are explained at the beginning of the glossary in *NION* III).

(1) In eastern Scandinavia the falling diphthongs /ei/ /au/ /øy/ were monophthongised to /e:/ /ø:/ /ø:/ respectively, e.g. O. Icel. *steinn* 'stone', *lauf* 'foliage', *dreyma* '[to] dream', O. Swed. *sten*, *løf*, *drøma*.

(2) Labial mutation (*NION* I, 3.1.7.1), although not infrequently attested in East Scandinavian runic inscriptions, is largely absent from Danish and Swedish vernacular manuscripts, e.g. O. Icel. *hǫfn* 'harbour' *kǫlluðu* 'called [3rd pl.]', O. Dan. *hafn*, *kallathu/o*.

(3) Front mutation (*NION* I, 3.1.7.2) is also lacking in the East in specific cases: (a) the present tense sg. of strong verbs, e.g. O. Icel. *kømr* 'comes', O. Swed. *kom(b)er*; (b) the past subjunctive of strong verbs and weak verbs of the *krefja* 'demand' and *hafa* 'have' types, e.g. O. Icel. *væri* 'would be', *hefði* 'would have', O. Dan. *vare*, *hafdhe*; (c) where the conditioning factors are /gi/ /ki/, e.g. O. Icel. *tekit* 'taken [supine]', O. Swed. *takit*; (d) where the conditioning factor is /z/ (which ultimately developed to /r/), e.g. O. Icel. *gler* 'glass', O. Dan. *glar*.

(4) In eastern Scandinavia there are more occurrences and more types of breaking (*NION* I, 3.1.7.3) than in the West, e.g. O. Icel. *ek* 'I', *syngva* '[to] sing', O. Swed. *iak*, *siunga*.

(5) /u/ often developed to /o/ in western Scandinavia while remaining unchanged in the East, e.g. O. Icel. *boð* 'message' 'command', O. Dan. *buth*.

(6) The Germanic diphthong /eu/ developed regularly to [ju:] in most eastern forms of Scandinavian, but in the West it became [jo:] immediately before /h/, /m/ and dental consonants (and occasionally in other contexts), e.g. O. Icel. *brjóta* 'break', O. Swed. *briuta*.

(7) Initial [w-] is lost in the West immediately before /r/, e.g. O. Icel. *rangr* 'crooked' 'wrong', O. Swed./Dan. *wrangær*.

(8) Nasal + /p/ /t/ /k/ commonly assimilates to /p:/ /t:/ /k:/ in western Scandinavia, e.g. O. Icel. *kroppinn* 'crooked', *brattr* 'steep', *ekkja* 'widow', O. Swed. *krumpin*, *branter*, *ænkia*.

(9) In eastern Scandinavia the *-sk* form of the verb (*NION* I, 3.6.4, 3.6.5.3) is simplified to *-s*, e.g. O. Icel. *skiljask* '[to] part [from]', *nefnask* '[to] call oneself' '[to] be called', O. Dan. *skiljas*, *nefnæs*.

(10) In western Scandinavia the 2nd pl. verb ending is *-ð*, in Sweden and eastern Denmark (Skåne) *-n*; in the rest of Denmark the consonant is lost, leaving the ending *-æ/-e*, e.g. O. Icel. *hafið* 'have [2nd pl. pres.]', O. Swed. *hauin*, (central and western) O. Dan. *hauæ*.

(11) In western Scandinavia the dat. pl. form of the suffixed definite article is *-num*, in Sweden and northern Skåne it is *-in/-en*, in Denmark otherwise *-num/-nom*, e.g. O. Icel. *steinunum* 'the stones [dat. pl.]', O. Swed. *stenomen*, O. Dan. *dyefflonom* 'the devils [dat. pl.]'.

The East/West division is by no means absolute (as items 10 and especially 11 indicate). Various western features are found in Danish manuscripts, especially those from Jutland (types of palatal mutation as in *slær* 'hits', O. Swed. *slar*, lack of breaking as in *æk* 'I', O. Swed. *iak*, 'o' rather than 'u' spellings as in *both* 'message' 'command', O. Swed. *buþ*). Nor can the language of Gotland easily be classified as

West or East Norse. In common with the former it retains the falling diphthongs, e.g. *bain* 'bone', *draumbr* 'dream', *droyma* '[to] dream'; on the other hand, it prefers /u/ even where O. Swed. and O. Dan. have /o/, e.g. *fulc* 'people', *lufa* '[to] permit', O. Swed. *folk*, *loua*. Other areas of the medieval Scandinavian world also have their linguistic peculiarities (as indicated above). Haugen offers an introduction to the variety in his 'Checklist of dialectal criteria in O[ld] Sc[andinavian] manuscripts (1150–1350)' (1976, 210–13).

Time as well as place can affect the language of medieval Scandinavian manuscripts. Around 1300 written Norwegian and Swedish still by and large retained the inflexional system inherited from North Germanic. By 1400, this system was in an advanced state of collapse. Danish succumbed earlier. Manuscripts from around 1300 show that Jutlandic apocope (loss of final vowels) and Zealandic reduction of unstressed vowels to /ə/ had already taken place, sweeping away the many inflexions dependent on the /a/ /i/ /u/ trichotomy (e.g. corresponding to O. Icel. *kallaða*, *kallaði*, *kǫlluðu* 'called [1st sg., 3rd sg., 3rd pl. indic.]' we find simply *kallæth* or *kallæthe*). Only in Skåne, where little or no reduction had occurred, does the language of the earliest Danish manuscripts regularly exhibit traditional case endings and verbal inflexions.

By the fifteenth century the influence of Low German had begun to make itself felt in Danish, Swedish and Norwegian manuscripts (introducing words such as *æra* 'honour', *handel* 'trade', *stolter* 'splendid' 'gallant', *bruka* 'use' and derivational affixes like *an-*, *be-*, *-aktig*, *-het*, Middle Low German *êre*, *handel*, *stolt*, *brûken*, *an-*, *be-*, *-achtich*, *-heit*). In Norway this influence resulted in part from the Swedicisation and ultimately Danicisation of the written language. So strong was the Danish input that by the time of the Reformation Norwegian had all but ceased to exist as a written medium.

Four samples of eastern Scandinavian are now provided, two from Sweden and two from Denmark. They have been selected for their linguistic (and generic) variety. Different geographical areas are represented, different stages in the development of Swedish and Danish and different styles. Unlike Old Icelandic and to some extent Old Norwegian texts, those from eastern Scandinavia are not customarily normalised. The manuscript spellings are thus retained here, although abbreviations are expanded without comment.

Bibliography

Michael P. Barnes, 'Language'. In *Medieval Scandinavia: an Encyclopedia*, ed. Phillip Pulsiano and Kirsten Wolf (1993), 376–78.

Michael [P.] Barnes, 'Language'. In *A Companion to Old Norse-Icelandic Literature and Culture*, ed. Rory McTurk (2005), 173–89.

Einar Haugen, *The Scandinavian Languages: an Introduction to their History* (1976).

Einar Haugen, *Scandinavian Language Structures: a Comparative Historical Survey* (1982).

Åke Holmbäck and Elias Wessén, *Svenska landskapslagar* 1 (1933).

Gunnar Knudsen, *Mariager Legende-Haandskrift Gl. kgl. Saml. 1586 4to* (Samfund til udgivelse af gammel nordisk litteratur 44, 1917–30).

Erik Kroman, *Danmarks gamle købstadlovgivning* 1, *Sønderjylland* (1951).

Rolf Pipping, *Erikskrönikan enligt cod. Holm. D 2* (Samlingar utgivna av Svenska fornskrift-sällskapet, part 158, 1921; reprinted as part 231, 1963).

Rolf Pipping, *Kommentar till Erikskrönikan* (Svenska litteratursällskapet i Finland 187, 1926).

Jerker Rosén, 'Erikskrönikan', *Kulturhistoriskt Lexikon för nordisk medeltid* 4 (1959), 28–34.

C. J. Schlyter, *Samling af Sweriges Gamla Lagar* 3 (1834).

Lars Vikør, *The Nordic Languages: their Status and Interrelations* (3rd ed., 2002).

Elias Wessén, *De nordiska språken* (1965 and later printings).

XX A: THE PROVINCIAL LAW OF UPPLAND

The age of this law is uncertain, but there are indications that parts of it may have existed in oral form in the late Viking Age. There are five medieval manuscripts. The text printed below — the preface to the law — follows Uppsala Universitetsbibliotek B 12 (from the first half of the fourteenth century), f. 1. The complete manuscript is published in Schlyter (1834), and a modern Swedish translation with extensive commentary is available in Holmbäck and Wessén (1933), see especially 7, 10–12. Many of the sentiments expressed in the passage about the purpose and role of the law (lines 5–10) are to be found in similar form in the prefaces to other Scandinavian provincial law texts.

Notes on the language

1. Monophthongisation of /ei/ /au/ /øy/ is marked throughout, e.g. *heþin* (11) 'heathen', *giøtæ* (3) 'of the Geats [gen. pl.]', *gømæs* (7) 'be observed', O. Icel. *heiðinn*, *gauta*, *geymast*.

2. Labial mutation is absent, e.g. *lagh* (1) 'law', *allum* (3) 'to all [dat. pl.]', O. Icel. *lǫg*, *ǫllum*.

3. Front mutation is absent in the past subj. form *warin* (10) 'were [3rd pl.]' and the supine (*aff*) *takit* (18) 'remove', O. Icel. *væri*, *tekit*.

4. The scribe writes 'v' rather than 'o' in *Gvþ* (1) 'God', cf. early West Norse *goð*, later *guð*.

5. The scribe writes 'iu' rather than 'io' in *þiuffnæþ* (24) 'theft', cf. O. Icel. *þjófnaðr*.

6. Historical [w] is shown in initial position before /r/, e.g. *wrangum* (9) 'wrongdoers [dat. pl.]', O. Icel. *rǫngum*.

7. The *-sk* verb form appears as *-s* throughout, e.g. *gømæs* (7) 'be maintained', *haldæs* (7) 'be kept', *skiptis* (20) 'is divided', O. Icel. *geymask*, *haldask*, *skiptisk*.

8. The 3rd pl. past subj. form *warin* (10) 'were' shows the *-n* ending typical of O. Swed. and the O. Dan. of Skåne (contrast O. Icel. *væri*). Final *-n* was generally lost in Viking-Age Scandinavian, but retained in certain forms in East Norse, cf. O. Swed. *øghon*, O. Dan. *øghæn* 'eyes', O. Icel. *augu*.

9. A characteristic feature of O. Swed. is the development of /d/ between /n:/ and /r/ and /l:/ and /r/, of /b/ between /m/ and /l/ and /m/ and /r/, and of /p/ between /m/ and /n/ and /m/ and /t/ (the linguistic term for this phenomenon is segmentation). Examples from the passage below are: *aldræ* (20) 'of all [gen. pl.]', *Fæmpti* (25) '[the] fifth', O. Icel. *allra*, *fimti*.

10. Characteristic of the O. Swed. of the province of Uppland is the use of '-æ' in unstressed syllables (especially endings) rather than '-a'. There are examples throughout the passage below, e.g. *sweæ* (3) 'of the Swedes', *wæræ* (5) '[to] be', *timæ* (11) 'time [dat. sg.]' 'era'. In other kinds of O. Swed. we find either '-a', or a mixture of '-a' and '-æ' dependent either on the quantity of the preceding stressed syllable or the quality of its vowel.

11. The inflexional system inherited from Germanic is still more or less intact in the B 12 manuscript of *The Provincial Law of Uppland*, though there are signs of incipient breakdown. The genitive is not necessarily found after *mellum* 'between' and *til* 'to', e.g. *mellum ræt ok o ræt* (6–7) 'between right and wrong', *til næfst* (8) 'for the chastisement', nor the dative after *aff* 'off' 'from' and *i* 'in', e.g. *aff . . . warþt raþ* (17–18) 'according to . . . our deliberations', *i. kristnu ræt* (14) 'in the Christian Law'. Acc. m. sg. *þæn* 'the' has been extended into the nom., e.g. *þæn fyrsti ær* (21) 'the first is'.

XX A: THE PROVINCIAL LAW OF UPPLAND

Gvþ siælwær skipaþi fyrstu lagh. ok sændi sinu folki mæþ moyses. ær fyrsti laghmaþær war. fore hans folki. Swa sændir ok en waldughær kunungær sweæ oc giøtæ. Byrghir son magnusæ. kununx. allum þem ær byggiæ mellum haffs ok sæw strøms ok øþmorþæ bok þessæ mæþ wigers flokkum. ok laghum. upplænzkum. Lagh skulu wæræ satt ok skipaþ almænni til styrls baþi rikum ok fatøkum. ok skiæl mellum ræt ok o ræt. Lagh skulu gømæs ok haldæs fatøkum til wærnær. spakum til friþær. æn o spakum til næfst ok ognær. Lagh skulu wæræ rætwisum ok snællum til sømdær. æn wrangum ok o snællum til rætningær. warin allir rætwisir þa þurfpti æi lagha wiþ. Laghæ yrkir war wiger spa. heþin i. heþnum timæ. Hwat ær wi hittum .i. hans laghsaghu ær allum mannum þarfflikt ær. þæt sætium wi[r] .i. bok þessæ. þæt o þarfft ær. ok þungi ær. at þæt uilium wi[r] utæn lykkia. Hwat ok ær hin heþne læt affat wæræ swa sum ær. i. kristnu ræt ok kirkiu laghum. þæt skulum wi[r] til økiæ .i. upbyriæn þæssæri bok. Ok wilium wir fylghiæ .i. laghum þæmmæ warum forfæþrum. Erikinum hælghæ. Byrghiri iarli. ok magnus[i] kunung[i] ok aff wari brysthyggiu. ok warþt raþ. hwat wir gitum til satt. ællr aff takit. sum allum snællum samþykkis a. þa skulum wir samæn sættiæ til þarwæ aldræ mannæ. ær byggiæ þær wir fyrmer saghþum. Bok þæssi skiptis .i. attæ laghæ balkæ. þæn fyrsti ær kirkiu balkær. ær man skal ‹sial› sinæ mæþ giømæ. Annær balkær ær um kunung. ok kununx eþsøre. ok skipwistir hans. ok um roþæræt. Þriþi balkær ær um giptæ mal. ok um ærffþir. Fierþi balkær ær um drap saer. ran. þiuffnæþ. ok fyndir. Fæmpti ær um iorþir. Sætti ær um løsøræ kiøp ok giæstning. Siundi ær bygningæ balkær. Attundi ok siþærsti ær um þingmal.

12, 13, 15, 17 *letters written but subsequently erased.* 21 *word omitted by scribe, supplied by Schlyter (1834, 7) from other manuscripts.*

XX B: THE TOWN LAW OF FLENSBORG

Apparently first written in Latin, this law was revised and put into Danish about 1300. The principal manuscript of the Danish text (now in Flensborg Stadsarkiv) stems from this period. The extracts printed below are found on ff. 1–2 (preface and *Vm arf*), 14–15 (*skipthiuf*, *skip i hauæn*). The complete text is published (without commentary) in Kroman (1951), 113–35, the sections below on pp. 113–14, 128.

Notes on the language

1. Monophthongisation of /ei/ /øy/ is marked throughout (except in the negative adverb 'ey' (6), cf. modern Danish and Swedish *ej*), e.g. *them* (5) 'them', *døør* (8) 'dies', (*han*) *gømæ* (19) '[let him] keep', O. Icel. *þeim*, *deyr*, *geymi*.

2. Labial mutation is absent in (*the*) *hafth* (6) 'they had', O. Icel. *þeir hǫfðu*. It is however marked in *børn* (13), *børnæ* (11) 'children', *logh* (13) 'law'. The product of labial mutation regularly develops to /ø/ in Danish when immediately followed by /l/ and /r/ (cf. modern Danish *øl* 'beer', *ørn* 'eagle'). N. pl. *logh* has exceptionally retained the mutated vowel (albeit probably as /o/); other neuter nouns with root /a/ exhibit the same vowel in sg. and pl., e.g. *land* 'country' 'countries', *blath* 'leaf' 'leaves'. Forms such as *oll* (8) 'all' do not reflect labial mutation, but rather rounding of /a/ immediately before /l:/ (common in manuscripts from southern Jutland), cf. *ollæ* (4), *olt* (20) 'all', O. Icel. *allir*, *allt*.

3. Front mutation is absent in the sg. pres. indic. forms *takær* (9) 'takes', *hauær* (11) 'has', *kummær* (32) 'comes', O. Icel. *tekr*, *hefr*, *kømr*. It is however found in *fææxr* (19) 'gets', *hæuær* (22) 'has', which is in keeping with the position in many Jutlandic dialects past and present (cf. above).

4. Breaking is absent from *stæl* (29) 'steals'. Jutlandic follows West Norse in being less prone to breaking than the generality of eastern dialects, cf. O. Icel. *stelr*, O. Swed. and central and eastern O. Dan. *stiæl*.

5. The scribe writes 'iu' rather than 'io' in *iutland* (5) 'Jutland', *skipthiuf* (28) 'ship thief', cf. O. Icel. *Jótland*, *þjófr*. Note, however, the forms *spiyt* (15) 'speer', *stiyp mothær* (22) 'stepmother', *nytæ* (23) '[let them] enjoy', which indicate the development /iu:/ > /iy:/ > /y:/ (cf. modern Danish *bryde* 'break', *dyb* 'deep', *nyde* 'enjoy', but also *Jylland* 'Jutland').

6. Nasal + /t/ is unassimilated in *wintær* (3) 'winters', cf. O. Icel. *vetr*. We also find 'nt' written where East as well as West Norse normally has '(t)t', e.g. *ient* (29) '[indef. art.]', *sint* (32) '[refl. poss.]', O. Icel. *eitt*, *sitt*, O. Swed. *et*, *sit*. These may be unassimilated forms too, but they could be analogical new formations in which the root morpheme (*i*)*en*-, *sin*- has been extended into the n. sg.

7. The *-sk* verb form appears as *-s* throughout, e.g. *byriæs* (1) 'begins', *skiftæs* (21) 'be divided', *økæs* (26) 'increases', cf. O. Icel. *byrjask, skiptask, eyksk.*

8. Characteristic of central and Jutlandic O. Dan. is the weakening of unstressed vowels: on Zealand and the other islands they tend to be reduced to [ə], commonly written 'e' or 'æ'; in Jutland word-final vowels are often apocopated (lost). The extracts below show both reduction to [ə] and loss, e.g. *liuær* (8) 'lives', *theræ* (26) 'their', *kunæ* (17) 'wife', *hafth* (6) 'had', *æfn* (15) 'means', *mell* (26) 'between', *scul* (29) 'are to', cf. O. Icel. *lifir, þeira, konu, hǫfðu, efni, milli, skulu.*

9. Jutlandic dialects often exhibit diphthongisation of /e:/ and /o:/. In the extracts below we find, e.g., *ien* (9) 'one', *gwoz* (20) 'property'. It is this diphthongisation that gives, for example, modern Danish *hjem* as opposed to Icel. *heim*, Swed *hem.*

10. The forms *iauæn* (9) 'equal', *gaghin* (27) 'gain' may reflect the syllabicisation of final /-n/ (cf. O. Icel. *jafn, gagn*), but it has also been suggested that these spellings could represent an early attempt to mark the glottal catch (*stød*), characteristic of many kinds of modern Danish.

11. Little of the inherited Germanic inflexional system remains in the Flensborg law text. With a few exceptions nominal and verbal endings are either apocopated or appear as *-æ*, *-ær*, *-æs* or *-s* (cf. the examples under item 8 above, and additionally *byriæs* (1) 'begins', *thers* (27) 'theirs', O. Icel. *byrjask, þeira*). Not only have many of the traditional inflexional distinctions disappeared, there has also been much analogical restructuring. We find, for example, *bymens* (1) 'townsmen's', *fathærs* (24) 'father's', *thers* (27) 'theirs', where the *-s* originally appropriate to the gen. sg. of certain nouns, pronouns and adjectives has been generalised as a possessive ending (O. Icel. *bæjar-manna, fǫður, þeira*); further: *klæthær* (10) 'clothes' and *børnæ* (21) 'children', where the plural morphemes *-r* and *-æ/-e* (the latter not uncommon in Danish) have been extended to neuter nouns which originally had no plural ending in Old Norse (O. Icel. *klæði, bǫrn*).

12. Grammatical gender no longer follows the pattern inherited from Germanic (and ultimately Indo-European). Masculine and feminine have largely coalesced, while words modifying certain neuter nouns are not marked for neuter gender, e.g. *thinnæ scra* (4) 'this legal code', O. Icel. *þessa skrá* (acc. f. sg.), *annæn kunæ* (17) 'another wife', O. Icel. *aðra konu* (acc. f. sg.), *ien par* (11) 'one pair', O. Icel. *einu pari* (dat. n. sg.), *hwær barn* (18–19) 'each child', O. Icel. *hvert barn* (nom. n. sg.). During the Middle Ages written Danish gradually loses the features that distinguish masculine and feminine gender, leading to the two-gender system of the modern standard language. Most Jutlandic dialects ultimately drop the neuter sg. *-t* marker in adjectives, while an area of western Jutland abandons the old gender system entirely, introducing a new distinction between countable nouns, which are common (m. + f.) gender, and non-countables, which are neuter. The confusion seen

in the extract below is presumably an indication of the way grammatical gender was developing in Jutland.

13. As early as medieval Danish we find that counting between 50 and 99 may be by the score, as it is in the modern language. Here *fiyrsin tiughæ* (2) denotes ‘eighty’, i.e. ‘four times twenty’ (modern Danish *firs*).

XX B: THE TOWN LAW OF FLENSBORG

Hær byriæs bymens skra af flænsborgh.

Fra wors hærræ aar, thusænd wintær. oc tuhundræth. fiyrsin tiughæ, oc fiyræ wintær. a fyrmer wor frugh aftæn.[1] aldærmen oc rathmen, oc ollæ bymæn i flænsborgh, lotæ scriuæ thinnæ scra, thær hærtugh woldemar af iutland gaf them. oc stathfæst mæth sin naath oc wold. for thi at the hafth ey fyr stathæligh skra.

Vm arf.

Af husbond døør i by, oc husfrugh liuær. i oll arf skift, oc af oll arf, hun takæ iauæn løt with aruing thær mest takær. Thær yuær ien full sæng. Af thry par klæthær, takæ hun then mæthælst. af tu par then krankær. af ien par, faangær hun ekki. Af hun hauær athælkunæ børnæ. the mugh krauæ theræ fæthærn, hwannær the wilæ. Enn liuær fathær, oc døør mothær. mæth engi logh, børn krauæ theræ mæthærn. tho at fathær takær annæn husfrø. Fathær scal tho giuæ hwær syn thre mark penning. skiold. swørth. oc spiyt. af æfn ær til.

Vm arf.

Thær fathær takær annæn kunæ. for brollæp. ellær brollæps dagh. fathær gif ut børn mæthærn.[2] ellær næfnæ gwoth witnæ til, mykæt hwær barn fæær til siit mæthærn. Oc han gømæ thet e mæth the wilæ. En for glømer han thet. tha skal olt hans gwoz, oc thet gwoz thær han fæk mæth hans kunæ skiftæs iauænt i tu. oc halft takæ hans børnæ. oc halft han mæth theræ stiyp mothær. Af hun hæuær børn fyr with annæn sin gift man.[3] the nytæ then samæ ræt, thær sagh ær. En brollups kost skal af fathærs løt ut gangæ. sum mothærs iorthæ færth. af ien barn løt.[4]

Vm arf.

E mæth arf ær mell fathær oc børn vskift. økæs theræ gooz, ellær nøkæs. gaghin oc skathæ wæræ oll thers.

skipthiuf

Hwo sum stæl i skip. skipmen scul ham sættæ i ient vbygd øland mæth tundær oc eldiærn. oc thrigi dagh cost.

skip i hauæn

Hwannær skip kummær i hafn. ænik skipman ma føræ sint gooz af skip, vtæn styræman, oc skipmenz orlof. 33

Notes

[1] 15th August, the festival of the Assumption. The Latin text of the law has *in crastino assumptionis beatae uirginis*, i.e. 16th August.

[2] 'Where the father takes another wife, the father is to distribute to the children the inheritance which comes from the mother before the wedding or the wedding day.'

[3] 'If she already has children by another husband . . .'

[4] 'But the wedding expenses are to be taken from the father's share, [just] as the mother's funeral [expenses are to be taken] from one child's share [of the inheritance].'

XX C: ERIK'S CHRONICLE (ERIKSKRØNIKAN)

Erik's Chronicle is a verse history of Swedish political affairs covering the period from the early thirteenth century until the election of Magnus Eriksson as king in 1319. Although the text was probably composed in the 1320s, the earliest extant manuscripts are from the second half of the fifteenth century. The genesis of *Erik's Chronicle* is poorly understood. Some have thought to see traces of Västergötland dialect in the text, and have connected the work to that part of Sweden, but in the forms in which we have the poem it is the late medieval character of the O. Swed. that is most striking. The extract printed below, lines 862–93 of the poem, is taken from p. 20 of Royal Library, Stockholm, MS D 2, dated 1470–80. The complete manuscript is edited in Pipping (1921), and there is a detailed commentary on *Erik's Chronicle* in Pipping (1926). See also Rosén (1959).

Notes on the language

1. Monophthongisation of /ei/ /øy/ is marked throughout, e.g. *swena flere* (5) 'many squires', *lôðst* (8) 'untied', O. Icel. *sveinar fleiri, leyst*.

2. Labial mutation is absent, e.g. *haffdo* (8) 'had', *allom* (11) 'all', *margh* (28, 32) 'many a', O. Icel. *hǫfðu, ǫllum, mǫrg*.

3. The scribe writes 'u' rather than 'o' in *skutin* (27) 'pushed aside', *brutin* (28) 'broken', O. Icel. *skotin, brotin*.

4. The scribe writes 'iw' rather than 'io' in the nickname *diwr* (21), O. Icel. *dýr* (<**deuʀa*), Faroese *djór*.

5. Segmentation of /d/ between /n:/ and /r/ and of /p/ between /m/ and /n/ is found (cf. passage A, Notes on the language 9), e.g. *andre* (5) 'other', *kompne* (3) 'come [pp.]', O. Icel. *aðrir* (< **annriʀ*, **anþriʀ*), *komnir*.

6. The vowels of unstressed syllables are mostly written 'a', 'e', 'o' as in modern Swedish, though 'i' and 'u' also occur, e.g. *thera* (8) 'their', *hallande* (18) 'Halland [dat. sg.]', *waro* (3) 'were', *bordhin* (27) 'the tables', *lupu* (30) 'ran [3rd pl.]' 'knocked', O. Icel. *þeira, Hallandi, váru, borðin, hlupu*. The rules governing the spoken and written forms of unstressed vowels in O. Swed. are complex, but by the second half of the fifteenth century 'a', 'e' and 'o' predominate in writing. The form *sagdo* in line 11 is presumably a scribal error, since the subject is singular.

7. M. nom. pl. *-r* is lost, e.g. *kompne* (3) 'come [pp.]', *andre slike* (21) 'other such [people]', *swena* (5) 'squires', O. Icel. *komnir, aðrir slíkir, sveinar*. This is a reflection of a general tendency in O. Swed. for historical [ʀ] (so-called 'palatal *r*') to be dropped in unstressed position immediately following

a vowel. The tendency is seen most clearly in certain texts from Östergötland and Småland, and seems to weaken in dialects further north and east.

8. There is evidence for the lengthening of short stressed syllables, a development that affected all forms of Scandinavian in one way or another between *c.*1200 and 1550, e.g. *samma* (2) 'same' (lengthened consonant), *wiid* (9) 'at', *maat* (9) 'food' (lengthened vowel), O. Icel. *sǫmu*, *við*, *mat*.

9. The inherited Germanic inflexional system has in large part been abandoned. This is not the result of the merger or loss of unstressed vowels as in Zealandic and Jutlandic Danish, but stems chiefly from a failure (of uncertain cause) to maintain the inflexional distinctions still potentially available in the language. Acc. replaces dat. in *gawo sik* (7) 'gave themselves', *aff sik* (8) 'from themselves', O. Icel. *gáfu sér*, *af sér*; acc. replaces gen. in *jnnan then samma tiidh* (2) 'within the same period', *mellom gardhin ok ena broo* (15) 'between the farm and a certain bridge', O. Icel. *innan* + gen. (normally), *(á/í) milli/millum* + gen.; indeterminate case replaces gen. in *til swerike* (22) 'to Sweden', O. Icel. *til Svíþjóðar*; dat. replaces acc. in *ælskade them* (26) 'loved them', O. Icel. *elskaði þá*; the demands of rhyme overwhelm the strong nom. m. sg. adjectival ending in, e.g., *goodh* (13) 'fine', *stark* (19) 'strong', O. Icel. *góðr*, *sterkr*; acc. m. sg. *then* has replaced nom. m. sg. *sa* (10) 'that' (a very early change in O. Swed., cf. passage A, Notes on the language 11), and acc. f. sg. *þa* (2) 'that' 'the', O. Icel. *sá*, *þá*.

10. Middle Low German influence is seen in the loan words *hælade* (13) 'warrior', *kamp* (14) 'battle', *bestoodh* (14) 'fought', *bleff* (32) 'remained' (cf. Low German *helet*, *kamp*, *bestân*, *blîven*). Note also the prefix *be-* (cf. Low German *be-*), which becomes productive in the mainland Scandinavian languages. The phrases *The danske* (3) 'the Danes' and *the vplænzske* (12) 'the Upplanders', with their preposed definite articles, are probably also Low German inspired (cf. O. Icel. *danir*, *upplendingar*).

11. Danish influence, not uncommon in late O. Swed., is found in the replacement of the reflexive pronoun and reflexive possessive by the corresponding 3rd pl. pronoun and possessive, e.g. *them* (25) 'themselves', *thera* (8) 'their', for *sik*, *sina(r)*.

XX C: ERIK'S CHRONICLE (ERIKSKRØNIKAN)

jNnan Etake war een striidh
tha jnnan then samma tiidh[1]
The danske[2] waro tha kompne tiit
herra benkt aff alsô ok palne hwit
Ok andre riddare ok swena flere
wæl hwndrada ôrss ok æn mere
Ok gawo sik alle godha trôst
ok haffdo thera plator aff sik lôôst
Ok satho wiid bord ok fingo sik maat
tha ôpte then man i træno saat
Ok sagdo them allom tidhande
at the vplænzske[3] komo ther ridhande
Herra wlff karsson een hælade goodh
huilkin kamp han ther bestoodh
mellom gardhin ok ena broo
han sagde ther aff æ til han doo
wæl twhundradhe ôrss waro thee
herra peder porsse aff hallande
een rasker hælade fromer ok stark
han war wt driffwen aff danmark
Ok offe diwr ok andre slike
the waro tha rymde til swerike[4]
Ok haffdo eth hertoghanom[5] eth hald
hertoghen lente them gotz ok wald[6]
Swa at the matto them wæl næra
ok ælskade them wæl ok haffde them kæra
bordhin wordo tha rasklika skutin
ok margh dôr sônder brutin
The hafdo summi latit sina hesta i stal
thera swena lupu hwar annan vm koll
Thera ôrss waro tha rasklika hænt
margh plata bleff ther ospent

23 eth (1)] *error for* aff '*from*'; *the scribe probably anticipated the following* eth.

Notes

[1] In 1277, following certain other acts of war committed by the Danes and the deposed Swedish king Valdemar Birgirsson in south-western Sweden.

[2] The Danish forces.

[3] The Swedish forces, fighting on behalf of the Swedish king, Magnus Birgirsson, younger brother of Valdemar.

[4] If Peder Porsse and Offe Diwr are to be identified with the Peder Porse and Uffo Dyre who were said to be among those responsible for the murder of the Danish king, Erik Klipping, we have to assume a chronological error in *Erik's Chronicle*, since the murder did not take place until 1286, nine years after the events portrayed here. There is evidence to suggest that at least some of those implicated in the death of King Erik fled to Sweden and obtained protection from King Magnus (Pipping (1926), 339–40; see also note 5 below).

[5] Before he became king of Sweden, Magnus bore the title 'duke'. He was elected king in 1275, but *Erik's Chronicle* has got events out of order (cf. note 4 above).

[6] Magnus gave the fleeing Danes succour (*hald*), granting them estates and power (i.e. fiefs).

XX D: THE MARIAGER BOOK OF LEGENDS

The Mariager Book of Legends is the (modern) title given to manuscript GKS 1586 4to (Royal Library, Copenhagen), a compilation of hagiographic literature and miracles translated into Danish from Latin, focusing in particular on the life and works of St Jerome (*c*.345–420). GKS 1586 4to dates itself to 1488, and states that it was written in the Birgittine monastery of Mariager, north-eastern Jutland, by brother Nicolaus Magni. Rather than Jutlandic, the language reflects the embryonic Zealandic standard that came increasingly to characterise late medieval written Danish, although various Jutlandic features can be found here and there throughout the manuscript. The extract printed below is taken from an apocryphal letter of St Cyril (*c*.315–86), Bishop of Jerusalem (*c*.349–86), to St Augustine (354–430), Bishop of Hippo (North Africa, *c*.396–430), and is found on ff. 97v–98r of GKS 1586 4to. The complete manuscript is published in Knudsen (1917–30).

Notes on the language

1. Monophthongisation of /ei/ /øy/ is marked throughout (except in the negative adverb 'ey' (12), cf. modern Danish and Swedish *ej*), e.g. *them* (3) 'them', *helighet* (4) 'holiness', *hørdhe* (11) 'heard [pp.]', O. Icel. *þeim*, *heilagleiki*, *heyrð*.

2. Front mutation is absent in the preterite subjunctive form *haffdhæ* (2) 'had' as is usual in East Norse, O. Icel. *hefðir* (though it is questionable how far a separate subjunctive mood is still a recognisable category in Danish at this late date).

3. Breaking is found in *iek* (8, 12) 'I', O. Icel *ek*. The original broken form is *iak* (thus O. Swed., cf. modern Swed. *jag*), but in Danish the [j] fronts the immediately following /a/ (modern Dan. *jeg*).

4. The form *sywffn* (14) for earlier *sjun* 'vision' 'revelation', O. Icel. *sjón*, *sýn*, seems to reflect a north-eastern Jutlandic dialect development whereby [ju:] > [yw].

5. The -*sk* form of the verb appears as -*s* in *lighnes* (5) 'resembles', O. Icel. *líkisk*.

6. The segmentation of /d/, /b/ and /p/ occurs in O. Dan. as well as O. Swed. (cf. passage A, Notes on the language 9), but in Dan. the development is in most cases reversed during the fourteenth century. However, /d/ sometimes remains between /n:/ and /r/, as in *andhre* (5) 'other' (<*annriʀ, *anþriʀ.).

7. The vowels of unstressed syllables are written '-e' or '-æ', both almost certainly reflecting some form of the central vowel [ə], e.g. *withæ* (1) 'know',

sændhe (4) 'sent', *sthoræ* (10) 'great', *ware* (11) 'were', O. Icel. *vita*, *sendir*, *stóru*, *váru*. Although the manuscript was written in Jutland, there are only occasional signs of the apocope of word-final vowels, as in the weak adjectival form *hedherligh* (15) 'honourable', O. Icel. *heiðarligi*.

8. Vowel + voiced velar spirant [ɣ] is normally diphthongised in medieval Danish. Following back vowels [ɣ] > [w], which is reflected in the forms *saffdh* (2) 'told', *saw* (< *sagh*, with analogical [ɣ]) (15) 'saw', O. Icel. *sagt*, *sá*.

9. In O. Dan. /p/ /t/ /k/ > /b/ /d/ /g/ medially between vowels and finally immediately following a vowel. This development is only sporadically marked in pre-Reformation writing, cf. *noghet* (< *nokot*) (3) 'something', *liighæ* (4) 'comparable', but *withæ* (1) 'know', *oc* (*passim*) 'and', *iek* (8) 'I', O. Icel. *nǫkkut*, *líkr*, *vita*, *ok*, *ek*, modern Dan. *noget*, *lig*, *vide*, *og*, *jeg*.

10. The inherited Germanic inflexional system has been almost wholly abandoned and replaced by something akin to the system of standard modern Danish. Morphological case is not much in evidence outside personal pronouns, and verbs are inflected for number and little else (this feature was finally discarded from the written language in the late nineteenth century). Lack of case inflexion can be seen in, e.g., *i thynæ breffwe* (3) 'in your letters', *aff mænneske* (11) 'by people', *for manghe daghe* (16) 'many days ago', O. Icel. *í bréfum þínum*, *af mǫnnum*, *fyrir mǫrgum dǫgum* (all dat.); there is no gender marking in, e.g., *thynæ breffwe* (3) 'your letters' (with analogical plural *-æ*/*-e*, cf. O. Icel. nom./acc. pl. *bréf þín*), *æren* (5) 'the glory' (f. indistinguishable from m.); the absence of personal inflexion from verbs is documented in, e.g., *thu haffdhæ* (2) 'you had', *Wij som withe* (9) 'we who know', O. Icel. *þú hefðir*, *vér sem vitum*. Preserved inflexional distinctions are, e.g., *war* (4) 'was', *ware* (11) 'were', *iek* (13) 'I', *mik* (16) 'me', *Wij* (9) 'we', *oss* (8) 'us'.

11. Middle Low German influence is seen in the loan words *ære*(*n*) (5) 'honour' 'glory', *bewiisthe* (6) 'demonstrated', *megtughe* (6) 'powerful', *thwiffwell* (7) 'doubt', *forklaræ* (12) 'establish' (cf. Low German *êre*, *bewîsen*, *mechtich*, *twîvel*, *vorklaren*). Note also the prefixes *be-* and *for-* and the suffix *-het* (Low German *be-*, *vor-*, *-heit*), which become productive in the mainland Scandinavian languages (as already here in, e.g., *helighet* (4) 'holiness', *sandhet* (8) 'truth', where *-het* is used to derive abstract nouns from native adjectives).

12. The orthography reflects a tendency to employ superfluous consonants, a usage which reached its culmination in sixteenth- and seventeenth-century handwritten Danish, e.g. *haffdhæ* (2) 'had', *skreffsth* (3) 'wrote', *thwiffwell* (7) 'doubt'.

XX D: THE MARIAGER BOOK OF LEGENDS

Kæresthe Augustine sigher sanctus Cyrillus Thu skalth withæ At manghe haffwe ther vndher paa ligherwiiss som thu haffdhæ saffdh them noghet nyth oc vhørligth Ther thu skreffsth i thynæ breffwe som thu sændhe mik. at jeronimus war liighæ i helighet johanni baptisthæ. oc andhre apostelæ Oc at han lighnes them oc i æren Hwicketh thu bewiisthe meth megtughe skæll oc vndherlighe sywffn Sanneligh ther er enghen thwiffwell vppa Mæn thet er alzwærdugsth at throo j all sannesthe sandhet oc gudelighet Oc wænther iek at oss skall enghen vndher oc thwiffwell hændhe ther om Wij som withe hans helgesthe leffneth. oc hans sthoræ vndherlighe jærthegnæ som aldrigh ware førre hørdhe aff mænneske Oc forthy at thynæ skæll ware swa sthoræ till at forklaræ thes sandhet Tha bør thet sik ey at iek skall ther till legghe noghre læthæ skæll oc eenfaldughe Thy will iek offwergiffwe them alle oc sighe aff een vndherligh sywffn som then hedherligh Cyrillus biscopp i alexandria saw som han withner i sith breff ther han sændhe mik for manghe daghe

XXI: EIRÍKS SAGA RAUÐA

There are various literary sources for our knowledge of medieval Norse visits to America (*Vínland*, *Markland*). As early as *c.*1073, Adam of Bremen writes in his *Gesta Hammaburgensis ecclesiae pontificum* (see pp. 62 and 66 above) that Sven Estridsson, the Danish king and one of Adam's main informants, 'also told me of another island discovered by many in that ocean'. Adam continues: 'It is called Wineland because vines grow there of their own accord, producing the most excellent wine. Moreoever, that unsown crops abound there, we have ascertained not from fabulous conjecture but from the reliable report of the Danes.' Half a century or so later, Ari Þorgilsson in his *Íslendingabók* alludes to the inhabitants of Vínland, the Skrælingar, in connection with traces of human beings found by Eiríkr rauði in Greenland (see p. 111 and note 30 to Text VIII above). An Icelandic geographical treatise (*landalýsing*) which may be as old as the beginning of the thirteenth century mentions Helluland (cf. lines 21–25 below), Markland (cf. lines 26–29 below) and Vínland and says that some people think that Vínland is an extension of Africa (cf. *HOIC* 104–06; *Alfræði íslenzk* I 1908, 12). The two 'Vínland sagas', *Grœnlendinga saga* and *Eiríks saga rauða* (respectively about 25 and 40 pages in the editions in the *Íslenzk fornrit* series) contain circumstantial, but often unreliable, accounts of various voyages said to have been made to Vínland. An Icelandic annal for the year 1347 records a visit to Markland by a party of Greenlanders that must have taken place at about that time (cf. *HOIC* 104).

It can be safely deduced from literary evidence alone that the Norse visited the American continent centuries before Columbus's voyages to it around 1500. In 1960, however, the Norwegian Helge Ingstad made the significant archaeological discovery of a Norse site at L'Anse aux Meadows on the northern tip of Newfoundland, and this he subsequently excavated in the following decade together with his archaeologist wife, Anne Stine Ingstad. The site at L'Anse aux Meadows consists of the remains of three largish halls and five other buildings, one of which was used for producing iron from local bog-ore. Radiocarbon analyses indicate a general dating to around the year 1000. It appears to have been occupied over a relatively short period of time and may have lain deserted for a year or more between visits. An important activity there seems to have been the repair of ships.

There is little or no archaeological sign at L'Anse aux Meadows of any crop or animal husbandry.

Few, then, now doubt that the Norsemen visited the mainland of the North American continent in the Middle Ages. The historical realities were probably somewhat as follows. The first visits can reasonably be dated to the period 980–1010 and it is quite possible that, as some written sources suggest, it was Leifr, son of Eiríkr rauði, or some other member of Eiríkr's circle, who made the first landings. Over the next three and a half centuries or so there would doubtless have been many voyages to North America, of only a few of which there is any record in the written sources. Most of these would have had their starting point in the Eastern Settlement of the Norse colony in Greenland (cf. notes 26 and 27 to Text VIII above) and many would probably only have reached the closest part of the mainland, Labrador, from where much-needed timber might be fetched. The finds at L'Anse aux Meadows confirm beyond doubt the presence of the Norsemen in Newfoundland. And it is entirely probable that they got further south, very possibly to the southern side of the Gulf of St Lawrence (and there found the wild grapes growing which gave rise to the name *Vínland*; cf. note 8 below). On the other hand, it is far less certain that they rounded the inhospitable coasts of Nova Scotia and penetrated further down the eastern coasts of what is now the U.S.A. In such areas as they did visit, they doubtless encountered members of the indigenous population, whether Inuit or Native American, whom they called 'Skrælingar' (cf. note 13 below). Some of the sources (e.g. the extract from *Eríks saga rauða* edited here) suggest that permanent agrarian colonisation was intended at least by Þorfinnr karlsefni Þórðarson. But while Þorfinnr may have been a historical figure who mounted a major expedition to Vínland (and whose son Snorri may indeed have been born in North America), the evidence of archaeology for actual settlement is virtually non-existent. Quite why the Norsemen failed to establish any permanent foothold in North America is difficult to say (cf. Perkins 2004, 62–63 and references there). The sources themselves suggest that the hostility of the Skrælingar played a major part in discouraging settlement by the Norsemen (cf. lines 153–54 below). This may have been a factor. But it was probably as much the length and tenuousness of lines of communication with the nearest Norse settlement in Greenland, itself small and fragile, that were decisive. At all events it seems likely that the last Norse voyages from Greenland to North America took place around or not long after 1350, and by the beginning of the fifteenth century the Greenland colony itself appears to have been in terminal decline.

As already indicated, it is *Eiríks saga rauða* and *Grœnlendinga saga* that give the most detailed medieval accounts of visits to Vínland. *Eiríks saga rauða* must have been written before *c.*1302–10, the date of the oldest text (in Hauksbók, AM 544 4to). There are certain reasons to suggest that this saga was first written no earlier than 1263, but these are not entirely decisive and some scholars believe that it may have existed, in some version or other, as early as the first decades of the thirteenth century (cf. *ÍF* IV 1985, 367–69; Perkins 2004, 34–36, 52–53). *Grœnlendinga saga* cannot be dated more precisely than to between about 1200 (the time that saga-writing is thought to have begun) and *c.*1387 (the date of the sole manuscript, Flateyjarbók). Although some of the same main characters appear in the two sagas and they both have accounts of voyages to Vínland as an important part of their narrative, there are also substantial differences between the stories they tell. In addition to an initial sighting by one Bjarni Herjólfsson, *Grœnlendinga saga* tells of four separate visits to Vínland, under the leadership of Leifr (son of Eiríkr rauði), Þorvaldr (also Eiríkr's son), Þorfinnr karlsefni and Freydís (said to be the daughter of Eiríkr) respectively. *Eiríks saga rauða* has no mention of the sighting by Bjarni Herjólfsson and tells of only two visits (an unplanned visit by Leifr in ch. 5 and Þorfinnr karlefni's expedition in chs 8–12). It is uncertain what relationship there is between *Grœnlendinga saga* and *Eiríks saga rauða* and which of them is the older. It is perhaps more likely that *Grœnlendinga saga* was written first and that it is, on the whole, truer to historical reality. *Eiríks saga rauða* appears to be more concerned with telling the life-story of Þorfinnr karlsefni and more particularly that of his wife Guðríðr Þorbjarnardóttir. But whichever of the two sagas is taken as the older, the possibility cannot be excluded that the author of the later of them knew the earlier in some way and used it as a source.

While the Vínland Sagas are the most detailed accounts of Norse visits to America, their limitations as historical sources must be emphasised. They were written at the earliest some two hundred years after the events they purport to describe took place. They contradict each other in various ways. They present a vague and confused picture of the topography of the lands in the West. Some of the place-names they mention are doubtless fictional and those that may be genuine are difficult or impossible to locate with any degree of certainty (cf. note 1 below). The descriptions given of the Skrælingar are distorted in certain respects (cf. note 13 below). Alongside the named persons in *Eiríks saga rauða* and *Grœnlendinga saga* who probably existed in reality (e.g. Leifr Eiríksson, Þorfinnr karlsefni Þórðarson), there are also a number who are entirely fictional. Thus the Þórhallr veiðimaðr of *Eiríks saga rauða* is an invented character (cf. line 9 and note 2 below); and doubtless the daughter of Eiríkr rauði called Freydís who appears both in *Eiríks saga rauða* and *Grœnlendinga saga* is also entirely fictional and the expedition she and her husband are said in ch. 7 of *Grœnlendinga saga* to have undertaken never took place; cf. Perkins (2004, 46–53). The narratives contain much exaggeration and the fantastic sometimes intrudes (cf. the story of Freydís in lines 132–42 and that of the uniped in lines 172–91 below). The aim of the authors was often more to tell a good story than to record history. As historical sources, then, the Vínland Sagas must be approached with a high degree of circumspection and their shortcomings never lost sight of. But with this said, it must also be stressed that the stories they tell and the picture they give of the lands in the West must often contain some kernel of historical truth, and an expedition to North America led by a historical Þorfinnr karlsefni very possibly really did take place.

For his account of Vínland and Þorfinnr karlsefni's expedition there, the author of *Eiríks saga* could well have had at least some genuine and accurate information, quite possibly in oral form. He may well have read *Grœnlendinga saga* (see above). It has been argued that he knew at first hand Adam of Bremen's *Gesta Hammaburgensis ecclesiae pontificum* (see above) and was influenced by it. He may also have been influenced by sagas (such as *Yngvars saga víðfǫrla*) which tell of Scandinavian expeditions in Russia and eastwards from there. The three verses which he incorporates into his narrative (see note 11 and lines 183–90) were probably not his own compositions and must therefore be ranked amongst the saga's sources for the passages in which they occur.

The excerpts edited here are from the saga now generally known as *Eiríks saga rauða* and its heading in 557 (f. 27r1) is *Saga Eiríks rauða*.

It is possible that in 544 the saga had the heading *Saga Þorfinns karlsefnis*, though if so it is no longer legible, and this could even have been its original name (cf. *ÍF* IV 1985, 338–41). Certainly the saga concerns itself more than with any other persons with Þorfinnr karlsefni, son of Þórðr hesthǫfði, and perhaps more particularly with Guðríðr, daughter of the Þorbjǫrn mentioned in line 16 below. Its ch. 3 tells of Guðríðr's arrival in Greenland with her father, ch. 6 of her marriage to Þorsteinn, son of Eiríkr rauði, and Þorsteinn's subsequent death. Ch. 7 introduces Þorfinnr karlsefni and relates how he sails to Greenland together with Snorri Þorbrandsson, Bjarni Grímólfsson and Þórhallr Gamlason (see lines 3–5 below); it also tells of Þorfinnr's marriage to the widowed Guðríðr. It has been related in ch. 5 how Leifr, son of Eiríkr rauði, went to Norway where King Óláfr Tryggvason bade him preach Christianity in Greenland. We are told in the briefest terms how, on his voyage back to Greenland, he unexpectedly came across lands before unknown, where grape-vines and self-sown wheat grew (*ÍF* IV 1985, 415). In Greenland he successfully preached the faith; further, there was much talk there of sailing in search of the country he had discovered. At the beginning of ch. 8, the scene is set at Brattahlíð, the home of Eiríkr rauði in Greenland after Þorfinnr's marriage to Guðríðr. It should be noted that the text of 557 is here, as elsewhere, somewhat corrupt and the start of a new chapter is not marked. Some of the characters who play a part in the subsequent narrative are only cursorily introduced or not at all (like Freydís, daughter of Eiríkr rauði and wife of Þorvarðr, for instance; see lines 132 and 162). On the historicity of the various characters in the saga, see Perkins (2004, 46–53).

Eiríks saga rauða is preserved in two vellums: (1) AM 544 4to (= 544), part of the important codex Hauksbók (cf. *MS* 271–72) named after Haukr Erlendsson (d. 1334) and written in the first decade of the fourteenth century. The text of *Eiríks saga* was written partly by Haukr himself and partly by two other scribes. (2) AM 557 4to (Skálholtsbók; = 557), probably written around 1420 by Óláfr Loptsson (d. *c.*1458). These two manuscripts present the saga in somewhat different forms. 557 offers us an often rather garbled text written by a careless and unpractised scribe, but one which is probably more faithful to the original of the saga than that of 544. 544's text (as has been shown in greatest detail by the Swedish scholar Sven B. F. Jansson in his 1945 monograph) appears to have undergone substantial rationalisation and revision by its three scribes, including both lengthening and shortening. For this reason, 557 (ff. 32v6–33v6; 33v25–35r12) rather than 544 is made the basis for the edition of the following excerpts from the saga (ch. 8 and chs 10, 11 and 12), though obvious errors are corrected and missing words supplied from 544 unless otherwise stated. The text of 557 is, however, in need of substantial emendation, and while this can often be carried out on the basis of the Hauksbók redaction (in 544), it has not been possible to eliminate all its illogicalities (especially the topographical ones). This should not be forgotten, and readers must reconcile themselves to some measure of inconsistency and obscurity remaining (e.g. at lines 146–48). In defence of the scribe of 557, it may be said that the manuscript he was copying was quite possibly difficult to read, and that some of the imperfections of narrative in his text may also have been found in it. The chapter divisions and chapter numbering are based partly on the manuscripts, partly on previous editions. The scribe of 557 made use of various abbreviations (e.g. for the personal name *Karlsefni*), which are here silently expanded.

Bibliography

Facsimile editions: Arthur Middleton Reeves (ed.), *The finding of Wineland the Good* (1890 and reprints). [Contains facsimiles with parallel transcriptions of *Eiríks saga rauða* from both AM 557 4to and AM 554 4to (Hauksbók) as well as of *Grœnlendinga saga* from Flateyjarbók]

Dag Strömbäck (ed.), *The Arna-Magnæan manuscript 557, 4to containing inter alia the history of the first discovery of America*, *CCIMA* XIII (1940).

Jón Helgason (ed.), *Hauksbók. The Arna-Magnæan manuscripts 371, 4to, 544, 4to, and 675, 4to* (1960).

Critical edition: the best critical edition of *Eiríks saga rauða* is that incorporated into Sven B. F. Jansson's study of its two main texts, *Sagorna om Vinland. I. Handskrifterna till Erik den rödes saga* (1945, 26–81).

Íslenzk fornrit edition: in the original issue of *ÍF* IV 193–237 (1935, reprinted with corrections 1957), which contained primarily *Eyrbyggja saga*, *Eiríks saga rauða* was edited mainly on the basis of AM 544 4to by Matthías Þórðarson, as well as *Grœnlendinga saga* based on its only manuscript, Flateyjarbók. In 1985, Ólafur Halldórsson produced a supplementary volume (*Viðauki*) with continuing pagination comprising a text of *Eiríks saga rauða*, now based on AM 557 4to, and a substantial introduction; the contents of this volume were also included as an appendix to the reprint of the 1935 edition. The whole is referred to here as *ÍF* IV (1985).

English translations: numerous translations of the two Vinland sagas into English exist. Both the following contain translations of *Eiríks saga rauða* based mainly on the version in AM 557 4to (as well as translations of *Grœnlendinga saga* and much background material).

Gwyn Jones, *The Norse Atlantic saga*, 2nd edition (1986).

Magnus Magnusson and Hermann Pálsson, *The Vinland sagas. The Norse discovery of America. Grænlendinga saga and Eirik's saga* (1965 and reprints).

Background reading: there is a huge body of secondary literature concerning the Norsemen in America. A comprehensive bibliography (best up to 1992) is Robert Bergersen, *Vinland bibliography. Writings relating to the Norse in Greenland and America* (1997). It should be noted that many contributions to the subject have been amateurish or biased or over-speculative and should be treated with circumspection.

Geraldine Barnes, *Viking America. The First Millennium* (2001).

William W. Fitzhugh and Elisabeth I. Ward (eds), *Vikings. The North Atlantic Saga* (2000).

G. M. Gathorne-Hardy, *The Norse Discoverers of America* (1921); 2nd ed. (1970) with a new preface by the author and a preface by Gwyn Jones.

Anne Stine Ingstad, *The Norse Discovery of America.* Volume I: *Excavations of a Norse Settlement at L'Anse aux Meadows, Newfoundland 1961–1968*, 2nd edition (1985). [The fullest account of the Norse finds at L'Anse aux Meadows, Newfoundland]

Shannon Lewis-Simpson (ed.), *Vínland Revisited: the Norse World at the Turn of the First Millennium. Selected Papers from the Viking Millenium International Symposium, 15–24 September 2000, Newfoundland and Labrador* (2003).

Ian McDougall, 'The Enigmatic *einfœtingr* of *Eiríks saga rauða*'. In *Frejas psalter. En psalter i 40 afdelinger til brug for Jonna Louis-Jensen*, ed. Bergljót S. Kristjánsdóttir and Peter Springborg, 2nd edition (1997, 128–32).

MS, under *America, Norse in*; *L'Anse aux Meadows; Maine coin; Viking hoaxes; Vinland Map; Vinland Sagas.*

Fridtjof Nansen, *In Northern Mists* I–II (1911).

Richard Perkins, 'The Furðustrandir of *Eiríks saga rauða*'. *Mediaeval Scandinavia* 9 (1976, 51–98).

Richard Perkins, 'Medieval Norse Visits to America: Millennial Stocktaking'. *Saga-Book* 28 (2004, 29–69).

Erik Wahlgren, 'Fact and Fancy in the Vinland Sagas'. In *Old Norse Literature and Mythology. A Symposium*, ed. Edgar C. Polomé (1969, 19–80).

Erik Wahlgren, *The Vikings and America* (1986).

Andrew Wawn and Þórunn Sigurðardóttir (eds), *Approaches to Vínland. A Conference on the Written and Archaeological Sources for the Norse Settlements in the North-Atlantic Region and Exploration of America. The Nordic House, Reykjavík, 9–11 August 1999* (2001).

Other works referred to:

Alfræði íslenzk I. Ed. K. Kålund (1908).

Kenneth Baitsholts, 'Humour, Irony, and Insight: The First European Accounts of Native North Americans'. In Lewis-Simpson (2003, 365–75).

Andrew Breeze 'An Irish Etymology for *kjafal* "hooded cloak" in *Þorfinns Saga*', *Arkiv för nordisk filologi* 113 (1998, 5–6).

Carleton S. Coon, *The Hunting Peoples* (1974).

Alan Crozier, 'Arguments against the **Vinland* Hypothesis'. In Lewis-Simpson (2003, 331–37).

Birgitta Wallace Ferguson, 'L'Anse aux Meadows and Vínland'. In Wawn and Þórunn Sigurðardóttir (2001, 134–46).

Helgi Guðmundsson, *Um haf innan* (1997).

A History of Norway and The Passion and Miracles of the Blessed Óláfr, tr. Devra Kunin, ed. Carl Phelpstead (2001).

Kevin McAleese, '*Skrælingar* Abroad—*Skrælingar* at Home?' In Lewis-Simpson (2003, 353–64).

Daniel Odess, Stephen Loring and William W. Fitzhugh, '*Skræling*: First Peoples of Helluland, Markland, and Vinland'. In Fitzhugh and Ward (2000, 193–205).

Ólafur Halldórsson, 'The Conversion of Greenland in Written Sources'. In Hans Bekker-Nielsen, Peter Foote, Olaf Olsen (eds), *Proceedings of the Eighth Viking Congress. Århus 24–31 August 1977* (1981, 203–16).

Richard Perkins, '*Potenti murmure verborum grandia cete maris in littora trahunt*'. In Heinrich Beck and Else Ebel (eds), *Studien zur Isländersaga. Festschrift für Rolf Heller* (2000, 223–30).

Haakon Shetelig and Hjalmar Falk, *Scandinavian Archaeology,* tr. E. V. Gordon (1937).

Sverrir Jakobsson, '"Black Men and Malignant-Looking". The Place of the Indigenous Peoples of North America in the Icelandic World View'. In Wawn and Þórunn Sigurðardóttir (2001, 88–104).

Birgitta Wallace, 'Vínland and the death of Þorvaldr'. In Lewis-Simpson (2003, 377–90).

XXI: EIRÍKS SAGA RAUÐA

Þorfinnr karlsefni Þórðarson's expedition to Vínland

‹Chapter 8›

. . . Ætluðu þeir Karlsefni ok Snorri at leita Vínlands[1] ok tǫluðu menn margt um þat. En því lauk svá at þeir Karlsefni ok Snorri bjuggu skip sitt ok ætluðu at leita Vínlands um sumarit. Til þeirar ferðar réðusk þeir Bjarni ok Þórhallr með skip sitt ok þat fǫruneyti er þeim hafði fylgt.

Maðr hét Þorva*rð*r. Hann var mágr Eiríks rauða. ‹Hann fór ok með þeim, ok Þorvaldr, son Eiríks.›

Þórhallr var kallaðr veiðimaðr.[2] Hann hafði lengi verit í veiðifǫrum með Eiríki um sumrum ok hafði hann margar varðveizlur. Þórhallr var mikill vexti, svartr ok þursligr. Hann var heldr við aldr, ódæll í skapi, hljóðlyndr, fámálugr hversdagliga, undirfǫrull ok þó atmælasamr ok fýstisk jafnan hins verra. Hann hafði lítt við trú blandazk síðan hon kom á Grœnland. Þórhallr var lítt vinsældum horfinn, en þ*ó* hafði Eiríkr lengi tal af honum haldit. Hann var á skipi með þeim Þorvaldi, því at honum var víða kunnigt í óbyggðum. Þeir hǫfðu þat skip er Þorbjǫrn hafði út þangat ok réðusk til ferðar með þeim Karlsefni, ok váru þar flestir grœnlenzkir menn á. Á skipum þeira var[3] fjórir tigir manna annars hundraðs.

Sigldu þeir undan síðan til Vestribyggðar ok til Bjar*n*eyja. Sigldu þeir þaðan undan Bjarneyjum norðanveðr. Váru þeir úti tvau dœgr. Þá fundu þeir land ok reru fyrir á bátum ok kǫnnuðu landit ok fundu þar hellur margar ok svá stórar at tveir menn máttu vel spyrnask í iljar. Melrakkar váru þar margir. Þeir gáfu naf‹n› landinu ok kǫlluðu Helluland.

Þá sigldu þeir norðanveðr tvau dœgr ok var þá land fyrir þeim ok var á skógr mikill ok dýr mǫrg. Ey lá í landsuðr undan landinu ok fundu þeir þar bjarndýr ok kǫlluðu Bjarney. En landit kǫlluðu þeir Markland, þar er skógrinn ‹var›.

Þá er liðin váru tvau dœgr, sjá þeir land ok þeir sigldu undir landit. Þar var nes, er þeir kvámu at. Þeir beittu með landinu ok létu landit á

1 *No chapter division or heading in 557.* 7 Þorvaldr *557.* 14 þá *557.* 18 fjórir tigir] *written* fjǫrutigi *557.* 20 Bjarmeyja *557.* 22 *spelt* 'kavnnavdu' *557.* 29 var] *editorial conjecture.*

stjórnborða. Þar var ørœfi ok strandir langar ok sandar. Fara þeir á bátum til lands ok f*und*u kjǫl af skipi ok kǫlluðu þar Kjalarnes. Þeir gáfu ok nafn strǫndunum ok kǫlluðu Furðustrandir,[4] því at langt var með at sigla. Þá gjǫrðisk vágskorit landit ok heldu þeir skipunum at vágunum.

Þat var þá er Leifr var með Óláfi konungi Tryggvasyni ok hann bað hann boða kristni á Grœnlandi[5] ok þá gaf konungr honum tvá menn skozka. Hét karlmaðrinn Haki en konan H*e*kja. Konungr bað Leif taka til þessara manna ef hann þyrfti skjótleiks við, því at þau váru dýrum skjótari.[6] Þessa menn fengu þeir Leif*r* ok Eiríkr til fylgðar við Karlsefni. En er þeir hǫfðu siglt fyrir Furðustrandir, þá létu þeir en*a* skozku menn á land ok báðu þau hlaupa í suðrátt ok leita landskosta ok koma aptr áðr þrjú dœgr væri liðin. Þau váru svá búin at þau hǫfðu þat klæði er þau kǫlluðu *k*jafal;[7] þat var svá gjǫrt at hattr var á upp ok opit at hliðum ok engar ermar á ok kneppt í milli fóta; helt þar saman knappr ok nezla, en ber váru ‹þau› annars staðar. Þeir kǫstuðu akkerum ok lágu þar þessa stund.

Ok er þrír dagar váru liðnir hljópu þau af landi ofan ok hafði annat þeira í hendi vín*b*er en annat hveiti sjálfsáit.[8] Sagði Karlsefni at þau þótt*u*sk fundit hafa landskosti góða. Tóku þeir þau á skip sitt ok fóru leiðar sinnar, þar til er varð fjarðskorit. Þeir lǫgðu skipunum inn á fjǫrð ‹e›inn. Þar var ey ein út fyrir ok váru þar straumar mikli‹r› ok um eyna; þeir kǫlluðu hana Straumsey. Fugl var þar svá margr at trautt mátti fœti niðr koma í milli eggjanna. Þeir heldu inn með firðinum ok kǫlluðu hann Straumsfjǫrð ok báru farminn af skipunum ok bjuggusk þar um. Þeir hǫfðu með sér alls konar fé[9] ok leituðu sér þar landsnytja. Fjǫll váru þar ok fagrt var þar um at litask. Þeir gáðu einskis nema at kanna landit. Þar váru grǫs mikil. Þar váru þeir um vetrinn ok gjǫrðisk vetr mikill, en ekki fyrir unnit, ok gjǫrðisk illt til matarins, ok tókusk af veið*a*rnar. Þá fóru þeir út í eyna ok væntu at þar mundi gefa nǫkkut af veiðum eða rekum. Þar var þó lítit til matfanga en fé þeira varð þar vel. Síðan hétu þeir á Guð, at hann sendi þeim nǫkkut til matfanga ok var eigi svá brátt við látit sem þeim var annt til.

33 fengu skjól *557*. 35 ok heldu *written twice in 557*. 39 Hekja *written* ‘hakia’ *or* ‘hækia’ *in 557*. 41 Leifi *557*. 42 *written* enu *557*. 45 bjafal *557*. hattr] hattrinn *557*. 50 vínker *557*. 51 þóttisk *557*. 53 fjǫrðinn *557*. 61 veiðirnar *557*.

Þórhallr hvarf á brott ok gengu menn at leita hans. Stóð þat yfir þrjú dœgr í samt. Á hinu fjórða dœgri fundu þeir Karlsefni ok B*jarn*i hann Þórhall á hamargnípu einni. Hann horfði í lopt upp ok gapði hann bæði augum ok munni ok nǫsum ok klóraði sér ok klýpti sik ok þulði nǫkkut. Þeir spurðu því hann væri þar kominn. Hann kvað þat øngu skipta; bað hann þá ekki þat undrask, kvezk svá lengst lifat hafa at þeir þurftu ekki ráð fyrir honum at gjǫra. Þeir báðu hann fara heim með sér. Hann gjǫrði svá.

Litlu síðar kom þar hvalr, ok drifu menn til ok skáru hann, en þó kenndu menn eigi hvat hval‹a› þat var. Karlsefni kunni mikla skyn á hv*ǫ*lum ok kenndi hann þó eigi. Þenna hval suðu matsveinar ok átu af ok varð þó ǫllum illt af.

Þá gengr Þórhallr at ok mælti: 'Var eigi svá at hinn rauðskeggjaði varð drjúgar*i* en Kristr yðvarr? Þetta hafða ek nú fyrir skáldskap minn, er ek orta um Þór fulltrúann. Sjaldan hefir hann mér brugðizk.'

Ok er menn vissu þetta vildu øngvir nýta ok kǫstuðu fyrir bjǫrg ofan ok sneru sínu máli til Guðs miskunnar. Gaf þeim þá út at róa ok skorti þá eigi birgðir.[10]

Um várit fara þeir inn í Straumsfjǫrð ok hǫfðu fǫng af hvárutveggja landinu, veiðar af meginlandinu, eggver ok útróðra af sjónum.[11]

. . . . . .

Chapter 10

Karlsefni fór suðr fyrir land ok Snorri ok Bjarni ok annat lið þeira. Þeir fóru lengi ok til þess er þeir kvámu at á þeiri er fell af landi ofan ok í vatn ok svá til sjóvar. Ey*r*ar váru þar miklar fyrir árósinum, ok mátti eigi komask inn í ána nema at háflœðum. Sigldu þeir Karlsefni þá til áróssins ok kǫlluðu í Hópi[12] landit. Þar fundu þeir sjálfsána hveitiakra þar sem lægðir váru, en vínviðr allt þar sem holta kenndi. Hverr lœkr var þar fullr af fiskum. Þeir gjǫrðu þar grafir sem landit mœttisk ok flóðit gekk efst; ok er út fell váru helgir fiskar í grǫfunum. Þar var mikill fjǫlði dýra á skógi með ǫllu móti. Þeir váru þar hálfan mánuð ok skemmtu sér ok urðu við ekki varir. Fé sitt hǫfðu þeir með sér.

66 Bjarni] barmaði *557*. 75 hvǫlum] hvalnum *557*. 78 drjúgarr (spelt 'driug*arr*') *557*. á *added after* ek *557*. 85 *Chapter division, no heading 557*. 88 eyjar *557*. 91 vín- *written twice 557*.

Ok einn morgin snemma, er þeir lituðusk um, sáu þeir níu húðkeipa[13] ok var vei*f*t trjánum af skipunum ok lét því líkast í sem í hálmþústum ok ferr sólarsinnis.[14] Þá mælti Karlsefni:

'Hvat mun þetta tákna?'

Snorri svarar honum: 'Vera kann a‹t› þetta sé friðartákn ok tǫkum skjǫld hvítan ok berum í mót.'[15]

Ok svá gjǫrðu þeir. Þá reru hinir í mót ok undruðusk þá, ok gengu þeir á land. Þeir váru smáir menn ok illiligir ok illt hǫfðu þeir hár á hǫfði. Eygðir váru þeir mjǫk ok breiðir í kinnunum ok dvǫlðusk þar um stund ok undruðusk. Reru síðan í brott ok suðr fyrir nesit.

Þeir hǫfðu gjǫrt b*ú*ðir sínar upp frá vatninu ok váru sumir skálarnir nær meginlandinu en sumir nær vatninu. Nú váru þeir þar þann vetr. Þar kom alls eng‹i› snjár ok allr fénaðr gekk þar úti sjálfala.

Chapter 11

‹E›n er vára tók, geta þeir at líta einn morgin snemma at fjǫlði húðkeipa reri sunnan fyrir nesit, svá margir sem kolum væri sá‹i›t ok var þ*á* veift á hverju skipi trjánum. Þeir brugðu þá skjǫldum upp ok tóku kaupstefnu sín á millum ok vildi þat fólk helzt kaupa rautt klæði. Þeir vildu ok kaupa sverð ok spjót en þat bǫnnuðu þeir Karlsefni ok Snorri. Þeir hǫfðu ófǫlvan belg fyrir klæðit ok tóku spannarlangt klæði fyrir belg ok bundu um hǫfuð sér, ok fór svá um stund. En er minnka tók klæðit, þá skáru þeir í sundr svá at eigi var breiðara en þvers fingrar breitt. Gáfu þeir Skrælingar jafnmikit fyrir eða meira.

Þat bar til at griðungr hljóp ór skógi, en[16] þeir Karlsefni áttu, ok gall hátt við. Þeir fælask við, Skrælingar, ok hlaupa út á keipana ok reru suðr fyrir land. Varð þá ekki vart við þá þrjár vikur í samt. En er sjá stund var liðin, sjá þeir sunnan fara mikinn fjǫlða skipa Skrælinga, svá sem straumr stœði. Var þá veift trjánum ǫllum rangsœlis ok ýla allir Skrælingar hátt upp. Þá tóku þeir[17] rauða skjǫldu ok báru í mót. Gengu þeir þá saman ok bǫrðusk. Varð þar skothríð hǫrð. Þeir hǫfðu ok valslǫngur, Skrælingar. Þat sjá þeir Karlsefni ok Snorri at þeir fœrðu upp á stǫngum, Skrælingarnir, knǫtt mikinn ok blán at lit ok fló upp á land yfir liðit ok lét illiliga við þar er niðr kom. Við þetta sló ótta miklum yfir Karlsefni ok á lið hans, svá at þá fýsti einskis annars en

97 veitt *557.* 106 búðir] byggðir *557.* 109 *Chapter division, no heading 557.* 111 þó *557.*

halda undan ok upp með ánni ok til hamra nǫkkurra. Veittu þeir þar viðtǫku harða.

Freydís kom út ok sá er þeir heldu undan. Hon kallaði:

'Því renni þér undan slíkum ‹a›uvirðismǫnnum, svá gildir menn er mér þœtti líkligt at þér mættið drepa þá svá sem búfé? Ok ef ek hefða vápn þœtti mér sem ek munda betr berjask en einnhverr yðvar.'

Þeir gáfu øngvan gaum hvat sem hon sagði. Freydís vildi fylgja þeim ok varð hon heldr sein, því at hon var eigi heil. Gekk hon þá eptir þeim í skóginn er Skrælingar sœkja at henni. Hon fann fyrir sér mann dauðan, Þorbrand Snorrason,[18] ok stóð hellusteinn í hǫfði honum. Sverðit lá hjá honum, ok hon tók þat upp ok býzk at verja sik með. Þá koma Skrælingar at henni. Hon tekr brjóstit upp ór serkinum ok slettir á sverðit. Þeir fælask við ok hlaupa undan ok á skip sín ok heldu á brottu.[19] Þeir Karlsefni finna hana ok lof‹a› happ hennar.

Tveir menn fellu af Karlsefni, en fjórir af Skrælingum, en þó urðu þeir[20] ofrliði bornir. Fara þeir nú til búða sinna ok íhuga hvat fjǫlmenni þat var er at þeim sótti á landinu. Sýnisk þeim nú at þat eina mun liðit hafa verit er á skipunum kom, en annat liðit mun hafa verit þversýningar.

Þeir Skrælingar fundu ok mann dauðan ok lá øx hjá honum. ‹Einn þeira tók upp øxina ok høggr með tré, ok þá hverr at ǫðrum, ok þótti þeim vera gersimi ok bíta vel.›[21] Einn þeira hjó í stein ok brotnaði øxin. Þótti honum þá øngu nýt, er eigi stóð við grjótinu, ok kastaði niðr.

Þeir þóttusk nú sjá, þótt þar væri landskostir góðir, at þar mundi jafn‹an› ófriðr ok ótti á liggja *af* þei*m* er fyrir bjuggu. Bjuggusk þeir á brott ok ætluðu til síns lands. Sigldu þeir norðr fyrir ok fundu fimm Skrælinga í skinnhjúpum sofanda ok hǫfðu með sér skrokka ok í dýramerg dreyra blandinn. Virtu þeir svá at þeir mundu gjǫrvir af landinu. Þeir drápu þá.

Síðan fundu þeir nes eitt ok ‹á› fjǫlð*a* dýra. Ok þann v*e*g var nesit at sjá sem mykiskán væri, af því at dýrin lágu þar um vetrna.

Nú koma þeir í Straumsfjǫrð ok er þar alls *gnótti*r. Er þat sumra manna sǫgn at þau Bjarni ok Freydís[22] hafi þar eptir verit ok tíu tigir manna með þeim ok hafi eigi farit lengra, en þeir Karlsefni ok Snorri hǫfðu suðr farit ok fjórir tigir manna ok hafi eigi lengr verit í Hópi en vart tvá mánuðu ok hafi hit sama sumar aptr komit.

154 en þeir *557*. 159 fjǫlði *557*. *written* vag *557*. 161 gnóttir] konar *557*. 164, 165 hafi] hafðir *557*.

Karlsefni fór á einu skipi at leita Þórhalls,[23] en liðit var eptir, ok fóru þeir norðr fyrir Kjalarnes, ok berr þá fyrir vestan fram ok var landit á bakborða þeim. Þar váru eyðimerkr einar. Ok er þeir hǫfðu lengi farit fellr ‹á› af landi ofan ór austri ok í vestr. Þeir lǫg‹ð›u inn í árósin*n* ok lágu við hinn syðra bakkann.

‹Chapter 12›

Þat var einn morgin. Sjá þeir Karlsefni fyrir ofan rjóðrit flekk nǫkkurn svá sem glitaði við þeim ok œptu þeir á. Þat hrœrðisk ok var þat einfœtingr ok skýzk ofan þangat sem þeir lágu. Þorvaldr, son Eiríks hins rauða, *sat við stýri ok skaut einfœtingr ǫr í smáþarma honum. Þorvaldr dró út ǫrina ok mælti:*

'Feitt er um ístruna. Gott land hǫfum vér fengit kostum en þó megum vér varla njóta.'

Þorvaldr dó af sári þessu litlu síðar. Þá hleypr einfœtingr á braut ok norðr aptr. Þeir hljópu eptir einfœtingi ok sáu hann stundum. Ok þ*ví næst* sem hann leitaði undan, hljóp hann út á vág einn. Þá hurfu þeir aptr. Þá kvað einn maðr kviðling þenna:

Eltu seggir,
allsatt var þat,
einn einfœting
ofan til strandar.
En kynligr maðr
kostaði rásar
hart of stopi‹r›.
Heyrðu, Karlsefni.

Þeir fóru þá í brott ok norðr aptr ok þóttusk sjá Einfœtingaland.[24] Vildu þeir þá eigi lengr hætta liði sínu. Þeir ætluðu ǫll ‹ein› fjǫll, þau er í Hópi váru ok ‹þessi› er ‹nú› fundu þeir. Fóru þeir aptr ok váru í Straumsfirði hinn þriðja vetr.

169 lágu inn í árósinum *557.* 171 *No chapter division or heading in 557.* 175–80 sat . . . aptr] Þá mælti Þorvaldr: 'Gott land hǫfum vér fengit.' Þá hleypr einfœtingrinn á brott ok norðr aptr ok skaut áðr í smáþarma á Þorvaldi. Hann dró út ǫrina. Þá mælti Þorvaldr: 'Feitt er um ístruna.' *577.* 180–81 því næst] *editorial conjecture*; þótti *557.* 192 *557 adds* at kanna *after* ætluðu. 193 þeir *before* fundu *557.* 194 vetr] *written* vintr *557. Cf. p. 275, no. 6 above.*

Gengu menn þá mjǫk sleitum. Sóttu ‹þeir› er kvánlausir váru í hendr þeim er kvángaðir váru. Þar kom til hit fyrsta haust Snorri, son Karlsefnis, ok var *h*ann ‹þá þrívetr› er þeir fóru á brott.[25]

Hǫfðu þeir sunnanveðr ok hittu Markland ok fundu Skrælinga fimm; var einn skeggjaðr ok tvær konur, bǫrn tvau. Tóku þeir Karlsefni til sveinanna[26] en hitt komsk undan ok sukku í jǫrð niðr. En sveinana hǫfðu þeir með sér ok kenndu þeim mál ok váru skírðir. Þeir nefndu móður sína Vætildi ok ‹fǫður› Óvægi. Þeir sǫgðu at konungar stjórnuðu Skrælingalandi. Hét annarr Avaldamon, en annarr hét Valdidida.[27] Þeir kváðu þar engi hús ok lágu menn í hellum eða holum. Þeir sǫgðu land þar ǫðru megin gagnvart *s*ínu landi ok gengu menn þar í hvítum klæðum ok œptu hátt ok báru stangir ok fóru með flíkr. Þat ætla menn Hvítramannaland.[28]

Nú kvámu þeir til Grœnlands ok eru með Eiríki rauða um vetrinn.[29]

197 hann] þar þann *557*. 205 línu *557*.

Notes

[1] This is the first mention of Vínland in *Eiríks saga rauða*. The subsequent account of Þorfinnr karlsefni's voyage contains various place-names, as follows: (a) (referring to Greenland and in addition to the term Grœnland itself): Vestribyggð (line 20; cf. notes 27 and 29 to Text VIII above), Bjarneyjar (lines 20, 21); (b) (referring apparently to lands in the west beyond Greenland): Vínland (lines 2, 4), Helluland (line 25), Bjarney (line 28), Markland (lines 29, 198) , Kjalarnes (lines 33, 167), Furðustrandir (lines 34, 42), Straumsey (line 54), Straumsfjǫrðr (lines 56, 83, 161, 194), Hóp (lines 90, 193), Einfœtingaland (line 191), Skrælingaland (line 203), Hvítramannaland (lines 206–07). 544 also refers to Írland it mikla (cf. note 28 below). In connection with the names listed under (b), two issues arise: (i) how far they were genuine place-names used for localities on the North American continent or islands off it, and (ii) how far any of those that are genuine can be identified with actual places or areas in North America. As to (i), we can be relatively certain that e.g. Markland was a genuine place-name and that e.g. Einfœtingaland was not (cf. note 24 below). Cf. also note 4 below. In connection with (ii), it should be noted that it is extremely difficult or impossible to locate any of the place-names which may be genuine with any degree of certainty. This applies, for example, to *Kjalarnes*, found both in *Eiríks saga rauða* and in *Grœnlendinga saga* ch. 4. On the other hand, it is quite likely that the place-name Markland was used for Labrador. And for some conjecture as to where Hóp could have been, see note 12 below. Cf. Perkins (2004, 55–57).

[2] Þórhallr *veiðimaðr* is obviously a fictional character. He conforms to the stereotype of the recalcitrant and often mischievous heathen who sometimes appears in the sagas and comes to bad end. One of his main roles in the narrative of *Eiríks saga rauða* is to act as a vehicle for two verses in ch. 9, which in turn have their own special function (cf. note 11 below). The word *veiðimaðr* could be used of both fishermen and hunters but was particularly used of whalers. Cf. Perkins (1976, 65–66, 70).

[3] Lack of concord between verb and subject is found also in lines 32 and 161; this is not all that uncommon in Old Norse when the subject

follows the verb, cf. Text XXIV, lines 4, 14–17, 28–29, 51–52 and note 2 below and *NION* I, 3.9.8.2.

[4] It seems unlikely that the word *Furðustrandir* was ever used by the Norsemen as a place-name for any locality or geographical feature in North America. The reason the author of *Eiríks saga rauða* had for placing these beaches of such length between Greenland and Vínland may have been to represent Vínland as much further south and thus much closer to Africa than it really was. This may have been in line with current geographical theory which regarded Vínland as an extension of Africa (cf. the geographical treatise (*landalýsing*) mentioned in the introduction, p. 287 above). This may also explain why the saga placed a uniped in Vínland; cf. lines 173–81 and note 24 below. But any certainty on a matter like this is impossible. See further Perkins (1976, particularly pp. 82–85).

[5] The account (in *Eiríks saga rauða* ch. 5) of King Óláfr Tryggvason (on whom see note 33 to Text VIII above) bidding Leifr preach Christianity in Greenland and of Leifr subsequently fulfilling this mission is in all probability entirely unhistorical. Cf. *HOIC* 100–01; Ólafur Halldórsson (1981).

[6] The adjective *skozkr* is sometimes used in Icelandic sources in the sense 'Irish' and this meaning may be intended here. *Skozkir menn* seem to have had a reputation for being fleet-footed; cf. *Eyrbyggja saga*, ch. 18 (*ÍF* IV 1985, 33) where we are told of a man called Nagli, described as *mikill maðr ok fóthvatr* and *skozkr at kyni*. Cf. Nansen (1911, I 339–43); Jones (1986, 283–85).

[7] Andrew Breeze (1998, 5–6) argues that *kjafal* is a corruption of an early Irish word *cochall* (itself from Latin *cucullus*) which has a sense of 'cowl, hood, hooded cloak'. On 557's reading *bjafal*, cf. *ÍF* IV (1985, 424, note 10), and its reading *vínker* (an error for *vínber*) in line 50 below.

[8] Adam of Bremen (see Introduction above), *Grœnlendinga saga* and *Eiríks saga rauða* all imply that grapes grew in the place called *Vínland* (Adam of Bremen calls it *Winland*) and Adam and *Grœnlendinga saga* (*ÍF* IV 1985, 253) more or less specifically connect the name given to

the country with the presence of grapes there. There has been much discussion of the grapes of Vínland. A number of scholars have argued that the Norsemen did not find wild grapes in North America and that their appearance in the sources must have some other explanation. It has, for example, been suggested that the accounts of grapes are purely literary borrowings and go back to accounts of the Insulae Fortunatae (or similar legendary places) in Isidor of Seville's *Etymologiae* and classical sources (cf. Nansen 1911, I 345–84; II 1–65). But such arguments are to some extent anticipated and countered by, for instance, Adam's own statement on this matter. Nor is there any good reason for believing that berries of some sort (rather then grapes proper) are referred to. And an interpretation of the first element of the name *Vínland* as originally the word *vin* f. (with a short vowel; cf. C–V 707) meaning 'pasture', may be confidently dismissed. Further, there is probably no good reason for rejecting the sources' statement on this matter. Wild grapes (e.g. riverbank grapes, *Vitis riparia*) do grow in eastern North America, at present as far north as the St Lawrence River and New Brunswick. In the more favourable climatic conditions of the Middle Ages they were perhaps to be found rather further north than they are today. They were remarked upon by some of the early post-Columbian explorers of the area, for example Jacques Cartier, who explored the St Lawrence in the 1530s (cf. Gathorne-Hardy 1921, 154–59; Jones 1986, 123–24). Thus the Norsemen could well have reached the areas where grapes grew. The references to self-sown wheat (*hveiti sjálfsáit* in line 50, *sjálfsánir hveitiakrar* in line 90; cf. Adam of Bremen's 'unsown crops') is more difficult to explain and there is no mention of it in *Grœnlendinga saga*. It is true that Cartier reports fields of wild cereals on the St Lawrence. But identification with any known North American plant appears rather uncertain. The suggestion that the accounts of wheat in Vínland were indeed literary borrowings from legends of the Insulae Fortunatae (or similar places) to pair with its grapes, which may have existed in reality, is not implausible. Cf. Perkins (2004, 59–60).

[9] Both *Eiríks saga rauða* and *Grœnlendinga saga* imply that the Norsemen took livestock with them on their expeditions to Vínland (cf. lines 95 and 119–20). There is, however, little or no archaeological evidence for this.

[10] The implication of the saga's account here is clearly that by composing poetry in honour of his patron Þórr (cf. *Þórr fulltrúinn*, line 79), Þórhallr has persuaded the god to strand a whale as food for the starving company. Certainly there is evidence elsewhere that praise-poetry was composed in honour of Þórr, that the god was thought of as something of a hunter and killer of whales and that he had the control over wind and wave necessary to beach a whale. But the Norsemen had various other forms of magic for luring fish and other sea-animals (e.g. seals) to land as well. For example, Adam of Bremen tells how the inhabitants of northernmost Norway employ 'a powerful mumbling of words' to draw whales to land. Nor was such magic the preserve of the Norsemen: for example, in Coon (1974, 129–30) there is a description of how a whale ritualist of the Nootka tribe of Indians (Vancouver Island) sought to get whales to drift ashore by a grisly process involving a human corpse. This he did after four days of ritual fasting in a remote shrine overlooking the sea from which whales could be seen. See further on this passage in *Eiríks saga rauða*, Perkins (2000, 223–30).

[11] In ch. 9 of *Eiríks saga rauða* (omitted in the present selection) we are told how Þórhallr veiðimaðr, apparently disappointed by the absence of wine at Straumsfjǫrðr, breaks away from the main expedition with nine others and heads north in search of Vínland. He is storm-driven by a westerly wind across to Ireland and there is brutally beaten and enslaved and dies. Before he sets sail, two stanzas in *dróttkvætt* are quoted, which Þórhallr is said to have declaimed. In the first of these, which the prose tells us was uttered as Þórhallr was carrying water on board his ship, he complains that despite being promised the finest drink, no wine has touched his lips; he has rather to wield a bucket. The second verse is an exhortation to put out to sea and to leave others boiling whales on Furðustrandir, though in the prose of the saga, it is in Straumsfjǫrðr that meat from the stranded whale is cooked. An older school of saga-criticism, which took the sagas far more seriously as history than is now customary, believed that these two verses were composed more or less under the circumstances described in the saga. They have even been claimed to be among 'the first recorded American poetry'. But in fact it is very unlikely that the occasion for the original composition of the verses was that

described in the prose of the saga and, as remarked in note 2 above, Þórhallr veiðimaðr is not to be regarded as a historical character. On the other hand, they were probably not composed by the author of the saga either and we can only guess at the circumstances of their origin. It is possible that the first verse was composed while the bailing of a ship was in progress. The second verse may have been used amongst groups of men engaged in hunting whales and processing their blubber (cf. Perkins 1976, 69–82). At all events, although the author of the saga probably formed his fictitious narrative partly to fit these verses, he also cunningly intended his audience to take them as corroboration of such details of his narrative as Þórhallr's disappointment at the lack of wine at Straumsfjǫrðr and the Furðustrandir of lines 34 and 42, which had their own special function in his account (cf. note 4 above).

[12] Place-names are often presented in this way in Old Norse writings (i.e. in the dative case preceded by the preposition normally used with them); cf. Text XV:33–34 above and *NION* I, 3.1.8 (p. 54).

While attempting to locate the various places mentioned in the Vínland Sagas is a hazardous business (cf. note 1 above), it is not impossible that Hóp was a genuine place-name and also not impossible that it referred to a locality on the south-western side of the Gulf of St Lawrence, more specifically around the mouth of the Miramichi River in New Brunswick. Here there are lagoons, sheltered from the sea by protective sandbars, to which the Old Norse word *hóp* might be applicable (see C–V 281; cf. Wallace 2003, 381 for an aerial photograph). It is in this area that some scholars would locate Vínland (e.g. Ferguson 2001). Wild grapes are found there, and also the place-name *Baie du Vin* apparently given by post-Columbian French settlers referring to them (cf. Crozier 2003, 336). A large concentration of Micmac Indians was also to be found there (cf. note 13 below). Nevertheless, no certain identification of Hóp can be made on the basis of these facts.

[13] With the arrival of these nine skin boats (*húðkeipar*) at Hóp, the Skrælingar are introduced into *Eiríks saga rauða* and later in the saga (lines 153–54) we are told that it is fear of Skræling hostility that causes Karlsefni and his band to abandon their attempt to settle in Vínland. The Skrælingar are mentioned in various other Old Norse

sources, including Ari's *Íslendingabók* (see Text VIII, lines 69–71), *Grœnlendinga saga* and *Historia Norwegiae* (see *History of Norway* 2001, 3). The etymology of the word Skrælingar is uncertain but it very probably had pejorative connotations. The Norsemen certainly used it of the Inuit (Eskimo) peoples they came into contact with in Greenland. But they doubtless also had some contact with Native American (American Indian) peoples as well as Inuit in the parts of the North American mainland (with Newfoundland) they visited, and they appear to have used the word also of them. The accounts of Skrælingar in *Eiríks saga rauða* and in *Grœnlendinga saga* may reflect such encounters. There seem to have been Dorset Inuit at least in Labrador at the time. And the Native American peoples the Norsemen might have come across could have been (the ancestors of) the Innu in Labrador, the Beothucks (now extinct) in Newfoundland or the Micmacs in Nova Scotia, Prince Edward Island and New Brunswick. Cf. Odess et al. (2000); McAleese (2003).

The Norsemen would have regarded the *húðkeipr* ('skin boat') as the traditional vessel of Skrælingar. One might here here think first of the umiaks of the Inuit rather than Indian canoes made of birch-bark. But both the Beothucks and the Micmacs seem to have had canoes covered with moose or deer skins and were also practised canoeists, and at least the Micmacs were traders and evidently owned canoes in largish numbers (cf. lines 110–11 and 122–23). See also note 30 to Text VIII.

Modern scholarship has expended much effort and ingenuity on attempting to square Norse accounts of the Skrælingar in the two Vínland sagas with what is otherwise known about the Inuit and Native Americans who inhabited these parts (cf. e.g. Gathorne-Hardy 1921, 173–95 for a traditional approach; and for a more modern one, Sverrir Jakobsson 2001). There is much that seems realistic in the saga's descriptions. For example, the account of trade between the Norsemen and Skrælingar (lines 112–18) seems fairly true to life. The Skræling interest in red cloth makes one think of the Beothuks of Newfoundland whose predilection for the colour red probably gave rise to the expression 'Red Indians'. The incident described in lines 149–52 gives quite a realistic picture of a person unacquainted with iron weapons (as both the Native Americans and Inuit of the area would have been; cf. lines 113–14). The *dýramergr dreyra blandinn* ('marrow from animal bones mixed with blood') which the five sleeping Skrælingar have with them in bark containers (lines 155–57) has been interpreted as some form of pemmican used as iron rations by certain Native American tribes while out hunting (cf. Gathorne-Hardy 1921, 179). Much less convincingly, the large sphere used as a weapon by the Skrælingar (lines 126–28) has been compared with some sort of ballista thought to have been used by an Algonquin people (cf. *ION* 219, note to lines 378–81). Unfortunately, the physical description of the Skrælingar in lines 103–04 (where 544 has *svartir* for 557's *smáir*) is hardly illuminating. And there are certainly various suspect elements in the accounts of the Skrælingar in *Eiríks saga*. For example, the names given to four of them in lines 201–03 were clearly invented on the basis of Norse name-elements or other European names (cf. note 27 below). The accounts of them in *Eiríks saga* could well be influenced by stories of exotic peoples encountered by Norsemen on their journeys east of Scandinavia (e.g. in Muslim countries). And when we find that the Skræling arrow which kills Þorvaldr Eiríksson in ch. 4 of *Grœnlendinga saga* is shot by a uniped in ch. 12 of *Eiríks saga rauða*, we see that the inhabitants of Norse America were in danger of joining the ranks of the fantastic peoples known to saga-authors from the learned literature of medieval Europe.

[14] As in other cultures, in the Old Norse world anticlockwise motion (cf. *rangsœlis*, line 123) had sinister or baleful associations. Conversely, clockwise motion (*sólarsinnis*) would have been regarded as auspicious and conducive to good fortune.

[15] We hear elsewhere of the display of white shields and red shields (line 124) as tokens of peace and hostility respectively (cf. the terms *friðskjǫldr*, 'peace-shield' and *herskjǫldr*, 'war-shield'); cf. also line 112 above and Text VI above, line 104 and note 11. But for red shields as 'peace-shields, see Shetelig and Falk (1937, 401).

[16] *en* (*er* in 544) here looks as though it might be being used as a relative pronoun; cf. *ÍF* IV (1985, 429, note 4); C–V 128. But in this instance at any rate, it is better regarded as anacoluthon ('— and Karlsefni and his people owned it —').

[17] This pronoun presumably refers to the Norsemen.

[18] It is not certain who is referred to here. It is possible that *Þorbrandr Snorrason* is an error for *Snorri Þorbrandsson*, mentioned earlier as Þorfinnr karlefni's partner and one of the leaders of the expedition (e.g. lines 3, 86, 100, 114). Certainly we never hear what eventually became of Snorri Þorbrandsson at the end of the saga (though cf. lines 161–65). Alternatively (but perhaps less probably), we must assume that Snorri Þorbrandsson had with him a son called Þorbrandr on the expedition and that it is he who is referred to here, although he has not been mentioned earlier (cf. Introduction, p. 291 above). See also *ÍF* IV (1985, 383–84 and 437); Perkins (2004, 50–51).

[19] This episode, in which Freydís appears to put the Skrælingar pursuing her to flight by slapping her naked breast with a sword, has mystified commentators. For discussion, cf. Barnes (2001, 27–30 and references).

[20] This pronoun refers to Karlsefni and his band; cf. Jansson (1945, 73, 163–64, 167).

[21] The words in brackets are supplied here from 544. Sven B. F. Jansson (1944, 144; cf. 73) regarded them as an addition by the redactor of the version in 544, but Ólafur Halldórsson (*ÍF* IV 1985, 430, note 11) is probably right in thinking that they (or words of similar meaning) were omitted by the scribe of 557.

[22] 544 has *Guðríðr*, which is perhaps more logical. Guðríðr Þorbjarnardóttir, wife of Þorfinnr karlsefni, plays a major part in both *Eiríks saga rauða* and *Grœnlendinga saga* and is in all probability a historical figure. She was mother of the Snorri who was born on this expedition (cf. lines 196–97).

[23] Cf. note 11 above.

[24] In chapter 4 of *Grœnlendinga saga* (*ÍF* IV 1985, 256), Þorvaldr, son of Eiríkr rauði, dies from an arrow-wound sustained in a skirmish with the Skrælingar; this account may even have some basis in historical fact (cf. Perkins 2004, 47 and 61). Here in ch. 12 of *Eiríks saga rauða*, it is a uniped who shoots the fatal arrow into Þorvaldr's entrails. The most plausible explanation for the introduction of this uniped is that

according to medieval Icelandic notions of geography Vínland was thought to be an extension of Africa and unipeds were believed to live in Africa (cf. Jones 1986, 285; Magnusson and Hermann Pálsson 1965, 15 and 39; Barnes 2001, 27–28; see p. 281 above). The verse about the uniped (lines 183–90) has been the subject of an essay by Ian McDougall (1997), who produces good reasons for believing that it is an adaptation of a riddle about a pen. The uniped (*einfœtingr*) represents the pen itself and the men (*seggir*) who chase it are the fingers of the hand holding it; the 'shore' (*strǫnd*) down to which the men chase the pen would be the bottom margin of the page or the writing surface in general. McDougall adduces parallels from other Icelandic and Old English riddles. The verse might have been introduced by the author of the saga to give support to the place-name *Einfœtingaland*, which is probably fictitious and may even have been invented by the author of the saga himself (cf. notes 1, 4 and 11 above). Þorvaldr's words in lines 177–78 resemble those attributed to Þormóðr Kolbrúnarskáld Bersason, mortally wounded by an arrow at the Battle of Stiklarstaðir (Stiklestad) (see *ÍF* XXVII 393; VI 276; *Hkr* 520–21; cf. also *ION* 219, note to line 434; Perkins 1976, 87, note 46).

[25] Snorri, like his father Þorfinnr karlsefni and mother Guðríðr Þorbjarnardóttir, may have been a historical figure and was quite possibly the first European known by name to have been born on the North American mainland, or at any rate in Newfoundland (cf. note 22 above; Perkins 2004, 64).

[26] This story, in which two Skræling boys are captured and taken back to Greenland, is perhaps not unrealistic. Jacques Cartier, the post-Columbian explorer of the St Lawrence, returned to France with two captured natives after his first voyage to these parts in 1534. For further similar instances, see Baitsholts (2003, 366 and references there).

[27] The names of the mother and father of the Skræling boys are inventions made up from Norse words or name-elements (cf. Barnes 2001, 30, note 81; Perkins 2004, 51–53). Vætildr: *vættr* f. means 'spirit'; (*h*)*ildr* is common as the second element in a number of Norse women's names (e.g. Bryn(h)ildr); Óvægir is related to the adjectives *óvægr*, 'unmerciful' and *óvæginn*, 'unyielding' (cf. the attested personal name

Óþyrmir related to *óþyrmir*, 'merciless man' and *óþyrmiligr*, 'unmerciful, harsh'). And the names of the two kings whom the boys say rule Skrælingaland, Avaldamon and Valdidida (in 557; Avaldidida in 544), are probably based on those of the king of Garðaríki, Valdamarr or Valdimarr, and his consort Allogía (mentioned, for example, in Oddr*ÓT* 23). It has been suggested that the boys' report that Skrælingaland was ruled by two kings may reflect the situation in Norway between 1261 and 1263: Hákon Hákonarson was king 1217–63, while his son Magnús was crowned in 1261 and died in 1280 (see Helgi Guðmundsson 1997, 63, note 42).

[28] 544 adds *eða Írland it mikla* 'or Ireland the Great' after *Hvítramannaland. Írland it mikla* is also mentioned in *Landnámabók* (*ÍF* I, 162; cf. *BS* 61). There we are told that it lay six days' sailing (*sex dægra sigling*) west of Ireland and near Vínland.

[29] The account of Þorfinnr's expedition to Vínland finishes here. The two following chapters (13 and 14) into which the remainder of the saga is conventionally divided tell how the ship captained by Bjarni Grímólfsson (cf. lines 5 and 162 above) sinks under dramatic circumstances (ch. 13), and of Karlsefni and Guðríðr's return to Iceland and their descendants. 544 concludes with a genealogy down to Haukr Erlendsson written in in Haukr's own hand.

XXII: ÓLÁFS RÍMA HARALDSSONAR

Óláfs ríma Haraldssonar was composed *c.*1350–70, and is preserved in the late fourteenth-century manuscript known as *Flateyjarbók* (GKS 1005 fol.). The poem is the earliest surviving example of what became the most popular literary genre in Iceland between the fifteenth and nineteenth centuries. *Rímur* are narrative poems based, in almost every case, on prose sources. They are sometimes referred to as 'metrical romances' in English; nearly eighty *rímur* survive from before 1600, and about half of these are based on *riddarasögur*, with about another quarter of the corpus based on *fornaldarsögur*. *Óláfs ríma* is one of only nine pre-1600 *rímur* based on *Íslendingasögur* or (as here) *konungasögur*. It is also an unusually short example of the genre: most *rímur* consist of several cantos or fits using different metrical forms, but *Óláfs ríma* consists of a single *ríma* of sixty-five stanzas. Unlike many later examples of the genre, *Óláfs ríma* does not begin with a *mansǫngr* (literally, 'love song'), a non-narrative introduction in the tradition of courtly love poetry.

Óláfs ríma is composed in *feyrskeytt*, the most common *ríma* stanza form. The first and third lines of each quatrain contain four stressed syllables, any two of which (other than the first and second) alliterate with one another. The second and fourth lines of the quatrain contain three stressed syllables, of which the first in each line alliterates with the two alliterating stresses of the preceding odd-numbered line. In addition, the quatrain rhymes *abab*; the *a* rhymes are monosyllabic and the *b* rhymes trochaic.

Foreign literary traditions influenced the development of the *rímur* (the name of the genre is related to French *rime*, and already in this first example of the genre there is some emphasis on courtesy (st. 31), and warriors are in one place (st. 24) referred to as *riddarar* 'knights'), but the influence of skaldic and eddic poetry is readily apparent, not least in the characteristically native poetic vocabulary employed, though there are also the loan-words *fánga, klókr* and *júngr* (Low German), *pín* (Old Saxon, Old English), *stríð* in the sense 'warfare' (Old Saxon). *Heiti* and kennings are more common in later *rímur* than in *Óláfs ríma*, but poetic diction employed in the poem includes fifteen *heiti* for 'king', and smaller numbers for 'man/warrior', 'battle', and 'sword'. The few kennings in *Óláfs ríma* are all two-element only and simple, conventional ones found frequently in skaldic battle-poetry; there are six for 'battle' (*randa glam* (st. 38), *darra él* (st. 41), *randa regn* (st. 46), *darra þing* (st. 54), and *odda hríð* and *málma leikr* (st. 55; maybe also *hjǫrva gnauð*, st. 56), one for 'sword' (*unda naðr*, st. 40), one for 'man/warrior' (*ǫrva meiðr*, st. 2), and one for 'breast' or 'heart, mind' (*hyggju strendr*, st. 19). As Vésteinn Ólason notes (1985, 9), the kenning *fálu hestr* ('horse of a giantess' = wolf) in stanza 41 is the only one in the poem to employ a mythological allusion.

Óláfs ríma is about an important saint, but the poet makes little use of the Christian skaldic diction developed in medieval Icelandic religious poetry; examples include *dróttinn himna hallar* ('Lord of the heavenly mansion'; st. 2), *himna gramr* ('King of heavens'; st. 51); note also *bragníngr allra þjóða* ('king of all peoples'; st. 65) and the description of Óláfr as *Kristz et bjarta blóm* ('the bright flower of Christ'; st. 62). But although the vocabulary of *Óláfs ríma* is influenced by that of skaldic poetry, the word order is much simpler, and according to Vésteinn Ólason 1985, 9, often 'comes close to that of the spoken language'.

The poem celebrates St Óláfr, King of Norway (r. 1015–30). It begins with general praise of his achievements, concentrates mainly on an account of events just before and during the Battle of Stiklastaðir, in which he was killed by rebellious subjects, and ends (after brief references to his burial, translation and posthumous miracles) with a request that the saint intercede for the poet. St Óláfr, protomartyr and patron of Norway, was a figure of immense religious and ideological importance in medieval Norway and Iceland. He was the subject of a wide range of written texts, including Latin hagiography and historical writing, skaldic battle-poetry, hagiographic skaldic verse, and prosimetric sagas (for a survey of early Norwegian and Icelandic texts about St Óláfr see Kunin and Phelpstead 2001, xxvi–xli). The high point of this textual tradition is Snorri Sturluson's *Óláfs saga helga*, originally composed as an independent saga and later incorporated in his *Heimskringla*. Snorri's saga provided the source material for *Óláfs ríma* and so it is the version of the saint's life referred to in the notes to the text below.

The continuing importance of St Óláfr in the later Middle Ages is attested by his prominence in *Flateyjarbók*, in which *Óláfs ríma* immediately follows Einarr Skúlason's *Geisli* (1152–53), the skaldic poem in praise of Óláfr composed to celebrate the establishment of an archiepiscopal see at his shrine in Trondheim. *Flateyjarbók* also includes a much-augmented version of *Óláfs saga helga*. The manuscript ascribes *Óláfs ríma* to Einarr Gilsson, who was briefly a *lǫgmaðr* (law-man, one of the two highest government officials in Iceland) in the north and west of Iceland in the late 1360s. It has been suggested that Einarr was a friend of Jón Hákonarson, the man who commissioned *Flateyjarbók*, and that *Óláfs ríma* might have been copied into *Flateyjarbók* from the poet's autograph manuscript (see Björn K. Þórólfsson 1934, 298–99; Rowe 2005, 299). *Óláfs ríma* and *Geisli* were added to the beginning of *Flateyjarbók* by its second scribe, Magnús Þórhallsson, *c.*1390. Rowe argues that the inclusion of *Óláfs ríma* in the manuscript 'underscores the points made by the inclusion of *Geisli*: the reader's focus should be on St Óláfr (and specifically on Óláfr as a martyr and saint, rather than as a king), and the manuscript should contain as many kinds of poetry as possible' (2005, 300).

This edition of *Óláfs ríma* has been normalised from Finnur Jónsson's text (1905, 1–9); for a facsimile of *Flateyjarbók* see CCIMA XX. One notable linguistic feature commonly found in the *rímur* that has been retained in this edition is the frequent apocope of the strong masculine nominative inflectional ending *-r*; other features of fourteenth-century Icelandic in general that are here retained are the diphthongisation or lengthening of short vowels before *-ng* and lowering of *á* to *ó* after *v* (except where *á* is required by the rhyme).

Bibliography

Ágrip af Nóregskonungasǫgum: A Twelfth-Century Synoptic History of the Kings of Norway, ed. M. J. Driscoll (1995).

Björn K. Þórólfsson, *Rímur fyrir 1600* (1934).

William A. Craigie, *Specimens of Icelandic Rímur from the Fourteenth to the Nineteenth Century/Sýnisbók íslenzkra rímna frá upphafi rímnakvedskapar til loka nítjándu aldar*, 3 vols (1952).

Finnur Jónsson, ed., *Rímnasafn: Samling af de ældste islandske rimer,* 2 vols, Samfund til udgivelse af gammel nordisk litteratur 35 (1905–22).

Peter A. Jorgensen, 'Rímur'. In *MS* 536–37.

Devra Kunin, tr., and Carl Phelpstead, ed., *A History of Norway and the Passion and Miracles of the Blessed Óláfr* (2001).

Elizabeth Ashman Rowe, *The Development of Flateyjarbók: Iceland and the Norwegian Dynastic Crisis of 1389* (2005).
Snorri Sturluson, *Heimskringla,* ed. Bjarni Aðalbjanarson. In *ÍF* XXVI–XXVIII; translated in *Hkr*.
Snorri Sturluson, *Óláfs saga helga*. In *ÍF* XXVII, II 3–415.
Vésteinn Ólason, 'Kveðið um Ólaf helga: Samanburður þriggja íslenskra bókmenntagreina frá lokum miðalda,' *Skirnir* 157 (1983), 48–63.
Vésteinn Ólason, 'Saint Olaf in Late Medieval Icelandic Poetry'. In Carol L. Edwards and Kathleen E. B. Manley, eds, *Narrative Folksong, New Directions: Essays in Appreciation of W. Edson Richmond* (1985), 2–17.

XXII: ÓLÁFS RÍMA HARALDSSONAR

Óláfs ríma Haraldzsonar er Einar Gilsson kvað

1. Óláfr kóngr ǫrr ok fríðr
átti Noregi at ráða;
gramr var æ við bragna blíðr,
borinn til sigrs ok náða.

2. Dǫglíng helt svó dýran heiðr
dróttni himna hallar;
eingi ský‹r›ir ǫrva meiðr
ǫðlíngs frægðir allar.

3. Mildíng hafði mentir þær,
er mestar vóru í heimi;
hvergi frægra hilmi fær
hvórki af gleði né seimi.

4. Fimm hefir kóngr kristnat lǫnd,
kann ek ǫll at nefna;[1]
gramr vill jafnan rjóða rǫnd
ok rángan úsið hefna.

5. Rán ok stuldi refsti hann
ok ræktar stjórn í landi;
hilmir lagði á heiðni bann
ok hefndi stórt með brandi.

6. Gramr nam lǫgmál setja svá
at seggir þol‹d›u valla;
dáligan lét hann dauða fá
dróttinssvikara alla.

7. Rekkar ýfðuz ræsi á mót
ok rétti harðla sǫnnum;
vóru kóngi heimsklig hót
hafin af sjálfs síns mǫnnum.

8. Hárekr var fyrir brǫgnum bystr,
búinn at stríða stilli;
Þórir hundr er þann veg lystr,
þriði var Kálfr enn illi.[2]

9. Kálfr var fyrr með kóngi sá
kærr í ǫllum ráðum;
nú er hann horfinn hilmi frá,
heiðri sviptr ok dáðum.

10. Þrændir geingu Þóri á hǫnd,
þeim var ljúft at herja;
háleysk þjóð vill rjóða rǫnd
ok ríkit kóngi verja.

11. Fylkir ríkr, frægr ok mildr
fréttir safnað þenna;
þá vill hilmir hraustr ok gildr
hvergi undan renna.

12. Bragníng lætr byrja ferð
bónda[3] múg í móti;
hann vill jafnan hræra sverð
ok herða skot með spjóti.

13. Siklíng hafði safnat þá
sínum gǫrpum snjǫllum;
lofðúngs kann ek lýði at tjá,
lángt bar gramr af ǫllum.

14. Hlýri kóngs var harðla júngr,
hann vil ek fyrstan nefna,
víst nam Haraldr[4] þykkju þúngr
Þrændum stríð at hefna.

15. 'Get ek ei hrotta hǫggit rǫnd,'
Haraldr talar við garpa,

'bindi menn við mína hǫnd
mæki þann enn snarpa.'

16. Rǫgnvaldr[5] var mildr ok merkr
með þeim kóngi góða;
Brúsa son nam brigða sterkr
brand í dreyra at rjóða.

17. Finnr Árnason[6] frækn ok hraustr
fylgir jǫfri sterkum;
Bjǫrn stallari[7] tryggr ok traustr
trúr vel ræsi merkum.

18. Sá var annar Árna mǫgr,
ýtar Þorberg kalla,
hann lét stálin stinn ok fǫgr
í sterkum hlífum gjalla.

19. Þormóðr var við Kolbrún kendr,[8]
kóngsins skáld it *fríða*,
sá berr hvassar hyggju strendr
hvar sem garpar stríða.

20. Náðuz menn í niflúngs flokk
nær sem risar at líta;
þeir hafa bragnar brynjurokk
brandi skorit enn hvíta.

21. Geingu fram fyr kóngsins kné
ok kvǫddu stilli enn teita;
buðu þeir bæði fylgd ok fé
frægum sjóla at veita.

22. Gramr réð spyrja garpa þá:
'Gerið mér heiti at inna;
trú skulu greina seggir svá
at satt megi til þess finna.'

19/2 fríða] *MS* dýra.

23. 'Opt hafa þegnar þrjózku hefnt,
þat mun eingi lasta;
Gauka-Þóri hafa gumnar nefnt
glaðan ok Hafra-Fasta.[9]

24. Treystum vér á mátt ok megn,
er margan riddara prýðir;
aungva hafa af Ásum fregn
okkrir sterkir lýðir.'

25. 'Taki þér heldr helga trú
himna kóngs með blóma,
virðar, kastið villu nú
ok verið með oss í sóma.'

26. Lýðir gerðu lykt á því
at leysa þenna vanda;
skírnarbrunn fara skatnar í
ok skynda Guði til handa.

27. Þrekstórr kom til þeingils maðr,
þann frá ek Arnljót[10] heita,
tók hann skírn ok gekk þó glaðr
grams í flokkinn teita.

28. Garpar fleiri at fylki renn[11]
en fyrðar mega þat telja;
siklíngr nam sæmdarmenn
sér til liðs at velja.

29. Kálfr hafði múga manns
merkta vǫllu víða;
níðíngligt var nærsta hans
niflúng þeim at stríða.

30. Bjálfa klæddiz hǫrðum Hundr
ok hans sveitúngar margir;
þat hafa geysigrimmligt undr
gert Búfinnar[12] argir.

31. Ræsir talar við Þorgils[13] þá,
þat var mest af prýði:
'Þér vil ek silfr í sjóði fá
þú seð með auma lýði.'

32. Þorgils hugsar þeingils mál:
'Þér innið framar hóti;
gef fyr þeira garpa sál
er gánga oss í móti.'

33. Herrinn drífr á hilmis fund
at heyja ímǫn stránga;
svó var þrútin þeira lund,
at þraut varð fram at gánga.

34. Múginn þessi geysiz gegn
gram með sárum vilja;
lǫgðu á orku ok allt sitt megn
jǫfur við land at skilja.

35. Á Stiklastǫðum var róman remd[14]
ríkum kóngi í móti;
þar vóru skǫpt með hǫndum hremd
ok hǫrðu kastað grjóti.

36. Hárekr eggjar herlið sitt,
heitr mǫrgum sóma.
'Lúki garpar geysistrítt
gram fyr harða dóma.'

37. Góða sverðit Hneitir hét,
hafði gramr til víga;
þar fyr margan þeingill lét
þegn at jǫrðu hníga.

38. Gumnar hlaupa geystir fram
grams fyr merkit væna,

reisa þannig randa glam
ok rísta skjǫldu græna.

39. Gellini tók at geysaz hart
ok gerði rómu stránga;
sannliga lét hann seggja mart
sáran dauða fánga.

40. Árna synir sinn unda naðr
einart drógu af magni;
kendiz ei svó klókr maðr
kæmi hlíf at gagni.

41. Þormóðr nam brytja bráð
bleikum fálu hesti,
varði kóng með dygð ok dáð,
darra él hann hvesti.

42. Þórir hundr þrautar gildr
þreif sitt spjót it snarpa;
laga var hann ok hǫggva mildr
við harða kóngsins garpa.

43. Þorsteinn hét sá er Þóri viðr
þar nam fram at gánga;
sá var kendr knarrarsmiðr,[15]
kominn í villu stránga.

44. Kóngrinn hjó til Þóris þá,
þat frá ek undrum sætti,
ekki beit hans bjálfann á,
brast sem grjóti mætti.[16]

45. Bjǫrn stallari bystr ok reiðr
barði Hund í móti;
síðan hné við sannan heiðr
seggr á Þóris spjóti.

46. Þorgeirr[17] vóð í randa regn,
ræsi náði at finna;
snarr réð kóngr þrjózkum þegn
þessi orð at inna.

47. ‘Þeygi gerir þú, Þorgeir, rétt
at þreyngir mǫnnum mínum;
lypta ek þér af lægri stétt,
lokit mun sigri þínum.’

48. Kóngrin hjó með Hneiti þá,
svó hrauð af eggjum báðum;
Þorgeir dauðr á lýngi lá,
lífi sviptr ok dáðum.

49. Þorsteinn réð á þeingils kné
þunnri ǫxi at sníða,
síðan lét hann fjǫr með fé
ok fell í ánauð stríða.

50. Bjǫrtum varp sér brandi frá
buðlúngs hǫnd in mæta,
sjóli bað með sǫnnu þá
sjálfann Guð sín gæta.

51. Þórir lagði í kóngsins kvið
kǫldum snótar ráðum;[18]
hilmis sál tók hæstan frið
himna grams með náðum.

52. Kálfr hjó til bragníngs bystr
batt sér þúngan vanda,
ramliga var hann á reiði lystr
ræsi þeim at granda.

53. Myrkri sló yfir menn ok hjǫrð
við mildíngs dýran dauða,

49/3 hann] *MS adds* líf.

litu þá hvórki lǫg né jǫrð,
lýð aflar þat nauða.

54. Þá kom Dagr[19] með dreingi sín
darra þíng at heyja;
margr hlaut við mikla pín
maðr af sút at deyja.

55. Æsilig var odda hríð,
undrum frá ek þat gegna,
mátti ekki meira stríð
af málma leiki fregna.

56. Hræðilig var hjǫrva gnauð,
harðar brynjur sprúngu,
dreingir feingu dapra nauð,
dǫrr á hlífum súngu.[20]

57. Stórt var þetta manna mót,
mest kom hjálp til bragna,
daufir feingu ok blindir bót,
bjúgir heilsu fagna.[21]

58. Þorgils geymdi þeingils lík,
þat fór heldr af hljóði;
maðr tók sýn fyr merkin slík
af mætu kóngsins blóði.

59. Fróni er huldr fylkir mætr
firðr nauð ok grandi;
líkami kóngs var mildr ok mætr
mánuðr tólf í sandi.[22]

60. Þeim kom virðum vóndzlig þraut
at vísis feingu reiði;
geislar skinu um grund á braut
grams af dýru leiði.[23]

61. Lýðir tóku upp líkama hans,[24]
lutu þá kóngi snjǫllum,
hár ok negl var heilags manns
hátt at vexti ǫllum.[25]

62. Hildíngs taka þá helgan dóm
halir í skrín at leggja;
nú er Kristz et bjarta blóm
ok blíðuz miskunn seggja.

63. Dróttni færði ǫðlíngr ǫnd,
ýtum líkam seldi;
nú er hann Guðs á hægri hǫnd
himins í æzta veldi.

64. Buðlúngs heiðr er bjartr ok ríkr
bæði um lǫnd ok geima,
fæddiz eingi fylkir slíkr
fyrri norðr í heima.

65. Reiðzt þú ei þó, þeingill, þér
þyrða ek vísu at bjóða;
biðr ek Óláf bjarga mér
við bragníng allra þjóða.[26]

Notes

[1] The conversion of five (or six) countries is attributed to St Óláfr's predecessor and namesake, Óláfr Tryggvason, rather than to St Óláfr in several Icelandic and Norwegian sources; the list (and number) of countries varies slightly: see, for example, *Historia Norwegiae* (Kunin and Phelpstead 2001, 21); *Ágrip* (1995), ch. 19; Oddr*ÓT*, ch. 52; and cf. Snorri's account of Óláfr Tryggvason's missionary endeavours in his *Óláfs saga Tryggvasonar* in *ÍF* XXVI, chs 47, 53, 73, 95–96.

[2] Hárekr ór Þjóttu, son of Eyvindr skáldaspillir, Þórir hundr ('the dog'), and Kálfr Árnason were prominent chieftains who led the rebellion against King Óláfr. Þórir hundr was, however, one of the first people to recognise Óláfr's sanctity after his death.

[3] Óláfr's opponents are usually characterised as *bœndr*, but the leaders of their army were of higher social status.

[4] Haraldr Sigurðarson, later known as *harðráði* ('hard ruler'), was king of Norway 1046–66. He was Óláfr's half-brother. On st. 15/3–4 cf. *ÍF* XXVII 364.

[5] Rǫgnvaldr Brúsason was the son of Earl Brúsi of Orkney. When King Óláfr settled a dispute between rival earls he required Rǫgnvaldr to remain at the Norwegian court in order to ensure that Brúsi kept to the agreement. Rǫgnvaldr remained there for many years; see *Óláfs saga helga* ch. 102; in *Haralds saga Sigurðarsonar* in *ÍF* XXVIII, ch. 1 Snorri tells how Earl Rǫgnvaldr helped Haraldr Sigurðarson to escape from the battle at Stiklastaðir.

[6] Two brothers of Óláfr's opponent Kálfr mentioned here supported the king, Finnr and Þorbergr (cf. stt. 18 and 40).

[7] Earlier in Óláfr's reign Bjǫrn stallari ('the marshal') had undertaken a diplomatic mission to try to make peace with the the king of Sweden. He had later visited the king in exile in Russia and reported on the state of affairs in Norway.

[8] The court poet Þormóðr Kolbrúnarskáld figures prominently in the last part of Snorri's *Óláfs saga helga* and is also a central character in *Fóstbrœðra saga*. Snorri records how he recited *Bjarkamál in fornu*

before the battle at Stiklastaðir and later died as a result of wounds received in the battle (*Óláfs saga helga* chs 208, 233–34). Þormóðr acquired his nickname after dedicating a poem to a woman called Þorbjǫrg kolbrún ('coal brow').

[9] Gauka-Þórir and Hafrafasti (Afrafasti in *Heimskringla* and most manuscripts of Snorri's separate *Óláfs saga helga*; Hafrafasti in Flateyjarbók) were brothers and robbers who decided to join Óláfr's army before the battle, but Óláfr would accept their help only if they first submitted to Christian baptism (*Óláfs saga helga* chs 203, 205).

[10] Arnljótr gellini (cf. stanza 39) was also required to convert to Christianity before Óláfr would accept his help in the battle: see *Óláfs saga helga* chs 141, 215.

[11] *renn* is presumably for *renna*, with the *-a* elided with the vowel at the beginning of the next line so as to preserve the rhyme.

[12] The Lappish inhabitants of Finnmark. Lapps were traditionally associated with sorcery. Þórir's protective magic cloaks are described in *Óláfs saga helga* ch. 193 (cf. ch. 228).

[13] Þorgils Hálmuson, a farmer at Stiklastaðir, fulfilled his promise to bury the king's body after the battle; cf. st. 58 below and see Snorri's *Óláfs saga helga* chs 210 and 236–38.

[14] The Battle of Stiklastaðir (or Stiklarstaðir) took place on 29 July 1030. Cf. note 18 to Text VIII above.

[15] In *Óláfs saga helga* ch. 222 Snorri tells how Þorsteinn knarrarsmiðr ('ship-builder') fell out with King Óláfr and was punished for his violent crimes by having a large ship he had built confiscated; Þorsteinn vowed to repay the king by being the first to strike him if he could get close enough in the battle against him. Snorri's account of the fatal blows inflicted on Óláfr by Þorsteinn, Þórir hundr and Kálfr Árnason is in *Óláfs saga helga* ch. 228.

[16] I.e. presumably the king's sword broke. But he is still using Hneitir at 48/1, and his sword is not said to be broken in *ÍF* XXVII 383–84.

[17] According to Snorri's account, Þorgeirr of Kvistsstaðir supported the rebels against Óláfr despite having earlier been elevated in social status by the king; see st. 47/3–4 and *Óláfs saga helga* chs 225, 227.

[18] Cf. the proverb *kǫld eru kvenna ráð* 'cold are the counsels of women' in e.g. *Njáls saga* (*ÍF* XII 292); and the episode in *Óláfs saga helga* ch. 123 (*ÍF* XXVII 213) where Sigríðr, Þórir hundr's sister-in-law, urges Þórir to stab the king with the spear that had killed her son Ásbjǫrn.

[19] Óláfr had exiled Dagr's father King Hringr of Heiðmǫrk from Norway, but on Óláfr's own return journey to Norway from exile in Russia he sent word to Dagr that if he were to regain Norway with Dagr's help he would grant him dominions as great as his ancestors had held there (*Óláfs saga helga* ch. 199). Dagr's renewal of the battle following Óláfr's death is recounted in *Óláfs saga helga* ch. 229.

[20] Craigie (1952, I 285) suggests that some verses may be missing between stanzas 56 and 57, where the story jumps to the evening after the battle when the first of the miracles took place (*Óláfs saga helga* ch. 236).

[21] Cf. Matthew 11: 5.

[22] Óláfr's body was secretly buried in a sandbank by the River Nið near Trondheim (*Óláfs saga helga* ch. 238).

[23] On the light from St Óláfr's grave see *Óláfs saga helga* ch. 238.

[24] The translation of Óláfr's body took place on 3 August 1031. His remains were enshrined in Trondheim, later the location of the Norwegian archiepiscopal see.

[25] The miraculous growth of the dead saint's hair and nails is recorded in many texts, including Snorri's *Óláfs saga helga* chs 244–45.

[26] The final prayer is presumably for the poet to be saved from the judgment of Christ on doomsday, which is a normal request, rather than from Christ himself.

XXIII: ENCYCLOPEDIC LITERATURE

PHYSIOGNOMY

The passage below is offered as an example of the kind of learned literature collected and edited by Kr. Kålund under the title *Alfræði íslenzk*. In line with Kålund's title, material of this type is often known as encyclopedic literature, specimens of which are to be found in Icelandic manuscripts from as early as *c.*1200, though the majority of the encyclopedic manuscripts that survive are from the fourteenth and fifteenth centuries. It must be stressed that the compilations in which such writing is found, in the Old Norse context, are not encyclopedias in the modern sense. The Middle Ages did indeed produce some influential Latin works of a truly encyclopedic nature in that their authors aimed at giving systematic and comprehensive accounts of lore concerning the whole world and its inhabitants; notable among these are the *Etymologiae* of St Isidore of Seville and the *Imago mundi* of Honorius Augustodunensis, the former being a work from the early seventh century that gained lasting currency throughout Europe, and the latter belonging to the first half of the twelfth century. The *Imago mundi* appears to have been especially popular in medieval Iceland: it is likely that there was a twelfth-century Icelandic translation of it, which has not survived; the fifteenth-century manuscript AM 685 a 4to contains a vernacular adaptation of the first part of the work; and AM 435 12mo, from which the passage below is drawn, refers to the work by name in the paragraph immediately before the one with which the present excerpt begins (*Alfræði* III 98). It can be said in general, however, that the Old Icelandic manuscripts which are compilations of encyclopedic literature function not as full descriptions of the world but as 'micro-libraries' (Clunies Ross and Simek 1993) consisting of unsystematised collections of works, or pieces of works, commonly dealing with such subjects as geography, the peoples of the world, the properties of stones, liturgical matters and computus (i.e. calculation, but in particular the art of calculating the correct dates of moveable feasts in the ecclesiastical year). AM 435 12mo, for example, includes sections on computus, the Icelandic calendar and the ceremonial of the Mass, but in addition its first fifteen folios are devoted to the subject of physiognomy.

As expressed pithily by the Peripatetic author of *Physiognomica,* long thought to be Aristotle himself, the basic proposition of the ancient and medieval science of physiognomy was that 'dispositions follow bodily characteristics' (Aristotle, *Minor Works* 1936, 85); in other words, the personality of a human individual can be perceived by observing the person's physical appearance. This idea had been endorsed by the real Aristotle in the *Prior Analytics* (70^b 7–38), which was available to the Middle Ages in a Latin translation by Boethius (*Aristoteles latinus* 1962, 5–139). The basis of physiognomy as understood by Aristotle was not simply the observation of human beings and their personalities but rather the drawing of analogies between humans and animals; as Ross's commentary on Aristotle's work (1949, 501) puts it, the methodology depends on 'the inferring of mental characteristics in *men* from the presence in them of physical characteristics which in some other kind or kinds of animal go constantly with those mental characteristics'. Remnants of this way of thinking can be seen in the references to bears, horses, sea-monsters, snakes, birds, goats and spiders in the passage below (lines 6, 60, 63, 66, 69 and 95–96). For the Middle Ages, perhaps the most influential writer on physiognomy was Marcus Antonius Polemon (*c*.88–144), whose work on the subject is lost in its original Greek form but survives in Latin and Arabic translations and in a later Greek paraphrase. It is Polemon who is the ultimate source for the material included in the Old Norse passage reproduced here. Contrary to the impression given by Kålund (*Alfræði* III xv), however, the more direct source for the passage is a later Latin work based on Polemon, the *Anonymi de physiognomonia liber*, or something quite like it; this fact is shown by the sequence of the topics discussed, which is radically different from that of Polemon, and by the close correspondence of many sentences. Details of the correlation between the Icelandic text and the Latin works are given in the notes below.

In other types of Old Norse literature, such as sagas of Icelanders and eddic poems, it is quite common for physical characteristics to be mentioned in ways that may imply some kind of significance for the personality or social status of the people who bear them. An interesting topic for further study would be that of the differences and similarities between the beliefs implicit in such references and the system of physiognomic lore outlined here. This is not the place to enter into such a study, but some pointers have been given in the accompanying notes.

The text is a normalised version of AM 435 12mo, folios 8r–13r, based on Kålund's transcription (*Alfræði* III 98–103). The manuscript, which has been dated to *c.*1500, shares its physiognomic material with another encyclopedic manuscript from Iceland, the Codex Lindesianus (John Rylands University Library, Manchester, Icel I; = L), c.1473, which has been described by Eiríkur Magnússon (1896–97). The passage includes a high proportion of unusual vocabulary, noted by Eiríkur (pp. 11–14) and Kålund (*Alfræði* III xvi–xvii), including *blauthærðr* (line 3), *fávitugr* (line 80), *fjórhyrndr* (line 32), *hugsanarmikill* (line 2), *ónæmi* (line 46), *rálítill* (line 38; here emended to *rólítill*), *stundanarmikill* (line 19), *útrauðr* (line 37), *þunnhærðr* (line 3) and *þykkhærðr* (line 4). The word *trítli* (line 39; MS *trillti*), which does not occur in L, is especially problematical; the reading given here is based on a suggestion made by Kålund (*Alfræði* III xvii).

Bibliography

Kr. Kålund with N. Beckman (vol. 2), eds, *Alfræði íslenzk*. 3 vols (1908–18).

Anonymi de physiognomonia liber latinus. In R. Foerster, ed., *Scriptores physiognomonici graeci et latini*. 2 vols (1893), II 1–145.

Marcus Antonius Polemon, *Polemonis de physiognomonia liber arabice et latine*, ed. G. Hoffmann. In R. Foerster, ed., *Scriptores physiognomonici graeci et latini*. 2 vols (1893), I 93–294.

Aristotle, *Minor Works*, ed. and tr. W. S. Hett (1936).

Aristoteles latinus III 1–4. *Analytica priora*, ed. L. Minio-Paluello (1962).

M. Clunies Ross and R. Simek, 'Encyclopedic Literature'. In *MS* 164–66.

E. C. Evans, *Physiognomics in the Ancient World* (1969).

Anne Holtsmark, 'Encyklopedisk litteratur'. In *Kulturhistoriskt Lexicon för nordisk medeltid*. 22 vols. (1956–78).

Eiríkur Magnússon, 'Codex Lindesianus', *Arkiv för nordisk filologi* 13 (1896–97), 1–14.

'Polemon'. In S. Hornblower and A. Spawforth, eds, *The Oxford Classical Dictionary*, 3rd ed (2003).

W. D. Ross, ed., *Aristotle's Prior and Posterior Analytics* (1949).

PHYSIOGNOMY

‹S›vá segja fornir frœðimenn, at eptir náttúrligu eðli sé karlmanna hugr skjótr ok ákafr í sinni fýst, iðjufullr ok hugsanarmikill, en kvenna hugr miskunnsamr ok óttagjarn.[1] Blauthærðir menn ok þunnhærðir sýna skjótt hugvit; þykkhærðir menn síngjarnir ok óhræddir. Þat hár er þrøngir mjǫk saman ok hrøkkr nǫkkut yfir enninu, sýnir grimman hug, ok því samþykkir hárferð á skógbjarnar hǫfði. Gulir lokkar, þykkvir ok nǫkkut ljósir, sýna mann ónæman. Døkkjarpir lokkar, ef þeir eru mátuliga þunnir, sýna góðsiðuga menn ok hœgt skaplyndi.[2]

Hǫfuð mjǫk mikit sýnir heimskan mann, en bǫllótt hǫfuð ok skammt óvitran ok óminnigan. Lítit hǫfuð ok yfir ofan svá sem slétt sýnir lausungar mark ok óvenju. Aflangt hǫfuð ok vaxit nǫkkut svá sem hamarr segir mann vera forsjálan ok athugasaman.[3]

Enni þat er mjǫk er mjótt, segir mann vera ónæman ok gráðgan; en þat er mjǫk er langt, segir litla skynsemðargrein. Kringlótt enni sýnir reiðan mátt. Lítit enni ok niðrlútt sýnir óframan hug ok lýtalausan. Ferhyrnt enni meðr mátuligum mikilleik sýnir mann mikilhugaðan með mikilli vizku.[4]

Ef brýnn eru þar til bjúgar sem þær koma saman viðr nefit, merkja gløggvan mann ok stundanarmikinn í ǫllum sínum gerðum; en ef þar verðr nǫkkut mjótt meðal, þat sýnir hryggan mann ok óvitran. En ef bjúgleikr brúnanna hne‹i›gisk niðr til augna ok beri niðr af mjǫk þykkvar kinnr, merkir vanrœktar hug. En ef brúna hár eru mjǫk lǫng ok mǫrg, þat merkir grimman mann ok mikilhugaðan.[5]

Augu þau sem bjar‹t›liga skína, segja til fagrferðugra siða; en ef þau eru óstaðfǫst, svá at þau renna stundum skjótt, en stundum sé þau kyr, merkja illa hluti válkask í huginum ok vera eigi fram komna.[6] Gul augu með skínandi birti merkja djarfan mann ok til illgerða vakran. Mikil augu skjálfandi ok svǫrt merkja drykkjumann ok kvennamann.[7] Augu hreinliga svǫrt merkja óstyrkan hug ok krap‹t›lausan. Svǫrt augu með rauðum dropum merkja réttlátan hug, dyggan ok hugvitran.[8] Þar sem í svǫrtum augum sýnask smádropar ákafliga rauðir ok nǫkkurir fjórhyrndir ok nǫkkurir bleikir, en aðrir gulir, ok hringar þeir, er liggja útan um sjáldrin, hafi á sér blóðslit, ok sé augun mikil ok birti sú sem fylgir sjáldrunum hrœrisk svá sem hrœrask sjáldrin, þvílík augu merkja

12 athugan saman

þann hug er um fram er allan hrædýra hátt, því at hvat er af óhœfunni má hugsat vera ór þvílíkum augum máttuligt at fremja, ok eigi munu varna við heimamannligu blóði. Þau augu sem eru mjǫk útrauð ok þó r*ó*lítil,[9] birta stillingarlausan ok ‹ó›stǫðugan líkam. Snǫrp augu ok snǫr í trít*l*i,[10] ef þau eru vát, sýna sannsǫglan mann, skjótan ok forsjálan í sínum gerðum. Þau augu sem optliga lúkask upp ok aptr, sýna óttafullan hug ok vanmegnan.[11] Augu mjǫk opin merkja heimsku ok óframa, en þau sem mjǫk eru lukt, merkja hrœriligan hug ok í ǫllum gjǫrðum sínum óstaðfastan.

Eyru þau sem hátt standa ok eru mjǫk mikil, merkja athugaleysi, heimsku ok óvizku; en mjǫk lítil eyru hafa illgjǫrða mark. Mjǫk kringlótt eyru merkja ónæmi, en aflǫng ok þrǫng merkja ǫfundar mark; þau sem liggja nær hǫfðinu sýna leti.[12]

Feitar kinnr ok mjǫk þykkvar merkja leti ok ofdrykkju, en þær er mjǫk eru þunnar merkja illgirni. Kringlóttar kinnr sýna ǫfund.[13]

Opnar nasir gefa af sér gleðimark ok styrktar, en þunnar ok langar óstaðfesti ok léttleika. Þat nef er niðr af enni ok fram er hvárki mjǫk hátt né lágt, heldr jafnt viðr sik ok rétt, sýnir af sér karlmannligt mark með staðfesti ok vizku. Nasir minni en hœfiligt er, er þjófa mark.[14]

Allt saman andlit, ef þat er kjǫtsfullt, þykkt ok feitt, merkir óþrifnaðar mark ok munhugðar. Bjúgleitt andlit vísar til undirferli ok vælar meðr slœgð.[15]

Þunnar varrir, ef hin efri er nǫkkuru meiri en hin neðri, sýnir mikilhugaðan mann ok sterkan; en þunnar varrir meðr litlum munni sýna óstyrkan hug ok slœgan. Ef varrir hanga nǫkkut svá niðr frá munninum, sýna óþrifnaðar mark, því at þat mark finnsk á ǫsnum ok hestum. Lítill munnr hœfir kvenna áliti og þeim hugum er kvennligir eru. Sá munnr er um fram hátt er víðr, sýnir mann gráðgan, ómjúkan ok ómildan, því at svá mikit gin hœfir sjóskrímslum.[16]

Haka sú er nǫkkut svá er lǫng, sýnir manninn miðr reiðan ok miðr skelfðan. Þeir sem hafa litla hǫku eru ómjúkir ok ǫfundsjúkir; þessa sagði meistari Plato hǫggormum líka. Nytsamligra manna haka er vel mátuliga mikil ok nǫkkut svá ferhyrnd. Sú haka er mjǫk er lǫng, sýnir prettóttan hug.[17]

Sú rǫdd er lík er fugla rǫdd eðr geita sýnir heimsku mark, en þeir er sína rǫdd hefja upp á fugla hátt, eru l*é*ttir ok auðveldir. Sú rǫdd sem er óstyrk ok nǫkkut grátlig, sýnir hryggan ok grunsemðarfullan hug. Þeira

38 rálítil 39 ‘trillti’ 70 littir

manna rǫdd er rennr í nefit, svá at nefit samhljóði rǫddinni, þeir eru lygnir ok illgjarnir ok fagna annarra illgjǫrðum.[18]

Langr háls ok þunnr merkir þann er illt hugsar. Kringlóttr háls sýnir hugar krapt ok líkams lítillæti. Skammr háls er mark þess er djarfr er. Sá háls er mjǫk berr sik réttan sýnir óvenju ok þrjótlyndi.[19]

Brjóst þat sem lengra er en kviðrinn, sýnir vitran mann.[20] Brjóst þat sem með kviðinum er hult miklu hári, merkir óstǫðugan mann útan siðlæti ok mildi. Brjóst þat er mjǫk er hult miklu kjǫti, segir ónæma menn ok fávituga, en ef eitt saman brjóstit hefir hárit, sýnir hugfullan mann.[21]

Þunnar herðar ok uppréttar vísa til þess manns er gjarna sitr um aðra.[22]

Armleggir, ef þeir eru svá langir at þá er maðrinn stendr með réttum líkama, taki lengstu fingr mjǫk til knjá, þó at aðrir fingr taki eigi jafnlangt, sýnir lítilláta menn ok styrka; en ef fingr eru ‹eigi› lengri en á mjǫðmina eða litlu lengra, sýnir illgjarna menn þá er fagna annarra illgjǫrðum.[23]

Mjǫk skammar hendr ok litlar sýna styrka menn ok vituga. Feitar hendr ok meir skammir fingr en hœfiligt er, birta mann ómerkan. Snúnar hendr ok þunnar sýna málgan mann ok gráðgan. Hvítir negl ok blautir, sléttir ok þunnir ok líttat rjóðir harðla vel skínandi, segja it hæsta hugvit; bjúgir negl sýna óvitra ok gráðga. Mjǫk samfelldir fingr sýna illgjarnan ok ágjarnan, en litlir fingr ok f*eit*‹i›r segja djarfan ok ǫfundsjúkan. Litlir fingr ok þunnir sýna hei‹m›skan mann.[24]

Þunnar ok þrǫngvar síður sýna hræddan mann, en kjǫtmiklar ok harðar sýna mann ónæman; því eru þær af spekingum kallaðar kǫngurváfum líkar.[25]

Sá hlutr fótleggjar sem undir knénu er, kallask at bókmáli sura; ef þar er fullt mjǫk, svá at þat þyngi fótinn, merkir mann stillingarlausan ok óhreinan. Blautar surae eru kvensligar.[26]

Feitir fœtr ok skammir sýna mjǫk óstyrkan mann, en mjǫk langir prettóttan, mjǫk þunnir ok skammir illgjarnan. Þeir er langa fœtr hafa ok stíga hátt ok langt, eru vanir at vera mikilhugaðir menn ok fljótvirkir. Sá er fljótliga gengr ok haldi sér þó svá aptr, lýtr niðr, sem hann beri allan líkamann bjúgan,[27] merkir ǫfundsjúkan ok slœgan. Sá sem hefir skamma fœtr ok berr þá skjótliga, er sagðr vera illgjarn ok óstyrkr.[28]

Svartr skinnslitr segir mann slœgan, en hvítr skinnslitr ok nǫkkut rjóðr segir styrka menn ok hugfulla. Ákafliga hvítr skinnslitr með bleikum merkir þrotnanda krapt ok óstyrkt af ofkaldri náttúru. Eldsligr skinnslitr

91 litlir] lit|litir *over line break* fœtr

með skínǫndum augum snýsk til œði. Meðalskinnslitr, hvítr ok svartr, ok 108
bregði á nǫkkut brúnu, sýnir mann með góðu hugviti ok góðum siðum.[29]

Notes

[1] For the probable source of this sentence see *Anonymi de physiognomonia liber* 4 (hereafter *Anon.*, all references being to section numbers).

[2] For the material on hair see *Anon.* 14, which includes the reference to the bear (*ursus*) whereas Polemon ch. XL specifies only a likeness to a wild animal (*similitudo ferae agrestis*). In connection with this topic it should be noted that hair curling over the forehead seems to have been regarded as an ugly feature in medieval Iceland, since in *Kormaks saga* (*ÍF* VIII 210) Steingerðr Þorkelsdóttir refers to this characteristic as the one blemish in the otherwise handsome Kormakr. An emphasis on particularly beautiful hair, however, is often taken to indicate points at which Old Norse literature has been influenced by European romance traditions, as in the case of the description of Sigurðr in *Vǫlsunga saga* (ed. R. G. Finch 1965, 41), which is probably based on a passage in *Þiðreks saga* (ed. Guðni Jónsson 1954, 255), the latter work being a translation of some German romance. See also the descriptions of various characters in *Trójumanna saga* (ed. Jonna Louis-Jensen 1963, 64–70), an Icelandic work that dates from the first half of the thirteenth century and is based on a well-known Latin text that the Middle Ages ascribed to Dares Phrygius; the passage gives prominence to the hair colour of each person mentioned, though it is not clear whether personality traits are to be inferred from the descriptions. Colouring, however, is definitely associated with social status, and hence character type, in the eddic poem *Rígsþula*, which has been dated as early as the eleventh century or as late as the mid-thirteenth and which gives black hair to the prototypical *þræll*, whereas it declares the original *jarl* to have been blond. It is most likely that nobility and beauty are the associations that the author of *Njáls saga* (*ÍF* XII 53) has in mind when he says that Gunnarr Hámundarson had thick golden hair, rather than the characteristic that could be inferred from the physiognomic text above.

[3] *Anon.* 16. See also Polemon XXX.

[4] *Anon*. 17. See also Polemon XXVII.

[5] *Anon*. 18. See also Polemon XLVIII.

[6] The material on eyes is a greatly abridged version of *Anon*. 21–44 (see also Polemon I) generally conforming to the sequence of topics in the Latin text but with interpolations. The sources of individual statements, where it has been possible to identify them, are indicated in the notes that follow. The two parts of the paragraph's first sentence are from *Anon*. 21 and 23 respectively.

[7] *Anon*. 23.

[8] This and the following sentence concerning black eyes are from *Anon*. 27, which includes references to wild beasts and the slaying of close kindred, which may be reflected in the references to *hrædýra háttr* and *heimamannligt blóð* in lines 35 and 37. In Old Norse literature there is an association between black eyes and Icelandic poets: in *Kormaks saga* (*ÍF* VIII 211) the eponymous skald says *Svǫrt augu berk* in a stanza replying to criticism of this feature made by a handmaid of Steingerðr Þorkelsdóttir, the object of the poet's love; and *Heimskringla* (*ÍF* XXVII 140) preserves a stanza by Sigvatr Þórðarson referring to *augun þessi íslenzk . . . svǫrtu*, apparently replying to a comment made by a woman in the court of Rǫgnvaldr jarl of Gautland, to the effect that Sigvatr has come with his black eyes to gain the gold ring that the jarl gives him. The latter exchange seems to be somewhat flirtatious, as is the comment in *Kormaks saga*; but it may also imply an accusation of avarice on the part of the poet, which would accord with the statement in *Anon*. 27, omitted in the Old Norse text above, that black eyes *lucri avidum indicant* 'indicate a person greedy for gain'.

[9] The MS reading *rálítill*, though it is explained by Eiríkur Magnússon as an otherwise unrecorded term meaning something like 'with rather indistinct corners' (*rá* f. corner), is more likely to be an error in the archetype for *rólítill*, which fits the context much better.

[10] The MS reading 'trillti' is not a known word in Icelandic, but Kålund in the introduction to *Alfræði* III (p. xvii) suggests a link with Norwegian *trilla*, *trilta* 'toddle, run', Modern Icelandic *trítla* 'mince,

trot'. Cf. also *trítill* 'top'; 'urchin'. It might then be dative of *trítill* m., meaning 'small movements', and here it has accordingly been emended to *trítli*. Alternatively the word might be **trilt* n., with the same meaning, and the text would then require no emendation.

[11] *Anon.* 41.

[12] *Anon.* 47. See also Polemon XXIX.

[13] *Anon.* 49. See also Polemon XXVIII.

[14] *Anon.* 51, but here the correspondence is closer to Polemon XXVI, which includes a reference to the mark of thieves. Note that in *Njáls saga* (*ÍF* XII 7) it is the eyes rather than the nose that can carry physical signs of a propensity to commit theft, since Hrútr Herjólfsson, on seeing Hallgerðr Hǫskuldsdóttir for the first time, asks *hvaðan þjófsaugu eru komin í ættir várar* 'whence thief's eyes are come into our family'.

[15] *Anon.* 50. See also Polemon XXVIII.

[16] *Anon.* 48, but the passage is closer to Polemon XXV, which includes a reference to crocodiles, corresponding to *sjóskrimsl*.

[17] *Anon.* 52 refers to snakes but not to Plato; Polemon XXIV does not mention either.

[18] The material on the voice corresponds to *Anon.* 78, though the Latin text refers to sheep rather than *geitr*. Polemon LII mentions neither sheep nor goats.

[19] *Anon.* 53–55, Polemon XXIII. There appears to be some confusion or corruption here as both Latin texts declare a short neck to be a sign of timidity.

[20] *Anon.* 63. See also Polemon XV.

[21] *Anon.* 73. See also Polemon XLIV.

[22] *Anon.* 58. This statement is not present in the corresponding passage of Polemon, XX.

[23] *Anon.* 59. See also Polemon XXI.

[24] *Anon.* 59–60. See also Polemon III–IV. Concerning the words *samfelldir fingr*, Kålund (*Alfræði* III xvii) declares that they answer to the phrase *digitos cum unguibus cohaerantes* 'joined fingers with nails' in Polemon IV; in fact, however, the sentence in which they occur is a rendering of *digiti cum coniuncti sunt et cohaerent, immundum hominem significant* 'when fingers are conjoined and cohere, they signify an impure man' (*Anon.* 60). The phrase *litlir fingr ok feitir*, in the emended text above, corresponds to *digiti . . . parvi et crassi* 'small and thick fingers' in *Anon.* 60 and provides a clear antithesis with *litlir fingr ok þunnir*, which correspond to *digiti . . . parvi et tenues* 'small and slender fingers'.

[25] *Anon.* 65. The Latin word corresponding to *kǫngurváfa* is *rana* 'frog'. This is not in Polemon, and it is possible that the Latin text used by the Norse compiler had a spelling for *rana* that he took for the Greek ἀράχνη 'spider', and he perhaps understood the simile to refer to thinness of limbs. At this point the Old Norse text omits material relating to the back, lower spine, pelvis, thigh and knee found in *Anon.* 66–70.

[26] *Anon.* 71 mentions σφυρα 'ankles' rather than *sura* 'calf'. The final sentence, to the effect that soft calves are womanish, corresponds to one in *Anon.* 72, which actually refers to feet. See also Polemon VII.

[27] '. . . and yet holds himself backwards, bowing down, so that he carries his whole body curved.' This rather confusing description appears to mean that the person bends himself in the middle with head and knees forward, putting his body in the shape of a C.

[28] The first sentence of this paragraph corresponds to one in *Anon.* 72; the rest relates to *Anon.* 75. See also Polemon V and L.

[29] *Anon.* 79. See also Polemon XXXVI. The phrase *með bleikum* (line 106) does not have a correlative in the corresponding sentences of either Latin text.

XXIV: KONUNGS SKUGGSJÁ

Konungs skuggsjá, or *Speculum regale*, was written in Norway, most probably in the 1250s, in the form of a dialogue between a father and his son, the former answering the latter's questions. It is in three parts, the first dealing with matters of interest to a merchant, the second with life at court and how a king's retainer should behave, and the third with the duties of the king, especially his duties as a judge. The work is anonymous, but it may safely be assumed that the author was a cleric closely associated with the royal circle, who probably wrote his 'king's mirror' for the enlightenment of King Hákon Hákonarson's sons, Hákon the Young (1232–57) and Magnús (1238–80), the latter of whom, Magnús the Lawmender, succeeded his father in 1263.

Konungs skuggsjá is preserved in some sixty manuscripts, both Norwegian and Icelandic; their interrelationship is discussed in Holm-Olsen 1952, 116–79 and Holm-Olsen 1987, 12–17. The text of the extract below reflects that of the so-called main manuscript, AM 243 b α fol., as edited in Holm-Olsen 1983, 48–49; it has also been collated with the relevant folios (62–64) of that manuscript as edited in facsimile by Flom (1915). The manuscript was written in Norway, most probably in Bergen, in *c*.1275 (Holm-Olsen 1983, xii). In the extract as edited here, Norwegian spellings and word-forms have been retained, as in the extract from *Fagrskinna* (cf. p. 65 above), though with the main differences that short, open *e* is represented by *ę* (corresponding to the long sound *æ*), and the Norwegian i-mutation of *au* by *øy* (often written *æy*).

The extract, from the second part of *Konungs skuggsjá*, is of great historical sociolinguistic interest for the light it throws on the uses of the singular, dual and plural forms of the first and second person pronouns (cf. *Gr* 3.2, 3.2.1) in the spoken language(s) of Norway and Iceland in the thirteenth century (cf. *Gr* 1.2). As Helgi Guðmundsson (1972, 39) notes: 'Of course the usage in question may not have been precisely the same in Iceland as in Norway, but in view of the close connections between the two countries at that time it cannot have been widely divergent.' The father is here advising the son on the appropriate uses of the pronominal forms. The plural is to be used in addressing the king (lines 3–4) or an influential person (57–58) or someone who deserves respectful treatment (61), such as a chieftain (72–75); this has become established as the custom among wise and courteous men (59–60). One should however guard against using the plural with reference to oneself when speaking to the king (4–6), or (it is implied) to anyone of higher rank than oneself, lest it be thought that one considers oneself the equal of such a person (82–84). Even when talking to an equal or to an inferior one should not seek to elevate oneself by speaking of oneself in the plural (84–86). Only a fool would refer to himself in the plural and to the king in the singular when addressing the king (4–6).

In other words, the first and second person plural forms, used respectively with reference to oneself and to the one addressed, are both felt to be honorific. Although in *Konungs skuggsjá* as a whole the father and son do not always follow in their own dialogue the father's recommendations as given here, as Helgi Guðmundsson (1972, 41) has noted, they do so in the extract itself: the son uses the plural in addressing the father (lines 22–23, 54), while referring to himself in the singular (22, 24, 50, 54), and the father addresses the son in the singular (1–10, 12–13, 25–26, 30, 47–49, 82–85), while also referring to himself in the singular (25–26, 29–32). It is true that the father uses first person plural forms at lines 28, 34, 40 and 42, but it seems clear that in doing so here he is speaking neither of himself as an individual, nor of just himself and his son, but of mankind (or at least Christendom) in general. When he is speaking of just himself and his son, on the other hand, he uses dual forms, as at lines 47 and 49. In this last respect, i.e. in using the dual to refer to just themselves, father and son are not entirely consistent, either, in *Konungs skuggsjá* as a whole, as Helgi Guðmundsson (1972, 46) has also noted, though Helgi's examples give the impression that the father is more consistent in this respect than the son. In the brief speech within the father's speech with which the extract opens, where the father is indicating to the son how the king should be addressed (lines 10–12), the father naturally follows his own rules in presenting the son as addressing the king in the plural and as referring to himself in the singular.

There is however one exception to the father's rule that a superior should be addressed in the plural, as the son diffidently points out to him (lines 15–24), i.e. that it is customary to address God in the second person singular. At lines 18–19 and 20–21 the son gives examples of what his experience has led him to regard as, respectively, the correct and incorrect uses of the personal pronoun in addressing the Almighty.

The father's reply, which is also somewhat diffident, since he claims that this is a matter more for theologians than for him (25–29), confirms by implication the accuracy of the son's observation in acknowledging that the question here raised deserves an answer (29–31). The father then explains this particular usage in terms of the singularity of the Christian God as opposed to other gods (32–39), an explanation which accords interestingly with one recently offered, in the context of the history of English but expressed in relatively general terms, by Smith (1991, 135). It may however be noted that Strang (1970, 139–40), also writing in the context of English while expressing herself in general terms, explains this usage by reference not to so much to the singularity of God as to His specialness. Once the use of the plural pronoun for polite address to a single person has been introduced into a language, she argues, it is likely to snowball, since in cases of doubt one would rather be polite than risk giving offence. The use of the plural to a single human superior would thus acquire the status of what Strang calls a central function, from which the use of the singular in addressing God, who is regarded as a special case, would become an exception.

In response to the question, asked by the son at lines 14–15 and again at lines 54–56, of why influential people should be addressed in the plural, the father justifies this on the grounds, firstly, that it is an old-established practice (57–61), and secondly that the plural form of address appropriately reflects the plurality of the responsibilities of those addressed. Chieftains, for example, are responsible for many more people than just themselves and their households (61–75), and the king does not function alone, but is surrounded by a retinue of counsellors (77–81). This explanation of the use of the plural in addressing a superior also accords interestingly with explanations by modern writers on language as to how this practice may have arisen. Pointing out that the polite use of the plural to refer to a single addressee 'seems to be very general in unrelated languages' (including Hungarian, Quechua, Tamil and many African languages), Brown and Levinson (1987, 198–99, cf. 202) suggest two possible motives for it: first, it provides the addressee with a 'let-out' in allowing him, theoretically at least, to interpret the address as not necessarily directed specifically at him; and second, it enhances his sense of status in treating him as the representative of a group rather than as a relatively powerless individual. Comparable to this second motive would be the motivation for the use of the high-status or 'royal' first person plural 'we', against the use of which, in the extract (lines 4–6, 82–86), the father advises the son, the implication being that it is appropriately used only by people of very high or responsible status.

Brown and Gilman (1960, 255–61) described the semantic evolution, as they saw it, of second person singular and plural pronoun forms, calling them respectively *T* and *V* (from Latin *tu* and *vos*) in French, English, Italian, Spanish and German, and maintaining that in these languages a set of norms crystallised in *T* and *V* usage at different stages between the twelfth and fourteenth centuries. This set of norms, which they called the power semantic, involved the downward and upward use of *T* and *V*, respectively, between people of unequal social status, and the use of *V* and *T* respectively between equals of the upper and lower classes. (A later development, they argued, was the solidarity semantic, whereby an intimate *T* came to be used between people not necessarily of equal status but sharing the same views and/or behaviour dispositions; they left unexplained, however, the use of *T* for addressing God.) Helgi Guðmundsson (1972, 60–61) noted examples in Old Norse-Icelandic of a distinction between ordinary (i.e. non-honorific) and honorific uses of the first and second person pronouns from as early as the tenth century (in skaldic poetry), attributing it to influence from Central and Southern Europe, while at the same time recognising it as a widely attested feature; he also showed (1972, 94–99) that, in Icelandic, an increased honorific use of the second person plural pronoun in the seventeenth century led to the need for an unequivocally defined 'ordinary' plural. As a result, the second person dual pronouns gradually acquired plural meaning, as did also, mainly by analogy, the first person dual pronouns. Thus the Icelandic dual pronouns lost their dual meanings and came to be used as ordinary plurals, whereas the old plural forms *vér*, *þér* etc. were reserved exclusively for honorific use. The resulting situation is reflected in present-day Icelandic by the use of *við* (< *vit*) 'we' and *þið* (< *þit*) 'you' in plural meanings, and by the genitive forms *okkar*, *ykkar* in the meanings 'our' and 'your' (pl.) respectively; honorific *vér* and *þér*, however, are now found for the most part only in the written language. Icelandic is unusual in using old dual forms in plural meanings, but a parallel development has taken place in Faroese (Helgi Guðmundsson 1972, 122–24).

Bibliography

Brown, Penelope and Stephen C. Levinson (1987), *Politeness: some universals in language usage.*

Brown, Roger and Albert Gilman (1960), 'The pronouns of power and solidarity', in *Style in language*, ed. by Thomas A. Sebeok, 253–76.

Finnur Jónsson, ed. (1920), *Konungs skuggsjá = Speculum regale udgivet efter håndskrifterne af Det kongelige nordiske oldskriftselskab.*

Finnur Jónsson, tr. (1926), *Kongespejlet: Konungs skuggsjá i dansk oversættelse.*

Flom, George T., ed. (1915), *The Arnamagnean manuscript 243 B α, folio at Det kongelige biblioteket, Copenhagen: the main manuscript of Konungs skuggsjá in phototypic reproduction with diplomatic text.*

Graves, Robert (1958), *The Greek myths.*

Hagen, Friedrich Heinrich von der (1836), 'Die deutschen Wochentagegötter', *Germania* 1, 18–38, 344–77.

Helgi Guðmundsson (1972), *The pronominal dual in Icelandic.*

Holm-Olsen, Ludvig (1952), *Håndskrifterne av Konungs skuggsjá. En undersøkelse av deres tekstkritiske verdi.*

Holm-Olsen, Ludvig, ed. (1983), *Konungs skuggsiá utgitt for Kjeldeskrift-fondet.* Second edition.

Holm-Olsen, Ludvig, ed. (1987), *The king's mirror: AM 243a fol.*

Larson, Laurence Marcellus, tr. (1917), *The king's mirror (Speculum regale – Konungs skuggsjá).*

Meissner, Rudolf, tr. (1944), *Der Königspiegel: Konungsskuggsjá aus dem Altnorwegischen übersetzt.*

Smith, Jeremy J. (1999), *Essentials of Early English.*

Strang, Barbara M. H. (1970). *A history of English.*

Strutynski, Udo (1975), 'Germanic divinities in weekday names', *Journal of Indo-European studies* 3, 368–84.

Svanhildur Óskarsdóttir (2005), 'Prose of Christian instruction', in *A companion to Old Norse-Icelandic literature and culture*, ed. by Rory McTurk, 338–53.

XXIV: KONUNGS SKUGGSJÁ

Faðir: . . . Nú kann svá til at bęra at konungr mælir til þín nǫkkur orð,[1] þá skalt þú þat varaz vandliga í andsvǫrum þínum at ęigi margfaldir þú ęngi þau atkvæði er til þín horfa, þó at þú margfaldir svá sęm til byrjar ǫll þau atkvæði er til konungs horfir.[2] En ęnn hęldr skaltu þat varaz, sęm fól kann stundum at hęnda, at ęigi margfaldir þú þau atkvæði er til þín horfa, en þú ęinfaldir þau er til konungsins horfa.

En ęf svá kann til at vęrða at konungr mælir til þín nǫkkur orð, þau er þú nęmir ęigi ok þarftu annat sinni ęptir at frétta, þá skalt þú hvárki sęgja 'há' né 'hvat', hęldr skalt þú ękki meira um hafa en kvęða svá at orði: 'Hęrra'. En ęf þú vilt hęldr spyrja męð fleirum orðum: 'Hęrra minn, látið yðr ęigi firi þykkja at ek spyrja hvat þér mæltur til mín, því at ‹ek› nam ęi gǫrla.' Ok lát þek þó sęm fæstum sinnum þat hęnda at konungr þurfi optar en um sinn orð at hęrma firi þér áðr en þú nęmir.

Sunr: Hvęr skynsęmð er til þęss at þá er bętr at ǫll atkvæði sé margfaldat, þau er mæla skal til ríkismanna, hęldr en ęinfaldat? En ęf maðr biðr bœnar sinnar til Guðs, er allum er fręmri ok hæri, þá eru ęinfaldat í hvęrri bœn ǫll þau atkvæði er til hans horfa, ok kvęðr svá at orði hvęrr er sína bœn flytr við Guð: 'Þú, Dróttinn minn, allsvaldandi Guð, høyrðu bœn mína ok miskunna mek betr en ek sé vę‹r›ðr'. En ęngan mann høyri ek svá taka til orðs: 'Þér, Dróttinn minn, høyrið bœn mína ok gørið bętr við mik firi sakar miskunnar yðarrar en ek sé vęrðr'.

Nú vęit ‹ek› ęi at allfróðlig sé spurning mín. En þó, męð því at þér hafið lofat mér at spyrja slíks sem mek forvitnar, þá vænti ek þó góðrar órlausnar sęm fyrr, þó at ek spyri bęrnskliga.

Faðir: Víst vil ek þat gjarna allt firi þér skýra er ek em til fœrr, en ęigi vęit ek hví þú forvitnar þętta mál svá gjǫrsamlega við mek at firi þat skal skynsęmð vęita hvęrsu atkvæðum er skipat í hęlgum bœnum, því at lærifęðr várir mundu þar kunna bętr svara um þá luti er til guðdómsins er en ek. En męð því at hvęr spurning lítr jamnan til svara, þá vil ek skýra þętta mál firi þér męð skjótri rœðu, svá sęm mér sýniz vænligast, ok vil ek því fyst svara er mér þykki ágætast vęra.

Nú ætla ek firi því svá skipat atkvæðum í hęlgum bœnum at hęldr sé ęinfaldat en margfaldat ákall guðlegs nafs, at allir þeir er á Guð trúa skili þat til fulls at vér trúum á ęinn Guð sannan, en ęigi á marga falsguða, sęm heiðnir męnn trúðu forðum á sjau guða. Kallaðu svá at ęinn guð stýrði himnaríki, en annarr himintunglum, hinn þriði þęssum heimi ok ávęxtum jarðar, hinn fjórði hǫfum ok vǫtnum, en hinn fimti vindum ok lopti, hinn sétti mannviti ok málspęki, en hinn sjaundi hęlvíti ok dauða.[3]

Nú skulum vér firi því gǫfga ęinn Guð, þann er allar skepnur þjóna, ok biðja til hans męð ęinfǫldu atkvæði, at ęi þýðiz flærðsamir guðar til várra ákalla firi þat at vér margfaldim atkvæði at fleiri væri guð en ęinn í ákalli guðlegs nafns.[4] Þęssir lutir ganga ok til at skammsýnir męnn mætti þat hyggja at fleiri væ‹r›i guð en ęinn ęf męð margfaldaðu atkvæði væri á hans nafn kallat, ok er þat réttliga tilskipat ok vitrlega at ęinfǫld trú ok heilǫg hafi ękki rúm eða villustíg at ganga af réttri þjóðgatu. Nú ęf þér skilz ęigi til fulls þęssi rœða, þá męgum vit ęnn flęira til finna. En ęf þęssi rœða má þek leiða til fullrar skilningar, þá męgum vit vęl víkja okkarri rœðu til andsvara um þá luti aðra er þú spurðir.

Sunr: Þęssir lutir skiljaz mér vęl ok þykki mér vęra bæði sannligir ok þó nauðsynlegir at firi því skal[5] hęldr ęinfaldaz en margfaldaz ǫll atkvæði til Guðs at hvárki męgi rétt trú spillaz firi margfalt atkvæði ok ęigi męgi slœgir úvinir undir þýðaz þat ákall er ęinfǫld trú ok rétt vísar þeim ífrá. En ek vil nú at þér skýrið þat firi mér er ek spurða um vęraldar ríkismęnn, hví ǫll atkvæði þœtti bętr til þeirra margfaldat en ęinfaldat?

Faðir: Þar er þó œrnu firi svarat, at firi þá sǫk þykki bętr vęra mælt til ríkismanna męð margfaldu atkvæði hęldr en ęinfaldu, at hœvęskir męnn hafa þat funnit firi andvęrðu, ok hęfir þat síðan snúiz til siðvęnju męðr allum vitrum mǫnnum ok hœvęskum þeim til sœmðar sęm við er mælt, ok til þęss er kominn at þiggja sœmðaratkvæði. En þętta ęfni funnu þeir til, er frá andvęrðu skipaðu þęssum atkvæðum, at ríkismęnn eru ęigi sęm ęinnhvęrr annarra, sá er firi sér ęinum bęrr áhyggju ok sínu hýski ok á firi fá męnn svǫr at vęita. En hǫfðingjar bęra áhyggju firi ǫllum þeim er undir þeim eru at þjónustu eða at vęldi, ok hafa þeir ęigi ęins manns svǫr í munni, hęldr ęigu þeir firi marga svǫr at vęita, ok ęf góðr hǫfðingi fęllr ífrá, þá er ęigi sęm ęins manns missi, hęldr er þat mikil missa allum þeim er af honum tóku upphald eða sœmðir, ok er sęm allir vęrði minni firi sér, síðan er þeir missa hǫfðingja síns, en þeir váru męðan hann lifði, nema því at ęins at sá komi annarr í stað er þeim sé jamvęl viljaðr sęm hinn er frá fell.

Nú męð því at hǫfðingjar halda upp męð mǫrgum hvártvęggja sœmðum ok andsvǫrum ok margfaldri áhyggju, þá er þat vęl til lęggjandi þeim til sœmðar at kenna þá męð margfǫldu atkvæði í allri rœðu frá því er til þeirra þarf at rœða er smæri eru ok minni firi sér.[6] En þęssir lutir eru þeir enn er þá váru til funnir eða hugleiddir, er þętta var fyrsta sinni til siðar tękit, at konungar eða aðrir ríkismęnn þá eru ęigi ęinir saman í ráðagerð sinni, hęldr hafa þeir męð sér marga aðra vitra męnn ok gǫfga; ok man þá svá sýnaz, ęf til hǫfðingja vęrðr mælt męðr margfaldu atkvæði, at þá sé ęigi til konungs ęins mælt, hęldr til allra þeirra er í ráðagerð eru męð hánum ok hans eru ráðgjafar. Ek gat þęss ok nǫkkut í hinu fyrra orði at þú skalt viðr því sjá at þú margfaldir annur þau atkvæði er til þín horfa, at ęigi virðir þú þek jamnan hinum er þú rœðir viðr ok meiri er en þú. En þó at þú rœðir viðr jammaka þinn eða minna mann en þú sér, þá bęrr þér ękki sjálfum at virða þik męð margfaldaðu atkvæði.

Notes

[1] *Nú* followed by verb and subject in inverted word order, even when the verb is not subjunctive, makes the opening clause conditional ('Now if it should come about that . . .'), and the main clause usually then opens with a correlative *þá* or *ok*. There are three examples of this in the extract from *Grágás*, XXVII:12, 16, 45 below.

[2] Lack of concord between subject and verb is not all that uncommon in Old Norse prose, but it is normally found only when the subject and verb are widely separated in the sentence and the verb precedes the subject (as in lines 16–17, where the lack of concord is between subject and participle, and 51–52), and especially when the subject consists of a sequence of conjoined subjects (see *NION* I, 3.9.8.2). There are examples in other texts in this book in I:26–27 (see commentary), XIX:23, XXI:18, 32 and 161. But it is remarkable that in this extract there are several examples of lack of concord where the verb does not precede the subject, as here and in lines 14–15 (where the lack of concord is again between subject and participle) and 28–29. Even though another of the principal manuscripts of this text, AM 243 a 4to, has regular concord in all these cases except the one corresponding to that of lines 28–29, where it has *horfir* instead of *er*, it seems unlikely that they are all the result of scribal error. Nor does it seem a possible solution to take the verbs in lines 4, 14–15 and 29 as impersonal, especially since *horfa* is clearly not impersonal in lines 3 and 17, and nor is *eru ęinfaldat* in line 16. What is further remarkable in this text is that the first three examples all concern the word *atkvæði* 'verbal expression', 'mode of address'. Since it is an abstract noun, the plural may not have been perceived to have any difference in meaning from the singular, and the grammatical plural may well have been taken by the scribe on occasion as a 'logical singular'.

[3] According to Finnur Jónsson ('Indledning', 1920, 60), it is the gods of classical (as opposed to Old Norse) mythology that are meant here; he tentatively suggests that the seven gods in question are, respectively, Jupiter, Sol, Liber (or Saturn), Neptune, Mercury, Apollo and Pluto. He also offers the alternative suggestion that the deities in question may be those associated with the days of the week, without, however, making it clear whether he is thinking of classical or Germanic deities in

this context. On the former, see Graves (1958, 15–17, 27–30, 258–60); on the latter, see Hagen (1836) and Strutynski (1975).

[4] The syntax of this rather tortuous sentence is not entirely clear. While *firi því . . . at* in lines 40–41 can be taken to mean 'for this reason . . . that', i.e. 'so that', 'in order that' and *firi þat at* in line 42 to mean 'because', 'as a result of the fact that', the second *at* in line 42 perhaps means 'as if', 'on the assumption that'.

[5] Cf. note 2.

[6] It is difficult to see how the last clause links to the rest ot the sentence, and if the *er* is relative, what the antecedent is. The meaning may be '. . . in every speech about what needs to be spoken to them (by those who) are lower in rank and of less importance' or '. . . in every speech about what needs to be spoken to them when they (the speakers) are lower in rank and of less importance'. On the other hand, Finnur Jónsson (1926, 84) and Meissner (1944, 121; though not Larsson 1917, 190) understand *frá* to mean 'as distinct from' and take *þeirra* as the antecedent of the particle *er* that occurs later in the line, giving a meaning something like '. . . in all speech, as distinct from (differently from?) the speech needed for addressing those who are lower in rank and of less importance'.

XXV: HAMÐISMÁL

Hamðismál is the last poem in the Codex Regius of the Poetic Edda, and its content forms the last episode in the legend cycle of Sigurðr and the Burgundian royal family, of whom Guðrún, Hamðir and Sǫrli are the last survivors.

It is probably one of the earliest surviving eddic poems, although in an anonymous traditional poem it is always possible that different stanzas may be of various dates and authorship. However, it has been convincingly argued by Magnus Olsen (1936, 123–30) and Ursula Dronke (1969, 214–17) that this poem is deliberately echoed several times in some skaldic verses attributed to Torf-Einarr, Jarl of Orkney, which probably date from around 890 (*Skj* B I 27–28). In celebrating his own revenge for the killing of his father by Hálfdanr, son of King Haraldr hárfagri of Norway, Einarr refers to himself as a *fjǫrðungr* 'quarter' of the force represented by himself and his brothers (Torf-Einarr st. 2/4), just as *Hamðismál* refers to the brothers decreasing their force at *þriðjungi* 'by a third' (line 55). This image of brothers forming equal fractions of an overall unit is not found elsewhere in ON verse. Immediately after this, Einarr tells his men to throw stones on the body of his dead enemy (st. 2/5–8) and then declares how glad he is that *geirar . . . bitu* 'spears bit' the ruler's son (st. 3/1–4). This looks like a deliberately ironic echo of Jǫrmunrekkr's recognition that *geirar ne bíta* 'spears do not bite' the brothers and they must be stoned (line 92); again, the combination of *geirar* with the verb *bíta* is not found anywhere else in ON verse. Finally, looking forward to further conflict, Einarr says that his enemies do not know *hverr ilþorna arnar / undir hlýtr at standa* 'who will have to stand under the heel-thorns (i.e. claws) of the eagle' (st. 4/7–8); this is probably indebted to lines 106–07 of *Hamðismál*, as we can see from the verb *standa*, which seems surprising in Einarr's verse but makes perfect sense in *Hamðismál*'s image of the heroes standing on the dead like eagles perching on the slain.

More tentatively, Dronke suggests (1969, 213–14) that some lines of *Hamðismál* may already have been familiar to the earliest known skaldic poet, Bragi Boddason (flourished *c*.850). Bragi's *Ragnarsdrápa* is a poem of thanks to his patron for the gift of a ceremonial shield painted with mythological and legendary scenes, one of which was the brothers' attack on Jǫrmunrekkr's hall (*Ragnarsdrápa* 3–6, *Skj* B I 1–2). One phrase in *Ragnarsdrápa* (3/5) resembles *Hamðismál* 83 (*rósta varð í ranni* 'there was tumult in the hall'), and the image of the *ǫlskálir* 'ale-cups' (*Ragnarsdrápa* 4/5–6, *Hamðismál* 83–84) rolling among the blood and severed limbs is similar in the two poems. However, both of these may have been commonplace elements that could be expected in any poetic description of this scene, and in other respects Bragi's account seems significantly different from the version in *Hamðismál*. For example, he seems to say that Jǫrmunrekkr was asleep when the brothers arrived in his hall. It seems most likely that *Ragnarsdrápa* and *Hamðismál* are independent of each other, and therefore that *Hamðismál* (or at least major elements of it) should be dated to *c*.890 or a little earlier.

Like some other early eddic poems (e.g. *Atlakviða*), *Hamðismál*, from the standpoint of the 'classical' Icelandic poetry of the late tenth century onwards, is rather irregular in metre, with stanzas and lines of varying lengths. Most of it is in the traditional *fornyrðislag* metre, 'the metre of ancient words (or deeds?)', with two stressed syllables in each half-line, usually with only one of those in the first half-line bearing alliteration. One stanza is in the radically different *ljóðaháttr* 'metre of (magic) songs', in which each pair of half-lines is followed by a single heavy half-line that alliterates only within itself (lines 102–05; see note 35). Some individual half-lines, while not technically irregular, show heavy concentrations of unstressed syllables including unstressed finite verbs (e.g. lines 21a, 62a). Line 66 has no alliteration at all, but this may be due to a nom. pl. noun or adjective having dropped out of the first half-line. Elsewhere, the alliteration does not always conform to the conventions of later Icelandic verse, and *hr-* is made to alliterate with *r-* in line 90, *hv-* with *v-* in line 100 (but with *h-* in lines 12 and 73) and *sv-* with *s-* in lines 9 and 32. The normal rule is that it is the first stressed syllable in the second half-line (i.e. the third in the whole line) that carries the alliteration, but in lines 77, 78 and 88 the alliteration is carried by the final stressed syllable of the line. This may be because the word order of these lines has been subject to scribal alteration. Line 32 has double transverse alliteration (*Hitt – hyggju, Sǫrli – svinna*), but this is probably a deliberate ornament rather than an irregularity. The poem is in a bad state of preservation, and many of these 'irregularities' may be the result of scribal corruption; others may be due to the early date of composition, when the rules may not have developed the strictness that became customary in later Icelandic poetry. Since the poem shows great brilliance in other respects, it is unlikely that they reflect the incompetence or carelessness of the poet.

The legend of the death of Jǫrmunrekkr grew out of the fall of the historical Ostrogothic king Ermanaric in 375 AD. According to his contemporary, the historian Ammianus Marcellinus (1935–39, Book XXXI, ch. 3; Hamilton 1986, 415), Ermanaric was

> a warlike king whose many heroic exploits had made him a terror to his neighbours. Ermanaric was hard hit by the violence of this unexpected storm (i.e. an invasion by the Huns). For some time he endeavoured to stand his ground, but exaggerated reports circulated of the dreadful fate which awaited him, and he found release from his fears by taking his own life.

Ammianus clearly does not tell the whole story of the historical events, and perhaps did not know the details, but the king's terrified suicide seems surprising, for his successors did not immediately collapse before the Hunnish onslaught, but organised an orderly retreat to the line of the River Dniester. This suggests that the historical Ermanaric may have been decrepit with age or physically disabled, though we have no contemporary evidence for or against this.

The next source on Ermanaric is the Ostrogothic historian Jordanes, who wrote his *Getica c.*550, basing his work on that of Cassiodorus (who was also of Gothic origin and wrote *c.*520, i.e. about 150 years after the events). Jordanes's account runs as follows (1882, 91–92, §§ 315–19; my translation):

> Hermanaricus King of the Goths had, as we related above, become the conqueror of many peoples, but while he was thinking what to do about the arrival of the Huns, the perfidious nation of the Rosomoni, whom he had then enslaved along with others, took this opportunity of betraying him. And so the King, stirred up with rage, ordered that a certain woman of that nation who is remembered by the name Sunilda should be tied to wild horses because of her husband's treacherous desertion of him, and that she should be torn to pieces by having them driven in different directions. In vengeance for their sister, her brothers Sarus and Ammius attacked Hermanaricus in the side with iron; wounded in this way, he dragged out his wretched life with a disabled body. Hearing of his miserable state, Balamber King of the Huns moved his forces into the territory of the Ostrogoths; certain Visigoths had also planned among themselves to separate themselves from alliance with the Ostrogoths. Meanwhile Hermanaricus, unable to bear either the pain of his wound or the incursions of the Huns, died at a great age and full of days in the one

> hundred and tenth year of his life. His death gave the Huns the opportunity to gain victory over those Goths who, as we have said, occupied the eastern region and were known as Ostrogoths.

This account introduces the prototypes of Svanhildr, Hamðir and Sǫrli and the sibling relationship between them, although it makes Svanhildr the wife of a rebellious tribal leader rather than of the Jǫrmunrekkr figure himself. It also gives her a manner of death similar to that in the poem, though not identical with it. Dronke (1969, 193–96) argues persuasively that there is no essential contradiction between the accounts of Ammianus and Jordanes, and that the latter could be substantially historical, but we have no real evidence either for or against this view. Despite his ferocious treatment of Sunilda, Jordanes seems, unlike the poet of *Hamðismál*, to admire Hermanaricus and to sympathise with him against both the Huns and the treacherous Rosomoni. This may explain why he says nothing of the suicide, which might have seemed dishonourable, and instead stresses the king's achievements and his great age. There is no reason to doubt that Sunilda may have been a historical woman, and the name Sarus was also known among the Goths (it was also the name of a commander of the Ostrogothic military forces in Ravenna *c*.500, see Randers-Pehrson 1983, 108), but it is a little suspicious that both Ammius and Sarus can be interpreted as functionally meaningful names. Ammius corresponds to OE *hama* 'skin' and ON *hamðir* may mean 'the one provided with a *hamr* (skin or form of another creature)' or 'the mail-coated one', and Sarus seems to be related to OE *searu* 'craftiness', 'skill', 'armour' and OHG *saro* 'mailcoat'. In *Hamðismál* the brothers seem to be immune to weapons, and in *Skáldskaparmál*, *Vǫlsunga saga* and Saxo Grammaticus, Guðrún provides them with armour or an enchantment that makes them invulnerable to weapons. If the names of the brothers mean 'the one with a skin' and 'the armoured one', they may have been invented to describe their role, in which case the names of the actual historical revengers, if they existed, have been forgotten, as the tribal name Rosomoni was soon to be.

It is clear that Svanhildr's affair with Randvér and the treacherous role of Bikki were not part of the story known to Jordanes, and there is no evidence either for the tragic killing of Erpr in his time. But Randvér, Erpr and Jónakr are all mentioned in *Ragnarsdrápa*, and by the time of the poet of *Atlakviða* (possibly *c*.900), Bikki must have become a byword for treachery, since Atli's treacherous warriors (in another story altogether) can simply be called *Bikka greppar* 'Bikki's men' (*Atlakviða* 14/3). At some time between *c*.550 and *c*.850, therefore:

1) Svanhildr became the wife of Jǫrmunrekkr himself;

2) Randvér (possibly 'shield-warrior') was invented to supply the young wife with sexual temptation along the lines of the Phaedra story;

3) Bikki (who as Becca King of the Baningas receives what looks like a blameless mention between Eormanric (Jǫrmunrekkr) and Gifica (Gjúki) in the OE *Widsið* 19) became the traitor who caused the lovers' deaths;

4) Erpr ('swarthy') was invented as the bastard brother who offers to help as hand helps hand or foot helps foot, but is murdered for his pains.

It is worth noticing that the poet of *Hamðismál* feels no necessity to tell the whole of this story. His focus is on the compulsion to heroic revenge and the mistakes of his two protagonists, and for this purpose Bikki could be completely ignored and the affair between Svanhildr and Randvér reduced to the mere fact of their violent deaths. So far as either he or Bragi tells the tale, they might have been falsely accused (as they are in Saxo's version of the story).

Later versions of the Scandinavian strand of the legend can be found in *SnE, Skáldskaparmál* ch. 42 (1998, 49–51), *Vǫlsunga saga* chs 40–42 (1943, 87–91; 1990, 106–09) and (in a more complicated form) in Saxo Grammaticus VIII, ch. x, 7–14 (1931–35, I 233–35; 1979–80, I 256–58). For the very different traditions of Ermanaric in Old English and Middle High German, see Brady (1943).

Bibliography

Sophus Bugge, ed., *Sæmundar Edda hins fróða* (1867).

Ursula Dronke, ed., *The Poetic Edda* I: *Heroic Poems* (1969).

Barent Sijmons and Hugo Gering, eds, *Die Lieder der Edda* I–III (1888–1931).

Ammianus Marcellinus, *Rerum gestarum libri qui supersunt*, ed. and trans. J. C. Rolfe, 3 vols. (1935–39); trans. Walter Hamilton as *The Later Roman Empire, A.D. 354–378* (1986).

Jordanes, *Getica*, ed. Theodor Mommsen (1882). In *Monumenta Germaniae historica, Auctores antiquissimi* 5, 1.

Vǫlsunga saga, ed. Guðni Jónsson in *Fornaldarsögur Norðurlanda* I (1943); trans. Jesse Byock as *The Saga of the Volsungs* (1990).

Morkinskinna, ed. Finnur Jónsson (1932); tr. T. M. Andersson and Kari Ellen Gade (2000). Islandica 51.

Saxo Grammaticus = *Saxonis Gesta Danorum*, ed. J. Olrik and H. Ræder, 2 vols (1931–57); Books I–IX trans. Peter Fisher and Hilda Ellis Davidson as Saxo Grammaticus, *The History of the Danes*, 2 vols (1979–80).

Beowulf, ed. F. Klaeber (1941).

Beowulf, tr. Seamus Heaney (1999).

Richard Hamer, *A Choice of Anglo-Saxon Verse* (1970).

Lex Burgundionum, in *Monumenta Germaniae historica, Legum Sectio* I, Vol. II.i (1892).

Theodore M. Andersson, 'Cassiodorus and the Gothic Legend of Ermanaric', *Euphorion* 57 (1963), 28–43.

Caroline Brady, *The Legends of Ermanaric* (1943).

Caroline Brady, 'The Date and Metre of the *Hamðismál*', *Journal of English and Germanic Philology* 38 (1939), 201–16.

Caroline Brady, 'Óðinn and the Norse Jörmunrekkr Legend', *PMLA* (1940), 910–30.

David Clark, 'Undermining and en-gendering vengeance. Distancing and anti-feminism in the *Poetic Edda*', *Scandinavian Studies* 77 (2005), 173–200.

George T. Gillespie, *A Catalogue of Persons Named in German Heroic Literature (700–1600)* (1973).

S. Gutenbrunner, 'Über den Schluss des Hamdirliedes', *Zeitschrift für deutsches Altertum* 83 (1951–52), 6–12.

Joseph Harris, 'Eddic Poetry'. In *Old Norse-Icelandic Literature: A Critical Guide*, ed. Carol J. Clover and J. Lindow (1985), 68–156. Islandica 45.

Ursula Hennig, 'Gab es ein "Jüngeres" Hamdirlied?', *Beiträge zur Geschichte der deutsche Sprache und Literatur* [Tübingen] 82 (1960), 44–69.

John Hines, 'Famous Last Words: Monologue and Dialogue in *Hamðismál* and the Realisation of Heroic Tale'. In *Learning and Understanding in the Old Norse World. Essays in Honour of Margaret Clunies Ross*, ed. Judy Quinn, Kate Heslop and Tarrin Wills (2007), 177–200.

L. M. Hollander, 'The Legendary Form of Hamðismál', *Arkiv för nordisk Filologi* 77 (1962), 56–62.

John McKinnell, *Meeting the Other in Norse Myth and Legend* (2005).

Magnús Olsen, 'Torv-Einar og Hamðismál', *Bidrag til Nordisk Filologi tillägnade Emil Olson* (1936), 123–30.

Justine D. Randers-Pehrson, *Barbarians and Romans. The Birth Struggle of Europe, A.D. 400–700* (1983).

Franz R. Schröder, 'Die Eingangsszene von *Guðrúnarhvǫt* und *Hamðismál*', *Beiträge zur Geschichte der deutsche Sprache und Literatur* [Tübingen] 98 (1976), 430–36.

Klaus von See, '*Guðrúnarhvöt* und *Hamðismál*', *Beiträge zur Geschichte der deutsche Sprache und Literatur* [Tübingen] 99 (1977), 241–49.

Tom A. Shippey, 'Speech and the Unspoken in *Hamðismál*'. In *Prosody and Poetics in the Early Middle Ages. Essays in Honour of C. B. Hieatt* (1995), 180–96.

E. O. Gabriel Turville-Petre, *Myth and Religion of the North* (1964).

XXV: HAMÐISMÁL

Spruttu á tái[1]   tregnar íðir
grœti álfa[2]   in glýstǫmu.
Ár um morgin[3]   manna bǫlva
sútir hverjar   sorg um kveykva.

Vara þat nú   né í gær,
þat hefir langt   liðit síðan;
er fátt fornara,   fremr var þat hálfu,
er hvatti Guðrún,   Gjúka borin,[4]
sonu sína unga   at hefna Svanhildar.[5]

'Systir var ykkur   Svanhildr um heitin,
sú er Jǫrmunrekkr   jóm um traddi
hvítum ok svǫrtum   á hervegi,[6]
grám, gangtǫmum   Gotna hrossum.

Eptir er ykr þrungit   þjóðkonunga,
lifið einir ér þátta   ættar minnar.

Einstœð em ek orðin   sem ǫsp í holti,
fallin at frændum   sem fura at kvisti,
vaðin at vilja   sem viðr at laufi,
þá er in kvistskœða   kømr um dag varman.'[7]

* * *[8]

Hitt kvað þá Hamðir   inn hugumstóri:
'Lítt myndir þú þá, Guðrún,   leyfa dáð Hǫgna,
er þeir Sigurð   svefni ór vǫkðu.
Saztu á beð,   en banar hlógu.

Bœkr[9] váru þínar   inar bláhvítu
ofnar vǫlundum[10]   — flutu í vers dreyra.
Svalt þá Sigurðr,   saztu yfir dauðum,
glýja þú ne gáðir;   Gunnarr þér svá vildi.[11]

20 *written* 'hugom stǫri', *i.e.* hugumstœrri?

Atla þóttiz þú stríða   at Erps morði
ok at Eitils aldrlagi   — þat var þér enn verra.
Svá skyldi hverr ǫðrum   verja til aldrlaga
sverði sárbeitu   at sér ne stríddit.'[12]

Hitt kvað þá Sǫrli   — svinna hafði hann hyggju —
'Vilkat ek við móður   málum skipta.
Orðz þikkir enn vant   ykru hváru.
Hvers biðr þú nú, Guðrún,   er þú at gráti ne færat?

Brœðr grát þú þína   ok buri svása,[13]
niðja náborna   lei*dd*a nær rógi.
Okr skaltu ok, Guðrún,   gráta báða,
er hér sitjum feigir á mǫrum;   fjarri munum deyja.'

Gengu ór garði   gǫrvir at eiskra.
Liðu þá yfir, ungir,   úrig fjǫll,
mǫrum húnlenzkum   morðz at hefna.

Fundu á stræti   stórbrǫgðóttan.
'Hvé mun jarpskammr   okr fultingja?'

Svaraði inn sundrmœðri;   svá kvaz veita mundu
fulting frændum   sem fótr ǫðrum.
'Hvat megi fótr   fœti veita,
né holdgróin   hǫnd annarri?'

Þá kvað þat Erpr   einu sinni
— mærr um lék   á mars baki:
'Illt er blauðum hal   brautir kenna.'
Kóðu harðan mjǫk   hornung vera.[14]

Drógu þeir ór skíði   skíðijárn,
mækis eggjar   at mun flagði.[15]
Þverðu þeir þrótt sinn   at þriðjungi —
létu mǫg ungan   til moldar hníga.

36 leiða.   49–52 *between 42 and 43*.

Skóku loða,   skálmir festu,
ok goðbornir   smugu í guðvefi.

Fram lágu brautir;   fundu vástígu
ok systur son[16]   sáran á meiði,
vargtré vindkǫld   vestan bœjar.
Trýtti æ trǫnu hvǫt,[17]   títt varat bíða.[18]

Glaumr var í hǫllu,   halir ǫlreifir,
ok til gota[19] ekki   gerðut heyra
áðr halr hugfullr   í horn um þaut.

Segja fóru   Jǫrmunrekki
at sénir váru   seggir und hjálmum:
'Rœðið ér um ráð,   ríkir eru komnir!
Fyr mátkum hafið ér mǫnnum   mey um tradda.'

Hló þá Jǫrmunrekkr,   hendi drap á kampa,
beiddiz at brǫngu,   bǫðvaðiz at víni;[20]
skók hann skǫr jarpa,   sá á skjǫld hvítan,
lét hann sér í hendi   hvarfa ker gullit.

'Sæll ek þá þœttumk   ef ek sjá knætta
Hamði ok Sǫrla   í hǫllu minni.
Buri mynda ek þá binda   með boga strengjum,
goðbǫrn[21] Gjúka   festa á gálga.'

Hitt kvað þá hróðrglǫð,[22]   stóð of hleðum,[23]
mæfingr mælti   við mǫg þenna:[24]

* * *

'. . . því at þat heita   at hlýðigi myni.[25]
Mega tveir menn einir   tíu hundruð Gotna
binda eða berja[26]   í borg inni há?'

Styrr varð í ranni,   stukku ǫlskálir,
í blóði bragnar lágu,   komit ór brjósti Gotna.

62 biðja. 81 hundruðum.

Hitt kvað þá Hamðir inn hugumstóri:
'Æstir, Jǫrmunrekkr, okkarrar kvámu,
brœðra sammœðra,[27] innan borgar þinnar.
Fœtr sér þú þína, hǫndum sér þú þínum,[28]
Jǫrmunrekkr, orpit í eld heitan.'

Þá hraut við inn reginkunngi,[29]
baldr í brynju, sem bjǫrn hryti:
'Grýtið ér á gumna, allz geirar ne bíta,
eggjar né járn Jónakrs sonu.'

'Bǫl vanntu, bróðir, er þú þann belg leystir:
opt ór þeim belg[30] bǫll ráð koma.
Hug hefðir þú, Hamðir, ef þú hefðir hyggjandi;
mikils er á mann hvern vant er manvits er.

Af væri nú haufuð ef Erpr lifði,[31]
bróðir okkarr inn bǫðfrœkni er vit á braut vágum,
v*e*rr inn ví*g*frœkni[32] — hvǫttumk at dísir —,
gumi inn gunnhelgi — gǫrðumz at vígi.'[33]

'Ekki hygg ek *o*kr vera úlfa dœmi,
at vit mynim sjálfir um sakask
sem grey norna,[34] þau er gráðug eru
í auðn um alin.[35]

Vel hǫfum vit vegit, stǫndum á val Gotna
ofan, eggmóðum, sem ernir á kvisti.
Góðs hǫfum tírar fengit, þótt skylim nú eða í gær[36] deyja.
Kveld lifir maðr ekki eptir kvið norna.'

Þar fell Sǫrli at salar gafli,
en Hamðir hné at húsbaki.[37]

Þetta eru kǫlluð Hamðismál in fornu.

94 *before this speech* Hitt kvað þá Hamðir inn hugumstóri: *(but the speaker here must be Sǫrli, since the* þú *in line 94 is certainly Hamðir).* 100 varr inn viðfrœkni. 102 ykr.

Notes

[1] The *tá* was a strip of beaten earth outside the main door and along the front of Norse houses. It was a traditional place for private conversations and could be used figuratively to refer to them, cf. *Morkinskinna* (1932, 89; 2000, 151): *ok heimtask nú á tá inir vitrustu menn, ok hafa tal milli sín* 'Some of the wisest men were assembled and took counsel'. Here it probably refers to the secrecy of the discussion between Guðrún and her sons.

[2] Sijmons and Gering (1883–1931, III.ii 428) take *grœti álfa* as a kenning for morning (because dwarves, who may be identical with 'dark elves', are turned to stone if the daylight touches them, as at the end of *Alvíssmál*), but no comparable kennings have been found. It is more probably a reference to the female family spirits (*dísir* or *fylgjur*, perhaps originally the spirits of dead ancestors; see Turville-Petre 1964, 221–31, and McKinnell 2005, 198–200) who were believed to preside over the fortunes of a household. Here they may be said to weep because of the coming extinction of the family. This statement contrasts with the more negative view taken by Hamðir and Sǫrli, who blame the *dísir* for having provoked their own killing of Erpr (see line 100). See also note 15 below.

[3] Early morning is a traditional time for brooding grief in Germanic literature; cf. *Beowulf* lines 2450–62 (1941, 92; 1999, 77–78); *The Wife's Lament* lines 35–36; *The Wanderer* lines 8–9 (Hamer 1970, 74–75; 174–75).

[4] According to the *Lex Burgundionum* (1892, 43) 'Law of the Burgundians' (*c*.500), Gibica (= ON Gjúki) was the founder of the Burgundian royal dynasty. In legend, Gjúki is the father of Gunnarr, Hǫgni and Guðrún, but only the first of these is clearly based on a historical person (King Gundaharius, killed by the Huns in 437; for sources, see Dronke 1969, 34–36). The figure of Guðrún may be indirectly derived from Ildico (= Hild), who according to Jordanes (1882, 123; §§ 617–19) was the wife whom Attila the Hun had just married on the night he died in bed of a nosebleed in 453. As Dronke demonstrates, a rumour soon grew up that Attila had been murdered by his new wife, and if her motive was assumed to be a Burgundian desire for revenge on the Hunnish king, it would be natural to give her name a

first element that began with G, like other Burgundian royal names. This explains why the heroine in German versions of the story is called Kriemhilt. But in ON sources, Grímhildr (literally 'mask-battle') becomes the name of the heroine's mother, and the almost synonymous Guðrún (literally 'war-secret', or perhaps 'god-secret') has been invented for the heroine herself, possibly because the extra character of the mother was needed to explain the magic potion that causes Sigurðr to fall in love with Guðrún and forget his previous love for Brynhildr.

[5] According to the cycle of legend related in the Poetic Edda and in *Vǫlsunga saga*, Guðrún was married three times, first to the hero and dragon-slayer Sigurðr, whom she loved and by whom she had Svanhildr; next to Atli (= Attila the Hun), whom she murdered, along with their two sons Erpr and Eitill; and finally to King Jónakr, the father of her sons Hamðir and Sǫrli. On the death of Svanhildr, see Introduction above.

[6] There were no paved military roads in Scandinavia. The important motif of roads and paths may have survived from earlier German or Old English versions of the story because of the idea that the stones finally 'take vengeance' for the blood of Erpr having been shed on them; see lines 43, 59 and 92.

[7] It was a traditional summer task of women on Norwegian farms to strip small branches from the trees during warm weather; twigs and pine needles were then dried and used for kindling and bedding, while deciduous leaves were fed to the farm animals (see Dronke 1969, 227).

[8] A stanza must be missing here, since line 21 implies that Guðrún has just compared her sons' courage unfavourably with that of her dead brothers Gunnarr and Hǫgni (for whose heroic death see *Atlakviða*). This lost stanza may have been used by the poet of st. 3 of the later poem *Guðrúnarhvǫt* (Dronke 1969, 146) which immediately precedes *Hamðismál* in the Codex Regius:

'Urðua it glíkir þeim Gunnari,	'You have not become like Gunnarr and his brother,
né in heldr hugðir sem var Hǫgni.	nor equipped with courage as Hǫgni was.
Hennar munduð it hefna leita,	You would have tried to avenge her
ef it móð ættið minna brœðra,	if you had the heart of my brothers,
eða harðan hug Húnkonunga.'	or the firm mind of the Hunnish kings.'

Most of this may in fact come verbatim from *Hamðismál*, as the following stanza of *Guðrúnarhvǫt* certainly does (cf. lines 20–24 of this edition of *Hamðismál*), but this cannot be regarded as certain. The only element in it which is probably not indebted to the lost stanza of *Hamðismál* is its reference to 'Hunnish kings' (probably an allusion to Sigurðr, who is of Hunnish origin only in later German and Norse tradition). But the lost stanza may have included the same implication that because they are not sons of her beloved Sigurðr, Guðrún places a lower value on the lives of Hamðir and Sǫrli than on that of Svanhildr. This would help to motivate their sense of rage at the way she taunts them into undertaking their suicidal venture, and the adjective *hugumstóri* 'mighty in courage' which is applied to Hamðir immediately afterwards suggests her unfairness in accusing them of cowardice (though it may also be a fixed epithet that was commonly attached to him; cf. line 85).

[9] Before the arrival of Latin literacy in the Germanic world there were no 'books' in the modern sense of the word. This is one of a number of instances in Old Norse where *bók* seems to refer to pieces of embroidered cloth (in this case bed-covers); cf. also *Sigurðarkviða in skamma* 49/7–8, where the dying Brynhildr offers *bók ok blæju, bjartir váðir* 'an embroidered cloth and coverlet, bright clothes' to any one of her maids who is prepared to die with her, and cf. the verb *gullbóka* 'to embroider in gold' in *Guðrúnarkviða II* 14/6. For the argument that the modern use of the word may be derived from a comparison of manuscript illumination with embroidery, see Dronke (1969, 228).

[10] Vǫlundr is familiar as the legendary master-craftsman of the Germanic world and the protagonist of *Vǫlundarkviða*, but the word occasionally appears, as here, as a common noun meaning 'craftsman' (cf. also *Merlínusspá II*, 7/2 and Snorri Sturluson, *lausavísa* 4/8; *Skj* B II 25, 89). It is not clear whether or not these instances are derived from the proper name, whose etymology is obscure (largely because it is difficult to derive ON *Vǫlundr*, OF *Galans* from the same root as OE *Wēlund*/*Wēland*, MHG *Wielant*). It is possible that they may indeed have different origins, with the common noun *vǫlundr* being related to ON *val*, *vǫl*, OHG *wala* 'choice' (cf. ON *velja* 'to choose'), hence 'one who makes choice things', while forms of the name with a long

front vowel could have come about by association with the noun *vél* 'device, trick'. In that case, the proper name *Vǫlundr* may be derived from the common noun rather than vice versa.

[11] In lines 21–27 Hamðir reminds Guðrún that the brothers she has praised were also the murderers of Sigurðr. As the compiler of the prose links in the Codex Regius points out at the end of *Brot af Sigurðarkviðu* (*PE* 201), there were various versions of how Sigurðr died. In *Brot* itself and in *Guðrúnarkviða I* the brothers kill him out of doors and report his death to Guðrún, but the poet of *Hamðismál* prefers the tradition shared by *Sigurðarkviða in skamma*, in which they kill him when he is asleep in bed with her. In *Sigurðarkviða in skamma* and *Vǫlsunga saga* the murder is actually carried out by Gothormr, the younger brother of Gunnarr and Hǫgni, who has not sworn an oath of foster-brotherhood with Sigurðr as they have. This may be an elaboration from a time later than that of *Hamðismál*, or this poet may simply have omitted it for the sake of brevity; whether they did the killing themselves or not, Gunnarr and Hǫgni were responsible for Sigurðr's death.

[12] In lines 28–31 Hamðir points out that Guðrún ought to realise that some revenges are too costly to the revenger to be worthwhile, as when she herself slaughtered Erpr and Eitill, her sons by Atli, as part of her annulment of their marriage following his murder of Gunnarr and Hǫgni. Ironically, Hamðir and Sǫrli will soon murder another Erpr, Jónakr's son by another woman, and one instance of the name may have been borrowed from the other. However, since its meaning ('swarthy', cf. OE *eorp* 'dark', ON *jarpr* 'brown') is appropriate to both of them (with Erpr in *Hamðismál* even being called *jarpskammr* 'the short brown man'), it is not possible to tell which if either is the original. The fact that the name lacks the vowel-breaking that was normal in this word suggests either that it fossilised at an early stage or that it has been borrowed from Old High German or Old Saxon, where this change did not take place (cf. OE *eorðe*, ON *jǫrð*, but OHG, OS *erda* 'earth').

[13] This phrase is curiously echoed in *Atlakviða* st. 39, which claims that Guðrún never wept for either her brothers or her sons. The tradition that Guðrún could not weep later became fixed (see *Brot*, closing

prose, and most of *Guðrúnarkviða I*), but it is not possible to say whether or not it already existed when *Hamðismál* was composed.

[14] In the Codex Regius, lines 48–51 are placed at the beginning of the encounter between Erpr and his brothers (before line 43 in this text), but this seems an obvious mistake, even though Hines (2007, 184–88) puts forward an argument in favour of the manuscript ordering of the lines. Line 43 clearly introduces the scene, which Hamðir and Sǫrli begin by decrying Erpr's offer of help (presumably because they regard him as an outsider and beneath them). His reply that he would help them as one foot or hand helps the other recalls versions of the story in which they later stumble on the way to carry out their revenge and realise the truth of his words (see *SnE Skáldskaparmál* ch. 42, *Vǫlsunga saga* ch. 44 and cf. Dronke 1969, 199–202). The poet may have omitted the latter half of this motif for the sake of brevity, and/or because it was so well known that it could be assumed from Erpr's words here. However, their killing of him is well motivated by his suggestion that they are cowardly (using what is probably a proverb). They have had to endure this damaging insult from their mother, but will not tolerate it from their bastard brother.

[15] The *flagð* 'ogress, giantess, hag' here may be either Hel, the female figure who presides over the world of the dead, or a malicious *dís* who wants to see the destruction of the family. If the first interpretation is right, the idea may be akin to that in *Ynglingatal* 7 (*Skj* B I 8), where Hel is said to enjoy (sexual) pleasure from the body of King Dyggvi. The second would suggest that the poet agrees with the view expressed by one of the brothers that the *dísir* provoked them to kill Erpr (line 100; but see line 2 above for a very different view, also in the mouth of the narrator).

[16] Strictly, Jǫrmunrekkr's son Randvér (see Bragi, *Ragnarsdrápa* 3, *c*.850; *Skj* B I 1) is their half-sister's stepson, but the emotional shock is reinforced by citing the sister's son relationship, which was particularly sacred in Germanic society. According to *Skáldskaparmál* ch. 42 and *Vǫlsunga saga* ch. 42, Svanhildr and Randvér were tempted into planning to marry each other by Jǫrmunrekkr's evil counsellor Bikki, who then informed on them, with the result that both were executed. In *Hamðismál* Randvér has evidently been wounded as well

as hanged, which may suggest an Odinic sacrifice; cf. *Hávamál* st. 138, *Gautreks saga* ch. 7 and Turville-Petre (1964), 47.

[17] Hanged and slain men are often indicated by reference to the carrion birds that feasted on them, but this is a strange example, because the crane is not a carrion bird. It should probably be understood as an abbreviation of some such kenning as *blóðtrani* 'blood-crane' (i.e. raven), cf. Óttarr svarti, *Knútsdrápa* 8/3 (*Skj* B I 274).

[18] The Codex Regius reading *biðja* 'to ask (for something)' makes no sense here, and is probably a scribal error for *bíða* 'to wait, linger'.

[19] *gota* is a poetic word, but may refer either to (Gothic) horses (a sense also found in a runic verse on the Rök stone, *c*.900) or to warriors (originally 'Goths'); in this latter sense it is used of the Burgundians in *Grípisspá* 35/6, *Brot* 9/4, *Atlakviða* 20/3, and Guðrún's mother Grímhildr is called *gotnesk kona* 'Gothic woman' in *Guðrúnarkviða II* 17/2. But in *Hamðismál* it seems unlikely that it refers to Hamðir and Sǫrli, since this would introduce an unnecessary confusion with Jǫrmunrekkr and his men, who actually are Goths and are referred to as such (though always with the alternative gen. pl. form *Gotna*) in lines 81, 84 and 105. The reference is probably to the sound made by the brothers' approaching horses.

[20] The vocabulary of this line is unusual and probably deliberately exotic, as part of the portrait of an arrogant foreign ruler. In ON *beiða* usually means 'to demand', but the context of *beiddisk* here seems rather to demand the sense 'stirred himself up', which is common in the corresponding words in OHG, OS and OE; the word here could either be a survival from an older version of the story in one of these languages or a deliberate exoticism introduced by this poet. The word *brǫngu* is found nowhere else in ON verse, but may be related to MLG *prank* 'battle, quarrel', and could be another foreign borrowing. The verb *bǫðva* is also found nowhere else, though it is obviously derived from the feminine noun *bǫð* 'battle', of which there are about fifteen examples in skaldic verse.

[21] The MS reading here could be interpreted either as *góð bǫrn Gjúka* 'good children of Gjúki' (Sijmons and Gering, Kuhn in *PE*, among

others) or as *goðbǫrn Gjúka* 'divinely descended children of Gjúki'. As Dronke points out (1969, 234) the latter is metrically more satisfactory, and is formally paralleled in Þórðr Særeksson's description of Skaði as *goðbrúðr* (*lausavísa* 3/6, *Skj* B I 304). Most Germanic royal families claimed divine ancestry, though in this context Jǫrmunrekkr may be mocking this claim.

[22] The word *hróðrglǫð* '(woman) pleased by glorious behaviour' is not found elsewhere, but for such similar compounds as *hróðrauðigr* 'rich in glory', *hróðrfinginn* 'devoted to glory', *hróðrfúss* 'eager for glory', see *LP* 286–67, and for *flugglǫð* 'rejoicing in flight' (a name for an arrow), see *LP* 143. *-glǫð* is also found as the second element in some female personal names (e.g. Menglǫð, the half-giantess who befriends the hero in *Orms þáttr Stórólfssonar*; and there is another Menglǫð in the late eddic poems *Grógaldr* and *Fjǫlsvinnsmál*), but there is no evidence that *hróðrglǫð* is a proper name here, though some editors have regarded her as the mother or mistress of Jǫrmunrekkr. Nor is it likely that it refers to Guðrún, as argued by Sijmons and Gering (1888–1931, III.ii 440), since this scene is taking place at Jǫrmunrekkr's court, far from the home of Guðrún (see line 39). The speaker seems to be simply an anonymous woman (or possibly one of the *dísir* of line 100) whose function is to admire the two young heroes.

[23] A *hleði* was a wooden shutter or sliding door to a *lokrekkja* 'closing bed, sleeping cubicle' in the hall; it was sometimes used by women as a way of peeping into the hall without being seen themselves (e.g. *Kormaks saga* ch. 3), and in this case it may explain how a woman in Jǫrmunrekkr's court can express a viewpoint that she would hardly dare to state openly.

[24] Several different emendations have been suggested here, to *við mǫgu sína* 'to her sons' (assuming that the speaker is Guðrún, see above), *við mǫg svinnan* 'to the wise young man' or *við mǫgþegna* 'to the young knights'), but the MS reading makes sense ('to that young man'), and should not be emended merely because it is surprising to find a singular here. It probably refers to Hamðir, the leader of the brothers.

[25] This line seems disjointed, with no explanation of its opening *því at* 'because'; a line has probably been lost before it. Both halves of

the line are metrically deficient. Some re-writings have been suggested: *því er þar hætta* 'one ought to desist from that (which) . . .'; *því átt at heita* 'you ought to promise that (which) . . .', *því áttat heita* 'you ought not to promise that (which) . . .' — all excellent suggestions, and improvements metrically, but for the fact that they are not what the MS appears to say.

hlýðigi: *-gi* is an originally emphatic particle used after a negative that came to be used as a negative particle when the *ne* was lost (e.g. **manngi** 'no one'). Apart from emendations, the only possibility for *hlýði* is that it is an otherwise unknown feminine noun meaning 'silence' (cf. **hljóðr** *adj*. 'silent'). The line might then be translated '. . . because they are vowing what would be no silence (i.e. not kept quiet) — sc. a famous deed', except that in this sense *heita* requires an object in the dative, not accusative case, and the line is probably corrupted beyond help other than emendation.

[26] The brothers are not literally trying to bind the Goths, but to kill them; *binda ok berja* seems to have been a generalised phrase meaning 'to gain complete victory over (someone)'.

[27] This word is tragically ironic in the middle of Hamðir's ill-advised speech of exultation over his enemy, since it contrasts with *sundrmœðri* (line 45) and thus reminds us of the crucial absence of Erpr from the revenge.

[28] For the motif of hands and feet, see lines 46–48 and note 14 above. Erpr's absence and Hamðir's vaunting delay the decapitation of Jǫrmunrekkr long enough to give him time to tell the Goths how to kill the brothers. They are invulnerable to weapons (see Introduction), so they can only be killed by stoning.

[29] *reginkunngi* is usually taken to refer to Jǫrmunrekkr's divine ancestry (cf. *reginkunnum*, referring to runes in *Hávamál* 80/3; *áskungar*, referring to the norns in *Fáfnismál* 13/4), and this must be part of the sense, but Dronke convincingly suggests that *reginkunnigr* here also has the sense 'knowledgeable about divine powers' and refers to the common belief that dying men could acquire supernatural perception (and the ability to curse their enemies effectively; cf. also *Fáfnismál*).

[30] *þann belg leystir* may refer to Hamðir opening his own mouth in lines 86–89, which offered the delay that enabled Jǫrmunrekkr to give the orders that led to the death of the brothers. But *belg* is only otherwise used in this sense in a proverbial metaphor for an old man as a bag from which words pour out, cf. *Hávamál* st. 134, and in line 95 the reference is certainly to Jǫrmunrekkr speaking in lines 92–93. Some editors have emended the first half of line 95 (Sijmons–Gering to *opt ór belg orðgum* 'often from a talkative bag'; Dronke to *opt ór rauðom belg* 'often from a red (i.e. bleeding) bag'), but neither seems necessary, even though Dronke cites a prose parallel in *Njáls saga* ch. 91. What Sǫrli means is that this particular 'bag' (i.e. Jǫrmunrekkr) often speaks words that have evil consequences. If *belg* in line 94 also means Jǫrmunrekkr, *er þú þann belg leystir* would have to mean 'when you left that bag free to speak'.

[31] It is not clear which brother is speaking here. Lines 94–97 are clearly spoken by Sǫrli; it makes sense for Hamðir to have the last word (i.e. lines 106–09); and lines 102–05 look like a rejoinder to the previous lines. One might see lines 98–101 as a continuation of the speech in which Sǫrli blames Hamðir and 102–05 as Hamðir's rather self-excusing reply (as I have done here). Alternatively, lines 98–101 may be Hamðir's belated realisation of his mistakes (as Dronke assumes), in which case lines 102–05 look like a conciliatory reply by Sǫrli. Unfortunately, one's view of the end of the poem seems likely to depend on which interpretation is adopted, and I can see no reliable way of choosing between them. Hines (2007, 183–84) suggests that the question is unimportant because the two brothers are finally merged into a single heroic personality.

[32] Codex Regius *varr inn við frækni* makes no sense; *vígfrœkni* 'bold in killing' (Neckel–Kuhn and Dronke) would be parallel in form and meaning to *bǫðfrœkni* in the preceding line, and thus seems preferable to *víðfrægi* 'widely famous' (Bugge and Sijmons–Gering).

[33] Sijmons–Gering and Dronke emend to *gǫrðumk* 'they made me', to produce a grammatical parallel to *hvǫttumk* in the previous line, but 'we forced ourselves to the killing' is quite possible for *gǫrðumz*. 'We prepared ourselves for a killing' also makes reasonable sense

(more or less the equivalent of 'we did do the killing'), and would acknowledge that even if the brothers were provoked by the *dísir*, they know that they must ultimately take the responsibility for Erpr's death themselves.

[34] 'Norns' bitches' are obviously she-wolves, though no exact parallel has been found. Dronke points out that the poet avoids suggesting that wolves are the Norns' 'steeds' because that would associate the Norns with giantesses and troll-women (such as Hyndla, who rides a wolf in *Hyndluljóð* st. 5).

[35] Unlike the rest of the poem, lines 102–05 are in *ljóðaháttr* 'the metre of (magic) songs' (see Introduction) which is also used in didactic or proverbial poems such as *Hávamál*. The different metre here has led to speculation that these lines may have been added by another poet, but the change of metre could be due merely to the content, which resembles proverbial advice (cf. *Fáfnismál*). On other metrical irregularities in the poem, see Introduction.

[36] *í gær* usually means 'yesterday', but Dronke suggests on the basis of one case in Gothic that it may here have an archaic sense 'tomorrow', or more generally 'some other day'.

[37] Dronke (1969, 190–92) sees a dichotomy between the attack in the hall and the fact that the brothers ultimately die outside the building, and concludes that lines 110–11 may be the work of another poet. But their deaths outside the hall can be explained in several other ways (e.g. they tried to fight their way out; they were rushed outside because it was easier to stone them there; they had to get outside so that the stones could complete their 'revenge'; see note 6 above), and her supposition seems unnecessary. Hines (2007, 193–96) suggests that *at salar gafli* and *at húsbaki* may refer to locations inside the hall, at its inner end, and so could imply that the brothers were killed inside.

XXVI: NJÁLS SAGA

Njáls saga (referred to in the manuscripts as *Brennu-Njáls saga* 'Saga of Njáll of the Burning') was probably written 1275–90. It is the longest and in many ways the greatest of the Sagas of Icelanders, combining several originally separate narratives and involving a large number of characters from all over Iceland, although the main events are located in the south-west of the country.

The two extracts reproduced here represent the climaxes of the first two parts of the saga: the extraordinary fight to the death of the great warrior Gunnarr, and the burning in his house of Gunnarr's friend Njáll and his sons. The feuds leading up to these events are largely disparate, but the two parts (which some have thought derive from two separate sagas) are linked both by the friendship and common desire for peace of the contrasting heroes, and thematically. This is clear from the overt comparison made, in the preamble to the burning at Bergþórshváll, between the burners and the more honourable attackers who had scorned to resort to the use of fire against Gunnarr (B, lines 60–66). The two parts of the saga are separated by the so-called *Kristni þáttr*, recounting the conversion of Iceland to Christianity, in which Njáll is given a leading (but no doubt fictitious) role; this section forms a pivot between the perspectives of the two parts, contrasting the noble pagan Gunnarr with his Christian, indeed almost saintly friend — whose killers are also Christian. The last part of the saga relates the lengthy quest of Njáll's son-in-law Kári, who survives the burning, to track down and kill the burners one by one, before he is finally reconciled with their leader Flosi.

This reconciliation is symptomatic of the fact that violence in the saga is more often a response to the demands of honour, in particular the duty of revenge, than the result of personal animosity. The leaders of both attacks are represented as upstanding men forced by these imperatives to take an action they regret. Flosi is a sincere Christian; Gizurr inn hvíti Teitsson, who leads the attack on Gunnarr, figures later in the saga as one of the first to bring Christianity to Iceland (a historical reality confirmed by *Íslendingabók*; his son Ísleifr was to be Iceland's first bishop). Gizurr is drawn into the feud by the need to avenge those reluctantly killed by Gunnarr. This theme is introduced to the saga by the sequence of incidents in which Gunnarr and Njáll struggle to maintain their friendship in the face of the attempts of their wives to draw them into a feud. Although they share a militant determination to protect their husbands' honour literally to the death, these women are contrasted by their attitudes to their marital situation: Bergþóra famously declares her determination not to be separated in death from the man she was married to when young (B, lines 163–64), whereas Hallgerðr proudly sacrifices each of her three husbands after a slight on her honour. Mǫrðr Valgarðsson too, described more than once as *slægr ok illgjarn* 'cunning and ill-disposed' (*ÍF* XII 70, 119), plays an unequivocally villainous role in both the first and the second parts of the saga, fomenting quarrels and acting as a ringleader in the attack on Gunnarr. He is said to be envious of Gunnarr, to whom he is related (their mothers were first cousins according to the saga's genealogy). Once again Christianity forms the fault-line between the morally upright and the disreputable, since Mǫrðr and his father, Valgarðr inn grái, are prominent among the opponents to the Conversion (ch. 102). Christianity changes the saga's perspective, but does not simplify it. The Christian burners are seen as more unscrupulous than their pagan predecessors who had attacked Gunnarr; and Njáll himself, though his death is infused with hagiographical overtones, remains bound by the ethic of revenge, choosing to die because he is too old to avenge his sons and will not live with shame. The overwhelming desire for harmony, shared by Gunnarr and Njáll even before the coming of the new faith, is set against the demands of the traditional code of honour, but this simple equation is complicated by conflicts of family loyalty, sexual desire and the ambiguous role of the law.

Njáls saga survives in nineteen medieval manuscripts (dating from between 1300 and 1550) as well as numerous later copies, demonstrating its popularity throughout its history (Einar Ól. Sveinsson 1953). None of these early manuscripts is complete and some are no more than fragments. The text used in these extracts is that of Reykjabók (*R*), the earliest extant manuscript, written around 1300. This and the manuscripts related to it cite more skaldic verse than the other manuscript groups, both in the body of the text and written later in the margins. The saga is also included in the fourteenth-century Möðruvallabók (*M*) (see pp. 42 and 198 above and Text XVIII), which has supplied some readings in the text. The chapter headings are those of *R*, written in a different but contemporary hand to that of the text, but the chapter numbers are those conventional in editions and translations.

Bibliography

Njála, udgivet efter gamle Håndskrifter. Ed. Konráð Gíslason et al. (1879–96).

Brennu-Njálssaga (Njála) Ed. Finnur Jónsson (1908). Altnordische Saga-Bibliothek.

Brennu-Njáls saga, ed. Einar Ól. Sveinsson (1954). *ÍF* XII. [Based on Möðruvallabók.]

Njáls saga: The Arnamagnæan Manuscript 468, 4to (1962). Manuscripta Islandica. [Facsimile of Reykjabók.]

Brennu-Njálssaga. Texti Reykjabókar. Ed. Sveinn Yngvi Egilsson (2004).

Njal's saga, tr. Robert Cook. In *CSI* III 1–220. Also published by Penguin, 2001.

Scriptores historiae Augustae, trans. D. Magie et al. (1922–23, reprinted 1991). Loeb Classical Library.

Jesse Byock, *Viking Age Iceland* (2001).

Ursula Dronke, *The Role of Sexual Themes in Njáls saga* (1981). Dorothea Coke Memorial Lecture.

Einar Ól. Sveinsson, *Studies in the Manuscript Tradition of Njáls saga* (1953). Studia Islandica 13.

Hjalmar Falk, *Altnordische Waffenkunde* (1914).

Lars Lönnroth, *Njáls saga: A Critical Introduction* (1976).

Ian Maxwell, 'Pattern in *Njáls saga*'. *Saga-Book* 15 (1957–61), 17–47.

Guðrún Nordal, 'Attraction of Opposites: Skaldic Verse in *Njáls saga*'. In *Literacy in Medieval and Early Modern Scandinavian Culture*, ed. Pernille Hermann (2005).

Evert Salberger, 'Elfaraskáld – ett tilnamn i Njáls saga'. *Scripta Islandica* 24 (1973), 15–24.

XXVI A: THE DEATH OF GUNNARR

Chapter 76: Atreið til Hlíðarenda

Um haustit sendi Mǫrðr Valgarðsson orð at Gunnarr mundi vera einn heima, en lið allt mundi vera niðri í Eyjum at lúka heyverkum. Riðu þeir Gizurr hvíti ok Geirr goði austr yfir ár þegar þeir spurðu þat, ok austr yfir sanda til Hofs. Þá sendu þeir orð Starkaði undir Þríhyrningi, ok fundusk þeir þar allir er at Gunnari skyldu fara, ok réðu hversu at skyldi fara. Mǫrðr sagði at þeir mundu eigi koma á óvart Gunnari nema þeir tœki bónda af næsta bœ, er Þorkell hét, ok léti hann fara nauðgan með sér at taka hundinn Sám ok fœri hann heim einn á bœinn.[1]

Fóru þeir síðan austr til Hlíðarenda, en sendu eptir Þorkatli. Þeir tóku hann hǫndum ok gerð*u* honum tvá kosti, at þeir mundu drepa hann, ella skyldi hann taka hundinn, en hann køri heldr at leysa líf sitt ok fór með þeim. Traðir váru fyrir norðan garðana at Hlíðarenda, ok námu þeir þar staðar með flokkinn. Bóndi Þorkell gekk heim á bœinn, ok lá rakkinn á húsum uppi, ok teygir hann rakkan á braut með sér í geilar nǫkkurar. Í því sér hundrinn at þar eru menn fyrir, ok leypr á hann Þorkel upp ok greip nárann. Ǫnundr ór Trǫllaskógi hjó með øxi í hǫfuð hundinum svá *at* allt kom í heilann. Hundrinn kvað við hátt svá at þat þótti þeim með ódœmum miklum vera, ‹ok fell hann dauðr niðr›.

Chapter 77: Víg Gunnars frá Hlíðarenda

Gunnarr vaknaði í skálanum ok mælti, 'Sárt ertu leikinn, Sámr fóstri, ok bút svá sé til ætlat at skammt skyli okkar í meðal.'

Skáli Gunnars var gerr af viði einum ok súðþaktr útan ok gluggar hjá brúnásunum ok snúin þar fyrir speld.[2] Gunnarr svaf í lopti einu í skálanum ok Hallgerðr ok móðir hans. Þá er þeir kómu at, vissu þeir eigi hvárt Gunnarr mundi heima vera, ok báðu at einnhverr mundi fara heim fyrir ok vita hvers víss yrði. En þeir settusk niðr á vǫllinn. Þorgrímr Austmaðr gekk upp á skálann. Gunnarr sér at rauðan kyrtil bar við glugginn, ok leggr út með atgeir á hann miðjan.[3] Þorgrími skruppu fœtrnir ok varð lauss skjǫldrinn, ok hrataði hann ofan af þekjunni. Gengr hann síðan at þeim Gizuri er þeir sátu á vellinu‹m›. Gizurr leit við honum ok mælti:

11 gerðu *M*, gerði *R*. 18 at *M*, er *R*. 19–20 *words supplied from M.*

'Hvárt er Gunnarr heima?'

Þorgrímr segir, 'Vitið þér þat, en hitt vissa ek, at atgeirr hans er heima.' Síðan fell hann niðr dauðr.

Þeir sóttu þá at húsunum. Gunnarr skaut út ǫrum at þeim ok varðisk vel, ok gátu þeir ekki at gert.[4] Þá hljópu sumir *á* húsin ok ætluðu þaðan at at sœkja. Gunnarr kom þangat at þeim ǫrunum, ok gátu þeir ekki at gert, ok fór svá fram um hríð. Þeir tóku hvíld ok sóttu at í annat sinn. Gunnarr skaut enn út, ok gátu þeir ekki at gert ok hrukku frá í annat sinn.

Þá mælti Gizurr hvíti, 'Sœkjum at betr, ekki verðr af oss.'

Gerðu þá hríð ina þriðju ok váru við lengi. Eptir þat hrukku þeir frá.

Gunnarr mælti, 'Ǫr liggr þar úti á vegginum, ok er sú af þeira ǫrum, ok skal ek þeiri skjóta til þeira, ok er þeim þat sk*ǫ*mm ef þeir fá g‹e›ig af vápnum sínum.'

Móðir hans mælti, 'Ger þú eigi þat, at þú vekir þá, er þeir hafa áðr frá horfit.'

Gunnarr þreif ǫrina ok skaut til þeira, ok kom á Eilíf Ǫnundarson, ok fekk hann af sár mikit. Hann hafði staðit einn saman, ok vissu þeir eigi at hann var særðr.

'Hǫnd kom þar út,' segir Gizurr, 'ok var á gullhringr, ok tók ǫr er lá á þekjunni, ok mundi eigi *út* leitað viðfanga ef gnógt væri inni, ok skulu *v*ér nú sœkja at.'[5]

Mǫrðr mælti, 'Brennu vér hann inni.'

'Þat skal verða aldri,' segir Gizurr, 'þótt ek vita at líf mitt liggi við. Er þér sjálfrátt at leggja til ráð þau er dugi, svá slœgr maðr sem þú ert kallaðr.'

Strengir lágu á vellinum ok váru hafðir til at festa með hús jafnan.

Mǫrðr mælti, 'Tǫku vér strengina ok berum um ássendana, en festum aðra endana um steina, ok snúum í vindása ok vindum af ræfrit af skálanum.'

Þeir tóku strengina ok veittu þessa umbúð alla, ok fann Gunnarr eigi fyrr en þeir hǫfðu undit allt þakit af skálanum. Gunnarr skýtr þá af boganum svá at þeir komask aldri at honum. Þá mælti Mǫrðr í annat sinn at þeir mundi brenna ‹Gunnar inni›.

Gizurr mælti, 'Eigi veit ek hví þú vill þat mæla er engi vill annarr, ok skal þat aldri verða.'

38 í *R*. 41 þrukku *R?* 45 skumm *R*. 53 út *M*, vítt *R*. 54 skulu vér *M*, skalt þú *incompletely corrected to* skulu þér *?R*. 65 Gunnar inni *Gráskinna*, *Bæjarbók*, *Oddabók*.

Í þessu bili hleypr upp á þekjuna Þorbrandr Þor*leik*sson ok høgg‹r› í sundr bogastrenginn Gunnars. Gunnarr þrífr atgeirinn báðum hǫndum ok snýsk at honum skjótt ok rekr í gegnum hann ok kastar honum á vǫllinn. Þá ljóp upp Ásbrandr, bróðir hans. Gunnarr leggr til hans atgeirinum ok kom hann skildi fyrir sik. Atgeirr renndi í gegnum skjǫldinn ‹ok í meðal handleggjana. Snaraði Gunnarr þá atgeirinn svá at klofnaði skjǫldrinn›, en brotnuðu báðir handleggirnir, ok fell hann út af vegginum. Áðr hafði Gunnarr sært átta menn, en vegit þá tvá. Þá fekk Gunnarr sár tvau, ok sǫg‹ð›u þat allir menn at hann brygði sér hvárki við sár né við bana.

Hann mælti til Hallgerðar, 'Fá mér leppa tvá ór hári þínu, ok snúið þit móðir mín saman til bogastrengs mér.'[6]

'Liggr þér nǫkkut við?' segir hon.

'Líf mitt liggr við,' segir hann, 'því at þeir munu mik aldri fá sótt meðan ek kem boganum við.'

'Þá skal ek nú,' segir hon, 'muna þér kinnhestinn,[7] ok hirði ek aldri hvárt þú verr þik lengr eða skemr.'[8]

'Hefir hverr til síns ágætis nǫkkut,' segir Gunnarr, 'ok skal þik þessa eigi lengi biðja.'

Rannveig mælti, 'Illa ferr þér, ok mun þín skǫmm lengi uppi.'

Gunnarr varði sik vel ok frœknliga ok særir nú aðra átta menn svá stórum sárum at mǫrgum lá við bana. Gunnarr verr sik þar til er hann fell af mœði. Þeir særðu hann mǫrgum stórum sárum, en þó komsk hann ór hǫndum þeim ok varði sik þá lengi, en þó kom þar at þeir drápu hann. Um vǫrn hans orti Þorkell Elfaraskáld í vísu þessi:[9]

Spurðu vér hvé varðisk
vígmóðr kjalar slóða
*Glaðstýr*andi geiri,
Gunnarr, fyrir Kjǫl sunnan.
Sóknrýrir vann sára
sextán við*a*r mána
hríðar herðimeiða
hauðrmens, en tvá dauða.

Gizurr mælti, 'Mikinn ǫldung hǫfum vér nú at velli lagit, ok hefir oss erfitt veitt, ok mun hans vǫrn uppi meðan landit er byggt.'

68 Þorleiksson *M*, Þorkelsson *R*. 73–74 *words supplied from M*. 95 glaðstýranda *M*; gnýstœrandi (*written* -adni) *R*. 98 viður *R*.

Síðan gekk hann til fundar við Rannveigu ok mælti, 'Villtu veita mǫnnum várum tveimr jǫrð, er dauðir eru, ok sé hér heygðir?'

'At heldr tveimr, at ek munda veita yðr ǫllum,' segir hon.

'Várkunn er þat,' segir hann, 'er þú mælir þat, því at þú hefir mikils misst,' ok kvað á at þar skyldi øngu r*æn*a ok øngu spilla. Fóru á braut síðan.

Þá mælti Þórgeirr Starkaðarson, 'Eigi megum vera heima í búum várum fyrir Sigfússonum, nema þú, Gizurr, eða Geirr sér suðr hér nǫkkura hríð.'

'Þetta mun svá vera,' segir Gizurr, ok hlutuðu þeir, ok hlaut Geirr eptir at vera. Síðan fór hann í Odda ok settisk þar. Hann átti sér son er Hróaldr hét. Hann var laungetinn, ok hét Bjartey móðir hans ok var systir Þorvalds hins veila, er veginn var við Hestlœk í Grímsnesi. Hann hrósaði því at hann hefði veitt Gunnari banasár. Hróaldr var með fǫður sínum. Þorgeirr Starkaðarson hrósaði ǫðru sári at hann hefði Gunnari veitt. Gizurr sat heima at Mosfelli. Víg Gunnars spurðisk ok mæltisk illa fyrir um allar sveitir, ok var hann mǫrgum mǫnnum harmdauði.

107 ræna *M*; ráða *R*.

Notes

[1] The dog Sámr (the name means 'dark-coloured') was a gift to Gunnarr from Óláfr pái (a major figure in *Laxdœla saga*), who claimed to have been given it on his journey to Ireland (ch. 70). It has been pointed out that, if this story were true, the dog would have been more than thirty years old when Gunnarr received it (Finnur Jónsson 1908, 156). Óláfr credits the dog with great intelligence in discerning between friend and enemy and a readiness to lay down its life for its master, effectively anticipating its role in warning Gunnarr of the attack.

[2] For the construction of the typical Icelandic farmhouse at this period, see Byock 2001, 358–68 (though the buildings discussed there are constructed of turf, as was usual, rather than the overlapping boards of Hlíðarendi). The *brúnásar* (referred to by Byock as 'rafter-bracing roof beams') were two beams running along the tops of the rows of interior pillars; these beams supported the rafters at the point where the pitch of the roof changed from steep to shallow, supporting the weight of the roof (especially heavy if made of turf) and allowing the use of shorter timbers for rafters. The *gluggar* were probably unglazed skylights in each side of the sloping roof just below the *brúnásar*.

[3] The *atgeirr* is an unusual weapon, apparently a large and heavy spear with a cutting edge on its head, like a halberd, used mostly for thrusting and hewing, but occasionally also thrown; Gunnarr's ability to do this demonstrates his unusual strength and skill as a warrior (Falk 1914, 62–83). Gunnarr wins the weapon in a battle against a Viking on his travels in the Baltic, and is said to carry it ever afterwards; it has special powers, making a resounding noise as an omen of its impending use in a killing (ch. 30).

[4] The saga's hyperbolic account of Gunnarr's fighting prowess includes special mention of his skill in archery: 'Hann skaut manna bezt af boga ok hœfði allt þat, er hann skaut til' (ch. 19); it is also referred to in ch. 17 of *Hœnsa-Þóris saga* (*ÍF* XII, 53 note 1).

[5] *Eyrbyggja saga* (ch. 47) refers to this incident, attributing this observation to Geirr goði. The mismatch between Gunnarr's intention to shame his opponents by injuring them with their own weapon, and his attackers' assumption that he has simply run out of ammunition, recognises his heroic status.

[6] Stories of bowstrings made of women's hair (and the use of these stories as illustrations of loyalty) can be found in classical sources, such as *Historia Augusta* from *c.*400 AD:

> Nor can we fail to mention the extraordinary loyalty displayed by the Aquileans in defending the Senate against Maximinus. For, lacking bow-strings with which to shoot their arrows, they made cords of the women's hair. It was said that this once happened at Rome as well, whence it was that the Senate, in honour of the matrons, dedicated the temple of Venus Calva (i.e. the Bald). (*Scriptores Historiae Augustae* III 377–78)

[7] See note 4 to the extract from *Laxdœla saga*, p. 205 above. Each of Hallgerðr's three husbands slaps her face, and in each case the humiliation leads to his death.

[8] Here a verse is added in the margin of *R*, introduced with 'Gunnarr kvað þá vísu'. This verse is included in an appendix in *ÍF* XII 477. For the marginal verses in *R*, thought to have been added to the manuscript by its earliest readers, see Nordal 2005.

[9] Þorkell Elfaraskáld is not known from elsewhere, and this is the only verse attributed to him. It has been suggested (Salberger 1973) that his nickname means 'poet of the traveller (*fari*) to the *Elfr* (the River Elbe, known as Göta älv in modern Sweden)', alluding to Gunnarr's exploits in Sweden as related in chs 29–30, where he acquires the *atgeirr.*

Verse in prose word order

Lines 93–100: Vér spurðu hvé Gunnarr, vígmóðr *Glaðstýr*andi kjalar slóða, varðisk geiri fyrir sunnan Kjǫl. Sóknrýrir vann sextán herðimeiða hríðar mána við*ar* hauðrmens sára, en tvá dauða.

XXVI B: THE BURNING OF NJÁLL

‹Chapter 127›

Nú er þar til máls at taka at Bergþórshváli, at þeir Grímr ok Helgi fóru til Hóla — þar váru þeim fóstruð bǫrn — ok sǫgðu móður sinni at þeir mundu ekki heim um kveldit. Þeir váru í Hólum allan daginn. Þar kómu fátœkar konur ok kváðusk komnar at langt. Þeir brœðr spurðu þær tíðinda. Þær kváðusk engi tíðindi segja.

'En segja kunnu vér nýlundu nǫkkura.'

Þeir spurðu hver sú væri ok báðu þær eigi leyna. Þær sǫgðu svá vera skyldu.

'Vér kómum at ofan ór Fljótshlíð, ok sá vér Sigfússonu alla ríða með alvæpni. Þeir stefndu upp á Þríhyrningshálsa, ok váru fimmtán í flokki. Vér sá‹m› ok Grana Gunnarsson ok Gunnar Lambason, ok váru þeir fimm saman. Þeir stefndu ina sǫmu leið, ok kalla má at nú sé allt á fǫr ok flaugun um heraðit.'

Helgi Njálsson mælti, 'Þá mun Flosi kominn austan, ok munu þeir allir koma til móts við hann, ok skulu vit Grímr vera þar Skarpheðinn er.'

Grímr kvað svá vera skyldu, ok fóru þeir heim.

Þenna aptan inn sama mælti Bergþóra til hjóna sinna, 'Nú skulu þér kjósa yðr mat í kveld, at hverr hafi þat er mest fýsir til, því at þenna aptan mun ek bera síðast mat fyrir hjón mín.'

'Þat skyldi eigi vera,' segja þau.

'Þat mun þó vera,' segir hon, 'ok má ek miklu fleira af segja ef ek vil, ok mun þat til merkja at þeir Grímr ok Helgi munu heim koma áðr menn eru mettir í kveld. Ok ef þetta gengr eptir, þá mun svá fara fleira sem ek segi.'

Síðan bar hon mat á borð. Njáll mælti:

'Undarliga sýnisk mér nú. Ek þikjumsk sjá um alla stofuna, ok þiki mér sem undan sé gaflveggrinn, en blóð eitt allt borðit ok matrinn.'

Þá fannsk ǫllum mikit um þetta nema Skarpheðni. Hann bað menn ekki syrgja né láta ǫðrum herfiligum látum svá at menn mætti orð á því gera.

'Ok mun oss vandara gert en ǫðrum at vér berim oss vel, ok er þat at vánum.'

1 *No chapter division in R. The preceding chapter heading is* Frá Flosa ok brennumǫnnum.

Þeir Grímr ok Helgi kómu heim áðr borðin váru ofan tekin, ok brá mǫnnum mjǫk við þat. Njáll spurði hví þeir fœri svá hverft, en þeir sǫgðu slíkt sem þeir hǫfðu frétt. Njáll bað øngvan mann til svefns fara ok vera vara um sik.

Chapter 128: Viðrtal Njáls ok Skarpheðins

Nú talar Flosi við sína menn: 'Nú munu vér ríða til Bergþórshváls ok koma þar fyrir matmál.'

Þeir gera nú svá. Dalr var í hválnum,[10] ok riðu þeir þangat ok bundu þar hesta sína ok dvǫlðusk þar til þess er mjǫk leið á kveldit.

Flosi mælti, 'Nú skulu vér ganga heim at bœnum ok ganga þrǫngt ok fara seint ok sjá hvat þeir taki til ráðs.'

Njáll stóð úti ok synir hans ok Kári ok allir heimamenn ok skipuðusk fyrir á hlaðinu, ok váru þeir nær þremr tigum. Flosi nam stað ok mælti:

'Nú skulu vér at hyggja hvat þeir taka ráðs, því at mér lízk svá, ef þeir standa úti fyrir, sem vér munim þá aldri sótta geta.'

'Þá er vár fǫr ill,' segir Grani Gunnarsson, 'ef skulum eigi þora at at sœkja.'

'Þat skal ok eigi vera,' segir Flosi, 'ok munu vér at sœkja þótt þeir standi úti. En þat afroð munu vér gjalda, at margir munu eigi kunna frá at segja hvárir sigrask.'

Njáll mælti til sinna manna, 'Hvat sjái þér til, hversu mikit lið þeir hafa?'

'Þeir hafa bæði mikit lið ok harðsnúit,' segir Skarpheðinn, 'en því nema þeir þó nú stað at þeir ætla at þeim muni illa sœkjask at vinna oss.'

'Þat mun ekki vera,' segir Njáll, 'ok vil ek at menn gangi inn, því at illa sóttisk þeim Gunnarr at Hlíðarenda, ok var hann einn fyrir. En hér eru hús rammlig, sem þar váru, ok munu þeir eigi skjótt sœkja.'

'Þetta er ekki þann veg at skilja,' segir Skarpheðinn, 'því at Gunnar sóttu heim þeir hǫfðingjar er svá váru vel at sér at heldr vildu frá hverfa en brenna hann inni. En þessir munu þegar sœkja oss með eldi ef þeir megu eigi annan veg, því at þeir munu allt til vinna at yfir taki við oss. Munu þeir þat ætla, sem eigi er ólíkligt, at þat sé þeira bani ef oss dregr undan. Ek em ok þess ófúss at láta svæla mik inni sem melrakka í greni.'

57 bæði] beðit *R*.

Njáll mælti, 'Nú mun sem optar, at þér munu‹ð› bera mik ráðum, synir mínir, ok virða mik engis. En þá er þér váruð yngri þá gjǫrðuð þér þat eigi, ok fór yðart ráð þá betr fram.'

Helgi mælti, 'Gerum vér sem faðir várr vill. Þat mun oss bezt gegna.'

'Eigi veit ek þat víst,' segir Skarpheðinn, 'því at hann er nú feigr. En vel má ek gera þat til skaps fǫður míns at brenna inni með honum, því at ek hræðumsk ekki dauða minn.'

Hann mælti þá við Kára, 'Fylgjumsk vel, mágr, svá at engi skilisk við annan.'

'Þat hefi ek ætlat,' segir Kári, 'en ef annars verðr auðit þá mun þat verða fram at koma, ok mun ek ekki mega við því gera.'

'Hefndu vár en vér þín,' segir Skarpheðinn, 'ef vér lifum eptir.'

Kári kvað svá vera skyldu. Gengu þeir þá inn allir ok skipuðusk í dyrrin.

Flosi mælti, 'Nú eru þeir feigir, er þeir hafa inn gengit, ok skulu vér heim ganga sem skjótast ok skipask sem þykkvast fyrir dyrrin ok geyma þess at engi komisk í braut, hvárki Kári né Njálssynir, því at þat er várr bani.'

Þeir Flosi kómu nú heim ok skipuðusk umhverfis húsin, ef nǫkkurar væri laundyrr á. Flosi gekk framan at húsunum ok hans menn. Hróaldr Ǫzurarson hljóp þar at sem Skarpheðinn var fyrir, ok lagði til hans. Skarpheðinn hjó spjótit af skapti fyrir honum ok hjó til hans, ok kom øxin ofan í skjǫldinn, ok bar at Hróaldi þegar allan skjǫldinn, en hyrnan sú in fremri tók andlitit, ok fell hann á bak aptr ok þegar dauðr. Kári mælti:

'Lítt dró enn undan við þik, Skarpheðinn, ok ertu vár frœknastr.'

'Eigi veit ek þat víst,' segir Skarpheðinn, ok brá við grǫnum ok glotti at.[11] Kári ok Grímr ok Helgi lǫgðu út mǫrgum spjótum ok særðu marga menn. En Flosi ok hans menn fengu ekki at gert.

Flosi mælti, 'Vér hǫfum fengi‹t› mikinn mannskaða á mǫnnum várum. Eru margir sárir, en sá veginn er vér mundum sízt til kjósa. Er nú þat sét at vér getum þá eigi með vápnum sótta. Er sá nú margr er eigi gengr jafnskǫruliga at sem létu. En þó munu vér nú verða at gera annat ráð fyrir oss. Eru nú tve‹i›r kostir til, ok er hvárgi góðr: sá annarr at hverfa frá, ok er þat várr bani; hinn annarr at bera at eld ok brenna þá inni, ok er þat stórr ábyrgðarlutr fyrir Guði, er vér erum menn kristnir sjálfir.[12] En þó munu vér þat bragðs taka.'

99 it *added after* sárir *R*.

Chapter 129: Bœjarbruni at Bergþórshváli

Þeir tóku nú eld ok gerðu bál mikit fyrir dyrunum. Þá mælti Skarpheðinn:

'Eld kveykvið þér nú, sveinar, eða hvárt skal nú búa til seyðis?'

Grani Gunnarsson svarar, 'Svá skal þat vera, ok skaltu eigi þurfa heitara at baka.'

Skarpheðinn mælti, 'Því launar þú mér, sem þú ert maðr til, er ek hefnda fǫður þíns, ok virðir þat meira er þér er óskyldara.'[13]

Þá báru konur sýru í eldinn ok sløkktu niðr fyrir þeim. Kolr Þorsteinsson mælti til Flosa:

'Ráð kemr mér í hug. Ek hefi sét lopt í skálanum á þvertrjám, ok skulu vér þar inn bera eldinn ok kveykva við arfasátu þá er hér stendr fyrir ofan húsin.'[14]

Síðan tóku þeir arfasátuna ok báru í eld. Fundu þeir eigi fyrr, er inni váru, en logaði ofan allr skálinn. Gerðu þeir Flosi þá stór bál fyrir ǫllum dyrum. Tók þá kvennafólkit illa at þola, þat sem inni var. Njáll mælti til þeira:

'Verðið vel við ok mælið eigi æðru, því at él eitt mun vera, ok skyldi langt til annars slíks. Trúið þér ok því, at Guð er svá miskunnsamr at hann mun oss eigi bæði brenna láta þessa heims ok annars.'

Slíkar fortǫlur hafði hann fyrir þeim ok aðrar hraustligri. Nú taka ǫll húsin at loga. Þá gekk Njáll til dyra ok mælti:

'Hvárt er Flosi svá nær at hann megi heyra mál mitt?'

Flosi kvazk heyra mega. Njáll mælti:

'Villt þú nǫkkut taka sættum við sonu mína eða lofa nǫkkurum mǫnnum útgǫngu?'

Flosi svarar, 'Eigi vil ek við sonu þína sættum taka, ok skal nú yfir lúka með oss ok eigi fyrr frá ganga en þeir eru allir dauðir, en lofa vil ek útgǫngu konum ok bǫrnum ok húskǫrlum.'

Njáll gekk þá inn ok mælti við fólkit, 'Nú er þeim út at ganga ǫllum er leyft er. Ok gakk þú út, Þórhalla Ásgrímsdóttir, ok allr lýðr með þér, sá er lofat er.'

Þórhalla mælti, 'Annarr verðr nú skilnaðr okkarr Helga en ek ætlaða um hríð, en þó skal ek eggja fǫður minn ok brœðr at þeir hefni þessa mannskaða er hér er gerr.'[15]

117 þar *written* þr *with superscript abbreviation for* ar *R*. 133 fyrr *written* f *with superscript* i (= firr *or* firir) *R*. 137 lofat er *written twice R*.

Njáll mælti, 'Vel mun þér fara, því at þú ert góð kona.'

Síðan gekk hon út ok mart lið með henni.

Ástríðr af Djúpárbakka mælti við Helga Njálsson, 'Gakktu út með mér, ok mun ek kasta yfir þik kvenskikkju ok falda þik með hǫfuðdúki.'

Hann talðisk undan fyrst, en þó gerði hann þetta fyrir bœn þeira. Ástríðr vafði hǫfuðdúk at hǫfði Helga, en Þórhildr kona Skarpheðins lagði yfir hann skikkjuna, ok gekk hann út á meðal þeira, ok þá gekk út Þorgerðr Njálsdóttir ok Helga, systir hennar, ok mart annat fólk.

En er Helgi kom út, mælti Flosi, 'Sú er há kona ok mikil um herðar er þar fór. Takið ‹hana› ok haldið henni.'

En er Helgi heyrði þetta, kastaði hann skikkjunni. Hann hafði haft sverð undir hendi sér ok hjó til manns, ok kom í skjǫldinn ok af sporðinn ok fótinn af manninum. Þá kom Flosi at ok hjó á hálsinn Helga svá at þegar tók af hǫfuðit.

Flosi gekk þá at dyrum ok kallaði á Njál ok kvazk vildu tala við hann ok Bergþóru. Njáll gerir nú svá. Flosi mælti:

'Útgǫngu vil ek bjóða þér, Njáll bóndi, því at þú brennr ómakligr inni.'

Njáll mælti, 'Eigi vil ek út ganga, því at ek em maðr gamall ok lítt til búinn at hefna sona minna, en ek vil eigi lifa við skǫmm.'

Flosi mælti þá til Bergþóru, 'Gakktu út, húsfreyja, því at ek vil þik fyrir øngan mun inni brenna.'

Bergþóra mælti, 'Ek var ung gefin Njáli. Hefi ek því heitit honum at eitt skyldi ganga yfir okkr bæði.'

Síðan gengu þau inn bæði. Bergþóra mælti:

'Hvat skulu vit nú til ráða taka?'

'Ganga munu vit til hvílu okkarrar,' segir Njáll, 'ok leggjask niðr; hefi ek lengi værugjarn verit.'

Hon mælti þá við sveininn Þórð Kárason, 'Þik skal út bera, ok skaltu eigi inni brenna.'

'Hinu hefir þú mér heitit, amma,' segir sveinninn, 'at vit skyldim aldri skilja meðan ek vilda hjá þér vera, en mér þikkir miklu betra at deyja með ykkr Njáli en lifa eptir.'[16]

Hon bar þá sveininn til hvílunnar. Njáll mælti við brytja sinn:

'Nú skaltu sjá hvar vit leggjumsk niðr ok hversu ek bý um okkr, því at ek ætla heðan hvergi at hrœrask, hvárt sem mér angrar reykr eða bruni. Máttu nú nær geta hvar beina okkarra er at leita.'

150 hana *M*.

Hann sagði svá vera skyldu.

Þar hafði slátrat verit uxa einum, ok lá þar húðin. Njáll mælti við brytjann at hann skyldi breiða yfir þau húðina, ok hann hét því. Þau leggjask nú niðr bæði í rúmit ok leggja sveininn í millum sín. Þá signdu þau sik ok sveininn ok fálu Guði ǫnd sína á hendi ok mæltu þat síðast svá menn heyrði. Þá tók brytinn húðina ok breiddi yfir þau ok gekk út síðan.[17] Ketill ór Mǫrk tók í móti honum ok kippti honum út.[18] Hann spurði vandliga at Njáli, mági sínum, en brytinn sagði allt it sanna. Ketill mælti,

'Mikill harmr er at oss kveðinn, er vér skulum svá mikla ógæfu saman eiga.'

Skarpheðinn sá er faðir hans lagðisk niðr ok hversu hann bjó um sik. Hann mælti þá:

'Snemma ferr faðir várr at rekkju, ok er þat sem ván er: hann er maðr gamall.'

Þá tóku þeir Skarpheðinn ok Kári ok Grímr brandana jafnskjótt sem ofan duttu, ok skutu út á þá, ok gekk því um hríð. Þá skutu þeir spjótum inn at þeim, en þeir tóku ǫll á lopti ok sendu út aptr. Flosi bað þá hætta at skjóta, 'því at oss munu ǫll vápnaskipti þungt ganga við þá. Megu þér nú vel bíða þess er eldrinn vinnr þá.'

Þeir gera nú svá. Þá fellu ofan stórviðinir ór ræfrinu.

Skarpheðinn mælti þá, 'Nú mun faðir minn dauðr vera, ok hefir hvárki heyrt til hans styn né hósta.'

Þeir gengu þá í skálaendann. Þar var fallit ofan þvertré ok brunnit mjǫk í miðju. Kári mælti til Skarpheðins:

'Hlau‹p›tu hér út, ok mun ek beina at með þér, en ek mun hlaupa þegar eptir, ok munu vit þá báðir í brott komask ef vit breytum svá, því at hingat leggr allan reykinn.'

Skarpheðinn mælti, 'Þú skalt hlaupa fyrri, en ek mun þegar á hæla þér.'

'Ekki er þat ráð,' segir Kári, 'því at ek komisk vel annars staðar út þótt hér gangi eigi.'

'Eigi vil ek þat,' segir Skarpheðinn. 'Hlauptu út fyrri, en ek mun þegar eptir.'

'Þat er hverjum manni boðit at leita sér lífs meðan kostr er,' segir Kári, 'ok skal ek ok svá gera. En þó mun *nú* sá skilnaðr með okkr

182 ǫnd *M*, hǫnd *R*. 213 nú *M*, þó *R*.

verða at vit munum aldri s*j*ásk síðan, því at ef ek hleyp ór eldinum, þá mun ‹ek› eigi hafa skap til at hlaupa inn aptr í eldinn til þín, ok mun þá sína leið fara hvárr okkar.'

'Þat hlœgir mik,' segir Skarpheðinn, 'ef þú kemsk á brott, mágr, attu mun hefna mín.'

Þá tók Kári einn setstokk loganda í hǫnd sér ok hleypr út eptir þvertrénu. Kastar hann þá stokkinum út af þekjunni, ok fell hann at þeim er úti váru fyrir. Þeir hlupu þá undan. Þá loguðu klæðin ǫll á Kára ok svá hárit. Hann steypir sér þá út af þekjunni ok stiklar svá með reykinum.

Þá mælti einn maðr er þar var næstr, 'Hvárt hljóp þar maðr út af þekjunni?'

'Fjarri fór þat,' segir annarr, 'heldr kastaði þar Skarpheðinn eldistokki at oss.'

Síðan grunuðu þeir þat ekki. Kári hljóp til þess er hann kom at lœk einum. Hann kastaði sér þar í ofan ok sløkkti á sér eldinn. Síðan hljóp hann með reykinum í gróf nǫkkura ok hvíldi sik, ok er þat síðan kǫlluð Káragróf.

214 sjásk *M*, 'saaz' *R*.

Notes

[10] The *dalr* is a depression in the hill (*hváll*) on which the farmhouse stood. It can still be seen, but is too small to have concealed the 100 men said (in ch. 124) to have taken part in the burning, together with the two horses of each (*ÍF* XII 325, note 3).

[11] Skarpheðinn is described as having an ugly mouth and protruding teeth (ch. 25), and his grin emphasises his threatening appearance at many points in the saga.

[12] The Christianity of the burners is emphasised by their having stopped at the church at Kirkjubœr to pray on their way to Bergþórshváll (ch. 126).

[13] Grani is the son of Gunnarr of Hlíðarendi, but is said to resemble his mother Hallgerðr in temperament (ch. 75).

[14] The use of the chickweed to kindle the fire that will burn Njáll and Bergþóra was predicted by an old servant-woman, Sæunn, but Skarpheðinn refused to remove it, since fate cannot be avoided (ch. 124).

[15] Þórhalla's father, Ásgrímr Elliða-Grímsson, and her brother Þórhallr (fostered by Njáll, who taught him law) later conduct the lawsuit against the burners.

[16] Þórðr, son of Kári and of Helga Njálsdóttir, has been fostered by Njáll (ch. 109).

[17] The ox-hide covering Njáll and Bergþóra provides a rational explanation for the undamaged state of their bodies when they are found, but this state is also used to imply an almost saint-like quality in Njáll (ch. 132).

[18] Ketill of Mǫrk is one of the Sigfússynir, and therefore among Njáll's attackers; but he is also the husband of Njáll's daughter Þorgerðr, who has left the house along with the other women of the household (line 148).

XXVII: GRÁGÁS

The name *Grágás* (literally 'grey goose') is a convenient if somewhat arbitrary label of obscure origin used collectively for the laws of the medieval Icelandic Commonwealth as preserved in a number of manuscripts. The two most important manuscripts are GkS 1157 fol. (also called Codex Regius or, as here, Konungsbók; = K) and AM 334 fol. (also known as Staðarhólsbók; = S). K is normally dated to *c.*1260, Staðarhólsbók to *c.*1280. Other manuscripts or fragments which preserve parts of *Grágás* include AM 315 d fol. (two leaves), written perhaps as early as *c.*1150–75 and one of the oldest Icelandic manuscripts in existence.

Compared with other laws of medieval Scandinavia, *Grágás* is a work of enormous size and detail. In Vilhjálmur Finsen's edition of 1852, the Konungsbók text of *Grágás* takes up some 460 pages; printed in the same series (also in 1852) with identical format and type, the next longest of the early Scandinavian laws, *Erik's law of Zealand* (cf. *MS* 384), covers only about 130 pages.

The contents of K may be roughly divided into fifteen sections, as follows (the symbol § is used for the chapters into which the texts of *Grágás* are divided in Finsen's editions): (1) *Kristinna laga þáttr* ('Christian laws section', §§ 1–19); (2) *Þingskapaþáttr* ('Assembly procedures section', §§ 20–85); (3) *Vígslóði* ('Treatment of homicide', §§ 86–112); (4) *Baugatal* ('The wergild ring list', § 113) (together with *Griðamál*, 'Truce speech', § 114, and *Tryggðamál*, 'Peace guarantee speech', § 115); (5) *Lǫgsǫgumannsþáttr* ('The lawspeaker's section', § 116); (6) *Lǫgréttuþáttr* ('The Law Council section', § 117); (7) *Arfaþáttr* ('Inheritance section', §§ 118–27); (8) *Ómagabálkr* ('Dependents section', §§ 128–43); (9) *Festaþáttr* ('Betrothals section', §§ 144–71); (10) *Landbrigðaþáttr* ('Land-claims section', §§ 172–20); (11) *Um fjárleigur* ('On hire of property', §§ 221–26); (12) *Rannsóknaþáttr* ('Searches section', §§ 227–33); (13) *Um hreppaskil* ('On commune obligations', §§ 234–36); (14) A section containing miscellaneous articles relating to such diverse matters as verbal injury by poetry or harm from tame bears, §§ 234–54; (15) *Um tíundargjald* ('On tithe payment', together with further miscellaneous provisions, §§ 255–68). The texts of K and S differ substantially. Staðarhólsbók does not have sections corresponding to (2), (4), (5), (6), (12), (13), (14) and (15) and the sections it does have appear in the order (1), (7), (8), (9), (11),

(3), (10). But sometimes matter in K in the sections absent in S is paralleled by matter in other sections present in S. Where the matter of the two texts is essentially the same, S is very often more detailed, better organised and has more 'modern' content than K. And both S and other manuscripts contain much matter not found in K at all.

A long tradition lies behind the preserved texts of *Grágás*, stretching back to oral recitations of what must have been essentially heathen law by the first lawspeakers at the Alþingi in the fourth decade of the tenth century (cf. Text VIII (c) and notes 19 and 21 to that text). The acceptance of Christianity in 999 must inevitably have led to profound changes in the law (cf. VIII:123–43). Further, in 1096 or 1097 a law of tithe was introduced (cf. VIII:150–68; *HOIC* 147–53). And in the period 1122–33, *Kristinna laga þáttr* was compiled and recorded in written form (cf. *HOIC* 160–69). Meanwhile, in the winter of 1117–18, at the home of Hafliði Másson at Breiðabólstaðr (in present-day Vestur-Húnavatnssýsla), some, at least, of the oral secular laws had also been committed to writing under the supervision of Bergþórr Hrafnsson, lawspeaker at the time, and other legal experts (cf. VIII:168–80; *HOIC* 89–93; *Laws* I 9–13). The result of these men's work was doubtless the book referred to in K § 117 (cf. *Laws* I 190–91) as *skrá sú er Hafliði lét gera* ('the screed which Hafliði had made'), called *Hafliðaskrá* by modern scholars, and it is generally supposed that the preserved manuscripts of *Grágás* (apart from *Kristinna laga þáttr*) go back in part ultimately to *Hafliðaskrá*. Law-making did not cease with the appearance of *Hafliðaskrá* and *Kristinna laga þáttr*, and texts of *Grágás* would have proliferated, developed and been expanded in various ways over the period after 1130, not least as a result of new legislation by the Law Council (*lǫgrétta*). After Iceland's submission to the Norwegian king in 1262–64, the main part of *Grágás* was superseded by *Járnsíða* in 1271 (itself replaced by *Jónsbók* in the early 1280s). *Kristinna laga þáttr*, however, remained in force in the diocese of Skálholt until 1275 and in the diocese of Hólar until 1354, and other sections of *Grágás* continued to be invoked in cases for which the much briefer *Jónsbók* provided insufficient guidance. It is uncertain how *Grágás* acquired the distinctly literary quality it has in contrast to that of the continental Scandinavian laws of the Middle Ages which are far more oral and primitive in their style. It could well have done so in connection with the first writing down of the laws in the second decade of the twelfth century (cf. Ólafur Lárusson 1958, 87–89; *Laws* I 14–15).

Grágás gives us a picture of numerous aspects of life, both everyday and ceremonial, in the medieval Icelandic Commonwealth. In many respects it presents a different and truer picture than many of our other sources (such as the Sagas of Icelanders). The passage selected here as a sample is the 'Lawspeaker's section' (*Lǫgsǫgumannsþáttr*), only preserved in K (pp. 83a17–84a14), where it is the shortest section (consisting of a single chapter, § 116). The lawspeaker would have been a central figure in public life in Iceland during the Commonwealth period and particularly prominent at the meetings of the General Assembly (*Alþingi*) held every summer at Þingvellir and attended by people from all over the country. He was elected for a term of three summers but could be re-elected. At the annual meetings of the Alþingi he had the important function of presiding at the Law Council, the foremost legislative body in the country. He also had the duty of reciting *Þingskapaþáttr* at Lǫgberg ('the Law Rock') every summer and the rest of the laws over the three-year period of his office. For a fuller account of the lawspeaker's position within the framework of the constitution of the Icelandic commonwealth, the student is referred to the chapter 'Form of government' in *HOIC* 35–93, supplemented by a reading of *Þingskapaþáttr* and *Lǫgréttuþáttr* as well, of course, as the passage edited here (see *Laws* I 53–38, 189–93, 187–88).

There were some 43 lawspeakers from the time of the institution of the Alþingi until 1271 and it is possible to draw up a complete list of them (see p. xliv above and Jón Sigurðsson 1886, 1–4) based on medieval sources such as *Íslendingabók* and lists in the manuscripts DG 11, which also contains a version of Snorra Edda (see pp. 15–21 above), and AM 106 fol., which also contains a version of *Landnámabók* (see pp. 261–66 above). The list extends from the shadowy Úlfljótr (cf. VIII:39–41) to Þorleifr hreimr Ketilsson (cf. III:44 above). It includes such notables as Þorgeirr Þorkelsson Ljósvetningagoði who, according to Ari Þorgilsson (VIII:116–43), played an important role in the conversion of Iceland to Christianity; Skapti Þóroddsson, who held the position longest of all (1004–30) and who must have had some hand in changes to the law resulting from the Conversion and also in the institution of the Fifth Court (*fimmtardómr*; cf. *HOIC* 70–74; *Laws* I 83–88, 244–45); the eleventh-century poet Markús Skeggjason (died 1107; cf. VIII:152 and note 51); and in the thirteenth century three prominent political and literary figures, all members of the Sturlung family, Snorri Sturluson and his nephews Sturla Þórðarson and Óláfr Þórðarson.

Apart from his official function as an authority on legal matters, the lawspeaker would have been a repository for much other information, not only current politics and gossip, but also history, lore and tradition. Indeed, the annual meetings of the Alþingi attended by people from all over the country and with the lawspeaker at the centre of its proceedings must have been a strong force for the preservation of a language that was hardly marked by regional differences and of a vigorous and dynamic oral tradition during the days of the Icelandic Commonwealth. This oral tradition would would have concerned the past as well as the present and would have become a rich source for thirteenth-century Icelanders writing about bygone times.

Bibliography

Facsimile edition: Páll Eggert Ólason (ed.), *The Codex Regius of Grágás*, *CCIMA* III (1932).

Critical editions:

Vilhjálmur Finsen (ed.), *Grágás. Islændernes Lovbog i Fristatens Tid udgivet efter det kongelige Bibliotheks Haandskrift* (1852; reprints 1945, 1974). [Text of K and various fragments, including AM 315 d fol.]

Vilhjálmur Finsen (ed.), *Grágás efter det Arnamagnæanske Haandskrift Nr. 334 fol., Staðarhólsbók* (1879; reprint 1974). [Text of S]

Vilhjálmur Finsen (ed.), *Grágás. Stykker, som findes i det Arnamagnæanske Haandskrift Nr. 351 fol. Skálholtsbók og en Række andre Haandskrifter* (1883; reprint 1974) [Texts of various minor manuscript sources; apparatus includes a detailed 'Ordregister' (in Danish) of technical vocabulary on pp. 579–714]

Popular edition: Gunnar Karlsson, Kristján Sveinsson, Mörður Árnason (eds), *Grágás. Lagasafn íslenska þjóðveldisins* (1992). [In modern Icelandic spelling; includes the whole of the Staðarhólsbók text (pp. 1–369) and parts of the text of K without parallel in S (pp. 371–480)]

English translation: *Laws of early Iceland. Grágás. The Codex Regius of Grágás with material from other manuscripts* I–II, tr. Andrew Dennis, Peter Foote, Richard Perkins (1980–2000). [= *Laws*. A complete translation of K, with 'Additions' from other sources (mainly S) which either amplify the contents of K or supply matter not found in it. Apparatus includes 'A guide to technical vocabulary'.]

Background reading:

Björn Þorsteinsson, *Thingvellir. Iceland's national shrine*, tr. Peter Foote (1987).

H.-P. Naumann, 'Grágás'. In *Reallexikon der germanischen Altertumskunde von Johannes Hoops, zweite . . . Auflage*, ed. Heinrich Beck *et al.* (1973–2008), XII 569–73.

Jón Sigurðsson, 'Lögsögumannatal og lögmanna á Íslandi'. In *Safn til sögu Íslands og íslenzkra bókmenta* II (1886), 1–250.

HOIC 35–93.

MS under *Alþingi*; *Goði*; *Grágás*; *Iceland*; *Laws 2. Iceland.*

Ólafur Lárusson, 'On Grágás – the oldest Icelandic code of law'. In *Þriðji Víkingafundur. Third Viking Congress, Reykjavík 1956* (*Árbók Hins íslenzka Fornleifafélags. Fylgirit, 1958*), ed. Kristján Eldjárn (1958), 77–89.

Beck, Heinrich, *Wortschatz der altisländischen Grágás (Konungsbók)* (1993). [A concordance of the Konungsbók text]

For maps of Þingvǫllr (with for instance the site of Lǫgberg marked), see *HOIC* 42, *Laws* I 281, Björn Þorsteinsson (1987), 9–11.

XXVII: GRÁGÁS

Lǫgsǫgumannsþáttr

Svá er enn mælt at sá maðr skal vera nokkurr ávalt á landi óru er skyldr sé til þess at segja lǫg mǫnnum, ok heitir sá lǫgsǫgumaðr. En ef lǫgsǫgumanns missir við, þá skal ór þeim fjórðungi taka mann til at segja þingskǫp[1] upp it næsta sumar er hann hafði síðarst heimili í. Menn[2] skulu þá taka sér lǫgsǫgumann ok sýsla þat fǫstudag hverr vera skal áðr sakir sé lýstar.[3] Þat er ok vel ef allir menn verða sáttir á einn mann. En ef lǫgréttumaðr nokkurr stendr við því er flestir vilja, ok[4] skal þá hluta í hvern fjórðung lǫgsaga skal hverfa. En þeir fjórðungsmenn er þá hefr hlutr í hag borit skulu taka lǫgsǫgumann þann sem þeir verða sáttir á, hvárt sem sá er ór þeirra fjórðungi eða ór ǫðrum fjórðungi nokkurum, þeirra manna er þeir megu þat geta at. Nú verða fjórðungsmenn eigi á sáttir, ok skal þá afl ráða með þeim. En ef þeir eru jafnmargir er lǫgréttusetu eigu er sinn lǫgsǫgumann vilja hvárir, þá skulu þeir ráða er biskup sá fellr í fullting með er í þeim fjórðungi er.[5] Nú eru lǫgréttumenn nokkurir þeir er níta því er aðrir vilja, fái engan mann sjálfir til lǫgsǫgu, ok eigu enskis þeirra orð at metask.

Lǫgsǫgumann á í lǫgréttu at taka, þá er menn hafa ráðit hverr vera skal, ok skal einn maðr skilja fyrir en aðrir gjalda samkvæði á, ok skal þrjú sumur samfast inn sami haf*a*, nema menn vili eigi breytt hafa.[6] Ór þeirri lǫgréttu er lǫgsǫgumaðr er tekinn skulu menn ganga til Lǫgbergs ok skal hann ganga til Lǫgbergs ok setjask í rúm sitt ok skipa Lǫgberg þeim mǫnnum sem hann vill. En menn skulu þá mæla málum sínum.

Þat er ok mælt at lǫgsǫgumaðr er skyldr til þess at segja upp lǫgþáttu alla á þremr sumrum hverjum en þingskǫp hvert sumar.[7] Lǫgsǫgumaðr á upp at segja syknuleyfi ǫll at Lǫgbergi svá at meiri hlutr manna sé þar, ef því um náir, ok misseristal, ok svá þat ef menn skulu koma fyrr til Alþingis en tíu vikur eru af sumri,[8] ok tína imbrudagahald[9] ok fǫstuíganga, ok skal hann þetta allt mæla at þinglausnum.

Þat er ok[10] at lǫgsǫgumaðr skal svá gerla þáttu alla upp segja at engi viti einna miklugi gørr. En ef honum vinnsk eigi fróðleikr til þess, þá skal hann eiga stefnu við fimm lǫgmenn in næstu dœgr áðr eða fleiri,

9 En] *The scribe first wrote* Ef *then altered it to* En. 15 fellr] *The scribe first wrote* er *then altered it to* fellr. 20 hafa] hafi *K*.

þá er hann má helzt geta af, áðr hann segi hvern þátt upp; ok verðr hverr maðr útlagr þremr mǫrkum er ólofat gengr á mál þeirra, ok á lǫgsǫgumaðr sǫk þá.

Lǫgsǫgumaðr skal hafa hvert sumar tvau hundruð álna vaðmála af lǫgréttufjám fyrir starf sitt.[11] Hann á ok útlegðir allar hálfar, þær er á Alþingi eru dœmðar hér,[12] ok skal dœma eindaga á þeim ǫllum annat sumar hér í búandakirkjugarði,[13] miðvikudag í mitt þing. Útlagr er hverr maðr þremr mǫrkum er fé lætr dœma, ef hann segir eigi lǫgsǫgumanni til ok svá hverir dómsuppsǫguváttar hafa verit.

Þat er ok, þá er lǫgsǫgumaðr hefr haft þrjú sumur lǫgsǫgu, ok skal hann þá segja upp þingskǫp it fjórða sumar fǫstudag inn fyrra í þingi. Þá er hann ok lauss frá lǫgsǫgu ef hann vill. Nú vill hann hafa lǫgsǫgu lengr, ef aðrir unna honum, þá skal inn meiri hlutr lǫgréttumanna ráða.

Þat er ok at lǫgsǫgumaðr er útlagr þremr mǫrkum ef hann kemr eigi til Alþingis fǫstudag inn fyrra, áðr menn gangi til Lǫgbergs, at nauðsynjalausu, enda eigu menn þá at taka annan lǫgsǫgumann ef vilja.

Notes

[1] I.e. some of the material from Þingskapaþáttr (Assembly Procedures Section, *Laws* I 53–138), and probably some of Lǫgsǫgumannsþáttr (The Lawspeaker's Section, *Laws* I 187–88) and Lǫgréttuþáttr (The Law Council Section, *Laws* I 189–93) too.

[2] I.e. *lǫgréttumenn* (members of the Law Council).

[3] I.e. the first Friday of the Assembly, which would have been the one between 19th and 25th June. Cf. *Laws* I 53–54.

[4] Opening a main clause that stands after a subordinate clause (especially one beginning with *ef* or *nú = ef*) with *ok* instead of *þá* is especially common in legal texts, but also occurs quite widely elsewhere (see lines 13, 17, 43 below and Texts II:21, XXI:38, and cf. Glossary under **ok**, **nú**, **ef**, **þá**[1] and *Gr* 3.9.9).

38 fyrir] *written twice in K at line-division.*

[5] The Skálaholt bishop had authority over the East, South and West Quarters, the Hólar bishop over the Northern Quarter. Cf. Text VIII, notes 54–55; *Laws* I 35–36.

[6] I.e. after the three years, a new lawspeaker will be appointed unless men do not wish to have him changed.

[7] Cf. *Laws* I 193.

[8] The *misseristal* would have been the calendar for the coming year. Cf. *Misseristal* (Calendar), *Laws* I 51 and 111–12.

[9] Ember Days (*imbrudagar*) are four groups each of three days at various times of the year observed in the Middle Ages as days of fasting and abstinence.

[10] Sc. *mælt* 'prescribed (that)' (cf. lines 25 above and 43 and 48 below; *Laws* I 12–13).

[11] The only source of Law Council funds (*lǫgréttufé*) that is mentioned in *Grágás* is payments for leave to marry within the remoter degrees of kinship (*Laws* II 55, 60–61, 81), but it may be that all licences had to be paid for. The lawspeaker was the only paid officer under the laws of the Icelandic Commonwealth.

[12] See *Laws* I 80 for an exception to this. It is also stated that he shares in fines imposed at the spring assembly he participates in, and that if he himself is fined for failure to discharge all the duties required of him, half is due to the man who prosecutes him and half to the judges of the case (*Laws* I 193). Cf. lines 48–51 below.

[13] We hear of two churches at Þingvellir during the commonwealth period, one in public ownership which collapsed in a storm in 1118, the other, known as *búandakirkja*, belonged to the local farmer and would have been a burial church (cf. *Laws* I 29, footnote 17). It is the churchyard of this latter which must be referred to here and which is often mentioned as the legally prescribed place for payments (e.g., besides here, *Laws* I 172, 205; cf. Björn Þorsteinsson 1987, 49–54).